The chronicle of
Crime

The chronicle of
Crime

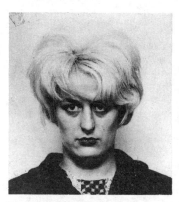

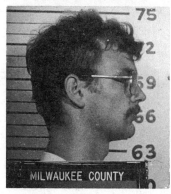

The infamous felons of modern history and their hideous crimes

MARTIN FIDO

CARLTON

Ce livre est dédié à Mercièle Tomassène, en amitié

THIS IS A CARLTON BOOK

Text and Design Copyright © Carlton Books Limited 1993, 1999

This edition published 1999

ISBN 1 85868 904 X

A CIP catalogue record for this book is available from the British Library

Design: Fiona Knowles
Project Editor: Martin Corteel
Project Art Director: Russell Porter
Picture Research: Kathy Lockley
Production: Sarah Schuman

Printed and bound in Great Britain

Author's Acknowledgements
This book could never have been completed in the time available without the assistance of Causeway Resources Genealogical and Historical Research, and my first debt of gratitude is to its founder and proprietor, Keith Skinner. He and I are also very grateful for the help of the staffs of the British Library, the British Newspaper Library, the Public Records Office, Penzance Public Library, the Metropolitan Police History Museum, and all in Room 216. Karen Lynn Sandel has sent useful data from across the Atlantic. Judith and Abigail Fido have confirmed by horrified giggling that my deliberate moments of bad taste have their desired effect for some.

Title page photographs: (top left) Myra Hindley; (top right) Charles Manson; (bottom left) Jeffrey Dahmer; (bottom right) Lizzie Borden

Contents

Introduction

THE WORST CRIMES against humanity over the last two centuries have probably been: transatlantic slavery; the attempted genocide of the American Indians; atrocities in the European colonial empires; the Nazi extermination camps; and the Soviet gulag. Belsen's Irma Grese, was probably a crueller woman than Myra Hindley; John Chivington (who headed the massacre and obscene mutilation of friendly Indian Black Kettle's people) more evil in the sight of God than Charles Manson.

But the men and women perpetrating these awful offences acted, or believed they acted, with the approval of their societies' legal codes. The author and publishers have decided that, for the purposes of this book, crime shall be defined as breach of the laws or mores of one's own time and country. International law, and the laws of natural justice are not, for our purposes, called in to convict even the worst outrages perpetrated with state approval.

It is difficult to know how to deal with terrorism. Today's terrorist is tomorrow's freedom fighter. A respected fellow of St Anthony's College, Oxford can now describe Irgun and the Stern Gang approvingly as partisans. So we have been sparing in the discussion of terrorist offences, tending only to include representative cases which, like the ongoing "troubles" in Ireland, or sabotage in America during the First World War, make some demonstrable impact on law-enforcement.

Chronicles include editorial opinions, whether they be old monks' approbation of saintly kings, or modern tabloid hacks assassinating the character of some easy target. *The Chronicle of Crime* includes a good deal of editorial pontification, giving the appropriate flavour of the times. It should be obvious that some of the predictions are blatantly wrong; and the author and publishers do not necessarily endorse any opinion expressed.

If certain personal opinions have made over-frequent editorial appearances, I apologize.

Chronicles have an appropriate style. In the nineteenth century this was often pompous and stuffy. In the twentieth it is often in execrable taste. These failings have been faithfully reproduced from time to time: largely to offer entertainment, but also, hopefully, to stimulate thought.

Martin Fido, Heamoor, 1993

Swindler Hadfield Caught: 'Pretty Mary' Avenged

The inn at Buttermere, in the Lake District, where wicked seducer Hadfield won Mary's love

Mary Robinson, the innkeeper's daughter

1803 **A**FTER MONTHS in which England has hoped for his capture, swindler John Hadfield has at last been taken, and his seduction of Mary Robinson is paid for.

Hadfield turned up in the Lake District last year, calling himself "the Honourable Augustus Hope", and living on credit by signing bills. He wanted to marry a local heiress, but his pose of aristocracy did not deceive the young woman's father.

Disappointed, Hadfield paid court to the Buttermere inn-keeper's daughter, Mary Robinson. Mary was flattered that a rich gentleman should pay court to her, but insisted on honourable matrimony.

Oh, her tears and shame when bills signed "Augustus Hope" were dishonoured and the rogue's flight revealed that he was plain John Hadfield, and already married! All of England pitied the girl who yielded to this false deceiver. All decent people will be pleased that the innocent Mary has been avenged and the bigamous bounder made to pay for the forged bills with his life.

Burglar Acquitted because of Improper Promise

1806 **L**ABOURERS John Maycock and John Pope exhibited a sudden access of wealth this August, appearing in new clothes. Hence the suspicion that they had murdered widowed Mrs Ann Maria Pooley, whose savings were taken from her house in Meymott Street off Blackfriars Road, London, by thieves who strangled her.

The constables hinted that Pope would not be charged if he implicated Maycock. So Pope told how he and Maycock had entered Mrs Pooley's house by removing a brick from the wash-house wall and drawing back the bolt. They hid there until the old lady came down in the morning, whereupon Maycock throttled her, and the two took £90 from the house.

When the judge learned how Pope's confession had been elicited he was furious, and ordered the man's immediate acquittal.

Maycock was not so fortunate, and has been hanged.

Murder and Indecent Mutilation of Young Harlot

1807 **N**INETEEN-YEAR-OLD Ann Webb, who came to London from the country a few years ago, found – as country girls since Hogarth's "Moll Hackabout" have done – that the streets of Covent Garden are paved with bawds waiting to entice would-be servants into a life of shame.

Ann was so enticed, and changing her name to Elizabeth Winterflood came under the protection of carpenter Thomas Greenaway.

This wretch, under the assumed name of "Weeping Billy" White, lives off women in Southwark. His cruelty and infidelities have driven one of his charges to suicide, and in August this year Miss Winterflood decided to dispense with his protection.

Dressed in virginal white, she stood at her "beat" on the corner of Higglers' Lane and Dirty Lane, where she was seen quarrelling with Greenaway shortly before midnight. At 2.00 am she was found lying on the ground, her legs indecently exposed and parted. She was dead, and her external genitals had been chopped off and thrown under a cart. This horrible mutilation is so extraordinary that the doctor summoned to examine the body failed to observe it until the mangled organs were handed to him.

Greenaway was charged with her murder, but Miss Winterflood's landlady and other women friends were so vehemently hostile to this vile procurer that the judge warned the jury against their prejudice.

In consequence "Weeping Billy" has been acquitted, though it is hard to see who else could have performed this horrible, vile and indecent crime.

Former Vice-President Burr Tried for Treason

1807 COLONEL AARON BURR, Vice-President of the United States of America from 1800 to 1804, has been tried in Richmond, Virginia, for arming a band of men with the treasonable purposes of conducting a war with Mexico, and persuading the states west of the Appalachians to secede from the Union.

Burr's political career has been in abeyance since 1804, when a warrant for his arrest was issued for the murder of fellow-politician Alexander Hamilton. We do not criticize the colonel for this act: the fact that he is an unscrupulous scoundrel, should not lead any right-minded gentleman to condemn him for shooting his opponent with a properly inspected duelling pistol under the observation of appointed seconds.

However, when last year Colonel Burr appointed General James Wilkinson his second-in-command, with finances to meet an advance guard of volunteers at Blennerhassett's Island and prepare to invest New Orleans, he showed he was bent on treason.

In the event, General Wilkinson changed sides and informed President Jefferson. Colonel Burr's assault down the Ohio River was a fiasco, and only the assistance of his admirer General Andrew Jackson permitted him to escape.

Taken in Virginia, he stood trial before Chief Justice Marshall – at a hearing in which judge, President and defendant seemed three hostile and competing interests.

In the event, General Wilkinson's initial acceptance of treasonable overtures could not be concealed; and Colonel Burr showed that he was not at Blennerhassett's Island precisely at the time when witnesses claimed.

The jury insisted that they found him Not Guilty only because he had not been proven guilty. Failing to win the complete exoneration he had wanted, Colonel Burr left the court a disgraced man.

Colonel Aaron Burr, found not guilty of treason against the Union, but deeply suspected

German Leaves a Trail of Death and Sickness

1809 ANNA SCHONLEBEN supported herself by prostitution after her husband's death, as she had since his drunkenness reduced them to penury. Alas, at 49, her charms no longer attracted the high-class clientele to which she restricted her favours. Early this year she changed trades and became housekeeper to a magistrate named Glaser in Pegnitz.

Herr Glaser was estranged from his wife, and Anna hoped to become his second spouse. To this end she acted as a conciliator, welcoming Frau Glaser back to her flower-bedecked marital home.

The happy reunion was short-lived: within four weeks, Frau Glaser succumbed to mysterious burning pains and died.

When matrimony did not ensue, because Herr Glaser was not attracted to Anna, she promptly went to work for Herr Grohmann, a 38-year-old bachelor lawyer. She was sure the 11-year age difference need not prevent their marriage, and was deeply offended when her master told her he was going to marry someone else. He died suddenly on May 8.

Anna soon found employment in the house of another lawyer, Herr Gebhard. Frau Gebhard was expecting a baby, and Anna tended her all through her confinement. Yet not seven days later, the mother died screaming that Anna had poisoned her.

Herr Gebhard's friends commented on the sudden deaths of others who had impeded or refused matrimony when Anna was in their service, and Gebhard dismissed her instantly. She accepted this meekly, thoroughly cleaning the kitchen and refilling the salt-box before she left. She also gave the baby a biscuit.

Half an hour later the baby was vomiting. So, later that night, were the servants. The salt-box was contaminated with arsenic.

Anna was traced to Bayreuth and committed to jail, where the authorities are trying to wring a confession from her.

Though her eyes sparkled and she gloated over a little cache of arsenic they found about her person, she insists that she is completely innocent of the poisonings in Pegnitz, and proceedings are at a standstill

MOUNTED POLICING REINSTITUTED

1809 The Bow Street Mounted Patrol has been reconstituted, and, it is hoped, will deter highway robbery on the outskirts of London, which has become a menace since the dissolution of Sir John Fielding's horse pursuit in 1765.

The new force is uniformed, with red waistcoats which have given them the nickname "Robin Redbreasts".

Their 70-strong brethren of the ordinary foot patrol, the "Bow Street Runners", still wear ordinary dress, and have as their first duty protecting His Majesty's person.

Two Families Battered: their Throats Cut

1811

MAIDSERVANT Margaret Jewell of Ratcliff Highway is lucky to be alive. Her master, hosier Timothy Marr, sent her to buy oysters at midnight on December 7. At 1.00 am the girl returned to find the door bolted against her, and no answer to her knock.

When a watchman helped her break in, they found Mr Marr battered to death by a seaman's maul left on the counter and with his throat cut.

The same horrible fate had overtaken his wife, his apprentice, and even his little baby as they lay in their beds!

Mr Marr's till was rifled. The villain had escaped through a window at the back of the house while Margaret looked for assistance. London was terrified.

A week later, landlord Williamson and his wife, of the King's Arms in New Gravel Lane, just down the road from the Marrs', were murdered. This time the murderer was seen. The Williamsons' lodger, 26-year-old John Turner, heard movements downstairs after he had gone to bed. He crept down in his nightshirt and spied a man in a bearskin coat rifling Mrs Williamson's bloody corpse. Turner fled and lowered himself out of his bedroom window. The murderer again escaped before help could arrive,

John Williams' body brought with his murder weapons for burial outside the Dolphin and Crown where Cable Street crosses Cannon Street New Road

but the Williamsons' 14-year-old granddaughter, Kitty Stillwell, escaped being murdered in her bed.

The parish constables now examined the maul left in Mr Marr's shop, and found the initials JP set in copper nails in the handle. This identified it as the property of Swedish sailor Johann Petersen, who was away at sea at the time of the murders. He had left his tools with John Williams at the Pear Tree inn, just round the corner from New Gravel Lane.

Williams was arrested; found to possess a bloodstained shirt which he could not explain, and a recent access of cash which he ascribed to gambling winnings.

He killed himself in Coldbath Fields Prison before he could be brought to trial, and was given, as is customary, a suicide's burial at a crossroads.

British PM Assassinated in House of Commons Lobby

1812

MR SPENCER PERCEVAL, the British Prime Minister, has been shot by a disturbed citizen, one John Bellingham, a merchant aged about 40 years.

Mr Bellingham fell foul of the authorities in Russia some years ago, and was committed to prison there. He appealed to Lord Levison-Gower, Britain's ambassadaor at the Czar's court, but His Excellency declined to take action. This appeal so annoyed the Russian authorities that Bellingham's prison sentence was doubled.

This second term of incarceration destroyed Bellingham's business, and he returned home a ruined man. From lodgings in New Millman Street he wrote letters outlining his grievances and seeking redress from government. Politicians, civil servants, even the Prince Regent received his appeals. All politely turned him down.

When Mr Perceval indicated that he could not take an interest in the case, Bellingham bought a pistol, skulked behind a pillar in the lobby of the House of Commons, and waited for the Prime Minister to appear.

Bellingham has been convicted of murder and hanged, but some unease is now felt, since his wits had apparently been turned by the wrongs he suffered, and it is not the mark of a civilized people to execute lunatics.

The new Prime Minister is Lord Liverpool, an opponent of reform, as indeed was his ill-fated predecessor.

The death of Mr Spencer Perceval

Defendant Challenges to Trial by Combat

" **NOT GUILTY. AND I AM READY TO DEFEND THE SAME WITH MY BODY.** " **Abraham Thornton**

QUOTE

1817

HOUSEMAID Mary Ashford and bricklayer Abraham Thornton left a dance at The Three Tuns Inn, Castle Bromwich, together after midnight on May 26. At about 4.00 am, Mary came cheerfully into her friend Hannah Cox's room to change out of her dance clothes before returning home.

Hannah noticed blood on Mary's gown: the girl had commenced her monthly courses.

At 6.30, Mary's body was found in a water-filled pit. Blood-spots and footprints suggested that she had been chased by a man who assaulted her violently, probably raping her, and then chased her again to the pit, where he drowned her. Abraham Thornton was fetched, and his boots fitted a preserved footprint exactly.

At his trial his counsel pointed out that the matching boot-print was made before the time of the struggle. Nobody had confirmed that Abraham had chased the girl again and drowned her. Abraham did not deny enjoying sexual connection with her, which he said was her desire as much as his, the rupture of her virgin hymen coupled with her menstrual flow causing the blood spots. The jury acquitted him.

Mary's brother William, however, discovered a statute of Henry VII by which he could reopen proceedings with a private prosecution within a year and a day.

He did so, only to be astonished when Thornton exploited the other half of the statute, and threw a glove on the floor of the court, while declaiming: "Not guilty. And I am ready to defend the same with my body."

For by the same unrepealed statute he could demand trial by combat; meaning that he and Ashford would be armed with staves and held in an enclosed ring to batter each other until Thornton yielded (to be hanged on the spot) or Ashford died, or daylight failed – at which point Thornton would be acquitted again.

Thornton's point of law was as valid, if obsolete, as Ashford's. The private prosecution was hastily withdrawn as a consequence of this stalemate. It now falls to Parliament to expunge this absurd, though interesting, antiquity from the statute-book forever.

Mary Ashford, Thornton's alleged victim

'Captain Lightfoot' Comes to America

1819

CAPTAIN LIGHTFOOT, the most famous highwayman since Turpin and Duval, has emigrated to America. He has achieved the traditional halo of romance by doffing his hat and saying to a young lady near Boston whom he spotted trying to hide her watch from him: "Ma'am, I do not rob ladies." He has, however, stopped coaches and travellers from Connecticut to Canada; he has even robbed Indians.

New England is as determined as Ireland and Scotland have been successively to terminate the career of this persistent menace.

Young Irish Squire Deceives and Murders Village Belle

1819

JOHN SCANLAN, lord of the manor of Ballycahane, near Limerick in Ireland, cast lecherous eyes on pretty 15-year-old Ellie Hanley. When the girl demanded marriage before yielding her maidenhead, John agreed. When Ellie prepared to elope with him, she stole the £120 savings of her guardian uncle.

The two were wed by an unfrocked priest. Scanlan believed the marriage was neither legal nor binding. He was shocked to learn, while honeymooning at Glin on the Shannon, that he was wrong and Ellie was his lawful wife.

Promptly he and his servant, Stephen Sullivan, set out to drown the "colleen bawn" (fair maiden), taking her rowing late at night. Their first attempt failed because Ellie thought Sullivan's raised club was a joke, and disconcerted the murderers by laughing merrily.

The second time, Sullivan clubbed her to death, stripped the body, and threw it in the river.

Ellie's body was washed up on September 6. Scanlan was caught and hanged near Ballycahane, despite his attempts to throw all the blame on Sullivan. The murderous boatman is still missing.

A dramatist's dream of Ellie Hanley rescued

IN BRIEF

1811

ANNA SCHONLEBEN (*see* 1810s) has been beheaded for poisoning. In April she was led to believe that a means of detecting arsenic in corpses had been discovered, whereupon she fainted and confessed.

Conspirators Kill Constable after Bombing Plot

1820

TWENTY OR SO muddle-headed revolutionaries devised a mad plan to throw grenades into Lord Harrowby's house in London on February 22, when they knew the Cabinet would be dining there. They intended to massacre the ministers and march on the Tower of London to declare themselves the new government. They imagined the Tower garrison would surrender to their makeshift pikes, and the soldiers would willingly join their uprising!

Fortunately, this absurd plot was known to the government, whose spies infiltrated the group. When the conspirators assembled in a cowshed in Cato Street, Marylebone, their hideout was surrounded by armed constables and soldiers. Unfortunately, the well-armed troops were directed to the wrong end of the street, and the lightly-armed Bow Street Runners entered the loft unaccompanied. Arthur Thistlewood, crack-brained leader of the conspiracy, recognized a Constable Smithers among the company as the officer who had once arrested him and could therefore identify him. He promptly shot at him before finishing him off with a sabre-thrust to the stomach.

In the confusion, Thistlewood and several other plotters escaped. He was taken at his lodgings in Little Moorfields the following day. Six of the leading conspirators were executed at Tyburn.

Arthur Thistlewood draws his sword to despatch wounded Constable Smithers

Friendly Crowd Turns Out for Thurtell's Execution

1823

AN UNUSUAL EXCHANGE of cheery greetings between a condemned man and an onlooker took place in England this January, as "the fancy" turned out to watch the hanging of one of their number for the murder of another.

As John "Tom" Thurtell mounted the scaffold, someone called out, "God Almighty bless you, Jack!", to which the doomed man responded, "All right, old chap."

Mr William Weare, a notable cardsharp and billiards hustler, was acquainted with Thurtell, William Probert and Joseph Hunt, with whom he played billiards at Rexworthy's Saloon off Whitehall. Mr Weare fairly consistently won. Thurtell, Probert and Hunt suffered a long losing streak.

So the three invited Weare to a weekend's shooting in Hertfordshire. Only they didn't tell him the game to be shot was himself!

In the event, Thurtell's pistol flashed in the pan when he tried to shoot Weare in their gig near Elstree. So he battered the sportsman's brains with the barrel and cut his throat with a penknife.

After Weare's pockets had been emptied, his body was taken to Probert's cottage, handily nearby, and put in a sack. The murderers dumped it in a pond, but then decided this was insufficient cover, and dragged it out again by dead of night to take it to a brook.

They were seen doing so, and identified when the body was later discovered.

Probert promptly turned King's Evidence. Thurtell and Hunt were convicted, but Hunt's sentence was commuted to transportation. Thurtell alone went to the gallows to an enthusiastic send-off by his fellow-sportsmen.

Neighbours Listen to Woman being Beaten to Death

1821

MATTHEW WELCH and Mary Baker lived together in Coal Yard, Drury Lane, London, though both were married to other people.

When Mr Baker came to visit his wife, Matthew and Mary quarrelled furiously after his departure. Mr Haffan, the parish constable, promptly led a deputation of neighbours into the house, threatening to lock Welch up for causing a disturbance. The infuriated man drove them out with a poker, and barricaded his doors. Then the Coal Yarders listened in horror to the sound of savage blows and curses, with terrible screams that finally died away until all was silence.

Not till dawn did they dare to break into the house. They found Mary Baker with her brains battered in while Welch appeared to have made good his escape through a back window.

It transpired that he coolly arrived at his real wife's house in Paddington to demand breakfast. Then he absconded, and his present whereabouts are unknown.

Mother's Red Barn Dream Reveals Daughter's Corpse

1828

THE ENGLISH village of Polstead believed their pretty "bad girl" Maria Marten went off last year with 21-year-old William Corder (four years her junior) for a marriage which should provide respectable cover for her next pregnancies. William claimed to have taken her to London and the Isle of Wight, yet Maria's loving parents received no word from their daughter. In April this year, Mrs Marten dreamed that Maria lay murdered in the the old Red Barn. The dream was prophetic! Maria's body was indeed found buried there, shot through the head.

William had arranged to meet Maria at the barn immediately prior to their original departure for London, having deposited women's clothes there; for some obscure reason, he insisted that she leave her gamekeeper father's cottage disguised as a man.

William Corder was arrested in London, during which time he had married and set up as a schoolmaster. He was tried and convicted at Bury St Edmunds Assizes, and hanged in August.

THE MURDER OF MARIA MARTEN

IN THE RED BARN AT POLSTED.
Containing the whole Account of the horrid Murder,
COMMITTED BY HER LOVER AND SEDUCER WILLIAM CORDER.
Which was revealed in a Dream by her Mother, and also a graphic
ACCOUNT OF HIS CONFESSION AND EXECUTION

R. MARCH & CO. ST. JAMES'S WALK, CLERKENWELL.

Horrid discovery of Maria Marten's body, buried in the Old Red Barn

Disgraceful Mistreatment of Orphan Apprentices

> ## DAMN HER! DIP HER AGAIN AND FINISH HER!
> **Ann Robinson**
> QUOTE

1829

ESTHER HIBNER'S embroidery business in London's Camden Town was run with orphan apprentices from the workhouse.

In January the grandmother of one of them, little Frances Colpitts, visited the establishment. She was told by Mrs Hibner and her daughter, another Esther, that the child had been "naughty" and could not see visitors. The indignant old lady complained to the parish beadle, who, in turn, went to the house to inspect the child.

He uncovered an appalling situation. The six little girls Esther had taken from the parish were starving, ragged, lousy and exhausted. Frances was seriously ill with abscesses on her lungs.

The children were taken back to the workhouse, and given broth to compensate for the starveling fare they had received in Pratt Terrace, comprising:

One quarter-pint of milk between the six of them with one slice of bread apiece for breakfast.
9 lbs of potatoes per week between the six of them.
One slice of meat every other Sunday.

Despite the generous supply of nourishment offered the children in the workhouse, Frances died within a few days. The two Hibners were tried for her murder, together with their forewoman, Ann Robinson.

It transpired that the children had been made to do fine embroidery work from 3.30 am to 11.00 pm every day.

The poor little mites were kept awake with almost hourly canings for slacking. They took their four hours nightly sleep huddled together on the bare floor under one blanket.

Frances Colpitts' serious injury occurred when the younger Hibner picked her up by the heels and dipped her head in a bucket of water, while Ann Robinson screamed, "Damn her! Dip her again and finish her!"

The jury had to decide whether the starvation or the dipping caused the death of this poor innocent child. In the former case, Mrs Hibner would be hanged; in the latter, her daughter and Ann Robinson.

In the event, the wicked and cold-hearted mistress has been condemned to death; her underlings will be transported.

IN BRIEF

1820 STEPHEN SULLIVAN, killer of the "colleen bawn" (*see* 1810s), caught and hanged.

1822 'CAPTAIN LIGHTFOOT', New England highwayman (*see* 1810s), captured 1821 and proved to be Irishman Michael Martin (46) who emigrated to Massachusetts in 1818 and returned to highway robbery after the failure of his brewery business and a love affair. Lightfoot escaped capture to become a popular hero, but was retaken and hanged in 1822.

Burke & Hare: The Edinburgh Bodysnatchers

William Burke

William Hare

Burke Hangs, Hare Cheats the Gallows

December 27, 1828

THE HANGING OF William Burke in Edinburgh's Grassmarket two days ago made Christmas merry for the citizenry. When his body was taken to Surgeons' Square for dissection, there was almost a riot as it seemed the multitudes who wished to see him served like his victims would be unable to gain access. Fortunately, the surgeons postponed the dissection for a day, allowing interested parties to file past and pay their disrespects.

When Burke's common-law wife, Helen M'Dougal, was released from custody on December 26, she foolishly went back to West Port where she was recognized and pursued by the infuriated populace. She would have been killed on the spot had she not been rescued by police.

There is considerable dis-

content that Burke's accomplice, William Hare, was released and smuggled to England in a coach after turning King's Evidence.

Demonstrations outside Dr Knox's house and lecture theatre include burning him in effigy. Edinburgh citizens agree with their philosopher and journalist "Christopher North" (Professor Wilson) that the anatomist must have known he was receiving murdered cadavers for his demonstrations. Since Knox's acerbic comments on his colleagues have made him unpopular with brother-surgeons, it is unlikely that he will be able to continue practising in the city.

Edinburgh's Fears of a Gang of Cannibals

Fears were raised last autumn that numbers of the poor and homeless were disappearing without reason. "Daft Jamie" Wilson, a sweet-natured beggar-boy, known by sight to all in the Old Town, was no longer seen on his normal rounds. Pretty young prostitute Mary Paterson ceased to cause drunken disturbances, and disappeared. The daughters of two old women, Abigail Simpson and Margaret Haldane, made themselves a regular nuisance enquiring after their missing mothers, until Mary Haldane herself vanished.

Rumour claimed that 32 of the city's vagrants were missing, and it was greatly feared that some monstrous family such as

the infamous Sawney Bean's was living secretly off butchered human flesh.

Unfortunately, the only people who could link a missing person with Burke or Hare were the associates of Mary Paterson, who last saw her in the room of Burke's brother Constantine, at Gibb's Close near Canongate. However, two bawds and a strumpet were not witnesses who would willingly come forward to the authorities with information.

The Gang Caught After Hallowe'en Festivity

The appalling crimes came to light on November 1 when Mrs Ann Gray, who had been lodging in Burke's room off West Port, went to fetch some clothes she had left behind. Mrs Gray is Helen M'Dougal's "stepdaughter" by a previous "marriage". She and her husband and child were unceremoniously turned out by Burke on Hallowe'en night because, he alleged, they had been quarrelling. He shifted them to Hare's lodging-house "Log's", at the bottom of Tanner's Close, in the west of the city.

When Mrs Gray returned that night to pick up a pair of stockings, she found the Burkes, the Hares and an old Irish vagrant who called herself variously Maggie or Margery Docherty, or Duffy, or Campbell, or M'Gonagal, singing and dancing in a neighbour's room. Mrs Gray

"Roond the wynd and doon the stair,
But and ben wi' Burke and Hare.
Burke's the butcher, Hare's the thief,
And Knox the boy wha buys the beef!"

Edinburgh children's rhyme

assumed that her family had been thrown out because the Burkes did not want to include them in their party.

Next day, when she went back for more clothes, Burke stopped her from looking in the bedstraw, and splashed whisky over it, effectively masking any unpleasant odour that might have been detected. When he left, Helen M'Dougal stayed sitting on the bed, apparently to prevent Mrs Gray from conducting any search. But when Helen left, Mrs Gray found an arm among the straw which she promptly showed to her husband. He uncovered old Mrs Docherty's body, and despite Helen's entreaties, the two went straight to the authorities.

The execution of William Burke, in the Grassmarket, Edinburgh. His was a fitting end: his body was sent for dissection after it was cut down

Burke Nearly Slips Through the Net

Since Burke enjoyed a good reputation as a poor, hard-working cobbler, Constable John Fisher was inclined to dismiss the accusations as malice. When he searched the room, the body was gone, and Helen M'Dougal plausibly explained bloodstains on the bedding with the story that a woman in her courses had slept there.

Helen also claimed that she had kicked Mrs Docherty out at 7.00 am for making indelicate advances to Burke. Her "husband" had already averred that the old lady left during the previous evening. Fisher took the couple to the police office to clarify this contradiction, and their story fell apart.

Enquiries established that Burke and Hare had taken the body to Dr Knox's dissecting rooms while the Grays were making their way to the police.

Hare Cracks

Regrettably, pathological examination could not prove that Mrs Docherty had not died in a drunken seizure as the villains claimed. Therefore, it became essential that one of them should turn King's Evidence if charges were to be brought.

Hare cracked first, and saved his neck by confessing. He told police that over the past year, he and Burke had killed 16 people and sold them all to Dr Knox's porter. They became "body-snatchers" when one of Hare's tenants died naturally, owing him rent. His body had fetched a remarkably good price.

Thereafter, they had induced the weak and sickly to imbibe liberal quantities of alcohol with them until they were feeble enough to be suffocated. This method of killing left no marks and the surgeon was apparently unaware that he had bought murdered specimens.

THE VICTIMS

AUTUMN AND WINTER 1827:
DESMOND, an old pensioner, died naturally, and sold to Knox for £7.10s.0d
MURDERED:
JOSEPH, a miller.
ABIGAIL SIMPSON, salt-pedlar and beggar of Gilmerton.
AN ENGLISH matchseller with jaundice, name unknown.

EARLY SPRING 1828:
A DRUNKEN OLD WOMAN, name unknown

9 APRIL:
MARY PATERSON, pretty but bibulous harlot.

LATE SPRING:
MARGARET HALDANE, old grassmarket beggar.
EFFY, an old West Port garbage-scavenger.
A DRUNKEN OLD WOMAN, name unknown.

MIDSUMMER:
A DRUNKEN OLD IRISHWOMAN, name unknown.
And HER DEAF-MUTE grandson.
A DRUNKEN OLD WOMAN, killed by Hare alone in Burke's absence.
MRS OSTLER, widowed laundry woman.
MARY HALDANE, Margaret's granddaughter, killed by Burke alone.
ANNE M'DOUGAL, cousin of Helen M'Dougal's former husband. Probably killed in lieu of Helen, whom Hare wanted to destroy.
"DAFT JAMIE" WILSON.
MARGERY DOCHERTY, aka Duffy aka M'Gonagal aka Campbell, lonely old Irishwoman.

First 'Peeler' to be Murdered on Duty

1830

SIR ROBERT PEEL'S new police force has its first martyr. PC John Long saw three men apparently estimating their chances of breaking into houses in the Gray's Inn Road, London. He followed them into Theobald's Road, Lamb's Conduit Street and Guildford Street, finally approaching them in Mecklenburgh Square. On being challenged, two of the men ran away. The third stabbed PC Long, who subsequently died.

The murderer was arrested and convicted under the name of John Smith, but he is now known to be a burglar called William Sapwell.

CITY OF LONDON TO FOLLOW PEEL'S SUIT

1832

Sir Robert Peel's "Metropolitan Police Force" have proved so successful since their creation in 1829 that the City of London is to create an identical force. In 1829 the Lord Mayor and aldermen insisted that their constables were already perfectly organized for disciplined law-enforcement, and Peel's Bill excluded the City from his force's jurisdiction.

However, the success of the "peelers" has persuaded the City fathers to uniform their own constables and place them under the direction of permanent magistrates' offices, exactly like the Metropolitan force.

A kindly member of Sir Robert Peel's new police force

French Poet, Murderer and Thief Guillotined

Lacenaire, French poet Jean François Gaillard

1836

MINOR POET Jean François Gaillard, who prefers to call himself "Lacenaire", was guillotined on January 10. Lacenaire was a vain and extravagant thief, imprisoned several times for larceny. He used an accomplice called Avril to help him rob and murder a middle-aged miser and his elderly mother. He enlisted another accomplice, François, to help him in an unsuccessful attempt to decoy and murder a bank messenger.

On their arrest, François and Avril, ordinary criminals both, made confessions implicating Lacenaire. This so outraged Lacenaire, an assassin who considers himself a cut-above the rest, that, without attempting to conceal his own guilt, he tried to ensure that his confederates went to the knife. He succeeded in dispatching Avril, but not François, who escaped with his life to spend it in penal servitude.

Lacenaire has been hailed as a romantic hero by some of his countrymen. We are assured, however, that his verse is facile: France has not produced a successor to criminal genius François Villon.

The authorities say Lacenaire went to the guillotine as a coward.

Woman's Body Scattered All Over London

1837 ON FEBRUARY 2 a workman found a pair of legs hidden in an osier field in London's Brixton. This completed the body whose first part, the headless torso, was found at the Pineapple Toll-Gate building development in Edgware Road last December. The head emerged in January, blocking a lockgate on the canal in Stepney.

The woman was identified as laundress Hannah Brown, who had been expected to marry James Greenacre on Christmas Day. On Christmas Eve, however, Greenacre informed her friends that the wedding was cancelled, as neither he nor Hannah had the money the other expected, and they could not afford to set up house together.

Hannah had not been seen since then. Greenacre's neighbours in Camberwell observed that he spent the week over Christmas working behind closed shutters, and then he, too, disappeared.

The evil Greenacre was finally discovered in bed in Lambeth with his mistress, Sarah Gale, who was wearing earrings belonging to Miss Brown.

It was shown, however, that Sarah had quietly moved out of the Camberwell house before Miss Brown came to tea on Christmas Eve and could thus only be charged as an accessory after the fact.

Greenacre claimed that a quarrel had taken place when he and Hannah each discovered the other to be penniless; both had believed themselves to be marrying advantageously. He had "accidentally" struck her with a silk-weaving roller, causing her to fall and kill herself by hitting her head. He had then panicked, dismembered the body and dumped the pieces in their far-flung resting places.

The jury did not believe his story and have sent this avaricious murderer to be hanged. His last letter from prison warns his children against the perils of greed.

The murderer Greenacre decapitates laundress Hannah Brown

Notorious Poisoner Convicted of Forgery

1837 LATE THIS SUMMER, Mr Charles Dickens and some friends had a surprise encounter with an old acquaintance as they toured Newgate prison in London. There, awaiting transportation to Australia, was Wainewright the forger who, as "Janus Weathercock" and "Egomet Bonmot", once contributed airy trifles to the *London Magazine*.

Wainewright was spotted and arrested by a former Bow Street Runner this summer, when he returned secretly to London from France, where he had been hiding for six years.

He was charged with defrauding the Bank of England by forging a power of attorney over his grandfather's property in 1829. His conviction and sentence to transportation discreetly overlook the fact that Wainewright is widely believed to have poisoned the old gentleman!

In 1830 he poisoned his mother-in-law, Mrs Abercrombie, and sister-in-law Helen, whose life he had insured. It was of Helen's murder that he remarked coolly, "Yes, it was a dreadful thing to do, but she had very thick ankles."

The insurance companies disputed the claim, and Wainewright lost the case after five years. Already his debts had exiled him to France, and there he avenged himself on the Pelican Insurance Company by poisoning a friend whom he had persuaded to take out a policy with them. This murder was almost one of disinterest, as the policy was not in Wainewright's favour!

This evil and heartless dandy will go to Van Diemen's Land instead of to the gallows where he rightly belongs.

Madman Leads Mob in Battle with Constables and Militia

1838 IN THE BRITISH REFORM BILL election of 1832, Canterbury Tories supported an eccentric Independent candidate who declared himself to be Sir William Courtenay, rightful heir to a disputed Kentish estate in Chancery.

"Sir William, the Canterbury Lion", was not elected, but became the hero of the mob. Within a year, however, this striking hirsute figure, with his flowing black locks and beard, was found to be insane and committed to an asylum.

By 1837 he had been identified as Cornishman John Nichols Tom, who disappeared in 1831 after twice undergoing treatment for madness. The Tom family gained an order for his release into their custody, but unfortunately "Sir William" denied all knowledge of them, and used his freedom to ride around Kent clad in a colourful velvet coat with epaulettes, stirring up subversion among good-hearted but simple agricultural folk.

In May this year he organized a band of 30 peasants, who followed his standard of a loaf of bread on a pole. Constable Daniel Mears came with his brother and an assistant to arrest this armed lunatic at Bossenden Farm, near Dunkirk, whereupon "Sir William" shot Nicholas Mears dead and roared out to his followers, "I am the Saviour of the World! You are my true lambs – every one of you. Though I have killed the body, I have saved the soul!" Then he forced the "lambs" to take up defensive positions in Bossenden Wood and await the arrival of more constables and a small body of militia. In the brief pitched battle that ensued, a soldier, a constable, "Sir William" and seven peasants were killed. The madman was buried hastily in an unmarked grave to prevent ignorant rustics making a martyr of him and renewing his ridiculous revolution.

Irish Murderer Exposed after Stealing Trousers

Daniel Good in his bricklayer's disguise

1842 A LONDON PAWNBROKER sold a pair of breeches to an Irish coachman this April, then summoned a policeman when his apprentice remarked that the customer had purloined a pair of trousers as he left the shop.

PC John Speed made a thorough search of the stables at Granard Lodge, Putney, where Daniel Good worked. He noticed Good throwing hay in one corner and went over to take a closer look. "Why, what is this? Here's a goose!" he exclaimed.

These words prompted Good to dash out of the stable, bolting the door from the outside. While the startled policeman waited for Mr Collingbourne's apprentice to unfasten the door, he turned back to the object in the hay.

"It's not a goose, it's a sheep," he remarked.

It was neither of these – it was

a woman's headless, limbless torso.

Enquiries soon elicited that she had been Daniel Good's common-law wife, Jane Jones, whom he intended to desert for 16-year-old Susan Butcher of Woolwich. Since Good is in his 50s, with a legal wife living in Spitalfields, and another deceased common-law wife, this meagre, balding Irishman's success as a lover is indisputable.

He disappeared for a week, but was taken by chance in Tunbridge Wells when a former Putney policeman recognized him working on a building site. It seems that Wells had removed Jane's property from her basement apartment in Marylebone; given it to his wife Molly in the East End (although they had apparently not seen each other for years); spent a night in Deptford with a nephew; and bought a suit of working man's fustians to pass himself off as a bricklayer's mate.

His feeble defence that Jane had killed herself, and that a mysterious matchseller had promised to dispose of the body, was unconvincing. The discovery of the noxious remains of Jane Good's entrails in the noisome coachman's box of the Granard Lodge landau sufficiently disproved Good's lies. With a severe reprimand from the judge for his incontinent womanizing still ringing in his ears, Good is to be hanged at Newgate.

> **WHY, WHAT IS THIS? HERE'S A GOOSE!**
> **PC John Speed**

The trial of Daniel Macnaughton

Attempt on Sir Robert Peel's Life by Madman

1843 SIR ROBERT PEEL'S secretary, William Drummond, was shot by a madman in London's Salopian Coffee-House between Downing Street and Whitehall, because the murderer, Daniel Macnaughton, believed Mr Drummond to be the Prime Minister himself.

At his trial it emerged that Macnaughton has for years suffered from delusions that "the Jesuits" or "the Tories" are conspiring to murder him, and he is liable to believe that anyone he sees on the streets is one of these persecutors. Edinburgh authorities have long known him as a madman, though they believed him harmless.

On learning that the prosecution was offering no rebuttal to this evidence, the court immediately ordered that Macnaughton must be found Not Guilty by Reason of Insanity, and after the hearing he was immediately dispatched to an asylum.

POSTSCRIPT TO MACNAUGHTON

While the courts are anxious not to repeat the scandal of mad John Bellingham's execution (*see* 1830s), the Queen is more concerned that madmen might be seen as licensed to take potshots at her Royal Person. She has demanded that the sentence be redefined as "Guilty, but Insane", and ordered the judges to reconsider the whole question of legal sanity.

Their retrograde ruling is that a lunatic may be convicted if it appears that he understood the nature and wrongness of his actions.

Electric Telegraph Traps Quaker Murderer

1845 ENGLISHMAN John Tawell is an abominable humbug! The 60-year-old attends Quaker meetings, wears the broad-brimmed hat and plain clothes of the Society of Friends, and lards his speech with "thees" and "thous".

Yet he impregnated his first wife before being compelled to marry her in 1803; was transported for fraud and forgery in 1814; and now awaits execution for murder. No wonder the Friends have never admitted him to full membership!

Tawell, whose second wife is a respectable Quaker lady, secretly kept a mistress and two children in Slough. Fearing that her existence might become known to his wife, he determined to kill her. He took a poisoned bottle of stout with him when next he went to visit her. He hoped to establish a false alibi of his being in the City of London at the time of the murder, leaving his overcoat in the Jerusalem coffee-house and timing his train journeys to perfection. But a neighbour who overheard Sarah Habler's death throes also saw an elderly Quaker leave her house. The vicar of Slough had the railway station telegraph Paddington to have police follow the first-class Quaker passenger when he disembarked. So now this pious hypocrite is to hang for his crime.

Tawell's arrest in the Jerusalem coffee-house

Lecherous Young Rake Kills his Friend

1845 THE BODY OF Eugene de la Rue, cudgelled to death, was found by a policeman outside the wall of Belsize Park, London. Soon he was joined by young Thomas Hocker, who did not recognize the body.

Yet suspicion was aroused when it was learned that Hocker was de la Rue's closest friend. The pair collected pornographic prints together and enjoyed orgies with housemaids and harlots.

Hocker's family realized that Thomas had lured Eugene to the lonely footpath with a forged note purporting to come from a girl friend who had found herself pregnant by him.

His motive was the theft of his friend's watch and purse, for de la Rue is a connection of the famous playing card manufacturers, whereas Hocker is a poor man.

Despite the young rake's foolish pretence that he can offer no proper explanation because he is romantically protecting a lady's name, he has been convicted and sentenced to death.

POLICE POSTSCRIPT TO GOOD

The week-long search for Good undertaken by disguised police officers left them always one jump behind, as they trailed him from Marylebone to Spitalfields to Deptford, and then completely lost him.

It has, therefore, been decided that in future there shall be a permanent body of plainclothes police to "detect" criminals, and not merely make arrests after the villains have been identified.

Bermondsey Murderers Caught in Edinburgh and Jersey

> ## I NEVER REALLY LIKED HIM.
> Frederick Manning

QUOTE

1845 FREDERICK AND Maria Manning lured their friend Patrick Connor to dinner at their tiny house in Bermondsey, London, this year, and killed him.

French-Swiss Maria urged him to come to the basement to wash and comb his hair. When he was on the bottom step, she put one arm round his neck and shot him. Frederick finished him off with a ripping chisel, remarking later, "I never really liked him." Then they buried him in the grave they had prepared in the kitchen.

The following day each tried to cheat the other. Frederick went out to sell off their furniture and abscond, returning to find that Maria had already disposed of hers and gone to Connor's house where she stole stocks and shares and two gold watches.

Maria was quickly caught in Edinburgh when she tried to cash in some railway shares. Frederick took longer to trace, because he had fled to Jersey.

Tried together, each tried to blame the other, and Mrs Manning burst into a furious tirade when she was convicted.

They were executed at Horsemonger Lane. Mrs Manning's black bombazine dress created so unfavourable an impression that haberdashers are having difficulty in selling the material.

Finding the body of Patrick Connor in Mrs Manning's kitchen

Harvard Professor Kills and Dismembers Colleague

1850 JOHN WEBSTER, Professor of Chemistry and Mineralogy at Massachusetts Medical College and occasional lecturer at Harvard University, was an academic with limited means but extremely luxurious tastes.

To support these, he borrowed considerable sums from a syndicate of colleagues, for whom retired Professor George Parkman acted as trustee. When Professor Parkman discovered that Professor Webster had raised further sums by mortgaging his valuable minerals collection, which was supposedly the syndicate's security, he began badgering Webster for repayment.

No one would ever have imagined that one professor might murder another had not Webster told false and improbable stories to a university porter called Littlechild which were supposed to indicate that Professor Parkman had been robbed and murdered by vagrants. Littlechild was already suspicious of Professor Webster's unusual sessions of late night work in his laboratory, with the boiler fully fuelled. He went to the authorities, and with their connivance, broke into Professor Webster's sealed lavatory.

There he and the police found calcined remains of a body whose false teeth proved it to be Professor Parkman. Webster confessed before his execution in August.

TRIAL
OF
PROFESSOR JOHN W. WEBSTER,
FOR THE
MURDER
OF
DOCTOR GEORGE PARKMAN.

REPORTED EXCLUSIVELY FOR THE N. Y. DAILY GLOBE.

PROFESSOR WEBSTER.

NEW YORK:
STRINGER & TOWNSEND, 222 BROADWAY.
PRINTED AT THE GLOBE OFFICE.

Professor John Webster

Dr Kirwan Saved from the Gallows

1852 THE IRELAND'S EYE tragedy this summer has resulted in Dr William Burke Kirwan's conviction for murdering his wife. Yet the complicated medical testimony would make his execution unsafe, so he has been sentenced to life penal servitude. The Kirwans visited the little island off Howth in June. Mrs Kirwan, a strong swimmer, was interested in bathing. The doctor wanted to sketch the landscape. Another couple who visited the island on the same day offered Mrs Kirwan a seat in their boat at 4.00 pm, but she declined, saying she would wait for her own boatman who was expected at 8.00 pm.

Shortly after 6.00 pm, cries were heard coming from a point on the island called Long Hole. When the boatman arrived, Dr Kirwan said he had not seen his wife for two hours. Her body was found at Long Hole. She lay on a sheet in her bathing costume. Blood had oozed from her ears and a wound on her breast. Medical examination established that she had died from asphyxiation, and had not drowned. Dr Kirwan's defence suggested that she had suffered a fit on entering the water, thus explaining her cries.

The prosecution preferred the view that the doctor had suffocated his wife with the wet sheet, hoping this would simulate drowning. They provided a motive in the person of a mistress by whom Kirwan has had seven children.

The doctor was convicted but reprieved from hanging.

Rugeley Poisoner Hanged for Killing Sportsman

1856 THE ENGLISH race meeting at Shrewsbury was spoiled for many enthusiasts last year by the death of one of their number, Mr John Parsons Cook. Cook's horse Pole Star won its race, but Mr Cook fell ill after the celebration supper. He was attended by his friend, Dr William Palmer. Dr Palmer also collected Cook's winnings – though these never reached the dead man's estate. When Cook's father asked for an investigation, it transpired that Palmer was deeply in debt; that he had taken Cook's betting book and altered it in his favour; and that he had fraudulently converted Cook's winnings for his own use.

At the post-mortem examination, Palmer had to be prevented from making clumsy attempts to contaminate the specimens being taken for analysis. The analysis found antimony in the body. There was very strong prejudice against the 32-year-old doctor, both in Shrewsbury, where racing circles resent this man's impudent evasion of his gambling debts, and in his home town of Rugeley, where a suspicious number of sudden deaths in his immediate circle is noted – to wit:

> Palmer's mother-in-law, whose fortune then reached Palmer through his wife.
> Palmer's four children, died in infancy, sparing him the expense of their upbringing.
> Palmer's wife, died after he had taken out insurance on her life.
> Palmer's brother, died after he had taken out insurance on his life.
> Sundry creditors and illegitimate children, bringing the possible total of Palmer's murders to 14!

To spare the defendant the opprobrious consequences of such gossip, he was tried at the Old Bailey. There he was found guilty of John Cook's murder, and he has been hanged.

Poisoner Dr William Palmer

THE PRIME MINISTER'S JEST

The citizens of Rugeley, England, disliking being known as the town of poisoner William Palmer, petitioned the Prime Minister asking for permission to rename the borough.

The Prime Minister willingly agreed, stipulating only that, like Lord Melbourne, he should have the town named after himself.

Rugeley will not be adopting the new name. It would not meet its purpose to be known forever as Palmerston!

Madeleine Smith Freed, Verdict: Not Proven

Madeleine Smith in the dock

1857 **A**LTHOUGH SCOTLAND has trembled over the wickedness of 21-year-old Madeleine Smith, this naughty charmer has not been convicted of murdering her lover Emile l'Angelier. The jury has rapped her over the knuckles with the Scottish "Not Proven" verdict.

Madeleine met 34-year-old seedsman's assistant Emile two years ago. Her wealthy architect father opposed the match, but the two became lovers secretly last year. The cache of her letters found in Emile's room leave no doubt that Madeleine revelled in her sin, and, like the most depraved of streetwomen, actually enjoyed the physical connexion to which she submitted her peson. Indeed, Emile consistently showed a more virtuous awareness that their coupling was wrong.

Early this year Madeleine tried to break off the liaison, accepting her father's choice of young businessman William Minnoch as a more appropriate suitor. But Emile would not let her go, and misled by Madeleine into believing that her mother knew and approved of their continuing courtship, threatened to tell Mr Smith that they had already known each other as husband and wife.

Madeleine started inviting Emile to stand outside her basement bedroom window for long conversations, and gave him cups of coffee and chocolate. It was after one of these occasions that Emile returned home feeling unwell, and died that night with enough arsenic inside him to poison 40 men!

Madeleine was shown to have purchased arsenic, using the false excuse that it was wanted to poison rats. She now says that she really wanted it for a face-wash, and did not like to reveal her vanity. It stood in her favour that she did not try to conceal the purchase once she had been arrested.

The jury is not sure whether or not she killed Emile l'Angelier - we have our own strong suspicions.

Emile l'Angelier arrives home full of arsenic

Successful Barrister is Crime Chief 'Jim the Penman'

1857 **E**NGLISH BARRISTER James Townsend Saward is known in The Temple as a most honourable counsel and advocate. He is known in the underworld as "Jim the Penman", the king of forgers!

Daily he wears wig and gown among his learned friends. Nightly he drinks with sinister scoundrels in secret taverns. He is equally at home in St James's or St Giles's.

This amazing double life has been sustained with skill worthy of a barrister. Saward is a brilliant forger: before signing someone else's cheque, he makes sure he has an example of their signature to copy. To this end he employs solicitors to collect pre-arranged debts, then forges his own debt-collector's signature on a specially obtained blank cheque!

Nor does he collect the money personally, but makes sure it passes from the bank to a hired messenger boy, and then through a chain of fellow-gangsters before it reaches him.

The ring he operates was trapped at Yarmouth this year, having mistaken the name in which they opened a false bank account.

The most astonishing "gentleman crook" of all time is to be transported to the harsher world of penal servitude in Australia.

Toddler Killed: Killer Dumps Body in Lavatory

POLICE HAVE still not solved the horrible murder at Road House, Trowbridge, England. On June 29 somebody took 4-year-old Francis Savile Kent from his cot, cut his throat, and dumped him in an outside lavatory.

Local police concluded it was an "inside job". Their competence must be doubted, however, as two of them contrived somehow to get locked in the kitchen for a couple of hours during which any villain might have destroyed evidence.

This is indeed what may have happened, as a half-burned bloodstained nightdress was found in the basement boiler. When the laundress reported missing one of three nightdresses normally sent for washing by Francis Savile's 16-year-old half-sister, Constance Kent, suspicion fell on her.

Constance, a difficult child, was arrested and charged with murder. However, as it seems impossible for her to have carried the heavy lad single-handed, the case was dismissed.

Two months later Elizabeth Gough, the nursemaid, was arrested. But she, too, satisfied the preliminary hearing of her innocence.

The case is utterly mysterious, and the police remain baffled.

Constance Kent, one of the main suspects in the baby in the lavatory killing

Vile Plot to Murder Sweetheart for Insurance

UNEMPLOYED FOOTMAN William Youngman persuaded Mary Streeter of Sussex, England, to accept his suit; published the banns at St Martin-in-the-Fields; and invited her to stay at his family's lodgings in Walworth. He also insured her life for £100. Between 5.30 and 6.00 am the morning after her arrival in Walworth, Youngman was found on the landing in his nightshirt with the stabbed bodies of his mother, his two little brothers and Mary around him.

His claim that his mother had perpetrated the massacre, and that he had finally succeeded in stabbing her when she attacked him, convinced nobody. His motive was unclear, however, until the insurance policy was discovered. It is assumed that Youngman was seen assaulting Miss Streeter, and promptly killed all the witnesses.

His continuing accusations against his dead mother did not avail him, and he has been convicted and hanged.

Soldiers' Outrage on Child: No Charges Brought

THE VIOLATION and murder of Elizabeth Slater in Holyrood Park, Edinburgh, was surely the work of soldiers. Eleven-year-old Elizabeth left her Canongate home secretly at about 2.00 am on August 19, taking a bundle of clothes with her. She had presumably prearranged a meeting with three Dragoons in whose company she was later seen. They were beating her and making her cry. At 4.00 am her body was found in an unspeakable state, the face blackened and marks of strangulation on her throat.

Two privates absent from barracks that night have been arrested, examined and released. It is now up to the authorities to find the scoundrels who perpetrated this vile outrage.

Reward Tempts Murderer to Make False Accusation

SCOTLAND YARD always suspected that ex-policeman James Mullins murdered Stepney property-owning widow Mary Emsley, for whom he had been doing some plastering. The offer of £300 reward for information led the man who police were sure had killed Mrs Emsley to turn up with a claim that he had seen Walter Emm, a rent collector, behaving suspiciously in the vicinity of the murder. Since Emm discovered Mrs Emsley's battered body, the CID followed up this information. Emm very rapidly proved his innocence, however.

Mullins ' story was obviously untrue; he claimed to have seen Emm inside a shed that he had not himself entered. The false step cracked Mullins' composure, and he was hanged for the murder in November.

Thousands Cheer NY 'Pirate' to the Gallows

NEW YORK'S STREETS, from the Tombs Prison to the dockside, were lined with cheering crowds as thief and murderer Albert Hicks went to the gallows.

"Hicksie" was a deadly villain who declined to work with the street-gangs infesting the city. Indeed, they kept well away from him, fearing for their mortal lives should Hicks find them trespassing on his turf.

Hicks robbed and murdered with impunity. The police could never prove his crimes against him. But this year, he incautiously wandered drunk into a "shanghai"

shop, and woke up to find himself forcibly enlisted as Ordinary Seaman on the sloop *E.A.Johnson*.

"Mutineer" Hicks promptly killed the captain and crew of two, cutting off their heads and throwing them overboard. "Pirate" Hicks stole everything portable from the vessel, and allowed the blood-stained sloop to drift.

But salvagers realized that foul play had occurred. When Hicks was eventually picked up, property of the captain and crew was found in his possession.

Hicksie's career, however, ended in something more like a raree-show than a solemn penalty.

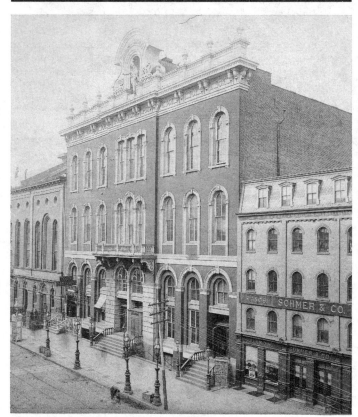

Tammany Hall, the Democratic Party's New York headquarters

THE NEW YORK GANGS

New York Police estimate that 30,000 men and women belong to the city's criminal gangs. The most notorious of these are:

PLUG UGLIES: Named for their "plug" (top) hats, stuffed with leather and rags to serve as helmets. Each Plug Ugly is at least 6ft tall and carries a brick or a bludgeon. Members wear hobnail boots to trample their victims, and many carry pistols. They have been active for 30 years.

BOODLE GANG: Originally robbers who raided food wagons, these toughs then acquired their own carts in which they descend on butchers in the Centre Market, snatching meat which they throw into their carts before racing away. This technique has now been transferred to bank messengers who are knocked down and lose their cash-satchels to gang members who then drive furiously away.

DAYBREAK BOYS: Lethal teenagers, some as young as 12 years. They kill for fun and scuttle ships in harbour. But they seem to have been much reduced in numbers since most of their leaders died in gun-battles with police last year.

DEAD RABBITS: Irishmen who do battle with a dead rabbit on a pole as their standard. Despite their claim to be a political association supporting Irish immigrant interests, there is no doubt that they control crime throughout the Lower East Side, except the Bowery. They are linked to sectional interests in Tammany Hall, the city Democratic Party headquarters.

BOWERY BOYS: Gangsters who also hold legitimate jobs, frequently in the fire service. Bitterly anti-Irish, they support Native American Party candidates whose policy is to repatriate immigrants. They fight the Dead Rabbits at weekends: one massive battle in 1857 left several gangsters on both sides dead. They also have links with Tammany Hall.

ROACH GUARD: Originally a vigilante group protecting shopkeepers in the Five Points area from the Dead Rabbits and the Plug Uglies, the Roach Guard has now deteriorated into just another mob of extortionist brawlers.

HARTLEY MOB: Ingenious thieves who use a hearse and a phoney funeral procession to transport stolen goods, or lull their enemies' suspicion before leaping into the fray.

GRABBER GANGS: Procurers luring girls into prostitution. The two main gangs are led by "Red Light Lizzie" and Hester "Jane the Grabber" Haskins.

GRADY GANG: Sneak thieves organized by receiver John D. Grady.

HOOK GANG: Waterfront pirates with a reputation for taking on vessels even when absurdly outnumbered.

Assault Reveals Couple's Crimes: Maids were Slaughtered

FRENCH MAID Marie Pichon went to Lyons in May to find work in domestic service. She was impressed by the soft-spoken peasant Martin Dumollard who introduced himself as factor of the Chateau at Montluel, and she accompanied him when he assured her of excellent wages.

As the two left the town and entered the country lanes leading to Montluel, Dumollard pounced and tried to strangle her.

IN BRIEF

DR THOMAS SMETHURST, convicted in 1859 of poisoning his mistress, Miss Banks, but reprieved and pardoned, has now completed his one-year sentence for bigamy. This man, who so narrowly cheated the gallows, now has the effrontery to start proceedings to prove his victim's will and secure her property.

But Marie was young and fit. She struggled free and ran back to the city. Next day the authorities traced Dumollard to his cottage, and uncovered a veritable peasant Bluebeard's Castle.

There were women's clothes in profusion; far more than Mme Dumollard could have come by honestly; and there were three bodies, all young women.

Mme Dumollard now confessed, revealing, to the horror of her examiners, that for ten years this wicked couple had lived by luring young women to their charnel-house of a cottage. Martin always pretended to be in search of domestic help and promised good wages and maybe an aristocratic employer.

Martin Dumollard, who took a sickening pleasure in personally killing young women, destroyed them. Then his wife stripped off their clothes, keeping what she liked and selling the remainder.

Dumollard showed several graves he had dug around the cottage. However, most of the victims he had simply flung into the river Rhone. The two go on trial in Bourg next year.

A contemporary French drawing of the Dumollard case

'Duck Bill' Hickok: the Falstaff of Nebraska

A FIGHT IN which three unarmed men were outnumbered and killed is undergoing transmogrification. Twenty-seven-year-old James Butler "Duck Bill "

Hickok, one of the winners, represents himself as the sole combatant against the "McCanles gang", in Rock Creek, Nebraska.

Forty-year-old Dave McCanles sold a house to the local freighting company, which was slow to pay. McCanles, something of a bully, went to demand the second instalment, taking a couple of unarmed ranch-hands and his 12-year-old son. At the office he was met by Hickok – nicknamed "Duck Bill" because of his sweeping nose which overhangs a protruding upper lip. There was already bad blood between the two, who had quarrelled over their disreputable interest in the same woman.

McCanles straightaway abused

manager Horace Wellman, ultimately using his fists. Whereupon Hickok, hiding behind a calico curtain, shot him in the back. Then Hickok, Wellman, Mrs Wellman and freight company employee, J.W. "Doc" Brink, ran out to McCanles' waiting ranch-hands. One was killed with a shotgun blast, probably by Mrs Wellman. The other was battered to death with hoes. The little boy saved his life by running away.

Hickok, Wellman and Brink were charged with murder, but it seems the case will never come to court. Meanwhile, Hickok is fabricating "nine men in buckram" out of Dave McCanles and his unarmed ranch-hands, who

have become the "McCanles gang" of "desperadoes, horse-thieves, murderers and regular cut-throats". Hickok claims to have faced them down, saying he was hit by 11 bullets during the fiercest gunfight one man ever undertook. He expects his unflattering nickname to change from "Duck Bill" to "Wild Bill" as soon as he finishes growing a sweeping moustache to cover his silly-looking mouth.

The facts are as we gave them. Hickok was one of three armed men and a woman who attacked three unarmed men and a child. Hickok's heroic act was to shoot a bully in the back without warning from a hiding place.

Pious Porter Defended by Priests, Prosecuted Once More

ANTONIO BOGGIA of Milan — whose name, as we can well believe, is said to be a corruption of Borgia! — stood trial for murder in 1855, when he was charged with killing a creditor. However, in priest-ridden Italy it proved impossible to convict a pious Catholic who regularly took the sacraments. "Their shaven reverences" insisted that Boggia was a good man, and the case was dropped.

This year a Milanese Alpine huntsman arrived home after an absence of two years, having been wrongly assumed dead. He went to Boggia's house where his mother resided, and was far from satisfied with the porter's account of her disappearance. The building was searched, and the mother's corpse was found.

Further search of a shack owned by Boggia disinterred the bodies of a blacksmith, a broker missing since 1855, and a woodcutter missing since 1853. It seemed Boggia had an unbroken record of settling his numerous debts by murder.

The priests are again clamouring for the release of their devout acolyte. Despite the irrefutable evidence of Boggia's villainy, they still insist that no man who serves Mass for them regularly is capable of heinous crime.

Once their influence would have saved this wicked man again, but the power of the Church in northern Italy has diminished over the past six years, and Boggia's head will be struck off in the main square of Milan.

Slade Uses Outlaw's Ears as Personal Jewelry

TEN YEARS AGO, Lodgepole Creek in America's unfederated Colorado territory put one Jules Beni in charge of the stagecoach post.

A succession of robberies wherein the bandits were clearly pre-informed about routes and schedules led to his dismissal and replacement by the fierce gunman Jack Slade.

In a shoot-out in 1859, Beni came off best, and nearly killed Slade with a shotgun. This year Slade at last got his revenge. He caught Beni and tied him to a wooden fence., then he spent a long time alternately drinking and firing shots into Beni's arms and legs.

When he finally despatched him, he cut the outlaw's ears off, and has since been using one as a watch fob. The other he sold to a like-minded representative of far western civilization.

'Bricktop' Kills her Man, Ignores his Ball-and-Chain

MARY "BRICKTOP" Jackson, the worst woman in New Orleans, has gone to prison for murder. Again! This 25-year-old strumpet, nicknamed for her red hair, entered prostitution when she was 13. She was evicted from New Orleans' notorious brothels for terrorizing other girls. She clubbed a man to death in 1856 for calling her a whore. She killed another the following year, arguing over the conclusion to a scientific dispute the two had as to which way he would fall if she stabbed his tall frame from the front. (She was right. He fell forward.)

In 1859, "Bricktop" and two other women knifed a man who objected to their foul language. In her short prison term for that offence, "Bricktop" encountered John Miller, temporarily serving as a jailer. Usually on the other side of the law, Miller had lost an arm and replaced it with an iron ball and chain attached to his stump; it constituted a horrifying weapon.

The pair worked the old trick known in the 18th century as "buttock and twang". Harlot "Bricktop" picked up punters and took them to dark corners, where bully-boy Miller attacked them with his ball and chain as soon as their breeches were down.

This year Miller took a whip to "Bricktop" to give her a thrashing. It was a mistake: "Bricktop" flogged him! She started by dragging him around the room by his own ball and chain. She bit his hand when he pulled a knife, then used the weapon to kill him.

IN BRIEF

SCOTSMAN ALLAN PINKERTON, who emigrated to America in 1840, opening the world's first "private detective agency" in 1850, has been appointed Chief of the Secret Service of the Army of the Potomac and made responsible for President Lincoln's security.

Jack Slade amuses himself killing Jules Beni

Glasgow Maid Killed by Thieving Friend

James Fleming, "the auld innocent"

ALTHOUGH SERVANT girl Jessie M'Lachlan's death sentence has been commuted to penal servitude for life, Scotland is still divided over this scandalous murder. Many believe that 75-year-old James Fleming was the true killer of Jessie M'Pherson.

Accountant John Fleming left his Glasgow home for the weekend, letting 25-year-old Jessie M'Pherson look after his old father. On Mr Fleming's return on July 7, the old man reported the maid missing from Friday evening. A cursory search discovered her half-dressed body beside her bed, savagely battered with an axe. There were bloody naked footprints on the floor.

Some of Jessie's clothes were missing as was some of the family silver. But the "thefts" seemed deceptive, as there were bloodspots on James Fleming's shirt. Also, how could he have failed to check her room when he missed her?

While Fleming was still in custody, some of the missing clothes and silver turned up in a pawnshop. The customer was 28-year-old Jessie M'Lachlan, a friend of

Jessie M'Pherson's. She told obvious and stupid lies about having been given the goods. Her feet fitted the prints on M'Pherson's floor. Old Fleming was released, and Jessie took his place.

Her lies did not help her in court, and she was convicted and sentenced to death.

Now she says that she actually witnessed the murder. She visited Jessie on the Friday night and found the old man (an uncouth peasant by comparison with his son) enjoying a dram in the servants' kitchen. M'Lachlan went out for more whisky and returned to find Jessie moaning as a result of being hit over the head with an axe by the old man, who was furious that she resisted his lewd advances. The "auld innocent" then finished his victim off, promising to pay M'Lachlan handsomely for keeping her mouth shut. The clothes and silver were supposedly part of that payment.

Unreliable as Jessie M'Lachlan seems, her story makes sense. Half Scotland believes the judiciary convicted her to spare the embarrassment of the murderous old lecher's respectable family.

Jesse M'Lachlan, the accused

Board of Guardians Clerk Poisons his Wife

MR RICHARD BURKE, highly respectable clerk to the Waterford Board of Guardians, Ireland, murdered his estranged wife during the summer.

The couple had been married for seven years, but spent little time cohabiting, Mrs Burke, retiring soon after the marriage to her property in Tipperary.

Early this year she learned that Burke had formed an immoral liaison with another woman, whereupon she visited him in Waterford, making clear her determination to seek legal maintenance through the courts.

Burke gave her £5, and thereafter visited her, expressing great concern about an indisposition that affected her. After his departure he posted her some medication, including a packet of salts.

These proved to be a mixture of Epsom salt, magnesia and strychnine, all purloined from the Waterford workhouse surgery. Mrs Burke died in agony within half an hour of taking a dose.

Despite the jury's recommendation to mercy on account of Burke's previous good character, and a moving declaration of innocence offered by Burke, there can be no doubt of his guilt. Passing sentence, Baron Deasy assured him that he had no possibility of reprieve from death.

All who know Mr Burke have expressed surprise that a man of his unblemished character should sink to the lowest levels of depravity. It would appear the late Mrs Burke recognized that latent villainy lurked under his smooth surface.

Black Sheep Kills Cousin who Thwarted his Allowance

MR WILLIAM HERDMAN was the black sheep of his respectable Belfast family. Despite education and opportunities, he sank to want, and became dependent on the benevolent gratuities of a rich female cousin. When his misconduct became intolerable, however, she insisted that he must never enter her house again, and would have to go abroad if she were to continue his allowance.

Herdman removed to the continent, but disliked being a "ticket-of-leave" man. On his return to Belfast, he formed the impression that another cousin, Mr John Herdman, was responsible for his disgrace. So he stationed himself about 100

yards from that gentleman's house, and, in full view of passers-by, shot him dead when he refused to enter into conversation with him.

An attempt by Herdman's wife to secure a reprieve has proved unavailing, and he is to be executed.

IN BRIEF

MARTIN DUMOLLARD (*see* 1861) guillotined for multiple murder. His wife sent to the galleys.

Quantrill's Robber Band Poses as Civil War Guerilla Unit

William Quantrill, schoolmaster turned bandit

THE CIVIL WAR raging in America allows crime to masquerade as derring-do. Before the outbreak of hostilities, bands of Kansas abolitionists copied John Brown by raiding slave territory in Missouri and forcibly freeing the negroes.

These "Jayhawkers" and "Red-legs" provoked reprisal raids by Missouri "Bushwhackers". Not surprisingly, some of these horsemen have stayed together as mounted guerrillas attaching themselves either to the Union or the Confederate cause

One-time schoolteacher turned horsethief, William Quantrill has seen how this cover can legitimize his crimes. His "Raiders" bid fair to prove one of the bloodiest bands in the war.

They fight under a piratical black flag – not the "Stars and Bars" of their alleged masters, the Confederate Army. They do not confront the Union Army directly, but confine themselves to night-time depredations on encampments and civilians, whose stock they loot and buildings they burn. Then, like the old Scottish borderers, they gallop away into the night.

Union generals do not recognize "Quantrill's Raiders" as a fighting unit, and have declared Quantrill an outlaw. Some southern generals endorse this view, and Quantrill's men risk being hanged out of hand without the benefit of a court-martial if they are captured.

Quantrill is a handsome but ruthless young man. His uncouth impudence was well instanced this year when he kidnapped for himself a mistress – 20-year-old Kate King – from her father's Kansas ranch. Unhappily, the young woman, with the weakness of her sex, found this "rough wooing" acceptable, and has willingly settled into a life of sin with this swashbuckling bandit leader.

Madwoman Kills her Ratcatcher Husband and Baby

TWENTY-FIVE-YEAR-OLD Rebecca Law of Starling Green near Clavering, England, astounded her mother on January 14 when she arrived weeping at her home in Langley, some three miles away, in the small hours of the morning. Mrs Law's dress was covered with blood, and she led her 6-year-old son by the hand. She had, she said, chopped up her husband, Samuel, then killed her 16-week-old baby, Alfred, with a hammer.

Investigation of the Laws' remote cottage confirmed this. Samuel Law, a dissolute ratcatcher, who had recently spent a month in prison, had been ferociously attacked with a billhook, and had over 100 deep cuts and slashes, mutilating his face, neck and shoulders.

Officials and the chaplain from the workhouse, where Mrs Law found relief during her husband's imprisonment, testified at her trial that she was melancholic and a religiomaniac; her own statements bore this out.

She had deliberately chopped up Samuel after they read the Bible together. In her statement she averred: "All the time I was hitting him there was a noise on the stairs. They kept on blundering up the stairs – I mean the devils – but I wasn't afraid."

The Lord Chief Justice suggested that the jury might wish to acquit her without hearing further proceedings. They did so, and she has been removed to an asylum.

> **ALL THE TIME I WAS HITTING HIM THERE WAS A NOISE ON THE STAIRS. THEY KEPT ON BLUNDERING UP THE STAIRS – I MEAN THE DEVILS – BUT I WASN'T AFRAID.**
> **Rebecca Law**

Lawrence, Kansas: pillaged and burned by "Quantrill's Raiders"

Southern Boy Bandit Disguised as Brothel Beauty

QUANTRILL'S RAIDERS (see 1862), the livestock thieves who pass themselves off as Confederate guerillas in the American Civil War, have gained a new recruit. Seventeen-year-old Jesse "Dingus" James robs under the direction of "Bloody Bill" Anderson, a ruffian who kills all his prisoners.

Anderson and Jesse dreamed up a new version of the "Trojan Horse" recently. Knowing that a house of ill-fame four miles outside Independence, Kansas, entertains Union soldiers, young James dressed up in a gingham dress and be-ribboned pink bonnet, mounted his horse sidesaddle and took his fresh, pretty young face to the brothel. He persuaded the madam that he was a saucy country-girl whose strict parents would not let "her" have beaux or "romp" with the boys, and claimed that "she" and 12 of her friends all wanted to come in and "play" with the soldiers that night. The old bawd, delighted at the prospect of fresh faces for her establishment, sent word to the soldiery. As a result, James and a dozen armed Raiders found a dozen unbraced and unprepared northerners in the brothel parlour when James's dulcet "lady's" voice secured them admission.

Young James's colleagues would have robbed the soldiers and let them go. The vicious pseudo-harlot, however, insisted that all their throats were cut. We cannot imagine that such a malign "Miss Nancy" will make much impression as a criminal once this dreadful war ceases to camouflage his villainy.

Jesse James, dulcet toned "lady" of Independence, and the bawd's boy

Mexican Bandits Shot, Beheaded — and Exhibited

THREE MEXICAN brothers have been killed after a robbery and murder spree against miners and prospectors in Colorado territory lasting two years. Vitorio, Felipe and Julian Espinosa claimed that six of their family died in the Mexican-American War. They announced their intention of killing 600 Americans in revenge.

By the middle of this year they had waylaid and killed 26 solitary travellers. Felipe then sent a message to the governor offering to abandon the campaign if he would grant the Espinosa 5000 acres of land and appoint them captains in the Colorado Volunteers. This impudent offer was immediately rejected and a reward of £2,500 placed on Felipe's head.

Early this year vigilantes cornered Vitorio Espinosa near California Gulch and hanged him. In the autumn, famous scout Tom Tobin led 15 troopers after Felipe and Julian. Tobin eventually cornered the pair at Indian Creek, and shot them forthwith. Then he cut off their heads as proof that he had got them and rode back for the reward.

He was paid part in cash and part in buckskins. The heads of the bandits are on display, pickled, as the sort of *objets d'art* which appeal to our far western friends.

Wigan's First Murder for 25 Years

SIXTY-YEAR-OLD John Barton was murdered near the peaceful English town of Wigan, which has not witnessed such a crime for 25 years past.

Barton was overnight fireman at Button Pit Colliery, Haigh. On Saturday, January 3, workmen discovered that he was not to be found. Examination of the boiler revealed clotted blood on the ashes and cinders in front of the furnace. This led to the discovery of bloodstains in Mr Barton's cabin, and the fear that he had been killed and his body carried down to the furnace to be burned.

When the fires were let out and the ashes raked through, it became clear that Mr Barton had indeed been burned there. All that remained of him were charred bone fragments, trouser buttons and nails from his boots. It is suggested that thieves assaulted him in his cabin and then, realizing their excessive violence had killed him, removed the body to the furnace for disposal. More than one man must have been involved, as no single individual could have raised the body to push it feet-first into the furnace mouth. The identity of the criminals remains a mystery.

Loose Woman Killed in Slum Lodging-House

THE HORRIBLE "St Giles's rookery" – perhaps the worst slum in London – has seen another ghastly murder. On April 9, a servant at no.11 George Street went into a room which was taken at 7.00 am that day by a young couple. On the bed she found 28-year-old Emma Jackson of Berwick Street, Soho, with her throat savagely cut. It was clear she had fought strenuously for her life.

Miss Jackson earned a decent livelihood as a shirtmaker, but every so often "cut loose" and disappeared from her family for a few days. At such times she would go and form immoral associations with strange and desperate men.

The lodging-houses of St Giles are notoriously available as houses of assignation when they are not in use as outright brothels.

Since nobody paid much attention to Miss Jackson and her escort when they took the room, the description of the murderer is hardly adequate. It seems likely that he came from her own neighbourhood of Soho, and he may have been a German baker.

Scotland Yard Detective Inspector Adolphus Williamson's best efforts seem unlikely to solve this atrocity in the infamous tents of wickedness.

St Giles's Rookery, probably the most infamous slum in London

LONDON'S CRIMINAL SLUMS

For 100 years the worst slum in London has been the ST GILES ROOKERY, west of St George's Church, Bloomsbury, identifiably depicted by the artist Hogarth in "Gin Lane".

The neighbourhood of CHADWICK STREET, near Westminster Abbey, shares St Giles's feature of holes knocked in party walls, enabling thieves to enter a terrace of houses at one end and escape via the other.

BRILL, lying north of King's Cross, is a region of squalid shacks bordering on brickfields and vast rubbish tips. Pickpockets and robbers abound here.

ALSATIA, south of Union Street, and "the Mint" around Mint Street, both in Southwark, were old haunts of highwaymen.

Pockets of squalor off SAFFRON HILL and HATTON GARDEN, from Hockley-in-the-Hole in the north to Field Lane to the south, house dog-stealers and receivers of stolen goods.

GOODMAN'S YARD, Whitechapel has become notorious for its violence and squalor.

Further north, the FLOWER and DEAN STREET area of Spitalfields has deteriorated badly since the collapse of handloom silk weaving.

Further north still, in BETHNAL GREEN and OLD NICHOL STREET, street bullies congregate.

The docklands are generally poor areas, where drunkenness abounds. Worse still is RATCLIFF HIGHWAY, the greatest centre of vice and crime, thronged with prostitutes, robbers, receivers, shanghaiers and, at the Limehouse end, opium dens.

Frontiersman's Dream Catches Prospectors' Murderers

WHEN HOTELIER Hill Beachy saw David Page, Chris Lowery and James Romaine ride into Lewiston, Idaho, he was absolutely horrified.

A few nights earlier he had dreamed that three men with exactly their appearance had murdered his old friend, muleteer Loyd Magruder, out on the trail. When he heard that they had been travelling with Magruder, he wanted them arrested, but felt that a vivid dream was not plausible evidence. When they left town, and he heard that Magruder's equipment had been found abandoned beside the trail, he pursued the three men to California.

Once he brought them back to Idaho, muleteer Bill Page, who had travelled with the party, testified that the three had indeed murdered Magruder, two prospectors, and four other muleteers who had been travelling together with a shipment of gold.

The three were convicted and hanged – and all because of one man's dream!

London Railway Passenger Robbed and Murdered

Lamentation of Franz Muller

Within a dark and dreary dungeon,
 In grief and anguish now I lie,
For a base and dreadful murder,
 In youth and vigour I must die.
Far from home, and far from kindred,
 In grief and sorrow I deplore,
Unhappy man, on a foreign land,
 I die at the age of twenty-four.

When I had done that dreadful murder,
 I sailed across the raging main ;
Justice followed poor Franz Muller,
 For the murder in the railway train.

That fatal night I was determined,
 Poor Thomas Briggs to rob and slay,
And in the fatal railway carriage,
 That night, I took his life away.
His crimson gore did stain the carriage,
 I threw him from the same, alack !
I ou the railway left him bleeding,
 I robbed him of his watch and hat,

When I poor Thomas Briggs did murder,
 I went across the briney sea,
And I was fully then determined,
 To reach New York, in America
My guilty soul was pierced with anguish,
 When the stormy winds did roar,
And justice ready was to seize me,
 Before I reached Columbia's shore,

Poor Briggs's goods was found upon me,
 Sufficient evidence, you see,

To bring me to the bar of Newgate,
 And hang me on the fatal tree ;
Oh ! was there ever such excitement,
 Or will there ever be again,
As there has been with poor Franz Muller
 For the murder in the railway train.

My noble counsel pleaded for me,
 And done their best my life to save,
A British jury found me guilty,
 I must lie in a murderer's grave ;
Numbers thought they'd not convict me,
 When at the bar they did me try,
Oh ! God above, look down in pity,
 My fate is sealed, and I must die !

Oh ! I must die a malefactor,
 In front of Newgate's dismal door,
In the midst of health and vigour,
 Aged only twenty-four.
I never thought the law would take me,
 When I sailed o'er the raging main,
All my courage did forsake me,—
 A murderer in the railway train.

Swift the moments are approaching,
 On the gallows I must die,
The cruel hangman stands before me,
 On the wretched tree so high,
I am full of grief and anguish,
 Full of sorrow, care, and pain,—
A warning take by poor Franz Muller,
 The murderer in the railway train,

H. Disley, Printer, 57, High-street, St. Giles.

A broadsheet sold at Müller's execution

THE ISOLATION of a first-class railway carriage has its disadvantages: it provides a suitably quiet location for robbery and murder! On Sunday, July 9, 70-year-old Mr Thomas Briggs travelled from his home in Hackney to south London, to pass the day with his daughter. On the same day, 25-year-old German tailor Franz Müller took the same route, for his regular appointment with a prostitute.

The two men returned home on the same train. Only Mr Briggs never arrived. His body was found on the line between Wick and Bow. His money and watch had been stolen. There were signs of a struggle in his compartment, and left there was a peculiar silk top hat of a new short design. Mr Briggs's hat was missing. There was, however, an unfortunate delay before the hat was identified.

Then a cab driver reported having described the new model hat to Müller, who announced his intention of getting one, and did so.

By the time this information reached the police, Müller was travelling to America on the SS *Victoria*. As the vessel was still at sea, police officers raced to New York by a faster ship, and arrested Müller when he landed. In his possession they found Mr Briggs's gold watch, and Mr Briggs's silk top hat, cut down about 2 inches at the brim and gummed together again to make it match Müller's own hat. He was brought back to London and convicted, confessing on the scaffold before a vast crowd at Newgate.

This sordid fellow has singularly influenced fashion. Young bucks are now adopting the "Müller cut-down" rather than the traditional "stovepipe" hat.

Dr Edmond de la Pommerais, poisoner

French Doctor Kills Mother-in-Law and Mistress

THREE YEARS AGO Edmond de la Pommerais was an impecunious young doctor in Paris. Then he married wealthy Mlle Dubisy, and used her money to establish a mistress; Madame de Pawr. In the same year, Mme de la Pommerais' mother died, and the doctor enjoyed a new access of inherited wealth.

Yet within two years he had squandered this fortune, and was again in need! He thereupon persuaded Mme de Pawr to join him in swindling an insurance company. The two insured her life for half a million francs. Then she agreed that de la Pommerais should help her feign a serious illness in the hope that the insurance company would change the policy for an annuity if it seemed likely that they were about to lose their client and their 500,000frs with hardly a premium paid. The plan apparently went wrong, as Mme de Pawr sickened appropriately, but then died. De la Pommerais signed the death certificate, giving cholera as the cause of death. He then demanded payment of her life insurance.

The company was suspicious, and had the body examined. The lady, they proved, had died of an overdose of digitalin. De la Pommerais was tried for her murder and that of his mother-in-law. Despite his protestations of innocence, has gone to the guillotine as he richly deserved.

'Making an Example' Proves 'Proper Punishment'

EARLY THIS YEAR, the Montana Vigilantes decided it was time to hang some associate of villains, who was not himself guilty of any crime, in order to frighten citizens out of socializing with known badmen. Since the roving outlaws carry out their depradations in the vicinity of townships where they enjoy the rowdy companionship of Wild West bar and brothel frequenters, it was thought shunning them would freeze them into neighbouring territory. So, a non-criminal roisterer should be executed as a warning against befriending robbers.

They picked one Frank Parish for this monstrous demonstration *pour encourager les autres*, but were spared the guilt of spilling innocent blood when at the last moment Parish confessed to not only drinking with bandits but to riding with them when they robbed stagecoaches and livestock.

To their intense disgust, the "law-enforcers" found they were hanging a guilty rather than an innocent man!

Death of a Badman

WHOEVER CROSSED Jack Slade died. Slade was happier with foul means than fair. Once, for example, he taunted a man who had drawn a gun on him with being afraid to face him in a fist-fight. When his exasperated antagonist threw the pistol aside and advanced in a pugilist's crouch, Slade promptly drew his own gun and killed him.

A story is told of Slade's repaying an insult and showing off his marksmanship by accurately shooting a man through a specified button of his coat at 25 yards.

This year the vigilantes of Montana are in high fettle. In March they gave Slade a warning to get out of town. The reckless bravo ignored it, judging himself a terror none would dare threaten seriously. On the evening of March 3, when he was drunk and shooting randomly around the streets, Slade was horrified to find himself grabbed, tied up and marched away for execution.

"My God! My God! Must I die? Oh, my poor wife, my poor wife! My God, men, you can't mean that I'm to die!" were the tearful last words of this cowardly killer of so many others.

OBITUARY

JOSEPH 'JACK' SLADE (1824-1864)

Died, in Virginia City, Montana Territory, of strangulation by a noose of hempen rope. The son of an Illinois congressman, Mr Slade fled to the western territories after killing a man in a quarrel. Here he came into his own as a determined killer, officially working in various capacities for the Central Overland stagecoach company in which he rose from driver to district supervisor.

Filial Love Saves Young Killer's Life... Once

LAST YEAR Haze Lyons, a young cowboy who joined Marshal Henry Plummer's "Innocents" in Virginia City, Montana, accepted the job of assassinating Plummer's deputy, Bill Dillingham, who refused to assist in criminality. Thus does the evil Plummer practise "crime enforcement" rather than law enforcement.

Lyons proved incompetent as an assassin, and was quickly caught, arrested and convicted on the spot by a miners' "court". But as the rope went around his neck, a bystander read out the young man's pathetic last letter to his mother. The hardy miners were moved to tears. They freed Lyons with a stern warning not to transgress again.

Alas, he did not heed their words but went straight back into Plummer's illicit service in Virginia City, where he was once again involved in nefarious activities early this year. He was taken and hanged without further ado. A popular ballad now laments the fate of the foolish young man who so loved his mother.

MONTANA VIGILANTES

Much of this year's striking law-enforcement has been the work of amateurs in the unfederated American territory of Montana. Plagued with bandits and robbers, the honest citizens and miners were outraged when they realized that sweet-talking charismatic Henry Plummer, who had got himself elected sheriff of Bannock and marshal of Virginia City, was using his law-enforcement offices as a base for controlling one of the worst gangs of bandits.

Around last Christmas, some of the most respectable young men in the territory joined with miners to extirpate the villains. They have had immense success.

They nail a mysterious warning reading "3-7-77" on the door of any man they suspect. Should he heed it and leave town, he will not be harassed. Should he brave it out, he will be hanged without question, a length of rope left around his neck to trail out of his grave as a warning to others.

Henry Plummer, law-breaking marshal

Lincoln Assassinated, Dies in the Hour of Victory

FIVE DAYS after General Lee's surrender confirmed the Union victory in the American Civil War, President Lincoln has been assassinated.

Mr and Mrs Lincoln went to Ford's Theatre in Washington to see *Our American Cousin* on April 14. During the play, the Washington policeman who was acting as the President's bodyguard went out to a tavern, leaving his post at the door of the Presidential box.

At 10.00 pm the 26-year-old English-born actor John Wilkes Booth made his way into the box. He was pale and drunk. He pulled a pistol and shot the President directly behind the ear. Then with a cry of "Sic sem per tyrannis!" (thus ever to tyrants), he hurled himself over the rail, in what was intended to be a swashbuckling leap on the stage. But his spur caught in the flag in front of the box and he fell heavily, breaking his leg. Though he escaped at that point, his injury prevented him from evading capture permanently among the demobilizing soldiers of Lee's army. He was

President Lincoln, accompanied by his wife and friends, is shot by John Wilkes Booth at the theatre on April 14

traced within 12 days to a tobacco shed near Port Royal, Virginia, and there, in a brief exchange of shots with Union soldiers, the assassin fell.

His body has been returned to England for burial – the home of his illustrious connections, John Wilkes the 18th-century radical MP and Lord Mayor of London, and the great Booth family of Shakespearean actors.

About a dozen men conspired with Booth to kidnap Lincoln before the war ended and drag him in chains to the Confederate capital of Richmond. When that plot collapsed with Lee's surrender, the scheme changed. Booth was intended to kill Lincoln while others killed the Vice-President and various cabinet members. But in the end Booth acted alone. Still, his co-conspirators have been arrested, and three of them have paid the penalty with their lives, alongside Mrs Mary Surratt in whose lodging-house they were taken.

SURRAT.   BOOTH.   HAROLD.

War Department, Washington, April 20, 1865.

$100,000 REWARD!

THE MURDERER

Of our late beloved President, Abraham Lincoln,

IS STILL AT LARGE.

$50,000 REWARD

Will be paid by this Department for his apprehension, in addition to any reward offered by Municipal Authorities or State Executives.

$25,000 REWARD

Will be paid for the apprehension of JOHN H. SURRAT, one of Booth's Accomplices.

$25,000 REWARD

The reward poster put on display after the assassination of President Lincoln

DUBIOUS LEGALITY OF ASSASSINS' EXECUTIONS

Since men should be convicted for crimes they have committed, and not ones they intended but did not carry out, Messrs Paine, Herold and Atzerodt probably should not have hanged as John Wilkes Booth's co-conspirators, because their intention was forestalled by Booth's drunken solo performance.

As for Mrs Surratt, she knew nothing whatsoever about her lodgers' felonious plans, and has been wickedly killed for the crime of keeping a boarding-house!

The whole trial of the "assassins" was marred by the pretence that the killing took place in time of war and so could be conducted by military rather than civil authorities. At times it seemed the prosecution was taking revenge on the Confederacy rather than presenting the illegal actions of three men and an innocent woman.

Glasgow Doctor Kills Wife and Mother-in-Law

AN ANONYMOUS letter to the Procurator-Fiscal led to Dr Edward Pritchard's arrest following the deaths of his wife Mary and mother-in-law Mrs Taylor in the spring.

Mrs Pritchard suffered a violent gastric upset at the beginning of February, and her mother moved into Pritchard's house to nurse her. It may be that this illness was genuine, giving Pritchard the opportunity he sought, for while his wife was ill the doctor purchased a quantity of aconite.

When Mrs Taylor also fell ill, Pritchard suggested to a colleague that she had overdosed herself with an opiate she took for her neuralgia. But the old lady died on February 25, and her daughter followed her to the grave some three weeks later.

Following the tip-off to the Procurator-Fiscal, the bodies were examined, and both ladies were found to have been poisoned with aconite.

Before his public execution in July, Pritchard confessed. He had impregnated a 15-year-old servant, and while urging her to keep quiet about this as he aborted her, he promised to marry her should his wife die. Whereupon he set about clearing the stage to carry out this promise.

Dr Pritchard, mother-in-law and wife killer

Constance Kent Confesses — Road House Mystery Solved

THE MURDER of 4-year-old Francis Savile Kent (*see* 1860) has been solved. His sister Constance, now 21 years old, has confessed that she killed the boy with her father's razor.

The lad was found in an outside toilet with his throat cut and a deep stab wound in his chest. Constance was the first suspect, but the case against her seemed impossible at the time. Now she says that she committed the murder to avenge her mother who was cruelly treated when her father transferred his affections to Savile's mother – the present Mrs Kent.

Constance has come under the influence of the Anglo-Catholic priest, the Rev. Arthur Wagner, and it was in making her Easter duties that she felt the need to confess to the reverend gentleman.

Opponents of Anglican papistry with its "man-millinery" and incense are appalled that auricular confession should lead to a conviction, and note that Constance's description of her crime includes the impossible and untrue claim that she inflicted the stab wound with a blunt-ended razor. But she has pleaded guilty, so no further investigation is warranted. Her death sentence, however, has been commuted to life imprisonment.

Authorities Refuse to Try the Right Brawling Italian

A BRAWL BETWEEN Englishmen and Italian immigrants in The Golden Anchor tavern on Saffron Hill, London, has led to the death of one man and the trials of two others for his murder.

Michael Harrington was stabbed in the mêlée, and when the constables arrived they arrested Serafino Pelizzioni who was lying stunned in the bar where he had been struck with a billiard cue. He and other Italians protested his innocence. He had, in fact, been summoned from another tavern as a respected immigrant whose influence might persuade his fellow countrymen to stop fighting. But neither the authorities nor an Old Bailey jury were prepared to accept their word that another Italian was responsible, and Pelizzioni was condemned to death.

Before he could be executed, Signor Negretti, the well-known metereological instrument-maker, financed a search for Gregorio Monzi, who was locally known to have wielded the knife. When Monzi was traced in the Midlands it transpired that he was quite unaware that Harrington had died after the affray. He willingly gave himself up admitting that he had struck with a knife during the fight.

But the authorities refused to re-open the case, and Mr Negretti had to a finance a private prosecution of Monzi. This proved successful, and Pelizzioni has at last been released.

Quantrill's Loot Opens Brothel for His Mistress

KATE KING, mistress of bandit William Quantrill who passed himself off as a "Confederate Guerilla" (*see* 1861) has become beneficiary of a will the fallen villain penned when he was captured by Union soldiers shortly before the Civil War ended.

Madame King has gone to St Louis where she has invested the money in opening a fashionable house of ill-fame. She has had business cards printed which she proposes to distribute at reunions of "Quantrill's Raiders", where she will be a regular guest of honour.

Visitors are warned not to speak ill of Quantrill on her premises, as she is ready with her pistol if she hears her former lover described as the vicious butcher he was!

Train Robbed — A New Crime for Modern Times

Since the train robbery in Indiana by the Reno gang on October 6, all American trains have now come under threat from highwaymen

THE RENO gang of Indiana have devised an entirely new crime; and since it earned $10,000, "train robbery" will probably overtake stagecoach robbery in highwaymen's esteem.

Brothers John, Frank, Simeon ("Slim") and William Reno have led a robber gang in the lawless west for some time. Hitherto their activities have comprised highway robbery, burglary, and hold-ups in saloon bars. But on October 6 they halted and boarded a train near Seymour, Indiana. Making their way to the express coach, they forced the guard to open the safe and removed the money. Then they mounted their horses, which were tethered beside the railway track, and galloped away across the prairie.

Mr Allan Pinkerton, whose "Private Detective Agency" now commands all his time since the war has ended, gives high priority to capturing the Renos. He hopes that depradations against American trains may be nipped in the bud.

Jersey Murderer Dies, Hell-Bound to the Last

THERE WAS nothing extraordinary about Francis Bradley's crime. This habitual young thief broke into elderly spinster Esther Le Brun's house at St Peter, Jersey, in the Channel Islands, and strangled her when she awoke.

It is, unfortunately, all too common for burglars to kill potential witnesses, though the peaceful Channel Islands are spared much of this type of crime.

Bradley was soon arrested, and his claim that blood on his clothes and hat came from abrasions suffered while he loaded bricks at the quay was easily disproved. In fact, Bradley had boasted to friends that he intended to rob a lonely cottage and cut off the occupants' heads with a hatchet.

But when he was sentenced, Bradley's true nature showed itself. In Jersey the Bailiff and judges cover their heads before passing sentence on a kneeling prisoner. Bradley refused to bow the knee, and had to be forced to the floor by "turnkeys" – a spectacle which caused a sensation in court, reducing several spectators to tears.

On hearing the sentence passed, Bradley burst into obscene swearing and profanity, before passing the printable remarks: "Infernal brigands, assassins, you are sentencing me to death for committing robbery. The One before whom I will shortly appear is just and knows that I am innocent."

This avowal, however, had the effect of persuading many onlookers of his undoubted guilt and they remarked that he deserved to die!

In prison he ate heartily, grumbling when he had to make do with four eggs for breakfast. He threatened suicide. And when he heard the scaffold being erected, he promised to be ready and waiting in Hell to make things hot for those who had compassed his death! Finally he refused to pray with the chaplain, and it was a relief to the whole island when he took the "drop" and departed this life on August 11.

IN BRIEF

LANCASHIRE MURDER SOLVED

The murderers of JOHN BARTON (*see* 1863) have been unexpectedly identified.

Following two false confessions, police this year published a description of the dead man's missing watch. This led its current owner to realize, with horror, that he had acquired stolen property.

When he revealed its source, police questioned a convict in Dartmoor, Thomas Grymes, who has now confessed that he and two others robbed and murdered John Barton three years ago.

THE REVEREND Mr Lindsey, Presbyterian pastor of Medina, N.Y., has refused the offer of release from prison on bail after a coroner's jury determined that his 3-year-old son's death resulted from chastisement by the father, without calling it murder.

On June 18 the child disobeyed its stepmother's command to say its prayers. Mr Lindsey thereupon took up a cedar shingle and beat the child for more than two hours. At the end of that time he called Mrs Lindsey, who told him the lad was dying. And die he soon did.

Lindsey now dares not enjoy his freedom, as less prayerful people long to beat this monstrous christian into his own grave.

Yard's Informers Round up Manchester Stamp Robbers

IN MAY, thieves broke into the Government Stamp Office in Manchester, taking cash and stamps to a value of £10,000. In cases of serious crime such as this, it is open to baffled provincial forces to turn to the Metropolitan Police for the assistance of their world-famous CID.

When Scotland Yard detectives were called in, they followed underworld information that the robbery had been perpetrated by brothers Tom and Bill Douglas and a man called Gleeson – a gang known as "The Countrymen".

Hearsay accusations could not be turned into charges, and the Yard could not act until a man named Charles Batt was arrested at Somerset House for trying to pass a stamp taken in the raid. Detectives watching him closely observed an ex-burglar known as "Peg-Leg Dick" Shaw pass him a wad of tobacco.

When Peg-Leg was questioned it transpired that he resents the criminal fraternity for allowing him to lapse into disregard after the loss of his leg. Provided the police would keep him drunk and listen to his woes, he was willing to inform on the men who had passed the stamps to the receiver Batt.

After one detective had suffered the real persecution of having this "nark" sleeping on his doorstep in a filthy and inebriated condition whenever he wanted a word, Shaw did at last supply information which enabled the police to arrest the "Countrymen" and convict them of their daring crime.

Bank Robbery: New Crime Devised in America

FEBRUARY 13, Liberty, Missouri. Another wholly new crime was perpetrated today by an unidentified band of former Confederate "guerillas". At 8.00 am, nine or ten howling riders galloped into town, and four dismounted at the bank. Inside, cashier Greenup Bird and his son William found themselves gazing down four revolver barrels.

The robbers forced the Birds into the vault, and swept the contents into a sack. Then they locked the Birds in and rejoined their companions to ride away.

But as they left town, one of the bandits casually shot 19-year-old college boy George "Jolly" Winmore, who was preparing to go to class with a valentine for his sweetheart.

This cold-blooded murder following open robbery of a bank by men who made no effort to disguise themselves, speaks volumes for the lawlessness of the central south western states since the disruption brought about by the late war.

Housekeeper Killed by Visitor She Expected — But Who?

CANNON STREET, in the City of London, buzzes with speculation about the sudden death of middle-aged Sarah Millson, housekeeper at the premises of Messrs Bevingtons the leather-sellers.

Mrs Millson, so far as is known, had led a blameless and uneventful life. She was sitting with fellow-servants during the evening when a knock was heard at the front door. Mrs Millson said she knew who it was and would let the visitor in. When she did not return, her worried fellow-servants went after her, and found the unfortunate lady beaten to death and lying in a pool of blood. It seems that she had removed her shoes before going to receive the mysterious caller.

This last point, taken in conjunction with her insistence on answering the door herself, suggests that she may have had some secret, if not guilty connection with the person she anticipated. Her friends and the authorities are at a loss to explain the tragedy.

Cannon Street, scene of the murder

Horrible Dismemberment of Child at Hampshire Village

THE PRETTIEST little 7-year-old English village girl, with long flaxen hair and cornflower-blue eyes, was found by horrified villagers in the following pieces:

HER BLOODY HEAD stuck on a hop-pole with the eyes gouged out and one ear torn off.
HER CHEST, severed at the diaphragm, with the heart scooped out.
HER ARMS, deposited separately, with two copper ha'pence pieces clutched in one hand.
ONE FOOT, dropped in a field of clover.
HER EYES, recovered from the nearby River Wey.
HER HEART, lying on its own.

It is assumed the river has taken all other remains. Her missing lower abdomen makes it impossible to say whether she had actually been interfered with.

The man responsible was solicitor's clerk Frederick Baker. He used his tea-break on a Saturday in August to walk through the meadows near the hop-field, and finding Fanny Adams playing with two friends, gave the girls ha'pence to run races for him; then sent the other two home while he took Fanny into the hop-field.

He appears to have battered the child with a large stone, and then cut her apart with his penknife. After which he went and had some beer and returned to his office where he wrote in his diary: "Killed a young girl. It was fine and hot."

He was unable to explain bloodstains on his cuffs. His suggestion that his knife was too small for butchering the child was countered with the observation that Fanny was a very small child. He was hanged at Winchester.

> **KILLED A YOUNG GIRL. IT WAS FINE AND HOT.**
> **Frederick Baker**
> QUOTE

Frederick Baker mutilates sweet Fanny Adams in the hop-field

Much Loved Creole Prostitute Murdered

VIRGINIA CITY, Nevada, has lost its favourite madam. The beautiful Creole, Julia Bulette, came to Nevada aged 27 in 1859. She entertained miners on her floor before her shack was completed, and rapidly became the most popular "game" in town. Soon she employed six girl assistants. Within a few years she opened an elegant house of ill-fame, with fresh flowers brought in daily, and imported French wines. As an honorary member of the City Fire Company she led the annual Fourth of July Parade from a firetruck. During the Civil War she pawned her jewels for the soldiers' medical fund, and turned her bagnio into a hospital.

Julia is said to have charged $1,000 for one night's enjoyment of her personal favours. But on January 20 she was found strangled in her bed, with most of her valuables rifled.

Furious enquiries by the heartbroken miners and civic dignitaries have so far failed to uncover the killer. Had they done so, he would without a doubt have been lynched on the spot.

As it is, Miss Bulette was given a splendid civic funeral and buried in a solid silver coffin. Every business in town closed for the day. The Metropolitan Brass Band headed a procession in which hundreds of weeping men attended this much-loved lady to the cemetery under festoons of black bunting, while their wives shuddered disapproval from behind shuttered windows.

And when Julia was finally buried, the whole town marched home again to the rollicking happy strains of "The Girl I Left Behind Me".

THE 'WILD' WEST

Three factors combine to give the American West the epithet "wild".

1. It comprises frontier territory; claimed from the Indians by the federal government, but not yet subject to internal state legislatures. Law-enforcement officers are elected from an unstable population comprising mining prospectors, cattlemen, pioneers and homesteaders, all of whom have headed West to improve their lot.

2. The late Civil War has left some young men dissatisfied with civilian life, and some defeated Confederates resentful of the federal government. So they live by robbing institutions like banks and railroads. Former "guerrillas" like the James and Younger brothers who rode with Quantrill's Raiders are adept at livestock theft.

3. Cattle raised in Texas and Kansas are driven huge distances to railheads for the the Chicago stockyards. The "cowboys" lead a demanding roving life and tend to celebrate like seamen ashore when they finish a drove and come into the poorly policed townships.

Australian 'Bushrangers' Murder Crown Commissioner

THE UNPOPULATED Australian "outback" is plagued, like the American West, by mounted robbers who attack mail-coaches. This year, two of them killed a brave passenger in an assault on the Bourke to Lower Macquarrie mail near Dubbo.

Mr J.G.Grenfell, former gold Commissioner of Forbes was travelling to take up his new post as Crown Lands District Commissioner for Albert. He was riding beside the driver and holding the reins while coachman Charles Stuart filled his pipe, when two men in white gauze masks with black rings around the eyes rode out of a patch of scrub, and ordered him to, "Bail up!" (an Australian term meaning put his hands up).

Mr Grenfell refused. He increased the horses' speed, and drew a small pistol with which he fired at the robbers. They rode ahead and fired back, ultimately putting a bullet in Mr Grenfell's thigh, whereupon Stuart brought the horses to a stand. Disregarding his injury, Mr Grenfell scrambled down and fired his pistol at the robbers again, so astonishing them that they fled.

Unhappily, Mr Grenfell's wound became infected and he died at Narramina despite the best available medical attention. (Naturally, small towns in the Australian bush cannot rise to the metropolitan standards.) But his example shows that courage may frustrate these desperadoes.

Brave London Shopkeeper Arrests Armed Robber

MR REARDEN of Church Lane, Bloomsbury, London, was just shutting up shop after midnight, September 29, when six well-known thieves, under the leadership of a notorious returned "transport" called Corrigan, entered the shop. Corrigan aimed a pistol and fired, but Mr Rearden fortunately stepped aside, and the bullet struck the landlady of a beerhouse. Still more fortunately for this innocent bystander, the ball rebounded from the steel of her corsets, leaving her severely shaken but otherwise unharmed. Their plan thwarted, the thieves immediately ran off.

The following afternoon Mr Rearden saw Corrigan enter Church Lane again. Without hesitation he seized the villain, disregarding the revolver in his hand. Corrigan was dragged to the police station where five bullets were found in his weapon.

Irish Terrorists Storm Police Van: Murder Sergeant

TWO FENIAN terrorists were released from a police van by their comrades at the cost of a police sergeant's life. "Captain" Healey came to England with "Captain" Deasy hoping to lead 28 fellow-Fenians from America in a rising. The 28 foot-soldiers, however, were arrested in Ireland.

Healey and Deasy were picked up in Manchester. As a prison van was taking them to jail, about 30 Fenians ambushed it. Peter Rice scrambled on to the roof, forced open a ventilator, and shot Sergeant Brett, the prisoners' escort. A woman prisoner was forced to take his keys and release Healey and Deasy, who escaped with Rice and the majority of the terrorists.

But police operations led to the arrests of Edward Condon, William Allen, Philip Larkin and Michael O'Brien, all of whom were convicted of murder, since they had co-operated in a felonious act which led to the death of a victim.

Condon, an American citizen, was reprieved and released following requests from the American Legation. But Allen, Larkin and O'Brien were executed on November 24.

The Fenian assault on the police van in Manchester

New Attempts to Check Irish Terrorists

FOLLOWING THE Clerkenwell Prison outrage, Scotland Yard is taking new measures to combat Fenian terrorism. Richard O'Sullivan Burke, second-in-command to the American terrorist "Captain" Healey (*see* 1867) was arrested in London last December, and placed in Clerkenwell Prison. Dublin Police warned Scotland Yard that an attempt would be made to release Burke by blowing up the exercise yard wall. The hour would be between 3.00 and 4.00 pm, and the attempt would be signalled to the prisoner by a white ball tossed into the air outside the wall.

It is hard to say who were the more incompetent, the infiltrated conspirators or the forewarned police. The former attempted a rescue on December 12, placing a barrel alongside the wall in full view of the public and a passing policeman, only to find the fuse was damp. They took their bomb away unmolested!

The following day they came back again, and successfully detonated their explosives. But Burke's exercise period had been changed, and he did not escape. Had not the general exercise time been altered, many prisoners would have been killed in the excessive explosion which destroyed

Bomb damage caused by Irish terrorists' assault on Clerkenwell prison

sixty yards of prison wall and several houses. In addition, 120 people were injured and 12 died.

Early this year, Michael Barrett was arrested in Glasgow and identified as the man who lit the fuse. He was hanged at Newgate on May 26.

The police apology for failing to prevent the explosion is that they expected it to come from a tunnel under the wall. The Home Secretary acknowledges that the Metropolitan Commissioner Richard Mayne blundered, but will not remove

him from office, as he retires in the course of nature next year.

Meanwhile two senior civil servants have been recruited from Dublin to work with the Home Office in keeping the police up to the mark in the checking of Fenianism in Britain.

Swain Batters Vicar and Shoots Servant — All for Love

AFTER VISITING his sweetheart in York, England, young Todmorden check weaver, Miles Weatherill, took home her likeness and half a jet necklace link as a love-token. His lady-love retained the other half as a charming emblem of the bond between them.

Then he went with four pistols and a small axe to Todmorden Vicarage. When the Rev. Anthony Plow appeared, Weatherill fired at him, but his pistol flashed in the pan without going off. Mr Plow wrestled with the youth and secured the pistol, whereupon Weatherill savagely battered him with his axe until the vicar fled, bleeding profusely.

Inside the vicarage, Weatherill shook off servants who tried to restrain him, and shot housemaid Jane Smith as she cowered in the dining-room; then attacked her with his axe. She died shortly after the assault. Upstairs, Weatherill

fired a pistol into Mrs Plow's pillow as she lay in bed. Then he beat her face and head with a poker, until the arrival of help summoned by Mr Plow. Weatherill was perfectly satisfied with his work, trusting that he had killed both the Plows. (Mr Plow, in fact, died days later.)

There was, it seems, a motive for the young man's inhuman barbarity. Like almost all respectable Christian employers, the Plows did not allow their young female servants to have "followers".

Apparently Jane Smith informed her employers that Weatherill was walking out with his sweetheart who was a fellow-servant. The virtuous Plows promptly dismissed the girl. Weatherill is content to hang for showing his detestation of moral servitude.

James and Younger Families Unite in New Gang

A DARING BANK robbery in Russelville, Kentucky, was the work of an alarming gang from the ranks of the former Confederate "Guerrillas".

In March this year, a tall handsome man calling himself "Mr Colburn" twice tried to exchange forged notes for large sums at Nimrod Long's Russelville Bank. On the second occasion, the Missourian, who described himself as a cattle dealer, was accompanied by a shabbier blue-eyed companion, who familiarized himself with the bank's layout.

It is now clear that "Mr Colburn" was actually Thomas Coleman ("Cole") Younger, a former Quantrill's Raider (*see* 1861). Younger was a dedicated Confederate whose post-war banditry has been lightened by charm and gallantry, especially if his victims are patriotic southerners.

His more charmless companion was fellow Quantrill raider Jesse James (*see* 1863) who, with his elder brother Frank, has been engaged in train and bank robberies since these crimes were devised three years ago.

On March 19, James and Younger came into town with five other men, and took hotel rooms. The following day the two went into the bank again, and Younger presented his third and last counterfeit bill. As it, too, was refused, the bandits pulled their guns and fired at Mr Long as he raced for the door. James's bullet creased his scalp, and the villain pounced on the bank manager, hammering his head with the pistol.

But Long fought back and made good his escape, calling for aid, while the bullets of the two desperadoes (who seem very poor marksmen) splintered the door-jamb behind him.

Younger and James helped themselves to $14,000 in currency. They loaded their booty onto a horse, while the rest of the gang rode wildly up and down firing at passing citizens. Finally the outlaws galloped away and split into smaller groups before a posse could be mounted to chase them.

If the James brothers have combined with Cole Younger and his brothers, we predict that the territories are in for a hot time!

Jesse James (right) and Frank James with their mother, Mrs Zerelda Samuel

Newspaper Editor Killed: Killer Acclaimed

AS MR H. RIVES POLLARD, editor of the *Southern Opinion* walked to the newspaper's office in Richmond, Virginia, a hail of shot from an upstairs window facing the building felled him. Mr Pollard died soon afterwards.

The assassin was well known to the whole town. Recently the *Opinion* had taken to printing salacious gossip and innuendo about leading ladies in Richmond society. When they printed such an attack on the daughter of the town's leading tobacco merchant, Mr W.H. Grant, the young lady's brother challenged Pollard to a duel. The editor refused. Young Grant then openly stated his intention of shooting the man who would neither retract nor defend his words. Evading police observation he took the room which became his vantage-point.

A coroner's jury has mendaciously attributed the murder to "a person unknown". Grant is a popular hero. And Pollard went to his grave without a single mourner at the funeral.

Cole Younger, partner of the Jameses

Thieves Strangle Lonely Birmingham Spinster

AT 7.00 pm on January 21, Mrs Bullock of Heneage Street, Birmingham, England, saw three men climb over the yard wall of her neighbour, Miss Mary Milbourne. They detected Mrs Bullock's presence, for one said: "There's a damn' woman and she will 'blow' on us!"

When police arrived, they found Miss Millbourne's house ransacked and her body at the top of the cellar steps. She had been manually strangled.

It seems certain that the robbers were aware of the large sum of £615 she had recently received. They were foiled, however, as she had deposited it with Messrs Lloyds' bank.

Despite Mrs Bullock's description of the men, Birmingham police hold out little hope of tracing them.

"THERE'S A DAMN' WOMAN AND SHE WILL 'BLOW' ON US!"
Murderer of Miss Milbourne

QUOTE

Murderer Turns Himself In after Eighteen Years

The execution of William Sheward, the wife-killer of Norwich

TAILOR **WILLIAM SHEWARD** killed his wife in 1851 – and got away with it! Her body was scattered in pieces around Norwich, England, and thought to be the remains of a very young woman. That eliminated Martha Sheward, whose husband told friends she had run away to London. Martha was 55.

Sheward was a drinker in an unhappy marriage. Martha feared ruin. William was certain that something would turn up, and his business could be placed on a sound footing with fresh capital.

Toward the end of 1851, Mr Sheward was visited by the local constable asking after Mrs Sheward. The tailor told him that he had no idea where she might be found in the metropolis. The constable re-

gretted this. Mrs Sheward had been left an inheritance of £300, but had to claim it in person.

Mr Sheward brooded for the next eighteen years, during which time he remarried and had two fine sons. But early this year, guilt and dismay overcame him. He went to the authorities and confessed that he had murdered his wife with his tailoring shears, and hers had been the scattered remains so erroneously identified as coming from a young person. He had killed her just three months before she would have inherited the fortune that might have saved their marriage and his business.

The unsympathetic authorities tried him for murder, and he was hanged at Norwich in April.

WILD BILL'S ALLEGED MARKSMANSHIP

While most western badmen are hopelessly poor shots, and rely on catching their victims at close quarters from behind, Wild Bill Hickok has been known to hit the human target he intended from a distance of 75 yards .

But his other alleged feats of marksmanship with his pistol are clearly suspect. Shooting the pip out of the ace of spades at 50 yards distance is quite beyond the capability of the clumsy long-barrelled pistols used by westerners. Spinning a silver dollar in the air and putting a bullet through it, is beyond the Newtonian capability of the two pieces of metal, which would simply dent each other if our hero ever succeeded in making them coincide.

Wild Bill Hickok Kills Again, in Nebraska

WILD BILL (formerly "Duck Bill") Hickok (*see* 1861) is back in the news. He has been using his guns in various parts of America's western territories, and successfully killed his friend Dave Tutt at a distance of 75 yards, in a quarrel over a woman. Bill's Falstaffian powers are undiminished, and Tutt is now "a savage outlaw"!

Early this year, Hickok was (remarkably) elected sheriff of Ellis County, Nebraska, and killed a genuine criminal. A drunken troublemaker called Sam Strawan took over a saloon, pitching most of the owner's glasses out on the street. Hickok mildly carried some back in, remarking: "Boys, you hadn't

ought to treat a poor old man in this way."

As the sheriff turned to the bar, Strawan started to draw his gun on Hickok's unguarded back. But Wild Bill spotted the move in the mirror, and shot Strawan before his gun was clear of its holster. Despite this achievement, he was voted out of office again in November. The brave sheriff was intolerably extortionate in the bribes he extracted from brothels and gambling-halls.

> "BOYS, YOU HADN'T OUGHT TO TREAT A POOR OLD MAN IN THIS WAY."
> QUOTE Wild Bill Hickok

Frenchman Murders Husband, Wife and Six Children

IN SEPTEMBER this year, the bodies of a decapitated woman and five children were found in a field outside Paris. She was identified as Mme Hortense Kinck of Roubaix, who had been enquiring after her husband Jean, at a Paris hotel on the 19th of that month. M. Kinck and his eldest son Gustave had disappeared.

Investigators traced a Paris cabdriver who told them a young man and a woman with five children had taken his cab past the Flanders Gate very late on the night of September 19. They stopped about a mile outside the city, where the adults and two of the children walked off into the night, leaving the other three to wait for them with the driver.

They told him the woman was their mother, and her friend M. Troppmann was helping them look for their father. After a little while the young man came back alone, took the children, and dismissed the cab.

Jean-Baptiste Troppmann was traced to Le Havre where he was attempting to escape the country. He was in possession of a great deal of Jean Kinck's property, and he told the police that wealthy brush manufacturer Kinck and Gustave had killed Mme Kinck and gone

Troppmann pulled from the water where he flung himself to escape the pursuit at Le Havre

into hiding on learning of her adultery. This story was rapidly disproved by the discovery of Gustave's body, close by where his mother and siblings had been buried. Finally, in November, M. Kinck's body was discovered in

Alsace. He had been poisoned with prussic acid.

It appears that Troppmann lured Kinck to an empty chateau proposing a counterfeiting scheme. In fact he had envied Kinck's wealth and success ever since meeting

him, and after killing him, sent a message in his name asking Hortense and the children to go to Paris.

Troppmann is now trying to explain away his actions and lies to the courts.

Paris Murderer Trapped by the Flow of Water

M. GUSTAVE MACÉ, the Parisian policeman, has proved murder by a triumph of deduction and experiment. When the legs of a missing craftsman named Bodasse were found in a well in the Rue Princesse, M. Macé noticed that they were professionally stitched into calico bags. And he

learned that the house using the well was often visited by a tailor named Pierre Voirbo, who farmed out work to a tailoress in the upstairs apartment.

M. Macé visited Voirbo who had been an acquaintance of Bodasse, and found some purloined securities of Bodasse's. He had no evidence that Voirbo had murdered Bodasse, but he was convinced the man had been dismembered in Voirbo's scrupulously cleaned room.

M. Macé thereupon tipped a small jug of water over Voirbo's tiled floor. Where the water collected, he had the tiles lifted. Underneath he found, as he anticipated, coagulated blood.

Voirbo confessed that he killed Bodasse when he refused to lend him money. Voirbo has now killed himself while awaiting trial.

'Bridget Fury' alias Delia Swift, Virago of New Orleans, Jailed

SINCE THE disappearance of Mary "Bricktop" Jackson after her release from prison seven years ago (*see* 1861), Delia Swift of Cincinnati has been the savagest virago in New Orleans. In the 1850s she and "Bricktop" terrorized sailors on the night-time streets. She soon earned the nickname "Bridget Fury".

In 1858 she received life imprisonment for murder, but the general amnesty of 1862 which returned Bricktop to liberty and dis-

appearance, also put Bridget back in business.

A few years ago she gave up robbing, pocket-picking and selling her unlovely body anonymously in the streets, and opened a brothel. Here she was arrested this year for robbing two Texan visitors. A fixed abode is not an advantage to a thieving whore!

Miss Fury has gone to prison again, and it is hoped she may emerge tamed and disappear like her hideous predecessor.

Rich Philanthropist Found Battered By Blasé Killer

ON JULY 28 this year, dissolute young Washington Nathan, who had spent most of the previous night drinking and fornicating with a young lady of the streets, went downstairs in his father's mansion on West 23rd Street, New York, for a glass of water to relieve his alcoholic dehydration.

Passing his father's bedroom he glanced in, and saw the wealthy philanthropist lying on the floor, his face and clothes covered with blood.

Benjamin Nathan, sometimes described as the richest man in New York, had been battered to death with a carpenter's fanged grappling-iron. There had been a struggle in the room before he yielded, and subsequently a safe had been forced open. The murderer's bloody handprint was on the wall, and a basin of water on the dresser showed that he had calmly cleansed himself before taking leave of his victim's body.

Suspicion instantly fell on Mr Washington Nathan, whose profligate extravagance has led to many quarrels with his father. But in this instance his vices served him well. Since Mr Benjamin died fully clothed he presumably encountered his killer before his normal bedtime. And at that hour young Mr Nathan was still in the arms of Venus, as the bad little lass willingly testifies.

So the case remains a mystery.

Trial by Acclamation: *Vox Populi* Gives its Verdict

AN EXTRAORDINARY example of the makeshift legal proceedings permitted in the unfederated American frontier territories took place in Iowa this August.

A man named Miller murdered a Mr Dunn and stole the money on his person. Miller was chased to Council Bluffs, arrested, and taken back to Ponca.

While he was in jail, a local clergyman, the Rev. Mr Beardshear, visited him, and Miller expressed his willingness to confess the entire crime. Mr Beardshear enthusiastically assembled three hundred people in the church, and Miller was brought before them in custody of the sheriff.

The congregation sang a hymn. They listened to a reading from the Bible. Mr Beardshear offered a prayer. And Miller stood before the company and admitted that he had robbed Dunn and killed him.

The Minister then put it to popular vote to decide whether or not Miller should hang. The assembly agreed that he should. Mr Beardshear donned full clericals to lead a procession out to the hastily constructed scaffold, and the unfortunate criminal was amateurishly executed, strangling slowly on the short rope, so that he twitched in agony for twenty minutes.

Americans place a high value on their democratic traditions. But we cannot help feeling that the advice of members of the bar and the directions of Her Majesty's judges, may better safeguard the interests of criminals and victims alike than a popular vote in a crowded church, after an emotional confession without examination! Although London's hangman, Calcraft, is notorious for his short drops, he does know how to hang on to his victims' legs to accelerate their demise and hasten their journey to meet their maker.

English Village Family Killed During Sunday Service

DURING MAY, the congregation at Denham parish church were puzzled when neither Emmanuel Marshall the blacksmith, his mother, his wife, nor any of their four daughters turned up for matins one Sunday.

The following evening neighbours discovered the explanation. Knocking unanswered at the Marshalls' door and finally breaking in, they perceived a frightful spectacle. Mrs Marshall lay dead in the hallway, her face completely battered. Two of her little girls lay dead at the bottom of the stairs. In the parlour, old Mrs Marshall sat dead in her chair, holding the body of the youngest child. The other daughter, it soon transpired, was staying with friends.

The immediate conclusion was that the unhappy Mr Marshall had destroyed his family in a fit of madness. But further searching revealed his body, equally battered, lying in his workshop. House and smithy alike had been locked and the keys removed. This proved fatal to John Jones, a drunken tramp seen hanging around Denham on Saturday evening. Police traced him to Uxbridge and Reading, and arrested him when they found him in possession of Mr Marshall's boots, watch and doorkey.

Jones denied everything, saying a stranger had given him these things. The claim availed him nothing, and hangman Calcraft executed him on August 8, when Jones surprised the public by remarking: "I am going to die for the murder of – what's his name? I forget. I am innocent."

A collection has been taken up to erect a memorial to the Marshall family in the village churchyard.

Rubbernecks gather for a good gawp at the site of the Marshall murders

Horrible Discovery at London Lost Property Office

ON SEPTEMBER 21, a box covered in light paper was sent by rail from Manchester to Carlisle, addressed to "Mr Newson, County Hall, Carlisle, To Be Left Till Called For."

On December 10, as it was still uncollected, the stationmaster at Carlisle sent it down to the Lost Property Office in Euston. There it was opened, and proved to contain the decomposed bodies of two children, wrapped in a copy of the *Manchester Guardian*.

Dr Joseph Hill, surgeon at the St Pancras Workhouse, carried out autopsy examinations, and reported that the children appeared to be twins, a boy and a girl, approximately nine months old at the time of their death. Their faces and heads are horribly mutilated, probably with a hatchet. But their death was caused by violent suffocation. They may also have been given chloroform or some other volatile poison.

This dreadful overkill of two innocent babes cannot, it seems, be brought home to any person. The railways' latest contribution to crime as a dumping ground for murder victims, seems even more horrible than their exploitation by violent robbers.

IN BRIEF

JEAN-BAPTISTE TROPPMANN (*see* 1869) guillotined for the murders of M. and Mme Kinck and their six children.

Swiss Porter Claims He Killed the Devil

TWENTY-THREE-YEAR-OLD Jacob Spinax came to Britain from Switzerland two years ago, and found employment as night-porter at Bruecker's Hotel, Christopher Street, London.

Spinax's conduct was covertly immoral: it sems he habitually smuggled prostitute Mary James into his room to consort with her, until he discarded her and transferred his attentions to her friend Cecilia Aldridge.

On Friday, December 15, his misconduct became overt. He went to a brothel in City Road, got drunk, and kicked up a row when he found his money had been stolen. A complaint to magistrate John Humphreys earned him a stern lecture on the folly of visiting houses of ill-fame, and an apparently chastened Spinax went back to Bruecker's for his usual night shift. He refused his deputy's offer to relieve him, and went down to his basement room.

At 8.30 in the morning the hotel was aroused by the sounds of smashing china and shouting from Spinax's room.

Mrs Bruecker went down to investigate, and found a wild and dishevelled Bruecker on the stairs who told her in German a lot of men led by the devil had attacked him, but he had beaten them off and killed the devil. He had not. He had killed Cecilia Aldridge, battering her terribly after a dreadful struggle.

It remains now for the courts to decide whether this formerly mild young man was drunk, mad or feigning hallucination to cover his crime.

City Road where murderer Spinax caused an affray in a brothel

The Dilessi Massacre

THE GREEK BANDITS who kidnapped Lord Muncaster's party of April 11 have assassinated their unfortunate hostages and made good their escape. It seems no serious attempt will be made to bring them to justice.

Lord and Lady Muncaster organized a picnic expedition to view the battle site at Marathon. Local militia were to escort them through the worst brigand territory, but their guide, none the less contrived to bring them unarmed and unprotected into the most dangerous plains.

After abducting the entire party, the bandits allowed the women and Lord Muncaster to make their way back to Athens to arrange a ransom. His lordship's repeated attempts to exchange himself for his friends have all been refused.

When it became apparent that they could not escape into Euboea with their captives, the brigands shot diplomats Edward Herbert and Alberto de Boyl, a young friend of Lord Muncaster, Frederick Vyner, and barrister Edward Lloyd in full view of pursuers near the town of Dilessi. Not even Prime Minister Gladstone's lack-lustre support for British interests abroad gave any expectation of such an outrage on Her Majesty's gallant subjects.

Greek bandits kidnap Lord and Lady Muncaster near Marathon

The Mad Spinster and the Naughty Doctor

Mad Christianna Edmunds pops poison in the mouth of Mrs Thomas Beard, her lover's wife

FOUR-YEAR-OLD Sidney Barker died in Brighton, England after eating peppermint creams his uncle bought him. Unsurprisingly, as they were filled with strychnine. He was not the first person to receive poisoned gifts.

Several people in the town received cakes through the post with teasing anonymous notes saying: "You will know who these are from."

One lady who claimed to have received such gifts was 42-year-old Miss Christianna Edmunds. But her doctor's wife had also received special cakes, labelled: "Those done up are flavoured on purpose for you to enjoy." When Mrs Thomas Beard's servants fell ill after eating some of the cakes, Dr Beard realized that a difficult patient with whom he had enjoyed a tender correspondence was trying to kill his wife.

Miss Edmunds fell in love with Dr Beard at first sight on Brighton promenade, and believed that her glance perpetrated a similar *coup de foudre* in the physician's breast. She took her ailments to him, and became his intimate correspondent. She also became difficult and jealous. When she realized that the doctor had told the police of the poisoned cakes sent to Mrs Beard, she sent out other lethal anonymous gifts, and hired boys to take poisoned chocolate creams back to the confectioner's shop on

QUOTE

" THOSE DONE UP ARE FLAVOURED ON PURPOSE FOR YOU TO ENJOY. "
Christianna Edmunds

the pretext that the doctored ones had proved to be the wrong size. Her hope was that the authorities would imagine some maniac was trying to poison all and sundry in Brighton. In fact, Miss Edmunds is the maniac! During her trial it became clear that severe hereditary insanity exists on both sides of her family, and her mother has never doubted that the poor woman is quite mad. In consequence she has been sent to an asylum for life, though some vengeful shopkeepers of Brighton would willingly have hanged the unfortunate lunatic who threatened to damage their holiday trade!

Evil New York Bar Closed After Seven Murders

THE "HOLE IN THE WALL" saloon, between Dover and Ward Streets, New York, has been closed. For 20 years this vile dive has been the most dangerous place in Fourth Ward. Strangers were mugged, beaten and thrown out on the street. Muggers who killed their victims were expected, as a matter of courtesy, to remove the body in a cart.

For many years, public order was maintained by one-armed Charley Mornell in partnership with a 6-ft English harridan called "Gallus Mag" (her "galluses" being the men's braces with which she kept her skirts up).

She punished troublemakers by biting off their ears, and kept the trophies pickled in alcohol behind the bar. One came from a man who rudely asked her age

The joint's most notorious fight was between two ruffians called "Slobbery Jim" and "Patsy the Barber", who quarrelled over 12 cents they had taken from a passing pedestrian they knocked out before drowning him in the harbour. Jim bit off Patsy's nose, before cutting his throat and kicking him to death.

But now the Hole in the Wall has gone too far, and the authorities have ended its evil days.

Famous Fossil Proved to be a Fraud

THREE YEARS AGO, William Newell of Cardiff, New York, "discovered" the fossil of a colossal man on his farm. He and his cousin George Hull exhibited it in a tent, claiming this was scientific evidence of the Bible's claim that once there were giants on earth.

Several scientists confirmed that the Cardiff Giant was a genuine fossil, though the president of Cornell University expressed doubts.

Last year, Mr P.T.Barnum, the showman, had a sculptor carve a replica, after the cousins refused to lease him the original for $60,000. Hull and Newell came to New York and started proceedings to prevent Barnum from showing his competing "giant".

But their action interested the press, and investigative reporters have proved that Hull employed a Chicago stonecutter to manufacture the original from gypsum, staining it with ink and sulphuric acid, giving it the appearance of great age.

So Barnum is in the clear: he is only exhibiting a copy of a fraud not the original as thought. It is Hull and Newell who have to explain themselves!

The ghastly murder of betrayed and jilted housemaid Jane Clouson on Eltham Common

Horrible Murder in Greenwich Outrages Citizenry

THE POOK FAMILY of Greenwich, London has been forced to move, so strong is local feeling against them. The populace is highly dissatisfied with young Edmund Pook's acquittal at his trial for the murder of Jane Clouson.

Seventeen-year-old Jane worked for the Pooks as a housemaid. It is not disputed that 20-year-old Edmund overcame her virtue, and the unfortunate girl found herself enceinte earlier this year. It is known that she hoped the young master would make an honest woman of her, and on the night of her death she was going to meet him. She was found later, crawling along Kidbrooke Lane beside Eltham Common with her head battered and one eye hanging from its socket. She died in Guy's

Hospital without giving a clear account of what had happened.

Circumstantial evidence against Edmund was strong. There was mud and blood on his trousers. A witness identified him as a man seen running from Kidbrooke Lane. A shopkeeper claimed to have sold him the bloodstained hammer found near the scene of the crime. But Edmund's claim to have spent the entire night in amorous longing outside the house of another young lady in Greenwich could not be positively disproved, and he benefited from a miniscule "reasonable doubt" in the jury's mind.

The Pook family still hopes that some one else may prove to have been Jane Clouson's murderer. The people of Greenwich hold no such expectation.

The Reverend Headmaster Turns Killer

THE REV. JOHN SELBY WATSON retired last year. For 25 years he was head of a grammar school in the Stockwell district of south London, building it up and improving its standards to the satisfaction of the governors. But as the Rev. Mr Selby reached the age of 66 enrolment started to fall, and the governors made him retire. The unfortunate man had no pension and no assistance from his church. He faced sudden poverty.

Some years earlier Mr Watson married an eccentric young Irishwoman, and Ann Watson did not take kindly to her husband's reduced circumstances. She berated him; taunted him, too, with the fact that the corpulent cleric no longer found himself able to carry out his marital duties in her bed. During one of these painful confrontations, the reverend gentleman seized his pistol and shot his wife. Then he shut himself in his room for two days and took a dose of poison, which failed to kill him. He has been found guilty of murder, but with a recommendation to mercy which has ensured that he will not be hanged.

It seems an awful warning to scholarly clerics against marrying high-spirited young women, and keeping loaded firearms in their bedrooms.

'Wild Bill' Strikes Wildly Again!

WILD (or "Duck") Bill Hickok has gone for his guns again. As Marshal of Abilene, Kansas, he mortally wounded a gambler named Dave Coe: then swung round, guns blazing, when he heard footsteps behind him. The great gunman thus despatched his deputy, Mike Williams, who was rushing to his aid! Abilene has expelled its trigger-happy policeman!

Prostitute Murdered in Great Coram Street

HARRIET BUSWELL, an unfortunate who plied for trade at the Alhambra Music Hall, Leicester Square, in the heart of London's West End, was found strangled in her bed in Great Coram Street on Christmas morning. An apple with a single bite taken from it lay on her dresser. It was hoped that toothmarks might identify her killer. But it seems these were made by the young lady herself.

On Christmas Eve, Miss Buswell was seen several times with a client: on an omnibus; at a restaurant; in a cab; and ascending the stairs of her lodgings. Several witnesses believed the man to be a foreigner, and a description assembled from their accounts was then circulated.

This elicited recognition from Ramsgate, where a German brig of emigrants intending to colonize South America put in for repairs shortly before Christmas. It seemed that the description matched Herr Wohlwebbe, the ship's engineer, who (among other officers and officials) took the opportunity to visit London over the Christmas holiday.

However, the witnesses who went to Ramsgate with a police inspector, failed entirely to identify Herr Wohlwebbe. Instead they declared the man they had seen was the Rev. Dr Hassell, the ship's chaplain, who voluntarily insinuated himself in the Identification Parade! Since Dr Hassell and his wife also spent the festive season in the capital, the police now have the embarrassing task of investigating a devout foreign Protestant pastor, accused of lewdly accosting and ultimately murdering a woman of the lowest moral standing!

IN BRIEF

THE BRITISH PARLIAMENT'S new Licensing Act has closed the Haymarket Night Houses. Kate Hamilton's in Coventry Street, Rose Barton's and Cooney's of Panton Street are no more. They may not trade after midnight, and young swells refuse to go earlier for overpriced champagne in the public rooms and a few minutes in a private room with a soiled dove.

Hence ladies like Harriet Buswell now meet clients in the Leicester Square music-hall foyers.

"Jubilee Jim" Fisk, murdered by Ned Stokes after row over a singer

Railway 'Robber Baron' Killed by Patrician Rival

JUBILEE JIM FISK made his fortune partnering Jay Gould in the Stock Exchange "theft" of the Erie Railroad. He made his popular reputation buying the New York Grand Opera House and making buxom singer Josie Mansfield his mistress.

Since Jim kept other chorus girls in other apartments, Josie had no qualms about sharing her favours with Social Register swell Ned Stokes. No harm need have been done, had not the two men quarrelled over business, during which dispute Fisk made uncomplimentary remarks about Stokes which appeared in the newspapers. Stokes sued for libel.

Fisk countersued, claiming that Stokes and Josie were blackmailing him. The popular press was delighted to report the story that the two men had fallen out over the appropriation of Josie's charms, as well as the disposition of money and bonds. Fisk's counsel gave Stokes a very hard time before the grand jury.

Over lunch on January 6, Stokes learned that he had been indicted and would stand trial as a blackmailer. Furious at this aspersion on his good name, he seized a revolver and went to the Grand Central Hotel where he shot Fisk in full view of the public.

Three murder trials followed. In the first the jury could not agree. In the second, Stokes was convicted and sentenced to death. When he won a third on appeal he had the conviction reduced to six years for manslaughter.

Sensational Ending to English High Society Libel Case

AFTER EIGHT DAYS in the High Court, Lady Twiss, wife of Professor Sir Travers Twiss, has abandoned her case, withdrawn her charges, and taken herself to the continent.

It is not disputed that solicitor Alexander Chaffers, after encountering Lady Twiss by chance, sent in bills for alleged past "services rendered". It is not disputed that when Lady Twiss refused to pay any more, Mr Chaffers told the Lord Chamberlain that it was he, Chaffers, who had paid for her past services when, as Marie Gelas, she had been a prostitute in Brussels.

Sir Travers and Lady Twiss denied the charge resoundingly, insisting that they met at the house of her father, Major-General Van Lynseele of the Polish army. Lady Twiss added that there was a Mme Gelas who had chaperoned her in Brussels. And when Chaffers insisted that there was no such chaperone, and Lady Twiss is an experienced strumpet whose cubicular arts have raised her to chaste court circles, she started proceedings for criminal libel.

The judge sympathized, telling Chaffers (as every gentleman must feel), that he will always be an object of contempt to honest and well-thinking men. But Lady Twiss's retreat in the teeth of victory suggests that the slippery solicitor was telling the truth – and milady was not! As the law now stands, Mr Chaffers' extortions are no offence if his charges were true.

We fear Sir Travers did a-wooing go in some murky frog-ponds!

Lady Twiss — Polish army officer's daughter or Belgian harlot? — with her husband and accuser

Crimean War Hero's Kept Woman Murdered

A LITTLE BIRD tells us that Lord Lucan, who ordered the Light Brigade to "Charge for the guns" at Balaclava, has lost the companion of his midnight hours. Mme Riel of 13 Park Lane, London, was not available to invite visitors to tea on April 7.

The following day, her body was found in a cellar pantry. A rope around her neck had apparently been placed as a handle to drag her body into concealment after she had been battered to death in the open space at the foot of the cellar stair.

Money was missing from the house. So was Belgian servant Marguerite Diblanc.

This woman, who was extradited from France to stand trial, confessed that she had struck Mme Riel down in a rage and killed her when she was given a month's notice but only a week's wages. The hot-tempered Belgian housemaid has been sentenced to life imprisonment.

But we understand that Mme Riel's rent was paid by Lord Lucan. That noble and gallant gentleman will now need another head to lie beside his own on his pillow.

BLACKMAIL, EXTORTION AND LIBEL

The cases of Lady Twiss and Ned Stokes highlight a gap in British law which appears to have been plugged in America.

Surely the extortion of money with menaces should be seen as criminal, even if the menace threatens the reputation rather than the pocket? Of course Lady Twiss ought not to have been presented at court if she was once a prostitute. But surely Mr Chaffers' action in extorting money for his silence should be seen as criminal as well as ungentlemanly?

In New York, Jim Fisk was able to suggest that Ned Stokes was bringing improper pressure to bear on him in a business dispute, and that this amounted to blackmailing extortion. And, although Fisk was undeniably a bounder and Stokes is a gentleman, he was winning his case.

British jurisprudence left Lady Twiss no redress but the libel laws, which apparently allow anyone who finds a skeleton in a closet to squeeze the owner dry.

We urge Parliament to rectify this situation.

Record-Breaking English Murderess Hanged at Durham

MARY ANN COTTON, hanged in Durham Prison on July 24, was a singularly bereaved lady. Twenty-one people in her immediate circle have died over the last 20 years.

A year ago, Mary Ann's stepson died. A doctor, made suspicious by the circumstances, refused to issue a death certificate until the child's body had been examined. Post-mortem analysis discovered arsenic.

Police learned that during the previous year Mary Ann's other stepson had died, as had: the boys' 39-year-old father, Frederick Cotton; a lover of Mary Ann's named Joseph Natrass; and Mary Ann's six-month-old baby. Mary Ann had no good explanation for her own purchases of arsenic. And went deservedly to the gallows.

But a survey of her life over the last twenty years shows that whenever this monster tired of a husband or lover – (and she had more of both than most) – the unfortunate fellow was likely to die; whenever she needed a small inheritance, an appropriate family member would pass away; whenever her children seemed too much trouble, the little darlings were fetched away to heaven.

Fourteen murders are confidently ascribed to this woman; a 15th is probable. So single-handedly she has committed as many murders as William Burke and William Hare did together some 40 years ago, and if but two more of her 21 suddenly-deceased relatives died at her hand, then she exceeds their conjoint total and will become Britain's worst mass killer, as she is certainly England's.

'Wickedest Man in San Franciso'

REPORTS IN the *Times* of London that "Ned Allen, the wickedest man in San Francisco" has died, may conceivably point to the fate of John Allen, heralded in *Packard's Monthly* ten years ago as "the wickedest man in New York".

Throughout the 1850s and '60s, "Allen's Dance House" on Water Street was one of the most depraved houses of ill-fame in the city. Allen and his wife employed 20 prostitutes who wore bells on their ankles – and precious little else to obscure their nether regions.

A former seminarian, and brother of three clergymen, Allen introduced hypocritical piety into his operation, placing Bibles and tracts in the cubicles where his girls entertained their clients.

As Allen included hymn-singing among his brothel's activities, it was not unduly surprising when ministers of religion took over the hall for prayer-meetings.

But Allen had not truly reformed. He was hiring fake "sinners" to the evangelists, and when he was exposed he disappeared yet again.

He has been variously reported as emerging in full wickedness in other places; and we wonder whether he has now come to a bad end in California or will he still be continuing his wicked ways.

Phoney Death Made Real After Failed Fraud

WHEN WINFIELD GOSS'S rented Baltimore cottage burned down in February, the inventor apparently failed to escape the conflagration, caused by an exploding oil lamp. Goss's brother-in-law William Udderzook had gone to a neighbour to borrow another lamp because Goss's was acting up.

Goss held a $25,000 life insurance policy, but the company delayed settlement, suspecting that the burned body in the cottage was a cadaver from a medical school. Dental examination suggested that it was not Goss.

In June, Goss's body was found in a shallow grave near Jennerville, Pennsylvania, where he had stayed at a hotel with Udderzook. Blood in their room led to Udderzook's arrest, and he confessed to murdering his brother-in-law who was threatening to expose their joint insurance fraud scheme when in his cups.

Murder at Smutty Nose, Norwegian Women Murdered

EARLY THIS YEAR, 28-year-old Louis Wagner, a fisherman of Portsmouth, New Hampshire, told friends he was so desperate for money he might murder for it. In March he did.

He rowed ten miles to Smutty Nose, one of the Isles of Shoals, where the Hontvet family lived. They had sheltered Wagner in the past after a disastrous fishing trip. He had stayed with them for a couple of weeks, coming to be regarded as a friend by the hospitable Norwegians; the island's only inhabitants.

The men of the family were away at sea, and Wagner broke into the house where their womenfolk slept. Karen Christiansen who woke up and mistook Wagner for her brother-in-law was felled with a single blow. Her sister Maren came running in and attacked the assailant. Then sister Anethe woke up and shouted, "Louis! Louis!" at the man she recognized.

Wagner seized an axe and silenced her. Maren ran outside while he killed Karen. Then, with the bodies of his former hostesses lying on the floor, Wagner cooked and ate a meal before ransacking the house, in which he found $20.

Maren spent the night looking for a boat with which to row to another island for help. Wagner rowed himself back to Portsmouth, where after a search a bloodstained shirt was found in his lodgings by the men Maren had aroused on nearby Appledore Island who came looking for him with the Hontven men.

Maren identified him positively at his trial in July, and Wagner's denials were weakened by the heavy blistering on his hands caused by 20 miles of rowing in one night.

German Family Robbed, Raped and Slew Wayfarers

The Benders' "hotel", where 20 or more travellers were murdered and thousands of dollars' worth of property was stolen

A man suspected of being Johann Bender

JOHANN BENDER'S lonely "hotel" on the prairy near Cherryvale, Kansas, was just a shack. A crude canvas curtain down the middle divided the "general store" at the front from the sordid "dining and bedroom" at the back. Visitors ate seated on a long bench with their backs to the curtain.

If they were strangers on the trail west, Johann's lively young daughter Kate held them in conversation, which she suddenly punctuated with a cry of, "Now!"

This signalled 60-year-old Johann or his son to swing a sledge-hammer against the curtain, cracking the traveller's skull. Then Frau Bender would join her revolting family in dragging the body into the tornado shelter under the building, where it was stripped and robbed.

Three years ago the Benders simply dumped their victims out on the prairies. But when the law prohibited leaving cattle carcases unburied, so that gatherings of vultures became an uncommon sight, prudence dictated burials around the hotel.

This year former army scout Col. A.M. York, came to Cherryvale looking for his brother who had disappeared on the trail.

Though the Germans disarmed his suspicions, they were unnerved and fled. Their disappearance was noticed, and the sinister Bender tornado shelter led the colonel's men to dig up the property.

The missing Dr York's body was found, along with nine others; also the body of a beautiful little girl who had been raped by both Bender men before being tossed alive into her father's grave.

The Colonel's party rode in pursuit of the "Hell Benders", and claim not to have found them.

It is believed, however, that the finest scouts in the southwest did catch this evil family, and exacted immediate condign punishment, hiding the bodies successfully.

The reward may be offered too late

New and Horrible Crime: Kidnapping Child for Blackmail

$20,000 REWARD

Has been offered for the recovery of Charlie Brewster Ross, and for the arrest and conviction of his abductors. He was stolen from his parents in Germantown, Pa., on July 1st, 1874, by two unknown men.

DESCRIPTION OF THE CHILD.

The accompanying portrait resembles the child, but is not a correct likeness. He is about four years old; his body and limbs are straight and well formed; he has a round, full face; small chin, with noticeable dimple; very regular and pretty dimpled hands; small, well-formed neck; full, broad forehead; bright dark-brown eyes, with considerable fullness over them; clear white skin; healthy complexion; light flaxen hair, of silky texture, easily curled in ringlets when it extends to the neck; hair darker at the roots,—slight cowlick on left side where parted; very light eyebrows. He talks plainly, but is retiring, and has a habit of putting his arm up to his eyes when approached by strangers. His skin may now be stained, and hair dyed,—or he may be dressed as a girl, with hair parted in the centre.

DESCRIPTION OF THE KIDNAPPERS.

No. 1 is about thirty-five years old; five feet nine inches high; medium build, weighing about one hundred and fifty pounds; rather full, round face, florid across the nose and cheek-bones, giving him the appearance of a hard drinker; he had sandy moustache, but was otherwise clean shaved; wore eye-glasses, and had an open-faced gold watch and gold vest-chain; also, green sleeve-buttons.

No. 2 is older, probably about forty years of age, and a little shorter and stouter than his companion; he wore chin whiskers about three inches long, of a reddish-sandy color; and had a pug-nose, or a nose in some way deformed. He wore gold bowed spectacles, and had two gold rings on one of his middle fingers, one plain and one set with red stone.

Both men wore brown straw hats, one high and one low-crowned; one wore a linen duster; and, it is thought, one had a duster of gray alpaca, or mohair.

Any person who shall discover or know of any child, which there is reason to believe may be the one abducted, will at once communicate with their Chief of Police or Sheriff, who has been furnished with means for the identification of the stolen child.

Otherwise, communications by letter or telegraph, if necessary, will be directed to either of the following officers of

PINKERTON'S NATIONAL DETECTIVE AGENCY,

Viz: BENJ. FRANKLIN, Sup't, 45 S. Third St., Philadelphia, Pa.
R. A. PINKERTON, Sup't, 66 Exchange Place, New York.
F. WARNER, Sup't, 191 and 193 Fifth Avenue, Chicago, Ill.
GEO. H. BANGS, Gen'l Sup't.

ALLAN PINKERTON.

Philadelphia, September 1st, 1874.

(POST THIS UP IN A CONSPICUOUS PLACE.)

Wm. F. Murphy's Sons, Stationers, Printers, 509 Chestnut St., Philada.

Pathetic appeal for information about kidnapped Charlie Ross

SINCE THE SUMMER, Mr and Mrs Christian K. Ross of Philadelphia have been in anguish over the unknown fate of their pretty four-year-old. Little Charlie Ross was stolen from his home on July 1, and an anonymous note demanded $20,000 for his safe return. It also warned Mr Ross not to go to the police.

Naturally the distraught father had already done so. But this may have led the suspicious criminals to break three elaborately arranged appointments to receive the ransom. They would, in fact, have been taken by police had they shown up.

In the meantime, New York detectives discovered that the handwriting on the ransom notes matched those of a known burglar, William Mosher. On December 13, Mosher and another man, Joey Douglas, were shot and fatally wounded while attempting a burglary in Brooklyn. Before he died, Mosher confessed that he and Douglas had indeed kidnapped little Charlie Ross. But he refused to say where the child was to be found.

Mr and Mrs Ross continue to hope beyond hope that their child is alive and well. New York police are doubtful. An ex-policeman named Westervelt is suspected of having been associated with Mosher and Douglas in abducting the child. But he is confessing nothing, and the fear is that the pretty little boy who has no further financial value to the villains who stole him must now be dead.

The Town That Dreads the Resurrection

ALTA TOWNSHIP, Utah territory, is different from the staid Mormon settlement in Salt Lake. The silver miners' settlement sports a sign reading: "Welcome to the Meanest Little Town in the West".

Its huge cemetery justifies the sobriquet. Despite avalanches and mining accidents, the largest contingent of bodies – well over 100 – are those who have died in gunfights.

Last year a smooth-tongued stranger came to town claiming that he had the mystical power to raise the dead. Terrified of the vengeance battles that would ensue if the gunslingers re-emerged, the miners collected a bribe of $2,500 to persuade this charlatan to leave!

Boy Condemned to Solitary Confinement — For Life!

FOURTEEN-YEAR-OLD murderer Jesse Pomeroy has been reprieved from hanging. But so dreadful are his offences that the court has ordered that he is to be held in solitary confinement for life: a penalty of unmatched inhumanity for modern times in America.

Pomeroy fell under immediate suspicion when 10-year-old Mary Curran disappeared in March, and 4-year-old Horace Mullen's body was found in the Boston suburb of Dorchester in April. Thirty-nine stab wounds disfigured the child, and his head was almost severed from his body.

Pomeroy had been released from West Borough Reform School in February, having served two years there for a series of crimes of monstrous cruelty to other children. The 12-year-old tied boys up and beat them unconscious. He stripped one naked and broke his nose with a board, knocking out several teeth. Another lad was tied to a telegraph pole and cut with a knife after he had been beaten. One victim's wounds were doused with salt water. Three were tortured with pins and knife-points.

Since those victims of 1871 and 1872 survived, they could describe their assailant, and Pomeroy, who has a hare-lip and a discoloured white eye, was swiftly arrested.

After Pomeroy had confessed to Horace Mullen's murder his mother, a grocer, moved house. The new tenant discovered Mary Curran's decomposing body in the cellar.

This dreadful child criminal is now paying a dreadful penalty.

Guillotined French Herbalist Poisoned Two Wives

AS A HERBAL pharmacist, Pierre-Desiré Moreau found an uncommon poison with which to dispatch his two successive wives. Copper sulphate. The first Mme Moreau, a penniless individual, died after a short illness, three years into her marriage. Nobody at the time thought anything of her husband's treating her. After all, most apothecaries treat their families when necessary. And a herbal apothecary seems a particularly safe purveyor of traditional remedies.

Yet now it is believed that Moreau did away with her, having his eye on a highly suitable replacement.

His second wife brought a substantial dowry with her, but only half of this passed directly to Moreau. The remainder was held in trust, only to pass to him in the event of her death.

When Mme Moreau fell ill early this year, she confided to friends that she suspected her husband was poisoning her. After her death, the body was exhumed and found to contain large quantities of copper. The first Mme Moreau was therefore disinterred and examined. She, too, yielded copper in abnormal quantities.

A pharmaceutical treatise in Moreau's shop had a passage on the toxic quality of copper sulphate marked, this was regarded as conclusive evidence and the 32-year-old herbalist was arrested.

Nobody doubted that this ambitious man's motive was the acquisition of the whole of his second wife's dowry. Instead, he has been guillotined, to the satisfaction of a large crowd which gathered for the execution in Paris on October 10.

Cannibal Mountaineer Caught, But Escapes Again

WHEN COLORADO mountain guide Alferd Packer turned up at Chief Ouray's Indian camp near Los Pinos in November last year, the chief advised him that the weather was too bad for him to continue into the mountains with his party of 20 travellers from Salt Lake City. Half the party took the chief's advice and turned back. The other half offered Packer a bonus to press on.

In February, the chief's wisdom was proved. Two of the Salt Lakers staggered into his camp, half-dead. They and two others had decided they could face no more of the blizzards: the other two had perished in attempting the unguided return.

In March, Packer returned to the camp, exhausted. He told how his party of five had abandoned him when he started suffering from frostbite and snow-blindness. Chief Ouray listened to his story of the terrible journey, and grunted: "You too damn fat!"

The wise old redskin's suspicions were taken up by others. Packer had money to burn; he had the knife and gun of one of his clients; and a Wells Fargo draft made out to another. He was placed tentatively under arrest.

When the snows cleared in April, excited Indians came into camp bearing strips of "human meat" they had found. Packer now made a rambling confession. He claimed that the oldest member of the party, Isaac Swan, had died. He contradicted himself as to whether he was murdered by outsiders or died of starvation. He claimed that the party had insisted on eating his flesh and dividing his money ($2,000). Thereafter they killed off the weakest until only Packer and Shannon Bell survived. And Packer luckily won their duel to the death.

An expedition to the mountains found the bodies and proved Packer's story to be self-interested lying. All but one of the men had been killed from behind, and the fifth had been shot after a struggle. Packer's camp remained, with a trail showing that he had gone back to the bodies repeatedly, stripping them of meat while he waited for the blizzards to ease.

But before this murderous cannibal robber could come to trial he escaped from captivity, and his whereabouts are now unknown.

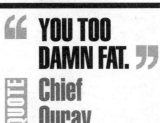

IN BRIEF

WILLIAM UDDERZOOK (*see* 1873) hanged for the murder of his brother-in-law Winfield Goss, asked to be buried near his victim "so that our spirits may mingle".

Brushmaker Takes Chorus Girl in Cab With Corpse

Businessman Henry Wainwright in the dock (left) between two warders during his trial for murdering his mistress

WHEN LONDON chorus girl Alice Dash stepped out of the Whitechapel Pavilion, she was flattered that businessman Henry Wainwright, invited her for a cab drive. Wainwright explained that he had to take some things from his old warehouse over the road down to Southwark, where he was renting space in Hen and Chickens building to store everything he could retain from the failure of his Whitechapel brushmaking company.

Wainwright was well known in the neighbourhood as a pious and popular amateur entertainer, giving improving monologues.

Elderly Alfred Stokes, long a Wainwright employee, handed up some parcels, and Wainwright lit a cigar to cover their unpleasant odour. Nor did the lady notice that Stokes chased the cab all the way to Borough High Street, trying to attract a policeman.

In the Borough, a policeman listened to the old man's story, and then asked Wainwright what was in the parcels. Wainwright immediately offered him £100 to go away and forget all about it!

Alice was arrested with her host when the policeman found rotting human remains in the parcels. But she was soon released as it became apparent that she knew nothing of the bankrupt brush manufacturer's doings.

Wainwright took Harriet Lane as his mistress in 1871. He set her up in various houses around the East End, and she bore him two children. But her extravagant drunkenness became more than he could tolerate, especially as his business began to collapse.

When Harriet disappeared last year, he told friends she had gone to Brighton, and then to the continent to marry a Mr Teddy Frieake. The friends continued to look after her children.

Wainwright's bankruptcy enforced his removal from his Whitechapel premises. Neighbours were already complaining of the smell emanating fom his Vine Court warehouse: and now it is clear that he had shot and battered Harriet, and buried her there.

His brother Thomas, who posed as Teddy Frieake to allay suspicion, and helped Henry dig and parcel up Harriet for the move, was given seven years' hard labour. The real Mr Edward Frieake, a former friend of the Wainwrights, was horrified to hear how his name had been abused.

Wainwright has been convicted and executed.

WAINWRIGHT'S EXECUTION

Whitechapel murderer Henry Wainwright went to the gallows bold and impenitent. He sat up through his last night on earth, smoking cigars and regaling his warders with naughty stories about his extensive love-life. And as he mounted the steps, he threw away his last cigar-butt, and said to the hundred or so people invited by the sheriffs to witness the hanging: "Come to see a man die, have you, you curs?"

Murder Case in Channel Islands Divides Jury

THE CASE OF Joseph Le Brun, hanged in Jersey on August 12, leaves a disquieting question in the mind. Le Brun was charged with killing his sister and injuring his brother-in-law near their home in St Lawrence last December. The trial was delayed to allow Mr Philippe Laurens, the brother-in-law, to recover from his injuries. And, to the end, he remained steadfast in his conviction that it was Le Brun who shot him and Mrs Laurens.

Yet Le Brun equally steadfastly denied it, charging his brother-in-law with being mistaken; asserting that he had no motive to harm his sister, and insisting that the only circumstantial evidence against him was his presence near the scene of the crime – which was unsurprising, since he lived thereby.

All this could be the hopeless denial of a guilty man. Yet the jury seemed indecisive in the face of this conflicting testimony, since they were unable to reach a unanimous verdict on the murder charge. They were, however, unanimous in convicting Le Brun of the attempted murder, and so he was hanged, still staunchly protesting his innocence.

Sympathy for James Boys' Mother after Bombing

LAST YEAR it seemed that some of the public in Missouri might at last recognize that the Jameses (see 1866) are not high-spirited ex-Confederate liberators, but sullen, brutal and murderous outlaws. In the course of the year the James-Younger gang killed three detectives and an unarmed bank cashier, and scalded to death the driver of a train they held up at Adair, Iowa, when the boiler burst as they turned it over.

Although farmers and smallholders admire the Jameses for robbing railroads, it is clear that the gang had gone too far. In the November elections, the newly formed "People's Party" which aims to woo commerce and investment back to the state, trounced the James-supporting Democrats.

This year Pinkerton's detectives learned that the James brothers were hiding out with their stepfather, Dr Samuel, in Clay County. On January 5 the decision was taken to flush them out.

A posse of Pinkerton's men surrounded the farm and tossed a fireball through the window. Dr Samuel quickly threw it on the fire, where it exploded violently. Dr Samuel was slightly injured. Mrs Zerelda Samuel, the James boys' mother, lost her right arm. Eight-year-old Archie Samuel died.

Jesse and Frank had already scented danger and left the place.

Public sympathy is now entirely on their side. Their own victims are forgotten in the outrage felt against Pinkertons for declaring brutal war on women and children.

Allan Pinkerton the famous detective

Italian Professor's Revolutionary Book About Criminals

THE MARCH OF science has made a great potential contribution to law-enforcement. Cesare Lombroso, Professor of Forensic Medicine and Psychology at Turin has published *L'uomo delinquente* ("The Delinquent") as the result of years of study, with countless phrenological measurements and detailed photographs of physical characteristics.

In a nutshell, Professor Lombroso says that criminals are born, not made. Instead of looking to wickedness or hardship as reasons for some men preying on others, the professor asserts that delinquency is a physiological abnormality: the delinquent is as precise an anthropological type as the Mongol or the Negro.

Professor Lombroso's careful observations describe the low sloping brow; the small close-set eyes; the somewhat simian appearance which warns that a man is a natural rogue.

Everyone may benefit from this major work. The police will no doubt train their eyes to spot marks of delinquency in the faces on the street. And all of us can protect ourselves more surely once we have learned to recognize a natural criminal by his tell-tale features.

Two criminals, drawn by Prof. Lombroso

Dance-Hall Hostess Makes Supreme Sacrifice

MOLLY BRENNAN, a 22-year-old dance-hall hostess at the Lady Gay Gambling Saloon, Sweetwater, Texas, has carved her niche in the annals of romance. Early this year, she was dancing with her latest beau, Bat Masterson, a civilian scout who works for the army. (Neither Bat nor Molly, we are reliably informed, normally restricted themselves to one love.) As the couple swooped and glided, the bar was stormed by Sergeant Melvin King of the 4th Cavalry.

A former lover of Molly's, he pulled his gun and fired at the couple as they separated. Molly immediately threw herself in front of her lover and received the bullet herself. As she fell, King fired again, shattering Masterson's pelvis. But the intrepid scout fired his own pistol, killing the sergeant and avenging his dying mistress.

Molly Brennan's memory is the toast of Texas, and gossips say Masterson was so moved by her sacrifice that he refused all offers of dalliance for a whole month after her death! (We can believe this: Bat's Shandeian injury came close to terminating his amatory career entirely!)

CRIMES OF THE NINETEENTH CENTURY

Murder or Suicide?
How did Charles Bravo Die?

Mrs James Cox (centre left) testifies at the inquest on Charles Bravo

THE SCANDAL almost outweighs the crime in the south London poisoning mystery – posing the question was there any crime at all? On April 18, as the household at The Priory, Balham, retired to bed, Mr Charles Bravo appeared on the landing, crying, "Florence! Florence! Hot water!"

His wife Florence, did not rouse. Her paid companion, widowed Mrs Jane Cox went to Mr Bravo's room and found him seriously ill.

Doctors over the next three days were convinced that Bravo had taken an irritant poison. But they could only prescribe an antidote if they knew what it was, and Bravo denied taking any drug at all, except a little laudanum rubbed sparingly on his gums.

Analysis of his organs after death discovered antimony. It transpired that he alone had drunk burgundy at dinner; also that the Bravos marriage had been unhappy, since Mrs Bravo resented the tight control her husband maintained over her fortune.

These points so exercised Mr Bravo's family and the public that an open inquest verdict was widely suspected of being a deliberate move to let Mrs Bravo escape. A second inquest was held.

At that, Mrs Cox electrified the nation by revealing that Florence Bravo had once been the mistress of famous hydropathic physician Dr James Gully, who moved to Balham to live near her. This time

the verdict was wilful murder, but the jury could not declare anyone guilty.

The difficulty is that while Florence and Dr Gully might both have been motivated to kill Charles Bravo, she had no access to antimony, and he had no access to The Priory. And it remains possible that Mr Bravo killed himself, knowing his wife never loved him.

Perhaps the most extraordinary suggestion is that frumpish, bespectacled Mrs Cox might herself have been the poisoner. The widowed lady has sons to support and was heavily dependent on her salary from Mrs Bravo. But Mr Charles Bravo was hopeful of dispensing with her services as a petty economy.

MRS BRAVO'S PAST

Before her liaison with Dr Gully, Florence Bravo was estranged from her first husband, alcoholic Captain Ricardo. He died of delirium tremens on the continent before his affairs could be arranged to exclude Florence from inheriting his fortune.

It may just be relevant that a small quantity of antimony was found in his body...

Cloaked Killer and Rapist Caught in Boston

WHEN 26-YEAR-OLD sexton Thomas Piper was observed taking 5-year-old Mabel Young into Warren Street Baptist Church, Boston, Massachusetts was at last freed from the terror that has hung over it since 1873.

For Mabel's raped and strangled body was found in the tower, and under questioning, Piper confessed that he had killed her and the other victims of the preceding years.

It all began on December 5, 1873, when a black-cloaked man clubbed Bridget Landregan to death, and was about to ravish her corpse when a passer-by scared him off. The same night, the man in the black cape battered and raped another young lady, who survived. The Boston Police Chief remarked to the press: "It is unseemly queer that only the nicest and most modest young ladies seem to get themselves raped."

Two more young ladies were subsequently killed, and others raped. Gentlemen abandoned the opera cape as a fashionable garment when Chief Savage ordered all caped men on the streets to be stopped and questioned.

Now the unprecedented scare is over, and those who wish to wear cloaks at night may again do so.

'Suburb of Hell' Destroyed in a Flash Flood

CALIFORNIANS can breathe a sigh of relief. Panamint City is no more. The single-street mining town came into being four years ago in a silver boom. Of all the west's wild towns it was the worst. Forty of its public buildings were gambling-hells; more were saloons; more still were brothels or prostitutes' cribs. In the brothels, men shot each other, wrangling over who got first go at new girls. Between two of the saloons, an iron sheet had to be installed between the walls to prevent shootouts in the Oriental from penetrating the lath and plaster and killing patrons next door in the Dexter (and vice versa)!

Wells Fargo refused to transport bullion from Panamint, so automatically were its coaches robbed. Eventually miners overcame this difficulty by welding their silver into vast balls that could only be rolled slowly down the roadway. Thus no robber could shift them quickly enough to evade capture. But the Heavens have spoken. Panamint City has been entirely washed away in a flash flood.

Attempt to Kidnap Lincoln's Body for Ransom

COUNTERFEITER Jim Kenealy and his gang dreamed up an extraordinary plot to secure the release of their master engraver, Ben Boyd, from prison. They set out to steal Abraham Lincoln's body from his mausoleum outside Springfield, Illinois, determined to hide it until Boyd was released and money turned over to them.

Fortunately an informer warned the Secret Service, and agents intercepted the gang just as they were extracting the coffin.

All escaped for ten days, but when they were arrested, Kenealy revealed his discovery that there is no law against stealing a buried body. The law rapidly used the loophole that had earlier been applied against British bodysnatchers, and convicted the men of attempting to steal a coffin!

Famous Western Gunslinger Shot

WILD BILL HICKOK IS DEAD. Dave McCall, a cross-eyed saddlebum, shot him as he played poker in Mann's Saloon, Deadwood, Dakota Territory. Hickok was studying his hand – pairs of aces and eights: a combination now known in the west as "Dead Man's Hand".

Hickok was reputed to be the best shot in the west. But when he joined Colonel "Buffalo Bill" Cody's "Wild West Show", his alleged parlour tricks of shooting the pip out of the ace of spades, or hitting a nickel spinning in the air, were actually beyond his powers, and he was reduced to delivering boastful Ned Buntline dialogue in silly minidramas. Since he was no actor, Hickok soon left the show and returned to the west where he was arrested several times as a vagrant.

This year he turned up in Deadwood with Martha "Calamity Jane" Cannarie, a big-boned prostitute from Fort Laramie who dresses in men's clothes. Hickok was living as a gambler, and feared that someone would make a name by shooting him. He surrounded his bed with crumpled paper so that any intruder should arouse him. And McCall was lucky to find him without his back to the wall and his eye on the door.

McCall claims to have avenged a brother whom Hickok had killed. A miners' kangaroo court instantly acquitted him of murder – so little do westerners think of their dead "hero".

Wild Bill Hickok

Stauntons Reprieved – Naughty Alice Goes Free

Louis Staunton and his mistress, Alice Rhodes

FOUR YOUNG PEOPLE appeared in the dock after 36-year-old Harriet Staunton died in lodgings at Penge on her way to the London Hospital in April, where her baby son had died of starvation and neglect a week previously.

Mrs Staunton was emaciated, filthy and lousy. Her mother, who always opposed her marriage, demanded an investigation. And when her 24-year-old husband, whiskered Louis Staunton agreed to postpone the funeral, he rapidly found himself arrested and charged with murder by neglect.

It transpired that auctioneer's clerk Louis married Harriet for her £3,000 fortune. As she was feeble-minded with distasteful habits, he soon ceased to live with her as man and wife, but not before making her pregnant. He took his sister-in-law Elizabeth's sister Alice Rhodes as his mistress, while brother Patrick (an unsuccessful artist) and Elizabeth looked after Harriet in Kent. For this service, Louis paid them £1.10s.0d per week.

Over the next few months, Harriet's mother and others formed the impression that she was being ill-treated and underfed. She was shut away in an upstairs room on her own, and visitors were not allowed to see her. When the baby died, the Stauntons panicked about Harriet's condition and sought speedy medical treatment for her, but they were too late.

Their conviction was greeted with universal approbation. But the law had to take cognisance of medical testimony that Harriet may have died naturally of meningitis, and they have been reprieved. The men will serve life sentences for her murder. Elizabeth Staunton serves a shorter sentence for manslaughter. Alice Rhodes, who is carrying Louis' natural child, has been released.

Louis Staunton is particularly penitent, accepting his punishment of life imprisonment as well and truly merited.

South London Man Beaten and Murdered Near Penge

WILLIAM SAUNDERS, a 34-year-old gas company labourer, was found on Sunday, March 25, kicked to death and thrown into a pond near Penge Cricket Club. He spent the previous evening drinking beer with his next door neighbour until 9.00 pm, after which his 45-year-old wife gave him a shilling and told him to go and amuse himself.

He was seen by a girl named Ann Winn, quarrelling with his lodger, young James Dempsey, at about 10.00 pm.

Dempsey is engaged to Jane Inman, Mrs Saunders' daughter by a former marriage, and being unemployed he, like Mrs Saunders and her six Inman children, was entirely dependent on Saunders.

Mrs Saunders, her eldest son Alfred Inman, and Dempsey all made unsatisfactory statements to the police. At first they claimed that Inman and Dempsey had been in-doors all evening. Later, as witnesses came forward who had seen them, they said that Inman had been drinking in the pub, and Dempsey had gone out briefly to buy some whisky, and they had forgotten this when first questioned by the police.

After a visit from Dempsey, Ann Winn, changed her story and said she really could not be sure now it was he she had seen with Saunders.

But since weeks have passed without Dempsey's and Inman's clothing being examined for mud or bloodstains, it seems unlikely that evidence will be assembled to prove the reasonable suspicion that these two young men killed William Saunders.

Hard Labour for Three Scotland Yard Men

CHIEF INSPECTOR Nathaniel Druscovitch, Chief Inspector William Palmer and Inspector John Meiklejohn have all received two years hard labour – the maximum sentence possible – after the longest criminal trial ever at the Old Bailey had found them guilty of corruption. Inspector George Clarke, who was acquitted, has resigned from the force.

The men were caught when brother-officers found extraordinary difficulty in arresting confidence tricksters Harry Benson and William Kurr this spring. The two had been detected in the "Royal Bank of London" fraud practised on the Comtesse de Goncourt. She had been persuaded that they were acting for a London gambler, whose success in backing horses meant bookmakers would no longer take his bets. She agreed to place large bets for him from Paris, and return his winnings in the form of cheques drawn on the "Royal Bank of London". When the Comtesse observed "Mr Montgomery's" success, she started backing his fancies with her own money, as the fraudsters hoped.

But when she needed to transfer yet larger sums to the "Royal Bank of London" and went for advice, it transpired that the bank, like the London bookmaker with whom the bets were placed, was a wholly imaginary entity consisting of some blank cheque forms and letterhead specially printed to deceive her!

Benson and Kurr escaped police attempts to arrest them in London and Glasgow, and were only taken by the Dutch police when they fled to Rotterdam.

Back in England Benson revealed that senior detectives had been in his pay since 1873. Meiklejohn was the first to fall, accepting payments from Benson with which to meet gambling debts, and warning him in return whenever the CID was on his trail.

The trial of the detectives: Benson testifies in convict uniform

Druscovitch joined the conspiracy next. Clarke and Palmer were the last to meet this Mephistophelean figure.

After this scandal, the whole detective force is to be reorganized.

Madame Pattia, the diva: victim of one of Benson's frauds

CRIMINAL INVESTIGATION DEPARTMENT

There have been permanent plainclothes policemen investigating crime in Britain since 1842, when the week-long disappearance of murderer Daniel Good aroused concern that hastily disguised policemen could not catch him. The senior detective officer, Superintendent Adolphus Williams, is unblemished by the Benson and Kurr scandal, and will remain in place. But a young barrister, Mr Howard Vincent, who has made a study of Paris police organization, has been called in to reform the section. He will become head of a new, permanent "Criminal Investigation Department" with direct responsibility to the Commissioner and the Home Secretary.

Mormon Bishop Executed 18 Years After Massacre

IN 1857, a large party of settlers entering Utah were attacked by Indians at Mountain Meadows. About 20 of them had been killed when Mormon Bishop John D. Lee, Indian agent for the territory, arrived with a group of horsemen. He halted the battle and offered to escort the wagon train to Cedar City.

As soon as the settlers had laid down their arms, Bishop Lee and his men joined the attacking Indians in turning on them. Of the 140 men, women and children in the party, only 17 children, too young to bear evidence, survived. Brigham Young, the redoubtable Mormon chieftain, feared that the Mormons' exclusivism and hatred of "Gentiles" would be severely punished if the truth emerged. He directed his people to withhold all assistance from the enquiry, although he discreetly excommunicated Lee and some of his lieutenants.

This year, the federal government at last amassed sufficient evidence to bring Lee to trial. He was convicted and executed by firing squad on March 23 at the site of the massacre.

These New York Gangsters are Like Pranksters

NEW YORK POLICE are acting to curb the "Molasses Gang". These thieves practice one crime only. They enter small stores, where one of them takes off his hat and asks for it to be filled with molasses, explaining that they are wagering on how much it will hold.

When the proprietor has filled the headpiece, it is clapped on his head and pulled down so that he is blinded by the streaming treacle. While he struggles to free himself, the gang robs his till and pilfers his wares at leisure.

South London Robber was Yorkshire's Missing Murderer

English Rancher Shot in New Mexico Trade War

PC Robinson struggles with the murderous, and inappropriately named, burglar Charley Peace

CHARLEY PEACE has been caught. The Banner Cross murderer, who disappeared in 1876, had taken up residence in Peckham as "Mr Thompson", organizer of domestic musical evenings where he played hymns on his violin. (His respectability was marred by the presence of Mrs Peace as "Mrs Ward, the house-keeper"; "Mrs Thompson" being another, younger mistress!)

At night Mr Thompson went abroad with his violin case full of housebreaking tools, and carried out audacious burglaries.

Two policemen spotted his flashlight in the darkened rooms of a Blackheath house at 2.00 am this October. They were joined by a sergeant, and kept watch until Peace emerged. PC Edward Robinson challenged him, and was shocked when the thief fired two pistol shots at him. Nevertheless, the constable grappled with Peace, receiving injuries in his arm and head from three further shots.

At the police station, Peace gave his name as John Ward. But as proceedings at the magistrate's court approached, police discovered that "Mrs Ward" had fled from Peckham, and "Mrs Thompson" confessed that her "husband" was really Charley Peace.

He has been sought by Sheffield police since November 1876, when he murdered Arthur Dyson. The Dysons were his neighbours in Darnall until Peace seduced Mrs Dyson and started treating her house as his own. The Dysons moved to Banner Cross to escape him, but he walked out of their new front door as they arrived with the moving van, saying, "I've come to plague you!"

And he did! slandering them throughout the neighbourhood until Mr Dyson swore out a warrant against him.

On November 29, Peace loitered outside the house until Mrs Dyson came out to the communal toilet at the end of the terrace. There he approached her. She screamed, and Dyson ran out, whereupon Peace shot him dead and ran off into the night.

Peace grovelled before the court in London and was spared the hangman's noose. He was sentenced to life penal servitude for the attempt on PC Robinson's life. He has yet to be tried in Yorkshire for the Dyson murder.

COMMERCIAL COMPETITION, beloved of classical economists, is carried to its logical bellicose conclusion in the American West. Businessmen and landowners hire armies of gunmen to shoot down their rivals. Businessman Lawrence Murphy of Lincoln, New Mexico, resented cattleman John Chisum challenging the cozy control of prices Murphy's "House" managed with the Sante Fe dealers and officials. When Murphy sold The House to ambitious merchants James Doland and James Riley, who tightened its monopolistic price-fixing, Chisum put up a strong challenge, aided by lawyer Alexander McSween, and English rancher John Tunstall. Tunstall privately hoped to take advantage of the cutthroat competition and secure monopoly powers in New Mexico himself!

But Doland and Riley persuaded a corrupt sheriff to issue a warrant for Tunstall's arrest, and the posse that went after him caught him on foot and gunned him down when he was unarmed.

Tunstall's ranch-hands, already physically threatened by Sheriff Brady and other House roughnecks, feel they are in a fight to the death for survival. They are led by a 19-year-old tearaway named William "Billy the Kid" Bonney, who has killed at least one man in a private quarrel. The ferocious "Kid" promises to make Lincoln County's strife as memorable as the conflict of York and Lancaster.

Bodysnatchers 'Kidnap' Millionaire's Corpse for Ransom

ALEXANDER TURNEY STEWART, multimillionaire merchant of New York City, who died in 1876, is not resting in peace! Buried in the graveyard of St Mark's-in-the-Bouwerie two years ago, Stewart was dug up again this year by greedy men with a strong commercial motivation.

The avaricious resurrection men who have taken possession of the captain of commerce's illustrious corpse have made known their demand for a ransom of at least $200,000 before they will consider returning it. Mr Tunney's family are negotiating with them via coded messages in the personal columns of the press, and it seems that this insalubrious crime will prove profitable to these heirs of Jerry Cruncher, the sack-'em-up men.

French Schoolmaster Drugs and Gases Wife

EUGENE CHANTRELLE'S career as a schoolmaster in England began in 1862. It was in tatters by last year. His dissipated ways inhibited parents from entrusting children to his care.

In 1868 Chantrelle seduced a 15-year-old pupil, Elizabeth Dyer. But he thereupon married her, and the couple had four children. The marriage was not happy. Chantrelle beat Elizabeth, and frequently said he would kill her, adding that he was clever enough to get away with it. Last year he did, and this year he didn't. (Kill her, that is, and then get away with it.)

Last year Chantrelle insured Elizabeth's life for £1,000. Soon afterwards, a servant found Mrs Chantrelle unconscious. Eugene tended her himself, and when medical help arrived there was a strong smell of gas in the room. Chantrelle claimed his wife had been overcome by fumes from a leaking gas pipe. But vomit on the bedclothes contained opium, and a post-mortem indicated that Mrs Chantrelle died of narcotic poisoning and not coal-gas.

Chantrelle never confessed, but he was known to have purchased a quantity of opium. He was hanged on May 31.

Best-Loved Outlaw in Texas Dies

AMBUSHED at Round Rock, Texas, popular outlaw Sam Bass was shot off his horse by Texas Rangers and mortally wounded. Bass was betrayed by gang member Jim Murphy, who fell to the lure of a huge reward for information. He was temporarily rescued by another comrade, Frank Jackson, who rode through heavy gunfire to carry him away to safety.

The next day Rangers found Bass dying under a tree. Following the traditional honour-among-thieves code, he refused to give information about his gang or their whereabouts, and died shortly after he had been found, on his 27th birthday.

Now the brief adventure of his life is over. But Bass is remembered in ballad: "Sam first came out to Texas, a cowboy for to be – A kinder-hearted fellow you seldom ever see."

Outlaw Sam Bass at the age of 16

OBITUARY

SAM BASS (1851-1878)

*S*am Bass came to prominence in 1876 when he gave up the life of an honest cowboy and joined two men in stealing cattle they had contracted to herd from Texas to Kansas. With their loot, the three went to Deadwood, Dakota territory, and opened a brothel described as "the most degraded den of infamy that ever cursed the earth".

Their own drinking, gambling and whoring sorely dented the joint's profitability, however, and the three recruited a gang to supplement their earnings by robberies.

A prize of $60,000 from a Union Pacific train enabled Bass to take his share of $10,000 and return to Texas, where his open-handedness made him a popular hero. He robbed in all corners of the vast state, and spent so freely that shopkeepers loved him.

Maid Boils Mistress — Sells her Fat as Dripping

KATE WEBSTER, a 30-year-old Irish domestic servant with several convictions for theft, resented being dismissed by her employer, Mrs Thomas of Richmond, London. So she disposed of her.

One Sunday this March, neighbours noticed Kate washing and cleaning Mrs Thomas's house instead of respecting the Day of Rest. On Monday, Kate visited Mr and Mrs Porter in Hammersmith: old friends she had not seen for fifteen years. They commented on her clothes and jewelry, and she said she had married well, and was now Mrs Thomas.

She asked their son Bobby to walk back to Richmond with her, helping with the heavy bag containing something about the size of a football she was carrying. Kate dropped the bag in the Thames off Hammersmith Bridge. But Bobby went home with her, and helped her fetch a heavy trunk out of the house and carry it to Richmond Bridge, where it too went in the river. Next day it turned up at Barnes Bridge, and proved to contain several bits of boiled woman.

Kate meanwhile was busily offering fresh dripping for sale in the neighbourhood...

Revisiting the Porters, she met publican John Church who found this big ugly woman attractive and put her reputation at risk by spending three nights in the house with her.

On the third day, Church and Porter were seen supervising van men removing Mrs Thomas's furniture. When neighbours remonstrated, they said they had Mrs Thomas's permission. To prove it they called Kate out of the house... and as neighbours exclaimed, "But that's not Mrs Thomas!" the murderess's imposture was exposed.

She fled forthwith, and made her way to Ireland, from which she was brought back to stand trial and undergo execution.

But the good people of Richmond don't like to think about the fresh dripping they bought from her...!

The execution of Irish domestic Kate Webster

Sheriff Ousted for Corruption after Triumphant Arrest

WILLIAM "BAT" MASTERSON, the sheriff of Ford County, Kansas, has been voted out of office, since his accounts show $4,000 spent on the care and feeding of prisoners over the last five months. As there were only seven jailbirds in his care, citizens refuse to believe public funds have been properly spent. The sum could hardly have been reached by serving the rogues unlimited turtle soup and caviar!

Yet only last year, Masterson led one of the West's most successful posses, bringing in James "Spike" Kennedy, heir to the massive King Ranch in Texas, for the murder of dance-hall hostess Dora Hand.

Dora was the leading madam of Dodge City, and the mistress of Mayor James "Dog" Kelley. Kennedy became infatuated with her, and after paying her lavish attention, was thrown out of the Alhambra saloon by the jealous mayor. Kennedy vowed revenge, and crept up on the mayor's wooden house at night to fire bullets through the wall into the bedroom.

By great misfortune, Dora, "the Queen of the Fairybelles" (as Dodge romantically names its harlots) was sleeping there alone, and the bullets struck her, killing her instantly.

Masterson took his good friend Wyatt Earp and several other gunslingers to trail the murderer, and when they saw him in the distance, the sheriff succeeded in knocking him off his horse with an excellent rifleshot. Earp then shot the horse.

Kennedy was taken back to Dodge, much chastened to learn that he had shot his lady-love and not her keeper. But his father's money hired lawyers who won him acquittal.

It is a little sad that, after such a success, one of the very few western lawmen who can fire a gun to useful effect has been exposed in lawlessness.

Bat Masterson, a corrupt but effective lawman

Charley Peace at Last Goes to the Gallows

> " IN MEMORY OF CHARLES PEACE WHO WAS EXECUTED IN ARMLEY PRISON... FOR THAT I DON BUT NEVER INTENDED. "
>
> QUOTE **Charley Peace**

BRITAIN'S WORST VILLAIN unhung isn't unhung any more. Charley Peace went to the gallows in Leeds for the murder of Arthur Dyson (*see* 1878) this February.

He did everything he could to save himself, even hurling himself from the window of the moving train which carried him from London to Yorkshire for his trial, after he had been granted momentary release from the escort to whom he was handcuffed when he expressed an urgent need to go to the lavatory. Throwing himself from the window he nearly died beside the track, in his handcuffs and convict's uniform.

He left a characteristically misspelled, self-serving and hypocritical memorial card for himself, which read: "In memory of Charles Peace who was executed in Armley Prison Tuesday February 25th 1879. Aged 47. For that I don but never intended."

Before his execution, Peace confessed to yet another murder; the shooting of PC Nicholas Cock in Manchester, who surprised him in the course of a burglary. This confession led to the immediate release of gypsy William Habron, who was serving life imprisonment for that killing! Peace, apparently, went to his trial and watched an innocent man approach the gallows for his crime.

It seems Peace always tied his pistol to his wrist so that it could not be forced from his grasp when he defended himself. He also enlivened his criminal career by stretching his hideous features into weird grimaces while in custody, so that no satisfactory description of him could be circulated.

For some unknown reason, this grotesque goblin of a man is being acclaimed as a "lovable rogue". When one has remarked that he embraced crime as a career after an industrial accident crippled him in his teens, and that he was a reasonably skilled amateur violinist and theatrical impressionist, one has said everything that can be proposed in his favour.

SQUALID PEACE, THE LAVATORY LOVER

Peace's career kept involving him in lavatorial crises. He was hiding in the outside lavatory when he surprised Mrs Dyson and shot her husband. And he tried to delay his execution by spending an inordinately long time in the prison WC before being led to the gallows. He grumbled that warders who urged him to come out needn't be in such a hurry; it was he and not they who was about to die!

'Fighting Pimp' Leaves City Where he was Marshal

WYATT EARP, deputy marshal of Dodge City, Kansas, has left the state and gone to Arizona. The reason, apparently, is that the brothels and saloons he ran with his brother James were no longer profitable. Though Earp has been a lawman for three years, he and his brother-officer, Bat Masterson, sheriff of Cochise County, are known as "the Fighting Pimps"!

Earp collected money from practically all the brothels south of the railroad tracks dividing Dodge. He was part-owner of a saloon run by his brother James, whose wife organized the brothel end of the business. His best-known piece of law-enforcement was shooting a drunken cowpoke called George Hoyt, who was trying to gun him down. Hoyt probably wanted the bounty put on Earp's head by Texan cattle-owners who suspected him of rustling!

The "Fighting Pimps" of Dodge City

'Bottle Imp' Disappears After Killing Chemist and Maid

M. LAGRANGE, pharmacist, of the Place Beauvau, Paris was found battered to death in his own cellar alongside his dead housemaid, Zelie Gaillot, on Monday, October 5.

It was clear who had committed the murder. The weapon lying beside them was a large iron pestle, which Lagrange's assistant, 21-year-old Arnold Walder used for exercising. Walder's blood-stained shirt lay in M.Lagrange's bedroom, from which his own shirts, together with his watch and 15,000 francs had been stolen. And in a letter posted from the Le Havre train, Walder confessed with an apology to Mme Lagrange.

Police promptly searched Le Havre and checked vessels leaving port. But the cunning Walder had doubled back to Paris, where initially he registered in a hotel under his own name!

Since then, four bottles have turned up in different canals and rivers around France, in which Walder's unmistakeable handwriting declares that he has committed suicide by drowning! The French public has no doubt he is alive and kicking, and grudging admiration for this elusive "Bottle Imp" is growing.

Irish Carry Out Sectarian Murders in Canada

THE BUTCHERY of a decent family in Lucan, Ontario, results from religious bigotry carried across the Atlantic. In this case, Catholic vigilantes murdered fellow-Catholics.

Sixty-nine-year-old James Donnelly was a devout Roman Catholic who, none the less, urged co-operation with Protestants. The potato famine of the 1840s drove him from Ireland. But Donnelly never concluded that all English Protestants were racial murderers.

This made him unpopular with more embittered immigrants. And he settled in a part of Canada dominated by the "Whiteboys" – extremist Irish Catholic vigilantes.

In the small hours of February 4, about 20 "Whiteboys" entered Donnelly's home, and killed him, his wife Johanna, and their children, Thomas and Bridget. Three miles away, another Donnelly was shot at his brother's house.

But the assassins were observed. The Donnelly's 11-year-old livestock boy, James Carroll escaped the massacre, and positively identified the leader of the invading brutes as James Carroll, the local constable.

The law-officer was brought to court with five others in October. But their fellow-bigots intimidated jurors, and no unanimous verdict was reached despite the clear and certain evidence of their guilt.

The bloodstained villains will be re-tried next year.

CATHOLICS AND CRIME

The Catholic community in England is not especially lawless, although the doctrine of universal membership, with Christ's salvation extended to even the most heinous sinners, entails the acceptance of some worshippers whose criminality would make them unacceptable to the Nonconformist sects.

As two cases this year show, Roman Catholic criminality in the Anglo-Saxon world is likely to be associated with political ideals. The Irish Fenians are not endorsed by their clergy, whose wish to be separated from Protestant England does not extend to approving of murder as a political weapon. Conversely, the Vatican's firm condemnation of godless Nihilism and Socialism may lead to violent anti-clericalism involving Catholics as the victims of violent crime.

Priest Arrests Sacrilegious Would-Be Assassin

ST PETER'S Roman Catholic Church, Hatton Garden, London (the Italian church), was the scene of an outrage on January 10. Father Adolphus Bakanowski was celebrating mass at 10.30 am, when 30-year-old asphalter Alexander Schossa walked in with his hat on, stood at a pillar near the sanctuary and said to the congregation, "Everybody leave!"

Then he fired a pistol at Father Bakanowski, who was at that moment elevating the Host. The altar-boy fled to the sacristy and locked its door behind him, so that Father Bakanowski could not enter.

Schossa fired several more shots at the priest, who ran to the centre of the church and made his escape through another door, followed by women worshippers.

Schossa then tore down candlesticks from the altar and trampled on the chalice. He wrenched open the door of the tabernacle, and pulled out the pyx which he battered. He scattered about 300 consecrated wafers around, and set fire to the altar cloths.

At this point, Father Henry Arkall came in. Schossa advanced on him, a pistol in one hand, a stiletto in the other. Father Arkall bravely seized his arms, and Elizabeth Brooks, the presbytery housekeeper, came to his aid, suffering severely cut hands in preventing Schossa from stabbing the priest.

Finally, with the help of some of the congregation, the villain was overpowered and delivered to the police.

Cardinal Manning preached at the church that evening. He referred to the desecration and ordered a Novena of Prayer. It seems that Schossa is a German-Swiss socialist who objected to an anti-nihilist pamphlet written by Father Bakanowski. He has admitted his intention was: "to kill the priest".

Cardinal Manning, Catholic Primate of England

Six People Shot in Coventry: All Survive

WATCHMAKER Oliver Styles went on a rampage in Coventry late in May. Entering the bar of the Half Moon Inn, Butts, he proceeded to the taproom where he drew a pistol and broke Henry Jennings' thigh with one bullet, and struck James Pellatt's hand with another.

In the bar, he fired a bullet into the landlady's back, and then escaped in the confusion.

Returning home, he shot his wife in the back, his mother-in-law in the temple, and his child in the arm.

Styles was arrested before he could commit further mayhem.

Fortunately all his victims survived. It appears that he was driven by jealousy, having become estranged from his wife.

Fruitless Detective Procedures in Manchester Murder

Shocking Discovery in Harley Street Cellar

A T ABOUT 7.00 PM on January 7, 19-year-old Jane Roberts, housemaid to Mr and Mrs Greenwood of Harpurhey, was heard screaming. Mr Greenwood was out at the time. Mrs Greenwood found the girl dead from a crushing blow to the back of the head. She thinks that two men made a rapid escape.

There were no footprints; no abandoned murder weapon; nothing was stolen; and there was no attempt to ravish Jane Roberts. The immediate assumption was that the motive must have been jealousy among the girl's clandestine followers.

The superintendent of police had a photographer take pictures of the dead girl's eyes, it being suggested that the image of her murderer would be fixed on her retina as she expired. Remarkable results suggesting this to be the case have been achieved with galvanized frogs in Italy. This experiment, however, proved inconclusive.

Visual technology was also used in lithographic facsimile reproduction of a letter received by Mr Greenwood on the morning of the murder. This asked him to meet the writer at The Three Tuns tavern that evening on business. When Mr Greenwood went, nobody kept the engagement, and it is suspected that this note was intended to lure him out of the house.

THE MURDERED GIRL SARAH JANE ROBERTS. (FROM PHOTO)

Manchester murder victim, Sarah Jane Roberts

With facsimiles displayed around Manchester, several people said the handwriting was identical to that on letters inviting people to subscribe to a scheme for assisted passage to Australia.

When the man who was touting this scheme left Harpurhey suddenly on January 9, police instituted a search for him.

Two weeks later 30-year-old Robert Haild was arrested in Plymouth, with Thomas Leycock. Haild had distributed the emigration information, and the two were brought back to Manchester. It was believed that Leycock had confessed to murdering Jane Roberts while Haild kept watch.

This story was lent colour by the lack of any obvious reason for Haild's suddenly deciding to leave England and emigrate to Australia. It seemed he might have helped Leycock take revenge on the girl.

But this proved false. It cannot be proved that Haild wrote the letter received by Mr Greenwood. Instead, Haild's wife and family produced positive alibi witnesses establishing his presence well away from the vicinity of Harpurhey at the time of the murder.

Despite the ingenious use of photography, lithography and handwriting comparison, the Manchester murder remains an impenetrable mystery.

The horrific discovery of the servant girl's battered body

U TTER MYSTERY shrouds the discovery of a woman's body in a cask, preserved in chloride of lime, in the cellar of no.130 Harley Street, London

The woman was about 45 years old, and her front teeth appear to have been sawn short. The house has been occupied by Mr Jacob Quintana Henriques for 25 years, and there is no question of his knowing anything about the matter. Nor is his butler, who made the discovery, in any way implicated.

The cask is of a kind used to deliver goods to the house. Mr Quintana Henriques has employed three butlers during the time he has lived there, and one of his previous servants may know something of the matter. But all investigations have so far proved fruitless.

The house of Mr Quintana Henriques

Ned Kelly: Australian Folk Hero and Bushwhacker

The Kelly Gang: (left to right) Steve Hart, Dan Kelly and Ned Kelly

Amazing Armour-Clad Bandits Let Bullets Bounce Off!

IN JUST TWO YEARS, Edward Kelly has become the most famous criminal Australia has ever known. And it will be many, many years before another Antipodean dims his memory.

After rising to notoriety with cop-killings and bank robberies at the end of 1878 and the beginning of 1879, the Kelly gang fell inactive for about a year. Then, in February 1880, farmers in Victoria suffered a series of most peculiar thefts. Somebody was pinching ploughshares!

Why?

A police informer explained. The Kelly gang were beating ploughshares into armour! Ned Kelly planned "to do something that will astonish the world!"

Irish Rebel May Have Planned State Coup D'Etat

Kelly has always bemoaned his father's Irish status and the supposed tyranny of English colonial rule. And he seems to have hoped he and his three companions might disable the Victoria State Police all on their own, permitting Irish settlers to throw off the "yoke" of colonial government.

At any rate, he declared: "I'm tired of running. We'll stand and fight! We won't give in."

To this end he forged the suits of crude armour, anticipating that the little band would stand up and pick off attacking police officers with impunity. To this end he tried to lure a mass force of police into a trap.

Murder of Aaron Sherritt

The Kellys knew their former associate Aaron Sherritt was giving police information about them. On June 26, Sherritt was hiding four officers at his shack near Beechworth. Joe Byrne and Dan Kelly abducted a drunk and forced him to knock on Sherritt's door and identify himself. When Sherritt came out, Byrne shot him dead.

It was assumed that the cops Sherritt was shielding would come to his aid, whereupon some of them would be killed: at least one survivor being spared to "escape" and rouse the main police force in Melbourne. In fact, the officers wisely refused to leave the shack. They all lived to pass on the bad news that the Kelly gang was fighting again, while Dan Kelly and Joe Byrne joined Steve Hart and Ned at Glenrowan.

The Kidnapping of a Township

In Glenrowan, the four gangsters simply took all the civilians in town prisoner, entertaining them royally as they held them in the hotel.

Glenrowan had no police station. It was vital to Kelly that any special train of police reinforcements for the beleaguered men

THE GANG

NED KELLY (1855–1880)
Eldest son of livestock thief "Red" Kelly. An excellent horseman, Ned Kelly had convictions for robbery; went straight for a time; then returned to cattle rustling until the police attempt to arrest him and Dan led to outlawry and the Stringybark massacre

DAN KELLY (1861–1880)
Ned's younger brother. Conviction for petty theft and "horse-borrowing". Leader of the sharply dressed "Greta mob" of poor farmer's sons when he joined Ned outside the law.

STEVE HART (1859–1880)
Another leading Greta mobster, he met Dan Kelly when in jail for "horse-borrowing". He and Dan became the muscle of Ned's gang.

JOE BYRNE (1857–1880)
Ned Kelly's best friend. Had literary turn of mind, but served six months for assault and cattle theft, in company with Aaron Sherritt who later betrayed the gang and was killed by them.

Before his final armour-clad shoot-out, Kelly's most amazing criminal innovation was the practice of holding huge numbers of hostages and entertaining them hospitably while robbery was taking place: twenty-two people at Euroa; the police of Jerilderie.

in Beechworth was bound to pass through it on the Belnalla and Wagaratta line.

Ned Kelly and Steve Hart made some railway workers rip up rails at a bend. They expected the police special to arrive and de-rail, leaving the policemen groggily at their mercy.

The plan failed because it took the police over a day to send their special. And by that time the gang's hands were so full with the 40 hostages in the little Glenrowan Hotel, that they failed to prevent one man from slipping out, and putting a home-made warning red signal on the line before the broken tracks. At 3.00 am a trainful of police disembarked at the signal, and advanced on the hotel. The Kelly gang were ready. They fired first and an officer fell. Then the police surrounded the building and poured bullets into it for fifteen minutes! They wounded many innocent hostages killing three. But not one of the Kelly gang.

The Man in Armour

In the darkness an astonishing figure lumbered out of the back door. Its head was the shape of a monstrous iron bucket, with a crude spade-like visor clumsily hinged over the face with nuts and bolts.

Below this, the man wore a frock coat, but his rivetted ploughshare breastplate showed dully underneath it. It weighed 97lbs, so the "knight" could only move slowly and awkwardly.

But Ned Kelly was moving out to the woods, where he expected rebellious hillmen to reinforce his beleaguered army.

While Ned was away, gang member Joe Byrne tilted his helmet visor up inside the hotel to drink a glass of whiskey. As

Ned Kelly, knight errant of the Australian Bush

he did so, a bullet struck him fatally in the groin. Dan Kelly and Steve Hart, assuming Ned had died, decided to run for their horses. They were too late, the police had shot them.

At dawn, Ned came back to the hotel. The hillmen who had promised to help him when the police train was wrecked never materialized. Ned could have escaped. Instead he came back to help his friends.

He advanced menacingly on the Senior Constable heading the police also, coincidentally, named Kelly. The astonished police officer fired repeatedly at the approaching tin monster,

and saw his bullets clang and bounce off the breastplate and helmet.

Until a charge of shot hit Ned in the leg, and he fell crying, "I'm done".

The arresting police asked why on earth he hadn't escaped once he was out. Ned's reply, in the tradition of the game and loyal bushwhacker was, "A man would have been a nice sort of dingo to walk out on his mates!"

Shortly before 10.00 am the police allowed the hostages to leave the hotel. Then, after some of the more desultory shooting at the two remaining gangsters, they set fire to the building.

They were too late. Dan Kelly and Steve Hart had killed themselves, realizing they were surrounded and helpless.

KELLY'S SHORT CRIMINAL HISTORY

1878

APRIL 15: Kelly family and friends injure a policeman in helping Dan resist arrest for rustling. Ned, possibly not present, and aggrieved at being charged with this. Dan escapes, and Ned joins him in outlawry.

OCTOBER 26: Ned and Dan, supported by Joe Byrne and Steve Hart of the Greta Mob, kill three policemen who try to arrest them at Stringybark Creek.

DECEMBER 12: Gang robs bank at Euroa, taking manger and his family back for a party at a nearby sheep station they commandeered, keeping 22 people there as comfortable hostages.

1879

FEBRUARY 10: Gang robs bank at Jerilderie, holding all police in station hostages and using their uniforms as disguise.

1880

JUNE 28: Final shoot-out at Glenrowan.

NOVEMBER 11: Ned Kelly is hanged.

Gunfight at the OK Corral

TENSION SPRANG UP over the past year between the Earp gang, in Tombstone, Arizona, and rowdy rustler associates of the Clanton family. Gambler-dentist "Doc" Holliday and the Earps had been robbing stage-coaches. When Wyatt Earp decided to pin the blame on three outlaws, he asked Ike Clanton to help by betraying the men. Ike agreed, but the plan went astray and the outlaws were killed.

At this point the Earps and the Clantons feared the exposure of their double-dealing, and mistrust between them grew.

On October 26, Marshal Virgil Earp learned that the Clantons were at an empty lot once used by the OK Ranch. He swore in Holliday as a deputy, and went with his brothers Wyatt and Morgan to the old corral, where he ordered Ike and Billy Clanton, Frank and Tom McLowery, and Billy Claiborne to surrender. The Clantons – none of them gunfighters – prepared to disarm, whereupon shooting broke out. It seems that Wyatt Earp fired without warning, injuring Frank McLowery.

Billy Clanton fired back, while Billy Claiborne ran for cover. Morgan Earp killed Billy Clanton. Ike tried to wrest Wyatt's gun away, only to be told: "Go on fighting or get away." Since Clanton was unarmed he, too, fled for shelter.

Doc Holliday blasted Tom McLowery with a shotgun, and turned his pistol on the injured Frank. Frank fired back, hitting the dentist's hip. But Morgan Earp despatched Frank McLowery with a bullet behind the ear. Billy Clanton went down shooting, and Wyatt joined Morgan in killing him.

The whole incident lasted about half a minute. It was, in effect, the murder of three unprepared men: the victory of the Fighting Pimps over the Rowdy Cowboys. Of such stuff is western heroism!

> **" GO ON FIGHTING OR GET AWAY! "**
> **Wyatt Earp**
> QUOTE

Tsar Alexander Asassinated in St Petersburg

ALEXANDER II, Tsar of All the Russias, died on March 13 when a bomb was hurled at him in the streets of St Petersburg.

The Tsar had just left his carriage to offer sympathy to the victims of a bomb flung a few minutes previously.

There had been three attempts to kill the Tsar over the last three years, but the authorities felt secure because they had just arrested the author of two of them.

The assassins appear to be "Nihilists", whose strange anti-philosophy denies that their actions or consciences are governed by familiar religious or moral codes.

Their preferred political theory is the equally extravagant "anarchism", which suggests that no government at all is necessary!

Death of Billy the Kid

IN 1878, young desperado William Bonney was working honestly as a cowhand for rancher Richard Brewer when he and all his co-workers were engaged by John Tunstall in the "Lincoln County War" (*see* 1878). On Tunstall's murder, Bonney swore, "I'll get every son-of-a-bitch who helped kill John if it's the last thing I do."

Despite this, "Billy the Kid" was a minor member of the 60-strong "army" that prosecuted the "war" on behalf of Tunstall's lawyer-partner, Alexander McSween. He did not become a leader until July 1878, when most of McSween's men deserted, and McSween himself was killed. During the intervening months, Billy was one of those who ambushed and gunned down Sheriff Brady in Lincoln, and one of a posse which killed three unarmed prisoners. With the leaders dead or bankrupted, the "war" ended, and the survivors agreed neither to fire nor inform on each other. But Billy broke this truce, betraying opposition gunmen to territorial Governor Lew Wallace.

His treachery backfired, and he was arrested and condemned to death for Brady's murder. But he escaped from jail by killing two sheriff's deputies. Finally on April 29, Sheriff Pat Garrett followed information to trail him to Fort Sumner and waited for the suspicious outlaw to creep in to a darkened bedroom, asking: "*Quien es?*" (Who is it?) He was shot before he could go for his guns.

THE FIVE CENT
WIDE AWAKE LIBRARY

"TRUE LIFE" OF BILLY THE KID

Billy the Kid: outlaw as hero

OBITUARY

'BILLY THE KID' (1859-1881)

AKA HENRY OR MICHAEL MCCARTY OR MCCARTHY AKA HENRY ANTRIM AKA WILLIAM H. BONNEY

Born in New York city, "the Kid" accompanied his mother to Indianapolis in 1865, and to Wichita, Kansas in 1870, where she married her second husband, William Antrim. In 1871 the family moved to New Mexico for Mrs Antrim's health, despite which she died of consumption in 1874.

Soon after her death, the Kid turned delinquent and joined Jesse Evans' desperadoes, adopting the name "William Bonney".

His youth and daring made him a popular hero for the last year of his life. He was free from racism, and spoke perfect Spanish among the Mexicans, whose dances he loved. Most of the community adored him, but his habit of sleeping promiscuously with their wives and daughters made him enemies, and two of these betrayed him.

President Garfield Dies of Bullet Wounds

Guiteau shoots dead President Garfield in the waiting-room at Washington railway station

PRESIDENT James A. Garfield, shot on July 2 at Washington Railway Station, by Charles Julius Guiteau, finally died on September 19.

During the election last year, Guiteau composed a campaign speech; posted a copy to Garfield, and distributed printed versions at meetings. When Garfield won, Guiteau believed that his "contribution" to the victory entitled him to be appointed ambassador to France! When his petitions went unanswered, he decided to kill the President.

His trial is taking weeks to complete, and has been adjourned over Christmas and the New Year to resume next year.

Second Railway Murder in England

PERCY LEFROY MAPLETON, emulating Franz Muller (*see* 1864), used a railway compartment for murder and robbery. Mapleton boarded the Brighton to London Bridge train on June 24, and disembarked at Preston Park. The ticket collector noticed his blood-stained clothes and a watch-chain hanging from his boot. Mapleton claimed that as the train entered Merstham Tunnel he heard a shot, before being knocked out by a blow over the head. When he came round, he was alone in the compartment.

The body of 64-year-old coin dealer Isaac Gold was on the line outside the Balcombe tunnel. He had been shot and stabbed in the neck.

Mapleton was in possession of rare German coins such as Mr Gold dealt in. He was arrested, and taken under police guard to his lodgings in Croydon. There, he walked in the front door, and

The Balcombe tunnel with insets of the murder site and the house where Mapleton lodged

straight out through the back door, while his escort waited for his return!

During the ensuing search for the missing man, a drawing of him appeared in newspapers in the hope that witnesses might identify him. In the event he was traced when he telegraphed for his wages.

He was tried and convicted this November, confessing before his execution.

Addict Doctor Poisons his Brother-in-Law

The trial of Dr George Lamson (seated in the dock and inset) at the Central Criminal Court

DR GEORGE HENRY LAMSON'S morphine addiction makes him an unreliable practitioner. Over the past few years he has fallen to writing bad cheques and pawning his instruments. His hope lay in his father-in-law's will, dividing money between his five children, to be received by each as he or she reached the age of maturity. If any died before inheriting, their share should be distributed among the others.

One living brother, Percy Johnson, was still only 18 this year. A crippled lad, with paralyzed legs, he was none the less popular at Blenheim House School in Wimbledon, south London, where he boarded.

On December 3 Lamson visited the school, taking a Dundee cake. Lamson accepted sherry from Mrs Bedbrook, the head's wife, and asked for sugar to add to it. Brought caster sugar, he pointedly stirred it with his pen-knife. Then he used the same knife to slice his Dundee cake and pass pieces to Percy and the Bedbrooks, taking one himself.

Finally, he took sample capsules from his bag, suggesting that Mr Bedbrook might find them useful for administering medicines. He filled two with sugar, gave one to Mr Bedbrook, and said to Percy, "Here, Percy, you are a swell pilltaker. Take this and show Mr Bedbrook how easily it may be swallowed." Percy was severely ill, and died the following day. When it was discovered that Lamson had bought aconitine on November 24, suspicion that he had poisoned his brother-in-law turned to certainty.

But how was it done? The sugar and sherry were innocuous: Lamson consumed both. Mr Bedbrook consumed sugar and a capsule. Everybody consumed cake cut with the knife that stirred the sugared sherry. How and in what was the poison administered?

The answer must lie in the cake. It seems likely that Lamson introduced aconitine into a minute area of the cake, ensuring that Percy's slice was the only doctored portion. All will, no doubt, be revealed at his trial next year.

> **TAKE THIS AND SHOW MR BEDBROOK HOW EASILY IT MAY BE SWALLOWED**
> **Dr G.H. Lamson.**

Policeman Killed Intercepting Burglar in Dalston

WHEN PC GEORGE COLES saw a young man acting suspiciously outside the Baptist Chapel in Dalston, London, opposite Messrs Reeves paint factory, he went to make an arrest. The young man pulled a pistol and fired two shots. One chipped stone from a house across the road. The other killed PC Coles. With that, the villain escaped into the fog.,

A set of tools, evidently intended to assist entry to the chapel through a basement window, was found behind the low wall fronting the chapel. But police have failed to identify PC Coles' murderer.

Jesse James Shot at Home

IN 1873, Pinkerton's Detective Agency was hired to track down the Jameses. Three years later the James–Younger gang folded, when only Jesse and Frank escaped after an attempted bank robbery in Northfield, Minnesota. For two years the brothers lived quietly.

But in 1879 Jesse recruited new gang members and returned to robbery. Last year the state of Missouri offered $5,000 reward for the capture or killing of Jesse or Frank.

Junior gang members Bob and Charles Ford made a secret deal with Governor Thomas Crittenden to assassinate Jesse for $10,000. When the brothers were invited to the house in Joseph, Missouri, where Jesse was living quietly as "Mr Howard", Bob Ford shot him while his back was turned and his gun-belt removed. The great outlaw had stood upon a chair to straighten a picture, like any ordinary small-town householder.

Outlaw Jesse James, at peace in death

OBITUARY

JESSE WOODSON 'DINGUS' JAMES (1847–1882)

Jesse James followed his brother Frank in joining Quantrill's Raiders (see 1863, 1864) during the American Civil War. His wounds were tended by his cousin Zerelda Simms, whom he married in 1874.

Subsequently, Jesse and Frank joined forces with fellow Quantrill alumni Cole and George Younger, probably inventing the crime of bank robbery (see 1866). They robbed banks and trains in Missouri, Kansas and Kentucky for the next three years.

James was remarkably popular with the public: partly because of his Civil War record, and partly because he stole from the railroads, which small farmers hate.

Mrs Pay Acquitted – So Who Did Kill Georgina Moore?

AFTER A SENSATIONAL trial exposing the love-life of building worker Stephen Moore, Mrs Esther Pay has been acquitted of killing his 8-year-old daughter Georgina.

The child's body was found in the River Medway close to Mrs Pay's parents' home, after Georgina had been missing for a week. Mrs Pay, a former fellow-lodger of the Moores, was one of the few people Georgina would have willingly accompanied from Pimlico in central London to Kent. Witnesses had seen a woman in a light ulster leading a small girl from Paddock Wood to Yarnley, where the body was found. And the prosecution speculated that Mrs Pay carried out an earlier threat to rob Moore of his daughter if he abandoned her – as he had done.

Mr Moore makes a practice of seducing, sometimes bigamously marrying, and then abandoning any willing ladies he meets!

But nearly all the witnesses were unable to identify Mrs Pay as the woman they had seen. Her parents swore she had not visited them over the period in question. And the jury apparently agreed that Mrs Pay had no motive to murder the child.

So if Mrs Pay didn't kill Georgina Moore, who did?

Belgian Brothers' Extraordinary Murder Plot

WHEN ANTWERP authorities received a letter in English from "Henry Vaughan", they learned, at last, the whereabouts of lawyer Guillaume Bernays, who disappeared 12 days earlier. Mr Vaughan confessed that he had run away after M. Bernays accidentally shot himself at a private meeting.

M. Bernays' body was found in 159 Rue de la Loi. Henry Vaughan's visiting cards lay here and there. But M. Bernays had been shot from behind. "Henry Vaughan's" handwriting was that of embezzler Leon Peltzer. And it was recalled that Leon's brother Armand had sacrificed his own fortune to save Leon and set him up in America. And Armand was so desperately enamoured of Mme Bernays that Bernays had barred him from his house.

Despite letters in Armand's possession suggesting that Leon was still overseas, the swindler was traced to Europe. Evidently he killed M. Bernays on his brother's behalf, since Mme Bernays was too virtuous to leave her husband.

A trail of letters and appearances by the disguised Leon made it seem that there really was an Englishman named Vaughan. But actually Armand devised the Byzantine scheme, and Leon perpetrated it, giving Armand an alibi for the time of the murder. The over-loving brothers have been sentenced to life imprisonment.

POSTSCRIPT TO JESSE JAMES

ON OCTOBER 5, Frank James walked into Governor Crittenden's office and surrendered, taking off his guns for the first time since he joined Quantrill's Raiders.

In November the Democratic Party refused to renominate Mr Crittenden for the governorship. His deal with "The dirty little coward that shot down Mr Howard" is so unpopular that his political career is over.

Child's Head Found at Apsley Castle

Apsley Castle in Wellington, Shropshire where the victim's head was found

SOME TIME AGO, a labourer named Mayers and his second wife were imprisoned for cruelty to Mayers' feeble-minded daughter by his first marriage. Since then Mayers has been employed as gardener by Mr Ogle of Apsley Castle, near Wellington, Shropshire. Neighbours believe the little girl (11 years old) was still sadly abused: she was frequently seen to be bruised, and always dressed in wretched clothing, cold and crying.

During January the child ran away to Shrewsbury, where railway officials found her and returned her home to her cruel father and stepmother at Apsley.

On February 11 a dog found her severed head in a pond in Apsley Park. It had been severely discoloured by heating – probably in an oven, with the purpose of rendering identification difficult – and then stitched into an alpaca wrapper with pink and white thread. Similar thread was found in the Mayers' cottage, together with the child's bloodstained clothes and bed quilt.

The wicked parents were promptly taken into custody, and a further search beside the pond discovered the poor child's legs, also wrapped in alpaca.

Shropshire regrets that due process of law must temporarily postpone the rightful execution of a couple who seem like something out of a bad fairy tale.

Hungarian President Murdered in Budapest

HERR VON MAJLATH, the President of the Hungarian senate, was murdered at his home in Budapest at the end of March. Not, however, by political terrorists – by burglars!

Some unemployed servants had united with unscrupulous colleagues who enjoy employment. Those in work admit those out of work to their masters' premises, and the gang had perpetrated a spate of robberies in Budapest.

Herr von Majlath's valet, Berecz associated with these rogues, and on March 28 he let two men called Spanga and Pitely into the house. When Herr von Majlath disturbed them, Spanga attacked him with a knife and Pitely strangled him with a rope. They stole nearly 2,000 florins from a safe, and some valuables.

A fourth associate named Javor, who supplied Spanga with the knife, was traced in an immense police trawl of over 100 possible informants.

Subsequently, on his testimony a search was instituted for Spanga, who was taken a week later enjoying the pleasures of a house of ill-fame in Presberg on the Danube.

Shortly afterwards Pitely was also arrested. And when these two confessed, implicating Berecz, he too finally acknowledged his part in the crime.

Tramp Sought by Police for Cheshire Murders

ELDERLY THOMAS EARLAM kept a common lodging house at Smallwood, near Congleton, Cheshire. The situation was a relatively lonely country road. But in that rural area the usual criminal activities are poaching and praedial larceny, and the occupants all felt themselves to be as secure as anyone in the kingdom.

Mr Earlham lived thriftily, and was believed to have considerable savings. Early this February, his house accommodated five people, all but one of whom were in employment and regularly left for their workplaces each and every morning.

The fifth was Thomas White, a tramp. When he left the house for the last time, late one morning, he left a scene of carnage behind him to be discovered by the returning lodgers.

Mr Earlam's housekeeper, Mrs Mary Moran, lay in the wash-house, writhing in agony with a fractured skull. Soon after being found she passed into unconsciousness and never recovered.

Mr Earlam lay dead in the passage between wash-house and kitchen, struck down with one terrible blow. His pockets had been torn open. Money and clean clothes were missing from the house, and the post office savings books of one of the lodgers.

White was seen hurrying away secreting a bundle at mid-day, and has since gone to ground. Police are confident, however, that he must still be in the county and they will trace him. There can be no doubt he is the murderer.

Too Many Children — So He Killed Them

TWENTY SIX-YEAR-OLD Londoner, William Gouldstone of Walthamstow is a hard-working abstemious blacksmith. He and his wife had three young sons until this August, when she gave birth to twins. The problem of supporting five children preyed on Gouldstone's mind, and neighbours observed that he became morose.

After the Bank Holiday he did not return to work, and when the twins were but one week old, he suddenly despatched all his off-spring.

The three toddlers, were forcibly drowned in a cistern containing but 14 inches of water. Then he burst into his wife's bedroom, and struck the twins at her breast with a hammer. As she screamed, he told her that she hadn't wanted the children, and now she should be single and happy.

At the police station he remarked, "I thought it was getting too hot to have five kids in about three and a half years, and thought I would put a stop to it." He added that he had "done it like a man"

and was "ready for the rope".

At his trial, evidence of insanity on both sides of his family was tendered, together with his workmates' observation that he

> ## " I THOUGHT IT WAS GETTING TOO HOT TO HAVE FIVE KIDS IN ABOUT THREE AND A HALF YEARS, AND THOUGHT I WOULD PUT A STOP TO IT. "
> ### William Gouldstone
>
> QUOTE

Home Secretary, Sir William Harcourt, who has reprieved Gouldstone

had often seemed suicidal. Even so, his statements showed that he knew what he was doing and knew that it was punishable by death, so he could not possibly be held legally insane.

Home Secretary Sir William Harcourt, however, insisted on his undergoing further medical examination after his conviction and sentence, and he has been reprieved from hanging.

IN BRIEF

JESSE POMEROY, sentenced at 14 to life solitary confinement, (*see* 1874) punctured a pipe in his cell, allowed the room to fill with gas; then struck a match he had acquired.

Pomeroy was blown out on to the corridor, shocked, but alive. Three convicts in the next cell were burned to death. And Pomeroy has been shifted to Charleston Prison.

Robbery in Arizona Turns to Massacre

THE ROBBERY of A.A. Castanada's general store in Bisbee, Arizona, ended in five deaths, and has provoked outrage that will not soon be quelled. Five masked men rode into the little

mining town on December 3. They wore long overcoats which concealed their rifles.

Two entered the store. Three stood guard outside. When the two in the store produced their rifles, customer J.C.Tappenier drew his guns. The robbers shot him down immediately. But the roar of gunfire attracted the townsfolk. As they hurried into the street to see what was going on, where the three look-outs opened a merciless fire on them.

Three men and a woman were killed; many others were wounded. And at last the robbers rode away with $3,000 cash and some jewellery.

A posse from Tombstone guided by local desert tracker Johnny Heath headed after them

as soon as it could be organized. It blamed its lack of success on Heath's deliberately circuitous trail. He was suspected of being in league with the robbers, especially when the rumour that he had once headed a gang himself was recalled.

Heath was taken back to Tombstone Gaol, and questioned. He confessed that he did indeed know the robbers' plans, and he identified them as Daniel Kelley, Daniel Dowd, "Tex" Howard, William Delaney and Comer Sample.

Excellent descriptions of all five have been telegraphed across the south west, and indignation at this massacre is so high that there is little doubt that they will be turned in sooner or later.

PC Coles' Murderer Caught: Left Bullets in Tree

PC GEORGE COLES, murdered outside the Baptist chapel in Dalston, London (*see* 1882) has been avenged at last. Police investigation following two lines of enquiry brought the crime home to Thomas Henry Orrock, a young man whose parents rent a pew in the chapel.

The first clue came from the burglar's tools abandoned outside the building. A chisel had crude letters marked on its handle forming the word "ROCK". Enquiries elicited that a tool-repairer believed the mark had been made when the tool was deposited for sharpening, and represented all that remained legible of the inscription "Orrock".

Further enquiries among young East Londoners produced witnesses who confirmed that Orrock acquired a pistol in 1872. Indeed, some lads had gone with him to Tottenham Marshes, where he fired shots into a tree.

Sergeant Cobb went to the tree; found the bullets; and extracted them. Forensic investigation proved them to be identical to the one that killed PC Coles.

All that remained was to find Orrock, who had disappeared. It was not long before he was traced to Coldbath Fields Prison where he was serving a short term for burglary.

Friends who accompanied him from pub to pub on the night of the murder confirmed that he had planned to rob the chapel. They had stayed in the pub at the end of the road, and did not, as Orrock anticipated, keep a look-out on his behalf.

With this evidence, Orrock was justly convicted, and at the comparatively young age of 21, he has been hanged.

THE MURDER OF POLICE CONSTABLE COLE AT DALSTON.

MRS SHEPPARD SAW THE SHOTS FIRED

ELIZABETH BUCKNELL

RICHARD BUCKNELL HEARD THE SHOTS FIRED AND SAW THE STRUGGLE ON THE GROUND

MURDER £200 REWARD

PARDON

THOMAS HENRY ORROCK THE PRISONER

Thomas Henry Orrock, murderer of PC Coles

Jonathan Wild (1682–1725)

THE GREATEST RECEIVER ever and King of Crime in 18th century London, maintained a respectable front by posing as the law-enforcing "Thief-Taker General of England and Ireland" with an office opposite the Old Bailey. Under this guise, he impeached thieves and presented evidence against them in court. Actually the threat of impeachment was his blackmail, forcing London thieves to deliver goods to him at his prices. Then, as a public informer, he would sell stolen goods back to their rightful owners if approached with a small fee.

A special Act of Parliament ended his career by making it an offence to take money for giving information about stolen goods, and Wild was hanged in 1725.

His fame brought him into John Gay's *The Beggar's Opera* as Mr Peachum, and Henry Fielding's novel, *Jonathan Wild the Great*, used his career to satirize the Prime Minister Walpole.

Jonathan Wild, "King of Crime"

Bandit Held at Razor-Point by Barber

DANIEL KELLEY, a leading perpetrator of the Bisbee Massacre (*see* 1883) has been caught in Deming, New Mexico and hanged. After the gang split up, Kelley arrived in Deming wearing several days' growth of beard. He went to barber Augustin Salas' shop to have his chin cleared of thick stubble, unaware that John Heath had confessed, and full descriptions of the robbers had been telegraphed over the southwest. As Kelley's stubble disappeared, his identifiable features emerged. Salas immediately clapped his razor's edge across the villain's Adam's apple and yelled for help. Kelley's fingers trembled toward his guns, but Salas "had the edge on him" and held it firm. So Kelley prudently preserved his throat for the rope.

Bank-Robbing Genius Killed for Seductions

BANK BURGLAR George Leslie has been found shot dead by unknown assassins outside New York City. His death resulted from his love-life. He has been dallying with colleagues' womenfolk: Jimmy Irving's sister and Mrs Shang Draper. It is believed that Irving the burglar and Draper the brothel-creeping sneak thief joined forces with three others to lure Leslie by a false trysting note to the lonely spot where they killed him.

New York Salon Hostess Opts to Jump Bail

MARM FREDERICKA MANDELBAUM has fled to Canada rather than face trial in New York. Abandoning her $21,000 bail bond, the 300lb 66-year-old hostess has packed an estimated $1 million dollars cash, and left forever the USA to which she immigrated in 1849.

After her husband Wolfe's death in 1874, Marm's career took off. She paid off Tammany Hall so that she could operate without let or hindrance. Like Jonathan Wild (*see* opposite) she ruled her city's theft industry, controlling burglars Bill Mosher and Joe Douglas, the kidnappers of Little Charley Ross (*see* 1874) as well as bank robbers George Leslie (*see* Obituary) and Ned Lyons, brothel sneak thief Shang Draper, cat burglar Sheeny Mike Kurtz, and thieves Johnny Dobbs and Jimmy Irving.

Marm's principles were strict: only 10 per cent of value for hot property. But her generosity was legendary: her dinner parties great occasions, where mayors and civic dignitaries rubbed elbows with prominent thieves.

Now the widow Mandelbaum is on the run. Incorruptible District Attorney Peter Olney by-passed New York's infamous Police Department, and called in Pinkerton's Detective Agency.

Pinkerton's men marked items in various stores, and caught Marm red-handed with bolts of silk stolen from Messrs Hearn and Sons. And an Aladdin's Cave of stolen furniture and jewels lay in her warehouses!

The mighty have fallen, even though she cannot be extradited to face trial. Tammany Hall is threatened by reformers, and Marm's lawyers have advised her to keep away from New York.

The events leading up to the arrest of the infamous Mother Mandelbaum

NEW YORK'S LADY CRIMINALS

Marm Mandelbaum's admiring imitators, who copied her social aspirations, include:

BLACK LENA KLEINSCHMIDT, "the Queen of Hackensack", pickpocket, sneak thief and blackmailer.

SOPHIE LYONS (wife of robber Ned), confidence trickster.

"QUEEN LIZ" and "BIG MARY", shop-lifters and tutors in Marm's Fagin-style school on Grand Street for young criminals.

Bisbee Massacre Informant Lynched in Tombstone

JOHNNY HEATH, the corrupt tracker who tried to mislead the posse chasing the perpetrators of the Bisbee Masacre (*see* 1883), is dead.

The Arizona legal authorities, (such as they are), felt that leniency should be extended to the man whose confession and descriptions have led to the arrests of the others (*see* Daniel Kelley). He was sentenced to life imprisonment and returned to Tombstone Jail.

But the citizenry felt the massacre was too heinous for such lenity to be acceptable. On February 22 they stormed the prison, and Heath was dragged out to a telegraph pole and unceremoniously hanged.

OBITUARY

GEORGE LEONIDAS LESLIE (1838-1884)

George Leslie, the greatest bank burglar of his times, was a wealthy brewer's son. He graduated in architecture from the University of Cincinnati, and a brilliant career was predicted for him. But he left the mid-west after his parents deaths in 1865, and turned to crime in New York.

As a criminal he was spectacular. He master-minded robberies that netted $786,879 (Ocean National Bank) and $2,747 7000 (Manhattan Savings Institution). He would travel long distances for good bauls. He was hired as consultant by gangs all over the country at fees ranging from $5,000 to $20,000. Leslie despised most of them. They lacked his cunning and self-control, which meant he would break in undetectably, and leave money in place if there was less than he expected, returning later for a better baul.

John Lee, The Man They Couldn't Hang

NINETEEN-YEAR-OLD John Lee is the luckiest man in England. He should have died on the scaffold, and nobody but Lee has any positive explanation why he didn't. Lee asserts: "It was the Lord's hand which would not let the law take away my life."

Miss Emily Keyse was found with her throat cut on November 15. The elderly spinster, once maid-of-honour at court, ran a strict household, and footman Lee found enforced abstemiousness and daily prayers irksome. When he broke the rules Miss Keyse cut his wages.

Lee was suspected of her murder, and convicted on thin circumstantial evidence.

But when hangman Berry put the noose round his neck, the scaffold's drop wouldn't respond to the lever. Lee was returned to his cell, and Berry tested the drop with weights. It worked perfectly.

A second attempt to hang Lee was made. Again the drop didn't budge, even though Berry stamped on it. Once again Berry thoroughly tested the mechanism, and once again the drop pitched weights down to the enclosure below.

Yet when Lee stood on the scaffold for the third time it proved impossible, yet again, to hurl him to perdition.

Lee was returned to his cell while the Governor contacted the Home Office. An order for Lee's reprieve was sent, and the young man started his sentence of life imprisonment.

> ❝ **IT WAS THE LORD'S HAND WHICH WOULD NOT LET THE LAW TAKE AWAY MY LIFE.** ❞ John Lee
>
> QUOTE

THE MURDER OF A LADY NEAR TORQUAY

THE PRISONER JOHN LEE

John Lee, the man who could not be hung despite being convicted of the murder of Emily Keyse

Immigrant Counterfeiters Caught Red-Handed

ACTING ON information received, Police Officers Caunter and Bolton went to no.7 Vine Court, Whitechapel Road, London, and, finding the door locked against them, forced an entrance. Inside they saw 21-year-old immigrant sawyer Morris Hertz holding a mould while another man ladled moulten alloy into it. On seeing them, Hertz cried, "*Raus!*" (look out), and his accomplice rapidly escaped. Hertz resisted arrest fiercely, and it required the help of passers-by to secure him. Thirteen counterfeit shillings were found in the room, and Hertz has got seven years hard labour.

British Army Pensioner Murders his Niece

ONE-TIME SOLDIER Thomas Boulton (47) had worked as a jeweller's assistant in Handsworth for the last 15 months, and lodged with his brother-in-law, Mr Bunting. His small army pension and his wages made him a very reliable tenant.

Boulton had always been on excellent terms with the Bunting family, apart from a little jealousy of a man who paid attentions to his niece Elizabeth. But no one was prepared for the horrid events when Mr Bunting bade them good night in April, and left Boulton and Elizabeth talking amiably together. In a short time the girl's screams attracted the family, who found Boulton standing over her dead body with a bloody hammer and knife in his hands.

In the confusion, Boulton escaped and was missing for five days. He was recognized and arrested after police had circulated copies of his photographic portrait.

At his trial, Boulton ascribed the crime to drink, adding, "I must have been mad." It seems that constant domestic proximity to the nubile nurse Elizabeth had aroused his lust, and he could not stomach her rejection. He was convicted and sentenced to death.

Burglars Injure Three Policemen, Kill a Fourth

WHEN LADY GRAHAME sent her maid for a handkerchief during dinner, the frightened Abigail returned to say the bedroom door was locked. Sir James Grahame and two footmen broke the door down, discovering that the maid had frightened burglars back down the ladder placed against the window. £400-worth of milady's jewels were missing from her bedroom.

The police cordoned off the Netherby area of Cumberland, and when Constables Roach, Johnstone and Fortune challenged four pedestrians, they found themselves the targets of pistol shots, which injured Roach and Johnstone. PC Fortune nevertheless chased the men, only to be kicked unconscious when he caught up with them.

One of the thieves escaped, and has never been identified. The other three appeared two days later at Plumpton Station asking about trains to London. They had missed the last, and went to the village inn where their London-accented presence aroused suspicions, and they soon hurried away.

But the landlord got a message to village bobby PC Byrnes, who ordered farmhands to collect staves and pitchforks and follow him. Alas, they had not arrived when he confronted the burglars, who shot him dead.

At 10.30 that night, guard Gaddes saw three men slip under the tarpaulin of a truck on his goods train as it pulled out of Penrith Station. He couldn't stop, as an unsignalled halt might cause an accident. He tried to get a message for police to be waiting at Tebay Station. He threw a note in his billycan into the cab of a passing up-train. But the driver and fireman had not passed the message on when Gaddes' train stopped at Tebay.

So the guard quietly called together stationworkers, telling them to bring staves and pieces of rail to the stowaways' truck. When ordered to come out, two of the men

Stationworkers surprise two of the Netherby Hall burglars at Tebay Station

popped from under the tarpaulin and started firing. But they could not hit the railwaymen, under the truck's steep sides. And when the gunmen leaned out to take better aim, they were struck down by the staves.

The third miscreant, however, escaped while the first two were being tied up. He was caught the next day, on another goods train. And with Lady Grahame's jewels discovered along their route the third man had followed toward Carlisle, the men were satisfactorily identified as the Netherby Hall burglars.

Anthony Rudds, John Martin and James Baker have been hanged for the murder of PC Byrnes.

Deserter Informs on his Aunt the Assassin

WHEN Sergeant-Major Charles Mercier, formerly of the French Dragoons, returned to Europe from America, where he had been on the run as a deserter for several years, his Aunt Euphrasia Mercier invited him to join the family at Villemonble, where, she assured him, the worldly fortunes of the Merciers had significantly improved since his last visit.

Indeed they had! Euphrasia Mercier now occupied the splendid mansion formerly owned by Mlle Eledie Menetret, an heiress whose servant-companion she had been. Running costs were met from Mlle Menetret's rents. It was said the old lady had retired to a convent abroad.

Charles deduced that she had been murdered. Tante Euphrasie promptly locked him in his room threatening to denounce him as a deserter. But his cousin Adele helped him escape, and the two went to the police.

Despite two of Euphrasia's sisters feigning madness to distract detectives, a search was carried out and a woman's body found buried in the grounds. There followed a protracted examination to determine just who the lady might be.

At the end of this year a false tooth proved it to be Mlle Menetret, and the case now passes from the police to the courts.

CHILDREN'S ASYLUM SCANDALS

Homerton Fever Asylum and the Eastern Asylum in London are under serious investigation at present. Vast quantities of burgundy and champagne had been purchased, allegedly prescribed for the children's wards! Nurse Eleanor Howard declared that one indent for 12 bottles of Beaune in one week had been altered from her order for two. Dr Collie, the medical superintendent, who signed all the orders, is under suspension, though he claims he never examined the forms he signed.

Asylum chaplain Edward Hudson's yet more serious claim that the Board of Management were aware that children were immorally interfered with has, however, been withdrawn under threat of libel proceedings. The Rev. Mr Hudson admits that he cannot substantiate his charges.

Pimlico Poisoning, Mrs Bartlett Goes Free

The trial of Mrs Bartlett, with (inset) Adelaide Bartlett and her shifty lover, Methodist minister George Dyson

PRETTY HALF-FRENCH Mrs Adelaide Bartlett did not poison her husband Edwin with chloroform on New Year's Day. So says a jury. The British public has delighted in the discovery of Edwin's alleged belief that every one should have two spouses; one for passionate adoration and one for platonic companionship. Like Mr Justice Wills, they have doubted Adelaide's claim that Edwin retained her for platonic companionship only, and agreed to forego the pleasures of the marital bed after one lone sexual encounter had brought the lady to pregnancy and miscarriage.

This story seems very fishy given that Edwin's wallet contained condoms and his sparse library included a manual of sexual advice for the married.

Nobody has accepted the story that young Methodist minister George Dyson received Edwin's encouragement to be his wife's passionate lover; to kiss and fondle her in his presence and write her love poems.

Indeed, had not Dyson been despicably willing to betray Adelaide and save his own skin, he would have stood in the dock beside her, since he admitted buying the chloroform that killed Edwin, using the false excuse that he wanted to clean grease spots off a suit.

The least likely story of all was Adelaide's insistence that she only wanted the chloroform to sprinkle on her handkerchief and wave under Edwin's nose whenever he forgot his pledge to respect her chastity, and started making advances!

Had Adelaide's acquittal depended on her own and Dyson's stories, she would have swung from the gallows ere now. But the doctors saved her. Edwin's stomach was certainly full of chloroform. The problem was how he could have drunk it, since it would have burned his mouth and throat. Pretty little Mrs Bartlett could not have forced it down him.

And so a "reasonable doubt" has restored this mysterious illegitimate child of Somebody Important in France to the anonymous wealthy friends who paid heavily for her to have the best defence possible. And science still wonders how she did it.

> **" NOW THAT IT IS ALL OVER, IN THE INTERESTS OF SCIENCE, MRS BARTLETT SHOULD TELL US HOW SHE DID IT. "**
> **QUOTE**
> **Sir James Paget**

Madman Shoots Wife Then Turns Gun on Himself

FOR THREE YEARS, clerk Arthur Egan, had been unable to work, being under the care of a lunatic attendant. His only money had come from subletting rooms in 13 Montague Street, Bloomsbury, London. This virtually dried up when his offensive manner drove away lodgers.

About two weeks ago the attendant was dismissed, and Egan attempted to care for himself. He concealed his condition sufficiently to buy a revolver without arousing suspicion, and on November 4, his maid, Lydia Chifney, found the Egans shot in their bedroom. Egan had fatally injured his wife before putting the pistol in his mouth and blowing his head apart.

Metropolitan Police Commissioner Resigns over Riot

A WORKINGMEN'S demonstration in Trafalgar Square resulted in windows being broken and buildings looted in Pall Mall, and might have destroyed shops in Oxford Street had not one police inspector taken a sergeant and 15 constables to disperse the howling, ugly mob.

Sir Edward Henderson, the Metropolitan Police Commissioner, was warned that there might be trouble. He placed 500 constables in reserve, but sent only a small force to the square, headed by elderly Superintendent Walker, who rapidly lost control of the situation as the crowd surged down Pall Mall. Confusing orders sent the reserves to the Mall, and the mob had reached Oxford Street by the time Inspector Cuthbert determinedly led his tiny band of officers out of Marylebone police station with batons drawn. Amazingly, the crowd fled before this puny force, and order was restored.

Henderson's head rolled none the less, his proffered resignation accepted without question by his superiors. Londoners are delighted that General Sir Charles Warren now takes charge of policing the capital.

THE NEW COMMISSIONER

While the British government's appointment of Sir Charles Warren to head "the Met" is transparently intended to bring military discipline to the policing of demonstrations, the general is also an intellectual and a detective in his own right.

His interest in archaeology, palaeography and biblical history has taken him to Egypt and the Holy Land. And in Egypt in 1882 he led the search for Professor Edward Palmer's missing party; establishing that they had been murdered by Egyptians, and tracking down the killers.

Bomb Outrage at Anarchist Meeting in Chicago

AN OPEN-AIR MEETING at the Haymarket, Chicago, on May 4, broke up in disarray when somebody hurled a bomb at approaching policemen. Seventy-six officers were injured and seven died. Nobody has the remotest idea who committed the crime. But the authorities arrested two of the meeting's platform speakers, August Spies, and Samuel Fielden, and issued a warrant for the third, Albert Parsons. In addition, five of the meeting's organizers were arrested and charged with conspiracy to murder.

When the case came to trial in June, Albert Parsons made a surprise appearance in court, and gave himself up voluntarily to take his place in the dock. The prosecution enflamed passions by quoting from subversive pamphlets written by the accused, though these had no bearing on the Haymarket bombing. The defence urged the jurors to stand up for Socialism!

Seven of the prisoners were sentenced to death and one to life imprisonment. Though three of the death sentences have been commuted, world-wide agitations are protesting against this travesty of justice, since the evidence shows that the defendants neither anticipated nor welcomed the atrocity for which they were tried.

RING DOWN THE CURTAIN.

The execution of Albert Parsons and three other Chicago anarchists

Poacher Kills Policeman and Hides with In-Laws

PC AUSTWICK of Dodsworth, near Barnsley, Yorkshire went to The Travellers' Rest Inn on July 31, expecting to meet local poacher, James Murphy. Murphy was indeed there and he exchanged high words with Austwick, finally pulling a pistol and shooting the constable, who died at his nearby home an hour later.

A two-week search for the murderer traced him to the home of his brother-in-law, a miner named Goss of Barugh Green. Two police superintendents and a detective went to arrest Murphy, but he pulled a gun on the detective and escaped again through a window. Mr and Mrs Goss were promptly taken in custody.

Murphy was caught two days later in a house on the outskirts of Barnsley, and though he fired his gun again at the officers who arrested him, he was at last captured and charged with murder.

Murder in Immigrant Slums: Greed Leads to Poisoning

WOULD-BE UMBRELLA manufacturer Israel Lipski of Stepney in east London, never got his slum-room sweatshop off the ground. For on the day he was to start the business, he caught sight of his fellow-lodger in Batty Street, 18-year-old Miriam Angel, lying in bed in the room below his.

Overcome by sudden lust, Lipski burst into her room and, it is believed, attempted to rape her. When he failed, he forced her to drink nitric acid. Then he hid under the bed, and tried to poison himself with the same acid.

Mrs Angel was dead, and young Lipski was not long believed to be a fellow-victim. Yet at his trial, he claimed to be just that, and attempted to accuse two labourers.

He did not persuade the jury. But his conviction worried the immigrant community, and certain newspapers. With a huge petition for mercy, the Home Secretary and the trial judge were at their wits' end whether or not to recommend a reprieve. Both believed Lipski had committed the murder. Both realized, however, that the evidence against him was

A drugged Israel Lipski is pulled from under the bed of murder victim, Mrs Miriam Angel. Lipski later confessed to poisoning her

not strong. They could be criticized whatever way they decided. At dawn on the day set for execution the two officials were still in an agony of indecision. Then, the glad news that Lipski had confessed to killing Miriam Angel was brought to them. He told the police that his motive had been robbery, not rape. But the officials were relieved to know they could hang him with a clear conscience.

The crowd outside the Stepney lodging house

Thief Left False Clues After Murdering Courtesan

FRENCH COURTESAN Mlle Regnault called herself Mme de Montille to clients. When she and her maid and little daughter were found murdered in their beds, letters signed "Gaston Geissler" lay in the room.

The concierge, who observed Mlle Regnault's visitors discreetly, letting them in and out by pulling a checkstring, gave a description of Geissler, who had been Mam'-zelle's visiting "friend" on the murder night. And a man answering to his description was arrested in Marseilles when he gave a prostitute a watch and jewels stolen from Mlle Regnault's room. Yet the man was an Italian named Henri Pranzini, and denied all knowledge of any Geissler, though he admitted knowing "Mme de Montille".

He hoped that Mlle Sabatier, yet another prostitute, would give him an alibi for the murder night. But she insisted she had spent the following night with him. And the discovery that Pranzini's handwriting is identical with the "Geissler" letters, and he once worked with a man named Geissler has sealed his fate.

Career of a Dentist Turned Gambling Gunslinger

ONE OF Doc Holliday's earliest killings was in Griffin, Texas, where he stabbed Edward Bailey over a card game. He was locked in the jail-less town's hotel, and escaped when his girlfriend, prostitute "Big Nose Kate", set fire to a nearby building as a distraction and helped him get away.

He became friendly with Wyatt Earp, and was always available when the "Fighting Pimp" needed a murderous gunman For Doc was an evil-tempered killer. From 1876 to 1879 he was associated with Earp, Bat Masterson and Luke Short in safeguarding their gambling and prostitution interests in Dodge City, Kansas.

In 1879 the gang was run out of town, and Holliday ran a saloon in Las Vegas, New Mexico, for a time, killing an ex-Army scout who tried to elope with one of the prostitutes he ran.

When the Earps took control of Tombstone in Arizona, Holliday became house-gambler at their Oriental Saloon. He also perpetrated stage-coach robberies.

Big Nose Kate informed against him when he beat her up once too often in 1881. The Earps cooled her off in a cell, and she withdrew the charge. But the scandal led to the notorious "Gun-Fight at the OK Corral" (*see* 1881), after which Doc married Kate so that she could never testify against him in court.

In 1883 Holliday surfaced again in Dodge City as a member of the infamous "Peace Commission" – in reality, a reorganization of the old Earp-Masterson mob which terrorized the citizenry into reinstating Luke Short's prostitution rackets.

After that triumph of evil over decency, Holliday drifted around the West, gambling and grumbling as his health declined, until in spring this year he entered a sanatorium and died from the TB that had ravaged him for so long.

OBITUARY

JOHN HENRY 'DOC' HOLLIDAY (1852-1887)

Died of consumption 8 November, in a Glenwood, Colorado, sanatorium. He had already lived twelve years longer than expected when he left Georgia to give his tubercular lungs the advantage the southwest.

Trained as a dentist, Doc Holliday preferred life as a gambling gunslinger. His last (and possibly accurate) words, as he drained his last whisky and looked down at his unshod feet, were: "Well I'm damned!" For he had fully expected to die in his boots.

Irish Doctor Kills Wife to Marry Nursemaid

IT IS NOT WISE, doctors, to sign your own wives' death certificates. It is still less wise to marry a pretty 21-year-old just a fortnight after your bereavement. Especially if you are 62, and your attachment to the girl has already aroused your late wife's indignation.

Dr Philip Cross of Munster did these things. He became so infatuated with Mary Skinner, his children's governess, that Mrs Cross dismissed her. Soon after which, Mrs Cross fell ill and died. Her husband certified the cause of death as typhoid fever. Her friends thought she died of his feverish passion for Mary.

The body was exhumed, and quantities of arsenic were found. The doctor was known to have purchased a large amount of the poison recently. He was arrested, and the second Mrs Cross, who never suspected the means by which her new bed was made vacant for her, refused to have anything more to do with her husband.

Dr Cross will be hanged early next year.

Police Search London for Murderer who Sat Tight

ON FEBRUARY 5, 31-year-old Thomas Currell quarrelled with his sweetheart Lydia Green, and shot her dead in her Hoxton home. He spent the following night south of Blackfriars Bridge, where he exchanged his bloodstained trousers. A day later he stole a coat from Flask Walk, Hampstead.

So mobile a runaway needed as many resources as the police could muster, and the public were invited to join the hunt. The police issued a woodcut of Currell, drawn from witness descriptions, and were inundated with reports that he was seen all over London.

Finally on February 15 Currell wrote saying he would give himself up in Islington. He did not do so, but was arrested in the vicinity shortly after failing to keep his appointment.

It transpired he had been in Islington ever since he left Hampstead, and had no fear of being taken since the woodcut is utterly unlike him. Three policemen who had him pointed out to them, but took no action, have been suspended.

Hell City

THE GOMORRAH of the Plains, previously a campground near Fort Dodge army barracks, sprang up in 1872 when it acquired a railway station. After this, it became a centre of booze and harlotry. "All they raise around Dodge City is cattle and hell," remarked one observer.

Railwaymen leaving their lamps outside whores' cribs gave the world its first "red light district". The enforcement activities of Short and Doc Holliday, which had nothing whatsoever to do with law-making, made the town's cemetery the first "Boot Hill".

Writer Ned Buntline came to Dodge, and romanticized its corrupt law-enforcers. Thus did the criminals Earp, Masterson, Short and Holliday become known as heroes!

So How Did All Those Deaths Happen?

AFTER HIS conviction for first-degree murder in 1886, and his associate John Dimmig's two trials, Dr J. Milton Bowers has been freed from the San Francisco jail which has been his home since 1885.

In that year, his third wife Cecilia died. Cause? Abscess of the liver. Age? Twenty-nine. Previous medical history? Excellent. Related history? The doctor's other wives both died suddenly and quite unexpectedly.

The insurance company dickered. Mrs Bowers was exhumed. She died of phosphorus poisoning. The doctor was convicted in March 1886 at a trial in which his brother-in-law, Henry Benhayon, gave hostile evidence.

The following year, Henry Benhayon died of potassium cyanide poisoning. A suicide note left by him confessed that he had killed his sister!

Did the authorities release Dr Bowers? They did not. The police investigated John Dimmig who had visited Bowers in his cell. A pharmacist identified Dimmig as the purchaser of some potassium cyanide.

Dimmig was tried for the murder of Henry Benhayon, but given the somewhat tangential circumstantial evidence, the jury found that they could not agree. He was re-tried in December, when he was acquitted.

So there is now no excuse for keeping Dr Bowers locked up. Another man has confessed to the crime of which he had been convicted. The doctor will walk free next year. But the police still believe he poisoned Henry Benhayon and Cecilia Bowers!

Hillbillies Family War Explodes, Massacre of McCoys

POOR APPALACHIAN mountaineers are the last exponents of southern family feuding. And the 15-year war between the Hatfields and the McCoys makes the Montagues and Capulets look like good neighbours.

The families took opposite sides during the Civil War (Hatfields, Confederate; McCoys, Unionist). In 1873 Randolph McCoy took Floyd Hatfield to trial for hog-stealing. The jury – half Hatfields, half McCoys – deadlocked, until a McCoy married to a Hatfield voted with his in-laws.

From then on McCoys would not let their boys court Hatfield girls; Hatfields threatened to kill McCoys, and, at last, a McCoy killed a Hatfield supporter who had made particularly vehement threats. And with that, war broke out. Anderson "Devil Anse" Hatfield is the most prominent general, commanding his troops

The feuding West Virginian hillbilly Hatfields. Devil Anse, seated second on the left

from a mountain hide-out, with a deep-dug underground shelter below his shack.

Nobody knows how many people have been killed in the feud. The McCoys shoot Hatfield Romeos from a distance if they meet with McCoy Juliets. The Hatfields go in for large-scale reprisals, killing three McCoy hostages by rustic firing squad after an election-day dispute in 1882 led to the death of Devil Anse's brother. The wild, ragged, bearded mountain-men are expert with the long barrelled rifle, and deadly but silent assas-

sins with the long-bladed knife.

Since the Hatfields largely live in West Virginia and the McCoys are a Kentucky family, the two states become embroiled whenever the McCoys appeal to their legislature to extradite Hatfields for murder.

The Hatfields resent the out-of-state law officers, who are more effective than native-born mountaineers in capturing feuders. This year Anse Hatfield mounted a massive raid on Randolph McCoys' home to wipe out his enemies once and for all. The gallant warriors succeeded in killing

one McCoy man, and two women – Randolph's wife and daughter. they also burned the house down.

This atrocity has brought Kentucky law enforcement officers into West Virginia for a determined drive against the Hatfields.

Those Appalachian residents who are not committed to one side or the other desperately hope that decimation of the Hatfields (who had substantially reduced the McCoy fighting forces) may cause the vendetta to wear itself out. It's no fun having your neighbours shootin' each other up all the time!

New Scotland Yard, as the photographer's camera may see it in two year's time

Brute Batters Chemist in Ripper's Third Street!

WITHIN ONE WEEK of Berner Street, St George's-in-the-East, being visited by the dreaded Jack the Ripper who killed Elizabeth Stride there (*see* Special), it was again the scene of murderous crime.

A brutal young robber named William Seaman broke into a chemist's shop, and on being disturbed, seized a hammer and savagely battered the chemist, Mr Simpkin over the head.

Both men were fortunate that the he survived. For Seaman, as coarsely stupid as he is bestially cruel, was quickly arrested. Had his victim died, he would assuredly have hung for a savage murder on an innocent man.

As it is, he has been given a long sentence of penal servitude, and it is to be hoped London will not be troubled by him again.

New Scotland Yard has its First Murder

LONDON'S FAMOUS old police headquarters in Scotland Yard at the top of Whitehall is now too small for the metropolitan force, and a new one is under construction on the Embankment.

As yet, only the foundations and cellarage of New Scotland Yard are complete. But already heinous crime has visited the site.

On the night of October 3, somebody climbed over the palings surrounding the work and made his way to a remote vault in the cellarage. Inside he left the headless, limbless body of a woman.

The arms of the same lady have been recovered from the Thames. The legs and head seem permanently lost.

There is speculation that this might have been another crime by the dastardly Whitechapel Murderer (*see* Special Section, Jack the Ripper). But police spokesmen insist that the case is entirely different, noting that the Ripper's victims are:

> **KILLED where they are found.**
> **THROTTLED before their throats are cut.**
> **MUTILATED abdominally and facially.**

The torso in New Scotland Yard, by contrast, was:

> **KILLED elsewhere and carried to the location.**
> **KILLED by some means that cannot be determined in the absence of the head.**
> **SUFFERED no abdominal mutilations.**

This, then, is the Whitehall Mystery of 1888. The Ripper's work is the Whitechapel Mystery.

Ladies of the Street Fight to the Death

NEW YORK GANGSTER Danny Lyons was an active pimp, running a sweetly named stable of three streetwalkers: Lizzie the Dove, Bunty Kate and Gentle Maggie. Last year he added a fourth to his team: Kitty McGown. This outraged her protector Joseph Quinn, and the New York underworld knew that vengeance was sworn and would be exacted when the two next encountered each other.

On July 5 last year, the men met and pulled pistols on each other. Lyons killed Quinn and after being tried, was hanged for the murder this year.

Kitty McGown and Bunty Kate went back to work with new protectors. But Lizzie the Dove and Gentle Maggie adopted widows' weeds, and abandoned their horizontal occupation for a period of mourning.

While grieving, they met in a Bowery bar, where a dispute arose as to which felt the bereavement the more deeply. Maggie "won" the argument in a way that was far from Gentle, plunging a cheese knife into Lizzie's throat.

Nor were the dying Lizzie's words Dove-like, as she told her rival, "I will meet you in Hell and there scratch your eyes out."

RATES FOR THE JOB

PIMP DANNY LYONS, hanged in New York this year, was also a bully-boy member of the Whyos street gang.

He volunteered to kill or injure on contract at the following rates:

Both eyes blackened:	$4
Leg broken:	$19
Bullet in the leg:	$25
"The Big Job":	from $100

Public Concern Over Mrs Maybrick's Conviction

Mrs Florence Maybrick, whose treatment at her trial for murder has caused great consternation

MR JUSTICE STEPHEN'S conduct of Mrs Florence Maybrick's trial at Liverpool in July is being widely criticized. His hostility to the 36-year-old American woman's adultery overshadowed the question whether or not she was also a murderess, and it appeared that the elderly jurist, who recently suffered some sort of stroke or seizure, did not grasp many important points.

Mrs Maybrick's husband James died this April, and nursemaid Alice Yapp opened, and read a letter her mistress wanted posted during his final illness. When she realized the recipient, Mr Alfred Brierley, had been Florence's lover, Miss Yapp passed it to James's brother, Michael, who, under a *nom-de-plume* is a composer of popular ballads.

The Maybrick family discovered quantities of arsenic in the house, and heard gossip that Florence extracted arsenic from flypapers and used it to doctor James's food. In fact, Maybrick's friends knew he took arsenic, strychnine, hyoscine and morphine as tonics and aphrodisiacs. A New Orleans brothel madam, aware of his habit of taking arsenic before intercourse, feared he would poison himself and die in one of her girl's arms during one of his visits to her establishment.

But the Maybricks' marriage had been unhappy since Florence discovered that James had a mistress in a separate establishment. When she retaliated by dallying with his friend Brierley, Maybrick beat her and cut her out if his will. And Mr Maybrick's brothers concluded she had killed him.

The authorities and now the jury have agreed with this opinion. Yet someone in the Home Office shares the general public's disquiet about hanging a woman whose husband regularly took poison. Mrs Maybrick's death sentence has been reduced to life imprisonment.

Arran Murderer Found to be of Unsound Mind

TWO HUNDRED Arran islanders participated in the search for London clerk Edwin Rose when he did not return from his holiday in July. They found his body on Goatfell, clubbed to death and hidden under a pile of rocks.

The search was on for young Scotsman "John Annandale", who had accompanied him to Arran. Islanders remembered Annandale returning alone and exhausted from Goatfell, and leaving on the ferry the following morning.

Annandale was identified as 25-year-old Glasgow pattern-maker, John Laurie, who ran away to Liverpool when he read in the newspapers of the body's discovery. While being hunted, he wrote to the press, "I smile when I read that my arrest is expected hourly." But arrested he was, preparing to board a train at Ferniegair.

He was tried in Edinburgh, and claimed that Rose had died from a fall, after which he had admitted robbing him. Pathological evidence, and his use of a false name told against him. He was convicted, but subsequently reprieved and committed to an institution.

> " **I SMILE WHEN I READ THAT MY ARREST IS EXPECTED HOURLY.** "
> **John Laurie**

SCIENTIFIC EXECUTIONS FOR AN AGE OF SCIENCE

New York State is changing the form of its death penalty. From next year, the hangman's noose will be abolished. In its place, the "electric chair" utilizing Mr Westinghouse's lethal 'Alternating Current' will pass 1,000 volts through the felon's body. Mr Edison's demonstrations on animals, supposed to warn the public against using Westinghouse Electricity, have satisfied the authorities that this will be swift, safe and humane.

The Last Years of Belle Starr

Belle Starr

I N 1883, cattle-dealers Sam and Belle Starr, for whom the government offered a $10,000 "dead or alive" reward, appeared before "Hanging Judge" Isaac Parker. As their actual offence was only receiving stolen livestock they drew short prison sentences. But while Belle was in jail the *Police Gazette* immortalized her as "Queen of the Bandits". When she came out, she joined a Wild West Show, and delighted audiences with a whooping attack on a stagecoach supposedly carrying Judge Parker!

When Sam came out, he shot one of Belle's new lovers, went into hiding, and re-emerged to resume receiving stolen livestock. In 1886 Belle was arrested again, but this time Judge Parker discharged her for lack of evidence.

Sam died in a shoot-out that Christmas. The last of Belle's subsequent succession of lovers was a Creek Indian outlaw named Jim July, whom she persuaded to surrender to the law at Fort Smith. It was returning from this errand that she was bushwhacked and killed on a lonely road near Eufaula, Indian Territory, Okla. It seems almost certain that the murderer was her 18-year-old son Ed Reed, who had suffered her attacking him with a bullwhip when she wasn't incestuously making love with him!

OBITUARY

MYRA BELLE STARR, NÉE SHIRLEY (1848-1889)

B orn in Missouri, Belle Shirley's association with the James Younger gang (see 1868) began when her brother Ed rode with them. In her teens, Belle bore Cole Younger an illegitimate daughter. Thereafter she shacked up with highway-robber Ed Reed and went to California with him where the couple had a son. In the early 1870s Ed and Belle moved to Texas, where he rustled cattle and she ran the ranch.

In 1874 Reed was killed by a lawman. Belle's subsequent lovers included her old flame, Cole Younger, until he was imprisoned in 1876. Later she married Cherokee Sam Starr, son of a famous horse thief. And it was under her final married name that she attained fame in the dime novels and Wild West Shows as supposed "Queen of the Bandits".

Male Brothel Exposed in Cleveland Street

Cleveland Street rent boy Algernon Alleys

M ISSING POSTAL ORDERS brought police to investigate the activities of Post Office messenger boys in Fitzrovia, London. When they were interrogated it came out that they had been staffing Charles Hammond's male brothel in Cleveland Street.

The vile procurers made accusations against prominent persons, hoping the fear of scandal might lead to charges being dropped. They were disappointed, but Lord Arthur "Podge" Somerset, decided to retire discreetly to Dieppe.

Lord Euston, by contrast, faced down his accusers. He declared that he had been handed a card promising *poses plastiques* (tableaux of naked women) in 19 Cleveland Street. When he visited the establishment and discovered its true nature, His Lordship insisted he left in a rage.

To the embarrassment of the authorities, the loathsome creatures tried to implicate a Very Important Person Indeed in their unnatural orgies. His name has been kept out of the press, but informed sources suggest to us that Home Office memoranda describe him as "P.A.V." – a formulation covering the identity of the Queen's eldest grandson, Prince Albert Victor. The Prince has hitherto been best known for his limited intellectual grasp, which has caused his parents some anxiety about his prospects as sovereign. Let us hope we have no more serious worries to entertain about this decendant of William II, Edward II and William III!

Brothel owner Charles Hammond

Dentist Seduces Child with False Occult Claims

D R ETIENNE DESCHAMPS, 55-year-old New Orleans dentist, "borrowed" 12-year-old Juliette Deitsch from her parents last year, claiming that his occult powers could trace pirate Jean Lafitte's lost treasure through the mediumship of a hypnotized child.

The hypnotic sessions continued for six months. Then, on January 3 this year, Juliette was found naked and dead in the doctor's bed. He lay beside her, severely injured by self-inflicted stab-wounds.

His claim that the child desired sexual intercourse (which took place whenever she came for "hypnotism") seemed doubtful, given that she had been chloroformed. The jury believed the prosecution's claim that Deschamps overdosed her deliberately because she threatened to expose him and returned a verdict of guilty of first-degree murder. The dentist has been sentenced to death.

Woman Kills Rival: Dumps her on Building Site

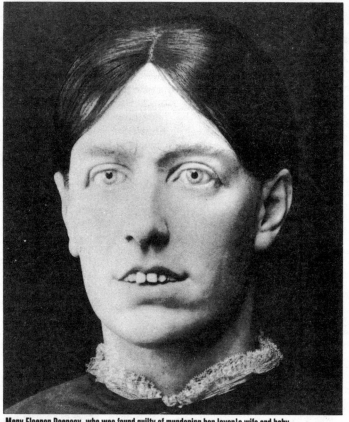

Mary Eleanor Pearcey, who was found guilty of murdering her lover's wife and baby

MRS MARY ELEANOR PEARCEY, a Gravesend businessman's kept woman in a bijou residence near Camden Town, London, had her own private light o' love. Frank Hogg held a key to her house, even after he was him-self married with a baby daughter. Mrs Pearcey remained friendly with Mrs Hogg until last Christmas, when the deceived wife realized what was going on.

On October 24, Mrs Pearcey extended an olive branch. She gave a boy sixpence to carry an invitation to tea to Mrs Hogg, and watched him deliver it.

Later that evening, neighbours heard screams from Mrs Pearcey's house. During the night, Mrs Pearcey was seen wheeling a heavily laden perambulator away from her home.

On the morning of October 25, builders in the neighbourhood of Swiss Cottage found a woman's body dumped on their site. Its head was battered and its throat cut. On a piece of waste ground in south Hampstead, a suffocated baby's body was found. Outside a house in Maida Vale, a collapsed perambulator lay on the pavement.

When reports of the body circulated, Mrs Hogg's family wondered if it could be she; for her disappearance the day before was mysterious. They persuaded Mrs Pearcey to accompany them to the police station, where they identified Phoebe Hogg. Mrs Pearcey's hysterical behaviour, however, drew police attention to her, and they visited her house.

They found bloodstains on her kitchen floor, on a poker, and on a knife. While they searched, Mrs Pearcey affected total unconcern, playing and singing to herself at her cottage piano. Asked about the blood in the kitchen she answered vaguely, "Killing mice... killing mice... killing mice."

Nobody believed her. It is clear that she murdered her rival; placed the body in the pram, which suffocated the unfortunate infant, and rambled for six miles, not discarding her victims until the pram broke down. Mrs Pearcey was hanged on December 23, deeply resentful that Frank Hogg did not offer her support throughout her trial.

> ## KILLING MICE... KILLING MICE... KILLING MICE.
> QUOTE **Mary Eleanor Pearcey**

Oxford Swell Turns Killer in Canada

CHARMING, HANDSOME Reginald Birchall, a graduate of Lincoln College, Oxford, descends from a line of distinguished churchmen. But as an undergraduate he headed the dissipated swell set, and on going down he bankrupted himself leading the fast life in London.

His first visit to Canada was in flight from the humiliation of bankruptcy proceedings. He called himself "Lord Somerset" and lived fraudulently on credit. He also discovered Blenheim Marsh near Princeton, Ontario, with its "bottomless pond" in which unwary travellers drown and lie un discovered.

Back in England, Birchall advertised for a partner to join him on a Canadian farm. Not one, but two ex-public school marks presented themselves, and Birchall greedily signed each on as his "sole partner" in return for a cash investment.

Inevitably, Mr and Mrs Birchall were unable to accompany both Frederick Benwell and Douglas Pelly to New York on the SS *Britannic* without the gulls meeting each other. Birchall told each the other was an intrusive nuisance, and hurried the party away to Buffalo.

There Pelly stayed to entertain Mrs Birchall while Birchall and Benwell went to look at the "farm". Birchall shot Benwell on the edge of Blenheim Swamp and cut all identifying markings from his clothes. He was, however, prevented by a fall of timber from dumping the body in the pond.

Back in Buffalo, Pelly easily accepted that Benwell had lost interest in the project. He accept-ed Birchall's invitation to visit Niagara Falls, where he twice formed the opinion that his companion intended to push him into the raging torrent, and was only prevented by the chance arrival of other wayfarers.

Birchall's entire plot fell apart when two woodsmen quite remarkably stumbled on Benwell's body. His identity was confirmed by Pelly when his cigar case, initialled FHB, was found in the woods. And smooth-tongued Birchall couldn't talk himself out of that!

The first old Lincoln man to be hanged in Canada dies on October 28.

First Use of Electric Chair May Be the Last!

WILLIAM KEMMLER, of Buffalo, New York, took a chopper to his woman, Tillie Ziegler, during a quarrel. He was the state's first convicted murderer to receive the new death penalty of electrocution (*see* 1889).

Indeed, his defence was financed by the Westinghouse

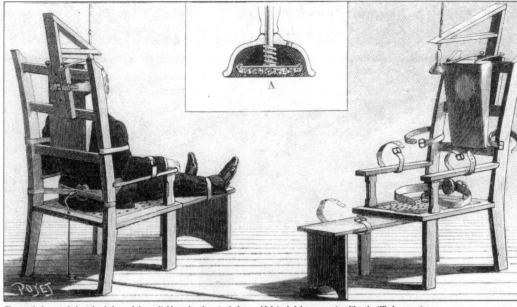

The newly-invented electric chair, and the switchboard and controls from which technicians execute with scientific incompetence

(Alternating Current) Electricity Company, which dreads the effect on sales should official executions prove their cheap power to be dangerous. Messrs Westinghouse need have no fears. The "scientific" execution was disastrously inefficient.

Kemmler was strapped into a solid wooden chair, and terminals were fastened to his limbs and head. Then a switch was thrown, and for 17 seconds, a massive shock of 1,300 volts pulsed through his body, which leaped, eyes popping in anguish, against the bonds. When the current was turned off, horrified doctors saw his chest expand, and breathing resume.

After a panicky conference, an-

other shock lasting 70 seconds was applied, which ended the unfortunate man's life. The poor wretch had been cooked by the current!

Few people believe this incompetent torture will be used

again. An efficient hangman using a calculated drop can end life instantly and painlessly. The electrician fries his victim with succesive agonizing jolts and not always successfully.

William Kemmler awaiting his cruel death

Police Chief Killed by Sicilian Secret Society

THE MURDER of New Orleans' Police Chief, David Hennessy, has uncovered an immigrant underworld. Mr Hennessy was investigating the criminal activities of two Sicilian immigrant families. Both belonged to the historic secret society "the Mafia", murderous extortionists exerting an evil stranglehold over Sicily.

Mr Hennessy discovered that the Provenzanos' and Matrangas'

extortion rackets control the New Orleans waterfront, and they were fighting each other for domination. He announced that he would produce evidence of this "Mafia" activity at the trial of two Provenzanos who murdered a Matranga.

On October 15, Mr Hennessy was shot down on the street. Sicilians are used to murdering their own policemen and judges with impunity, and imagine they can do the same in America.

They are wrong. Nineteen "mafiosi" have been rounded up, and 60 witnesses will testify against them.

With luck, Mr Hennessy's tragic death will keep this vile corruption out of America.

THE MAFIA

This secret society has, within living memory, only existed for the purpose of brigandage and extortion. Yet it dates back centuries, and purports to be an alliance to protect native peasants against foreign rulers.

Mafiosi call themselves "Men of Respect" (meaning "Pay our Demands or We'll Maim You") and protect themselves from reprisals by the code of *omerta* (Silence – or You'll be Killed.)

The "Honourable Society" are actually coarse and despicable ruffians.

Male Body in Cask Nearly Auctioned

A CASK ADDRESSED to Messrs Beresford Bros, Racine, Wisconsin, was held in a warehouse at New York harbour when it was found that no such company existed. It would have been auctioned later in the year, had not the Danish consul asked for it. A Danish businessman named Phillipson, under investigation for fraud in Copenhagen this April, admitted under questioning that he had killed a debt collector named Meyer, packed him into a cask, and despatched it to an imaginary address in America. When the New York cask was opened, there was Mr Meyer, neatly folded up in plaster-of-Paris.

Some speculative buyer might have suffered a nasty surprise had the unopened cask been auctioned as intended!

CRIMES OF THE NINETEENTH CENTURY

Eleven Gangsters Lynched After Bent Trial

The lynch mob breaks into the prison at New Orleans to kill the mafiosi

THE TRIAL of the 19 Sicilian "Mafiosi" charged with murdering Police Chief Hennessy last year (*see* 1890) proved a travesty of justice. Witnesses and jurors alike were bribed and intimidated. Sixteen defendants were acquitted; the jury disagreed over the other three.

Amid huge popular protests, the authorities held all the defendants in custody while they decided what to do. As the murderous extortionists lay in prison, several thousand people, led by prominent citizens, marched on the jail. Eleven mafiosi whose guilt had clearly been proved at the trial which acquitted them were dragged from their cells. Two were hanged on the street outside the jail. Seven were executed by makeshift firing squad in the women's yard of the prison. And two who got away and hid in a dog kennel were shot there where they lay like dogs.

The lynching party included a large number of respectable black citizens. This is a unique occasion in southern history – the lynching of white men by black men, with the full approval of the white bourgeoisie.

DAVID HENNESSY, SUPERINTENDENT OF THE NEW ORLEANS POLICE
Who was killed by Italian Assassins at the instigation of the "Mafia"

Police Chief David Hennessy

Student Indicted for Murdering Secret Wife

CARLYLE HARRIS, a 22-year-old medical student in New York, has been leading a secret life. He gambles. He frequents the company of bad women. And last year he contracted a secret marriage to 18-year-old Helen Potts who, at the time of her death this February, was still a pupil at boarding school.

Miss Potts – or Mrs Harris – was herself somewhat "fast and loose". Harris had necessarily performed an abortion on her; or so he told her uncle, who definitely performed another! With such wickedness locked in her heart, no wonder the girl did not rest easy in her bed! To counter her insomnia, Harris gave her quinine capsules with one-sixth of a grain of morphine. Helen died at school on February 1. Doctors attending her noticed that the pupils of her eyes had reduced to pinpoints, and deduced that she had taken morphia. After her death, a lethal quantity was found in her body.

Harris confidently asserts that the dose he gave was safe and sensible, and could not possibly have caused death.

But his secret dissipation and his dishonourable malarkey with the once innocent schoolgirl tells heavily against him.

The District Attorney's office believes that this young man regretted having tied himself to one woman, and after a year found himself tiring of her. He has been indicted for murder by a Grand Jury, and goes on trial next year.

East End AntiSemitic Ruffian Sent Down

A **NASTY** incident near Euston Square casts an evil light on the "Blind Beggar Gang", (named for their favourite Bethnal Green tavern), the doyens of London's East End criminals.

These pickpockets, bullies and extortionists disdain to rob their impoverished home neighbourhood. Instead they frequent racetracks and the West End, and some of their exploits have shown a touch of humour. We admit to chuckling over the impudent "Blind Beggar" mobster who mounted the steps of the Carlton Club on election night, cheering to the echo a victorious Tory candidate. And as the gratified politician accepted a pat on the shoulder from his sharply dressed supporter, so did he lose his watch and chain!

But now the mob's wicked cruelty has been exposed. Early this year, several of them were travelling on the underground railway, when elderly Mr and Mrs Fred Klein boarded their compartment at King's Cross. The mobsters began jeering at them and making offensive antiSemitic remarks. The Kleins disembarked at the next station, and walked away down Gower Street. But the unpleasant young hooligans followed them, and one, Paul Vaughan (who uses the alias Paul Ellis) jabbed at Mr Klein with his umbrella.

Quite by accident, the ferrule penetrated his eye, and Mr Klein fell to the pavement, injured. The brave mobsters ran away terrified. And as soon as the law began to ask questions, "dishonour among thieves" prevailed, and the others "shopped" Vaughan to save their own skins.

It was a frightening lesson for the young swaggerer to find himself remanded to prison charged with causing Grievous Bodily Harm.

Were it not for the death of Mr Klein and the suffering of Mrs Klein, we should rejoice still more that Vaughan has been given a long sentence of hard labour for manslaughter, and will spend at least seven years sledge-hammering rocks in the cold rain of Dartmoor.

Woman Found Murdered Under London Railway Arch

A **T 2.20** in the morning of St Valentine's Day, PC Ernest Thompson found a token of disjointed love lying in "Swallow Gardens", a sordid railway-arched passage between backstreets behind the Royal Mint. 26-year-old Frances Coles lay on her back with her throat cut. Her hat was beside her; a second hat was pinned to her skirts. As PC Thompson tended the dying woman, he heard footsteps running away toward Cable Street and the docks.

Enquiries soon established that Coles had spent much of the previous 48-hours with a violent ship's stoker named Sadler, but they had quarrelled earlier in the day, and he had turned up covered with blood at her lodgings asking for her. He was found by police, drunk and bloodstained outside the Mint about 20 minutes before the dying woman was discovered. Furthermore, he tried to sell his seaman's knife the following day.

There seemed a strong case against him, especially when three railway carmen – "Jumbo" Friday and two brothers called Knapton – confirmed seeing a couple standing in Swallow Gardens shortly after 2.00 am. Friday said the woman was Coles and the man looked like a stoker.

But the case collapsed when courting couple Thomas Fowles and Kate McCarthy declared they were the pair canoodling in the archway. And as they recognised the Knaptons and "Jumbo" their evidence seems conclusive.

Much to their regret, the police have been forced to release Sadler.

The "Jack the Ripper" scare

Cannibal Banquet for Black Georgians

W **HEN A** black man makes good in Washington, Georgia, the community honours him. When he has gone away poor and returned rich, he is welcomed into the ranks of Afro-American wealth with a sumptuous public feast.

So prosperous black citizens ordered a celebratory banquet at Lizzie Hughes' Cook-house when one of their number came home in triumph after several years' absence.

The meal was excellent, though the only meat served was markedly pale, lean and firm-fleshed, tasting something like veal. When the diners congratulated Mrs Hughes and asked her what the meat was, the woman's little daughter replied, before her mother could speak, "My sister."

She then told of watching her mother kill, butcher and cook her own child that afternoon. A doctor confirmed that the bones were human. And only the arrival of the police prevented summary justice from being executed on Mrs Hughes.

RIPPER SCARE CONTINUING

Despite police assurances that the Whitechapel Monster has not struck since November 1888 (*see* Jack the Ripper Special), almost every murder in London's East End is still hailed as another appearance of the fiend.

So seriously does this affect police work that Frances Coles' murder site was personally inspected by the Metropolitan Assistant Commissioner (Crime) Dr Robert Anderson, CID Chief Constable Melville Macnaghten, Superintendent Arnold, Head of H Division (Whitechapel), and Inspector Reid, Head of H Division CID.

A preposterous array of top brass for one insignificant crime! And all because the press cry up the case irresponsibly to sell newspapers!

Dr Cream Hanged: He Poisoned Five Prostitutes

CROSS-EYED CANADIAN physician Thomas Neill Cream had an extraordinary hobby. Giving strychnine capsules to prostitutes! A hobby that was to cost him his life.

He came to London last year, after a prison sentence in Illinois where he was convicted of poisoning a patient whose wife he was seducing.

In Lambeth, Cream picked up streetwalker Ellen Donworth and was seen leaving her room in Duke Street, shortly before she collapsed on the pavement in Waterloo Road. The client she knew as "Fred" had given her poison.

Unfortunately police investigated the wrong man. Cream wrote letters purporting to come from "H.W. Baynes, barrister", one of which suggested that the heir of bookseller W.H.Smith intended to poison Ellen Donworth, and another offered Baynes's services for his defence.

Next Cream poisoned Matilda Clover. Her doctor assumed she had died of delirium tremens. But Cream wrote more anonymous letters accusing Lord Russell and Dr William Broadbent of poisoning Matilda, and the diagnosis was corrected.

On a quick visit to Canada early this year he had flysheets printed warning guests at the Metropole Hotel that Ellen Donworth's killer was among them. He was never to use these.

On his return he poisoned Emma Shrivell and Alice Marsh. His accusatory letters this time led to his arrest, as they were sent to the father of one of his fellow-students at St Thomas's Hospital in the 1870s. The family recalled that Cream fitted the description of the man seen leaving Ellen Donworth's room.

Cream's conviction became certain when prostitute Lou Harvey told of spending a night with him, but avoiding taking the mysterious pills he tried to force on her.

Cream was hanged in London on November 15.

Popular crime journal depicts Doctor Cream's last hours

Otay Mesa Murders: Injun Joe Hanged Despite juror's Doubts

JOHN AND ANNA GEYSER farmed a homestead in beautiful Otay Mesa, high in the Sierras near San Diego. Half a mile away, their nephew Fred Piper ran another farm. On October 12 Fred's daughters were riding across the mesa seeing a friend home, when they heard blows and shouts from the Geyser farm. They cantered home, and Fred Piper and his son sauntered across to see what was going on. In the dusk they saw two bodies sprawled in front of the house which they agreed were drunken Indians. In the Geysers' darkened bedroom a moving light was hastily extinguished as the Pipers called out.

A small man escaping from the house was caught and fiercely beaten by the Pipers. It was Joseph "Injun Joe" Gabriele, who had been digging a cistern and clearing soil for John Geyser. That afternoon, he and two other Indians had bought wine at a nearby plantation. Joe slept off his heavy boozing in the barn, and then, he said, came over to see where Mr and Mrs Geyser were.

They were dead. They were the bodies outside the house. Injun Joe was almost lynched by angry homesteaders.

His trial, however, was little better. His counsel never made clear that his story was consistent with the evidence, and the two missing Indians (who had certainly been drinking with him that afternoon) might have committed the murders while Joe slept. He didn't appeal for the mistrial to which Joe was entitled when one juror protested against the sentence.

Joe was just another injun. And they hung him.

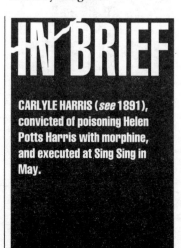

IN BRIEF

CARLYLE HARRIS (*see* 1891), convicted of poisoning Helen Potts Harris with morphine, and executed at Sing Sing in May.

Eye-Drops Used to Disguise Pin-Point Pupils

DR ROBERT BUCHANAN read about murderer Carlyle Harris (see Feature Box) and told a barman he could do better. If Harris had given Helen Potts eye-drops of atropine with her overdose of morphine, her pupils would have dilated to normal size, and nobody would have suspected poison.

Journalist Ike White learned of this conversation when investigating the fascinating fact that the recently widowed doctor had been married to a brothel madam. The second Mrs Buchanan (formerly Annie Sutherland) ran a house of assignation in Newark, New Jersey, and owned $50,000.

This fat, ugly woman jumped at the doctor's offer of respectable matrimony in 1890. But after only two years marriage, this pathetic woman, desperate for acceptance in the community, for which she subsequently died.

Two fellow-physicians agreed with Buchanan that the lady had suffered an apoplexy.

The doctor then went to Nova Scotia and remarried his first wife; a wealthy manufacturer's daughter whom he had divorced when he met Annie Sutherland.

Ike White learned that Buchanan's drunken boast was endorsed by the medical profession: acute morphine poisoning can only be distinguished from apoplexy by the pin-point pupil retraction in the former case. So Buchanan's tipsy indiscretion puts the doc in the dock, accused of murdering his wife.

Mrs Marie Deeming, murdered by her husband at Rainhill

Liverpool Murderer Caught in Australia

FREDERICK DEEMING left England last October, and turned up in Australia using a false name and passing himself off as a gentleman. His actual station and skills were those of a plumber and gas fitter.

In March this year, the authorities were called in over an unpleasant smell emanating from a house Deeming had been occupying under the name of Albert O. Williams. The smell proved to be the body of "Mrs Williams", cemented under the kitchen hearth.

"Williams" was traced to Sydney and arrested, and when his identity and recent immigrant status were established, the Home Office was asked to find out what they could about his activities in England.

They turned out to be worse than his wife-murder in Australia.

Cemented under the kitchen floor of Deeming's former house at Rainhill, Liverpool, were the bodies of his previous wife and four daughters. He had apparently cleared them out of the way tidily before moving on to his new life on the other side of the globe.

Full details of how and why Deeming committed the Rainhill murders may never be known, for the Australians quickly tried and executed him for his activities in Melbourne. A persistent rumour that he confessed to "the last" Jack the Ripper murders has been denied by his solicitors.

Nevertheless, the Australian police have sent his death mask to Scotland Yard, feeling that Deeming's is a peculiarly fine specimen of the ape-like skull Professor Lombroso assigns to the natural criminal (see 1875).

War in Wyoming Over Wire Fencing

A "WAR" IN Johnson County, Wyoming, may herald the end of the "Wild West". The days of all-powerful cattlemen dominating the ranges seem to be over.

Three years ago, rich stockmen controlled law and land throughout the territory. When a prostitute called Ella "Cattle Kate" Watson sold her favours for stolen stock, the cattlemen hanged her, and then falsely spread it to newspapers all over the country that she was a Bandit Queen.

This year they declared that Wyoming homesteaders had formed a band of rustlers known as the "Red Sash Gang", and they organized an army to wipe them out. While there are undoubted rustlers and desperadoes in the mountain hide-outs, the stockmen's first victims were two ranchers, killed in cold blood.

This aroused the county. Desperadoes and farmers united to drive off the stockmen's army, who in the end had to be rescued by US cavalry.

It seems that the cattlemen's real grievance is the spread of fixed ranches, with barbed wire fencing which restricts the great cattle ranges. Both cowboys and rustlers may now find their palmy days are over

Lizzie Borden: Gave Her Parents Eighty-One Whacks

Does Miss Lizzie look a fiend? Asks Defence Counsel

Borden Parents Brutally Killed by Unknown Assailant

AFTER A 13-DAY TRIAL, Miss Lizzie Borden walked free, acquitted of savagely killing her father and stepmother with an axe. Ex-Governor Robinson of Massachusetts, conducting her defence, played down the tricky questions of just where Lizzie was, and when, and why, as a mysterious intruder entered the Borden house and battered, first Mrs Abbie Borden, and then her husband Andrew.

Instead, the governor stressed Miss Lizzie's gentility, and the unlikelihood of the quiet, slightly plump, slightly pop-eyed spinster being so unladylike.

Public opinion, originally hostile to Miss Lizzie, swung strongly in her favour as she faced trial for her life. But now she has been acquitted, the fickle world is turning against her again, and she may anticipate a somewhat isolated life with her sister Miss Emma in Fall River, Massachusetts.

Discovery of the Bodies

About 10.30 am, August 4, 1892, businessman Andrew Borden returned to his home and lay down on the sofa for a nap.

Soon after this, Miss Lizzie called the maid, Bridget Sullivan, with the dreadful news that someone had broken in and killed her father.

Mr Borden had been struck ten times with an axe as he lay in his shirtsleeves. His blood was splashed over the wall and the sofa.

Neighbours coming to help asked where Mrs Borden was. Bridget Sullivan had not seen her since her mistress gave her orders to wash the outside windows early in the morning. Miss Lizzie said she had gone out to visit a friend – she did not know who.

As the neighbours crept upstairs to look in the bedroom, they saw the frightful spectacle of Mrs Borden lying beside the bed in a pool of her own blood. She had been battered 19 times with the axe, an hour or more

before her husband's death.

The screen door to the porch was unlocked. Anybody could have walked in. But neither Bridget nor Miss Lizzie had seen or heard anyone.

Where Were the Two Survivors During the Crimes?

As the only possible witnesses, Bridget Sullivan and Lizzie Borden had to account for their movements that morning.

Bridget had gone all round the house washing windows, as Mrs Borden had ordered. She must have been outside the house and out of view of the door when Mrs Borden was killed.

Then she retired to her room at the back of the house to lie down, as she was feeling sick in the sweltering hot weather.

She was there when Mr Borden died, and emerged from there when Miss Lizzie called her.

Miss Lizzie had also spent the early part of the morning in her own room at the back of the house. Mrs Borden's death had occurred in the front bedroom.

When Mr Borden came home, Miss Lizzie was in the loft over the barn in the garden, looking for some pieces of iron to make fishing sinkers for a riverside picnic at the weekend. She sat there a little time as she ate an apple. When she came back into the house she found her father's body.

Police Search Finds Murder Weapon

The police searched the house for anything suspicious. On neither Miss Lizzie's clothes nor Bridget Sullivan's did they find blood.

Andrew Borden, battered to death on his sofa

> "Lizzie Borden took an axe
> And gave her mother forty whacks;
> And when she saw what she had done
> She gave her father forty-one."
>
> **Children's rhyme.**

But in the basement they found a household chopper. It had been cleaned and lightly scoured with ashes fom the boiler, despite which it seemed to carry bloodstains. It could certainly have inflicted the Bordens' injuries, and thus pointed to a murder by someone inside the house with knowledge of its equipment and layout.

That left four possible suspects:

1. MISS EMMA BORDEN – staying with friends some distance away at the time of the murders. She might just have travelled home and back during the morning, but it seemed utterly improbable.

2. MR JOHN VINNICUM MORSE, middle-aged relative and houseguest of the Bordens. He went out to town early in the morning, and appeared in the garden shortly after Mr Borden's body was found. His composed action of picking windfall pears and ignoring the excitement aroused some suspicion at first, but he easily established a complete alibi.

3. BRIDGET SULLIVAN. Police found nothing suspicious whatever in her account of her morning's doings. Nor did any of her subsequent actions seem in any way untoward.

4. MISS LIZZIE BORDEN. Her account gave grave cause for suspicion.

The Brilliant Defence

Miss Borden's defence was perfectly suited to a New England jury. Governor Robinson is above all a gentleman, and quietly, without flamboyance, he saw that Miss Lizzie was treated as a lady.

Her "fishy" story about the apples and iron in the loft was simply accepted, as one accepts a lady's vagaries.

Her burned dress, it was delicately insinuated, had suffered contamination from a lady's monthly complaint: something no lady could possibly mention in public.

And so the gentlemen of the jury did the gentlemanly thing, and took the lady's word for everything.

But, as the children's rhyme shows, ladylike Lizzie will for ever live in the popular mind as the woman who "took an axe and gave her parents many whacks!"

ANOTHER SUSPICIOUS CIRCUMSTANCE?

The day before the murders, Mr and Mrs Borden were sick. This has been attributed to a joint of mutton which had been reappearing on their table variously prepared throughout the whole very hot week.

But that same day, Miss Lizzie tried to buy prussic acid in several stores. She said she wanted it to moth-proof a cape...

THE CASE AGAINST MISS LIZZIE

Her relations with Mrs Abbie Borden were bad. Miss Lizzie resented her stepmother inheriting any of Andrew Borden's property.

Early on the morning of August 3 she was wearing a blue dress. Later in the day she was wearing a brown one. The change was never properly explained.

A few days later she was seen to be burning the blue dress in the boiler, making the excuse that it was stained.

Whereas Bridget's story of her movements was corroborated at points by people who had seen her washing the windows, Miss Lizzie could produce no supporting witnesses.

Her story of visiting the loft was an obvious fabrication because:

1. The loft floor was carpeted with undisturbed dust.
2. There were no apples in the loft and no apple core was found.
3. There were no pieces of iron in the loft, and never had been.
4. Fishing sinkers are lead, not iron, anyway.
5. Nobody had ever heard of Miss Lizzie Borden fishing before, on church picnics or any other occasions!

The Borden house: to its left the undisturbed barn and loft where Lizzie pretends to have been

Tutor 'Not Proven' to Have Murdered his Pupil

Monson shakes hands with his counsel

TUTORIAL COACH Alfred Monson tried to become a financier when he took charge of 17-year-old Cecil Hamborough. Cecil's landowner father's property was heavily mortgaged, and he was in the hands of a moneylender. Monson tried to buy out Major Hamborough, but lacking the resources only made himself unwelcome to the Major.

With young Cecil completely under his influence, Monson moved to Ardlamont, Scotland, where he leased a house which, for fraudulent purposes, he pretended Cecil had purchased. He also insured Cecil's life for £20,000, and persuaded the lad, after some difficulty to make the policies payable to Mrs Monson.

In August this year, Monson tried to make the policies fall due. He went fishing with Cecil, and somehow the rowing-boat they were in overturned. Cecil was lucky not to drown. He went rabbit shooting with Cecil – and an unlucky accident meant that Cecil received a full charge of shot and died.

Monson raced home to report that Cecil had accidentally shot himself. Neither the gun, the ammunition nor the position of the wound were consistent with his story, and the attendant physician asked whether there was any insurance involved.

Insurance company investigators thought that the whole affair suspicious, and Monson found himself charged with murder and attempted murder.

He was lucky on two counts. The judge was favourable to him, and stressed that it was not the duty of the defence to prove innocence. And since he was in Scotland, it was open to the jury to bring in the stinging non-acquittal verdict Not Proven.

The holed hull planking alleged to have caused the deliberate capsizing of Cecil Hamborough's boat

Anarchist Assassinations Terrorize in Paris

THE POLITICAL EXTREMISTS who call themselves "Anarchists" have been carrying out a terror campaign in France over the past few years, flinging bombs at notables and officials whenever occasion arises. Their motives are threefold. They wish to show their distaste for private property by destroying houses and goods. They wish to break down social order, hoping to start another Revolution. In these respects they are imitating their Russian confreres.

But they also want revenge on French officialdom.

Their rage was triggered by police action in Clichy, a Paris suburb where police broke up a demonstration on May Day 1892, and five of the demonstrators complained that they were beaten by officers while resisting arrest.

A few months later, infernal machines destroyed the houses of the judge and the public prosecutor at their trial. Police announced that their principal suspect was a young man with a scarred hand, and when a café waiter noticed that he was serving such a man, he quietly had the police summoned.

It took ten men to overpower the fiercely struggling revolutionary: an anarchist named Ravachol. He declared that he was indeed responsible for the bombings, and they were undertaken to avenge the demonstrators of Clichy. Ravachol quickly became the idolized toast of the anarchist world. Happily, police quenched this adulation for a terrorist when they discovered that he lived by burglary and in the course of his crimes had committed several murders.

Another bomb, placed in a mining company office after Ravachol's execution, killed a policeman who removed it. And this May, a man called Vaillant hurled a home-made contraption of a saucepan containing old nails and gunpowder into the Chamber of Deputies. He was speedily executed.

'Rose of Cimarron's' Lover Escapes in Gun-Battle

ON SEPTEMBER 1, US marshals learned that a notorious gang of outlaws led by Bill Doolin were carousing at the little town of Ingalls in Oklahoma territory. A strong posse used a covered wagon as their Trojan Horse to gain unsuspected entry into the town, and might have arrested the band, had not they been spotted as they crept out of cover.

The resulting gun-battle was a disaster for the law. Three deputies were killed, and all but one of the badmen escaped.

The romantic highlight was the escape of handsome George "Bitter Creek" Newcomb. He was almost invisible in the dust kicked up by a hail of deputies' bullets. With his leg wounded and his ammunition spent, he seemed certain to be taken, when a young girl known as the "Rose of Cimarron" dashed into the eye of the storm, handed Newcomb a fresh gun-belt, and fired at the marshals, covering Newcomb with her body while he reloaded.

It is said this "Rose" was young Rosa Dunn, whom Newcomb seduced when she was a child.

It is alternatively suggested that she was tough western prostitute Rose O'Leary.

But it is also hinted that the whole story of Rose of Cimarron is a myth, and Newcomb escaped by sheer good luck!

$5,000.⁰⁰
REWARD
FOR CAPTURE
DEAD OR ALIVE
OF
BILL DOOLIN
NOTORIOUS ROBBER OF
TRAINS AND BANKS
ABOUT 6 FOOT 2 INCHES TALL, LT. BROWN HAIR,
DANGEROUS, ALWAYS HEAVILY ARMED.

IMMEDIATELY CONTACT THE
U.S. MARSHAL'S OFFICE, GUTHRIE, OKLAHOMA TER.

Police poster for wanted bandit Doolin

Angry Policeman Beats his Girlfriend to Death

PC GEORGE COOKE had a stormy relationship with prostitute Maud Merton. The London policeman paid her rent and let her pass him off as her husband. But he beat her when they quarrelled, and earlier this year, her complaints led to his being transferred from Bow Street to Acton.

On June 7 she found out where he was, and tackled him on his beat outside Wormwood Scrubs Prison. The two were heard quarrelling at 11.00 pm, and Miss Merton declared her intention of staying through the night and plaguing him even if his partner, PC Kemp, came and joined him.

The couple walked over the Scrubs and there Cooke drew his truncheon and smashed in the side of her face. He hit her again as she lay on the ground and pressed his foot on her throat until she was dead. He remarked later, "I thought nothing of killing her. I have been much happier since she was dead than I was before."

He joined PC Kemp back at the prison, and the two were very jolly all night for the remainder of their beat duty.

The Home Secretary does not agree with the defence submission that an efficient officer must be forgiven for brutally battering a mere harlot if she annoys him, and Cooke has been hanged!

> **" I THOUGHT NOTHING OF KILLING HER. I HAVE BEEN MUCH HAPPIER SINCE SHE WAS DEAD THAN I WAS BEFORE. "**
> QUOTE **PC George Cooke**

Pinkerton's Catch Hedgepeth, Aristocrat of Western Badmen

OUTLAW MARION HEDGEPETH, captured by Pinkerton's agents in San Francisco this year, is not the usual unwashed saddle-scuffed western ruffian. Short, but immaculate, Hedgepeth usually wears a beautifully cut suit and tailored overcoat, with his hair neatly pomaded under a bowler hat. Traditional gunslingers have occasionally made the mistake of thinking him an easy mark. At least one paid for this with his life, shot down by the dexterous Hedgepeth who drew, fired and hit his man – all after the enemy had his gun drawn and ready to fire.

After Jesse James's death (*see* 1882), Hedgepeth and his friends Albert Sly, Lucius Wilson and "Illinois Jimmy" Francis ("The Hedgepeth Four") inherited the James gang's mantle as leading train robbers. Their huge haul of $50,000 from a robbery at Glendale, Missouri, enabled them to split up and enjoy a respite from work, and it was during this pleasant break that Hedgepeth was taken.

The authorities in Missouri are seeking a long sentence for him, and if he is convicted, it is likely that the old "Wild West" will have changed beyond recognition by the time he re-emerges.

In the meantime, Missouri lawyers are shocked that his cell is a mass of flowers sent in daily by the adoring female population, who long to see this handsome and dapper villain acquitted and returned to the community.

IN BRIEF

DR ROBERT BUCHANAN, charged with murdering his second wife, was convicted after a cat was poisoned in court with morphine and its pupils dilated with atropine.

The doctor is strenuously appealing.

Bookkeeping Womanizer Kills Pregnant Girl

James Canham Read and his Mitcham mistress: a tangled love-life ended in tragedy

JAMES CANHAM READ'S women included his legitimate wife (who bore him 8 children), Mrs Ayriss and her unmarried sister Florence Dennis, and at least one other lady, who lived at Mitcham in south London.

Florence caused Read, a bookkeeper at the Royal Albert Dock, the greatest problem. She was but 18 when he seduced her two years ago, and early this year she found herself to be pregnant. She informed Read, and in the summer wrote asking him what he intended to do. Read arranged to meet her at Southend in June, after which Miss Dennis was not seen again.

Mrs Ayriss, knowing something of the tangled love-life in which she was involved, telegraphed Read asking what he knew about her missing sister. Read replied that he had not seen Florence for 18 months – a claim that could easily be refuted.

Apparently Read realized he was now in serious difficulties, for he stole some money from his employers and went into hiding with the lady at Mitcham. While he was there, Florence Dennis's body was discovered near Southend, a bullet through her head. The hunt was on for Read, and he was traced when he wrote to his brother.

Read claimed that his June visit to Southend had entailed his meeting Mrs Ayriss to whom he gave money for Florence. He further claimed that the father of Florence's forthcoming child was a soldier. Unfortunately for him, Florence had confessed all to her parents and declared that Read was the father.

Read called no evidence to support his story at his trial, and was hanged on December 4.

Chicago Brothel Doubles Staff for World Fair

VINA FIELDS' house of ill-fame on Custom House Place, Chicago, has for several years been the largest in the city, employing 40 girls. For this year's World's Fair, however, Vina has doubled the number, and trade is booming.

Vina is a black lady, and all her girls are black, though her clientele is exclusively white. It is normal for black harlots to be wickedly exploited by American brothel madams, but Vina pays her women an excellent percentage of the take, and in return they accept the extraordinary discipline which has made her house safe and successful.

Every three days Vina holds a court of enquiry. Girls who have been drinking, soliciting from the windows, lounging around the rooms in a state of disordered undress, or otherwise misbehaving, are fined or given domestic duties to perform. Serious offenders are dismissed. It is Vina's proud – and true – boast that no client has ever been robbed or cheated in her house.

In addition, Vina uses her personal wealth to alleviate the sufferings of others. She supports her own poor sisters and their husbands in the "Jim Crow" south. And with a notably severe winter setting in, she has opened her house to the homeless of Chicago in the evenings, providing free meals for the destitute. As many as 200 men at one time have eaten from her benevolence.

Mr W.T. Stead, editor of the *Pall Mall Gazette*, has been visiting Chicago and its infamous red light district to collect material for his continuing crusade against prostitution and the white slave trade. And yet even he remarks, "She is probably as good as any woman can be who conducts so bad a business."

Murder of Night Watchman at the Café Royal

NIGHTWATCHMAN Marius Martin was shot at London's Café Royal during the night of December 5-6. He was found lying inside the staff door leading out to Glasshouse Street.

It appears that someone hid in the building after the establishment closed with the intention of despatching him. Staff believe that the gentlemen's lavatory was still occupied at the time when the last of them left for the night.

Martin was a sour-tempered man who made many enemies by reporting waiters and cooks if he suspected them of leaving the building with left-over food.

IN BRIEF

RAVACHOL REMEMBERED
After the assassination of French President Sadi Carnot, stabbed in Lyons by the Italian anarchist Caserio, Mme Carnot received through the post a photograph of the executed anarchist murderer Ravachol (*see* 1893) inscribed, "He is avenged."

THE GRAFTON STREET MURDER
LATEST INCIDENTS IN THE CASE

"THE MAN TRIED TO STRANGLE ME. YOU CAN SEE THE MAN'S—"

"WHAT'S IN THAT TRUNK?"

HE FELL OVER ON TO THE FENDER

THE TRUNK.

MARIE HERMANN.

MARIE HERMANN MAKING HER STATEMENT IN HOLLOWAY-GAOL

Elderly harlot Marie Hermann perpetrates "the most terrible murder of the age" on lecherous punter Henry Stevens

Elderly German Prostitute Kills Cabman

MARIE HERMANN came to England as a German governess. There she married and had three children, but was left penniless when her husband died.

Unable to return to teaching, Mrs Hermann bravely took to the London streets to support her children, and in her heyday was known around the Haymarket as "the Duchess" for her classy manners.

But old age had made her trade less remunerative, and early this year she lived and worked from cheap lodgings in Grafton Street. On March 17, however, she enjoyed a sudden access of good fortune. She took and furnished better lodgings in Upper Marylebone Street, bringing with her a heavy trunk which, she declared, contained "treasures of hers".

Her neighbours were suspicious and informed the police, who found the trunk contained the body of retired 70-year-old cabdriver Henry Stevens. He had been battered to death. Marie claimed that he had tried to force himself on her without paying, and was actually strangling her when she managed to seize the poker and hit him. Mr Stevens' son dismissed the story as poppycock, saying his father would never have gone with a prostitute, and £50 he had been carrying was missing.

Things looked black for Frau Hermann until she reached the Old Bailey. But her counsel, a brilliant young barrister named Edward Marshall Hall, who had never conducted a murder defence before, successfully showed that bruising on her neck and abrasions on Stevens' elbow fully supported her story. He further established that Stevens' house is a brothel, and young Mr Stevens cohabits with one of its working girls. Finally, in a brilliantly theatrical peroration he moved himself, his client, and many onlookers to tears. Mary Hermann, originally accused of "The Most Terrible Murder of the Age", has received a short sentence for manslaughter.

Extraordinary Case of Murder by Hypnosis

POLICE INVESTIGATING the death of 27-year-old Kitty Ging, whose body was found in Minneapolis with a bullet behind the ear on December 3, have uncovered a bizarre story that the most sensational novelist might hesitate to invent.

As soon as the body was found, a lawyer went to the district attorney's office to report that one of his clients, a Mr Adry Hayward, had approached him earlier in the year for advice about her. Mr Hayward said that his brother Harry had tried to persuade him to assassinate Miss Ging. It appeared that Harry held two large insurance policies on her life, and hoped to establish a cast-iron alibi while someone else killed her. When Adry Hayward indignantly refused, Harry said he would try to use the services of a simple-minded handyman called Claus Blixt who was easily influenced. Mr Adry Hayward also reported that his brother appeared to be trying to hypnotize him while they talked.

The lawyer dismissed the story as absurd until Miss Ging was in fact murdered. Under questioning, Blixt has revealed that Harry Hayman constantly practised hypnotism on both him and Miss Ging. Under the hypnotic spell, Miss Ging made over money to Hayward for him to invest, and took out the life insurance policies. Blixt had also been "hypnotized" to set fire to a property owned and insured by Miss Ging, for which arson he was paid.

Harry Hayward has his cast-iron alibi for the murder, he was at the Minneapolis Grand Opera House at the time when Kitty died. It seems certain, however, that Blixt was induced to kill her, either by hypnotic influence or by the promise of cash.

The investigation continues.

Oscar Wilde was Not 'Posing as a Sodomite'

LONDON'S MOST successful playwright, with two brilliant comedies running simultaneously, now lies a discredited convict. Oscar Wilde's indiscreet friendship with Lord Alfred Douglas perturbed Lord Alfred's father, the Marquess of Queensberry, three years ago. The Marquess, a sportsman who has done much to legitimize prize-fighting, was appalled that his son might be less than manly. And while Mr Wilde's charm could have soothed the marquess, Lord Alfred provoked disharmony.

When *The Importance of Being Earnest* opened this February, the Marquess went to St James's Theatre to create a disturbance. Turned away, he went angrily to Mr Wilde's club, and left his card with the mis-spelled inscription, "To Oscar Wilde posing as a somdomite." "Bosie" Douglas is foolish and litigious, and he egged Mr Wilde on to sue the Marquess for criminal libel.

When the case came on in November, Mr Wilde could not explain his familiarity with grooms and newspaper boys.

Realizing that these Miss Nancies were going to give evidence of his indecencies with them, Wilde broke down and withdrew his case.

That night he was himself arrested and charged with criminal misconduct. After two trials, he has been jailed for two years: the longest sentence possible, and one which Mr Justice Wills believes all right-thinking men and women must find utterly inadequate punishment for men so dangerous to society that they actually toy with one another's genitals.

Mr Oscar Wilde, now exposed as an unspeakable pervert

THE BLACKMAILERS' CHARTER

Wilde has been convicted under the Criminal Justice Act of 1885, a routine bill, to which Radical MP Henry Labouchere added an apparently insigificant amendment, laying down two years imprisonment as the penalty for homosexual acts.

Fortunately the Act had to receive the assent of our Gracious Queen who, herself a woman, noticed that this implied women might commit indecencies with women: something she knew to be untrue. So the penalties for such wholly imaginary "Sapphic love" were withdrawn.

It was, nevertheless, observed that so many evil men deliberately give themselves over to voluntary animality with other men, that the Labouchere Amendment constitutes a blackmailers' charter!

Gang's Terrible Reputation in Just Two Weeks!

RUFUS BUCK and four other Creek Indians with black blood, formed a criminal gang on July 28 and were captured by Creek mounted policemen on August 10.

In those 13 days the savage adolescents held up stores and ranches, raped women, killed a deputy marshal because they didn't like the way he looked at them, shot a black boy in cold blood because his employer had taken up their challenge to outrun their guns and succeeded, threatened to drown a mother's babies if she didn't let them rape her.

The Creeks pleaded with the law to let the tribe carry out Indian justice on them, Hanging Judge Parker (*see* these pages) insists that he will be their nemesis.

Either way, we wager they will not survive the next year!

Killer of the Hangman's Daughter Reprieved

TO THEIR disappointment the citizens of Fort Smith, Arkansas, are not about to learn whether their famous hangman George Maledon can hang a man badly and leave him twitching. George's daughter Annie started a love affair with married Frank Carver. George couldn't hang Frank for that.

But when the liaison involved a quarrel, and somebody pulled a gun, and Annie died with a bullet in her back – well, that put Frank in front of "Hanging" Judge Parker (*see* 1889).

Since 1875, George Maledon and Isaac Parker have been a great team in Arkansas and the Indian territory, where the saying runs: "Parker sentenced the man, and Maledon suspended sentence."

Parker was particularly keen to see Carver suspended, as Annie had played with his own little boys as a child. He and Maledon and the whole community, therefore, were furious when a higher court overturned the sentence of death.

So now we'll never know what George Maledon might have done to the man that killed the hangman's beautiful daughter.

> ## "PARKER SENTENCED THE MAN, AND MALEDON SUSPENDED SENTENCE."
> **Anon**
>
> QUOTE

Doctor Built Murder Hotel for World Exposition

DR HERMANN WEBSTER MUDGETT, alias H.H. Holmes, has been arrested at last after a pursuit across America and Canada during which this monstrous villain wiped out all the children of his dupe Benjamin Pitzel, leaving buried bodies for his pursuers to find. Still more remarkably, the evil genius concealed from both Mrs Pitzel and the current Mrs Holmes that the other existed and he was travelling with both! By the end of the journey he had also reunited with the original Mrs Mudgett, whom he deserted years ago!

Police have sought Holmes earnestly since his short-term cellmate Marion Hedgepeth (*see* 1893) revealed that Holmes cheated him of his share of an insurance scam. The swindle entailed insuring Pitzel under a false name, and claiming he died in a laboratory explosion. All the plotters understood Holmes would provide a disguised cadaver to be found in the wreckage. As police discovered, he poisoned Pitzel instead!

The identification of the body by Holmes and one of Pitzel's children was rendered tragically convincing by the child's genuine grief.

Further investigation of this horse-thief, bodysnatcher and general swindler showed that he was a bigamist who regularly killed superfluous wives and mistresses; and, most astonishing of all, he constructed a hotel for the Chicago World's Exposition last year in which every room was monitored by secret electric bells; many could be rendered airtight and have poison gas pumped into them; and chutes transmitted bodies to a two-tier cellar for dismemberment and incineration.

How many people Holmes killed and robbed in his various schemes is unknown. He has admitted to 20 or 27. Others estimate 40 to 100. Sensationalists suggest 200!

However many it be, H.H. Holmes is probably America's all-time master-criminal.

Naked Trysts in Emmanuel Baptist Church

W.H. "THEO" DURRANT was a Sunday School teacher and Christian Endeavour Society member by day. By night he went to San Francisco's most depraved brothels for the peculiar perversion of having a pigeon stabbed at the height of his ecstasy, to feel its blood spurt over him.

On April 12 Durrant was seen entering Emmanuel Baptist Church with 20-year-old Minnie Williams. Two hours later he was at a Christian Endeavour Society meeting. She was not.

When her disappearance caused alarm, it was recalled that Durrant had been seen entering the church with 18-year-old Blanche Lamont nine days earlier, some hours before she, too, disappeared.

The church was thoroughly-searched, and the two girls' naked bodies were at last found in the belfry. It appeared that after sex with the two ladies Durrant strangled them and mutilated their bodies with a knife.

Blanche, it seems, died for resisting the fiend's attempt to ravish her. Yet Minnie died although she had happily sported naked with her lover and enjoyed his attention in the sacred premises.

The jury unanimously found Durrant guilty of murder on their first ballot.

Murderer Durrant carries victims to belfry

IN BRIEF

DR BUCHANAN (*see* 1892) executed for the morphine poisoning of his wife.

CLAUS BLIXT sentenced to life imprisonment, and Harry Hayward executed, for the murder of Kitty Ging (*see* 1894). Hayward, flamboyant to the end, secured suspension by a red rope on a red scaffold, though refused permission to wear red clothes.

Jack the Ripper: The Whitechapel Murderer

Panic spreads all over London with the double killing of Elizabeth Stride and Catherine Eddowes

Mystery Killer Knifeman Terrorizes London Slums

EVEN IN 1889, rumour in the East End had it that agitator Albert Bachert had been told by police that the murderer had drowned. And in 1890, before his resignation Metropolitan Police Commissioner James Monro stated publicly that he had "decidedly" formed a theory on the case, adding that, "when I do theorize it is from a standpoint and not upon any visionary foundations."

Even so, no Metropolitan Police officer has favoured the press with their suspect's name. Chief Constable Melville Macnaghten of the CID, who keeps horrifying photographs of the murderer's hideously mutilated victims in his office, privately tells acquaintances of three final suspects, one of whom he has concluded was certainly the Ripper. But he adds that he will never reveal his name.

Mr Macnaghten also clears up one more mystery for Ripper hunters. While his colleagues were claiming that the murderer was already dead, several more gruesome killings took place. Mr Macnaghten now reveals that only five murders attributed to the villain were the work of the same man: the others were not connected.

The Early Murders

London first realized that a terrifying killer stalked the streets on August 31, 1888. Then, two carters walking to work past a gloomy Whitechapel warehouse, found prostitute Mary Ann Nichols lying in the gutter. Not only was her throat cut, but a grisly gash in her abdomen laid open her intestines. Some astute detectives linked her slaying with those of Martha Tabram, three weeks previously, and Emma Smith on Easter Monday.

Within eight days the monster had struck again, cutting Annie Chapman's throat, and inflicting mutilations so indecent that the coroner had women and children cleared from the inquest before allowing the doctor to describe them in detail.

After a short respite of three weeks, two appalling murders occurred within fifty minutes of each other. Disturbed before he could mutilate Elizabeth Stride in Berner Street, the killer made his way to Mitre Square in the City of London and struck down Catherine Eddowes.

The Fiend Taunts His Hunters

From now on, the gaps between murders became longer and longer. But there was no cessation of panic, since the criminal let the public know how he gloated over his misdeeds.

"Dear Boss," he wrote to the Central News Agency, "I keep on hearing the police have caught me but they won't fix me just yet ... I love my work and want to start again ... My knife's so nice and sharp I want to get to work right away ..." and he signed this red-inked missive with the name by which he wanted to be

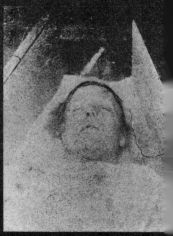

Ripper victim: Mary Ann Nichols

Years of anxiety end as file is closed and world-wide murder hunt is terminated. The Whitechapel murderer is no more. The fiend who terrorized East London for two years has died, according to the Metropolitan Police. Sources close to Chief Inspector Donald Swanson, who headed the enquiry, report that he says the mysterious Jack the Ripper was a man who is now dead.

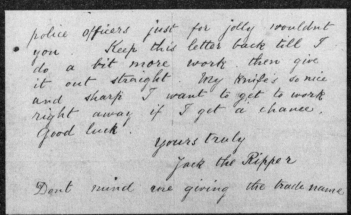

police officers just for jolly wouldnt you. Keep this letter back till I do a bit more work. then give it out straight. My knife's so nice and sharp I want to get to work right away if I get a chance. Good luck.

yours truly
Jack the Ripper

Dont mind me giving the trade name

An extract from the "Dear Boss" letter signed in red ink by "Jack the Ripper"

known – Jack the Ripper.

Since then, letters in the same handwriting have been received at Scotland Yard and in newspaper offices, along with other communications which, police think, include a number of hoaxes. But Mile End building contractor Albert Lusk, who headed a local vigilance committee of respectable businessmen, received the most sickening mail of all. Along with a jeering letter, the maniac sent him a parcel containing half a human kidney. This, it was alleged, came from the City of London victim, Catherine Eddowes, and the killer boasted of having fried and eaten the other half!

Police medical advisors tried to throw cold water on this sensation by calling it a student hoax. But the public was not impressed. Panic spread all over London, and the Queen herself urged the Home Secretary to take more decisive action.

was found by a rent-collector. She lay on her bed in the wretched room where she entertained depraved clients.

Her last and worst visitor cut her throat. Then he cut all round her neck, but failed to decapitate her. He cut all the flesh off her chest, down to the ribcage, and scored between the ribs. He cut away much of her eyebrows, nose, cheeks and ears. He carved surface flesh off her left thigh, and totally exposed the bone in her right thigh.

The poor woman's abdominal wall was removed and left in three huge flaps of flesh on a table. The abdominal cavity was emptied, and all the organs were found on the bed: on, under and around the body. Her heart was pulled out of her chest, but he failed to extract her lungs.

This unspeakable butchery left the room splattered with blood. Nobody who saw this appalling spectacle wishes to talk about it in length.

The Worst Crime of All

November 9, 1888, the day of the Lord Mayor's Show, saw the most unspeakable crime of the series. Mary Jane Kelly's body

Three More Murders

After that fearful savagery there was a long lull. Indeed, Chief Constable Macnaghten gives it as his private opinion that the

murderer's indulgence in unrestrained slaughter triggered a brainstorm which led him to commit suicide.

None the less, there were three further murders which some have attributed to the dreaded Ripper.

Rose Mylett was found dead in a builder's yard in Poplar High Street in Christmas week, 1888. (Police insist, contradicting the inquest verdict, that hers was a natural death.)

"Clay Pipe" Alice Mackenzie was found up an alley in July 1888 with her throat stabbed and some abdominal injuries. (Commissioner Monro declared that this was not the work of the Ripper.)

Frances Coles was found bleeding to death from a cut throat under a railway arch in February 1891. (Police brought charges against a ship's fireman called Sadler, who was cleared at the magistrates court.)

Since then, there have been no further atrocious murders of this kin, though public speculation as to the miscreant's identity remains intense.

Who Was He?

The first important suggestions came from police doctors. It was reported that the Ripper was left-handed, and that he had some medical or butchering skills. A noted alienist remarked that he must have somewhere to clean himself up, from which he deduced that he was a gentleman and not a slum dweller. The immigrant community suspected a mad Russian medical student, believed to have been recently released from incarceration in France. Local prostitutes thought he was a man – possibly a Jewish immigrant – who threatened them on the streets, and one such suspect was actually arrested and cleared.

VICTIMS

April 3, 1888
EMMA ELIZABETH SMITH
Osborn Street, Whitechapel

August 7, 1888
MARTHA TABRAM
George Yard, Whitechapel

August 31, 1888
MARY ANN NICHOLS*
Buck's Row, Whitechapel

September 8, 1888
ANNIE CHAPMAN*
Hanbury Street, Spitalfields

September 30, 1888
ELIZABETH STRIDE, *LONG LIZ**
Berner Street,
St George-in-the-East

September 30, 1888
CATHERINE EDDOWES*
Mitre Square, City of London

November 9, 1888
MARY JANE KELLY*
Dorset Street, Spitalfields

December 20, 1888
ROSE MYLETT, *LIZZIE DAVIES*
Clarke's Yard, Poplar High St

July 17, 1889
ALICE MACKENZIE,
CLAY PIPE ALICE
Castle Alley, Whitechapel

February 13, 1891
FRANCES COLES
Swallow Gardens,
Royal Mint St, E1

* These are the only real Ripper victims, police now say

Baby Farmer Put Murdered Infants in River Thames

Mrs Amelia Dyer, baby farmer

FIFTY SEVEN-YEAR-OLD Mrs Amelia Dyer, a devout Church Army member, looks a motherly soul in her bonnet and shawl. For 15 years mothers have entrusted babies to her care – especially if the babies were "shameful bundles" the mothers could not acknowledge.

But last year Mrs Dyer made a mistake and assumed Miss Doris Marmon did not want to see her child again when she did. The difficulties and delays led to the temporary arrest of Mrs Dyer's daughter and son-in-law in Willesden in north-west London, where the dear old soul had received the sweet little poppet. For the poppet's clothes were still in Arthur and Polly Palmer's house.

But baby Marmon had been found in the Thames at Reading. Strangled. Mrs Dyer lived at Reading.

By the time the police traced her, a total of seven babies had been fished out of the Thames. Mrs Dyer apparently imagined she was one of many good souls passing the little innocents into the arms of the river, for she said reassuringly, "You'll know all mine by the tape around their necks."

Infamous though baby farmers are for their cruelty, the police were relieved that by this token they found no one else's victims.

Despite a resolute and convincing defence of insanity, supported by irrefutable evidence that Mrs Dyer has been in and out of asylums for the past ten years, she has been convicted and will hang on June 10.

> " **YOU'LL KNOW ALL MINE BY THE TAPE AROUND THEIR NECKS.** "
>
> **Mrs Amelia Dyer**

QUOTE

Double Murder in Turner Street, Stepney

YOUTHFUL DETECTIVE-SERGEANT Wensley of H Division, Whitechapel, London, has made his name in the Turner Street murders case. Called to no. 33, on the corner of Turner and Varden Streets, Wensley found a small crowd. Uniformed constables reported a man's body inside the front door and a woman stabbed upstairs. But they saw no trace of any intruder.

Mr Wensley himself says the "detection" was extremely simple. He went to the bedroom and observed a newly-made hole in the ceiling. He stood on a chair to look through it and saw a man disappearing through another newly-made hole in the roof. He alerted his colleagues.

The intruder emerged to see police thick among the crowd below him and escape impossible. So, cursing the bystanders as Jews, he launched himself into the air and dropped 40 feet, breaking both thighs.

He proved to be William Seaman, recently released from prison for his murderous assault on a Berner Street chemist (*see* 1888). His Turner Street victims were 77-year-old John Goodman Levy and his housekeeper Mrs Gale. It was widely believed that Levy had amassed a fortune as a receiver of stolen goods, and kept it on the premises.

Seaman was convicted, sentenced and hanged in short order, sharing the scaffold with Albert Millsom and Henry Fowler (*see* these pages).

Watch What You Drink in Chicago

ANOTHER DANGER for the unwary in the Windy City lies in the drinks served at the Lone Star Saloon and the Palm Garden on Whiskey Row. For the barkeeper running these two joints is a guy named Mickey Finn, who owns the recipe to a voodoo mixture that is overwhelming in alcohol and water.

Take one of Mickey Finn's specials, and you'll start talking silly and reeling about the room, until you pass into a deep slumber.

Then you are carried into a back room, where Mickey dons a bowler hat and a clean white apron to search you for valuables. He will also remove any good clothes you own and replace them with filthy rags, before dumping you in an alley. When you wake up, you won't remember a thing.

So never take a drink from Mickey Finn!

IN BRIEF

H.H. HOLMES, executed for the murder of Benjamin Pitzel (*see* 1895) after publishing a highly inaccurate confession claiming that the Devil was present at his birth.

THE RUFUS BUCK GANG (*see* 1895) executed, one of them leaving a maudlin and misspelled poem to his mother in his cell, which moved flinty old Judge Parker to tears!

Muswell Hill Burglars' Toy Lantern Helps in Arrest

QUOTE

> **"IT'S THE FIRST TIME IN MY LIFE I'VE BEEN A BLOODY PEACE-MAKER!"**
>
> **William Seaman**

MR HENRY SMITH of Muswell Lodge used to fill his grounds with spring-guns and alarms. These practices did not ultimately protect the timorous householder; rather they persuaded the criminal fraternity that he must have something worth stealing.

On February 14 Mr Smith was found dead in his kitchen. He had been tied up and his head slashed with penknives – the work of brutal thieves who subjected him to cruel questioning.

Near Mr Smith's body was a child's toy lantern; an odd piece of burglar's kit, but certainly not something belonging to the house. It appeared to be the only clue.

Albert Millsom and Henry

Violent Henry Fowler, the infamous Kentish Town criminal, fiercely resists detectives arresting him in Bath

Fowler, well-known Kentish Town criminals, had been seen in the vicinity, and enquiries proved that they had left London for destinations unknown. When Millsom's young stepbrother was shown the lantern he immediately identified it as his, and the hunt was on.

The pair were traced to Bath,

and Fowler proved to have passed a banknote stolen from Mr Smith's safe.

Under interrogation, Millsom admitted the robbery but blamed Fowler for the murder. This led to ill-feeling between the pair, and Fowler tried to attack Millsom at their trial.

In turn, an odd scene occurred at their execution, where multi-murderer William Seaman (*see* opposite page) was hanged with them and placed between them on the scaffold. Seeing irony in this situation, he remarked: "It's the first time in my life I've been a bloody peacemaker!"

Muswell Lodge, home of the security-conscious Mr Henry Smith

Chicago Gang is Just Two Women!!!

POLICE IN CHICAGO refer to it as the "Kitty and Jenny gang", and note that it has carried out at least 100 serious and violent robberies each year for the last seven years. Yet the "gang" is two people, and both are women!

Kitty Adams came to Chicago around 1880 and soon became known as "The Terror of State Street". She worked as the only

white prostitue in a black brothel for a time, learning, among other things, the defensive value of a cut-throat razor – something she always carried thereafter. She has been known to excise the ears of a difficult lover!

Jennie Clark, a younger and prettier prostitute, teamed up with her in 1886. They have a crib in the Levee, Chicago's red light district.

But their real joy is the "badger game". Jenny's looks will pick up a client and lure him down a dark alley where Kitty springs out and holds a knife to his throat while Jenny empties his pockets. And woe betide the mark if he screams or struggles!

This year, however, a bold man identified them and brought charges. Kitty promptly jumped bail. But Jenny appeared for her trial, to hear Mr Justice Goggin deliver the astonishing judgement: "Any man who goes down to the Levee deserves to get himself robbed. Case dismissed." With that, the fugitive warrant against Kitty evanesced, and the two are back on the street, luring and robbing.

Famous Actor Murdered at Stage Door

William Terris in "Days of the Duke"

A TERRIBLE SCENE occurred at the entry to London's Adelphi Theatre in Maiden Lane, used by actor-manager William Terris as his personal stage door. As the handsome hero of melodrama walked briskly up for the evening performance on December 16, a gaunt figure raced across the road from under the awning of Rule's Restaurant; a knife flashed; and Mr Terris lay bleeding on the step.

Fellow-actors helped him to a sofa in the green-room, but he had not long to live. As the tragic news was telegraphed from theatre to theatre, all the stages of the West End observed a brief silence in his memory.

The assassin made no attempt to escape, but strode vaingloriously up and down the street muttering words to the effect that he was glad of what he had done and Terris deserved it. Then the police arrived, and he meekly handed over his knife. When they offered him food

he burst into tears, saying, "I'm so hungry".

It turns out he is Richard Prince, an eccentric Scottish actor known as "Mad Archie". He harboured delusions that his talents were undervalued, and some colleagues mischievously played up to his insane conviction that Mr Terris enviously restricted him to walk-on parts.

In fact, it was as an act of charity that Mr Terris employed Prince at all, his mental condition making him a very poor actor. And when the time came that Prince could not be put on the stage at any price, Mr Terris still gave him hand-outs and free theatre passes.

It seems that the refusal of a pass Prince peremptorily demanded at another theatre turned the poor fellow's wits, and he concluded that Mr Terris was conspiring against him.

There can be no question of Richard Prince hanging for the crime. He is obviously quite mad, and will be detained at Her Majesty's pleasure.

The assassination of Mr Terris by "Mad Archie" Prince

Wife's Passion and Poison in Yokohama

THERE IS something in tropical ex-patriate life conducive to most un-English passions. Thus the British consul in Yokohama has the unwelcome duty of trying a fellow-countrywoman for conduct that might befit the demon-lady in a Kabuki drama.

Toward the end of last year, Mr Walter Carew, an English businessman, fell ill and no treatment would settle his bilious stomach. Later, a Japanese chemist sent his doctor a note reading: "Three bottles of arsenic in one week". This was what he had supplied to Mrs Carew and this, it transpired, was killing her husband.

Mrs Carew claimed that she ordered the arsenic solution for her husband as the only medicine to afford relief for an undiagnosed illness to which he was prone. But love-letters in her home showed that she was involved in a liaison with a young bank clerk. She had complained to this inno-

cent that her husband mistreated her, and discussed leaving Walter Carew. Her complaints aroused the young man's ardour, and he seemed to contemplate eloping with Mrs Carew, should she be free and willing to go.

Apparently under the impression that *tu quoque* is an acceptable defence, Mrs Carew has produced letters purporting to show that her husband was also entangled in an adulterous liaison. But a Japanese handwriting expert declares that these are the forged work of Mrs Carew herself.

And so in the New Year, the British Consul in Yokohama will perforce take on the unexpected role of Judge in a steamy murder trial under the oriental sun.

French 'Ripper' Taken: Blames Mad Dog Bite

ON AUGUST 4, a woman walking through woods near Tournon was attacked by a tramp. Her husband responded to her cries and between them they overpowered the rogue and turned him in to the police.

Joseph Vacher was charged with offending against public decency and given a three month sentence. But all the time the authorities wondered whether they had at last captured the maniac who had ravished, murdered and mutilated seven women and four youths over the past four years. Vacher had just emerged from an asylum when the killings began, having been incarcerated for a year after attacking a girl and trying to shoot himself.

At first Vacher denied all complicity in these mutilating sex-murders. But now he has blurted out that he committed them all in moments of frenzy. He declares he was bitten by a mad dog when he was a child, and has suffered from infected blood ever since.

It falls to the French courts to decide whether this man is sane enough to stand trial for the horrible multiple murder.

Vacher, the French Ripper

'Jig-Saw Puzzle' of Body in New York Harbour

A MAN'S CHEST, abdomen and legs were found separately this June, wrapped in red oilcloth in New York harbour and the Harlem River. Fitted together, this "jigsaw puzzle" formed one man, minus his head.

His manicured hands and a scrap of tissue excised from the chest identified him as masseur Willie Guldensuppe, who had born an identifiable tattoo at the point from which skin had been removed.

Guldensuppe lived with midwife Anna Knack and was one of her many lovers. Investigators found blood in the soakaway drainage system around her house.

Mrs Knack caved in under questioning and agreed to turn State's Evidence. According to her story, another lover, Fred Thorn, was jealous of Guldensuppe and shot him. The body was then dismembered in the bath and wrapped in oilcloth after the telltale tattoo was excised. The head was embedded in plaster of Paris to ensure its sinking, and the lot dumped into the harbour.

Among the many interesting features of this sordid story is the discovery that plaster of Paris forms a satisfactory sinking weight, and does not disintegrate under the action of the tides.

Since Mrs Knack admits to helping dispose of the body, she will be charged as accessory after the fact, while Fred Thorn faces indictment for murder.

Chicago Butcher Turns His Wife Into Sausages

ADOLPH LUETGERT, Chicago's main sausage manufacturer, was a phenomenal lover, with many mistresses and a convenient bed located at his factory for occasional dalliance.

But the 250-lb German immigrant's wife Louise found his infidelities intolerable.

In May, Louise's brother went to the police to say she had disappeared. Since Luetgert had made passionate demands that the police institute an all-out search for his missing dog some time previously, Captain Hermann Schluetter found it suspicious that he had not reported Louise's absence.

A search of the sausage factory turned up human bone fragments and Louise's wedding ring in one of the vats. Circumstantial evidence indicates that Luetgert stabbed her, boiled down the body, and put it through the sausage grinder. He has been sentenced to life imprisonment, and the citizens of Chicago are very cautious about buying sausages!

Another Train Murder — But No Robbery: No Rape

BARMAID Elizabeth Camp was found dead under a seat in the evening train from Houndsworth to London's Waterloo station. The bloody pestle that killed her lay on the line near Putney.

Police believe the killer was a moustachioed, bloodstained man, who briefly appeared in the Alma Tavern just after the train left Putney.

They believe he was a demented vagrant who was recently committed to an asylum and possessed a false moustache. But as they are prohibited from disguising him in the moustache for an identity parade, they cannot put their theory to the test.

Discovery of Miss Camp's body under a London train seat

'Red Hot Mama' Kills Lover's Wife

FAT, PLAIN, and very, very sexy: that's Cordelia Botkin of San Francisco! In 1896, when she was 42, Mrs Botkin lured journalist John Presley Dunning away from his wife to join her in low-life whoring and gambling. Mrs Dunning went to live with her parents in Delaware. For two years she has received threatening anonymous letters, warning her not to attempt reconciliation with her husband.

This year, journalist Dunning was hired to report the Spanish-American War. Cordelia evidently feared that removal from her presence might lead him to rejoin his wife. Mrs Dunning received a postal parcel containing candies and a lace handkerchief. A note read "With love to yourself and baby - Mrs C."

Mrs Dunning did not spend too long puzzling over the identity of "Mrs C". She and her sister, Mrs Joshua Deane, ate the candies.

That night they both died. The sweets had been heavily dosed with arsenic. It was possible to trace the candy back to Cordelia Botkin, who had also bought a lace handkerchief and some arsenic. Furthermore the anonymous notes sent to Mrs Dunning over the past two years appear to be in her hand.

The jealous murderess has been sentenced to life imprisonment. And the press has dubbed this ugly but enticing sensualist "the Red Hot Mama".

Living Like Animals in Slumland

BRUTAL SLUMLAND domestic life appeared in uncontested evidence at Thomas Daley's trial for murdering his common-law wife Sarah Ann Penfold in Chatham, Kent.

On June 3, Daley came home drunk and went to bed. Toward 10.00 pm Sarah Penfold came home, also drunk. She complained incoherently that she had been "dragged", had fallen over chairs and ended up on the floor.

Daley tore her clothes off when she refused to undress, and put her to bed. During the night she arose repeatedly to drink water. The third time she knocked the jug over, spilling water over the room. Daley thereupon got up and hit her with the poker. When she fell to the floor he jumped on her, trampled her and kicked her. This calmed his temper a little, but as she did not answer him, he returned to kicking her.

It then occurred to him that she might be dead, so he dragged her to a chair. Feeling shaky with drink and violence by this time, he went back to bed and slept.

At 6.30 in the morning he called a neighbour to say Sarah Ann might be dying. The neighbour found the naked corpse hanging over a chair with injured eyebrows, cheek and mouth; bruised arms; and a huge bruise on the abdomen. There was blood all over the room.

The jury was so convinced of Daley's guilt that they did not need to retire to consider their verdict, and pronounced him guilty from the box. When the judge reproached Daley with ill-using a woman who had been good to him, he replied improbably:

> " **SHE WAS A GOOD WOMAN. I TRUST THAT ALMIGHTY GOD WILL GIVE ME POWER TO SEE HER AGAIN.** "
> **Thomas Daley**

New York Knickerbocker Club Poisonings

ON DECEMBER 23 this year, Harry Cornish, athletics director of New York's posh Knickerbocker Club, received a bottle of Bromo-Seltzer anonymously through the mail. Mr Cornish thought some friend was having a little joke with him, hinting that he might be tempted to excessive-bibulous celebration at Christmas.

On December 28, Mr Cornish's landlady, Mrs Katherine Adams, complained of headache. Mr Cornish offered her a dose of Bromo-Seltzer, which she gratefully accepted and drank off, complaining however that it tasted surprisingly bitter. Mr Cornish took a tiny sip, but detected nothing.

Mrs Adams thereupon went into convulsions and died. Mr Cornish is seriously ill. The Bromo-Seltzer contained mercury cyanide.

Club members then recalled that this was the second recent sudden fatality associated with the Knickerbocker, and in both cases there was a suspicious association with Mr Roland B. Molineux.

Mr Henry C. Barnett died suddenly in November, and it was widely suspected that he had received poison through the mail. Mr Barnett had been paying attentions to Miss Blanche Cheeseborough, who married Mr Roland B. Molineux very shortly after Barnett's death.

Mr Molineux also disliked Mr Cornish intensely, as everyone knew. Matters came to a head recently, when Mr Cornish bested Mr Molineux in a weight-lifting contest, and Mr Molineux resigned from the club when the committee refused to dismiss Mr Cornish.

Roland B. Molineux, a brilliant, socially successful and charming chemist, who was cited as co-respondent in a divorce case at the tender age of 15, now stands strongly suspected of poisoning two of his fellow club-members.

Policemen Enter House Without Preventing Murders

AT ABOUT 7.30 in the evening on February 5, police sergeants French and Darnall were told that a row was going on at no. 115, Brick Lane, London. The sergeants went into the pitch-dark building, and waited for a candle before proceeding upstairs. While they hesitated, shots rang out and two people were fatally injured.

The upper part of the house was let to 27-year-old Marta Wysocka, whose husband is in America. During his absence she sublet rooms to immigrant bamboo-workers, and contracted a close friendship with 39-year-old Frederick Kareczewski. This aroused disapproval among his friends and Marta's fellow-lodgers. Frederick claims he feared they would beat him when he visited Marta, and so carried a revolver.

When Marta and her roommate Ada Karinski shut themselves into the brothers Teodor and Clement Kuzmierovich's room, Frederick shouted at them, "Come out all of you and I will shoot the lot of you!"

He then fired through the door panels, injuring Ada and fatally wounding Marta. On breaking in, he put his pistol to Teodor Kuzmierovich's throat, and as Ada and Teodor struggled to wrest the weapon from him, it discharged, killing Clement.

So the police sergeants who had been called to put an end to the disturbance arrived on the scene to find confusion and dead bodies.

IN BRIEF

W.H. "THEO" DURRANT, executed, after many appeals, for the belfry murders (*see* 1896). Durrant's sister will delay her first professional appearance as an artistic exotic dancer and use the name Maud Allan rather than present the spectacle of a murdering rapist's kin.

JOSEPH VACHER (*see* 1897) guillotined on December 31 for murder. His head was handed over to scientists for examination.

FRED THORN (*see* 1897) electrocuted for the murder of Willie Guldensuppe. Anna Knack sentenced to 15 years imprisonment.

English Jury Frees Infanticide Maid

MAIDSERVANT Alice Button murdered her newborn baby on December 28 last year, but lack of proper evidence has resulted in her leaving Chelmsford court unconvicted. Alice's employer, Mrs Smith of Grays, realized she was pregnant, but said nothing.

When Alice went upstairs saying she felt ill, Mrs Smith and her sister-in-law asked how she was, and were told Alice had given birth to a stillborn infant. But later Alice confessed, "I've told you a lie. It's a baby and I've tied a string round its neck to prevent its breathing."

There was indeed a dead baby with a knotted string tightly pulled around its neck, and the doctor surmised it had died of strangulation or haemorrhage.

But in court he could not swear to the child's having had a separate existence before the ligature was placed around its neck; so the prosecution asked for the murder charge to be changed to manslaughter. The judge instructed the jury that there was no evidence of concealment of the birth. Confused by these changes, the jury set Alice free.

> **" I'VE TOLD YOU A LIE. IT'S A BABY AND I'VE TIED A STRING ROUND ITS NECK TO PREVENT ITS BREATHING. "**
>
> QUOTE **Alice Button**

Brick Lane, Spitalfields, where police arrived too late to stop a bloody affray in which two people were killed and a third was wounded

'Educated Elzy' of 'The Wild Bunch' Imprisoned

AS THE "Wild West" yields to industrial mining, settled farms and railheads beside cattle ranges, a few adventurers still try to keep the buccaneering spirit of the last 30 years alive.

Principal among these are the "Wild Bunch" of Wyoming. They hide out in the mountains at "Brown's Roost" and the "Hole in the Wall". They emerge to steal livestock or rob a train from time to time. And they are generally good-humoured and lively. While some of them are dangerous if crossed, the true leaders of the bunch, "Butch Cassidy" (George Leroy Parker) and Elzy Lay, are simply adventurous young men

without the bloodthirstiness that hitherto characterized Western badmen.

Thirty-one-year-old Lay is so intelligent and well-informed that the bunch assert he went to college in Boston. Whether Lay has any education, we cannot say, but he has never set foot in Boston in his life.

Lay and Cassidy are close friends. When the exigencies of outlaw life split them up, Cassidy usually rides with Harry "Sundance Kid" Longbaugh, and Lay with the brothers Sam and "Black Jack" Ketchum.

The Ketchums are as stupid a pair as have ever emerged in West-

ern crime. "Black Jack" beats himself over the head with his own pistols when annoyed with himself.

On June 11 this year, Lay joined the Ketchums in their final attempt to rob the Texas Flyer Express at Twin Mountains, New Mexico. The robbery was a disaster because it was the Ketchums' fourth assault on the same train in the same place in the last seven months! Naturally, it was well guarded, and the gang was surprised and fled in disarray.

Lay was cornered and arrested in Carlsbad, New Mexico after the gang split up. Sentenced to life imprisonment, this spirited young man offers unusual hope of possible rehabilitation.

'Peculiar People' Permitted Prayer in Place of Physic

THE "PECULIAR PEOPLE" are one of Britain's smallest religious sects, and they look set to stay that way. Frederick and Eleanor Norman are devoutly "Peculiar People", and when their daughter Grace fell ill, they followed the tenets of their persuasion and set their face against summoning medical help. When the child died, the medical profession noted angrily that proper treatment might have saved, and certainly would have prolonged Grace's life.

The Normans found themselves in the Old Bailey this July, charged with murder by negligence. They addressed the jury themselves rather than through counsel, explaining that their interpretation of the Bible prohibits putting faith in man rather than God. Therefore they prayed over Grace and called in a female elder of the sect to lead them in prayer.

Others who are persuaded of their own "Peculiarity" testified (as appears to be the case) that the Normans were devoted, if peculiar, parents. One even suggested that they loved Grace too much, wherefore God had taken her away from them!

The jury saw no criminal intent in all this prayerful neglect, and the Normans have been acquitted, leaving "Peculiar" parents free to go on yielding up their children to God and the grave rather than Great Ormond Street.

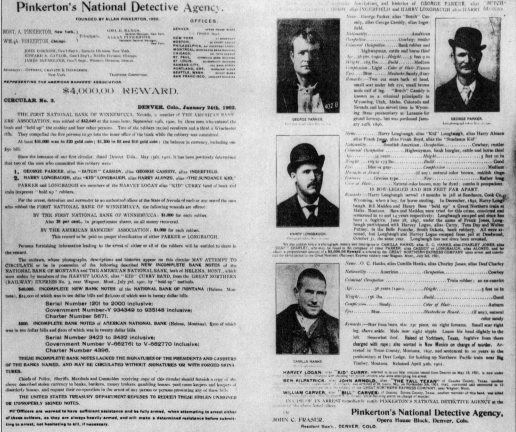

Pinkerton's "wanted" poster for the "Wild Bunch", with pictures of some of the gang

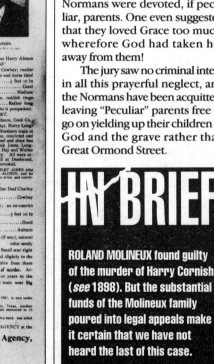

IN BRIEF

ROLAND MOLINEUX found guilty of the murder of Harry Cornish (*see* 1898). But the substantial funds of the Molineux family poured into legal appeals make it certain that we have not heard the last of this case.

Crime Pays Less than 10 Per Cent of Value

IN JANUARY, Sir Samuel Montague, MP for Tower Hamlets, dismissed William Henry Gibson, the butler at his Kensington home, for habitual drunkenness. On Gibson's departure, an inventory of property under his care was checked. Four hundred pounds' worth of silver plate was missing.

Gibson confessed that he had stolen this. His brother Arthur had persuaded him to pilfer the goods to back horses. Arthur and his common-law wife, charwoman Elizabeth Gray had pawned the silver in Earl's Court, realizing a mere £40!

Elizabeth Gray was sentenced to nine months' hard labour, and the Gibson brothers to 18 months apiece.

The pawnbroker was reprimanded by the Recorder for not having exercised the discretion expected of one who had been in the business 16 years. But he restored the property to Sir Samuel and is not charged with receiving.

British Financier Dies, Halting Fraud Trial

THE COMPLICATED Coolgardie Mine and Iron King Gold Mines case that has been inching its way through the Old Bailey was brought to a sudden halt at the end of the year as the principal defendant, Sir Alfred Kirby - whose persistent absence on pleas of ill-health has looked so evasive for the last seven months - actually died!

The auditors, Messrs Fring, concerned with winding up the Coolgardie Mine Company which ceased to trade last year, found that the original purchase of the mine in Australia in 1896, was made with shares duplicating stock already issued. And Sir Alfred's was the signature on all the fraudulent share certificates.

In his absence, counsel and other directors have tried to throw all the blame on the company solicitor. But Sir Alfred's constant failure to appear in court bore all

The White Feather Mine at Coolgardie, centre of the great stock fraud

the appearance of guilt.

Now Kirby is dead, and so, unlucky man, must bear the suspicion surrounding his business dealings with him into eternity. He can never be convicted or acquitted.

The Great Keely Motor Co. Water Power Fraud

JOHN KEELY had a workshop; he had equipment with impressive pumps and gauges; he persuaded four leading businessmen that his scheme to produce power from water without the expense of converting it to steam was a good investment.

The Keely Motor Co. was set up with their capital and know-how, and was soon trading on stock markets around the world. Other investors sank large sums into the project, widowed Clara Jessup Moore putting half a million dollars into the company.

The Scientific American declared the claims to be bunkum, and published calculations demonstrating the impossibility of producing energy in Keely's

manner. But the "hard-headed realists" of the business world were sure they knew better than "ivory tower academics", and before long John Jacob Astor was trying to buy in for $2 million, so confident was he of being on to a winner!

For 24 years this charade has run, with never a locomotive quite making it to the rails. And now the inventor is dead, his laboratory flung open for inspection.

And his experimental machines? All are powered by a hidden air compressor. Secret springs and valves allowed Keely to run motors as he felt inclined. The carny barker has sold his biggest collection of top-level suckers. The academic "theoretical" scientists are completely vindicated.

OBITUARY

JOHN E. W. KEELY (1827-1898)

Greatest of confidence tricksters, John Keely, who died peacefully at his home in Philadelphia this year, robbed robber barons and mulcted millionaires by persuading them to invest in his Keely Motor Co.

Now he is dead the greedy investors are shown to have put their money into so much wind!

Keely began his career as a carnival barker. He moved his deceptions to a higher plane in 1874, when he announced that he would soon produce power from water with far greater efficiency than the steam engine. Indeed, he claimed that he would be able to supply locomotive energy to draw a 30 carriage train at 60 mph for an hour and a quarter from just two pints of water!

And he has lived comfortably for the last 24 years on that claim!

The Wild Bunch Active in Texas

The "Wild Bunch", all dressed up and ready to captivate Mme Porter's harlots. (Left to right) standing are Carver and Logan. Seated are the "Sundance Kid", Ben Kilpatrick, and "Butch Cassidy"

PINKERTON'S, the American Detective Agency, reports the appearance in Texas of the infamous train robbers, "The Wild Bunch".

Active in Wyoming some years ago, the gang had fallen on hard times, and their leader, "Butch Cassidy" (George Parker), almost negotiated himself a free pardon. But with negotiations at a critical stage, it seems that an appointment was missed. Cassidy believed he was betrayed, and responded by robbing another train. So clemency offers were withdrawn.

That train robbery netted a beggarly $50.40. The gang compensated by relieving the First National Bank of Winnemucca, Nevada, of over $33,000 – a robbery made memorable by the fact that one of their number, Bill Carver, had an encounter with a skunk on the way in, and he stank to high heaven!

This was mentioned in posters advertising their descriptions. So it is surprising that five cowboys galloped away from Winnemucca, one of them smelling like a polecat, only to reappear at a photographer's studio in Fort Worth for a group portrait in the dress of fashionable sporting gents!

The robbers then headed for San Antonio, and hid for three months at Madame Fanny Porter's Sporting House. Here, "Kid Curry" (Harvey Logan) formed an attachment to Lillie – one of Madame Fanny's most attractive girls. Lillie was disappointed when her fancy man headed for Idaho without her, and she told Pinkerton's of the gang's doings.

Cassidy used his holiday to master the art of bicycle-riding, at which became proficient. Then the gang perpetrated one last train robbery, taking with them Bill Carver's lady-love, a half-Indian named Laura Bullion. She probably held the horses while they took $40,000 from the freight car.

With that, the Wild Bunch disappeared. Pinkerton's knew just where they'd been for three months, but not where they were now!

Child-Killer is Century's First Woman on Gallows

LOUISE MASSET, hanged January 9, is the new century's first executed murderess. This merciless creature stripped and battered her son with a large stone from her garden in Stoke Newington, London, dumping the body in the ladies' lavatory at Dalston Junction Station.

Thirty-six-year-old piano teacher Louise bore Manfred out of wedlock four years ago and placed him in care at Tottenham. Recently, 19-year-old Eudore Lucas came to reside next door to her, and the woman immediately entered into an immoral relationship with him. In October last year, she arranged a weekend in Brighton with her paramour. On 27th she collected Manfred, saying that his father was to take him over. The little boy showed signs of distress when seen with his mother at London Bridge Station around mid-day. His body was found at 6.30 pm. The murderess, meanwhile, went to Brighton and enjoyed her dalliance!

When Miss Masset was arrested, she told a story of having placed Manfred with two baby-farmers' from West London. She claimed to have handed the boy over at London Bridge, with £12 for his upkeep.

But before her execution, she confessed. She claimed she killed Manfred to spare him the abuse that all too often confronts the illegitimate.

But it is believed she really wished to rid herself of the obstacle to her vain ambition to captivate and hold young Eudore Lucas.

Swindler Arrested for Strangling Wife on Beach

AN ARREST has at last been made in the Yarmouth Beach Murder. On September 22, a woman's body was found lying on the sand, strangled with a bootlace. A courting couple passed the spot the previous night and saw a man and a woman lying there; but they interpreted the moans the woman emitted as an act of public indecency.

Over the last two-and-a-half months, police have identified the dead woman as Mrs Herbert Bennett, wife of a ne'er-do-well London clerk, who employed her in several nefarious schemes, including the sale of faked antique violins.

Further investigation showed that Bennett previously brought her to Yarmouth on August Bank Holiday, apparently testing the route and hotels he would use for his murder visit. On September 21 he came down from London alone, subsequently staying at another hotel, apparently wearing a false moustache. It seems certain that he inveigled his wife to the beach to murder her, especially as he was in possession of the gold chain she was seen wearing in her hotel on the night of the killing.

Observation of Bennett's movements in London prove that he was initiating a liaison with a young parlourmaid named Alice Meadows, and no doubt this explains his wish to detach himself from the wife who bore him a baby, yet whom he compelled to live in separate lodgings for the last few months of her tragically short life.

The case comes to trial early in the New Year.

Genteel Ladies Open World's Most Luxurious Brothel

TWO KENTUCKY heiresses have embarked on an extraordinary occupation for ladies, investing their money in the purchase of "Madam" Lizzie Allen's mirrored brothel on Dearborn Street, Chicago.

For five years the house has been run by Miss Effie Hankins, but the Misses Minna and Ada Everleigh have made it the greatest bordello in the world. They have decorated Gold, Silver, Copper, Moorish, Red, Green, Blue, Oriental, Chinese, Japanese and Egyptian Parlours, all sound-proofed. Each room has a fountain jetting perfume. In addition the house boasts a library, an art gallery, a ballroom, and three orchestras. Occasionally, butterflies are released to fly around the premises.

The house harlots are required to be sober and dress in evening gowns to meet their clients on a proper social footing.

Nothing like this has been seen since the closing of Kate Hamilton's Leicester Square nighthouse in 1872.

Minna Everleigh, a high-class brothel keeper who entertained her clients in style

THE YEAR OF THREE ASSASSINS

In addition to Bresci's successful murder of "King Humbert the Good" the new century has seen two other attempts on royal lives.

In Paris, a young Belgian named Sipido fired on the Prince of Wales as he was arriving at the Gare du Nord in June. And in November an Algerian anarchist named Salsou fired at the Shah of Persia as he drove through the city in his carriage.

Fortunately neither of these did any harm. Sipido appears to be more of a pro-Boer than a true anarchist, and in any case has been found to be insane.

King of Italy Shot by Anarchist

The trial of King Umberto I's assassin

ON JULY 29TH, King Umberto I of Italy was assassinated as he travelled by carriage to a villa in Monza. An anarchist named Bresci pushed forward and fired three pistol shots into the king, who fell back on his cushions, saying: "I think it is nothing". By the time he reached the villa the King was dead.

> ## I THINK IT IS NOTHING
> King Umberto

Bresci planned his murder after a state of emergency in Milan led to artillery being turned on a crowd. He practised target shooting at Prato, and punctured the tips of his bullets with scissors to make them more deadly.

He has expressed no remorse and in August, a Milan court sentenced him to a life of penal servitude and solitary confinement.

Huge Cache of Corpses Uncovered in New York

A "MURDER STABLE" has been uncovered at no.303 East 107th Street, New York, where 61 bodies were buried. Most are Italian immigrants known to have received threatening "Black Hand" extortion notes before their disappearance. One has been identified as the 18-year-old son-in-law of gang leader Giuseppi Morello. It is believed that he was tortured and killed because he intended to inform on the gang's counterfeiting activities.

The premises belong to the notorious Ignazio "Lupo the Wolf" Saietta, feared as a leading extortionist. But Lupo may get away with his claim to be an absentee landlord who knows nothing about the use to which his stable was put, as the "Black Hander" has sufficient influence with local authorities to halt any further investigation.

THE BLACK HAND

This greatly feared Italian-American secret society probably does not exist. Although threatening notes adorned with skulls, daggers and inky paw-prints have been received by numerous citizens, in the few cases where the extortionists have been traced, they have proved to be lone individuals cashing in on publicity given to what American newspapers call the "Dirty Mitt".

Italians are naturally fearful of murderous blackmailing secret societies, since Naples has long been terrorized by the Camorra and Sicily by the Mafia. But there is no evidence that these groups have joined up to form a larger ring. The Morello gang is probably the largest single group involved in writing Black Hand threats. They are also trying to control the New York waterfront, with its opportunities for theft, smuggling and labour racketeering.

Closely allied with the Morellos are the notorious "Lupo the Wolf" and his brother-in-law Ciro Terranova, who is gaining a monopoly of the profitable artichoke trade by intimidating retailers into buying from him at inflated prices.

'Black Jack' Ketchum Decapitated on the Gallows

AFTER SEVERAL YEARS' delay, Thomas "Black Jack" Ketchum has at last been hanged for his part in the fourth Twin Mountains train robbery, in 1899. But the hangman at Santa Fe misjudged the length of the drop. Ketchum's head was torn from his shoulders as he fell.

"Black Jack" and his brother Sam were possibly the stupidest outlaws associated with the "Wild Bunch" and other villains who hid at the Wyoming mountain lair, the "Hole in the Wall". Their first train robbery took a mere $50 from No.1 train, the Twin Flyer at Twin Mountains, New Mexico. Yet the Ketchums made three more assaults on the same train in the same place, so that inevitably a posse was waiting for them at their fourth attempt. In the shoot-out the gang was dispersed and Sam lost his life. "Educated Elzy" Lay, their most intelligent associate, and the closest companion of "Butch Cassidy", was also arrested (*see* 1899).

Black Jack then made a mad attempt to hold up a train at Folsom singlehanded! The conductor and the express agent outnumbered and outgunned him, and seriously injured his right arm

> ## "I'LL BE IN HELL BEFORE YOU START BREAKFAST "
> ### Black Jack Ketcham
> QUOTE

as they drove him off. His trail of blood and weakened state enabled Pinkerton's men to capture him the following morning. He went to his death cheerfully, minus his right arm, and helped the hangman to adjust the noose with the words: "I'll be in Hell before you start breakfast".

Butch Cassidy and the Sundance Kid Visit New York

BUTCH CASSIDY (George Parker) and the "Sundance Kid" (Harry Longbaugh) spent February this year in New York City, squiring a mysterious lady known as Etta Place.

She appears to be Longbaugh's light-o'-love, since the couple passed themselves off as "Mr and Mrs Harry D. Place" when they had what looks like a honeymoon portrait photograph taken at De Young's Studio on Broadway. The train robbers also visited Messrs Tiffany's, where they bought the young lady a gold watch. Miss Place also underwent private treatment for some mysterious female complaint in atop-notch hospital All three stayed at Mrs Taylor's fashionable boarding-house on West Twelfth Street.

Miss Place is rumoured to be the daughter of an English aristocrat who owns acres of land; said, too, to have been a schoolteacher until "Sundance's" charms lured her away from the classroom. Both stories are improbable, and she seems more likely to be an active prostitute: the class from which all other "Wild Bunch" camp followers have been drawn. She seems to have made their acqaintance during the gang's holiday at Miss Fanny Porter's sporting house in Texas, and may have been one of the daring young women who went with them on train robberies. She can certainly ride and shoot, and is believed to have accompanied her two gallants by boat to South America at the end of their month in the city.

President McKinley Assassinated in Buffalo, N.Y.

AFTER NINE DAYS, President McKinley has died from the anarchist's bullet that struck him in Buffalo, N.Y.

> ## I DONE MY DUTY!
> ### Leon Czolgosz

The President was shaking hands with visitors to the Pan-American Exposition on September 6, and smiled warmly as a dark-haired man with a bandaged hand reached the head of the line. When 28-year-old Leon Czolgosz was a few feet from the President, he pulled out the pistol his false dressing concealed, and fired twice at Mr McKinley.

"I done my duty!" was the killer's vainglorious cry as his victim staggered backwards. One of the President's guards immediately felled the assassin with a smashing blow to the face. The stricken President cried weakly: "Go easy with him, boys!" But the bullet had done its foul work, and Mr McKinley has succumbed to gangrene in the pancreas.

Secret Service investigations this spring followed rumours that anarchist gangs had decided to kill Mr McKinley. But all organized groups disavowed any such intent, warning however, that disaffected lone individuals might threaten the President's life. Czolgosz appears to be just such an individual, having been denounced in the anarchist journal *Free Society* as a dangerous crank who might even be a police spy. So the ominous warning that "only a single heartbeat separates Teddy Roosevelt from the White House" is entirely justified and Americans must come to terms with an intellectual aristocratic cowboy who knows how to "rough ride" as President.

> ## GO EASY WITH HIM, BOYS!
> ### William McKinley

The late President McKinley, a safe conservative Republican

Child Murdering Carpenter Caught by Chemist's Microscope

LUDWIG TESSNOW, accused of murdering four children, has been charged after a new scientific process establishes that blood on his clothes was definitely human, and not, as he claimed, animal.

Tessnow, a carpenter fom the Baltic island of Rugen, was arrested in 1898 when the bodies of schoolgirls Hannelore Heidemann and Else Langemeier were found hacked to pieces near Osnabruck. He insisted that red marks on his clothing were wood dye stains, and this could not be disproved.

This July, the mangled bodies of the Stubbe children, Hermann (8) and Peter (6) were found on Rugen, shortly after they were seen talking to Tessnow. He again claimed that marks on his clothes were wood stains and cattle blood. But Dr Paul Uhlenhuth has found out how to identify blood with scientific certainty, even distinguishing human from animal stains, and Tessnow will go to trial.

The assassination of President McKinley at the Pan-American Exposition, Buffalo, N.Y.

IN BRIEF

HERBERT BENNETT, the Yarmouth beach murderer (*see* 1900), convicted and hanged on March 21.

ADOLPH BECK, swindler, imprisoned in 1896, who has persistently claimed that he is not the "John Smith" or "Lord de Willoughby" for whose crimes he was convicted, has completed his sentence.

Hung Jury Leaves Peasenhall Murder A Great Mystery

AROUND MIDNIGHT on June 1, a brutal murder was committed in the little Suffolk village of Peasenhall. Rose Harsent, resident domestic to the local Congregationalist deacon and his wife, was left lying in a pool of her own blood on the kitchen floor; a broken paraffin lamp dismantled around her. Her throat had been cut and an unsuccessful attempt was made to burn the body.

When she was found to be six months pregnant, and an anonymous note by her bed showed that some man had made a secret assignation with her that night, suspicion fell on local Methodist worthy William Gardiner, observed engaging in licentious familiarities with the 23-year-old the previous summer by two peeping toms.

A medicine bottle from Gardiner's house and a copy of the local paper to which he subscribed were discovered in the kitchen. And despite offering an alibi supported by his wife and next-door neighbour, Gardiner was put on trial.

The village has always been certain "Holy Willy" was guilty. He is a fine craftsman (a carpenter and wheelwright) but not especially popular as the foreman at the seed drill works which employs most villagers. Rose Harsent, by contrast, was a great favourite. A good-natured girl, much admired by the young men of Peasenhall, she was not severely criticized for her adulterous liaison.

Young barrister Ernest Wilde won great acclaim for his spirited defence of Gardiner. He roundly condemned the prurient curiosity of the young men who spied on Rose and Gardiner's naughty tryst, and established that another young man living next door to the girl pursued her with lascivious letters (which, it must be remarked, the unhappy young lady accepted in the lewd spirit in which they were offered).

But although Mr Wilde demonstrated a lamentably low state of morality in rural Suffolk, suggesting that more than one man may have wanted to father a child on Rose, he had not proved his client's innocence. The jury could not agree, and Gardiner is scheduled for retrial early next year.

SENSATIONAL CRIME IN SUFFOLK.
A VILLAGE GIRL'S MYSTERIOUS DEATH.

The front page of *Police News*, 1902, showing the sensation caused by The Peasenhall Murder

Mutiny and Murder on the *Veronica*

SEVERITIES INFLICTED on the largely foreign crew of the barque *Veronica* last December resulted in the deaths of seven men at sea and the execution of two more at Walton Prison, on June 7 this year.

A German seaman named Rau sparked off mutiny. He disliked the authoritarian discipline of First Mate Alexander MacLeod. Rau prided himself on his own seamanship and resented reproof.

When the ship was becalmed in the south Atlantic, Rau approached the youngest of the crew with his proposals. At midnight on the first Sunday in December the mutineers killed Mr MacLeod and two loyal seamen and threw them overboard. They locked Captain Alexander Shaw and the second mate in the cabin. They prepared a lifeboat. When all was ready the two captive officers were released. The mate sprang overboard and swam alongside the ship where the mutineers shot him. The captain was chased around the vessel with an axe, and finally shot. The seven survivors sank the *Veronica* and took to the lifeboat.

Rau prepared the story that a storm had injured one crewman and swept MacLeod overboard, whereupon the captain had promoted him to acting Second Officer. Then they were to say the ship caught fire and the entire crew took to the two lifeboats: Captain Shaw commanding one and Rau the other.

As the mutineers headed for the coast of Brazil, two of their number proved incapable of remembering the prepared story and were incompetent in handling the boat. So they, too, were murdered.

When the remaining five arrived in South America their story was accepted as a sea tragedy. Returning to England it became apparent that the negro sea-cook was afraid of his former shipmates, and eventually he confessed. Flohr, one of the two boys from the *Veronica*, gave way under interrogation and confirmed the cook's story. Rau and his co-conspirators, Smith and Monsson were put on trial in England. All were convicted, but Monsson was spared the gallows on account of his youth.

Many shipboard disturbances result from mutinous foreign seamen who fail to understand English orders. Perhaps it is time the merchant marine was crewed by Englishmen.

McCoy and Others Jailed for Street killing

ONE OF THE worst gang-fights in the East End for many years has culminated in prison sentences for the leaders of the infamous "Bessarabians".

These Jewish hooligans have terrorized the streets for some time, threatening passers-by and extorting money with menaces from the weak.

Their fortunes took a turn for the worse a couple of years ago, however, when they tried to take over the Odessa Cafe run by Mr Kikas. He fearlessly picked up a chair and drove out the unwelcome visitors. In his honour, a new

gang named itself the Odessians.

In the summer this year the two gangs clashed in the York Minster pub behind the London Hospital. Knives were pulled, and an Odessian named Henry Brodovitz was fatally injured.

At an Old Bailey trial in November, three of the leading Bessarabians, Max Moses, Samuel Oreman and Barnett Brozevishky, all received long sentences of penal servitude for manslaughter.

Moses, incidentally, is better known by the name "Kid McCoy". He adopted this name to enhance his reputation in his professional boxing career.

Ironically the American middle- and welterweight champion Henry Selby, who pioneered the use of the ring name, has been known as "the real McCoy" ever since he knocked out a drunken saloon bar brawler, who refused to believe he was the champion in person until McCoy knocked him into oblivion and he recovered from his concussion. Max Moses is not the real McCoy!

The Death Sentence for Pretty Kitty Byron

A MOST PATHETIC case tried before Mr Justice Darling has resulted in conviction and a death sentence for 23-year-old Kitty Byron.

This unfortunate young woman stabbed her lover, stockbroker Arthur Reginald Baker, at Post Office Court, Lombard Street, on the day of the City of London's Lord Mayor's Show.

The previous night, the two had quarrelled furiously in their lodgings and their landlady gave them notice.

The following morning, Baker offered to get rid of Kitty if the landlady would let him stay on, and when the maid reported this ungallant offer to the young woman, she said roundly: "I'll kill him before the day is out." She then bought a

large knife, and did so.

Her youth and distress won her many sympathizers in court, especially when she trembled and almost collapsed as the judge unfeelingly tapped the murder weapon on his desk. But there could be no doubt of her guilt, and this comely young woman must now pay for her sins with her life.

I'LL KILL HIM BEFORE THE DAY IS OUT.

Kitty Byron

Newgate's Scaffold Reaps its Last Victim

DEMOLITION WORK is to start on Newgate Prison, the great bastille of London which has held so many famous prisoners over the last eight hundred years. In its place, on the corner of Old Bailey and Newgate Street, a new Central Criminal Courts building is to be erected.

This means that George Woolfe, cowardly killer of his girlfriend Charlotte Cheeseman early this year will achieve the unenviable distinction of being the last man hanged at Newgate.

Woolf was arrested by the police after trying to join the army and escape to the South African War.

The young east Londoner killed his jilted sweetheart, Miss Charlotte Cheeseman, in the spring when it appeared he would be compelled to marry her. Woolf took her for a walk on Tottenham marshes where he strangled her.

Regrettably, the Newgate gallows' last fruit was a petty and squalid villain.

A cell in Newgate. No longer will the condemned await the gallows in these grim surroundings

IN BRIEF

NURSE JANE TOPPAN, 48, has confessed in Massachusetts to murdering over 30 of her patients with morphine.

Investigators believe the true figure is nearer 100. Despite her insistence that these were sane mercy killings, she has been sent to a Criminal Lunatic Asylum.

ROLAND B. MOLINEUX, freed last year after his second trial for the murder of Harry Cornish (*see* 1898) is now reporting other people's murder trials for the newspapers.

But his wife, the former Blanche Cheeseborough, is now threatening to leave him. So if he *did* also murder Henry C. Barnett on her account, 'twas of no avail in the long run.

Seducer Lives Life of Orgiast on Spinster's Fortune

FOR FOUR YEARS, Samuel Dougal thought murder would never out, as he wrote cheques on his victim's bank account. This theft ultimately led police to arrest him, dig up Moat Farm near Saffron Walden and discover his terrible secret.

In 1898 the middle-aged, but virile, Dougal met 55-year-old spinster Miss Camille Holland. She was charmed by this twice-widowed ex-soldier. He was charmed by her possession of a fortune of £7,000 and cultivated her acquaintance.

The following year, disregarding propriety, the couple moved into the lonely farmhouse. Before long they quarrelled, as lusty Mr Dougal began to seduce the housemaids. Miss Holland ordered him to pack up and leave - yet it was she who disappeared from the neighbourhood.

For the next four years Dougal enjoyed himself in his remote sanctum. He returned enthusiastically to the practice of seducing the domestic staff, and took up the peculiar practice of bicycling with them in the nude.

A succession of strange women stayed at the farm and the neighbourhood was scandalized.

Then came the enquiry into Miss Holland's steadily diminishing bank account and Dougal fled to London.

After Dougal's arrest, police dug up the farm and uncovered Miss Holland's mouldering body wrapped in sacking and buried in a drainage ditch. She had been shot through the head.

Dougal was convicted at Chelmsford in June, and hanged on July 14, ridding the country of this deceitful felon.

Edwards launches his cowardly assault on Mrs Darby and child

Whole Family Killed and Buried: Shop Stolen

AT THE END of last year, neighbours in Camberwell were surprised when Mr William John Darby, his wife and baby disappeared from their grocery. True, the shop had been advertised for sale, but the Darbys had not said they had sold it before their disappearance on December 1.

On December 23rd, a grocer named Garland from Victoria Park, East London, went to see a man in Leyton calling himself Fox, who expressed an interest in buying Mr Garland's shop. Before the conversation had gone very far, Mr Fox attacked Mr Garland with a sash weight. The elderly grocer screamed and broke a glass panel in the front door, effectively summoning assistance.

Police examining Mr Fox's house found William Darby's business stationery, and when they dug up Mr Fox's garden, they found the entire Darby family buried there. Mr Fox had battered all three to death with his sash weight, and then carted them and their furniture back to Leyton.

Fox's real name was Edgar Edwards. He had a criminal record and had only recently come out of prison, when he began his short murderous career. There is evidence of insanity in his family, and his lawyers tried to exploit this in his defence, though their client refused to plead. After being convicted, Edwards said: "Let 'em get on with it as soon as they like," and on hearing the death sentence passed he burst into gales of laughter. Finally on the scaffold, his last words to the chaplain were:

" I'VE BEEN LOOKING FORWARD TO THIS LOT! "

QUOTE

Edgar Edwards

MISS HOLLAND AND DOUGAL MET THROUGH AN ADVERTISEMENT.

Samuel Dougal makes the acquaintance of Miss Holland

Murderous Baby Farming Women Hanged

THE EXECUTION of cruel baby farmers, Amelia Sachs and Annie Walters has been greeted with satisfaction.

For some years now, Mrs Sachs has run a small private lying-in hospital at her converted suburban home, Claymore, in East Finchley, London. As a trained midwife she provided an efficient service and called in doctors for assistance with difficult deliveries.

But her speciality was a follow-up service, offering long- or short-term foster-care for parents unable to cope with their newborn offspring immediately. She would also negotiate adoption for unmarried girls who could not care for their children at all.

In these last cases, the babies were delivered to Mrs Annie Walters in Islington. This uncouth and uneducated woman lodged with a policeman and his wife, to whom she presented herself as a short-term foster-mother, thus explaining the constant appearance and disappearance of newborn babies in her charge. Her landlady thought Mrs Walters was very fond of the infants, though she was suprised when Mrs Walters left a "dear little girl" with her to be changed, and the baby proved to be a "dear little boy".

But Mrs Walters repeatedly claimed that "a beautiful lady" stopped her carriage in the street and asked to adopt the dear little baby the foster-mother was carrying. This led her landlord to follow her one day as she went to look for an adoptress.

Mrs Walters was seen to go to Whitechapel, and there shove the baby's corpse into a remote rubbish tip. Enquiries proved that she was frequently seen in Spitalfields pubs carrying babies. And when she was arrested she was carrying a feeding bottle full of lethal chlorodine.

Since Mrs Sachs was clearly aware that her aide was not allowing the children to survive, both women perished on the gallows in January.

Bigamist Publican who Buried Barmaids

PUBLICAN George Chapman, hanged on April 7, habitually married his barmaids, who equally habitually died. In 1897, Mrs Shadrach Spink with whom he was living as man and wife, died. In 1901, barmaid Bessie Taylor died under the name of Mrs Chapman. Last year Maud Marsh followed her to the grave, but the doctor refused to issue a death certificate for a second "Mrs Chapman" in the space of 20 months.

All three women were exhumed and found to have died of tartar emetic poisoning. None was really Mrs Chapman, as this Polish immigrant (real name Severin Klosowski) was almost certainly married previously to a Polish woman he deserted. Chapman is believed by retired Detective Inspector Frederick Abberline to have been Jack the Ripper!

IN BRIEF

THE HOME SECRETARY has commuted the death sentence passed on Kitty Byron (*see* 1902) to life imprisonment.

AFTER A sensational second trial, William Gardiner, charged last year with the murder of Rose Harsent, (*see* 1902) has been freed without being found either guilty or innocent. A second jury was unable to agree on a verdict, and the Crown has decided to proceed no further with the case.

Hardest Punished Prisoner in USA Freed from Solitary

San Quentin, notorious top-security prison

AMERICA'S MOST NOTORIOUS prisoner, Ed Morell, has been released from the lifetime of solitary confinement laid down for him at San Quentin, and returned to the general prison population. Morell was a populist outlaw in the 1890s, helping those who by-passed the law to fight off the depradations of big railways and landowners. But for "stealing" a police officer's revolver while helping a brother outlaw escape, he was sentenced to life imprisonment. The injustice led Morell to make escape attempts, and in San Quentin he was given such brutal punishments as "the San Quentin overcoat" – a coffin-shaped all-over straitjacket, and "the lime cell" – a torture chamber created by slaking chloride of lime on the walls to create a burning mist.

His final term of life solitary was awarded by the corrupt and brutal governor Martin Aguirr, who has been dismissed. His reforming replacement, and prison captain John C. Edgar are now working for Morell's permanent release.

1904

CRIMES OF THE TWENTIETH CENTURY

Adolph Beck Again After Conviction, Double is Caught

SWINDLER ADOLPH BECK, who protested his innocence of the frauds on women for which he was convicted in 1896 (*see* 1901) was arrested again when a similar sequence of deceptions began. In one of these the criminal used the alias "Lord Willoughby" – the name under which Beck was said to have passed false cheques and defrauded a lady of her jewels eight years ago. Beck has always claimed that another man, known as "John Smith" was the true criminal. Police said Beck and Smith were one and the same.

But no sooner was Beck back in prison than "John Smith" was arrested, and those witnesses who identified Beck now confess their error.

It is true that the two men look remarkably alike. But the really shocking information is that the authorities knew all the time that they were two different men. Medical examinations in prison had established that "Smith" is circumcised, and Beck is not. It seems that the police and Home Office took the view that since Beck had a criminal record anyway, it was not important whether he had committed the particular crimes with which he was charged!

We are confidently assured that Beck will very soon be freed with handsome compensation. It is likely, too, that a Court of Criminal Appeal may be established, to prevent such miscarriages of justice in future.

Adolph Beck, the criminal wrongly convicted of another man's misdemeanours

Horrible Rape and Murder of German Child

AFTER A TWO DAY search for the missing child, the torso of 9-year-old Lucie Berlin was pulled from the River Spree, Germany on June 11. Her head and limbs had been cut off and she had been raped.

Police enquiries at the slum tenement where she lived focused on the flat of prostitute Johanna Liebestruth, immediately above the Berlin family. It was common gossip that Theodore Berger, who had been living off Fraulein Liebestruth's immoral earnings for many years, had finally consented to marry her. The lady explained why. She spent the three days prior to the discovery of Lucie's body in prison, and returned to find her suitcase missing. Berger admitted entertaining another prostitute in Miss Liebestruth's absence, and giving her the suitcase. He agreed to marry his longstanding mistress in compensation.

Berger, denied all this – especially after the badly bloodstained suitcase was discovered in a canal. The child's head and legs were found in the same canal.

At Berger's trial it transpired that the little girl had come up to Liebestruth's flat while he was there in his mistress' absence, and thoughtlessly stood on her head. The sight of her legs inflamed the brute, who tried to assault her; strangled her when she struggled; then raped and dismembered the body, taking the parts to the waterside in the suitcase, which he abandoned there.

IN BRIEF

Paedophile child-murderer Ludwig Tessnow, (*see* 1901) has been hanged at Greifswald.

Florence Maybrick (*see* 1889) has been freed after serving 15 years of her life sentence. She has returned to her native America.

William Kirwan, controversially convicted of the "Ireland's Eye" murder, has died. He was released from prison in 1879.

An International Conference at Paris has agreed to the formation of a Central Authority to suppress the "White Slave" trade. It has agreed that White Slave Trafficking includes all procurement or enticement of a woman to gratify the passions of another even when the woman gives her full consent.
Scotland Yard is appointing 12 officers to permanent duty in this Suppression of Vice. They will co-operate with the National Vigilance Association in watching railway stations for runaway girls, and liaise with continental police forces.

Leading Gangster Goes to Sing Sing

NEW YORK'S premier street-gang leader, 31-year-old Monk Eastman, has been jailed for ten years. After dominating the Lower Manhattan saloons and dancehalls for a decade, the ugly tough gratuitously robbed a pedestrian who happened to be under the protection of Pinkerton's Detective Agency. The minder fired a pistol and Eastman ran straight into the arms of a policeman.

Corrupt Tammany Hall politicians who have used this brute's strong-arm services in the past are now glad to see him out of the way.

Eastman was famous for the gallantry that always made him take off his brass knuckles before blacking a lady's eye!

116

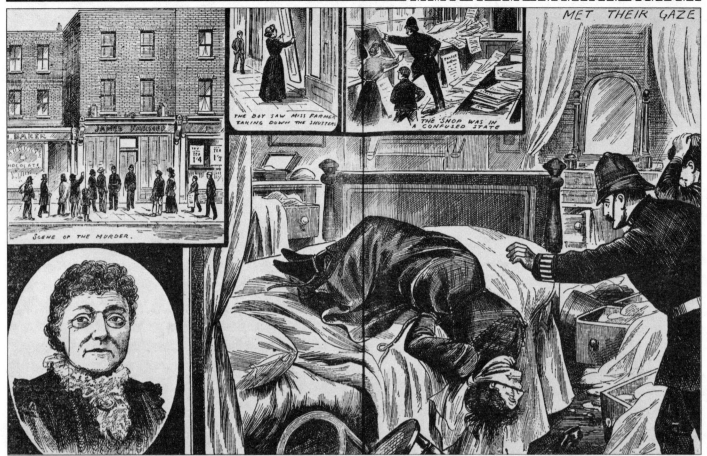

MET THEIR GAZE

THE BOY SAW MISS FARMER TAKING DOWN THE SHUTTERS

THE SHOP WAS IN A CONFUSED STATE

SCENE OF THE MURDER.

The dreadful discovery of the robbery and murder of Stepney businesswoman Miss Matilda Farmer

London Robber Confesses Before Hanging

ANY DOUBTS about the conviction of Conrad Donovan and Charles Wade were resolved when, as they went to the scaffold, Donovan said he had not meant to kill the old lady.

Miss Matilda Emily Farmer, newsagent and tobacconist of 478 Commercial Road, Stepney, was found lying face-down on the floor of her premises with her hands tied on October 12. She had choked on a gag in her mouth. Her false teeth and one shoe were beside her, and her jewelry was missing.

Miss Farmer had been well known in the neighbourhood for owning and wearing jewels.

A Sunday school teacher subsequently identified Donovan and Wade as two men he had seen lurking suspiciously about the premises two nights prior to the crime.

Although there was probably no intention on their part to kill Miss Farmer, the law is quite clear that accidental killing in the course of committing a felony wherein the perpetrators predetermined to use force is murder. Donovan and Wade have now paid the supreme penalty.

Second Jury Deadlocks over Floradora Girl

NEW YORK is agog over Nan Patterson's trial. The 22-year-old chorus girl from Floradora divorced her husband and became the mistress of wealthy socialite gambler Frank "Caesar" Young. Their attempts to elope to Europe were foiled by Young's wife, and in June as the two were riding along Broadway in a hansom cab, bystanders heard a shot ring out, and, at the same time, Miss Patterson's voice exclaiming: "Look at me, Frank. Why did you do it?"

Miss Patterson thereupon di-rected the cab to a drugstore, and thence to Hudson Street Hospital. But Young proved dead on arrival. The two had been quarrelling over Young's agreement to go to Europe with his wife the following day, and Miss Patterson – either falsely or under a genuine misapprehension – told him she was pregnant. She claims that he committed suicide when she challenged his acceding to Mrs Young's request for a marital holiday.

Prosecutors allege that she shot him in sheer fury before he could frame an answer. Gunsmiths argue that he could not have held the pistol that killed him, given the position of the wound in his head.

Miss Patterson's first trial in November was broken off when a juror died. The December trial has now ended with the jury deadlocked, unwilling either to acquit her of the charge or find her guilty, although Miss Patterson has not changed her story to meet the evidence against her. It remains to be seen next year whether a third jury can survive the excitement and bring themselves to convict this very attractive young lady.

Tiny Thumbmark Hangs Two Male Murderers

AN OLD BAILEY jury has agreed that a tiny fingermark on a tin box shall be sufficient evidence for capital conviction! In March this year, Mr and Mrs Thomas Farrow who kept a paint shop in Deptford High Street were found battered. Mr Farrow was dead in the parlour. Mrs Farrow, unconscious in bed, only survived four days. Their cashbox had been rifled. Two men were seen running from the premises before dawn. They wore stocking masks, and police checked their files of local criminals.

Suspicion fell on Albert and Alfred Stratton, brothers from the Creekside area of Deptford, with records for burglary and housebreaking. But the circumstantial evidence against them was flimsy: Alfred's lady love testified that the brothers had been out all night, and Alfred had subsequently destroyed his coat and dyed his shoes.

Then, using a new technique, the police examined the cashbox; detected a thumbmark; and had it photographed and enlarged. The brothers' fingers were inked and they were forced to make impressions of their fingerprints on clean paper. These, too, were photographed and enlarged, and experts then demonstrated that the mark on the cashbox was identical with the print of Alfred's right thumb. These same experts also confirmed under oath that no two people's fingermarks are identical. In the light of this evidence the jury was able to convict. In future, criminals had better beware! Their lightest touch on a smooth surface will betray them.

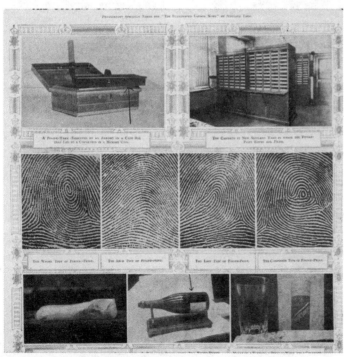

Scotland Yard's new fingerprinting technique was used on the cashbox in the Stratton case

HOW FINGERPRINT DETECTION CAME TO LONDON

Scotsman Dr Henry Faulds first solved a crime by "fingerprinting". He was working in Japan in 1880 when a neighbour's house was robbed by a thief who left sooty fingermarks on the walls. Faulds compared these with the fingers of a man who was arrested and declared them to be different. A second arrestee proved to have fingertips that matched the soot patterns, and Faulds' evidence convicted him.

Faulds published an account of his "scientific detection" in *Nature* and Sir William Herschel added that he had used fingerprints instead of signatures from illiterate labourers in India.

Sir Francis Dalton classified the different patterns of ridges on fingertips, naming the variations "loops", "arches" and "whorls".

The Argentinian police first used fingerprint evidence in a murder case, extracting a confession from Francesca Rojas in 1892 by showing that the bloody fingermark near the bodies of her dead children matched her own print.

Fingerprinting has come to Scotland Yard through Major Edward Henry, the new Commissioner of Metropolitan Police. He used the technique when in Bengal, and introduced it to London on his appointment as Assistant Commissioner (Crime) at Scotland Yard in 1903.

This year Major Henry was promoted to Commissioner on Sir Edward Bradford's retirement, and a single fingerprint has already hanged a pair of murderers! We venture to prophesy that this minute scrutiny of the most ephemeral smudges and discolorations bids fair to become a mighty weapon against crime.

'Bluebeard' Bigamist Sets Record for Murdering Wives

GERMAN IMMIGRANT Johann Hoch, who lived well by marrying often, has been arrested in New York and sent back to Chicago for trial.

The "Stockyard Bluebeard" bigamously married at least 55 women, deserting his brides as soon as he had relieved them of their possessions. One woman testifies that he crept from her bed during the night, removing her gold false teeth from the glass of water on the bedside table!

But at least 15 of Herr Hoch's lady wives did not survive matrimony. These women's bodies have been exhumed and examined, and all contain arsenic.

The insouciant Mr Hoch expressed no surprise, pointing out that undertakers' embalming fluid is richly charged with the poison. His claim is true, but unfortunately for him, his penultimate "wife", Mrs Marie Walcker of Chicago, was embalmed and buried by an undertaker using a new technique and a fluid which contains no arsenic whatsoever! For this reason the "Stockyard Bluebeard" goes back to the city of the stockyards to face his trial and fate.

The great ladykiller offers all men a formula for success with women: "The average man can fool the average woman if only he will let her have her own way at the start" is his maxim.

> ## " THE AVERAGE MAN CAN FOOL THE AVERAGE WOMAN IF ONLY HE WILL LET HER HAVE HER OWN WAY AT THE START "
>
> **Johann Hoch**

MAN COMBINES BIGAMY AND TRUNK MURDER

George Crossman combined bigamy with "trunk murder". When his tenant complained of the bad smell coming from a trunk under the stairs in his house in Queen's Park, London, Crossman agreed to remove the "box of size" that had "gone bad". When a policeman approached him as he removed it, he ran away and cut his throat. The box proved to contain Ellen Sampson, the fifth "Mrs Crossman", packed in cement.

Mystery of the Girl Found Dead in a Tunnel

COMPLETE MYSTERY surrounds the death of Sophia Mary Money, whose body was found in the Merstham Tunnel on the London to Brighton Railway line at 11.00 pm on Sunday, September 24.

Pretty Miss Money worked at a dairy on Lavender Hill, and was regarded by her employers as a reliable and respectable young woman with a good character and no followers. Yet her actions on the day of her death imply a secret life that confounds all who knew her.

Permitted the afternoon off work, Miss Money told a friend she was going for a walk. At a sweetshop in Lavender Hill she remarked that she was going to walk to Victoria. Yet instead of doing so, she made her way to East Croydon, where she was seen furtively boarding the 9.33 train from London Bridge to Brighton. As this train passed the Purley Oaks signal box, the signalman was startled to see a man struggling with a woman in one of the compartments. And at 11.00 pm Miss Money's body was found.

It does not appear that she was pregnant, which might have provided a clue to the mystery. The police are completely baffled, and nobody has managed to put forward any helpful suggestion concerning Miss Money's last day on earth.

There was no evidence of immodest outrage on the girl, nor had she apparently been robbed. Her brother Robert, who identified the body, insists that the family have no suspicion of any sinister associates in her life.

IN BRIEF

THE THIRD NAN PATTERSON jury has deadlocked (*see* 1904), and the chorus girl has been freed. She will not be prosecuted again for the murder of "Caesar" Young.

Wife Murderer Hides Body in Trunk

CHEMIST'S ASSISTANT Arthur Devereux found that even if two can live as cheaply as one, three cannot ... and five certainly cannot! Life as a married man with three children entailed serious financial hardship. In January he bought a large trunk and some morphine and chloroform.

Somehow he persuaded his wife and their twin children to drink the poison. Then he sealed his three victims into the trunk with an airtight mixture of glue and boracic acid, and deposited them at a warehouse in Harrow, England, before moving to Coventry with his surviving son. Mrs Devereux's mother successfully traced her son-in-law's movements and tracked down the bodies to the warehouse. Police apprehended Devereux, who has been convicted and hanged.

Society Sex Scandals Behind New York Killing

Killer Drowns Pregnant Obstacle to His Engagement

WHILE NEW YORK reels at the impossibility of convicting Nan Patterson for the murder of her playboy lover (*see* 1905), yet another Floradora chorus girl features in a high society murder.

On June 25, the rich and famous sipped their bubbly in the roof restaurant of Madison Square Garden as the new musical *Mamzelle Champagne* unfolded before them. Suddenly, 34-year-old railway heir Harry Thaw walked over to where millionaire architect Stanford White was dining and shot him in cold blood, saying: "He deserved it. He ruined my wife."

Shocking facts emerged at Thaw's trial. In 1902, when Miss Evelyn Nesbit was 16, she was plucked from the chorus line by big, heavily-moustached Stanford White who took her to his apartment, plied her with drugged champagne, and seduced her.

> ## "HE DESERVED IT. HE RUINED MY WIFE."
> ## Harry Kendall Thaw
> QUOTE

After that she joined him in bizarre sexual pursuits: swinging high on a velvet swing with some of her clothing removed; dressing up as a little girl for him to fondle; letting him take indecent photographs of her. Nor was she the solitary victim of his lusts. White introduced other young chorus girls to his velvet swing.

Last year Miss Nesbit left White and married Thaw. Her new husband had peculiar tastes of his own, liking to tie her to the bed before thrashing her with a dog-whip. She found that she could escape his frenzy by telling him how White had abused her. Thereupon Thaw redirected his rage to the seducer, and insisted thenceforth that Evelyn should only refer to White as "The Beast", "The Bastard", or just "The B".

Thaw's millionaire mother is spending a fortune to denigrate White, and present her son as the eccentric defender of a maiden's honour. She says she will spend $1 million to save his life. Thaw faces trial next year.

FACTORY FOREMAN Chester Gillette (22) wanted to marry money. In Courtland, New York, the upper crust knew that Chester was the nephew of the prosperous skirt-manufacturer who employed him. So society ladies let the young man court their daughters, and Chester had every hope of seeing his ambitions realized.

Until Grace "Billie" Brown told him she was pregnant. Farm girl Billie came to Courtland to work as a secretary for $6 a week, and cheating Chester found her more accommodating than the beautiful socialite to whom he hoped to become engaged. When he declined to answer Miss Brown's letters, she became desperate and threatened to expose him. Whereupon Chester asked his uncle for a week off and took Miss Brown upstate to Utica, and thence to a hotel on Big Moose Lake.

On July 11 Chester hired a rowing-boat and took Miss Brown for a picnic lunch on the lake. That evening he was seen walking through the woods, dripping wet and carrying a suitcase. At 9.00 pm he registered as "Carl Graham" at another inn, where he asked whether there had been any report of a drowning in the lake.

The following day Miss Brown's body was found floating. She had been battered to death before being thrown in. The murder weapon – a tennis racquet – was found buried by the lake shore.

At his trial, Gillette claimed first that Miss Brown had attempted suicide and thrown herself into the lake, and then that the rowing boat had capsized and the lady struck her head against the hull. He could not explain his own failure to rescue her, although he is a competent swimmer.

The jury found him guilty, and he has been sentenced to death.

Harry Thaw, killer of his wife's former lover

Evelyn Nesbit Thaw, the girl who swapped a velvet swing for a dog-whip

Fake Prussian Captain Runs Off with Town Treasure

EVEN THE "All-High" Kaiser Wilhelm II of Germany could not contain his laughter when he heard of the exploits of Wilhelm Voigt, the "Captain of Köpenick".

In October this year, Voigt, an unemployed shoemaker with a petty criminal record, came into possession of a Prussian Guards' officer's uniform.

Swiftly realizing that the official Prussian mind respects authority before common sense, and identifies authority with uniforms, Voigt promptly dressed himself as a captain and marched out till he encountered a couple of grenadiers. He ordered them to accompany him, and took his small troop to the burgomaster's office in Köpenick.

There he informed the burgomaster and the town treasurer that they were under arrest on suspicion of some defalcation, and would be sent to Berlin for examination.

He had them open the town treasury, and extracted the large sum of money therein for "official examination". He sent the civic officials by train to Berlin, escorted by his faithful grenadiers.

Then Herr Voigt took the civic money, slipped away, discarded his uniform and disappeared for a week.

His exploit has entertained the whole of Germany hugely, and he is unlikely to suffer a severe penalty for a crime which bears so much resemblance to a delightful practical joke.

Wilhelm Voigt stands trial for his Köpenick caper

Sherlock Holmes' Creator to the Rescue

SIR ARTHUR CONAN DOYLE has taken up the cause of a young man released from prison this year. George Edalji, Parsee son of the Rector of Great Wyrley, Staffordshire, was accused of mutilating sheep and cows around the village in 1903, and sentenced to seven years' penal servitude.

Now he is out on parole, and the creator of Sherlock Holmes believes that he was "framed" by xenophobes in the neighbourhood. It transpires that obscene letters signed, "Shapurji Edalji" (the name of George's father) were received in the village in 1893, and 10-year-old George was accused of writing them. Sir Arthur has a handwriting expert's opinion that this is impossible, and hopes to clear the young man of all blame for his alleged offence.

Sir Arthur Conan Doyle: graphologist's skills may clear accused's name

Lustful Prophet's Killer Slain By His Own Sister

JOSHUA CREFFIELD, whose killer has just been murdered by his own sister, set up as a preacher in 1903. His mission in Corvallis, California, appealed almost exclusively to women, and the frenzied services climaxed when, with a cry of, "Begone vile clothes!" the prophet would strip off his raiment, and his disciples followed suit. When photographs of Creffield indulging in lewd practices began to circulate in Corvallis, the prophet was tarred and feathered and run out of town.

Creffield twice married a young Corvallis disciple named Maude Hunt, the intercalated divorce coinciding with a period when he was sued for adultery in Portland. Early this year he left Portland for Newport, Oregon, calling down God's curse on Seattle and San Francisco. His followers believe that this caused the San Francisco earthquake. In Newport on May 7, a man named George Mitchell shot him dead on the street, and was acquitted of the charge of murder when the jury learned that Creffield had deflowered both Mitchell's sisters simultaneously.

On July 2, Esther Mitchell shot her brother through the head as he stood in a queue at the railway station. She has subsequently been found insane and sent to an asylum.

IN BRIEF

BIGAMOUS BLUEBEARD Johann Hoch (*see* 1905) was hanged at Chicago in February.

Joy as Wood is Acquitted of Camden Town Murder

AFTER a tense trial, London is rejoicing that Mr Edward Marshall Hall has secured a young commercial artist's acquittal on the charge of murdering Phyllis Dimmock in September.

Railway dining-car attendant Bert Shaw returned to his flat in Camden Town on the morning of September 12, to find his common-law wife, Miss Dimmock, lying in bed with her throat cut.

Mr Shaw was apparently unaware that Miss Dimmock plied her trade as a prostitute around local public houses during his absence on night-trains.

A letter in the lodgings signed "Bert" invited Phyllis to meet the writer at the Eagle public house on September 11, and a postcard in the same writing signed "Alice" included a caricature of a winking sun to illustrate its invitation to a meeting at the Rising Sun.

When this was publicized, a young prostitute named Ruby Young recognized the drawing as the handiwork of one of her clients, Mr Robert Wood.

But Wood asked her to keep quiet about it. She, however, mentioned it to a journalist friend, and thus Wood was then traced.

Mr Marshall Hall succeeded in persuading the court that identifying witnesses, who recognized Wood's distinctive gait as that of a man leaving Miss Dimmock's house in the early hours of September 12, are unreliable since they saw their suspect under exceedingly dim street lighting.

And Wood himself made an excellent impression in the witness box, leading to his popularity throughout the metropolis.

The police have no further suggestions to offer as to the commission of the crime. Given the extent to which Wood has benefited by Mr Marshall Hall's famous eloquence and the jury's exercise of a very slender "reasonable doubt".

We should perhaps see him as an extraordinarily lucky young man to have escaped the gallows, rather than very unfortunate to have had his sordid love-life exposed in the harrowing circumstances of a murder trial.

Phyllis Dimmock, the murdered prostitute of Camden Town

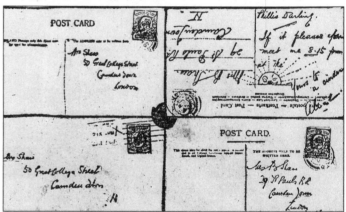

The stylish drawing that revealed Wood's contact with Phyllis

IN BRIEF

THE JURY in the Thaw case (*see* 1906) cannot agree, and he will stand trial again next year. His mother has said she will spend more than $1 million to secure her son's freedom.

Irish Swindlers Caught with Body in Trunk

VERE AND MARIA GOOLD, the Monte Carlo trunk murderers, have been arrested in Monte Carlo, despite the lady's attempt to bribe a police officer.

These seedy Irish adventurers have been living in Monaco using the assumed titles of Sir Vere and Lady Goold. (True, Goold is in line for a baronetcy, but he has not yet succeeded to it.) Not for the first time, "Lady" Goold has been living off her wits, while her (third) husband drifted in an alcoholic stupor.

The couple were close to penury at the beginning of this year. Then they met Madame Levin, a rich old Swedish lady, who lent Maria £40. No amount of wheedling, however, could persuade her to increase the loan, and by August she was pressing for repayment. Maria invited her to tea at the Goold's shabby lodgings, and while "Sir" Vere held their guest in conversation, "Lady" Goold crept up from behind and battered Madame Levin with a poker. Then she cut her throat, decapitated her and cut off her legs. The torso was packed into a trunk labelled for Charing Cross, London; the head and limbs into a carpet bag. A visitor that evening was told that gore all over the apartment was the result of Vere's being taken ill and vomiting blood.

The following day the Goolds fled the principality and deposited the trunk in Left Luggage at Marseilles. A clerk who noticed blood oozing from it sent to their hotel asking what it contained. "Lady" Goold haughtily responded that it was poultry, and ordered him to despatch it to London. The clerk went to the police instead, and Maria's offer of 10,000 francs to Inspector Pons ensured her arrest.

Fraudulent Will Beneficiary Kills the Wrong People

RICHARD BRINKLEY murdered the wrong people in an attempt to cover up his own fraud. Some time ago the greedy carpenter met 77-year-old Mrs Johanna Blume in Fulham, London and determined to acquire her property.

He persuaded her to sign a will in his favour by folding the form and declaring it was a collection of signatures for a seaside outing. By the same ruse he persuaded Henry Heard and Reginald Parker to sign it as witnesses.

When Mrs Blume died early this year, her granddaughter contested the will and her solicitor began proceedings. Realizing that examination of the witnesses would lead to his exposure, Brinkley decided to eliminate them. He went first to Parker's house, on the pretext of discussing a dog for sale. He took with him a bottle of stout, laced with prussic acid.

While the two men were outside looking at the dog, Parker's landlord, Mr Beck, came in with his wife and daughter, and seeing the opened stout on the kitchen table, the three refreshed themselves from it. Mr and Mrs Beck died in consequence, and their daughter was seriously ill.

Scientific examination of the disputed will showed that three different inks were used for the three signatures. And Brinkley's denial of all knowledge of the problems did him no good.

Although he did not intend to kill the Becks, he had formed the felonious intent to kill. He will therefore be hanged at Wandsworth on August 14.

Heroic New York Cop Murdered in Sicily

JOSEPH PETROSINO, scourge of the Black Hand in New York, has been murdered in Sicily. The police detective first hit the headlines when he uncovered the "Murder Stable" of "Lupo the Wolf" (*see* 1901). He established at that time that there was no such formal organization as "the Black Hand", although various extortionists used the term in their threatening notes. He also realized that Lupo (Ignazio Saietta) and fellow Sicilians in the Morello gang had brought the Sicilian "Mafia" with them to New York, and operated its reign of terror among the Italian community under cover of the mutual help organization, the *Unione Siciliano*. He was unable to charge Saietta on that occasion, but did succeed last year in bringing charges against Lupo and an accomplice known as "Petto the Ox" together with Giuseppe Morello and a restaurateur named Inzarello, for the brutal murder of a counterfeit distributor named Benedetto Madonia who wished to leave the gang. Alas, the charges could not be made to stick because intimidated witnesses withdrew their testimony in court.

As an Italian-American, Petrosino was always acutely aware of the danger posed to the community by the bands of extortionists and blackmailers who have gained a firm footing in Calabria and Sicily. Finding witness intimidation taking place in New York, he persuaded his superiors that liaison with their Italian counterparts was necessary to prevent the bandits from importing more of their violent and lawless ways.

Lt Petrosini went to Sicily this year to organize Italian-American police co-operation against the bandits, and was shot down in broad daylight outside the Palermo courthouse by a leading mafioso.

Murdered Whiteley was a Hypocritical Sex Orgiast

ALTHOUGH THE late William Whiteley's friends pretend that his murderer was completely unconnected with him, the public disagrees and is delighted that Horace Rayner has been reprieved.

The young ne'er-do-well made his way into the millionaire Department Store founder's office earlier this year and, after a short quarrel, shot him dead and then turned his gun on himself, though he only succeeded in mutilating his face hideously.

At the trial it emerged that Mr Whiteley enjoyed three-in-a-bed intercourse with Rayner's mother and her sister, and the young man, rightly or wrongly, believes himself to be Whiteley's son. Since the "Universal Provider" made much of his evangelical virtue, there is little distress among the wide public at the manner of this humbug's passing.

Horace Rayner: parricide?

William Whiteley: murdered millionaire with a secret sex-life

Widow Advertised for Husbands – Killed Forty

Belle Gunness, multiple murderess of husbands on her lonely Indiana farm

WHEN THE Gunness farm near La Porte, Indiana, burned down during the night of April 28, Joe Maxon, the hired hand, was apparently the only person to survive. The bodies of the widow Gunness's four children were found in the basement, together with a headless woman, presumed to be Mrs Gunness, since her false teeth lay alongside.

Suspecting arson, police arrested recently sacked hired hand, Ray L'Amphere, whose unrequited passion for Mrs Belle Gunness had led her to make several complaints about him. But once in custody L'Amphere's statements started police digging around Belle's pigsty.

They unearthed the remains of 14 men. And that was less than half of it! L'Amphere estimates that the widow murdered at least 42 people over the last four years, including her 14-year-old adopted daughter Jennie Olson, who told authorities back in 1904 that she saw Momma Gunness beat out Poppa Gunness's brains with a cleaver. At the time, Belle's alternative story was believed: that a meat grinder fell off a high shelf on to the unfortunate Peter Gunness's head.

Fat, ferocious and fiftyish, Widow Gunness advertised for matrimonially interested men willing to help her pay off the mortgage on the farm. They came with their savings. And Belle rapidly disposed of them. She drugged their coffee, or chloroformed them, and finished them off with her trusty cleaver.

Recently, she seems to have panicked when the brother of one of her missing suitors enquired about his disappearance. Belle drew up a will and paid off one of her mortgages. Then came the fire.

Did Belle perish in it? No part of the head except her false teeth has been located. The burned body appears to have stood five inches shorter and weighed fifty pounds less than Belle. Moreover it did not burn to death, but was poisoned before the fire consumed it .

It seems that Mrs Gunness lured some poor vagrant to her farm and killed her to conceal her own escape. The wicked widow is still at large, somewhere, possessed of a small fortune.

Recovering the bodies from the basement where Belle killed her children

Tragedy of a Retired Couple

ON AUGUST 24, Major General and Mrs Charles Luard set out at 2.30 from their home, Ightham Knoll in Kent, for an afternoon walk. The 69-year-old general proposed going a couple of miles to his golf club to fetch his clubs in preparation for a holiday. His wife was only accompanying him for half a mile, as she expected a visitor for tea. They strolled through Fishpond Woods to a summerhouse known as the Casa, where Mrs Luard stopped and the general went on.

At 3.15, local people heard three shots. The general got home at 4.30, and was surprised to find his wife was not there. He entertained the visitor in her place, and then went back to the Casa to look for her. Mrs Luard lay on her face in the summerhouse. She had been struck on the head with a blunt instrument, and then shot twice. Her rings had been pulled off her fingers; a pocket cut away from her dress.

There can be little doubt that some vagrant or hoppicker committed this crime, but police have failed to link anyone known to be in the area with it.

Somewhat deplorably, local rumour suggested that the general himself destroyed his wife. Lonely and depressed by cruel anonymous letters, the general took his own life by lying in front of a train on September 18.

IN BRIEF

THE SECOND trial of Harry Thaw (*see* 1906) has produced a verdict of Not Guilty by Reason of Insanity, and Thaw has been sent to Matteawan Asylum for the Criminally Insane.

Wild Chase over Tottenham Marshes — Two Killed

ON SATURDAY morning, Latvian anarchists Paul Hefeld and Jacob Lepidus made a daring wage-snatch at factory gates in Chesnut Road, Tottenham. They shot at the delivery driver, penetrating his leather coat, but missing his body; grabbed the wages bag; and shot a hole in the car radiator so that it was unable to pursue them for any distance.

Police from nearby Tottenham Station quickly responded to the gunfire. Lepidus and Hefeld ran, firing their pistols, and killed 12-year-old Ralph Joscelyne as he dived for cover behind a car. When they approached the marshes, they were nearly over-taken by PC Tyler, who bravely confronted them. They shot him dead at pointblank range.

The chase continued for six miles; some police following on bicycles, one armed with a cutlass. They ran past the reservoir, where a party of duck-shooters joined the pursuit. Some rounds of duckshot took effect, but the light peppering did not stop the villains.

At Chingford Road the anarchists hijacked a tram. Police commandeered a milk-van to follow them, but the fugitives shot the pony dead. Undeterred, police stopped a tram going in the opposite direction and ordered the driver to reverse after the robbers.

At Forest Road, Lepidus and Hefeld abandoned their tram. They seized a greengrocer's cart, but made little progress as they omitted to release the brake. When they allowed the wheels to rotate, the sudden spurt careered them into the ditch, and a wheel came off.

They ran on to the River Ching, and there, almost trapped in a narrow path beside a high fence, Lepidus found he could go no further and shot himself.

Hefeld raced on to some newly built cottages, where he shooed a frightened family out of their house and pelted upstairs to lock himself in the bedroom.

Police courageously followed him, but a last shot rang out before they burst into the room. Hefeld used his final bullet to kill himself.

The two men fired over 400 rounds during the chase. The stolen money has not been recovered, and police think it must have been thrown to an accomplice at the start of the chase. They have no explanation for sooty handmarks Hefeld left over the kitchen of the house where he died.

A police photograph of the last redoubt of Latvian desperado Paul Hefeld. The caption reads: "Oak Cottage, Hale End. The final scene in the Tottenham Tragedy ..." The window of the room in which the second assassin committed suicide is marked with a cross.

Actor Slays Wife and Transports Torso

BOSTON HUSBAND-AND-WIFE acting team Chester and Honora Jordan will never again delight New England audiences. Early in September, Mr Jordan purchased a knife, a hacksaw and a pair of shears. A couple of days later he was transporting an unusually heavy trunk around the city. A cab driver mentioned this to police, who traced Jordan, and doubted his claim that the trunk contained clothing, given its weight and the vile smell it emitted.

Pressed further, Jordan confessed that it held his wife's torso. He had pushed her down some stairs to her death; then dissected her and attempted to burn the head and limbs.

Tragic Discovery of Missing Schoolgirl from London

THE SEARCH for missing child Maria Ellen Bailes has come to a distressing conclusion. When she failed to return from school in Islington, London, her parents informed the police, and sympathetic neighbours went with them around the district helping to hunt for the 11-year-old schoolgirl.

The following day a large parcel was found in a gentlemen's convenience at the Elephant and Castle. This turned out to contain the unfortunate schoolgirl, whose throat had been cut.

It is not known how the murderer could have managed to lure or transport her all the way from north to south London.

Did this Sinister German Really Kill?

OSCAR SLATER, the 37-year-old German Jew extradited from America and convicted of the murder of Miss Marion Gilchrist last December, has been reprieved.

On December 21, Miss Gilchrist's maid, Helen Lambie, returned from an errand to find a neighbour outside her mistress' apartment door, from where he had heard some commotion. As Miss Lambie entered the flat, a respectably dressed man walked calmly out and ran down the stairs.

Miss Gilchrist was found battered to death with a chair leg. Parts of the flat had been turned over, but the only item missing from Miss Gilchrist's extensive collection of jewellery was a crescent-shaped diamond brooch.

On Christmas Day, police learned that Slater had tried to sell a pawn ticket for just such a brooch. When they went to his lodgings on Boxing Day, they learned that he had just sailed for America.

Slater is a man with an infamous reputation who has, among other things, lived off the immoral earnings of women. Police followed him to New York where Helen Lambie and other witnesses, who had seen a man leaving or in the vicinity of the building, all more or less positively identified Slater.

Slater has consistently denied knowing anything about Miss Gilchrist, but his counsel dared not let him give evidence on his own behalf.

Nevertheless, sufficient doubt exists in this case that Slater's death sentence has been commuted to life imprisonment. Sir Arthur Conan Doyle, who is taking up the cudgels for Slater, observes that the brooch pawned by Slater has been traced: he pawned it a month before the murder, and it was not Miss Lambie's. Furthermore, his journey to America was long pre-arranged, and not, as police suggested, a guilty flight to evade the long arm of the law.

It is to be hoped there has been no miscarriage of justice.

Oscar Slater, a shady character dubiously convicted of murdering Miss Marion Gilchrist

Two Extortionist Pimps Murder Drunken Sailor

THE CONVICTION of Morris and Marks Reubens for the murder of William Sproull has clarified the law on premeditation in murder cases.

Second mate McEarchen of the freighter *Dorset* was found drunk and incapable in London's Whitechapel Road. When he reported that he and his friend, second engineer Sproull, had been attacked in a house in Rupert Street, Whitechapel constables repaired to that sordid alley of brick shacks, and found Sproull dying in a gutter.

A trail of bloodstained three-penny-bits from his pockets led back to the house used by prostitutes Ellen Stevens and Emily Allen, where they and their pimps, Morris and Marks Reubens were cowering.

The gang's claim to know nothing about Sproull collapsed when a search revealed Morris's bloodstained pocket-knife hidden behind the stove. McEarchen testified that after he and Sproull had gone to the house with the girls for an immoral purpose, the brothers sprang out to accuse them of molesting their "wives", and Marks threatened the seamen with a hippopotamus-hide whip. When McEarchen and Sproull fought back, Morris pulled his knife and stabbed the engineer.

The judge decided that this was premeditated murder, since the clasp-knife had to be opened before it could be used, and the short period of opening proved intent to injure.

Despite pleas from the dock in the name of their "poor old mother", the brothers will hang.

'Sisters in Black' Arrested: Who Killed Daughter?

THREE SOUTHERN US gentlewomen, who always dress in black, seem to have contrived the murder of several of their relatives.

Virginia, Caroline and Mary Wardlaw, daughters of a judge, have made a point of living close to each other, and watching their children intermarry and die – profitably.

Caroline married a Colonel Martin, and bore one daughter: Ocey. Mary married a Mr Snead, and gave birth to two sons, John and Fletcher. Unmarried Virginia became an educator, presiding first over Montgomery Female College, and subsequently Soule College, Murfreesboro, Tennessee.

In 1900, after Mr and Mrs Snead had separated, young John Snead eloped with a student from Montgomery College. He was pursued, brought home, and two days later discovered burning to death behind the Wardlaw house. This was said to be suicide, and Mrs Mary Wardlaw Snead collected $12,000 insurance money.

In the rumour-filled aftermath the sisters separated, and Mrs Martin rejoined her husband in New York. Soon afterwards, their landlady discovered Colonel Martin dying with acute stomach pains, while Ocey, filthy, half-starved and in rags, watched from her bed. Mrs Martin collected $10,000 insurance money.

Mrs Martin and Mrs Snead then reunited with Miss Wardlaw at Murfreesboro, and Ocey married Fletcher Snead. He soon allowed himself to be packed off to Canada, while Ocey remained under the care of her mother and aunts.

On November 19, Ocey was discovered drowned in a bathtub in East Orange, New Jersey. Her condition was again half-starved. When police discovered that she had recently been insured for $32,000 they arrested the "Sisters in Black" who appear to live by killing their nearest and dearest.

Butch Cassidy and Sundance Kid Killed in South America

REPORTS are coming in from South America that "Butch Cassidy" (George Parker) and "the Sundance Kid" (Harry Longbaugh), leaders of the old "Wild Bunch" of cattle thieves and train robbers, have been shot dead after a long gun battle with a company of soldiers.

Since their escape from New York, in 1901, the pair have been operating in Bolivia and Argentina, helped by Longbaugh's lady-love, Etta Place.

The reports of the circumstances in which they died are confused, however. Some authorities say that Parker and Longbaugh were shot by a company of cavalry called in by the San Vicente police in Bolivia when the two strangers who had ridden peacefully into town were recognized; others say that a company of Uruguayan soldiers trapped them in the act of robbing a bank at Mercedes. By this latter account, Etta Place was killed with the men.

OBITUARY

GEORGE LEROY PARKER ALIAS 'BUTCH CASSIDY' (1866 –1909)

Son of a Mormon rancher in Utah, George Parker adopted the surname of a rustler called Cassidy who led him into bad ways before he was 20. The nickname "Butch" came from a spell working as a butcher's boy. After imprisonment for some cattle-rustling and bank robbery, Butch moved to Wyoming where he teamed up with outlaws who were outliving the old Wild West to form the Wild Bunch. From their mountain hideouts "Brown's Hole" and the "Hole in the Wall" they enjoyed an adventurous life of good-natured criminality.

Butch's fame as the last of the great outlaws is not diminished by the fact that he never killed a man.

His reported death in two countries at once is quietly disputed in some quarters, and it is possible that he is back in the USA living respectably under the pseudonym William Thadeus Phillips.

Mysterious Murder of English Businessman

MYSTERY SURROUNDS the murder of Mr George Harry Storrs, a successful building contractor, at his home, Gorse Hall, outside Stalybridge, England.

The Storrs family were attacked by an unknown assailant on September 10, who fired a random shot through their sitting-room window. Mr Storrs had an alarm bell fitted to his roof, and a test proved that police respond promptly to its tolling.

November 1, however, was the day of local elections, and it was some time before the authorities could react to the alarm's violent peal. Early in the evening, a man armed with a pistol forced his way past the maid in the kitchen and entered the sitting room, where Mr Storrs grappled with him. Mrs Storrs seized his pistol, and ran upstairs to ring the alarm bell. Before help could arrive, the man had stabbed Mr Storrs fatally and escaped through the scullery.

Though Mr Storrs lingered for some time, he gave no clue as to who his assailant might be. A ne'er-do-well cousin of Mr Storrs, Cornelius Howard, who has amassed several convictions for burglary, was arrested and identified as the intruder by Mr Storrs' womenfolk. But since Mr Storrs himself had not named Howard and the young man had a plausible alibi, the case against him has been overturned.

Police are still searching for the real murderer.

Cornelius Howard, cleared of murder

Siege of Sidney Street — Robber-Murderers Die

Peter the Painter: escaped from the siege at Sidney Street, Stepney, in east London

AN EXTRAORDINARY train of events led Home Secretary Winston Churchill and a company of guardsmen to the battle in Sidney Street, Stepney, in London which it is hoped, will end the depradations of the anarchist gangs associated with "Peter the Painter" and Fritz Svaars.

Earlier this year, Latvian anarchists led by George Gardstein planned a robbery at Harris's jeweller's shop in Houndsditch. They were overheard tunnelling their way into the shop by night from an empty house at the rear, and when police arrived, the foreign subversives shot their way out, killing three policemen and injuring two.

In this unspeakable violence, however, they also injured their leader fatally, and Gardstein died in hiding a few days later.

The remainder of the gang scattered. But it finally reached authority's ear, that two or three were holed up in 100 Sidney Street, and would probably resist arrest with more gunfighting.

Police surrounded the building under cover of darkness, and tried to evacuate all innocent ten- ants and neighbours. The two anarchists attempted to hold the landlady hostage, removing her skirt on the assumption that a devout Jewish lady would not face the public in her underclothes.

They were mistaken. She fled as soon as their attention was distracted, and the siege began. When Detective Sergeant Leeson was injured, the guardsmen were called in. Firing at and from the house continued for several hours, until it was seen to be ablaze

It is not certain whether the anarchists started this conflagration themselves. In any case, both men perished. One had been shot, and died well before the signs of their surrender. The other, believed to be Fritz Svaars, dodged from window to window, keeping up a fusillade of bullets singlehanded until he was overcome by smoke and fumes and had to surrender.

But "Peter the Painter" had escaped.

Armed police marksmen take aim at No.100 Sidney Street

ANARCHISTS IN LONDON

Anarchists have been a serious social problem in Europe for the last 30 years, since many of them adopted the policy of haphazard terror and assassination to "destabilize bourgeois society".

No crowned head seems safe from their pistols and bombs, and no respite from their activities can be predicted until they have stirred some cataclysmic upheaval in Europe.

Technically the terrorist anarchists are a very small section of a minority group within the international revolutionary movement, which embraces constitutional "Fabian" socialists at one end, and the violent revolutionary extremist Social Democrats at the other. Russian political exiles and the immigrant Jewish community in the East End have introduced these doctrines to England, and special sections of the police keep a wary eye on the dangerous Social Democrats in Stepney.

Guardsmen take over from police to conclude the amazing gunfight in the East End

White Slave Trafficking Gang Smashed

ANTONIUS CELLIO and Alexander Berard have been sentenced to long terms of hard labour in a case generally seen as the most important blow ever struck against the vile traffic in human flesh, perpetuated by greedy and immoral pimps.

Last year Cellio and Berard were living off the immoral earnings of women in New Zealand. Cellio controlled Cecilia Rae, his common law wife; Berard ran Maria Vernon, a 17-year-old photographer's assistant. It was the latter who, apparently, expressed the desire to visit both Paris and London.

The men arranged passages for Buenos Aires, where they registered their women in a brothel, thus giving themselves a "working holiday" and paying their travel expenses.

It seems that the young ladies found the discipline unappealing and cut short their stay after a week. The four then travelled on to Paris, where Cellio and Berard cajoled three *filles de joie* to join them in London.

As it happened, police were keeping a strict watch on West End prostitutes and pimps. Detectives noticed Cellio and Berard meeting their women and visiting flats where they placed them. The two men also took coffee with their infamous fellow-countryman Max Kassell, who runs a vice ring.

Eventually some of these unfortunate young women agreed to give evidence against the two pimps. "Mrs Cellio" made good her escape, taking swift passage to Australia. But the French girls were picked up and placed in the care of the National Vigilance Association.

Sad to say, when their exploiting masters had been convicted, only Maria Vernon showed any continuing signs of penitence, and asked for repatriation. The French girls demanded release from the NVA, and on being returned to Paris positively refused to be placed in the care of a convent, indicating quite clearly that they intend to resume their rudely interrupted lives of sin.

East End Gangs Clash and Crash

POLICE ARE confident that the two leading gangs of extortionists and receivers in London's East End have collided in such a way as to end their power.

Gentile Arthur Harding's mob had sworn a vendetta against Jewish "Darky the Coon" Bogart's gang, and "the Coon" was so frightened that he asked for police protection.

When Bogart was surrendering to his bail at Old Street magistrates' court this year, the "Vendetta" mob were awaiting him, and armed men with knives and clubs swiftly surrounded Bogart and his principal lieutenants as they approached Old Street.

But the police were forewarned and sealed off the entire area. Before the gangsters could create their usual mayhem, squads of uniformed men raced in and arrested them all.

It is confidently assumed that the shame of having recourse to police protection will terminate Bogart's power in the underworld, and Harding should serve a long enough prison sentence to ensure that he is little danger to the public when he emerges.

Mysterious Death of Music-Hall Actor

MYSTERY SURROUNDS the death of actor Weldon Atherstone in an empty basement flat in Battersea, London, two floors below the residence of his mistress, Elizabeth Earl.

Mr Atherstone was found just outside the ground-floor flat door, shot through the head. He was carrying a homemade cosh in his back pocket and wearing carpet slippers. His boots were inside the empty flat. Nobody knows what he was doing there, or how he came to be killed.

IN BRIEF

JOHN ALEXANDER DICKMAN has been hanged for the robbery and murder of wages clerk, John Nisbet, on a slow train through Northumberland, England, this March.

THE THREE "SISTERS IN BLACK" in the Ocey Snead murder case (*see* 1909) have come to different ends.

MISS VIRGINIA WARDLAW went on hunger strike and starved herself to death in jail.

MRS CAROLINE MARTIN was convicted of the murder of her daughter, but certified insane.

MRS MARY SNEAD was acquitted.

The three appear to be a unique instance of educated ladies of breeding improving their income by murder.

Ada Everleigh, quality Madam

World Famous Brothel Closed

FOLLOWING BRITISH evangelist Gipsy Smith's crusade through Chicago's red light district last year, authorities have closed the famous Everleigh sisters brothel (*see* 1901).

Miss Minna Everleigh cheekily remarked of the crusade:

> **WE ARE GLAD OF THE BUSINESS OF COURSE.** Minna Everleigh

QUOTE

When the sisters followed that impertinence with the issue of an illustrated brochure, advertising their wintertime steam heating, and summertime electric fans, the authorities decided enough was enough, and closed the house.

The gracious lady procuresses have gone into retirement in New York.

Dr Crippen: No escape for Wife-Murderer

Simpering Belle Elmore on the music-hall stage

A Second-Rate Soprano

CRIPPEN'S WIFE Cora was last seen on January 21, 1910 when she and Crippen entertained their friends, retired "musical acrobats" Mr and Mrs Martinetti. Mrs Crippen herself had attempted a singing career, appearing as one "Cora Motzki" in operetta, and as "Belle Elmore" in various music-halls. (She was christened Kunigunde Mackamotzki, so she had every excuse for adopting a stage-name!)

Belle Elmore's singing career was a flop. Ultimately she restricted herself to serving as treasurer of the Music Hall Ladies' Guild, a charity which brought her into contact with great stars. The Guild's office in New Oxford Street also brought her into contact with the quiet typist Miss Ethel Le Neve, who worked for her husband. Crippen was hawking patent medicines and acting as a dentist's anaesthetist in the same building. As he qualified as a homeopath in his native America, the BMA would not license him to practise medicine in Britain.

Where's Belle?

Two days after the dinner with the Martinettis, Crippen brought the Ladies' Guild a note with Belle's resignation and apologies. She had to return to America to see a dying relative.

When friends asked how Belle was getting on, Crippen reported that she was ill, and finally, that she "passed on of pneumonia up high in the mountains of California".

Variety artistes were shocked, however, when the bereaved doctor brought his secretary to the Ladies' Guild Ball wearing Belle's diamond brooch. Neighbours in Hilldrop Crescent, North London, were shocked that Ethel had moved in with him. Friendly enquiries in California revealed that nobody knew anything about Belle's visit, illness and death. Gossip culminated in a tip-off to Scotland Yard, and Inspector Walter Dew went down to New Oxford Street to see the doctor.

Duping Dew

Crippen easily deceived the good-natured detective. He confessed that the story of Cora's death was false. He explained that she had run away with a younger man, and he felt so humiliated that he had put about the story of the sick relative and Cora's ultimate demise.

Dew accepted this story completely. Had he made enquiries, he might have found plausible support for it. For Cora frequently cuckolded her husband. (We do not say she "deceived" him, for she was contemptuously open about her liaisons with younger, stronger men from the music-hall world, and made the wretched Crippen clean their boots when they stayed at Hilldrop Crescent.)

At Crippen's invitation, Dew searched 39 Hilldrop Crescent. Apart from a litter of unwashed clothes in the kitchen, where Crippen (and Ethel) seemed to be living permanently, he saw nothing amiss. And the case would have been closed, had not

Ethel Le Neve in her shipboard disguise

Respectable Dr Crippen

Dew returned to New Oxford Street on July 11 to confirm the exact date of Belle's departure for his report.

Headlong Guilty Flight

Crippen had gone. Ethel had gone. They left no forwarding address and no explanation. Dew's suspicions were reawakened. For the next two days he searched the house from top to bottom. And at last he rapped his stick on the brick floor of the basement and heard it ring hollow. The floor was taken up, and pieces of flesh were discovered, wrapped up in a pair of pyjamas.

Belle had been found. Crippen's flight was explained. The widely publicized man-hunt was on.

Dr Harvey Hawley Crippen, whose flight, arrest and trial have held the world spellbound since July, was hanged at London's Pentonville Prison on November 23. The previous week his lover, Ethel Le Neve, was acquitted of complicity in the murder of his wife. Crippen's last request was that a photograph of Ethel should accompany him in his coffin.

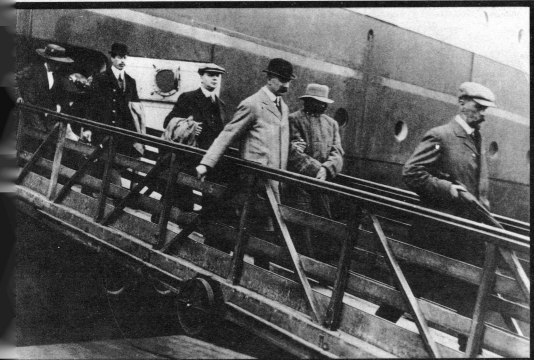

You're nicked: detectives escort the wanted man down the gangplank of the *Montrose*

Immoderate Affection

As the papers reported the nationwide man-hunt, Captain Henry Kendall of the liner *Montrose* was perturbed by the appearance of unnatural passions between two of his passengers who claimed to be Mr John Philo Robinson and his 16-year-old son. As they stood behind a lifeboat, Captain Kendall saw what seemed a shocking display of homosexual ardour. "The younger one squeezed the other's hand immoderately. It seemed to me unnatural for two males, so I suspected them at once" said the good captain.

But on re-examining his newspaper the captain changed his mind. He whited out Crippen's spectacles and moustache in a newspaper photograph, and the likeness of Mr Robinson was before him. Captain Kendall tested his theory, inviting the Robinsons to dine at his table and observing Master Robinson's suspiciously feminine shape. He called, "Mr Robinson" to the pair on deck, and noted that the passenger made no immediate response to his name. And when Master Robinson's trousers split down the beam-end and the young man fastened them with a safety pin, the captain was positive.

The World Follows the Chase

The *Montrose* is one of the first vessels equipped with Marconi's radio-telegraph, and Captain Robinson used this equipment to tell his owners he believed Crippen and Le Neve were on board. The owners told the police and the press, so that the public knew all about the daring escape and the amateur detective captain. The public learned about Ethel's trousers, and heard when Captain Kendall found ladies' underwear in the Robinsons' cabin.

Scotland Yard immediately despatched Inspector Dew by the *Laurentic*, a faster vessel that would reach Montreal before the *Montrose*. And so when Crippen landed and was arrested, the world's press was there to witness this first murder case cracked by the Marconigram.

The Trial

Crippen's defence was a plea of complete ignorance of the flesh in his cellar. But young pathologist Bernard Spilsbury proved that a fringe of pubic hair matched Belle's known coloration, and a scar matched her operation wound from an illegal sterilization. Traces of hyoscine in the remains showed how she had been poisoned. And Crippen had recently bought an unusual quantity of the drug. No one knows how Crippen disposed of the rest of the body. But no one doubts his guilt.

Steinie Morrison in the dock before magistrates as a Snelwar's Restaurant waiter (left) testifies to his carrying an iron bar on the night Beron was killed

Clapham Common Murderer to Live

HANDSOME BURGLAR Steinie Morrison will not hang. British Home Secretary Winston Churchill, has commuted his sentence for the murder of Leon Beron to life imprisonment.

Last New Year's Eve, Morrison spent the evening at a Polish cafe in Whitechapel, talking to Beron – a local slum landlord and, it is whispered, stolen-goods receiver's agent. A waiter at the cafe insists that a parcel Morrison left with him felt like an iron bar. Morrison swears it was a flute.

Subsequently Beron and Morrison were seen in Whitechapel Road, after which Morrison's landlady confirms he went home and retired to his room.

The following morning Beron's battered body was found miles away on Clapham Common, his face carved with waving lines that might imitate a letter "S". Three cabmen reported taking men answering the description of Morrison and Beron between Whitechapel and Clapham, and one who looked like Morrison, from south London to Finsbury Park.

Morrison disappeared from his lodgings and when arrested on January 8, said he had been spending the time with a new girlfriend – a lady of the streets – in Lambeth.

At his trial he persuaded another girlfriend, 16-year-old Jane Brodsky, whom he seduced last year (much to her own satisfaction), to provide him with a false alibi. This was exposed in court, and coupled with Morrison's criminal record swayed the jury against him.

Nevertherless, his conviction seems unsafe. He might merely have identified Beron to confederates who committed the actual murder: he might even, as he claims, have had nothing whatever to do with the man's removal to Clapham.

Although Morrison calls himself a socialist, the police do not endorse the popular belief that the murder is associated with recent anarchist outrages, or that the "S" on Beron's face accuses him of being a spy.

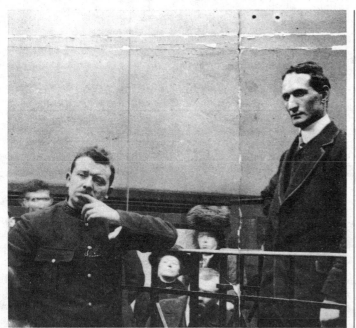

Steinie Morrison, fastidiously dressed burglar, in the dock at Bow Street

Doctor Deliberately Gave Patient Diphtheria

A DOCTOR HAS been exposed in Petrograd (the former St Petersburg) of using his skill to murder. Patrick O'Brien de Lacy, a resident of the city, divorced his wife in order to marry wealthy Mademoiselle Burturlin. It was Mademoiselle's fortune rather than her face which attracted him, however, and he planned to murder every member of her family who stood between him and his father-in-law's estate!

A Dr Panchenko accepted 360,000 roubles to inoculate members of the Burturlin family with poison. When Mrs O'Brien's brother died of blood-poisoning, suspicion was aroused, and at length Dr Panchenko confessed to substituting a preparation of diphtheria for the young man's anti-cholera medicine.

Although the moving force in the conspiracy was de Lacy, it seems that Dr Panchenko's is the name that will live in the annals of crime.

He is most unusual in abusing his skills murderously for a fee, instead of killing on his own account, as one would expect.

North London Landlords are accused of Poisoning Tenant

FREDERICK AND MARGARET SEDDON have been arrested for the murder of their lodger, Miss Eliza Barrow, and will go on trial at the Old Bailey next year.

Miss Barrow, a 49-year-old spinster, took the upper rooms in Seddon's Crouch Hill house in July last year, after a quarrel with her relatives. With her she brought a small boy, Ernie Grant, who had been in her care since the death of his mother some years previously.

Mr Lloyd George's sensational budget this year frightened Miss Barrow, who feared that single people like herself, entirely dependent on their invested capital, might soon find themselves unable to make ends meet. Seddon, a senior insurance agent, made some calculations, and told Miss Barrow that he could make her an annuity and allow her to live in his house rent free for the rest of her life if she made her capital over to him. Accordingly Miss Barrow transferred to him about £3000 worth of India stock and two houses in Camden.

She only lived to collect one payment of the annuity. During the gastro-entiritis epidemic this summer, she seemed one of the worst afflicted, and died after several days' vomiting and diarrhoea. Seddon promptly had her buried in a pauper's grave, taking a small commission from the undertaker for introducing the business.

When Miss Barow's cousins the Vonderahes learned that she was dead, they protested that Seddon had not informed them and asked him about her money. Seddon claimed that he had written to them and rudely told them Miss Barrow left nothing. The Vonderahes became suspicious and had Miss Barrow exhumed, whereupon the body was found to contain arsenic.

On being arrested, Seddon said indignantly: "What a terrible charge – wilful murder! It is the first of our family that has ever been charged with such a crime!"

Following evidence that Mrs Seddon had been cashing £5 notes that undoubtedly came from Miss Barrow's cashbox, and endorsing them with a false name and address, she followed her husband into custody.

Police claim that Seddon's daughter Maggie purchased arsenic in the form of fly-papers from the local chemist.

> ## " WHAT A TERRIBLE CHARGE – WILFUL MURDER! IT IS THE FIRST OF OUR FAMILY THAT HAS EVER BEEN CHARGED WITH SUCH A CRIME! "
>
> Frederick Seddon

Appeal Spares Pimp who Stabbed his Girlfriend

ENGLAND'S RECENTLY formed Court of Criminal Appeal has saved its first victim from the gallows. The jury found Charles Ellsome guilty of murdering Rose Render.

The 22-year-old labourer had been living with the 18-year-old waitress for some time and, according to her father, forced her into prostitution to earn money for him. In the small hours of the morning of August 21, a Clerkenwell man on his way home heard a woman's voice scream, "Don't, Charles, don't!" from Wilmington Square. And at daylight Rose's body was found, stabbed to the heart.

It was shown that Ellsome had bought a long-bladed knife that day, and a fellow prisoner reported that Ellsome had confessed the murder to him, saying, "She drove me to do it."

The Appeal Court takes the view that Mr Justice Darling's summing-up did not stress the caution with which the jury should treat Ellsome's alleged confession. For this reason they have overturned the conviction.

None the less, their own view is made fairly clear by their observation that in ordering Ellsome's release they are not expressing any view as to his guilt or innocence.

Mysterious Deaths at Lancaster Castle

THE LANCASTER CASTLE poisoning case has come to an inconclusive end with Miss Edith Bingham's acquittal.

In January this year, Mr William Bingham died, after thirty years service as caretaker and guide at the English castle. His son, Mr James Bingham, was appointed to take his place, and he asked his unmarried sister Margaret to come and act as his housekeeper. A few days after joining him, she died.

Mr Bingham then invited another sister, Edith, to take her place. But Edith proved extravagant and unreliable, so he soon replaced her.

On August 12, Mr Bingham died after eating a meal Edith had prepared. He proved to have succumbed to arsenic poisoning. Exhumation of the bodies of William and Margaret Bingham proved that they too had ingested large quantities of the poison.

Edith Bingham was tried for all three murders, but no clear motive can be shown for her poisoning her father and sister; nor does any evidence show how she could have administered it.

So the question remains: who killed the Binghams?

IN BRIEF

Thieves have stolen the famous Mona Lisa from the Louvre, cutting it from its frame while the gallery was closed for cleaning. Their purpose is obscure, as so famous a painting could not be sold at any art market in the world.

Seddon to Die: His Wife Acquitted

The Seddons seated in the witness-box at their trial

AFTER A tense trial which the British Attorney-General, Sir Rufus Isaacs, prosecuted with icy fervour, Seddon is to hang while his wife goes free (*see* 1911).

> **I PRAY YOU AGAIN TO MAKE YOUR PEACE WITH THE GREAT ARCHITECT OF THE UNIVERSE.**
>
> **Mr Justice Bucknill**

Seddon made a very bad impression in the witness-box, although he answered almost every question clearly, and without evasion. But Sir Rufus had little difficulty in making him appear a cold human being whose primary concern was to justify all his financial transactions. Feeling in court was that Seddon and his victim, Miss Barrow, were a pair of money-grabbing misers who tried to over-reach each other.

On hearing his wife's acquittal, Seddon leaned toward her, and said, "You're well out of this." His own conviction did not, apparently, lead him to despair.

On hearing his sentence declared, Seddon delivered a short speech explaining yet one more financial point in his favour, and then made a desperate Masonic sign, which almost unnerved Mr Justice Bucknill, who still recovered sufficiently to say: "Our brotherhood does not encourage crime. On the contrary it condemns it. I pray you again to make your peace with the Great Architect of the Universe."

Mrs Seddon, by contrast, said little in her own defense, and offered no explanation for passing Miss Barrow's £5 notes under a false endorsement. But the jury felt sorry for her as she seemed to be dominated by her husband.

An enormous petition shows that the public is by no means satisfied in this case. Seddon's and Miss Barrow's alleged meanness is contradicted by the alacrity with which each in turn voluntarily accepted financial responsibility for the orphaned Ernie and Hilda Grant. Ernie confirms that they were always kind to him, unlike Miss Barrow's relatives, who appear to have hung around her money like so many vultures.

The chemical test for arsenic made on Miss Barrow's body is an entirely new process, and Professor Willcox concedes that the minutest error in measurement would make a quite disproportionate difference to the final calculations. Finally, Seddon's lower middle class vulgarity was easily made to look sinister by the smooth barristers confronting him.

Yet this unfortunate man will undoubtedly hang.

'The Hooded Man' Identified and Convicted

THE HOODED MAN, George McKay, whose girlfriend knew him as John Williams, has gone to the gallows after offering his new-born baby a piece of bread.

Cat-burglar Williams was spotted on the portico of Countess Szataray's house in Eastbourne, Sussex, and shot Inspector Arthur Walls dead when he ordered him to come down.

The following day police learned that Williams, a London resident, was the criminal they wanted, and he was arrested and brought to Eastbourne with his head hooded to prevent witnesses from seeing him before the identity parade. In the event, none of them was able to identify him.

But Williams' pregnant girlfriend, Florence Seymour, directed police to the point on the beach where he had hidden the murder weapon.

She was refused permission to marry her lover in prison, but when she took her new baby in to see his father before he was hanged, Williams gave the child a piece of prison bread with the words:

> **NOW NOBODY CAN SAY THAT YOUR FATHER HAS NEVER GIVEN YOU ANYTHING.**
>
> **George McKay aka John Williams**

Open Murder Under Blazing Broadway Streetlamps

The Metropole Hotel, Broadway, where Herman Rosenthal (inset) had his last meal

THE HEADLINE of the *New York World* for July 16 screamed: GAMBLER SAYS POLICE LIEUTENANT WAS HIS PARTNER.

At 1.00 am, that same gambler, Herman "Beans" Rosenthal bought a copy of the first edition and sat down to a steak in his favourite resturant, the Hotel Metropole on Broadway.

With his betting outfit on West 54th Street doing badly, and his corrupt political protector Tim Sullivan dying, Rosenthal found the greedy extortion of Police Lieutenant Charles Becker more than he could handle.

So he was exposing Becker to journalist Herbert Bayard Swope who, in turn, fed the information to District Attorney Charles Seymour Whitman. And the D.A.'s office hoped the revelations would enable them to crush corruption in New York.

In a secret meeting with Whitman, Rosenthal promised that he would testify before a Grand Jury, describing police collaboration with Manhattan gamblers and criminals. And he evidently calculated that his personal ties with leading gangster Jack Zelig (who has headed Monk Eastman's mob ever since Eastman's imprisonment in 1904), coupled with the publicity he was receiving in the press, would protect him from sudden death.

Rosenthal was wrong. As he left the Metropole at 2.00 am and walked into the brilliant lights and crowded pavement of Broadway, a voice cried, "Over here, Arnold."

With that four men sprang from the shadows, pistols blazing, and killed him at pointblank range.

They escaped in a Packard limousine that was easily traced, as it has often been hired by mobsters. Even so, a bystander who took the car's number had great difficulty in persuading police to accept it from him. It is clear that New York Police Department contains powerful officers who do not wish to see this crime properly solved.

> **I WANT ROSENTHAL CROAKED!**
> **Lt. Charles Becker, NYPD**

As of December, the four young thugs who did the actual shooting – Harry "Gyp the Blood" Horowitz, "Lefty" Louie Rosenberg, Jacob "Whitey Lewis" Seidenschmer, and "Dago" Frank Cirofici – have been tried, convicted and sentenced to death. However, the District Attorney's office is still struggling to find evidence to bring to trial their commander-in-chief, Big Jack Zelig, and the crooked policeman Charlie Becker who, it is believed, is the one to have ordered the murder, with the words: "I want Rosenthal croaked!"

Illicit Liaison Ends with Bullets in Taxicab

EDWARD HOPWOOD'S love affair with actress Florence Dudley ended twice over on September 28. In the morning the lady – real name Florence Alice Bernadette Silles – learned two unacceptable facts.

Hopwood was already married. And the police wanted him for passing bad cheques. Horrified at the notion of bad publicity and an uncertain future the actress, (appearing at the Tivoli Theatre), told Mr Hopwood their relationship was over.

In the afternoon Hopwood took a taxi with her to Fenchurch Street Station, London, pleading for forgiveness. When this was not forthcoming, he drew a pistol and shot her. Then he turned the gun on himself.

He did not die, however, but was nursed back to life to stand trial and die on the gallows in December.

The Merstham Tunnel Murder: New Sensational Information

A SENSATIONAL SUICIDE and murder in the English seaside town of Brighton recalls the mysterious murder of Sophia Money in the Merstham Tunnel (*see 1905*).

A man calling himself C R. McKie shot his wife and three children in their boarding house; then set fire to his petrol drenched room before shooting himself. His sister-in-law escaped, screaming, just before the massacre began.

It turns out that McKie, who also passes himself off as "Captain Murray" and pretends to be a barrister's son, is actually Sophia's brother Robert, who identified her body when it was found. He had enjoyed liaisons with both Mrs McKie and her sister in Clapham, having children by each of them. Now financially at the end of his tether he decided to destroy himself and all his dependents.

Lovers Kill Their Spouses in Agra, India

FAMILY LIFE in the sub-tropical climate of Anglo-India may have all the fervid passion of Mr Rudyard Kipling's romances, it seems.

Illicit associations that cross racial boundaries and involve English women and Eurasian men may produce consequences as sinister as those depicted in the author's inappropriately named *Plain Tales from the Hills*.

In 1911, 42-year-old Eurasian Dr Henry William Clark of Agra in India formed a liaison with 35-year-old Augusta Fullam, wife of an army auditor. The guilty couple decided to get rid of their unwanted spouses. Clark sent Mrs Fullam arsenic for her husband's soup, but the dose proved ineffective. Clark then offered to treat his rival for "heatstroke", and injected him with the alkaloid poison gelsemine. When Fullam died in October 1911, Clark signed the death certificate and nobody suspected anything but heatstroke.

Last December the lovers rid themselves of Mrs Clark. Four native assassins broke into the house and hacked her to pieces. They were quickly caught and executed.

Clark drew attention to himself and his lover by explaining his absence from the house truthfully. He was dining with Mrs Fullam. A search of her house uncovered a tin box full of love letters from the doctor and a few abusive letters to Mrs Clark.

With the contents of this box and a little pressure to persuade Mrs Fullam to testify against her lover, the prosecution had no difficulty in securing a death sentence for Clark. He was executed on March 13. Mrs Fullam was saved from sharing his fate because she is pregnant. She has therefore been imprisoned.

IN BRIEF

HARRY THAW, millionaire murderer of fellow-millionaire Stanford White (*see* 1906) has escaped from Matteawan Asylum to Canada. Extradition proceedings are being started.

LEO FRANK, Jewish manager of a pencil factory in Atlanta, Georgia, has been convicted of the murder of 14-year-old Mary Phagan, an employee.

THE MONA LISA has been recovered safely (*see* 1911). Louvre employee Victor Peruggia claims that he took it as an act of Italian patriotism. He may, however, have been the accomplice of an unidentified swindler who "sold" it six times over to dishonest American collectors, supplying each with a forgery they dared not take to the police!

Triple Killer Gives Himself Up to Save Father

GANGSTER ORESTO Shillitoni, "The Paper Box Kid", gave himself up in June when he heard that his father had been arrested. On May 3, New York police officers Charles Teare and William Heaney moved in to stop two men fighting on the street. One of the combatants thereupon pulled a gun and shot both policemen and his antagonist, a well-known gangster named John Rizzo. All three died.

Over 100 policemen were assigned to the hunt for Oresto Shillitoni, but he successfully disappeared until, in June, an eye-witness suggested that Shillitoni's father had been implicated.

When the elder Shillitoni was arrested, "The Paper Box Kid" in fear for his father's life, turned himself in so he could make a statement clearing his father.

He now goes on trial for the murder of the policemen and his fellow criminal.

Oresto Shillitoni, "The Paper Box Kid" who murdered two policemen and a fellow gangster

Killer Caught by Lure of Soccer

WANTED MURDERER George Ball was an anonymous figure until he went to watch his Merseyside team play. Then he was recognized from photographs that had been flashed across the city's cinema screens all week.

Ball worked at a tarpaulin shop, and resented the authority of 40-year-old manageress Miss Christine Bradfield. On December 10, Ball stayed late at work and indecently assaulted Miss Bradfield in the room behind the shop, before battering her with an iron pipe when she scratched his face severely in retaliation. The loathsome killer then sewed her body into a sack.

The night was windy, and at about 10.00 pm one of the shop's shutters blew down, denting the hat of a passing seaman walking his girl. Eighteen-year-old Samuel Eltoft came out of the shop to replace the shutter, and summoned Ball, who reimbursed the seaman. A few minutes later, the young couple watched Ball and Eltoft push a handcart bearing a heavy bundle away down the windy streets.

Miss Bradfield's body was found in the canal next day. Enquiries quickly indicated that only her shop clerks could have been responsible. Eltoft soon told the police what had happened. But Ball disappeared until his arrest outside the soccer ground.

The two men go on trial for murder next year.

Ordained Priest was Forger, Conman and Murderer

FATHER HANS SCHMIDT of St Boniface church in New York, is one of the most remarkable criminals who ever lived. He was born in Germany in 1881, and led a dissolute student life at Mainz Seminary, despite which he was ordained in 1904. Soon after, he forged himself a doctoral certificate. He also forged other degree certificates for fellow priests. When this became known, Father Schmidt was unfrocked.

In 1909 he came to America and used forged documents to win an appointment at St Francis Church, Trenton, N.J., transferring from there to St Boniface.

At the same time he used forged documentation to practise as "Dr Emil Moliere of Paris, France". He used this identity in swindles involving forged patent medicine companies' stock.

Under the alias "George Miller", Schmidt operated a counterfeiting plant on West 134th Street, turning out $10 and $20 bills. He also forged blank death certificates which he intended to use for a continuing career of murder.

Murder brought him into police hands in the first place. The bisected torso of Anna Aumuller, presbytery housekeeper of St Boniface's church, was found in the Hudson River, and identified by a birthmark on the chest.

The parish priest revealed that

Saw, twine and butcher's knife, used by Father Schmidt for disposal of his mistress, Anna Aumuller

he had sacked Aumuller the previous year because he suspected her of a romantic entanglement with Father Schmidt.

Schmidt confessed that he had gone through a form of marriage with Aumuller. He claimed to have killed her "because he loved her" and because "sacrifices should be consummated with blood". Cynical police believe that he killed her because she had become pregnant.

Schmidt has been sentenced to die in the electric chair.

Chicago's Red Light District is Closed

CHICAGO AUTHORITIES have closed the Levee – the city's infamous red light district – which contained what may be the world's highest concentration of houses of ill fame. Two years ago, evangelist Gipsy Smith led a crusade against immorality in the Levee, but the only consequence was the closure of the Everleigh Sisters sporting house. Now the authorities have closed all the other brothels, disregarding warnings that vice will simply move to the suburbs. Biggest loser is gangster "Diamond" Jim Colosimo, who runs clubs and brothels throughout the Levee.

DIAMOND JIM COLOSIMO'S EMPIRE

COLOSIMO'S CAFE: Luxurious setting with showgirls and "jazz" music. Gambling upstairs.
HOUSE OF ALL NATIONS: Brothel boasting girls from any country you can name.
THE BUCKET OF BLOOD: Combination saloon bar and brothel.
BLACK MAY'S: Black prostitutes for white punters. Occasional obscene circus acts.
THE CALIFORNIA: Pick your girl from the selection wearing transparent chemises in the windows. All cost $1.
BED BUG ROW: "25 cent cribs" with black prostitutes for all comers.

Father Schmidt in court: the first ordained Catholic priest to suffer execution in the USA

The Chicago pimp "Diamond" Jim Colosimo

French Minister's Wife Murders Journalist, but is Acquitted

MADAME HENRIETTE Caillaux, second wife of the French Minister of Finance, has been acquitted to public acclaim after shooting Gaston Calmette, editor of *Le Figaro*.

Caillaux's pacific policies were unpopular with the French public this spring, and his position was

Calmette, goaded French minister

made weaker by a scandalous divorce, during which his first wife produced sensational love letters her husband had written to Henriette.

In March, *Le Figaro* published one of these letters, and Caillaux threatened to confront the editor. Henriette believing her husband had actually gone armed to confront Calmette, rushed out to stop him. But, unable to find him, she bought a gun herself, and went to the editor's office. After a short altercation, Mme Caillaux shot the journalist dead.

Her trial in July opened with the public firmly hostile to her. But as evidence emerged that Calmette had been involved in anti-French propaganda, the tide turned. It is possible, too, that a French jury was influenced by the fact that Mme Caillaux is a noted society beauty. In any case, she walks free as a patriotic assassin.

Madame Henriette Caillaux, acquitted of the murder of the editor of *Le Figaro*

New Zealand Axe Murders: German's Hunnish Brutality

WHEN WAR broke out this year, Arthur Rottman, a German seaman on a New Zealand ship, was interned and sent to work at Joseph and Mary McCann's farm in Ruahine. The McCanns allowed him to celebrate Christmas merrily, and on December 27 he awoke with a hangover and failed to go out to milk the cows. When McCann up-

braided him, Rottman lost his temper and split the farmer's head open with an axe. Then he attacked Mrs McCann and her infant son the same way.

After his orgy of murder, Rottman delivered milk to a nearby dairy in the usual way, and then caught a train to Wellington where he found employment at a construction camp. Rottman saw newspaper accounts of the "Ruahine Axe Murders", and asked co-worker, William Kelly, to tell no one where he was. Kelly, however, promptly informed the police.

Rottman claims that he was still so drunk when he awoke on December 27 that he had no idea what he was doing. He goes on trial in the New Year.

South African Bandit in Romantic Death Drama

SOUTH AFRICA'S leading desperado shot himself and his wife in a cave on Kensington Ridge this September. Twenty-eight-year-old William Foster fell into criminal company some years ago when he and two companions were arrested for stealing three donkeys they found wandering in the desert. Sentenced to a month's imprisonment in German South West Africa, Foster nurtured deep resentment and emerged with a taste for alcohol and a loathing of the law. Over the next few years he built up

a criminal record, though his offences were minor until he planned a major jewellery theft, hoping to marry on the proceeds. His arrest earned him 12 years' hard labour, but he escaped after 9 months.

His girlfriend had married him while he was in jail waiting for his trial, and as Mrs Peggy Foster she now joined him in a career of robbing, escaping and shooting pursuers. Foster was recognized as South Africa's most wanted man when he and two fellow-villains were finally trapped on Kensington Ridge. One of the three committed suicide. Then Foster's family, including Peggy, went into the cave to persuade him to give himself up. Soon the family emerged. But Peggy stayed to die romantically with her beloved husband.

Boy Strangled on London Train: Father Cleared

FIVE-YEAR-OLD Willie Starchfield's little body rolled up and down the railway carriage between Chalk Hill and Dalston all one afternoon, until a passenger noticed the child's hand under a seat.

Willie's mother left him in the care of a neighbour during the morning, but returned to find the babysitter distraught as the boy had not returned from a simple errand.

Two passers-by told police they had seen Willie in the company of a man, and one of them subsequently identified Willie's father, newspaper-seller John Starchfield, as the man in question.

Mr and Mrs Starchfield have been acrimoniously separated for some time, and the father's alibi for the day – that he had spent much of the time resting on the bed in his lodging-house – seemed inadequate.

Charges were brought, but Starchfield's solicitor mounted a vigorous defence before magistrates, presenting evidence that other witnesses had seen Willie unwillingly abducted by a woman, and persuading the witness who had identified Starchfield that she was not really sure of her identification at all.

The case has been dismissed, and it seems likely to remain a mystery.

John Starchfield (foreground) bows his head at the inquest on his son Willie

Murderer Preaches, Retracts, Confesses on Scaffold

> ❝ **THIS IS THE HAPPIEST DAY OF MY LIFE** ❞
>
> **Henry Spencer**

HENRY SPENCER (34) aroused suspicion in Wheaton, Illinois, when he was seen withdrawing all his fiancée's savings from the bank. As he tried to leave the town by train, the local sheriff accosted him and took him away for questioning.

Spencer, who claimed to be a salesman, turned up in Wheaton earlier in the year, and paid assiduous court to Allison Rexroat, a woman much older as well as much richer than himself. After

the couple announced their engagement, Spencer took her for a picnic in the country. And it was on his return – alone – from this pleasant outing that he was seen helping himself to the lady's savings.

Miss Rexroat was a respected local resident, so bank tellers and customers alike wondered why she had permitted a comparative stranger to the town such freedom with her assets. Some of them had already suspected the young man's motives.

Under questioning, he insisted that he did not know where Miss Rexroat was. But a farmer had seen the couple on a hillside, and a search in the area led to discovery of the lady, her head battered by a hammer. Shortly after, Spencer confessed.

At his trial, he alleged that the confession had been beaten out of him. The jury was unimpressed, and he was convicted and sentenced to death.

His execution was a remarkable occasion. Hangings are still

open to the public in Wheaton, and a vast crowd came to see the murderer die. Spencer declared that he had embraced religion and was a reformed character. "I've joined the ranks of God's children," he averred, and springing up the scaffold, he cried: "This is the happiest day of my life!"

Finally, as the drop fell, he withdrew his confession with the words: "I never harmed a hair on her head. So help me God!"

> ❝ **I NEVER HARMED A HAIR ON HER HEAD. SO HELP ME GOD!** ❞
>
> **Henry Spencer**

IN BRIEF

ORESTO SHILLITONI has been found guilty of the New York triple murder (see 1913) and sentenced to death.

ESCAPED MILLIONAIRE lunatic killer Harry Thaw (see 1906, 1913) has been extradited from Canada and returned to New York. His mother's lawyers, however, have secured him a retrial which will take place next year.

GEORGE BALL has been convicted and executed for the murder of Christine Bradfield (see 1913). His young accomplice Samuel Eltoft has been imprisoned for 4 years.

Murdering Monster Dies a Coward's Death

GEORGE JOSEPH SMITH, the "Brides in the Bath" killer was dragged to the scaffold on August 15, wailing to the executioner: "I am in terror!"

Smith's career ended in January this year when Charles Burnham of Aston Clinton, England, spotted a news item describing the death of Mrs John Lloyd (née Margaret Lofty) in Highgate. The lady drowned in her bath only a few days after her marriage. Mr Burnham was interested, because his daughter Alice had died at Blackpool in exactly the same way. Her husband, a Mr Smith, had made life very unpleasant for the Burnhams as he tried to extract Alice's trust fund from them. Mr Burnham drew the attention of the police to the coincidentally similar deaths.

So too, did Alice Smith's Blackpool landlord, Mr Joseph Crossley.

Police quickly established that Smith had a long record as a petty thief, swindler, bigamist, and confidence trickster preying on lonely spinsters. They also discovered that Alice Burnham was not the first of his wives to end their lives drowned in a bath.

In 1912 Smith reunited with Beatrice (Bessie) Mundy, a respectable spinster whom he had married bigamously in 1910, and rapidly deserted when he believed he could only secure £138 of her £2,500 inheritance.

After the reunion, Smith and Bessie exchanged wills in each other's favour. Five days later Bessie was found drowned in her bath.

Smith profited by his three murders to the tune of about £3,800, and would have made a further £700 on Margaret Lofty's life insurance had not the company withheld payment.

He had invented a plausible accident, and found an almost perfect means of murder. He hanged himself by his greed.

> ## I AM IN TERROR!
>
> QUOTE **George Joseph Smith**

George Joseph Smith with Bessie Mundy, his first "bride in the bath"

One Month's Jail for Honeymoon Killer

EPILEPTIC PORTER CHARLTON has been released from custody after serving just 29 days in prison for the murder of his wife in 1910. Young Charlton, then 21, married fierce-tempered actress and heiress Mary Scott Castle and took his markedly older bride on holiday to Italy. The marriage was stormy, and Charlton soon battered Mary to death and disposed of her remains in a trunk in Como.

He confessed willingly on his return to America, and a three-year delay ensued while Italy and the USA wrangled over which should try him. In 1913 he was extradited to Italy, but further delays and the outbreak of war put off his trial until October 18 this year.

After all that waiting, with Charlton's epilepsy in evidence, he has served just one month for his murder.

Mobster Takes Top Job in Windy City Brothels

DIAMOND JIM COLOSIMO has summoned his nephew, Johnny Torrio, from New York to help him run his Chicago flesh empire (*see* 1912). Torrio, who is handy with a knife, began his career as "Terrible John", the bouncer at Nigger Mike's place in Manhattan. He has been a sort of Fagin to young Italian delinquents, organizing a gang of juveniles in the Five Points district and watching their talent and appetite for crime grow.

Torrio has the makings of a gang in this youthful and impressionable group. Since opening his own place near Brooklyn Navy Yard, he has become known as "The Brain", and constantly talks about running criminal enterprises like big businesses.

As a directorial partner in Big Jim's brothels, Johnny the Brain has now got his finger into some of the biggest pies around.

Corrupt Police Lieutenant Follows Hoods to the Chair

THE PUBLIC slaying of gambler Herman Rosenthal on Broadway (*see* 1912) has at last been brought home to New York Police Lieutenant Charlie Becker – the man whose corruption Rosenthal was exposing.

Becker joined the police in 1893 by bribing Tammany Hall Democrats' East Side boss, "Big Tim Sullivan". Gangster Monk Eastmann (*see* 1904) introduced the two. Becker quickly made himself notorious by beating up a prostitute who had refused to sleep with a brother officer.

In 1912, when Sullivan succumbed to his last illness, Becker took over the gambling and prostitution houses from which the City boss had extorted bribes, and sharply increased the amounts he demanded. Rosenthal, a former protegé of Sullivan's, was outraged when Becker's greedy demands outran his ability to pay, and started talking to journalist Herbert Bayard Swope. As the scandal hit the New York press, Rosenthal was a marked man.

He was gunned down in full view of the public on Broadway, and despite some deliberate police obfuscation of the investigation, the four gunmen were arrested and electrocuted.

It has taken another four years for District Attorney Charles Whitman to bring the electric chair to Charley Becker, the man everyone knows told a hired assassin: "Walk right up to him and blaze away at him and leave the rest to me. Nothing will happen to anyone that does it. Walk up to him and shoot him before a policeman if you want to, and nothing will happen."

Whitman's integrity in conducting the case led to his election as state Governor last year. So it was no surprise to anyone that he did not exercise his prerogative of mercy, and Becker has died in the "hot seat".

> ## " WALK UP TO HIM AND SHOOT HIM BEFORE A POLICEMAN IF YOU WANT TO, AND NOTHING WILL HAPPEN. "
>
> QUOTE **Lt. Charles Becker, NYPD**

IN BRIEF

NEW ZEALANDER Arthur Rottman has been executed for the Ruahine axe murders (*see* 1914).

AT HIS THIRD trial for the murder of fellow-millionaire Stanford White, (*see* 1906) escapee criminal lunatic Harry Thaw has been found Not Guilty and declared cured of his insanity. His mother's expenditure of millions has finally secured this lethal sadist's freedom.
Thaw's first action on regaining control of his affairs was to open divorce proceedings against Evelyn Nesbit, the girl whose relations with Stanford White led him to shoot the architect. He denies fathering her child, Harry Russell Thaw.

FRANK JAMES, elder brother and fellow outlaw of the notorious Jesse, has died after living a respectable life as a horse-handler and farmer for over 20 years.

SCOTLAND YARD is dissolving its small squad investigating the White Slave Traffic.
In the ten years since the International Protocol came into effect (*see* 1904) not one single case has occurred of a woman being forced or tricked into travelling abroad for an immoral purpose. The Metropolitan Police can no longer afford to devote 12 officers to helping the National Vigilance Association try to persuade girls out of a sinful, but quite legal, way of life.

Innocent Jew Convicted, Reprieved, Then Lynched

A LYNCH MOB calling itself "the Knights of Mary Phagan" broke into Milledgeville Prison Farm on August 17. They dragged out 31-year-old Leo Frank, serving a life sentence for the murder of Mary Phagan (*see* 1913) and hanged him before a blazing cross.

Frank was convicted, largely on the evidence of semi-literate black janitor James Conley, who said he had often seen Frank committing perverse sexual acts with young girls, and that Frank had ordered him to take Mary's body

Lynching in the southern states: the racist murders that encouraged a mob to kill Leo Frank

from his office to the basement where it was found.

Subsequent evidence that Conley himself was a habitual practitioner of the perversions of which he accused Frank, and almost certainly the actual murderer, led State Governor John Slaton to commute Frank's death sentence. But anti-semitic Georgian rednecks then murdered this innocent man who was already serving a life sentence for a crime he never committed.

Drama at Palace as Rasputin is Murdered

RASPUTIN, "the Mad Monk", who has been called the power behind the Russian throne, was brutally murdered by a group of aristocrats on December 15.

Gregoriy Efimovich Novikh "Rasputin" was an uneducated peasant holy man from Siberia. He preached, prophesied and practised faith healing. He is reputed to have enjoyed sexual orgies with female followers, saying that one must sin to be forgiven. His power lay in his charisma. He was introduced to the court when the Tsarina despaired over the haemophilia which threatened her son's life. Rasputin's hypnotic therapy proved effective in staunching any minor bleeding which might have proved lethal to the Tsarevich, and the empress demanded the constant presence of this healer.

Although Rasputin's personal corruption went no further than occasional drunkenness and sexual adventures, and his political influence never amounted to more than gaining petty posts for friends and clients, he was deeply resented by the aristocracy. Some blamed him for failures of imperial policy. At one point he was exiled, but the Tsarina demanded his return.

This December, a group of aristocratic thugs led by Prince Yussoupoff decided to rid the court of the contaminating peasant. They invited Rasputin to dinner, and discovered that he was so strong it was difficult to assassinate him. They gave him drugged and poisoned sweets. Rasputin ate them greedily and asked for more. They pulled a pistol and shot him. He advanced furiously on them. They bludgeoned him, and still he fought back. They dragged him to a car, drove him out to the frozen river, and forced him under the ice to drown. And with superstitious arrogance, they offered to the world their incompetence as proof that Rasputin was supernaturally evil!

He was not. He was not a monk. (He was married.) He was not mad. He was not the Romanoffs' *eminence grise*. He was simply a peasant faith healer, murdered by snobbish brutes who couldn't stand a common man outranking them at court.

Rasputin, the Siberian faith healer Gregoriy Efimovich Novikh

Thaw Again! Now He Ravishes a Boy

MAD, MURDEROUS, millionaire molester Harry Thaw, was back in the dock this year. He was finally acquitted last year of the murder of Stanford White (*see* 1906), following three trials, two sanity hearings and an escape to Canada, all financed by his doting mother.

Now this New York sadist, long known for the pleasure he takes in whipping young women, has changed the object of his lust. Early this year he kidnapped 19-year-old Frederick B. Gump, beat him, and sexually molested him.

He was tried, and once again found insane. But Mrs Thaw poured out her dollars and achieved another sanity hearing. This time Thaw was declared sane, and then it transpired the Gumps were now going to drop all charges.

Mrs Thaw is said to have paid them $500,000 to leave her loathsome offspring at large.

Meanwhile Evelyn Nesbit, the former Mrs Harry Thaw, on whose account the millionaire murdered Stanford White, has herself dipped into the Thaw millions again.

After some years appearing in vaudeville as "The Girl on the Red Velvet Swing" – the infamous sex-toy she sat in at Stanford White's apartment – she announced last year that she was expecting, and the father was ... her ex-husband Harry Thaw! She claimed to have bribed guards to let her into Matteawan Asylum for a post-marital dalliance.

Highly improbable as Evelyn's story seems, Mamma Thaw has again handed over the cash to defence lawyers to keep her evil son out of trouble.

TRIPLE-MURDERER Oresto Shillitoni (*see* 1913) tried to escape death by shooting Sing Sing guard Daniel McCarthy one week before his execution date. He was electrocuted as scheduled on June 30, regardless.

Sabotage in USA Munition Works

ALTHOUGH THE USA is not involved in the Great War, its studied neutrality does not satisfy agents of the Hun, who have started dynamiting Uncle Sam's munitions works.

A security guard at the Black Tom freight yard in New Jersey was startled to see a small conflagration under a railroad truck filled with explosives. Despite his sounding the fire alarm, an enormous explosion destroyed the entire freight yard filled with munitions destined for sale to the Allies. Three people were killed.

Hungarian immigrant Michael Kristoff was reported as behaving suspiciously, and actually confessed to the sabotage when informally questioned by a US agent. But before he could be arrested, Kristoff disappeared.

Since then, the Mare Island Navy Yard in California has been destroyed in a similar explosion. This time sixteen innocent people were killed.

Fire raging at Black Tom freight yard, New Jersey, an act of Hunnish sabotage against neutral America.

Husband Kills Wife and Lover: Then More

HUNGARIAN POLICE, hunting for hoarded petrol, went to a house in Czinkota after it was reported that conscript soldier Bela Kiss (42), who had died of wounds in Belgrade, had collected large petrol drums in 1912, saying it was patriotic to store fuel.

But the seven drums Kiss had collected contained no fuel. Each held the garrotted body of a woman. Further searches turned up more drums, two of which contained the bodies of Kiss's young wife Maria and her lover Paul Bihari. Kiss had claimed the two eloped in 1912.

It transpires that Kiss advertised in the matrimonial columns as "Professor Hoffmann". When optimistic widows and spinsters met the "professor", bringing their savings and jewels to start a new life with him, they ended their present life rather smartly, and went into storage in Czinkota.

From the number of advertisements Kiss placed, and the answers he received, it is thought there must have been substantially more than seven victims killed and robbed. Certainly he is one of the greatest mass murderers who ever lived.

Despite the original report that Kiss was dead, it is now believed that he switched identity tags with a fallen comrade, and the mass murderer is at large, somewhere in the field of war.

Jury Rocks with Laughter at Murderous Doctor

DR ARTHUR WARREN WAITE charmed the jury all the way to the verdict. Handsome, stylish and witty, with a first-class tennis player's lithe frame, he made them laugh as he told of his difficulties in murdering his millionaire parents-in-law.

When his mother-in-law, Mrs John E. Peck, came to stay with the young dentist in New York after the New Year, he took her driving in pouring rain with the windscreen open. Mrs Peck declined to catch pneumonia. He put ground glass in her marmalade. He sprayed her throat with cultures of anthrax, diphtheria and influenza. Mrs Peck had never looked better. Finally he gave her an overdose of veronal, and nursed her lovingly through her final illness, insisting that she be cremated on her death.

Later this year, when widowed Mr Peck came to visit his son-in-law, the old gentleman was treated to water in his galoshes and a car-ride with a wet passenger seat. He was offered concoctions of typhoid, pneumonia and diphtheria in his puddings. He was given damp sheets. Finally he was given a massive dose of arsenic. And when even that failed to kill the robust old gentleman, Waite suffocated him with a pillow!

Suspicious relatives refused a second cremation and had the body examined. The arsenic was discovered, and charming Dr Waite, who intended killing his wife next, to use her inherited money in supporting his expensive society mistress, has charmed his way to a death sentence.

French Butcher Hid His Mistress' Head and Hands

Voisin's basement kitchen: scene of butchery

BRILLIANT DETECTIVE work by Inspector Frederick Wensley of the CID has solved London's Regent Square mystery. On November 2, a road-sweeper found a sack containing a woman's headless, handless torso, wrapped in a sheet in Bloomsbury Square. Another bundle contained legs of the same woman, with some elegant French underwear. The sheet bore the laundrymark IIH, and a piece of paper with the torso had the words, "Blodie Belgiam" scrawled on it. Pathologists suggested that the dissection showed a degree of skill.

From the clue of the underwear, and the appearance that the scrawl misspelled the word "Belgium", Wensley directed his men to check laundries for one which had washed the sheet, asking especially about French or Belgian women. This identified the woman as 32-year-old Emilienne Gerard, in whose kitchen an IOU for £50 signed by Louis Voisin was found.

Voisin, a butcher, lived in nearby Cleveland Street. He had been Mme Gerard's lover, but also enjoyed the favours of Berthe Roche, who was with him when police came making enquiries.

Wensley then asked Voisin to write the phrase "Bloody Belgium". Voisin reproduced exactly the spelling errors left with the body.

The Inspector was now sure the paper had been left to mislead police into imagining that the murderer was some Englishman who resented our being dragged into a continental war on behalf of France and Belgium.

A search of Voisin's basement kitchen uncovered bloodstains and one of Mme Gerard's earrings, caught in a towel. A cask of alum in the coal cellar contained her head and hands.

Police deduce that Mme Gerard came round to Voison's rooms during the frightening Zeppelin raid of October 31, only to find him ensconced with Berthe Roche. A quarrel ensued and the two killed her. Both will be tried for her murder.

Man on Death Row Hugs Victim's Picture

DUTCHMAN PIET VAN DE CORPUT, awaiting execution in Sing Sing, has obtained a picture of the woman he killed, which he says he will take with him to the electric chair before he meets her again in heaven.

De Corput, a sailor, enjoyed a drunken leave in New York in the autumn of 1915. During this time, widowed Barbara Wright was suddenly attacked on the street by a man who stabbed her with a long-handled knife, and ran away.

Police investigation suggested the killer was John Hendricks, a Dutchman who roomed in the same house as Mrs Wright and pestered her. New York was plastered with pictures of his face, to no avail.

When they picked him up a year later, after he had reverted to his real name of Piet van de Corput, they discovered he had been in the city all the time, once complaining at a police station of being mugged.

Eye-witnesses easily identified de Corput, and he rejected his lawyers' suggestion that the identification parade had in any way been mishandled. The jury took only a few minutes to reach a guilty verdict.

Navy Yard Saboteur Trapped in Mexico

THE MARE ISLAND Navy Yard saboteur (*see* 1916) has been caught. Kurt Jahnke, a German in Mexico City, developed the habit of drinking with Mexican army colonel Paul Altendorf. He did not realize that Altendorf was in the pay of Washington, keeping an eye on enemy aliens in the neutral country. During one drunken conversation Jahnke admitted that he had both forewarned the authorities that Mare Island would be bombed, and perpetrated the crime. He explained that he gave the warning to divert suspicion from himself.

Altendorf offered to help Jahnke make his way illegally over the border into the USA, but, of course, betrayed him to secret service men who arrested the Kaiser's explosives and sabotage expert in Nogales, Arizona.

IN BRIEF

THE DISTINGUISHED BRITISH barrister Mr Edward Marshall Hall KC, has been knighted, and becomes Sir Edward.

Greedy Dr Hyde has no Jekyll Side

AFTER THREE trials, Dr Bennett Clarke Hyde has been freed. Although he almost certainly killed three people in 1909 and intended to kill four more, his lawyers have raised the point that he cannot be tried four times for the same offence.

Hyde's wife Frances was the niece of her husband's second victim, millionaire Thomas Swope of Kansas City. The doctor wanted to become executor of the old man's will and obtain control of his estate. To that end he offered Swope's nominated executor, James Hunton, the outdated treatment of "bleeding" when he became poorly. In fact, Dr Hyde bled and poisoned his patient to death, which he then registered as apoplexy.

Distressed by the loss of his old friend, 82-year-old Mr Swope himself fell ill. Hyde tried unsuccessfully to have others suggest to the old man that his doctor would make a very good administrator for his estate. Despite this failure, he poisoned the old man with strychnine and cyanide – a cunningly chosen cocktail in which each toxin cancelled the symptoms of the other.

By Mr Swope's will, Mrs Hyde inherited $250,000. But the greedy doctor, wanted to eliminate the other five nephews and nieces and inherit their share as well. Four of them soon fell ill, and Hyde diagnosed typhoid. When Christian Swope died in November, the family nurse went to Frances Hyde to voice her suspicions. Mrs Hyde was furious and sacked the nurse, going also to her lawyer to complain.

The lawyer recommended that another doctor should treat the surviving Swope nieces and nephews, whereupon they rapidly recovered.

Now suspicious family members obtained exhumation orders for Hunton and Swope, whose bodies proved to be full of strychnine and cyanide. Hyde was put on trial and found guilty.

But his wife employed able lawyers who won a retrial on a technicality. Toward the end of that trial, a juror fell ill and a second mistrial was declared. It was believed at the time that there was nothing wrong with the juror only that he had been bribed. A third trial resulted in a hung jury – and again bribery was suspected.

Now it is clear that the scheme of going through three trials was intended to secure the doctor's release.

He will not, fortunately, practise medicine again.

Lloyd George, British Prime Minister, was intended victim of harebrained plot

Mad Scheme to Kill Lloyd George

A LUDICROUS PLOT to assassinate British Prime Minister Lloyd George has come to light. Mrs Wheeldon, a widow in Derby, holds strong Suffragette, Socialist and Pacifist beliefs. In her Suffragette days, she discussed the possibility of assassinating Mr Lloyd George by poisoning a nail in his boot. With the Prime Minister prosecuting the War energetically, she decided to move from theory to action.

Using a simple code, she wrote to her son-in-law Arthur Mason, a chemist exempted from conscription as his work is of national importance. Mason willingly sent her phials of strychnine and curare. And Mrs Wheeldon turned to two deserters she was hiding for assistance in conveying the poison to the Prime Minister.

Unknown to her, the deserters were really government agents. Mrs Wheeldon and the Masons have been sentenced to varying periods of penal servitude.

Dr Hyde and his loyal wife Frances; guilty verdict overturned on a technicality

Axeman Terrorizes City: Italian Grocers the Victims

THE CITY of New Orleans is in a panic as a mad axeman cuts a devastating swathe through the Italian community. He strikes small grocers and their families. He kills them while they sleep. He enters by removing a panel from the back door. And he leaves his axe behind him.

In the spring, Mr and Mrs Joseph Maggio, who lived above their small grocer's shop, were found hacked to death in their bed. The murder weapon, a bloodied axe, was outside their back door. It yielded no fingerprints. A panel neatly chiselled from the door showed how the murderer had made his entry.

In June, Louis Besumer and his common-law wife Harriet Lowe were attacked. Both were taken to hospital with head injuries, and Mrs Lowe was believed to have murmured that she thought Besumer might be a German spy.

As he is Polish and not Italian, the police accepted this suspicion, and for a few days he was held under arrest.

One month later Mrs Lowe died, mumbling that Louis had struck her with an axe, and Besumer was re-arrested. He was released the following day, as the axeman struck again that very night, injuring pregnant Mrs Edward Schneider as she lay in bed. She caught sight of her assailant before he hit her, and says the axeman is a tall, heavily set white man.

On August 10 the axeman fatally wounded Joseph Romano. As usual he chiselled out a door panel and left his weapon nearby. But for the first time, whether by accident or design, he had struck a barber and not a grocer.

New Orleans police and pressmen recall that three Italian grocers and their wives were killed in axe murders in 1911. The perpetrator was never caught. They believe the same man is now terrorizing the city.

Nobody has a clue as to his motive: is he an anti-Catholic anti-foreign redneck, possibly in the grocery trade, who resents Italians competing in his market? Is there some personal connection between all the victims? Or are these murders part of a campaign of extortion by one of the Italian criminal secret societies? The Mafia was certainly present in New Orleans at the end of the last century, when outraged citizens lynched several of them (*see* 1890).

IN BRIEF

LOUIS VOISIN and Berthe Roche were tried for last year's murder of Emilienne Gerard (*see* 1916), and Voisin was executed in March. Mme Roche was sentenced to penal servitude as accessory after the fact.

Husband Killer Paroled After Two Convictions

WILLIAM BRANSON, twice convicted of assisting his lover, Anna Booth, in the second-degree murder of her rancher husband in the state of Oregon, has been paroled.

The killing took place in October 1915. Branson was convicted the following year and sentenced to life imprisonment. This conviction was overturned on appeal, and Branson was again tried and again convicted.

But the state parole board believes that Anna Booth actually pulled the trigger, and Governor Olcott is impressed that another man has since confessed to the murder of the rancher. Since that new suspect was immediately sent to a lunatic asylum, it is not clear why his confession should have secured Branson his liberty.

Ex-Soldier Rapes and Kills Girl

NELLY TREW left her home in Eltham, England, on June 16 to visit the library, and never returned. The following morning the 16-year-old's raped and strangled body was found on Eltham Common.

Close to the corpse lay a bone coat-button with wire rather than cotton twisted through the holes, and a Leicestershire regimental badge shaped like a tiger.

David Greenwood who lived about 100 yards from the scene of the crime normally wore such a badge on his overcoat. When workmates, reading about Nelly's fate in the papers, asked him where his badge had gone, he gave inadequate explanations. When police interviewed him, they noticed that all the buttons had been removed from his overcoat.

On this circumstantial evidence, Greenwood was tried for the "Button and Badge" murder. His defense was very weak respecting the evidence against him. His claims to have sold the regimental badge over the weekend, and to have used his overcoat buttons to mend his lathe were completely refuted. But the medical aspect of his defence served him well.

Greenwood was invalided home from the trenches recently, and his lawyers claim that he is no longer strong enough to perpetrate rape and murder on a fit young woman. This did not impress the jury, but the fact that the young man was severely shell-shocked in defending his country counted heavily in his favour. Greenwood was found guilty with a strong recommendation to mercy. And the Home Secretary has commuted his death sentence to life imprisonment.

The badge and the button that trapped murderer Greenwood

Philandering Doctor's Wife Slain By His Playmate

" I DID NOT DECEIVE HER OR LEAD HER ON. OTHER WOMEN HAVE CARED FOR ME, BUT I WAS MARRIED AND THEY KNEW THEIR LIKING FOR ME WOULD COME TO NOTHING PERMANENT. SO THE AFFAIRS USUALLY FADED AWAY. "
Dr David Roberts

The trial of Grace Lusk, Waukesha, Wisconsin, for the murder of Mrs David Roberts

NAUGHTY DR DAVID ROBERTS of Waukesha, Wisconsin, is a dangerous man in an illicit liaison. The married doctor plays around constantly, and never expects his playthings to ask for more than a little dalliance. When Grace Lusk pulled out a pistol and shot the doctor's wife, he wept as he exonerated himself.

Mrs Roberts tried to hasten Grace Lusk's fading. She visited the lady and tendered the warning that one of the doctor's previous lovers had died in an attic after an operation. After this peculiar veiled threat, she expressed her own unfavorable opinion of Miss Lusk's value to the doctor as a mistress. When Miss Lusk found the personal observations unbearable, she shot Mrs Roberts dead with a .25 pistol. Her attempt to kill herself immediately failed.

She has been convicted of second degree homicide and sent to prison.

Grace Lusk

Double Murderer Caught on Second Insurance Claim

ARRESTED IN France on August 21, swindler Henri Girard must have believed he had long got away with murder. In 1909 he persuaded broker Louis Pernotte to give him power of attorney. He also insured Pernotte's life for 316,000 fr. In 1912 he put a culture of typhus bacilli in Pernotte's drinking water. And as Pernotte lay sick, he prepared a syringe of camphorated chamomile which he persuaded Mme Pernotte to inject into her husband. At the same time he remarked, like a conjuror: "You observe that I have nothing in my hands."

Even so, no suspicion was aroused, and Pernotte's death was attributed to an embolism.

After this, Girard tried unsuccessfully to poison M.Mimiche Duroux. He had better luck with widowed Mme Monin, who died fifteen minutes after eating a mushroom Girard gave her at a Paris Metro station. The Phoenix Insurance Company, with whom Girard had insured the lady's life, was suspicious. And M.Girard is now in custody trying to explain the fatalities to a *juge d'instruction*.

1919

CRIMES OF THE TWENTIETH CENTURY

French Ladykiller Landru Killed 200 Ladies

WIDOWER WITH TWO CHILDREN, AGED FORTY-THREE, WITH COMFORTABLE INCOME, AFFECTIONATE, SERIOUS AND MOVING IN GOOD SOCIETY, DESIRES TO MEET WIDOW WITH A VIEW TO MATRIMONY.

Henri Desiré Landru

Landru, the French Bluebeard

BALD-HEADED, bushy-browed and spiky-bearded, Henri Desiré Landru may yet be the world's greatest ladykiller. In both senses. Shortly before the war he discovered the lure of matrimony and thereafter he preyed on lonely, middle aged women, promising to marry them.

Landru entrapped his victims through advertisements in the newspapers. A typical Landru snare read: "Widower with two children, aged forty-three, with comfortable income, affectionate, serious and moving in good society, desires to meet widow with a view to matrimony."

Many women responded to such appeals and many were fascinated since Landru radiated a voracious sexual appetite.

Landru was caught this year because of his greed two years ago. After the disappearance of 47-year-old widower Mme Buisson on August 10, 1917, he turned up at her apartment with a forged note demanding her furniture. Mme Buisson's relatives knew she had been corresponding with this man for two years and intended to marry him. Since they heard no more from him after the lady disappeared, Mme Buisson's sister was interested when she saw Landru strolling down the Rue de Rivoli on April 11 this year, with a pretty young woman. She informed detectives, who trailed Landru to a villa in Gambais.

There they found a notebook with a classified list of 283 women and voluminous correspondence from these ladies – nearly all of whom have disappeared!

They also found a quantity of women's clothing and possessions, much of it identifiable as belonging to women last known as being "engaged" to this creature. In the stove, they found human bone ash.

It seems that Landru began his activities using a villa at Vernouillet as his base, moving to Gambais in 1916 when he felt he had killed two victims dangerously close to each other. Neighbours have commented on the number of women who visited him and the noxious smoke that poured from his chimneys after the visitors had "left".

CATEGORIES OF WOMEN CORRESPONDENTS

The French Bluebeard's notebooks listed his prospective victims under the following cynical headings:

1. To be answered poste restante.
2. Without money.
3. Without furniture.
4. No reply.
5. To be answered to initials poste restante.
6. Possible fortune.
7. In reserve. For further investigation.

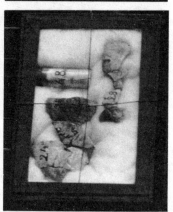

Human bones found in Landru's villa

Elderly Doctor Murders Wife: Hangs Himself

SIXTY-SEVEN-YEAR-OLD Dr Walter Keene Wilkins, convicted earlier this year of his wife's murder, has hanged himself in Mineola Jail.

The old couple lived on Long Beach, Long Island, and Mrs Wilkins died there on the night of February 27. Police found the doctor tending his dying wife in the driveway when they responded to his emergency call. He told them that he and Mrs Wilkins had surprised a gang of housebreakers when they returned home from New York City, and the lady had been attacked.

Shortly after that, Mrs Wilkins' lawyer received a copy of an invalid will, dated 1915, in which she left two bequests to her husband. Her previous will, of 1903, disposed of her assets so that the doctor gained nothing.

Meanwhile police were puzzled at finding Mrs Wilkins' false teeth and gloves inside the house. It seemed odd that she went to the city without them. It was further noted that Dr Wilkins' hat-brim was stained with blood, and the picture-wire binding the abandoned lead cosh which had been the murder weapon was identical with wire found in the house.

Dr Wilkins promptly disappeared. When he resurfaced in Baltimore, he was arrested. His fingerprints matched those on the lead cosh. A tie-pin he claimed the housebreakers had stolen was found in his overcoat pocket. And he was found guilty of first degree murder.

Shellshock Victim Shoots Lover: Was it for Gain?

FREDERICK HOLT, a shell-shocked army lieutenant who was discharged from the War in 1918 suffering from depression and amnesia, has been arrested and charged with the murder of Mrs Harriet Breaks. Her body was found in sandhills near Blackpool on Christmas Eve. She had been shot three times.

Holt's revolver and gloves were found nearby, and footprints matching his trailed to and from the scene of the crime.

Holt met Mrs Breaks, who was separated from her husband, soon after his return to England. The two have been living together ever since. Although Holt's mental state earns him some sympathy, it is noted as suspicious that he recently insured Mrs Break's life for £5000, and stood to gain from her will.

It is interesting that neither of the pair were normally known by their given names. Holt called himself "Eric", and Mrs Breaks was known as "Kitty".

The trial of Frederick Holt

Child Murderer Acquitted, then Reconvicted

A MAN may be too drunk to intend murder – but he's never too drunk to intend rape! So, at least, think Lord Chancellor Birkenhead (the former Mr F. E. Smith) and his fellow British Law Lords, sitting on the appeal of Arthur Beard.

On April 25 this year, Beard, a nightwatchman, raped and strangled 13-year-old Ivy Lydia Wood in Hyde, Cheshire. Mr Justice Balhaiche sentenced Beard to death when the jury brought in a verdict of guilty.

But Beard's counsel submitted to the Court of Criminal Appeal that his client was drunk when he killed Ivy and could not have formed the deliberate intention of committing murder. The Court

upheld the appeal and overturned the guilty verdict.

Now the Crown has taken the matter up to the Law Lords and the Learned Peers have concluded that he was quite sober enough to form an intention of rape and since the victim of that felony died in consequence, the original charge of murder stood, together with the guilty verdict.

Lord Birkenhead has ruled, however, that Beard should not be executed, since he was given the delusive hope of the now overturned Appeal Court decision. Despite this clemency, Lord Birkenhead is notoriously intolerant of nonsense, and certainly hopes never again to hear drunkenness pled in mitigation of a felony.

'So Sorry, Officer, We've Just Had a Murder'

POLICE CALLED to 13 Holland Park Avenue, London, were surprised to be greeted by an imperturbably gentlemanly family, who agreed that neighbours had heard gunshots; refused all offers of assistance in tidying up, and regretfully announced that a murder had taken place.

The house is Sir Malcolm Seton's, and he lent it to his cousin Miles. Miles had been visited by his friends, Dr and Mrs Norman Rutherford. The pair were on the verge of separating, and Dr Rutherford, knowing that his wife had consulted Miles Seton, resented his having apparently advised her to leave the marriage. He went further, and jumped to the conclusion that Miles was his wife's lover. So he shot him.

Dr Rutherford was severely shellshocked during the War, and this has made his personality unstable and edgy for some time. He has been committed to Broadmoor.

The scene in court, with Mrs Rutherford's maid in the witness-box (left)

Dr Rutherford in uniform during the Great War

IN BRIEF

BASEBALL'S WORLD SERIES – the US national championship final – was fixed this year. Eight players from favourites Chicago White Sox conspired with gambling boss Arnold Rothstein and others to lose to the underdog Cincinatti Redlegs.

The Redlegs won, and the bookies cleaned up.

Ex-Officer Light Cleared: So Who Killed Bella?

THE ACQUITTAL of former British army officer Ronald Vivian Light on the charge of murdering 21-year-old factory worker Bella Wright is a triumph for the great defender, Sir Edward Marshall Hall.

Bella's body was found beside her bicycle in a Leicestershire lane last year. A bullet had passed cleanly through her head and lay nearby. She was not robbed or sexually assaulted.

Enquiries established that a man on a green bicycle rode with her when she visited her uncle at Gaulby, and went away with her, though she had only just met him. A search for this well-spoken squeaky-voiced man, in his thirties or forties was unsuccessful until, this February, a dismantled green bicycle was dragged up from a canal, and near it a pistol holster containing ammunition identical to the bullet beside Bella's body.

A serial number on the bicycle frame identified it as one bought in 1910 by Cheltenham schoolmaster Ronald Light. The holster, too, was identified as his army-issue property.

Light claimed to have sold the bicycle and to know nothing about the holster.

But in court he confessed that he had been lying. He had, he said, been panicked by newspaper assertions that the green bicycle's owner was the murderer. He had, indeed, met Bella and lent her a spanner. They parted before she went to the lane where the body was found.

Light gave his evidence clearly and cogently, persuading the jury, if not the judge. In addition, Sir Edward showed that the clean wound in Bella's head was not such as would be expected if she had been shot from close range. Marshall Hall suggested that a spent or riccocheting bullet from a rook-rifle fired at a distance had killed the girl.

But assuming Light to have been justly freed, considerable mystery still surrounds the girl's death.

Ronald Light in the dock: the bicyclist schoolmaster accused of killing Bella Wright

Man Shot: Is this the End of the Axeman?

MRS MIKE PEPITONE, who saw the mad axeman of New Orleans (see 1918) after he killed her husband, has shot dead Joseph Mumfre in Los Angeles, and declares that he was the monster.

The axeman's carnage raised terror to new levels last year. In March he injured Mr and Mrs Charles Cortimiglia and killed their two-year-old daughter. Mrs Cortimiglia claimed to recognize him – or rather, them: Iorlando and Frank Jordano, rival grocers from the same street. Both were convicted on Mrs Cortimiglia's sole testimony in May, and released in September when she confessed it was a pack of lies.

Three more people were attacked during 1919, the last being grocer Mike Pepitone whose wife found him dead in bed, and saw the axeman rush past her.

After their experience with Rose Cortimiglia, police are loth to accept Mrs Pepitone's identification of Mumfre, and she has been given ten years' imprisonment for homicide. But Mumfre spent time in prisons around New Orleans, and the axe murders always took place when he was free and his whereabouts couldn't be determined.

New Orleans hopes its panic is now over.

Daughter says She Also Drank the 'Poisoned Port'

IN HIS second triumph of the year Sir Edward Marshall Hall has won acquittal for Kidwelly solicitor Harold Greenwood. The Welshman was suspected of poisoning his middle-aged wife with weed killer.

Dr Willcox the pathologist testified that there was arsenic in Mrs Greenwood's remains. Parlourmaid Hannah Williams swore that Mrs Greenwood was the only person to drink from a bottle of port Greenwood fetched from the pantry for lunch.

But Sir Edward easily established that a barely competent local GP prescribed a morphine and arsenic tonic to Mrs Greenwood, poorly labelled and in dangerous quantities, so that she might have taken it in mistake for a sedative or digestion mixture. Mrs Greenwood's daughter swore under oath that she too had drunk port from the suspect bottle, which has not been recovered.

Greenwood seems to have been the victim of tattling neighbours who resented his marrying a pretty young woman soon after he was widowed.

Brutal Murder on the Crumbles

SEVENTEEN-YEAR-OLD typist Irene Munro was found dead in shingle at the Crumbles, near Pevensey, Sussex, on August 19. Her face had been savagely battered.

Witnesses saw her walking in that direction that afternoon accompanied by two young men. All three seemed happy and companionable.

The men were soon identified as Jack Field and William Gray, unemployed ex-servicemen from Eastbourne, where Miss Munro was on holiday. Field was a lad of 19. Gray was an older married man.

Both men denied having been with Miss Munro at all. They attempted unsuccessfully to have another young lady give them a false alibi. Gray approached a fellow-prisoner while on remand awaiting trial, asking him, too, to say that they had been with him and nowhere near the Crumbles on the afternoon of 19 August. The convict refused, and these attempts to obstruct justice did the men great harm.

Nevertheless, the jury brought in a surprising recommendation to mercy. This may be because evidence suggests that Miss Munro was a sexual "tease" who enjoyed leading older men on. In any case it did not help: the men will be hanged in the New Year.

Examining the scene of Irene Munro's murder

Confusion outside Colosimo's restaurant after the slaying of owner "Diamond Jim"

Chicago Slaying of 'Diamond Jim' Colosimo

PIMP "DIAMOND JIM" COLOSIMO has been shot dead in Chicago by unidentified gunmen. He had gone to a meeting arranged by his lieutenant Johnny Torrio (*see* 1915) but "Johnny the Brain" never showed up.

Brooklyn mobster Frankie Yale just happened to be in Chicago at the time, and fits the description given by witnesses of one of the gunmen. The witnesses, however, refuse to identify Yale when confronted with him.

It seems that Torrio and former Brooklyn hoodlum Alphonse Capone arranged the killing because Diamond Jim was slow to take advantage of the Volstead Act passed on January 1. This makes the sale and consumption of alcoholic beverages illegal throughout the USA, and gangsters see immense profits awaiting them as they take over the distribution of liquor.

But Diamond Jim, recently married to a much younger woman, was content to draw profits from brothels and gambling, and put no effort into fighting off competitors.

Torrio and Capone have now taken over Colosimo's enterprises, with the "Four Deuces" at 2222 Wabash Avenue as their headquarters.

In addition to gambling and brothel facilities, this building has cells and torture rooms where the mobsters can punish their enemies.

Second Welsh Solicitor Accused of Poisoning Wife

MAJOR HERBERT ROWSE ARMSTRONG (52), solicitor and clerk to the court at Hay-on-Wye, will pass through the dock of his own court in the New Year, charged with murder.

Earlier this year the major was unable to return moneys held in escrow for a client of rival Hay-on-Wye solicitor, Oswald Martin. While Mr Martin was pressing the major for restoration of these funds, he received a box of chocolates anonymously through the post. A friend who ate one was sick, and Mr Martin threw the remainder away.

Shortly after this, the major invited his rival to tea, ostensibly to discuss their business differences. When his housekeeper brought in a plate of scones, the major selected one and passed it to his guest, with the words: "Excuse my fingers, Mr Martin!"

Mr Martin ate the scone, and was extremely ill. His doctor analysed his urine, and it contained arsenic.

When the police were informed, they noted that Mrs Armstrong, a dominating woman who henpecked, and humiliated her tiny husband, died suddenly last year after an illness which always improved when she was in residential care, but worsened when she returned to her husband for nursing. Arrangements were made to exhume her body and analyse the contents.

In the meantime, the unfortunate Mr Martin had to fob off a positive barrage of invitations to tea from the major!

Finally, on New Year's Eve, the major was arrested as there were large quantities of arsenic in Mrs Armstrong's body. At the time of his arrest, the major had a little packet of arsenic in his pocket and 19 more have been found distributed around his house. He claims that he prepares individual doses of poison to kill individual dandelions on his lawn, and finds it handy to carry them around with him in case a weed suddenly catches his attention.

Local opinion is that the major was inspired by the acquittal of brother-solicitor Harold Greenwood (*see* 1920).

Pathologist Dr Webster (left) and Armstrong's family doctor, Dr Hinks

IN BRIEF

HENRI GIRARD (*see* 1918) still awaiting trial for the murders of Louis Pernotte and Madame Monin, has swallowed a germ culture and died in prison. He told his guards, "I will always be misunderstood - abnormal, as I have been called - and for all that, I am good, with a warm heart."

US Anarchists Murder Two in Wage-Snatch

IN A CASE reminiscent of Britain's Tottenham outrage (*see* 1908), robbers at Braintree, Massachusetts on April 15 killed a cashier and guard at the Slater and Morrill Shoe Company, and made off with a $16,000 pay-roll.

The villains escaped in a car, which police believe they recognized a month later. The men in charge of it, Nicola Sacco and Bartolomeo Vanzetti, were arrested and found to

Bartolomeo Vanzetti and Nicola Sacco between guards

be illegally in possession of firearms. They also turned out to be anarchist immigrants and members of a group of subversives already viewed with suspicion by police. Vanzetti has been charged with another robbery in the vicinity, and both men go on trial for the Braintree shootings next year.

There is considerable hostility to the anarchists in New England, as law-abiding citizens hoped the anarchist outrages of the years before the Great War had been brought to an end by that carnage.

Now Alcohol Prohibition Triggers Crime Wave

FEARS THAT last year's Volstead Act prohibiting the sale and consumption of alcohol in America would lead to large-scale criminal activity have proved justified. All over the country, most notably in New York and Chicago, gangs of organized criminals have taken over the production, import and distribution of liquor.

Criminal gangs have always been a more serious problem in America than in Britain. Most states prohibit prostitution and gambling, which has led to successful criminal organizations supplying these perennial pleasures. Local author-ities, police, and even some of the judiciary have long been corrupted by "racketeers" (nicknamed for their attendance at noisy dances or "rackets" sponsored by City Hall in New York at the end of the last century). But the mobs never dreamed of winning the wholesale power to corrupt entailed by making it a crime to drink a glass of beer. Now senators, cabinet ministers and the highest reaches of the establishment are all engaged in commerce with known criminals, and it may, in the long run, prove impossible to eradicate this cancer from the body politic.

PROHIBITION SLANG

The criminalization of drinkers in America has taught the whole nation a new criminal slang. We offer a glossary:

SPEAKEASY: An illegal bar, entered by giving a password.

BOOTLEGGER: A supplier of alcohol. Deriving from frontiersmen who smuggled illegal whisky to Indian reservations in their boots.

HIJACKER: A bootlegger who steals another's shipment of liquor.

RUM-RUNNER: An importer of alcohol, using varying smuggling techniques.

RUM ROW: A line of ships, just outside US territorial waters, purveying wholesale alcohol to rum-runners in speedboats.

ALKY COOKING: Making small quantities of alcohol in home-made stills for sale to bootleggers. Particularly common in the Italian section of New York, where Cita Terranova "the Artichoke King" has hundreds of tenement dwellers distilling for him.

BATHTUB GIN: A noxious spirit distilled in the home from almost any fermentable mash available, usually for home consumption.

NEEDLE BEER: The legal alcohol-free beer, given a kick by injecting a hypodermic syringe of industrial alcohol – a seriously toxic drink.

Boy Sex Maniac Acquitted: Then Kills Again

WITHIN 14 days of his triumphant acquittal for the murder of Freda Burnell in February, 15-year-old Harold Jones struck again, raping and murdering Florence Irene Little, whose bloodstained body was found in his attic.

Eight-year-old Freda disappeared on February 5, having last been seen being served by Jones in the Abertillary, Wales, seed-shop where he worked. The following day her body was found nearby. She had been strangled, and an attempt had been made to rape her. Her handkerchief was found in the back of the seedshop, and after enquiries, Jones was charged with her murder.

There was great public rejoicing when the lad was cleared and went free.

But rejoicing changed to horror two weeks later when 11-year-old Florence Little's body was discovered. Jones had cut her throat after tearing her clothes in his vicious assault.

Jones confessed to this murder, giving as his reason "a desire to kill". After his trial at Monmouth, he also confessed to the murder of Freda Burnell.

This adolescent monster is too young to hang, and will be detained at His Majesty's pleasure.

Harold Jones, lethal sex maniac, outside the Welsh seedshop where he worked

Canadian Theatre Millionaire Missing: Is He Alive?

ON DECEMBER 2, 1919, Toronto theatre magnate Ambrose Small sold his holdings for $1 million and disappeared. That Christmas, Small's secretary, John Doughty, also disappeared after taking $100,000 of bonds from Small's bank deposit boxes. It was assumed that Doughty murdered Small, but no body was found and Doughty could not be traced.

This November he turned up in Oregon. He has confessed to stealing the bonds, but he apparently knows nothing of Small's disappearance.

Local opinion now suspects that Small's devout widow got rid of her adulterous husband to secure his money for her beloved Church.

Surburban Stabbing After Letters of Passion and Poison

Edith and Percy Thompson on holiday, in happier days before her love for Bywaters led to his death

ON OCTOBER 3, Percy and Edith Thompson were returning home in Ilford, Essex, after the theatre, when a young man rushed out and stabbed Mr Thompson. Mrs Thompson, hysterically distressed, said she had no idea who the assailant could have been.

But when Chief Inspector Frederick Wensley learned that neighbours were scandalized by 29-year-old Mrs Thompson's liaison with 22-year-old ship's clerk Frederick Bywaters, he arranged to have Bywaters arrested and Mrs Thompson brought to a police station where she could glimpse her lover in an-

other room. Immediately Mrs Thompson betrayed her complicity by crying: "Oh, why did he do it? I did not want him to do it!"

Bywaters' lodgings contained scores of letters Mrs Thompson had written to him. Many discussed poisoning Percy, and even claimed that Edith had put ground-up light bulbs in his food.

The two stood trial in

December. Mr Justice Shearman, expressed the strongest distaste for their adulterous liaison.

After two hours deliberation, the jury convicted both. Bywaters is justly found guilty; he told police he attacked Thompson because: "He never acted like a man to his wife. He always seemed several degrees lower than a snake."

But Mrs Thompson, who moaned, "I am innocent! I am innocent!" on hearing the verdict, may be correct in strict law. Even Lord Chancellor Birkenhead notes that, while she undoubtedly willed her husband's death and probably conspired to bring it about, the assault which killed Percy – the actual murder with which she was charged – was unplanned, unpremeditated, and an unwelcome suprise to her.

Unless there is a reprieve, the two will be executed in the New Year.

Prostitute Killer, True, Goes to Broadmoor

THERE IS public disquiet over the reprieve of Ronald True, convicted of murdering prostitute Gertrude Yates (who operated under the name "Olive Young") in her basement flat in Fulham, London.

Miss Yates' maid saw True when she came to work on the

morning of March 6, and accepted his story that he had taken Miss Yates a cup of tea in bed. Shortly after True left, the maid discovered that the bed contained pillows, and Miss Yates' body lay in the bathroom. She had been battered with a rolling pin and strangled with her dressing-gown cord.

True left a visiting card in the flat, and was easily traced to a music-hall that evening. *En route* he had pawned some of Miss Yates' jewellery and changed his bloodstained clothing.

He offered the extraordinary defence that he has a "double" named "Ronald Trew", who goes around London bouncing cheques and committing petty frauds and thefts for which True is held re-

sponsible. True says Trew killed Miss Yates.

The universal conclusion is: "Not true. Not Trew. True."

But True's conduct had been unbalanced for years. He was thrown out of the Royal Flying Corps during the War because of his eccentric behaviour. His estranged wife found him too mad to live with. The Home Secretary has therefore reprieved him, and sent him to Broadmoor.

Still, many people wrongly suspect that he escaped the noose because he is the black sheep of a middle-class family, and his victim was a humble prostitute; whereas Henry Jacoby was hanged as a working-class boy who impertinently murdered a lady.

Ronald True, mad murderer of Gertrude Yates

Radical MP and Newspaper Magnate Jailed for Theft

THE GAUDY career of Horatio Bottomley (62) has ended with a prison sentence for fraud. Bottomley, who never denied his origins as an illegitimate workhouse child, rose through his journalistic skills. He founded the *Hackney Hansard* in 1884, and the *Financial Times* in 1888. Soon after that he was charged with peculations in connection with the collapse of his £1 million local Hansards empire. He defended himself brilliantly and won acquittal.

In 1906 he founded the popular paper *John Bull*, and became Hackney's Liberal MP.

In 1908 he was prosecuted for manipulating the crash of his Joint Stock Institute. Again he defended himself with brilliant success, winning the congratulations of the court. Still, in 1912 he was bankrupted and had to leave Parliament.

He reinstated himself by making recruiting speeches during the War, and his journals promoted competitions and lotteries in aid of the war effort.

Now it has been proved that Bottomley pocketed the funds of at least one of these – the £900,000 Victory Bond Club. And he has been sentenced to seven years' penal servitude.

Not even his worst enemies accuse Bottomley of hypocrisy, however. When an office boy was brought to him charged with stealing a one-shilling postal order from a competition entry, Bottomley tolerantly remarked:

> **HE'S GOT TO START SOMEWHERE!**
> QUOTE Horatio Bottomley

Horatio Bottomley, publisher, politician, and peculator, playing at patriot during the War

Hotel Servant Batters Old Lady in Bed

EIGHTEEN-YEAR-OLD pantry boy Henry Jacoby told police exciting stories that might have come from the "tuppenny bloods" he loved, when they questioned staff at Spencer's Hotel, Portman Street, London, about the death of Lady White. The elderly widow was found battered in her bed on March 15. Jacoby talked of hearing intruders in the night, and of creeping along corridors after them.

In the end, shrewd questioning by Inspector George Cornish of Scotland Yard elicited a confession. Jacoby planned to rob a guest's room, and armed himself with a hammer left by workmen carrying out repairs in the hotel. When he found Lady White awake, he killed her, and then washed the hammer before returning it to its place.

Despite his youth, the murderous pantry-boy was hanged on June 5.

Henry Jacoby, hotel porter affected by crime

Terrorist Irish Assassins Fell War Hero

FIELD MARSHAL Sir Henry Wilson was shot down on his Belgravia doorstep by Irish terrorists Reginald Dunn and Joseph O'Sullivan as he returned from unveiling the new War Memorial at Euston Station. The general drew his dress sword – the only weapon he had with which to defend himself – but was powerless against the assassins' bullets.

The two were chased down Ebury Street, and had to seize first a cab, then a victoria to try to escape, since O'Sullivan had a wooden leg. The infuriated crowd eventually seized them, and they would have been lynched on the spot had not the police come to their rescue.

IN BRIEF

MAJOR HERBERT ROWSE ARMSTRONG (*see* 1921) hanged for the murder of his wife.

HENRI DESIRÉ LANDRU (*see* 1919) guillotined for the murders of at least 30 women.

CHAUFFEUR THOMAS HENRY ALLAWAY, hanged for murdering Irene Wilkins whom he lured to Bournemouth, England with a false advertisement.

ERNEST WALKER (17) sent to Broadmoor for motiveless torture and murder of 14-year-old Raymond Charles Davis, a District Messenger Co. page boy.

Madame Fahmy Freed: Shocking Story of Perversions

Mme Fahmy, Parisian adventuress

A T THE height of a thunderstorm during the night of July 10, shots rang out from a luxury suite in the Savoy Hotel, London. Servants found Madame Marguerite Laurent Fahmy standing over the body of her husband, Prince Ali Fahmy Bey, a smoking pistol in her hand.

The marriage had been unhappy. Mme Fahmy is a Parisian adventuress, who won wealth and status when she captivated the young Egyptian millionaire diplomatist. But life in romantic Egypt proved frightening and sordid. The prince bullied her. He was more interested in men friends than his wife. It was widely believed that he enjoyed an unnatural relationship with his sinister secretary, Said Enani. She feared for her life when forced to travel up the Nile with the prince's devoted and gigantic black bodyguard. The prince used Madame Fahmy sexually as though she were an unnatural male lover: an abuse which gave her distressing ailments in an embarrassing place.

It was Mme Fahmy's hope that their visit to Europe might result in a separation, and she could return to Paris for surgery on her injured fundament. But quarrels continued, culminating in the prince's death in their hotel.

Sir Edward Marshall Hall triumphantly secured the lady's acquittal. He demonstrated that her Browning pistol was so complicated that her story of accidentally firing it under the impression that she was removing the bullet from the chamber could easily be true.

Unfortunately, he also laid great stress on Mme Fahmy's marrying an Egyptian pervert, and seemed to suggest that all Egyptians subject their wives to "oriental" vices. This has resulted in a strong diplomatic protest from the Egyptian Embassy.

But Madame Fahmy at last walks free.

Inspector Crosse at Fahmy's inquest

Woman Kills Boy: Uses Daughter to Conceal Body

M YSTERY SHROUDS 30-year-old Susan Newell's murder of a Glasgow newspaper boy. Nobody doubts that she was justly hanged on October 10 for killing 13-year-old John Johnston. Nobody can imagine why she did it.

Mrs Newell and her 8-year-old daughter Janet were given lifts by a lorry and a car whose drivers saw them pushing a heavy handcart carrying a bundle. As they left the car, a passer-by saw a head and hand loll out of the bundle, and called the police.

Mrs Newell tried to blame her husband, with whom she had quarrelled. When that failed she made no further useful statement. Janet testified to helping her mother put the boy in the bag.

Mason Reprieved in Brixton Taxi Case

A TANGLED TRAIL, starting with a gold-topped walking-stick incorporating a pencil-case, and proceeding through a prostitute's rooms, has led 22-year-old Alexander "Scottie" Mason to conviction for murder.

In the evening of May 9, two men struggled in Baytree Road, Brixton, London. Three shots rang out. One man fell; another jumped over a wall and escaped through the back gardens of Acre Lane.

The dead man was London taxi-driver Jacob Dickey, who had brought a fare from Victoria Station. Beside his body lay the peculiar walking-stick, identified as the property of a thief called James Vivian who lived with his girlfriend, prostitute Hetty Colquhoun, in Pimlico. Vivian acknowledged the stick, but said that he had lent it to his friend, Canadian army deserter "Scottie" Mason.

Mason confirmed this when first approached, telling a story that was initially supported by Vivian and Hetty. He said he and Vivian intended to rob a house in Brixton, and ordered a "bent" taxi-driver to supply a getaway car. They were surprised when the "straight" Dickey drew up, and shocked when a passenger got out, fought with him, finally shooting him. Vivian and Mason ran off in different directions, and Mason agreed that it was he who passed along the Acre Lane gardens. But Vivian changed his story under interrogation, claiming that he did not join Mason as planned, because of a tummy upset. Mason protested that Vivian's "illness" was feigned to quiet Hetty's anxiety about her boyfriend going on a robbery. But the police accepted Vivian as a prosecution witness when he added that Mason came home dishevelled, saying he had killed a taxi-driver.

Although the jury found Mason guilty, the Home Secretary would not hang the man on such accomplices' lies, and his death sentence was commuted to life imprisonment.

Mother's Dream Uncovers Her Son's Murder

A FTER HIS mother dreamed that he lay at the bottom of a well, Eric Tombe's body was actually found in a well. Tombe, missing since April 1921, had been shot through the head. The well is at the stud farm in Kent, England, which he ran with fellow ex-officer Ernest Dyer from 1919 until a fire destroyed it in the month Tombe disappeared.

The insurance company refused to reimburse Dyer, declaring the fire was fraudulent. Tombe's clergyman father discovered that Dyer had forged his son's signature to a power of attorney over his affairs.

In November last year, Dyer shot himself in a Scarborough Hotel, when detectives came to question him about a petty fraud on a local newspaper.

Now, ten months after the murderer's suicide, his victim of three years ago has been mysteriously found.

Ernest Dyer, murderer and suicide

Murdered 'Model' May Have Been Blackmailer

Dot King, murdered New York courtesan

N EW YORK is rife with speculation over the murder of "model" Dot King. Her body was found in bed in her comfortable apartment on March 15. An empty bottle of chloroform stood beside her. Her arm had been twisted behind her back and her telephone removed as far from her reach as its cord allowed.

Dot's maid confirmed that pyjamas under the pillow belonged to her wealthy friend "Mr Marshall", who often stayed. Dot's friends, it transpires, envied her this wealthy "Sugar Daddy", who gave her $10,000 in the bank and $20,000 worth of clothes and jewelry – a fortune for a young woman who was a poor chauffeur's wife only a few years ago.

The search for "Mr Marshall" ended when Philadelphia millionaire J. Kearsley Mitchell came forward and confessed that he was Dot's lover and protector. He also proved conclusively that he had no hand in her death.

Speculation next turned to the possibility that Dot had other lovers, and attempted to blackmail one of them. But while this sensation delights New York, police note that all Dot's jewels are missing. They believe she was the victim of a burglar who merely intended to render her unconscious with chloroform, but accidentally administered a lethal excess.

The case remains open.

IN BRIEF

EDITH THOMPSON and FREDERICK BYWATERS (see 1922) hanged for the murder of Percy Thompson.

ALBERT BURROWS, unemployed labourer, hanged for murdering his mistress and her two children in 1920, and a 4-year-old boy he sexually assaulted this year. All the bodies were found in old Derbyshire mineshafts.

CECIL MALTBY, bankrupt tailor, shot his mistress in the bath at his Baker Street neighbourhood home; covered it with boards off which he ate meals for three months, until police broke in and he shot himself.

Millionaires' Sons Kill 14-year-old Boy for Fun

THRILL-KILLERS Nathan Leopold and Richard Loeb have been saved from execution. In a brilliant display of trial tactics, Chicago lawyer Clarence Darrow pleaded the two boys guilty to avoid having their crime described to a jury, and in a two-day hearing before Judge John Calverley persuaded him that the boys were emotionally retarded and disturbed, and it would be barbaric to execute them. While his clients smirked and giggled, Darrow's eloquence and humanity won the day against all odds.

Leopold and Loeb, respectively 18 and 19 years old, are the brilliant homosexual sons of millionaires. University of Chicago students, they have been influenced by Nietzsche's philosophy and think themselves "supermen". They planned to demonstrate their superiority by committing the perfect crime.

In May this year they kidnapped 14-year-old Bobby Franks. They gagged him, and killed him with four blows of a chisel to the head. Then they left the body in their unlocked hire-car while they ate a five-course meal in an exclusive restaurant.

Replete, they poured hydrochloric acid over Bobby's face to impede identification and hid the body in a lonely culvert. They typed a ransom note demanding $10,000 which they posted to Bobby's father, and followed it up with another signed "George Johnson" which they left on a train. But by the time this one was delivered, Bobby's body had been found.

They were easily caught. Leopold's spectacles slipped out of his breast pocket at the culvert. The frames were a specially crafted horn-rim design

Nathan Leopold (*left*) and Richard Loeb, rich spoiled and brilliant students who murdered Bobby Franks to prove their cleverness

only supplied to three customers. A stolen typewriter was recovered from the lake where they had thrown it, and proved to be the one which typed the ransom notes. District Attorney Richard Crowe was sure he would send these boys to their death, and public opinion had no sympathy for the self-important spoiled brats.

You may be interested to know that in the event that I am sentenced to death upon the gallows (as appears quite likely) I shall take steps to attempt to "pierce the veil" altho I personally am convinced that no after life exists. I at least will be prepared for the exigency in case I be mistaken.

This letter, written by Leopold after his arrest, is unlikely to sway public opinion

THE LAWYERS

Ironically the rich and reactionary boys have been saved by a lawyer who is a well-known socialist egalitarian. Rumpled and warm-hearted, Clarence Darrow loathes the death penalty, and refuses to take fees from poor clients who are not being given a fair chance. The Leopold and Loeb families, as arrogant as their sons, have quibbled about paying his well-earned $100,000 fee for saving the boys' useless lives, and Darrow is unlikely to see more than the $30,000 they have grudgingly handed over.

By contrast to the agnostic Darrow, Catholic District Attorney Richard Crowe, who prosecuted with self-righteous moral fervour, is part of the corrupt political establishment of Chicago, and endorses the activities of murderous bootlegging gangsters. Crowe wants to execute rich kids who kill for fun, but happily associates with rich men who kill to preserve the profits of their crimes.

Free Enterprise Heroes Rob the Taxpayer Rotten

THE SCANDAL-RIDDEN administration of President Warren Harding, who died last year, is likely to be remembered more for its corruption than its legislation.

Harding himself did not have his hand in the till. But his weak good nature was summed up his father, who said, "If Warren was a girl he'd always be in the family way. He just can't say no." So he provided no leadership to check the excesses of the venal "Ohio gang" who had secured his presidential nomination.

President Harding's mentor and Attorney-General, Harry Daugherty, orchestrated most of the mulcting of public funds, siphoning off vast sums from the Veterans' Administration and putting a price on Federal jobs and judgeships.

But Albert Fall, Harding's Minister of the Interior, has been resoundingly caught out taking bribes. In 1920 he noted that the naval oil reserve field at Teapot Dome, Wyoming, was being drained by nearby commercial drilling. He therefore sold off the field, and another at Elk Hills, California, to private enterprise.

Now it emerges that these oilfields were sold to Fall's friends at a gift price without competitive tender. Oilmen Edward Doheny and Harry Sinclair stand to make $100 million on the deal, and the taxpayer loses.

And Fall? He received $100,000 in used notes delivered in a little black bag!

The cabinet minister will go on trial for corruption alongside his crooked "free market" oil friends.

Severed Head Opens Its Eyes in the Flames

ONE-TIME fraudster Patrick Mahon had gone straight for the last two years. But the good-looking Sunbury sales manager was suspected by his wife of womanizing. When Mrs Mahon found a Waterloo Station Left Luggage ticket in his pocket she gave it to a friend in the railway police. When the policeman opened the case, he found bloodstained clothes and a butcher's knife.

Mahon had promised typist Emily Kaye that he would leave his wife and elope with her to South Africa. To this end he relieved her of her savings. When the pregnant Miss Kaye demanded that the elopement be put into effect, he invited her for a "love experiment" in a beach cottage at the Crumbles, Sussex (where Field and Gray killed Irene Munro (*see* 1920)).

There he killed Miss Kaye and dismembered the body for burning. The cottage was filled with cut-up flesh and bits of bone ash. Mahon's most horrifying moment came when he burned the head during a thunderstorm, and saw, by a flash of lightning, the eyes open up in the heat of the fire!

Despite his claim that Miss Kaye's death was an accident, the jury didn't believe him and Mahon was hanged on September 9.

Hangover Cure Proves Deadly

MRS MABEL JONES met red-bearded radio technician Jean Pierre Vaquier in Biarritz last summer, and enjoyed a holiday dalliance with the 46-year-old Frenchman.

This February Vaquier turned up on St Valentine's Day at the Joneses' Blue Anchor Hotel in Byfleet, Surrey, to resume the relationship. Mrs Jones was no longer so keen, and Vaquier decided to get rid of her husband. He bought strychnine in London, claiming it was for wireless experiments. He signed the poisons book as "J.Wanker", and returned to Byfleet to administer his poison.

Mr Jones drank the strychnine in his bromo salts to cure a hangover on March 29. The doctor who attended his last moments spotted strychnine crystals by the bar and had them analysed.

Vaquier was convicted and hanged in August.

Jean-Pierre Vaquier, self-styled "Mr Wanker"

Homosexual German Butcher Sold Human Meat

BUTCHER, MEAT SMUGGLER, petty thief, police informer, homosexual and paedophile, 45-year-old Fritz Haarman was not suspected of murder and cannibalism until two police enquiries converged this June.

Skulls found in the river at Hanover in May led to the recovery of bones from 27 bodies. These apparently came from missing boys who had been sleeping rough near the railway station.

In June, a boy from the station accused Haarman of indecent assault. When police searched his rooms, they found identifiable possessions of the lads who had gone into the river.

Haarman confessed, implicating his homosexual lover Hans Grans. The two had butchered their victims and sold the flesh as horsemeat.

IN BRIEF

THE US MINISTRY OF JUSTICE'S corrupt and incompetent Bureau of Investigation is to be restructured under young civil servant J. Edgar Hoover.

He promises a complete transformation. The Federal Bureau of Investigation, as it will now be called, will only employ agents with degrees in law or accountancy.

Their personal appearance and habits will be strictly monitored. No lapses from the highest standards will be tolerated.

Innocent Under-Age Girls Lured to Filthy Orgies

ON OCTOBER 15, police at East Grinstead heard that a young girl was being held against her will at Pippingford Park, Sussex, England. When PC Mills investigated, he spotted the girl cowering beside the Eastbourne Road at Witches' Corner. She informed detectives that she had been hired as resident kennel-maid by 37-year-old broker Hayley Morriss, and had been terrified when he came into her bedroom and made improper suggestions.

It turned out that Morriss and his housekeeper Madeline Roberts (22) made a practice of employing young girls whose real function was the gratification of Morriss's lust. If they objected, Miss Roberts urged them to comply. But many innocent virgins were seduced by Morriss's offers of expensive presents.

The two employed a woman friend in London who pretended she ran an employment agency in Jermyn Street, where they recruited girls. They also hired girls from the Employment Registry Office in Brighton.

On one occasion, seeing two girls walking along the Brighton Road, they stopped their Rolls-Royce and Roberts persuaded the girls, against their better inclination, to accept a lift. They were taken to Pippingford Park and invited to enter employment there, which they refused.

It is impossible to say how many girls this infamous pair has corrupted, but three at least were under 16, one of whom was Roberts's own younger sister!

One week after they were charged with procuring for an immoral purpose, sexual assault, and carnal knowledge of women under the age of 16, Morriss and Roberts married, presumably to avoid giving evidence against each other.

The two should have been tried this December, but Mrs Morriss has produced doctors' certificates showing that she is unfit. The case has been deferred until next year.

So horrible are these offences that Sir Edward Marshall Hall has made an exception to his normal role, and accepted the prosecution brief.

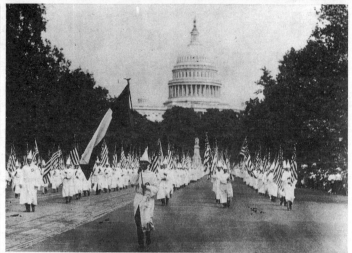

Ku Klux Klansmen from 22 states parade down Pennsylvania Avenue, Washington

KKK Grand Wizard Rape Leads to Woman's Suicide

D.C.STEVENSON, charismatic Ku Klux Klan "Grand Wizard" of Indiana, has been convicted of murdering 28-year-old Madge Oberholtzer whom he kidnapped, stripped, beat and raped in the private berth of a railway sleeping-car last year.

Miss Oberholtzer was permitted by her captor to buy some medication to alleviate her pain, but actually bought six bismuth of mercury tablets which she took in an attempt to commit suicide.

When she became extremely ill, the Klansmen returned her to her parents, explaining her injuries as the result of a road accident.

Miss Oberholtzer died this year, and the courts have made a landmark decision that death following a suicide attempt may be charged as murder against the person whose felonious conduct brought about the suicidal impulse.

Stevenson's abominable action has halted the growth of the murderous Klan, which had hitherto passed itself off as an organization for the best in white Protestant manhood.

Teeth and Ear Betray the Wrong Corpse

FRAUDSTER CHARLES SCHWARTZ decided to fake his own death in the destruction by arson of his Berkeley, California chemistry laboratory. With this in mind, he murdered evangelist Warren Gilbert Barbe and doctored the body to resemble his own.

He burned off part of Barbe's chest where he himself had a scar, punctured the different coloured eyeballs and extracted two teeth where he had lost two.

After the building exploded, investigators swiftly observed that "Schwartz's" corpse was different in a number of small but significant ways. The corpse had a mole on the ear which the fraudulent chemist did not have, and its missing teeth had been recently extracted.

Finding himself hunted for murder, Schwartz committed suicide in the Oakland boarding-house where he was hiding.

White slaver Hayley Morriss and his wife Madeline Roberts, who offered girls dubious employment

Popular 'Public Enemy No.1' Charged with Murder

IN AN ATTEMPT to undo the popularity they were giving a criminal, the newspapers began labelling Gerald Chapman "Public Enemy Number One".

> ## " DEATH ITSELF ISN'T DREADFUL BUT HANGING SEEMS AN AWKWARD WAY OF ENTERING THE ADVENTURE. "
> ### Gerald Chapman

Like many popular villains, Chapman wins admiration for his daring and athletic escapes. In 1921 he robbed a mail truck in New York City by leaping from a moving car on to the truck's running board, and holding a gun to the driver's head. (That venture netted $1,424,129, the largest haul on record.)

He took an up-market apartment in New York, and became known as "the Count of Gramercy Park". When he was betrayed by an informer, he flabbergasted in-terrogators by saying, "Sorry, gentlemen", and diving out of a 75ft high window. He was swiftly recaptured, however, when a cleaning woman signalled that he had wriggled down a ledge to another open window.

He escaped from Atlanta penitentiary after feigning illness by drinking disinfectant. Retaken and shot in the process, he none the less escaped again within six days.

But on October 12 last year he participated in a robbery in Connecticut accompanying an in-experienced criminal who shot a policeman as they made their getaway. Taken and held under tight security, Chapman has been charged with murder, and seems likely to be executed.

In his cell he has composed epigrams, including the remark: "Death itself isn't dreadful but hanging seems an awkward way of entering the adventure."

PUBLIC ENEMIES

Chicago has adopted this term for its Crime Commission's list of "Persons who are constantly in conflict with the law."

The first, published in 1923, led off with Al Capone, followed immediately by one of his body-guards, and his brother Ralph.

Chicken Farmer Beheads and Buries 'Pregnant' Fiancée

WHEN 23-YEAR-OLD Elsie Cameron set off from London last December to visit her fiancé Norman Thorne in Crowborough, Sussex, she intended to make him act on her bad news. For although Norman and Elsie had pledged to refrain from premarital intercourse, Elsie claimed to be pregnant.

She wasn't. But the plain and bespectacled girl desperately wanted to marry Norman, and rightly suspected that he had met another more attractive young lady.

Norman's claim that she never arrived at his "farm" (a shack surrounded by chicken-runs) did not ring true with the neighbours' recollections of seeing Elsie carrying her suitcase from Crowborough Station. When police dug up the farm, they found her decapitated body.

Now Norman claimed that Elsie had hanged herself in his absence. He panicked on finding the body, and quickly buried her among the hens.

He was too late with this new tale, and medical arguments about the nature of marks or folds on her neck did not save him from hanging at Wandsworth on April 22.

Norman Thorne poses at the chicken farm where he killed Elsie Cameron

Johnny 'The Brain' Quits Chicago Mob

JOHNNY TORRIO (see 1915) has retired. The 43-year-old gangster negotiated a truce between rival gangs distributing alcohol in Chicago in 1920, which broke down two years later. Last year Torrio's gang murdered his rival Dion O'Bannion. This year Hymie Weiss, originator of the "one-way ride", ambushed Torrio who was seriously injured. The millionaire gang leader has made over his empire to Al Capone and gone abroad.

IN BRIEF

FRITZ HAARMAN (see 1924) has been beheaded for the murder of 27 boys in Hanover. He expressed surprise that there were so few, believing he had killed at least 40. He did, however, deny one murder with which he was charged, loftily asserting the boy was not pretty enough for him!

Murder of Minister and Chorister Still a Mystery

Mrs Jane Gibson, "the Pig Woman", testifies from her sickbed at the Hall-Mills trial

ON SEPTEMBER 16, 1922, the bodies of the Rev. Edward Wheeler Hall (42) of St John's Episcopal church, New Brunswick, New Jersey, and choir singer Mrs Eleanor Mills (34) were found under a crab-apple tree in lonely De Russey's Lane. Both had been shot through the head, and Mrs Mills' throat had been cut. Love letters from the singer to the minister were scattered around.

This year, the Halls' maid told police that Mr Hall had said he intended to elope with Mrs Mills. The authorities, accused in the popular press of letting the minister's widow and her family buy off witnesses, finally decided to prosecute Mrs Eleanor Hall (53), her two brothers Willie and Henry Stevens, and her cousin Henry Carpender.

Star prosecution witness was Mrs Jane Gibson (56), the "Pig Woman", who raised pigs around her delapidated shack at the bottom of the lane. On the night of the murder she rode her mule up and down the lane, first looking for suspected predators, then looking for a moccasin she dropped on her first sally. She said she saw four people around the tree, threatening and beating Mr Hall and Mrs Mills. She heard one call another, "Henry".

Unimpeachable witnesses proved that Henry Stevens was away on a fishing trip that weekend. Mrs Gibson's mother sat in front of her, muttering, "She's a liar! She's a liar!" Mrs Hall gave calm and dignified evidence on her own behalf, though her icy disbelief that there could have been any impropriety between her husband and Mrs Mills strained credulity. And Willie Stevens, though eccentric, was sufficiently definite in his account of his movements that night to satisfy the court that he had no hand in the murders. All four defendants were cleared.

Since Mrs Mills' husband, the church sexton, was decisively cleared in the original investigation, it is very hard to imagine who wanted to execute the guilty couple.

Fingerprint expert Fred Drewer studies Willie Stevens' fingerprints

Tragedy of Respectable Inscrutable Immigrant

A RESPECTED LEADER of the Chinese community in Liverpool has been hanged for the wilful murder of his wife and two daughters last December. Lock Ah Tam (53) came to Britain as a seaman and opened a club in Liverpool. He was successful, generous and good-natured, and the authorities used him as a mediator with the immigrant community.

In 1918 he was struck on the head with a billiard cue while stopping a brawl. After that his character changed. He became morose and took to drink. His business deteriorated, and last year he was bankrupted.

On December 1 he hosted a birthday party for his son, behaving graciously while guests were present. But once the family were alone, Lock went into a blinding rage. His son hurried away to fetch the police, but in his absence Lock deliberately shot dead his wife Catherine and their daughters Cecilia (18) and Dorothy (20). Then he calmly telephoned the police and told them what he had done, waiting patiently for them to come and arrest him.

Sir Edward Marshall Hall argued movingly for temporary insanity. But the jury could not believe that the oriental stoicism with which Lock summoned his own arrest was the act of a lunatic and they found him guilty.

Woman Steals Worthless Junk: Then Kills Owner

LEEDS PROSTITUTE Louie Jackson persuaded nightwatchman Arthur Calvert to marry her in 1924 by pretending to be pregnant. In March this year the baby still had not arrived, and Louie told Arthur she was going to stay with her sister in Dewsbury, Yorkshire, for her confinement.

In fact she lodged in Leeds with eccentric widow Mrs Lily Waterhouse. While there she adopted the baby of an unmarried teenage mother, and took it to Arthur in triumph. She also took some worthless cutlery and household items.

Mrs Waterhouse had already notified the police that she thought her lodger was stealing from her. When they found the landlady battered to death in her home, they arrested Louie, who confessed to having previously killed another man for whom she worked as housekeeper. She was hanged at Strangeways in June.

'Pistols at Dawn', But There Was Only One Gun

Student's Mother Shot Investigating His Thefts

Mrs Alfonso Smith whose jealous husband shot her lover but was acquitted of murder

ALFONSO AUSTIN SMITH joins the long line of men and women saved from the gallows by Sir Edward Marshall Hall. The old Etonian, who served in the British Army with distinction in the War, was distressed when his wife fell in love with his close friend John Derham. Smith wrote to Derham: "You damned swine, I only wish you had the courage to meet me." Despite this operatic utterance, Derham came to Whitstable, Kent in April, responding to a telegram Smith sent in his wife's name, and accompanied the Smiths from a hotel to a villa where they were staying.

There they quarrelled, and Mrs Smith's sister rushed into the drawing room on hearing a shot at 11.00pm. She found Smith on the floor and Derham beating him with a revolver, while Mrs Smith tried to pull the two apart.

But it was Derham who had been shot in the abdomen, and subsequently died.

Marshall Hall persuaded the jury that the killing was accidental, caused when Smith tried to shoot himself and Derham tried to pull the gun away from him. He probably did not convince Mr Justice Avory, who imprisoned Smith for a year for possession of an unlicensed firearm.

> **"YOU DAMNED SWINE, I ONLY WISH YOU HAD THE COURAGE TO MEET ME."**
> **Alfonso Austin Smith**

DONALD JOHN MERRETT (18) is a bad student. His wealthy widowed mother sent him to Edinburgh University so that he could live at home with her. But Donald neglected his studies and spent time when he should have been at lectures in the arms of tea-dancers.

He also kept himself in funds by forging cheques in his mother's name.

On March 17, after breakfast, Mrs Merrett puzzled over her accounts following a letter fom her bank manager saying she was overdrawn. There was an explosion, and Donald called the maid, saying, "My mother has shot herself."

There was a head wound behind Mrs Merrett's ear and she was taken to hospital where she recovered sufficiently to say that she remembered Donald fiddling around irritatingly behind her, before there was a bang, and everything went black. She died after three weeks.

Donald insists that she shot herself when worried by her financial position. But now it is known that he fraudulently created the overdraft, he is to go on trial for forgery and matricide.

IN BRIEF

HAYLEY MORRISS (*see* 1925) given two years' hard labour, and Mrs Morriss four months, for white slaving. Counsel protested that the defendants could give no evidence because Mrs Morriss was ill. But Mr Justice Avory, in one of the most hostile summings-up since Judge Jeffreys, dismissed this as flimsy excuses which didn't deceive him.

GERALD CHAPMAN (*see* 1925) executed for the murder of a policeman by a confederate in the course of a felony in Connecticut.

Villa Stella Maris where sudden death prevented marital break-up

Donald John Merrett: matricide

'Granite Woman' and Her 'Putty Man' to Die

BORED HOUSEWIFE Ruth Snyder met prissy corset salesman Judd Gray two years ago. Then and there they went to his office, where Ruth took her clothes off to try on a foundation garment. There and then they became lovers.

"Lover Boy" and "Momsie" coupled in Manhattan hotels until, by 1926, Ruth wanted to get rid of her husband Albert. Ruth insured his life for $100,000 and tried to kill him. He didn't die when she left the gas on. He didn't die when she knocked him off their motorboat. He didn't die when she gave him poison for his hiccups, though Judd later remarked: "I told her that was a helluva way to cure the hiccups!"

This spring, "Granite Woman" told her "Putty Man" that he must help her kill Albert. When Judd demurred, she threatened no more cuddles. Lover Boy caved in.

On April 17 Judd hid in the Snyders' spare room while they were out. Ruth came whispering in to him at 2.00 am. The two made love before getting down to business.

Judd took a sash weight, went in to Albert's room, and crashed it on the sleeping man's head. Albert woke with a roar, and seized the corset salesman. Ruth raced in to finish the job herself. She hit Albert a felling blow with the weight and then looped picture-wire round his neck to strangle him. She ordered Judd to bring a bottle of chloroform, and her trembling lover splashed it on Albert's face. With Albert dead, the two ransacked the house, and Judd tied Ruth up to suggest that burglars had done the deed.

The police were not convinced when they found Ruth's "stolen" jewellery hidden in a mattress.

The two tried to incriminate each other. Ruth claimed that her overwhelming allure led men to do things she would never have wanted. Judd claimed that he had gone along unwillingly with a plan which Ruth ultimately carried out.

Both have been condemned to death and will be executed in the New Year.

Mrs Ruth Snyder listens nervously to the evidence against her being given in court

FUNERALS HELD For Gray, Mrs. Snyder

— Story on Page 3

WHEN RUTH PAID HER DEBT TO THE STATE!—The only unofficial photo ever taken within the death chamber, this most remarkable, exclusive picture shows closeup of Ruth Snyder in death chair at Sing Sing as lethal current surged through her body at 11:06 Thursday night. Its first publication in yesterday's EXTRA edition of THE NEWS was the most talked-of feat in

"Granite Woman" meets her death in the electric chair

Oscar Slater Freed: A Great Triumph for Sir Arthur's Unremunerated Campaigners

OSCAR SLATER, convicted of the Glasgow murder of Miss Marion Gilchrist (see 1908), has been freed and awarded £6,000 compensation. This ends the long campaign led by Sir Arthur Conan Doyle and Scottish criminologist William Roughead.

The witnesses who identified Slater at the trial in 1909 have all been shaken. Helen Lambie, the maid who saw the murderer walk out of Miss Gilchrist's flat, is, in Sir Arthur's opinion, lying to protect someone. Miss Barrowman, who supposedly saw Slater outside the flat, admits that police showed her a photograph of him before her identification. The third witness, Mr Arthur Adams, never swore to more than a "close resemblance".

Slater refuses to reimburse Sir Arthur for any of the campaign's expenses from his £6,000.

Gorilla Killer Caught and Convicted in Canada

AFTER A YEAR'S reign of terror, the "Gorilla murderer" has been caught in Canada. In February last year, Mrs Clara Newman of San Francisco was strangled by a man with a monkey-face and ape-like arms to whom she let a room. Over the next six months he killed four more middle-aged California landladies. All were stripped and raped after they had been killed.

In October three landladies died in Portland, Oregon. In November he killed one in San Francisco and another back in Portland. In December the attack moved to Council Bluffs, Iowa, and then on to Kansas City where both Mrs Germania Harpin and her 8-month-old daughter were strangled.

A woman was killed in Philadelphia in April: another in Buffalo in May. Two sisters (raped together) died in Detroit in June, and then Mary Sietsome of Chicago became the last victim in the USA.

On June 8, flower girl Lola Cowan disappeared in Winnipeg. On June 9 Mrs William Patterson was raped and killed in her home in that city. While the Winnipeg victims were not landladies, the pattern of strangulation and a ravished corpse matched the American Gorilla murders.

In Regina, 200 miles from Winnipeg, the killer attacked a woman in a rooming-house who screamed and escaped. The police were informed, and the Gorilla murderer was seized at the edge of town.

The police had in custody 30-year-old Earle Nelson, a man who vanished for seven years after raping his estranged wife in a hospital ward in 1919. He was tried and convicted promptly, and will be executed in the New Year.

IN BRIEF

DONALD MERRETT (*see* 1926) has been Not Proven guilty of his mother's murder, after pathologist Bernard Spilsbury and gunsmith Robert Churchill testified that Mrs Merrett could have shot herself. He has, however, been imprisoned for forgery.

NICCOLA SACCO and BARTOLOMEO VANZETTI have been executed for the Braintree robbery murder (*see* 1920). Worldwide protests followed the almost universal belief that they are innocent and have been railroaded by viciously reactionary Massachusetts authorities.

New York Mobster Shot Dead, Bodyguard injured

GANGSTER Jacob "Little Augie" Orgen was shot dead in New York in October. His body-guard, Jack "Legs" Diamond, was injured.

Augen was a labour racketeer, offering thugs to employers or unions to beat up strikers or black-legs. His lieutenant Louis "Lepke" Buchalter urged him to infiltrate union locals, so as to control their subscriptions and pension funds. But Orgen was not interested.

Since Buchalter associates with the new generation of hood-lums like "Lucky" Luciano and Meyer Lansky, who co-operate across ethnic boundaries that have hitherto separated mobs, it may be that Augen's labour interests will now gain some Italian input. His bootlegging and narcotics trade is inherited by Diamond.

Woman's Body in Charing Cross Trunk Identified

SKILLED DETECTION solved London's Charing Cross trunk murder this summer. The malodorous deposit in Left Luggage contained a butchered woman's body wrapped in pieces of cloth. One bore a laundry mark; another an embroidered greyhound. The first led to a Mrs Holt, who employed a succession of maids over the last few years; the other to the Greyhound Hotel, where one of Mrs Holt's former maids, Minnie Bonati, worked. And Minnie had disappeared.

Meanwhile, a taxi-driver reported taking a man with a trunk to Charing Cross from an office in Rochester Row. When police visited the office it was deserted. The tenant, Mr John Robinson, had left no forwarding address.

But his waste paper basket contained a bloodstained split match-stick. And a woman came forward saying that she was meeting Robinson at the Greyhound Hotel.

The matchstick and the cloth from the Greyhound cracked Robinson's claim to know nothing of Minnie Bonati. He finally claimed that she had approached him at Victoria station, come to his office, and tried to extort money. When she attacked him he pushed her away, and she fell, striking her head.

But pathologist Bernard Spilsbury established that Minnie was suffocated as well as struck over the back of the head. Robinson was convicted and hanged in August.

The trunk left at Charing Cross station, containing the body of Minnie Bonati

Essex Policeman With Eyes Shot Out, Villain Arrested

THE HORRIFYING murder of village bobby PC Gutteridge may be solved. His body was found in a country road between Ongar and Romford in September. He had been shot twice, and then his eyes had been shot out. (It seems the killer believes the legend that a dead man's eyes retain the reflection of the last person they saw.)

Tyre marks and scraping on the grass verge indicated that Gutteridge had stopped a car when he was murdered. And the car itself soon turned up, abandoned in Brixton. It was the property of Dr Lovell of Billericay, stolen from his garage during the night. There was blood on the driver's side and an empty cartridge case on the floor. But not a single fingerprint.

Since the car was abandoned in South London, police suspicions quickly fastened on Guy Browne, a Clapham garage owner with a long record of convictions for housebreaking, car theft and general thuggery. But there was no evidence to link him with the crime.

Then, at the end of the year, a robbery took place in Sheffield, and a witness took the getaway car's number. It belonged to a known Sheffield criminal, and on being apprehended he admitted his responsibility, and told police that Browne had been his confederate. He also revealed that Browne had confessed to him that he and a villain named William Kennedy murdered Gutteridge.

With that statement on record, the police had the necessary evidence for a warrant to search Browne's premises. In the garage they found a box of old-fashioned black powder cartridges – just the unusual type that had been found in Dr Lovell's car. A Webley revolver belonging to Browne proved to be the weapon that fired it. Browne has been arrested.

An intensive search is under way for Kennedy, a petty criminal who also has convictions for indecent exposure. The authorities hope to secure an early arrest so that the two men may be tried together early next year.

The body of murdered Police Constable Gutteridge was found on the left of this stretch of road between Ongar and Romford

Guy Browne

William Kennedy

Youth Murders his Employer the Priest's Housekeeper in Ireland

FATHER JAMES MCKEOWN, an Irish country village priest, employs a housekeeper and a handyman-chauffeur. Last year he had servants who disliked each other. When 36-year-old Mary Callan, the housekeeper, disappeared with her bicycle on May 16, Gerard Toal the chauffeur expressed no concern.

It was thought she had visited her mother, but the old lady had not seen her. Chauffeur Toal claimed she left the house after giving him dinner.

Mary seemed to have absconded permanently, and Fr. McKeown hired another housekeeper. Then, early this year, parts of a woman's bicycle, which Toal confessed he had stolen, were found in his room.

In April Fr. McKeown sacked the young man. Toal announced that he was going to Canada, but was in fact arrested for theft in Dundalk 10 days later.

At this point police made a thorough search of the presbytery and garden, and found women's clothing and more bicycle parts in the ash-pit. Finally Mary Callan's decomposed body was found in an abandoned water-filled quarry nearby.

Toal confessed that there had been a violent quarrel between the two in May 1927, but swore that her death was accidental. The trial judge advised the jury against bringing in a verdict of manslaughter, however, and the 18-year-old was hanged in Dublin on August 28.

Why Did Chung Yi Miao Kill His Bride?

Dr Chung Yi Miao

" IT IS TERRIBLE! MY WIFE ASSAULTED, ROBBED, MURDERED! "

Chung Yi Miao

CHUNG YI MIAO and Wei Sheung Siu took their honeymoon in the Lake District, one of England's beauty spots. The couple were married in New York after Chung received his Doctorate of Law degree in Chicago. Wei Sheung, one year older than her husband, was also wealthier, and travelled with £4,000-worth of jewellery.

On June 19 they went for a walk from which Chung returned alone. He told hotel staff his wife had gone shopping in Keswick.

A farmer found Mrs Chung's body by a path along the river. She had been strangled and there may have been some attempt to assault her sexually.

Immediate suspicion focused on some unidentified oriental visitors who had been seen in the district – quite a rarity in those parts. But Chung brought suspicion on himself when the police informed him of his wife's death, and he blurted out: "It is terrible! My wife assaulted, robbed, murdered!" although these possibilities had not been mentioned.

Suspicion turned to certainty when Wei Sheung's valuable rings were found in his suitcase. Hotel staff knew she had been wearing them when she went out.

Dr Chung was hanged at Strangeways on December 6, but his motivation remains a mystery. The prosecution suggested that he was sexually frustrated. The press thought he might have discovered that his wife would never bear children. But his landlady's family in Chicago have also seen sinister orientals visiting the young man they knew as charming and gentle. And they wonder whether he was under pressure from some Chinese secret society to assassinate a young woman whose marriage to him, for some reason, did not meet with their approval.

Revolting Kidnapping and Murder in California

A HORRIBLE KIDNAPPING and murder took place in Los Angeles at the end of last year. 23-year-old student Edmund Hickman took 12-year-old Marion Parker from a wealthy suburb, and sent her father notes, headed "DEATH" and signed "THE FOX", demanding a ransom of $7,500.

When Mr Parker handed over the money at the edge of town, Hickman, who was holding the child wrapped in a blanket, said he would leave Marion further down the road. Mr Parker found his child strangled and with her limbs cut off.

Hickmann was arrested in Seattle. During his trial this year he twice attempted, or feigned attempts at suicide. He tried to convince the jury that he was insane. But they convicted him, and he was hanged at San Quentin in October.

Californian kidnapper and murderer Edmund Hickman, "The Fox"

Adulterous Minister Cleared of Wife-Slaying

REVEREND RONALD GRIGGS, a young Methodist minister in Omeo, Australia, married a girl from his home in Tasmania when he graduated from Melbourne Theological College. But in the spring of 1926 he became attached to Methodist farmer John Condon's 19-year-old daughter Lottie. Ethel Griggs, pregnant with the couple's first child, protested. But Griggs paid no attention, and in December he and Lottie became lovers.

Last year Ethel paid a summer visit to Tasmania, and fell sick on her return to Omeo. She died shortly after. Recurrent rumour forced an exhumation and the discovery that repeated doses of arsenic had been administered.

Griggs went on trial for her murder this March, but the jury could not agree. He was re-tried the following month, and acquitted. His strong motive and definite opportunity to commit the murder do not cancel the possibility that Mrs Griggs poisoned herself in despair at the loss of her husband's affections.

IN BRIEF

Historic Year: Massacre, 'Peace Conference', Capone Jailed

THIS AMAZING YEAR in the history of organized crime, opened with the brutal St Valentine's Day Massacre in Chicago; proceeded to a gangsters' "Peace Conference" in Atlantic City, and concluded with Al Capone himself behind bars for the trivial offence of carrying a concealed weapon in Philadelphia!

On St Valentine's Day, five Capone hit-men, disguised as police, marched openly into a garage on North Clark Street, Chicago, disarmed the five North Side Irish gang members who were there, lined them against the wall together with a garage mechanic and a mob-fan dentist who happened to be present, and machine-gunned the lot. The North Siders' leader, George "Bugs" Moran, was lucky to be absent: indeed, the hit only took place because the assassins mistook his finance manager for the boss himself entering the garage.

Two months later, Capone attended the three-day conference in Atlantic City where mobsters from all over America debated the future organization of crime in the event that alcohol prohibition does not long survive next year's elections. Sicilian "Lucky" Luciano and Jewish Meyer Lansky of New York were key figures, pressing home the message that their co-operation had proved fruitful, and their fellow-villains should abandon ethnic rivalries that bring the gangs bad publicity – as witness the St Valentine's Day massacre! Capone's old mentor Johnny Torrio came out of retirement to support proposals which match his long-term policy that criminal organizations should co-operate as business syndicates with shared interests.

Notably absent, however, were Moran, and the two principal New York gang leaders, Joe "the Boss" Masseria and Salvatore Maranzano. These two have been waging the "Castellamarese Wars" in New York for two years, named for Masseria's Sicilian home town, Castellamare del Golfo. Technically, Luciano, Frank Costello and Joe Adonis are Masseria lieutenants, while Albert Anastasia and Joe Profaci serve Maranzano. But the younger men describe their bosses as "Mustache Petes", and privately despise their pointless struggle to be esteemed as "Boss of all Bosses".

Capone's surprising arrest in Philadelphia the day the conference ended, May 16, was orchestrated by himself. It is not clear whether he wants the safety of a short prison sentence while Moran feverishly tries to avenge his fallen henchmen, or whether the conference itself ordered Al to take a short rap as public expiation for the extravagant outrage on St Valentine's Day.

The Boardwalk, Atlantic City, N.J., taken over by mobsters for three days in May while they negotiated a national settlement to end gang wars

Man in Blazing Car Was Not Who He Seemed

ON NOVEMBER 27, an Opel car belonging to 26-year-old Erich Tetzner was found burning after a crash near Regensburg, Germany. The charred body trapped in the driving seat was assumed to be Tetzner.

But a company with which Tetzner had recently taken out a large insurance policy had the body examined and discovered it was much smaller than their client, and there were no traces of soot or carbon monoxide in the lungs and blood, as would be expected had the unfortunate driver expired in the inferno that had engulfed the vehicle after the crash.

The investigators suspected that Tetzner was still very much alive but in hiding somewhere. So, Frau Tetzner was placed under observation. In December she received a telephone call from France, which proved to be from Tetzner. He was arrested in Strasbourg, and has confessed to killing a hitchhiker and burning the body to defraud the insurance company.

Crook Slays Garage Manager after Frauds

THE MURDER OF Southampton garage manager Vivian Messiter was finally wrapped up in December with a guilty verdict passed on prime suspect William Podmore.

Messiter had been brutally battered about the head and his body concealed behind oil drums in the Wolf's Head Oil Company Garage for two months before it was discovered in January. The police also found in the garage an accounts book with pencil indentations from ripped-out pages showing false sales and commission credited to one "W.F.Thomas". This individual, a recent employee of the garage, had not been seen in Southampton since the disappearance of Messiter late last year. Investigations revealed that he was actually a man called Podmore with a substantial criminal record.

Podmore was charged with fraud and convicted; then, when the details of the fraud had been more fully established from the accounts book, he was tried for and convicted of the additional charge of murder. He will be hanged in the New Year.

The garage in Southampton where Mr Vivian Messiter's body lay for two months

Hundreds Attend Open-Air Trial in California

THE TRIAL of Eva Rablen for poisoning her deaf husband Carroll aroused so much interest in Columbia, California, that hundreds swarmed to the trial. The little town is not accustomed to receiving so many visitors, and the tiny courtroom was bulging at the seams just with the news hounds wanting a sniff of the case. Deciding that justice must be seen to be done, Judge J.W.Pitts adjourned to a large open-air pavilion in the town centre.

The defendant was a glamorous and outgoing young woman who enjoyed a lively social life. She adored partying and especially dancing. Not so her older husband Carroll, who was as unsociable and withdrawn as she was gregarious and fun-loving. He did not try to curb her activities, however, and tolerated her dancing with other men. At a dance in Tuttletown this April, Eva fetched her husband a cup of coffee as he stood on the sidelines. He had hardly time to say that it tasted bitter before he fell writhing to the floor, and died soon after.

Carroll's father believed Eva had poisoned her husband for his $30,000 insurance policy, and when a strychnine bottle was found in a cupboard in her house, she was arrested. The bottle had been sold to a woman calling herself Mrs Jo Williams who said she wanted it to poison gophers. But an autopsy turned up no trace of poison in the body. Judge Pitts sent the case on to a higher court.

Before Eva could come to trial, she learned that another pathologist had succeeded in tracing strychnine in Carroll's stomach as well as on the dress of a woman she had passed while coffee spilled from the cup. She changed her plea to guilty and entered San Quentin Prison in June.

Respectable Surburban Family Deaths from Arsenic

WITHIN THE space of a year, three members of the same family from Croydon in Surrey, England, have died of arsenic poisoning.

In April 1928, retired colonial officer Edward Creighton Duff took to his bed on returning from a fishing trip, and died shortly after. His death was ascribed to a weak heart. His wife brightly suggested that a bottle of beer he "snaffled" from the larder might have gone bad and strained his system.

In February this year, Mr Duff's unmarried sister-in-law, Vera Sidney, also died suddenly. She, too, was believed to have strained her heart – by cranking her car with a starting handle. This was surprising because Miss Vera was a hearty and sporty spinster, a masseuse by profession, well up to the exertion of cranking her car.

But when Miss Sidney's widowed mother Violet died the following month, there was no mistaking the signs of arsenic poisoning. Exhumation and analysis proved that Mr Duff and Miss Sidney had died of the same cause. Mrs Duff and Miss Sidney's brother Tom, a concert entertainer, live in the same neighbourhood, but have not been affected.

Nobody has any grudge against the family, and they do not share servants. Suspicion falls on Mr Tom Sidney and Mrs Duff, both of whom use arsenical weedkillers and are known to have been in and out of their relatives' houses. Yet the authorities cannot discover a likely motive for either to murder their blood relatives. Unless some striking new evidence emerges, it seems unlikely that charges will be brought against anyone, and this curious case will remain open.

IN BRIEF

GUY BROWNE and WILLIAM KENNEDY were convicted and executed in April for the murder of PC Gutteridge (see 1928).

Monster Longs to Hear His Own Blood Gushing

PETER KÜRTEN, the Düsseldorf monster, ended his life with a grisly ambition. Facing beheading in Cologne, he asked the executioner: "After my head has been chopped off, will I still be able to hear at least for a moment the sound of my own blood gushing from the stump of my neck? That would be the pleasure to end all pleasures." All Kürten's pleasures ended on July 2.

In August 1929 Düsseldorf realized it had a murdering maniac in its midst. A 26-year-old housemaid escaped from being stabbed with scissors by a man whose advances she refused, shortly after the bodies of a 14-year-old girl and her 5-year-old sister were found. Citizens then recalled that another housemaid, a 9-year-old girl, and a drunken man had all been found stabbed to death with scissors earlier in the year.

Before long, Kürten had killed two more young women and another child, changing his weapon to a hammer.

These were not his first murders. By his own account, he deliberately drowned a child when he was six, and almost strangled his girlfriend when he was 14, discovering in the process that it was even more satisfying than the cruelties he loved to inflict on animals.

He spent half his adult years in prison for theft and arson. In 1913 he killed a 13-year-old girl in her home. He dropped his initialled handkerchief on that occasion, but suspicion fell on the child's father, Peter Klein.

He was caught on May 14. He offered to see 21-year-old Maria Budlick home, and took her to his flat where he gave her a meal. Then he led her to a public park and tried to rape her. Failing in this, he asked if she remembered how to reach his home, and released her when she claimed to have forgotten.

Maria led police there, and to the amazement of Kürten's wife, who had never suspected him, he was arrested.

Kürten killed at least 23 people in the course of his murderous career. He was charged with the murders of nine

Peter Kürten, the monster of Dusseldorf

Homosexual Ex-Gigolo Murders Mother for Insurance

The crowd at Maidstone jail for the execution of Sidney Fox

SIDNEY FOX and his 61-year-old mother were swindlers. They travelled around hotels in England, passing dud cheques and flitting off without paying their bills. At 31, Sidney was past working as a gigolo or a rent-boy.

In April last year he insured Mrs Fox's life for £3,000. In October, just as the second premium was due, the pair were staying in the Hotel Metropole at Brighton. Guests were astonished when the trouserless Sidney ran downstairs screaming that his mother's room was on fire and she was in danger.

Mrs Fox was dead in her badly charred armchair before the gas fire. But there were signs that the conflagration had been deliberately started with old magazines.

And at his trial in March, Fox could not explain why he closed the door to shut the smoke (and his mother) in, rather than dragging her out.

This nasty perverted individual at last got his just deserts in April, when he was hanged at Maidstone jail .

Panzram Dies: Was He the World's Worst Criminal?

CARL PANZRAM (39), hanged this year, had been incorrigible since his first conviction for being drunk and disorderly at the age of ... eight!

He was hardened at Minnesota State Training School where he burned down the warehouse in 1905. On leaving, he embarked on a career of burglary, arson and sodomy, punctuated by prison sentences and escapes. He spent the War in prison, escaping in 1918 to South America where he committed a spectacular arson on an oil rig.

His biggest haul came in 1920 when he stole $40,000 in bonds and jewels from ex-President Taft's home. He bought a yacht, and murdered the men who refitted it for him. He went to Africa where he sodomized and murdered a 12-year-old boy, and threw six native porters to crocodiles.

Back in America he wrote, during a prison sentence: "I have murdered 21 human beings. I have committed thousands of burglaries, robberies, larcenies, arson, and last but not least I have committed sodomy on more than 1,000 male human beings."

Imprisoned again in 1928, Panzram threatened to kill the first man who bothered him. This proved to be civilian laundryman Robert Warnke, whom Panzram killed with an iron bar in June 1929.

The authorities quickly tried and sentenced this villain who had committed enough crimes for 20 men. Panzram reviled reformers who opposed his execution, saying: "I wish you all had one neck and I had my hands on it."

The burnt out Morris of Alfred Arthur Rouse, the infamous "blazing car killer"

Blazing Car Man Wanted to Escape Girlfriends

THIRTY-SEVEN-YEAR-OLD salesman Alfred Arthur Rouse has too many wives, girlfriends and paternity orders out against him. He decided to end it all by "dying".

> ## IT LOOKS AS THOUGH SOMEONE IS HAVING A BONFIRE UP THERE.
>
> QUOTE **Alfred Arthur Rouse**

On Guy Fawkes' night two young men going home from a dance in Northamptonshire, England, saw a man emerge from a ditch. They asked him about a blaze visible further down the road, and the man said: "It looks as though some one is having a bonfire up there."

The young men hurried to the flames and found a fiercely blazing Morris car with a body in the front seat. The number-plates identified the car as Rouse's.

Presumably, Rouse intended to disappear quietly after the car was found, leaving it to be assumed he had died in the fire. Thus he would escape the problem of having 80 intimate women friends.

But as he was seen near the fire, his plan failed. Rouse made his way to Wales and stayed with one of his lady-loves, finally coming forward when newspapers reported that police wanted to interview him.

Rouse himself does not know who the victim was – just an old tramp he gave a lift. He goes on trial for his murder next year.

Brave Old Lady Refuses to Name Killer

EIGHTY-TWO-YEAR-OLD Margery Wren has taken her murderer's secret to the grave. The old lady was found bleeding in her shop at 6.00 pm on September 20, but gamely went on serving. Asked what had happened, she claimed to have tripped over her tongs. This

> ## I DO NOT WISH TO MAKE A STATEMENT.
>
> QUOTE **Margery Wren**

was nonsense: she had been battered repeatedly about the head and face.

She made contradictory statements to investigating officers, claiming variously that a man had attacked her; two people had attacked her; she had simply fallen down; nobody had hit her; she had no enemies.

Finally she said: "I do not wish him to suffer. He must bear his sins. I do not wish to make a statement." And on September 25 the old lady died, without giving a clue to her murderer's identity.

IN BRIEF

ERICH TETZNER *(see* 1930) executed on May 2 for murder of unidentified hitch-hiker.

Murder Mystery: Are You Mr Qualtrough, Mr Wallace?

William Herbert Wallace — innocent man or clever murderer?

TRIED FOR the murder of his wife, convicted, and freed by the Court of Appeal, William Herbert Wallace (52) features in one of the most puzzling mysteries outside the pages of detective fiction.

He arrived at his chess club in Liverpool on January 19 to receive the previously telephoned message that a Mr R.M. Qualtrough of 25 Menlove Gardens West wanted to see him the following night on business. Wallace, an insurance salesman, spent the early evening of 20 January fruitlessly searching the Menlove Gardens development, only to find there was no such address. (Menlove Gardens North, South and East all exist, but there is no Menlove Gardens West.) When he crossed the city and returned home, his wife lay battered to death in the front room. A small sum of money had been taken.

Police discovered that "Mr Qualtrough's" call to the club was made from a public kiosk outside Wallace's house when he left home. They speculated that Wallace set up the false appointment to give himself an alibi. They over-ruled a milkboy who claimed to have seen Mrs Wallace alive after Wallace had left the house. They thought Wallace had stripped and worn only an old macintosh (which lay under Mrs Wallace's head) to avoid bloodstains. But they were unable to suggest a motive for Wallace.

Despite the jury's verdict, the Court of Appeal has freed Wallace, declaring, uniquely, that the verdict ignored the facts in the case. So did chess player Wallace craftily plan his moves ahead? Or did some intruder come in and murder the lady?

'Legs' Diamond Shot in Lover's Apartment

LEGS DIAMOND, the gangster they couldn't nail, has been gunned down in hiding. Killers caught him at the apartment of his girl-friend, Kiki Roberts, in Albany, New York.

The gangster's troubles began after he took over "Little Augie" Orgen's rackets in 1927. He opened the Hotsy Totsy Club on Broadway, where he openly killed rival Red Cassidy in 1929. Before evidence could be given, the barman and three customers were murdered, and four more people, including the hat-check girl, disappeared. Diamond was not charged with the killing.

In 1930 he declared war on "Dutch" Schultz, who had tried to acquire some of his interests. This year he declared that he wanted some of Joey Fay's nightclubs and some of "Waxey" Gordon's boot-legging contracts. "Legs" was personally at war with some of New York's biggest criminals.

Yet he feared nothing. Bullets injured him in 1924, 1927, 1930, and last April. He survived every time, and came to believe he was truly invincible.

On 18 December, unknown killers proved him wrong.

"Legs" Diamond, after a bootlegging conviction

OBITUARY

JACK 'LEGS' DIAMOND (1896-1931)

*L**egs Diamond earned his nickname as a youthful and nimble smash-and-grab thief. Soon after the end of prohibition, Diamond went to work for racketeer "Little Augie" Orgen, and ran some small bootlegging operations. After Orgen's death (see 1927), Diamond took over his bootlegging and narcotics.*

Spruce, slim and good-looking, double-crossing Jack Diamond is mourned by no men, but many women, including his wife and showgirl Kiki Roberts.

Consumptive Lustful Beauty Kills Rivals: Found Insane

SEXY 25-YEAR-OLD Winnie Ruth Judd, wife of a rich, elderly California doctor, shared a bungalow in Phoenix, Arizona with two other young women, having been sent to the desert for her chest.

In October she decided that her housemates were stealing her boyfriends, and shot dead Agnes LeRoi (30) and Helga Samuelson (23). She also shot herself in the hand to suggest that she had been attacked.

She packed the bodies into a large trunk, and took a train to Los Angeles, where baggage clerk Andrew Anderson suspected that she was smuggling illegally shot venison in her meat-smelling, blood-sticky luggage.

Winnie hid for three days in a disused sanitorium. She gave herself up on reading a newspaper appeal from her husband.

At her trial in Arizona, Winnie claimed that Agnes and Helga had attacked her and the killings had been self-defence. The plea failed and she was sentenced to death.

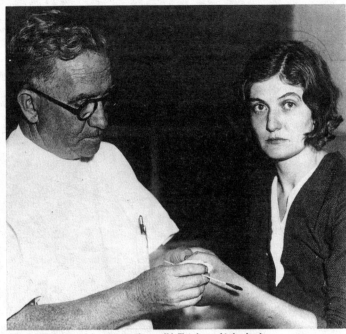

Winnie Ruth Judd receiving treatment for a self-inflicted wound to her hand

Prison doctors, however, are sure she is insane. At a special hearing, the lady put on an extraordinary display of insanity. Her sentence was commuted, and she has been sent to an asylum.

An Oxford Mystery Quickly Solved

VACUUM-CLEANER salesman Henry Seymour murdered 54-year-old Mrs Annie Kempson in Oxford in Ausgust simply to steal whatever he could find.

Mrs Kempson was found with her head battered and her throat slit. Nearby landlady Mrs Andrews told police Seymour had stayed in her house before the murder. He took with him a brand-new hammer and chisel. The hammer was found, carefully washed, in a suitcase Seymour left in an Aylesbury hotel in lieu of payment. Finally, Seymour himself was traced to Brighton and put on trial for Mrs Kempson's murder. He was hanged in December.

Death by Fire in Deserted Border Moors

THE HORRIBLE death of 28-year-old Evelyn Foster on lonely moorland between the towns of Otterburn and Newcastle in northern England remains a mystery.

Evelyn, daughter of a charabanc and car-hire operator, picked up a fare in Otterburn on the evening of January 6. The man said he wanted to go to Hexham to catch a Newcastle bus.

Late that evening a bus driver discovered the blazing wreck of Evelyn's cab on the moor. Near it lay the badly burned young woman herself. She claimed that the fare had forced her to stop, raped her, then poured inflammable liquid over her and the car and set fire to them before letting the vehicle roll on to the moorland.

Before Miss Foster died of her injuries, she declared, "I have been murdered". Yet her story cannot be squared with the fact that the car was driven carefully onto the moorland before it was set alight. And the passenger she alleged to have picked up that evening seems to have vanished into thin air despite an intensive hunt for him.

Was this, the police wonder, an insurance scam that went wrong?

Sir Patrick Saves Socialite with His Trigger Finger

Michael Scott Stephen, murdered lover of Elvira Barney

> ## I'LL TEACH YOU TO ARREST ME, YOU BLOODY SWINE!
> QUOTE **Elvira Barney**

SOCIETY LAWYER Sir Patrick Hastings has saved drunken socialite Mrs Elvira Barney from the gallows. In the small hours of May 31, neighbours in classy Williams Mews, in London's Belgravia, heard a shot, and then Mrs Barney's voice sobbing: "Don't die, chicken, don't die!"

(That's what they they *thought* they heard. Mrs Barney's actual words were: "Don't die, Mickey!")

A doctor arrived at the flat to find 24-year-old Michael Scott Stephen dead and fully clothed in the bedroom. He could see from the bed, however, that Stephen and the rather blowzy 27-year-old Elvira had been sleeping together earlier.

Mrs Barney, daughter of government auditor Sir John Mullins, reacted with contemptuous hauteur when police arrived, and were unconvinced by her story. She said that she and Stephen had been to a nightclub with guests from a cocktail party the previous evening. On their return a quarrel began, and Stephen picked up her pistol to shoot himself. As she struggled to stop him, the gun went off and Stephen fell, mortally wounded.

"I'll teach you to arrest me, you bloody swine!" screamed the "bright young thing" as she realized she was going to be charged with murder or manslaughter.

Neighbours described an occasion when Mrs Barney appeared naked in her bedroom window and fired her pistol at Stephen in the mews below, crying: "Laugh, baby, laugh for the last time!"

But she never changed her story one iota. And Sir Patrick, exercising great stamina, clicked her pistol's trigger repeatedly at the court ceiling after a gunsmith testified that it took a 14lb pull, languidly remarking that it didn't seem difficult to him. So, at the cost of a sore finger, the great advocate persuaded the jury that his client was innocent. And Mrs Barney continues on her merry boozy way.

> ## DON'T DIE, CHICKEN, DON'T DIE!
> QUOTE **Elvira Barney**

Mrs Elvira Barney, enjoying an outing after her acquittal

Woman Kills Two Husbands, One Son

NURSE DAISY DE MELKER, hanged in South Africa this December for three murders, almost got away with two of her crimes. In 1923 her first husband, William Cowle, died after 14 years of matrimony. His doctor diagnosed a stroke, and Mrs Cowle inherited the bulk of his estate and £1,700 insurance.

In 1927 she married again. Robert Sproat did not last the year. He died leaving his widow £4500. Again, a stroke was diagnosed.

In 1931 Daisy married former rugby star Clarence de Melker. The following year, her step-son Rhodes Cowle was approaching his 21st birthday and looking forward to receiving an inheritance left by his father. Daisy bought some arsenic and gave him that instead.

His sudden death aroused suspicion at last. The chemist from whom a "Mrs Sproat" had bought arsenic recognized her as Daisy de Melker. Exhumation of her husbands showed they had died of strychnine poisoning.

Mrs de Melker did not confess before dying, but her guilt is not in doubt.

Ex-Policeman Cuts Ex-Fiancée's Throat

EX-POLICEMAN Maurice Freedman hoped to marry young typist Annette Friedson. But her family were not impressed by unemployed Maurice's hand-to-mouth existence, and even Annette wondered when he would divorce his wife as he promised.

At the beginning of this year she broke off with him. On January 26 Freedman followed her to work and cut her throat in the vestibule of her City of London office. Then he hurried away toward the East End.

There was some confusion about the murder weapon. A safety razor blade mounted in a stick was found abandoned in a bus. It was spotted with blood of Annette's group, yet Freedman swore he had taken his cut-throat razor intending to kill himself, and it accidentally slashed Annette as she tried to pull his hand away. Then he threw the razor into the canal.

This didn't matter as far as the court was concerned. Freedman had wielded a razor, and Annette had fallen dead.

Freedman, too, has died. On the gallows.

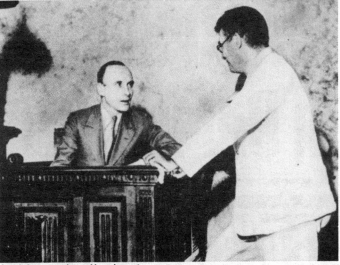
Captain Lancaster gives evidence in court

When Dead Men's Doctors Do Agree . . . the Jury Doesn't

PETER QUEEN might be thought to drive women to drink. He married early, but left his wife when she became an alcoholic. In 1930 he began a relationship with Christina Gall, who was employed as a maid by his father. But Chrissie, too, loved the bottle, and Mr Queen Sr dismissed her.

Chrissie went to live with friends who tried to wean her off drink. Peter joined them, to live with Chrissie as man and wife.

But the drinking depressed him, and the sinfulness of their relationship tormented his Glasgow Presbyterian soul. This summer the couple set up house on their own.

In November, Peter rushed into a police station, and said: "I think you will find my wife dead. I think I have killed her."

Or so the police aver. Queen maintains he said: "I don't think I've killed her."

Pathologists Sir Bernard Spilsbury and Sir Sydney Smith both agree. The young woman was found strangled in bed with a length of washing line. But Smith and Spilsbury saw no sign of any struggle, and think Chrissie killed herself when drunk.

The jury disagreed and convicted Queen with a strong recommendation to mercy. He has been reprieved from the gallows and sentenced instead to life.

Air Aces in Love Triangle Shooting

AERONAUT WILLIAM LANCASTER and Australia's woman air ace, "Chubbie" Miller, made a record-breaking flight from London to Australia in 1927. Whereupon, disregarding convention and their respective spouses, they became lovers as well as flying partners.

Last year they played the aerobatic circuses of America, and then Lancaster went on a trip to Mexico. While he was away, "Chubbie" fell in love with writer Charles Haden, and wrote to Lancaster saying she and Haden intended to wed.

Lancaster returned to Miami, and there was a stormy scene before the three retired to separate beds. During the night Lancaster roused Chubbie from sleep with the words: "Haden has shot himself."

Indeed the writer was in bed with a bullet through his head, a pistol beside him, and a suicide note in his typewriter. But the authorities didn't believe that he had done it himself.

Lancaster was tried for his murder in August, and owed his acquittal largely to "Chubbie's" impassioned testimony to him as "one of the finest men she knew". But the couple have split up again after coming back to England, and their aero-nautical partnership seems to be over.

IN BRIEF

The election of Frank Delano Roosevelt as US President and the end of alcohol prohibition will change the face of organized crime in America. Gangsters will have to return to their traditional enterprises: extortion, gambling, prostitution, loan-sharking, labour racketeering, and narcotics, now the profitable liquor trade falls back into legitimate hands.

Two Trunk Murders Found in Brighton by Police

Tony Mancini, the London gangster

IT TAKES A SIGNOR TO SLASH YOUR FACE

Italian villain Tony Mancini is really British Cecil Louis England. The Mediterranean monicker is a *nom-de-guerre*. Since 1923, Darby Sabini and his brothers Charley, Harry and Joe, heads of the Clerkenwell Italian mob, have been London's leading gangsters. They inherited the race-track extortion interests of the East End's old "Blind Beggar Gang" (c.1880-1905) after the collision between "Darky the Coon's" mob and Arthur Harding's "Vendetta" mob (*see* 1910) left East Enders too weak to prevent a Clerkenwell take-over.

The Sabinis fought off the Midlands "Brummagen" mob and protected themselves against "Darky the Coon" Bogart by hiring their own East End "Yiddishers". In 1923 they defeated a mutinous combination of Yiddishers and "French" Italians under the Cortesi brothers, since when the Sabinis have ruled.

They rule with razors, knives, coshes, and brass knuckles. They inflict fearful injuries on bookmakers who resist their extortion and rivals who encroach on their territory. And they are the principal employers of criminal thugs.

Mancini's assumed name suggests that today's ambitious villain must claim Italian descent. We know the Russian Ballet forces assumed names on home-grown dancers, so that young Alice Marks and Patrick Kay become Alicia Markova and Anton Dolin. But our thugs, likewise, must now be "signori" it seems!

N JUNE, someone in Brighton deposited a woman's torso in a trunk at the station. To date she has not been identified and her killer has not been traced.

But while searching the town, police found another body in another trunk, abandoned by Tony Mancini, a London gangster, who frequently changed rooms over the previous weeks, taking his increasingly smelly trunk with him.

The body was quickly identified as Violette Kaye (real name Violet Saunders), a London exotic dancer and prostitute, who accompanied Mancini to Brighton. Although he worked as a waiter, he was essentially living off her immoral earnings.

On May 10, Violette turned up drunk at the Skylark Cafe and accused him of having other women. That was the last time she was seen.

Mancini says he arrived home and found her battered to death. He assumes she was murdered by a client. But he was sure that his record for violence would count against him, and so he travelled with her body for the next two months.

Mr Norman Birkett, defending Mancini, made an impassioned plea to the jury not to judge his villainous criminal record, but to look at the facts of the case, which fitted Mancini's story.

The jury obliged, and a flabbergasted Mancini greeted his acquittal with the words:

> ## " NOT GUILTY, MR BIRKETT? NOT GUILTY, MR BIRKETT? "
>
> QUOTE **Tony Mancini**

The trunk containing Miss Kaye, as Mancini abandoned it

Tough Bandit Taken: FBI Claim He Called Them 'G-Men'

GEORGE "MACHINE-GUN" KELLY has been arrested in Tennessee for kidnapping millionaire Charley Urschel. Kelly, an amiably incompetent bootlegger during prohibition, was given a machine-gun and told to become tough by his bride, Kathryn Shannon. She couldn't make him competent though, and when Kelly and Albert Bates burst in upon Mr and Mrs Urschel playing bridge with another couple, they had no idea which of the two men was their intended victim. They abducted both, before it occurred to them to examine the men's wallets for ID papers.

When the $20,000 ransom had been paid, Kelly stood up to his wife at last, and refused to kill Urschel, pointing out that it would be bad for future business.

J.Edgar Hoover's FBI puts it about that when they made the arrest, Kelly screamed: "Don't

shoot, G-Men! Don't shoot!"

It is said the puzzled federal agents learned on this occasion that the term "G-Men" describes themselves, America's most feared law enforcers. The story appears to be a publicity-seeking canard, however. The term G-Men has been used to describe Secret Service agents for many years. Also, "Machine-Gun" Kelly was actually arrested by Memphis City detectives, to whom he said: "I've been waiting for you all night."

George "Machine-Gun" Kelly

Builder Killed Billiards Partner in Staged Suicide

A FIRE IN the locked Camden shed which London builder Samuel Furnace used as an office led to a widely publized manhunt in January. When firemen broke in, they found a charred corpse sitting at the desk, and an unburned suicide note reading: "Goodbye to all. No work. No money. Sam J.Furnace."

It made sense, as Furnace's business was failing. But the body proved to be that of Walter Spatchett, a young rent-collector and billiards partner of Furnace. The nation was alerted to the search for the missing builder.

He was caught in Southend when he sent a message to his brother-in-law asking for clean shirts. He claimed his pistol had gone off by accident when he was quarrelling with Spatchett, and he had panicked.

Police doubt this story, as Furnace had Spatchett's watch and cash. But he poisoned himself in prison before it could be tested in court.

Lover Terrorizes Mistress: Kills Husband in Inferno

ERNEST BROWN, a 35-year-old groom on Frederick Morton's remote Yorkshire farm, Saxton Grange, became Mrs Dorothy Morton's clandestine lover until his possessiveness and jealousy soured the affair. The groom also resented Morton's

re-appointing him in an inferior position after he walked out and then asked for his job back. He was so angry, he threatened to wreck the place.

On September 5, while Morton was out, Brown had a furious row with Mrs Morton and knocked her to the ground. Then he locked her and housekeeper, Ann Houseman, in the house, cut the telephone wires, and mounted guard outside with a shotgun which he fired off alarmingly from time to time, saying he was shotting at rats. The two women retreated to a bedroom and locked themselves in.

When Morton drove home in the small hours, Brown shot him, and then left him in his car in the garage which he set alight. Mrs Morton and her housekeeper escaped through a window and hid in fields while the fire raged.

Brown has been arrested and charged with murder.

Helping His Father-in-Law to the Grave

REGINALD HINKS (33), vacuum-cleaner salesman and handbag snatcher, has long hoped to inherit money from his 85-year-old father-in-law. Dismissing the male nurse who tended the senile old gentleman, Hinks took personal charge, and tried to hasten Mr Pullen's demise with stringent dieting.

He secured £900 of the old man's money, and bought a house in Bath. But cautious solicitors kept the rest of Mr Pullen's wealth away from him. Hinks took his father-in-law on long walks, and abandoned him in traffic-filled streets. Mr Pullen declined to die.

On December 1, Hinks said he found the old gentleman with his head in the gas oven, and re-

marked that "any bruise" on the back of his head was caused as he pulled him out.

Such a bruise was indeed evident, but. it had been inflicted before Mr Pullen died of gas poisoning. Hinks goes on trial for the old man's murder next year.

IN BRIEF

AIR ACE WILLIAM LANCASTER, cleared of murder last year (see 1932) has disappeared on a solo flight to South Africa.

Capone Goes to Alcatraz

Al Capone, Chicago "business man" who prided himself on his appearance

In 1919, Torrio sent for 20-year-old Capone to join him in the Windy City.

Johnny "The Brain" realized that Prohibition meant big bucks for bootleggers, and he and Capone took drastic steps when the elderly Colisimo refused to throw his influence behind the new business.

Capone and Torrio pioneered a murder method that would become a hallmark of organized crime. To avoid incrimination themselves, they hired an out-of-town killer – their old Brooklyn friend Frank Yale – who came to Chicago and shot Colisimo, while his treacherous aides established firm alibis.

With Big Jim dead, Torrio and Capone owned the largest string of brothels and gambling-houses in the city, and set about building up their bootlegging business. Torrio, a man before his time, negotiated agreements with other criminals, establishing spheres of influence and gang monopolies in different districts. There was plenty of profit for everyone, he reasoned, and the illegal alcohol trade would get a bad name if it was disfigured by gang fights.

Johnny Torrio, Capone's mentor

swooped and closed the brewery down. When Capone learned that O'Bannion had deliberately arranged the fiasco and had every intention of going on as a bootlegger, O'Bannion was advised to make peace with him but the Irishman merely responded: "Oh, to hell with the Sicilians." He had signed his own death warrant.

In November Frank Yale revisited Chicago, and led Capone hit-men Albert Anselmi and John Scalise in assassinating O'Bannion in the back room of his own florist's shop.

Hymie Weiss then commanded the O'Bannion gang, and despite telling newspapermen: "Al's a real pal. He was Dion's best friend, too," it was war to the knife.

In 1925 Johnny Torrio was shot as he stepped out of his car, And although he survived, "The Brain" took himself rapidly into retirement in Italy.

Capone now headed the biggest mob in Chicago on his own.

The Weiss gang tried a new murder technique devised by George "Bugs" Moran. Cruising slowly past Capone's car in their own limousine, they raked it with pistol and shotgun fire. The chauffeur was injured, but Capone escaped unharmed.

In 1926, a convoy of 11 cars drove past Capone's headquarters, the Hawthorne Inn in

AL CAPONE'S NICKNAMES

Dubbed *Scarface* by the press – he had three heavy scars on the left of his jaw, inflicted by Frank Galluccio in a quarrel over a girl when both men were in their teens. Al hates this nickname.

Called *Snorky* by his intimates – underworld slang for "well-dressed".

Pioneering Contract Murder and Syndication

CAPONE'S criminal career started in his native Brooklyn when he joined a teenage gang, managed by the adult criminal Johnny Torrio.

In 1915, Torrio went to Chicago to mange his uncle "Diamond Jim" Colisimo's gambling and prostitution empire.

The Beer Wars

Torrio's fragile peace collapsed within nine months. Far from being a model city of peaceful criminal organization, Chicago became a byword for the worst excesses of gangland warfare.

The most vicious of the "Beer Wars" was that between the Torrio-Capone mob, based in the suburbs of Oakland and Cicero, and the Irish North Side mob headed by Dion O'Bannion.

In 1924, O'Bannion double-crossed Torrio and Capone. He announced his retirement, and sold them a brewery. On the night of the transfer, police

Master Criminal Al Capone has been transferred to Alcatraz, the US Federal Government's new escape-proof penitentiary off the coast of California. Here he will endure a more humiliating regimen than the pettiest pimp or pickpocket behind bars. The ganglord who ruled Chicago for a decade has been toppled by the law. "Mr Big" is made small.

Cicero, and poured over 1,000 bullets from machine guns in it. One gangster and one woman passerby died, but Capone escaped again.

A month later he eliminated Hymie Weiss, using his own favourite ploy: crossfire from the windows of two rented rooms overlooking Weiss's doorway.

St Valentine's Day Massacre

War raged on, with "Bugs" Moran leading the northsiders until, in 1929, Capone men perpetrated the St Valentine's Day Massacre.

Disguised as raiding police officers, five Capone men wiped out five Moran toughs, a motor mechanic, and an optometrist who just liked to hang out with crooks, in a garage. Moran escaped because the Capone lookouts mistook his business manager, Al Weinshank, for the gangleader, and signalled the raid to start on his arrival. Although he threatened fearful revenge, the brutal slayings had ended Moran's effectiveness.

From now on, Al Capone, Chicago's "Mr Big" ruled the city without any serious challenge.

The Bloodiest Murders of All

Although Capone liked to present himself as an ordinary businessman whose commodity just happened to have been made illegal, he was personally brutal if crossed.

His worst atrocity was the killing of John Scalise, Albert Anselmi and Joe "Hop Toad" Giunta when they treacherously planned to betray him.

Capone gave them a superb banquet and proposed loving toasts to them. Then, when the meal was over, he had their arms pinned, and seizing a baseball bat broke every bone in their bodies he could reach, before they were mercifully despatched with bullets in the head.

'Mr Big' Rules — OK?

He threw his guns behind the mayoral election campaigns of Republican "Big Bill" Thompson, a corrupt and asinine clown who cheerfully let mobsters give orders to City Hall.

In 1928 the Capone mob overdid their electioneering. In the infamous "Pineapple" elections, they threw so many bombs and threatened so many canvassers that the electors revolted. There was twice the normal turn out, and the Republicans were routed.

It was the beginning of the end of Capone's popularity.

Downfall of the Big Man

From 1930, Al Capone was targetted by a team of Inland Revenue agents, who disregarded his claim that he had almost no income and proved that he had withheld declarations and evaded payments totalling millions.

Federal Judge Wilkerson got round the Capone mob's attempt to pervert the course of justice by substituting a brother judge's panel of jurymen for his own at the last minute.

Capone was sentenced to 11 years' imprisonment and ordered to pay $80,000 in fines and costs – the heaviest sentence ever handed down for tax offences. As he started his sentence, Capone commented sourly to his cell mate: "Imagine, some creep gets me on a damn tax rap. Ain't that a helluva deal?"

Secure in Alcatraz, Capone's reign in Chicago finally ended.

HOW AMERICA'S WICKEDEST CRIMINAL WON POPULARITY

1. He sold alcohol in defiance of silly and hated Prohibition laws.
2. He maintained a high profile as a benefactor to hospitals and charities.
3. He and his mob dressed smartly in suits, spats and fedora hats.
4. He always appeared perfectly washed, brushed, shaved, talced and manicured in public.
5. He made spontaneous generous gifts to beggars, shoeshine boys, news vendors and the like.
6. He attended and supported popular sporting events.
7. He masqueraded as forgiving, employing the man who scarred him as a bodyguard.
8. He attended his victims' funerals, pretending grief and staying unshaven during the mourning period.
9. He had real personal charm, and rather heavy dark good looks.
10. He persistently denied all wrong doing.

The scene in which five of Capone's henchmen, masquerading as police officers, perpetrated the "St Valentine's Day Massacre"

Life and Death of the Greatest Bank-Robber

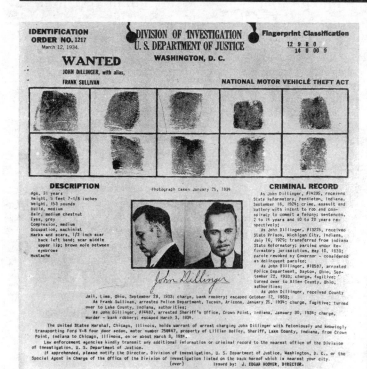

FBI description and fingerprints of most-wanted man, John Dillinger

JOHN DILLINGER, the superstar bank robber, was given an unfair sentence for his first offence. As a delinquent Navy deserter in 1924, he and an accomplice injured a grocer in an armed robbery. Assured that a guilty plea would bring a light sentence, Dillinger actually drew ten years. His older accomplice got two, and the injustice rankled.

In prison, Dillinger met future accomplices Harry Pierpoint and Homer Van Meter. He also mastered Prussian immigrant Baron Lamm's principles of bank robbery: military style pre-planning, with reconnaissance and timed and tested getaway routes.

When Dillinger was released in May last year, he committed two successful bank robberies, and used the proceeds to smuggle guns into prison so that Pierpoint, Van Meter and others could break out and join him. They returned the compliment, springing Dillinger from jail in Ohio, where he had been arrested. In the course of this jailbreak, Pierpoint shot a sheriff, and Dillinger won public affection by saying in disgust, "Did you have to do that?"

After a number of bank robberies, the gang was caught in January. Dillinger was imprisoned in Indiana from where he made his famous "wooden gun" jailbreak, threatening warders with a dummy pistol whittled from a washboard. (Privately police believe this was a cover story, and a real gun was smuggled in.) His new gang included the vicious killer "Baby Face" Nelson. In a fatal shoot-out with FBI men in Wisconsin, the trigger-happy Nelson killed an agent, and the FBI's retaliatory fire killed one bystander and wounded two others. Comedian Will Rogers commented wryly: "Well, they had Dillinger surrounded and was all ready to shoot him when he come out, but a bunch of other folks come out ahead, so they just shot them instead."

Dillinger and Van Meter underwent plastic surgery to alter their faces and fingerprints. This proved completely unsuccessful.

When he went into hiding in Chicago, his current girlfriend's room-mate, Ann Sage, betrayed him to the FBI, partly for a £10,000 reward, and partly for remission of the deportation order against her for brothel-keeping. When she went to the Bioscope movie theatre with Dillinger and his mistress on July 22, she wore an identifiable red dress. As the three came out, waiting agents shot Dillinger dead.

OBITUARY

JOHN HERBERT DILLINGER (1903-34)

Public Enemy Number 1 Dillinger's popularity owed much to his good looks; much to his humour (disguising bank reconnaissance as film-making, for example); much to his flirtatious manner with elderly ladies in banks he robbed; and much to his sexual reputation as a man who was never a single night without an adoring woman in his bed.

Most of all one questions why a man who never killed innocent bystanders, and may not even have been personally responsible for the deaths of policemen in his shoot-out escapes from ambush, was described as a more serious "public enemy" than Al Capone's goons.

Gamekeeper's Daughter Uses Vermin Poison on Husband

ETHEL LILLIE MAJOR'S marriage went sour when her husband, Arthur, discovered that her younger "sister" was actually her illegitimate daughter. This year Arthur started a correspondence with another woman. Ethel complained to her doctor, her solicitor, and the Chief Constable of Lincolnshire. Arthur spat out a piece of sandwich Ethel had given him for lunch, saying, "That woman is trying to poison me." Then he and workmates watched, horrorstruck, as a sparrow which pecked at the abandoned food keeled over and died.

Arthur publicly refused accountability for Ethel's debts. On May 24 this year he died after a short illness.

Anonymous letters to the police advised that pets in the neighbourhood had died after eating corned beef Ethel had prepared for her husband. When she was questioned by police, she gave herself away by mentioning that he had been poisoned with strychnine before the substance was identified by them as the agent responsible for his death. It was shown by the prosecution that she had access to her gamekeeper father's small stock of poisons. On December 19 Mrs Major was duly hanged.

ERNEST BROWN, hanged for the murder of Frederick Morton (*see* 1933).

REGINALD HINKS, hanged for the murder of James Pullen (*see* 1933).

VIENNA, SYLVESTRE MATUSCHKA, Hungarian businessman, convicted of causing two train crashes with 22 fatalities. Apparently this satisfied him sexually. Death sentence commuted.

The bullet-riddled car in which Bonnie Parker and Clyde Barrow died

Texas Rangers Gun Down Bonnie and Clyde

KINKY, BLUNDERING, vicious, folksy, greedy, sentimental and murderous – Bonnie Parker and Clyde Barrow were all these things. The Texas robbers never hit anything bigger than grocery stores and the smallest small-town banks. Yet they killed 13 people in their clumsy getaways over the last four years. Ace getaway driver Clyde was forever piling into ditches and hitting lampposts.

They snapped each other obsessively with their Kodak Brownie, and Bonnie wrote greetings-card doggerel about their love: yet young William Daniel Jones who travelled with them for a bit was sexually abused by both poofter Clyde and nympho Bonnie.

It was Jones's successor, Henry Methvin, who finally had enough and turned them in to the Texas Rangers. After the Barrow gang was surrounded in July last year at Dexter, Iowa, and Clyde's brother Buck was killed, Methvin and his family arranged to betray Bonnie and Clyde's movements.

At Gibland, Louisiana, Texas Ranger Frank Hamer led the ambush party which trapped the pair on May 23, and Bonnie and Clyde perished in a hail of gunfire.

Mother-in-Law is No Joke

DR ALICE WYNEKOOP (62) is a well-known Chicago physician and philanthropist. But her adored son Earle is a disappointment: a tipsy womanizer.

Some years ago Earle married violinist Rheta Gardner. A neurotic hypochondriac, she did little to stabilize him and resented his obsessive attachment to his mother, with whom the couple lived.

On November 21, Dr Wynekoop called a hospital to say something terrible had happened to Rheta. Police found the young woman's naked body on Dr Wynekoop's examination table, a bullet through her breast and chloroform burns around her mouth.

Dr Wynekoop lamely suggested that intruders had killed Rheta, but after taking a lie detector test confessed that she had done it. She claims that hypochondriac Rheta asked for an anaesthetic, and she administered chloroform, realizing suddenly that she had accidentally given an overdose. So she shot her daughter-in-law to put her out of her misery.

Earle has tried to save his mother by confessing to the murder, but there is no doubt that he was on a train travelling west at the time.

Flippin' Kid: Murdering Neighbour Fakes Child's Rape

ABERDEEN HOUSEWIFE Jeannie Donald was annoyed by 8-year-old Helen Priestley from upstairs in her tenement. The child would ring her doorbell and run away shouting, "Coconut!" when Jennie's permanent wave frizzed badly.

On April 20 the child disappeared. After a wild goose chase involving a man in a car, said by a mischievous little boy to have abducted her, Helen's body was found next day in a sack under the tenement stairs. She appeared to have been raped. But pathologists determined she had been suffocated and then assaulted with a stick to simulate rape. Hairs and cinders in the sack could be traced to the Donald kitchen.

Helen's heart condition means she might have died accidentally if Jeannie had caught her and given her a good shaking. But deciding to plead Not Guilty to murder rather than Guilty of manslaughter, Mrs Donald has said nothing about what really happened, and stoically accepted the life sentence she has been doled out.

Preserved Skin of Flayed hand Gives Print

THE GRUESOME discovery of the glove-like skin of a dead man's hand led to the conviction of Edward Morey for murdering vagrant Percy Smith.

Smith's body, flayed by five weeks' immersion in the Murrumbidgee River near Wagga Wagga, Australia on Christmas Day last year, is quite unidentifiable. The "glove", from which prints could taken, was discovered on the bank.

Smith was seen in Morey's company. When Morey's property yielded a bloodstained axe and clothing, he was arrested.

During the trial, prosecution witness Moncrieff Anderson was shot by his retarded wife, who had fallen in love with Morey and pretended that her husband had really killed Smith; then himself been shot by intruders.

Both Morey and Lillian Anderson have been convicted of their respective killings, and they face life imprisonment.

Alma Rattenbury Kills Herself: Stoner Reprieved

THREE DAYS after escaping conviction for murdering her husband, Alma Rattenbury has killed herself. Her sacrifice wins a reprieve for her lover, George Stoner.

Alma, a talented musician, married middle-aged Francis Rattenbury in 1928. They had two children. Their marriage became shaky after they moved to Madeira Villa, Bournemouth, where Rattenbury started drinking and the two slept in separate bedrooms. Last year they advertised for a chauffeur-handyman. They had difficulty retaining men in service, since 31-year-old Alma made improper suggestions to them.

Eighteen-year-old George Stoner was open to such suggestions, however, and was soon coming to Alma's bedroom at night where, as a shocked court heard, they made love while Alma's little boy slept in the same room.

On March 24 police were summoned to Madeira Villa, where Rattenbury was in his armchair, streaming blood from a battered head. Alma was extremely drunk.

She confessed confusedly to having killed her husband. But as she was also trying to kiss a policeman, her statements seemed worthless.

At 8.00 am, after a fitful night's sedated sleep, she made a confession which was accepted. She was charged with attempted murder: a charge which changed to murder when Rattenbury died in hospital.

Meanwhile Stoner told Alma's maid that he was responsible, and indicated where he had abandoned the murder weapon – a mallet. She told the police, and Stoner joined his lover in prison.

The two shielded each other, until Mrs Rattenbury allowed her defence to tell what seems to be the true story: that Stoner came up to her bedroom after she had retired and told her he had battered her husband.

Stoner was sentenced to death. Mrs Rattenbury was acquitted, but severely reprimanded for her immorality. Now she has walked into a river and stabbed herself. And the Home Secretary has ended this tragic bloodbath by reprieving Stoner.

Shark Spits Out Murder Victim's Arm

AUSTRALIAN DRUG-SMUGGLERS, forgers and extortionists Patrick Brady, Reg Holmes and James Smith have been busy trying to murder each other this year.

In April, Smith's unmistakeable tattooed arm, was spat out by a recently captured shark in an aquarium. Smith had last been seen in company with Patrick Brady, who denied killing him, but implicated Smith's employer, Holmes.

Holmes denied knowing Brady, let alone having criminal dealings with him and Smith. But two days later police caught him trying to escape from Sydney in a speedboat. There was a bullet wound in his head, and now he confessed to knowing Brady whom he accused of murdering Smith.

Brady was arrested. But two days before Smith's inquest opened, Holmes was found shot dead in his car. With the star witness gone, Brady's prosecution failed.

Sydney, Australia starts to look like Chicago, Illinois!

Why Schultz Had to Die

The body of "Abbadabba" Berman

DURING PROHIBITION "Dutch" Schultz held the Bronx beer monopoly: then branched out into the profitable "policy" or "numbers" racket – a street betting operation in which punters venture almost impossible odds to predict a random combination of three digits that changes daily. Jacob "Abbadabba" Berman has found ways of fixing the odds to give the gangs even more of the takings, and is said to be the only man Schultz paid well.

"Dutch" only became violent over money, lethally so as fellow mobsters "Legs" Diamond and Vincent "Mad Dog" McColl found to their cost.

When "Lucky" Luciano and Meyer Lansky put together the "Syndicate" which has governed organized crime ever since Joe Masseria and Salvatore Maranzano died, Schultz was too powerful to be left out. He never accepted Luciano's view that leading criminals should keep a low profile.

This year he crossed the syndicate. Special Prosecutor Thomas Dewey has been appointed to crush organized crime. Schultz's Democrat friends in Tammany Hall could not protect him when Republican Dewey bit into his profits. The Syndicate categorically refused to assassinate Dewey. So "Dutch" insisted he would do it himself, planning to shoot him in a call-box he habitually uses on his way to work.

The Syndicate saved Dewey by killing Schultz and Berman. Arthur Flegenheimer died in hospital on 25 October, after being gunned down while using the urinal at a restaurant in Newark, New Jersey. What a way to go!

OBITUARY

ARTHUR FLEGENHEIMER ALIAS DUTCH SCHULTZ (1902-35)

One of the most successful and disliked of New York gangsters "Dutch" Schultz adopted his monicer because it is short enough for newspaper headlines (unlike his real name, Arthur Flegenheimer) and "the Dutchman" liked to read about himself.

Schultz was notoriously tight-fisted. Other gangsters dress expensively. He bought the cheapest suits, and said: "I think only queers wear silk shirts."

Joy as Lindbergh Baby Kidnapper Executed

Kidnapper Bruno Hauptmann

THREE YEARS ago America was shocked when the baby son of national hero, pioneer solo transatlantic aviator Charles Lindbergh, was kidnapped and murdered. The child was snatched from its bedroom, which the kidnapper had reached by using a make-shift wooden ladder. After intricate arrangements, an intermediary transferred $50,000 in marked notes and $20,000 in gold bonds to an unknown man with a German-accent. The baby was found dead.

Probably the villain suspected the ransom might trap him, as none of the notes or bonds appeared in circulation until this year, when it was announced that the bonds issued to him were to be withdrawn and should be cashed immediately.

New Jersey carpenter Bruno Hauptmann was promptly caught trying to pass one of the specially numbered ransom bonds at a garage, and despite his claim that he was only looking after the loot for a friend who had recently died in Germany, he has been sent to the electric chair.

Wood from Hauptmann's attic went into making the ladder (though Hauptmann denied that the rickety structure was his handiwork). While there is a strong possibility that Hauptmann's dead friend was deeply involved, it is unlikely that Hauptmann himself was innocent as he claimed to the last.

WANTED
INFORMATION AS TO THE WHEREABOUTS OF

CHAS. A. LINDBERGH, Jr.
OF HOPEWELL, N. J.
SON OF COL. CHAS. A. LINDBERGH
World-Famous Aviator

This child was kidnaped from his home in Hopewell, N. J., between 8 and 10 p. m. on Tuesday, March 1, 1932.

DESCRIPTION:

Age, 20 months	Hair, blond, curly
Weight, 27 to 30 lbs.	Eyes, dark blue
Height, 29 inches	Complexion, light

Deep dimple in center of chin
Dressed in one-piece coverall night suit

ADDRESS ALL COMMUNICATIONS TO
COL. H. N. SCHWARZKOPF, TRENTON, N. J., or
COL. CHAS. A. LINDBERGH, HOPEWELL, N. J.

ALL COMMUNICATIONS WILL BE TREATED IN CONFIDENCE

COL. H. NORMAN SCHWARZKOPF
Supt. New Jersey State Police, Trenton, N. J.

March 11, 1932

The Lindbergh kidnap tragedy, three years ago

Bloody Ma Goes Down, Guns Blazing

THE BLOODY BARKERS have been eliminated. They were the only mid-western bank-robbing gang to stand comparison with the great city gangs.

Ma (Arizona "Kate") Barker shielded her sons Herman, Lloyd, Doc and Fred from the law, and provided hide-outs for them. She distributed bribes to officials and, according to the FBI, masterminded their robberies.

One by one the boys have been arrested, until only Doc and Freddy remained at large, and the very able criminal Alvin "Creepy" Karpis took command of the gang, organizing the kidnapping of millionaires William Hamm and Edward Bremner.

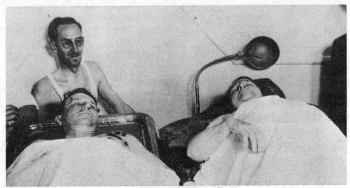

The bodies of Fred and Ma Barker in the morgue at Oklawaha, Florida

In January, Doc was traced through his women and arrested. Eight days later, Freddy and Ma (64) were caught in Florida, where both died after a four-hour shoot-out in which "Arizona Kate" allegedly wielded a machine-gun.

IN BRIEF

DR ALICE WYNEKOOP (see 1934), convicted of murdering her daughter-in-law and sentenced to life imprisonment.

KENNETH NEU, failed actor-singer who killed a homosexual theatre-owner and stole his suit; also an elderly stranger. Neu went to the gallows carolling his own composition:"I'm fit as a fiddle and ready to hang!".

Albert Fish: Itinerant Child Murderer and Cannibal

The cruel unflinching stare of manic mass murderer Albert Fish

Cannibal Child Murderer Executed

ON JANUARY 16, 1936, prison officers brought a little old man with grey hair and a straggly moustache to the electric chair. He looked gentle and meek, although by most estimates he flogged and tortured over a hundred children and killed at least four – possibly 15. He did not look excited, although he once said: "What a thrill that will be, if I have to die in the electric chair. It will be the supreme thrill – the only one I haven't tried."

He did not look mad, although few psychiatrists would suggest that this man was normal: a man who ate human flesh and excrement; drank human urine and blood; stuffed 27 needles into the genital area of his own body; lit fires of toilet paper in lavatories; prayed all hours of the day; and was once observed yelling: "I am Jesus! I am Jesus!" over and over again.

It took two shots of electricity to kill him. It often does. But on this occasion, reporters suggested that the needles in his body shorted the circuit the first time.

Albert Hamilton Fish, at 66 the oldest man ever executed in Sing Sing, and pretty certainly the maddest, is dead.

Trapped by Handwriting After Six Years

Fish was arrested in 1934 for the murder of 11-year-old Grace Budd six years earlier. He was caught because in November that year he suddenly wrote to Mrs Budd telling her how he had killed and eaten her child. It was the work of a sick man who relished reliving his crime and fantasizing about others. Yet he may have intended to give some crude solace in his final obscenity: "I did not fuck her tho' I could of had if I wished. She died a virgin." (Later he would tell a psychiatrist this was untrue.)

New York Missing Persons' Bureau knew this unsigned letter really did come from the mysterious "Frank Howard" who took little Grace "to a party" on May 27, 1928, never to be seen again. Its handwriting matched that of Howard's on a telegram form he had made out to the Budd family.

There was no address or signature, but an engraved monogram on the envelope traced it to a batch which had been left in a rooming-house on East 52nd St, New York. And the landlady there said that her former tenant, a Mr Albert Fish, called regularly to pick up cheques from his son. The next time he did so, detectives arrested him.

The Murder of Grace Budd

Albert Fish met the Budd family when they advertised requesting summer farm work for their 18-year-old son Edward. Fish (who planned to murder and eat Edward) presented himself as "Frank Howard" a Farmingdale smallholder, and the Budds were impressed with his good manners and shabbily correct black three-piece suit. They agreed that Edward should go with him the following week.

On the day Mr Howard came to collect Edward, however, he saw little Grace. With a swift change of plan, he proposed taking her to a children's party he said his sister was giving on Columbus Avenue. They would stay a couple of hours before he returned for Edward.

In fact, he took the excited child by train to a deserted house in Westchester County. There he sent her to pick flowers outside while he undressed upstairs. Then he called her in, grabbed her when she screamed at his nakedness, and strangled her.

He stripped the body and

He played with urine and ate faeces. He enjoyed sex with women or men, using or being used. When he couldn't get needles to stick in his groin, he used sharpened chicken bones from his prison dinner. Children spanked him, and *Albert Fish ate children!*

butchered it with what he called "implements of hell": a butcher's knife, a meat cleaver and a saw. He took the head and threw it away in waste ground behind the house. He wrapped up a forearm to take away and eat. And before dressing, he stuffed his own rectum with cotton wool soaked in lighter fuel, and ignited it. The fierce pain delighted him and gave him an orgasm.

Over the next nine days he returned to the house regularly collecting further joints of Grace to take home. Finally he threw the bones and "the implements of hell" where he had thrown the head. After his arrest, police recovered them, encrusted and worn away.

This is the crime for which Albert Hamilton Fish was tried and executed.

Fish is hauled down to the police station to help New York police with their enquiries into the murder of Grace Budd

The Life and Times of Albert Fish

Fish's hazy memory of dates and places makes it difficult to be precise. He travelled a lot, and committed offenses (included murders) which cannot now be placed.

1870 Born in Washington DC.
1875 Father died; Albert placed in orphanage. Unhappy there. Bedwetter until age 15. Sexually excited by witnessing and receiving bare-bottom spanking inflicted by woman teacher.
1885 Left orphanage. Dropped name "Hamilton". Became housepainter.
1898 Married 19-year-old girl who may have shared mild sadomasochistic tastes. Went on to have six children with her.
1902 First conviction. Stole $800 from store where he worked as maintenance man on hearing it was about to go bankrupt. Spent 2 years in Sing Sing.

1917 Wife left him, removing all furniture. Fish proved excellent caring father to the children, who remained with him.
1920 Became obsessed with religion. Regular Episcopalian church-attender for remainder of life. Knew Bible thoroughly, though misquoted and concentrated on punitive texts.
1927 Murdered and ate Billy Gaffney.
1928 Murdered and ate Grace Budd. Arrested in Manhattan and the Bronx for petty larceny. Suspended sentences.
1929 Married (bigamously) Myra Nicholas in Ohio (one of at least 3 bigamous marriages he contracted). During the one-week "marriage", before he deserted her introduced her children to games involving spanking him.
1930 Arrests for vagrancy and sending obscene letters through the mail. Sent to Bellevue Psychiatric Hospital for observation. Doctors concluded odd but sane, and released him.

1931 Started to live by himself rather than with family.
1933 Began having difficulty finding work.

1934 Arrested.
1935 Tried for murder of Grace Budd.
1936 Executed.

THE ALBERT FISH COOKBOOK

Fish described his feast off 4-year-old Billy Gaffney in 1927 thus:

I split the cheeks of his behind open, cut off his monkey and pee wees and washed them first. I put all in a roasting pan, lit the gas in the oven. Then I put strips of bacon on each cheek of his behind and put in the oven. Then I picked 4 onions and when the meat was roasted for about 1/4hr., I poured about a pint of water over it for gravy and put in the onions. At frequent intervals I basted his behind with a wooden spoon. So the meat would be nice and juicy.

In about 2hr. it was nice and brown, cooked thru. I never ate any roast turkey that tasted half as good as his sweet fat little behind did. I ate every bit of the meat in about four days. His little monkey was as sweet as a nut, but his pee wees I could not chew. Threw them in the toilet.

Parsi Doctor Kills Wife and Maid

WHEN PARSI Dr Buck Ruxton's (or Bikhtyar Rustomji's) American common-law wife Isabella Van Ess disappeared in September last year, along with the family nursemaid Mary Rogerson, the doctor reported that she had deserted him and taken the pregnant maid for an illegal abortion.

Since the Ruxtons' relationship had been passionate but stormy, no one was particularly surprised, although Miss Rogerson's parents protested that he must be lying about their daughter.

At the end of the month, pieces of two human bodies were found wrapped in newspapers beside a Scottish river when floodwaters receded.

One piece of paper was a special Morecombe and Lancaster edition of the *Daily Graphic*. Lancaster police knew of the two missing women.

Pathologists proved that one body was Isabella's by superimposing an old photograph of her head upon a picture of a skull taken from the same distance, and angle. It was evident, too, that the murderer had destroyed separately identifiable parts of the body like Isabella's thick ankles.

Neighbours now recalled Ruxton's giving away bloodstained clothing and carpets after frenzied house-cleaning at the time of the disappearances.

His denials in the witness-box made no impact on the powerful circumstantial evidence against him, and the murderous Dr Ruxton confessed to the murders before he was hanged in April.

Love and Murder in Rustic Slum Setting

SEMI-LITERATE Charlotte Bryant enjoyed coarse couplings with bucolic lovers at her slummy farm in Dorset, England. Her husband Frederick seemed unconcerned, even when married gypsy Leonard Parsons moved in with the Bryants.

But Charlotte wanted more room for Parsons, and gave her husband arsenic weedkiller. The gormless woman was surprised to be charged with murder when Frederick died as a result of her ministrations

She seemed incapable of understanding the proceedings against her. Parsons was little better. Nor was he much concerned, as he caroused cheerfully in a pub while Charlotte awaited hanging on July 15.

Dead Pimp Found in St Albans

IN JANUARY a man's bullet-ridden body was found dumped by the roadside near St Albans in England. His fingerprints identified him as "Red Max" Kassell, a Latvian pimp active in England since the trial of his fellow-countrymen Cellio and Berard (*see* 1910). Recently he had been using a Canadian passport and passing himself off as "Emil Allard".

Chief Inspector Richard "Nutty" Sharpe, Scotland Yard's expert on racetrack gangs and white slavers, picked up rumours that Kassell had actually died in Little Newport Street, Soho. A piece of broken window-glass led him to no. 36 where the removal of a bobbled fringe from Suzanne Bertron's curtain caught his eye, and the curtain was found to contain traces of blood.

Despite claims that Kassell is "the Vice Czar of London", the middle-aged pimp was probably dependent on one elderly prostitute at the time of his death. He borrowed money from Suzanne Bertron's pimp, Roger Vernon (aka Georges LaCroix), and the two men quarrelled in Bertron's room when Vernon tried to reclaim it. On realizing he had killed Kassell, Vernon telephoned a friend, Pierre Alexandre, who helped him drive the body to St Albans while Bertron and her maid cleaned up the room.

Vernon and Bertron fled to Paris, where the authorities refused to return them to England. Vernon was sent to Devil's Island from which he escaped: Mme Bertron was acquitted. Alexandre, who, like Kassell and Vernon uses a Canadian passport, was tried in England and sent to prison.

CANADA AND THE WHITE SLAVE TRAFFIC

The French Canadian passports in the Max Kassell murder case point to the true nature of the "White Slave" traffic. Contrary to popular legend, women are never kidnapped in Europe and shipped out to a life of shame in South America. Inspector "Nutty" Sharpe states categorically that procuresses drugging innocent girls with hypodermic needles have never existed. The only known case of a "well-dressed lady" offering girls sinister lifts in her big car is that of Madeline Roberts (*see* Hayley Morriss, 1925), and no harm whatsoever came to the girls who accepted the lift.

But active prostitutes wanting to cross international borders to practise their profession are hindered by immigration authorities. So gangs of pimps help women move as they wish and find them flats. Since most foreign women wishing to work in London are French, there is a considerable trade in forged Canadian passports allowing them to enter as French-Canadian Empire citizens. And that is the serious business of "White Slavery" in London.

"Unlucky" Luciano goes to jail

'Lucky' Luciano Jailed for Pimping

SPECIAL PROSECUTOR Thomas Dewey has made his most important arrest in the war on New York's organized crime. "Lucky" Luciano has been convicted of living off immoral earnings and given an extravagant 30 to 50 years sentence.

Obviously this reflects the known extent of Luciano's massive crime empire, and not the miserable offence of running a couple of prostitutes for which he has been convicted. Indeed, the underworld's claim that he got "a bum rap" is most likely true. It is impossible to imagine the elegant and managerial Luciano personally forcing women onto the streets and seizing their pathetic earnings, as was claimed at the trial.

But few people will care how it was done, rejoicing that this syndicate head is behind bars.

FBI Director Makes His First Arrest... Incompetently

STUNG BY JEERS that America's top policeman had never made an arrest, J.Edgar Hoover, director of the FBI, arrested Public Enemy No.1, Alvin "Creepy" Karpis in person.

Karpis, surviving leader of Ma Barker's gang of bank-robbers and kidnappers (*see* 1935) cheekily robbed a train after Ma's death. "Creepy" knew it would enfuriate Hoover to see the revival of a crime believed to have been put down at the turn of the century.

Karpis is, however, an unusually competent criminal. Ma and her boys were typical mid-western no-hopers until he came to command them. Had he been able to find robbers and kidnappers worthy of his leadership, he might have posed a real threat to law and order on the open prairies.

When agents trapped Karpis in New Orleans and surrounded his car, they were ordered to hold him until Mr Hoover could be summoned personally to make the arrest.

It is alleged that Mr Hoover stopped Karpis from grabbing a rifle on the back seat of his car. But Karpis's Plymouth coupé doesn't have a back seat.

As a final touch, when Mr Hoover ordered his men to put the handcuffs on Karpis, it turned out that nobody had brought any!

But the arrest has been loudly publicized, and J.Edgar Hoover hopes it will soon be forgotten that he is really a lawyer-bureaucrat, and not a gun-toting "agent".

IDENTIFICATION ORDER NO. 1218
March 22, 1934.

DIVISION OF INVESTIGATION
U.S. DEPARTMENT OF JUSTICE
WASHINGTON, D.C.

Fingerprint Classification
13 1 R 5
1 0 7

WANTED

ALVIN KARPIS, with aliases,
A. CARTER, RAYMOND HADLEY, GEORGE HALLER, ALVIN KARPIS,
EARL PEEL, GEORGE DUNN, R. E. HAMILTON, RAY HUNTER.

KIDNAPING

DESCRIPTION
Photograph taken May 19, 1936.

CRIMINAL RECORD

RELATIVES:

FBI wanted order for Public Enemy No. 1, Alvin "Creepy" Karpis

"Nurse" Waddingham

Children's 'Uncle Fred' Kills Mona

Frederick Nodder, the children's "Uncle Fred"

On January 5, 10-year-old Mona Tinsley of Newark, England, failed to arrive home from school. Reports of a man taking her on a Retford bus led back to lorry driver Frederick Nodder, who once lodged with the Tinsleys and was known to their children as "Uncle Fred".

He had called himself Frederick Hudson when living with the Tinsleys, who were quite unaware that under his real name he had a police record, dating back to the search for him to enforce a paternity order for his illegitimate child.

Nodder was blessed with rather prominent "staring" eyes, which made his identification easy when a schoolboy reported seeing such a man waiting at a Newark bus stop with a little girl, and a passenger remembered seeing the pair on the bus.

Under interrogation he admitted to accompanying the child on the bus, and claimed that she had asked him to take her to her aunt in Sheffield. He said he put her off at Worksop with her fare money and instructions on how to reach Sheffield.

She never got there.

In March, Nodder was sentenced to seven years' imprisonment for abduction, the judge commenting severely that Nodder alone knew what he had done with the little girl, but time might reveal the truth. This seemed unlikely because an extensive search, in which rivers and canals had been dragged and dumps sifted, had yielded no clues.

In June, Mona's strangled body floated to the surface of the River Idle. The same judge passed the death sentence, saying, "Justice has slowly but surely overtaken you."

IN JANUARY, Frederick Nodder killed. In April, he seemed to have got away with it. In June, Nemesis at last caught up with him. In December, he was hanged.

Murderer's Scheme to Incriminate His Landlord

ARTHUR PERRY, convicted of murdering his wife and sentenced to death this November, has had his trial overturned. Perry now goes for re-trial next year. It seems that when Perry decided to kill his 20-year-old wife Phennie, he plotted that 39-year-old Arthur Palm, who sublet a room to the Perrys, should be incriminated.

He acquired samples of Palm's handwriting, and wrote a letter to Phennie in which Palm appeared to say he would kill the girl if she refused to let him have sex with her. Since Palm is a responsible chainstore salesman, and deacon at a Black Baptist church, Phennie was astonished. She showed the letter to her husband, who said he would deal with the problem.

On July 1, Phennie Perry took her baby with her to a bingo hall in Jamaica, New York. From there she should have gone to her sister's. But Perry waylaid her and battered her to death with an iron purloined from Palm's apartment. Beside the body he also left papers from Palm's dresser, a shirt-pocket ripped from one of Palm's garments, and a left shoe with a hole in it.

The papers led police straight to Palm's apartment, and the torn shirt and matching right shoe were found there. But Perry was taken into custody as well, since Palm had an unshakeable alibi for the previous night.

A handwriting expert declared that the threatening letter from "Palm" to Phennie had actually been written by Perry. Forensic tests found that one of Perry's socks was stained with mud and blood in exactly the position of the hole in Palm's shoe. And Perry found himself in the dock where he belonged.

Doctor, Witch and Actor Team Up To Kill

AN ASTONISHING gang of insurance-scam murderers has been caught in Philadelphia. Over the last five years, the Bolber-Petrillo ring has probably killed at least 50 people.

Dr Morris Bolber and his cousin Paul Petrillo stumbled into lucrative murder when Mrs Antony Giscobbe, one of Bolber's patients, complained of her husband's infidelities. Bolber sent Petrillo to seduce her, and propose that they murder Tony for his $10,000 life insurance.

A natural death was easily arranged. When Tony staggered home drunk for a good night's sleep, his wife left the window over his bed open to admit the rain. Soon Tony was dead of pneumonia, and Dr Bolber and Mrs Giscobbe were each the richer by $5,000.

Bolber and Paul now put their scheme on a regular business footing, and recruited another cousin, amateur thespian Hermann Petrillo. His job was to impersonate each uninsured victim and take out a policy. The gang's subtlety was best shown in the "on-the-job" accident (with double indemnity arranged for a roofer. Before pushing him off a roof, they put filthy postcards in his hands, to suggest that he was carelessly distracted by the luscious naked lovelies.

Carino Favato, "the Witch of Philadelphia," was the gang's next recruit. This sinister "faith healer" had poisoned three of her own husbands, and sold poison to other women. She helped identify clients. The gang was caught when an ex-convict approached Hermann Petrillo with a proposal. Hermann was not impressed, and said: "Dig up somebody we can murder for some insurance and you can make some dough with us." The humble villain was appalled, and went to the police. Under arrest, the gang all informed on each other. The Petrillos have been executed for their crimes; the Doctor and the Witch sentenced to life imprisonment.

Mass Killer-Robber Caught in Paris

GERMAN-BORN Eugen Weidmann, who killed five people in Paris in the course of robberies, has been caught just in time to stop him graduating to kidnapping.

His first victim was American Jean de Koven, whom he strangled and buried early this year. Jeannine Keller suffered similar treatment. Joseph Couffy, a car-hire driver, was shot on the Paris-Orléans road in September. Businessman Roger le Blond was killed in his car a few weeks later, and estate agent Raymond Lesobre died in an empty house, around which he was supposedly showing an English client. Weidmann, a fine linguist, passed himself off as French or English at will.

The police received information that a man named Sauerbrey was involved, and went to his house near Saint Cloud. M. Sauerbrey fired a pistol at them when he learned what they wanted. He was overpowered, and proved to be Eugen Weidmann.

With an accomplice named Million and two others who planned to team up as kidnappers, Herr Weidmann is now explaining to a *juge d'instruction* why he kept the cars of Couffy and Lesobre. He has admitted to all five murders.

The execution of the Paris murderer and robber, Eugen Weidmann, outside St Pierre Prison

Rich Brat Thought He Could Avoid Murder Charges

TWENTY-YEAR-OLD sex maniac Alexander Meyer had a rich daddy, and so he thought he could get away with murder. In 1935 he shot at two young Philadelphia girls who rejected his advances. He was sent to a Reformatory for that.

In January this year he assaulted and nearly killed 15-year-old Jeannie Waterson when she re-fused to have sex with him. A little later he drove through country lanes in Pennsylvania in a stolen truck which he later confessed to having taken "for the sole purpose of running down and killing a girl."

Near Coatesville he saw 16-year-old Helen Moyer. He ran her down. He drove her (still living) to an empty farm and raped her. He threw her (still living) down a well.

He threw two sticks of dynamite after her and destroyed the well. But Jeannie Waterson identified him, and his daddy's money didn't save him. Meyer went to the electric chair in July for Helen Moyer's murder.

> **I TOOK THE TRUCK FOR THE SOLE PURPOSE OF RUNNING DOWN AND KILLING A GIRL.**
>
> QUOTE **Alexander Meyer**

IN BRIEF

ERNEST WALKER, (*see* 1922) detained at His Majesty's pleasure for the pointless murder of messenger-boy Albert Davies, has been released from Broadmoor.

At the time of his conviction, Walker was reprieved on grounds of youth rather than insanity. He is still only 33.

Man Says He Killed Blackmailing Prostitute Unwittingly

TWENTY-SEVEN-YEAR-OLD George Brain borrowed his firm's green Morris Eight van on July 13. Near Wimbledon Common, London, he was distracted by 30-year-old prostitute "Irish Rose" Atkins and offered her a lift.

George couldn't remember exactly why he did this, for almost immediately (he said) he suffered a blackout, prompted by fury when Rose demanded money from him, saying she would tell the St Pancras boot wholesalers for whom he worked that he had been out pleasure-driving in their van.

The police filled in the blanks for him: he had stabbed Rose, battered her over the head with a starting handle and then run the van over her body. He had also taken four shillings from her bag.

Two days later George's employers reported his disappearance with £32. His van, left in a workmate's garage, was blood-stained. Its tyres fitted the marks on Rose's body and its colour matched witness descriptions of a vehicle seen in the area of the murder.

After his photograph was published, George Brain was spotted by a schoolboy at Sheerness. He went on trial in November, and was hanged in December.

Prostitute "Irish Rose" Atkins, one of George Brain's victims

A Miscarriage of Justice Feared

MRS MARGARET DOBSON (67) was found, stabbed, on a cart track on January 18. For 30 years she and her husband have farmed near Wolviston, Durham, England.

Suspicion fastened on 21-year-old Robert Hoolhouse, who fitted a vague description of a loiterer seen near the scene of the crime. Hoolhouse's face and hands were scratched; his coat had blood and hair on it.

Five years ago his family quarrelled with Mr and Mrs Dobson, and were evicted from their tied cottage. The labouring family had to move to a village four miles away, and Robert, 16 at the time, did not pretend to have loved the Dobsons.

His legal advisers felt there was no case against him. Farm workers' faces and hands are scratched by briars: their clothing picks up blood and hairs in animal husbandry. Resentment of a high-handed landlord in 1933 was a thin motive for murder in 1938. A footprint near the body was definitely not Hoolhouse's.

For these reasons, counsel called no witnesses in Hoolhouse's defence. It seemed better to have the last word with the jury – something only permitted if no defence witnesses are called.

The strategy failed, and despite a petition with over 14,000 signatures, Hoolhouse has been hanged. But the public is not satisfied that justice has been done.

Kidnapper Trailed from Wisconsin to Los Angeles

BURGLAR John Henry Seadlund turned his incompetent hand to kidnapping last year, and wound up a double-murderer with FBI chief J.Edgar Hoover flying to California for his arrest.

With accomplice James Gray, Seadlund picked an expensive-looking car in Illinois, swerved his own vehicle in front of it, and ejected the owner at gunpoint, leaving the chauffeur to raise the alarm.

Charles P.Ross, a Chicago businessman, was taken to Wisconsin and forced to write a note asking for a $50,000 ransom to be raised. This note, and one that succeeded it, were passed to the FBI.

The Bureau gave their usual advice: meet the demand first; let them try to catch the criminals after the victim was secure. But the notes yielded fingerprints. The typewriter on which they had been written was new, and the store which sold it gave a description of the as-yet unidentified Seadlund.

The ransom was delivered in marked bills, and these started turning up in a trail that led to Los Angeles.

On January 14 the FBI surrounded Santa Anita racetrack, where Seadlund was arrested. He then broke down and confessed to having murdered both Mr Ross and James Gray, and directed officers to the buried bodies in Wisconsin, where he had hidden them

Seadlund went to the electric chair in the spring.

Pretty Fraudster Killed Protector and Relatives

Emil Marek, self-mutilator

EXECUTED ON December 6, Austrian Martha Marek lived her adult life on the proceeds of fraud and murder. Born in 1904, Martha Lowenstein was a foundling. At age 15 she worked in a dress shop where she was spotted by department store owner Morris Fritsch, who adopted her, seduced her, and improved her style by sending her to finishing schools.

In 1924 Fritsch died, leaving young Martha his fortune. She married engineeer Emil Marek, and the two raced prodigally through Fritsch's money.

To restore their finances, they took out a £10,000 insurance policy and staged an accident. Emil went to hospital with an almost severed leg: his axe had slipped while he was cutting a tree, he said.

The limb had to be amputated, but the insurance company refused to pay up when the surgeon testified that it had taken three blows to reduce the leg to its damaged condition. Frankly, the doctor could not conceive of a man who had hit his leg once with an axe accidentally taking another couple of swipes at it!

The Mareks bribed a nurse to say the surgeon himself had made the additional cuts. When this was exposed, they drew four-month jail sentences for witness-tampering.

In 1932 when the Mareks were near destitution, Emil died, supposedly of tuberculosis, and Martha collected a small insurance payment. Soon after that her little daughter Ingeborg died.

At this point Martha became companion to her rich aunt, Suzanne Lowenstein, and inherited her house and estate when the old lady died. Yet again Martha proved recklessly extravagant. By this year all that remained of Suzanne's wealth was the house, in which Martha took lodgers.

She faked the theft of some paintings to defraud her insurance company again, but was quickly remanded to jail for this. When news of her arrest reached a young man whose mother had died as Martha's tenant, he reported his suspicions to the police. The exhumed body contained the rare poison thallium. So, it proved, did the bodies of Suzanne and Ingeborg and Emil and Moritz Fritsch. Martha's still-living son was rescued from slow poisoning in the nick of time before his mother fell to the executioner's axe.

Martha Marek, with her adoptive sister Paula Lowenstein (behind)

Mr Hoover and President Share New Deal Interest in Publicizing FBI

FBI CHIEF J. Edgar Hoover is receiving extraordinary personal publicity as America's top cop. He and President Roosevelt have converging interests in his propagandized fame. "Law and Order" is a part of the New Deal which will not be attacked for "creeping socialism" as the President extends federal police powers, and so Mr Roosevelt is keen to see Federal crime-busting widely publicized.

Mr Hoover, for his part, wants this publicity personalized. For he is a holdover from earlier Republican administrations, and does not want to lose his job to a Democratic partisan.

President and Director alike therefore welcome popular publicity for J. Edgar as a machine-gun-waving tough denouncing the "rats" and "scum" he arrests, even though this distorts the office-bound bureaucrat's real achievement in establishing a skilled force of highly educated professionals.

IN BRIEF

ARTHUR PERRY (*see* 1937), convicted and executed for wife-murder after re-trial. Police remark that this ill-educated black man perpetrated one of the most cunning and calculated murders on record. A rare true life crime that matches detective fiction and almost led to a wrongful conviction.

'Mad Butcher' is Dead, says Top Policeman

CLEVELAND POLICE chief Eliott Ness believes that the "Mad Butcher of Kingsbury Run", who has terrorized the city for four years, is now dead.

Ness was originally head of the group of prohibition enforcement agents known as "the Untouchables". Cleveland appointed him Director of Public Safety in 1935.

In September that year, two decapitated men were found near ramshackle Kingsbury Run. Four months later a headless prostitute was found hacked to pieces in the same neighbourhood.

Three more headless and mangled men were found in 1936. In 1937 a headless, dismembered black woman was dumped under a bridge in a sack. A man killed later in the year was hacked to pieces.

Last year saw three more murders: two men and a woman.

In August last year, Mr Ness made a bold decision. Nearly all the victims were prostitutes or vagrants from the East 45th Street and Kingsbury Run warren of shacks and shanties. Mr Ness cleared the inhabitants out and burned the slum to the ground. And with his hunting-ground obliterated, the mad butcher stopped killing.

Ness didn't stop hunting him, however. He deduced from the number of male victims that the murderer was probably homosexual. He had to be big and strong enough to overpower his victims.

He had to have a car to transport their bodies. He had to live on his own in a house clear of inquisitive neighbours. And he had to have sufficient money to maintain his house and car.

Investigations ultimately uncovered a man who fitted the model: a big, sullen, withdrawn and hostile homosexual. Mr Ness interviewed him repeatedly, hinting that he was trapped. The suspect, in turn, nursed his feeling of superiority to the investigators by almost admitting the offences.

Until he cracked – but not to the police. He committed himself to a mental home, where he died this year.

Mr Ness is quite sure this man was the "Mad Butcher".

Eliott Ness, Cleveland police chief

'Brick Moron' Kills in LA: Executed in Chicago

THE MYSTERIOUS "Brick Moron", caught and executed in Chicago this year, rampaged pointlessly through two cities, using a different name in each.

The first brick killing took place in Chicago in 1936, when a young cocktail waitress was beaten in the hotel room where she lived with her 7-year-old son. The killer scrawled, "Black Legion Game" in lipstick on the dressing-table mirror. And he left a beautiful set of his fingerprints which showed that he was Robert Nixon, an 18-year-old black delinquent. But Nixon vanished.

In Los Angeles, a young black man called Thomas Crosby started amassing a record, with arrests for purse-snatching and suspicion of auto theft. A brick-murderer also began working in the city. He killed twice in March, and again in April. All victims were women killed in their own homes, with the last victim's 12-year-old daughter also battered to death. The clumsy stupidity of these pointless killings led to the assassin being dubbed "The Brick Moron".

In May last year, Mrs Florence May Johnson, a fireman's wife in Chicago, was killed with a brick. Soon after that, Chicago police picked up Nixon, and it was not long before he had confessed. Then the Los Angeles Police Department spotted the similarity between the Chicago brick murders and the killings in their own city. Exchanged fingerprints confirmed that Robert Nixon and Thomas Crosby were one and the same. Chicago tried the young man and electrocuted him this June.

Robert Nixon (aka Thomas Crosby), the moronic brick killer of Chicago and Los Angeles

'Bugsy' Siegel Nearly Murders Hitler's Chiefs

THE NEW YORK mobs have sent Benjamin "Bugsy" Siegel to California, and the good-looking blue-eyed mobster is making an impact in Hollywood social circles.

Long-time associate of Syndicate financier Meyer Lansky, with whom he ran the "Bug and Meyer Mob" in the early 'twenties, Siegel provided the muscle and violence while Lansky was the brain. As this pair of Jewish criminals saw the wisdom of co-operating with Italian rivals, Lansky hired out Bugsy's killing abilities to "Lucky" Luciano, and "the Bug" led the hit team which rubbed out "Joe the Boss" Masseria, leaving Maranzano with the delusion that he would now be the Sicilian "Boss of all Bosses".

George Raft, a boyhood friend, shows Ben Siegel around the stars' social circuit (and they never call him "Bugsy" if they value their health: the nickname both describes his paranoid "Bughouse" rages, and provokes them if he hears it!) Siegel proved this year

that he has the aplomb to circulate in society; accept a summons to commit murder; return after having killed to "charm the panties" off starlets at the party he briefly abandoned. This happened when he got a message that the boys wanted "Big Greenie" Greenberg killed. Bugsy took off with Frankie Carbo and Allie Tannenbaum; saw to the killing personally; and returned to the Hollywood lovelies.

His most bizarre exploit since, has been a trip to Italy with current girlfriend, Countess Dorothy DiFrasso. This shady lady is a friend of Mussolini, and persuaded Siegel to visit Il Duce offering him a revolutionary new explosive.

Whilst exploring European Fascist society, Ben was also introduced to Göring and Goebbels. Seems our boy didn't care for Hitler's head goons – well, he is Jewish! Unfortunately Dorothy's pleas persuaded him not to bump them off on the spot as he proposed. Pity. She really isn't a very nice gal.

Gangster Ben Siegel: friends call him "Benny Blue Eyes", others call him "Bugsy"

Top Crime Czar Arrested: Faces Life in Prison

IF YOU thought it was great when Special Prosecutor Tom Dewey sent "Lucky" Luciano down for pimping (*see* 1936), what do you say to Louis "Lepke" Buchalter – arrested for narcotics conspiracy with a lifetime's-

worth of prison sentences ahead?

Lepke jumped bail when he heard Dewey was gunning for him, but the labour racketeer and New York crime "family" boss got double-crossed twice over.

First, Luciano, still wheelin' n' dealin' from his comfy cell in Dannemora Prison, decided time had come for Lepke to be pressured. He got a message slipped to him that J. Edgar Hoover, no less, would do a deal: let Lepke turn himself in to the Feds, and a lighter sentence than Dewey's would come down.

Second, Hoover and street-smart journalist Walter Winchell played Judas. They picked up Lepke in a car, and immediately gave him the bad news. They were turning him in to Federal authorities and Dewey!

Guess ol' J. Edgar's strict Presbyterian integrity don't extend to the members of the criminal fraternity he calls "bums and rats"!

Young Girl's Murder Still Unsolved

THE FILE on Pamela Coventry is still open. The 11-year-old was found, raped and strangled, in fields near her Essex, England, home this January.

A hand-rolled cigarette-end made from used tobacco lay by the body, which was trussed with electric cable. Police quickly traced 28-year-old Leonard Richardson who rolls his own with used tobacco;

owns electric cable like that used on Pamela; and was home off work on the day of the murder.

But Richardson has been completely co-operative, and an Old Bailey jury was directed by the judge that they had not heard evidence on which to convict him. Richardson walks free, and Pamela's murderer is still sought by the police.

New York Crime Investigations Uncover Murder Inc.!

Louis "Lepke" Buchalter, boss and racketeer

New York Special Prosecutor Tom Dewey (second from right) gives a press conference on his recent crime-busting activities

SPECIAL PROSECUTOR Thomas Dewey's work against organized crime in New York has been taken over by Burton Turkus. Spectacular results are coming from informer Abe "Kid Twist" Reles.

To escape conviction for the 1938 murder of informer "Whitey" Rudnick, Reles is informing on all and sundry – "singing like a canary" in underworld parlance. And he knows what he's talking about!

Reles was one of a gang of professional killers who met at Matilda's Cafe in Brooklyn. Run by Brooklyn crime boss Albert Anastasia, these men took contracts to kill dispensable villains and informers in other parts of New York city and the USA.

Learning of this assassination by outside contract (an old underworld method of keeping "the home team" out of trouble with safe alibis), the press have dubbed Anastasia's mob "Murder Inc."

Reles' revelations go back a long way. It seems that Bugsy Siegel, Vito Genovese, Joe Adonis and Albert Anastasia shot Joe "the Boss" Masseria (fingered by his lieutenant "Lucky" Luciano) in 1931, and four Jewish gangsters "rubbed out" his successor, Salvatore Maranzano shortly after this.

These two murders enabled Luciano and Meyer Lansky to divide up New York's crime operations between them, their gangs co-operating and so eliminating the murderous rivalry that was such a feature of underworld life in the Prohibition period.

Most sensationally of all, Reles ties crime boss and labour racketeer Louis "Lepke" Buchalter to the 1936 murder of one-time trucker Joe Rosen.

Lepke is already in secure custody for narcotics offences (*see* 1939). For the first time ever, one of the true heads of organized crime faces capital charges and the very real possibility of being sent to the electric chair for his many crimes.

English "Lady" Takes off Glove to Shoot Lover

FLORENCE RANSOM is an English lady who was caught because an English lady should never be seen without her gloves – even if she's gone out to murder. Florence became the lover of Lawrence Fisher of Matfield in Kent some time ago, and was delighted when he left his wife and family to move in with her at Piddington, near Bicester in Oxfordshire. But on July 9 she decided that Mrs Fisher's survival was inconvenient, and went down to Kent to pay a social call. She persuaded Mrs Fisher and her 19-year-old daughter to come out into the garden, where she shot them. When the housemaid came out to see what was going on, Florence shot her, too. Then she returned to Piddington. But she had dropped one of her kid gloves, which was traced. Adjudged guilty but insane, Florence was spared the hangman and transferred to Broadmoor after her trial.

Corpses Turn Morgue Attendant into Mad Killer

WORKING AS janitor in the morgue of New York's Mount Sinai Hospital made Wilhelm Johanssen unbalanced. He couldn't stop thinking about dead bodies, and after a few drinks he had blue flashes and had to kill someone – or so he said.

In October 1933 he had a drunken quarrel with his ex-wife, who threw a flowerpot at him. He carved her up with a boning knife and fled to Brooklyn. There, with his name changed to Harry Gordon, he remarried before going to California and settling in Long Beach, where his new wife Lydia opened a flower shop.

Harry's new job as merchant seaman often took him up the coast. In April 1935 he picked up prostitute Betty Coffin in San Francisco and checked into a waterfront hotel with her as "Mr and Mrs H. Meyers". Next morning the naked body of "Mrs Meyers" was found beaten, strangled and mutilated with a razor.

In June this year, prostitute Irene McCarthy's naked body was found in a hotel in 4th Street, San Francisco. She had been slashed with a weapon and strangled with a belt. To Lydia Gordon's astonishment, her husband was arrested as the "Mr Wilkins" who had checked in Irene as his wife the night she died. Since his arrest, Harry has confessed to all three murders.

Incestuous Father of Five Kills Wife

AFTER DELAYS and appeals, 61-year-old William Spinelli of Los Angeles has finally been executed for the murder of his wife, Rose, in 1938. Rose, who worked as a maid in Beverley Hills, supported William and their five children, while her unemployed husband loafed around and drank. They quarrelled frequently, especially over his incestuous relations with their daughters, one of whom is thought to have borne him a child.

On December 20, 1938, one of the Spinelli daughters called the police to say that her mother was missing. Detectives found blood all over the bathroom and bedroom. Spinelli said he had cut himself. He showed them a letter dated December 12 in which Rose said she was eloping to South America.

Forensic scientists concluded that no one could have survived losing all that blood, and Spinelli was arrested. Enquiries in the neighbourhood revealed that on the day Mrs Spinelli disappeared, William kept a fire burning in the incinerator for five hours, and made several trips out of the house carrying heavy packages.

After a gas station operator revealed that Spinelli had persuaded him to write "Rose's" departure letter, and Spinelli's son told of being threatened by his father when he asked questions about the incinerator and Rose's disappearance, Spinelli finally confessed. He had killed his wife with a hatchet during one of their quarrels; then left a note for the family before going out to a restaurant to fortify himself for the long job of getting rid of the body.

Californians wryly note this as the murder year of the Spinellis, with Julia (see above) also sentenced to death in their state.

Middle-aged Crime Queen Taught Kids to Rob and Kill

JUANITA SPINELLI (51), bizarre "headmistress" of a crime school in California, has been convicted of murdering a pupil. "The Duchess" (as fellow-convicts call her) is a half-Sioux Indian who became the mistress of Detroit hoodlum Michael Simone, until she grassed on a strikebreaker and fled to San Francisco to avoid gangland vengeance. There she organized kids in their late teens and early 20s in a succession of flaky crimes: stealing cars, housebreaking, robbing small businesses. When there was no other work on hand, they were expected to roll drunks.

In April this year, three of the kids held up a barbecue stand. Twenty-three-year-old Albert Ives, panicking when the owner reached for his hearing aid, shot him dead. The robbery netted two paper bags full of meat, which the kids thought were stuffed with money!

Juanita was furious; angrier still when 18-year-old Robert Sherrard, a gang member with a history of mental disorder, looked as if he was going to give them all away. She had Sherrard knocked out with a Mickey Finn and dumped in the Sacramento River to drown. Then the gang fled to Reno, Nevada.

There Ives took fright at her threats that he would be next to go and, doing what she had warned him against, confessed to the police. When taken into custody the Duchess showed only contempt for Ives and others who informed. She has been convicted and sentenced to death, along with Simone, whom she had imported from Detroit to captain her juvenile mobsters, and one other gang member.

California convicts have petitioned the Governor not to break a 100-year-old state tradition of not executing women.

WOMEN AND THE GALLOWS IN CALIFORNIA

In 1851 a beautiful Mexican hooker called Juanita stabbed a rowdy but popular miner who tried to force himself on her.

A miner's kangaroo court convicted her, but was criticized internationally for faking evidence by dipping her clothes in blood; kicking out a young lawyer who had been allowed to start a speech in her defence; and driving away a doctor who reported her to be pregnant.

Concern about the state's good name after that scandal had inhibited any further executions of women.

Orgiast Aristocrat's Shooting Excites Planter Society

Lord Erroll's crashed car

THE POINTED QUESTION, "Are you married or do you live in Kenya?", relevant to adulterous white settlers, has been given added significance by the trial of Sir "Jock" Delves Broughton for the murder of Lord Erroll.

Broughton, a 59-year-old wealthy big-game hunter and race-horse owner, married pretty young gold-digger Diana Caldwell in London last year. On arrival in Kenya, Lady Broughton discovered that ne'er-do-well planter Lord Erroll was younger, more aristocratic and better looking than her morose and often tipsy husband. Erroll's vices were more fun, too: he organized sex orgies and seduced every good-looking Englishwoman who came near him.

Early this year, Erroll and Diana told Broughton they wanted to marry. With astonishing complacency, Broughton agreed to settle £5000 on his departing wife, and negotiated a three-month delay.

On January 25, all three went to the Muthaiga Country Club. At 1.30 Broughton came home drunk and went to bed. At 2.30 Erroll drove Diana home and set off in his car toward Nairobi. At dawn his body was found behind the wheel, three miles away. There was a bullet through his head, and white pipeclay marks on the rear seat where his killer's shoes had rested. The bullet had been fired from a pistol of Broughton's which he and Diana had both used for target practice. It went missing from his house the previous week.

The question for detectives was whose white shoes? Broughton's tennis shoes? (Burned, apparently.) Diana's dancing shoes? (No scuff-marks on them.)

Broughton was arrested and charged, but, given his age and general infirmity, it was inconceivable that he could have climbed from his bedroom window to hide in the car, and thereafter run three miles home to be seen in his dressing-gown at 3.30. The trial ended with his acquittal, but the murder continues to titillate settler society.

Lord Erroll, playboy planter

Diana Broughton, wife of defendant "Sir Jock"

Murderer Leaves Name as well as Fingerprints

HAROLD DORIAN TREVOR has been a small-time thief and fraudster for most of his 62 years. Not a very successful one: he has spent time in jail for passing himself off as monocled "Sir Charles Warren" or "Commander Crichton" in various swindles.

Still, he might have known better than to leave his real name and a set of fingerprints when he turned to murder!

Elderly Theodora Greenhill had a room to let in north Kensington. Dorian presented himself as a tenant and proffered a deposit. Mrs Greenhill seems to have got as far as writing "Received from Dr H.D. Trevor the s..." when she was struck over the head with a beer bottle and strangled at her writing bureau. The phoney title did not mislead police: Trevor's fingerprints were found on the beer bottle, the dressing-table and Mrs Greenhill's ransacked money box. He has been arrested in Rhyl and goes on trial in the New Year.

IN BRIEF

'DUCHESS' JUANITA SPINELLI (*see* 1940), first woman ever executed in California.

Who Dropped the Canary Out of His Cage?

ABE "KID TWIST" RELES is dead. The 34-year-old killer whose testimony has blown the roof off organized crime in New York fell 75 feet from his window in the Half Moon Hotel, Coney Island, where a constant guard of six policemen watched him night and day.

Stoney-faced, the guards say they just weren't looking when it happened. Stoney-faced, the NYPD says it was either suicide or an escape attempt, pointing to a couple of sheets tied together. Stoney-faced, Mayor William O'Dwyer says that the capital case assembled against "Lord High Executioner" Albert Anastasia, head of Brooklyn's crime family, has died with Reles, and the promising murder charges in preparation for "Bugsy" Siegel must be dropped as well.

It is whispered that crime syndicate "Prime Minister" Frank Costello shelled out $50,000 in bribes to ensure that Reles died before Anastasia and Siegel could tread the path of Louis "Lepke" Buchalter.

For the crime family boss and labour racketeer has been sentenced to death on Reles' testimony. Never before has one of the top gang leaders faced the electric chair. It remains to be seen whether Lepke's money, friends and influence will somehow intercede with appeals and delays, or whether he will die with his shoes on, like so many of his enemies.

Abe "Kid Twist" Reles

Kiwi Farmer Shoots Six Before Being Shot

NEW ZEALAND'S biggest manhunt has ended with seven people dead, one of whom was dangerous killer Eric George Graham. Graham's dairy farm started to fail last year, and the more he lost money, the more he withdrew into himself and blamed his neighbours. On October 7 he threatened two of them with a rifle, and they informed the police.

Constable Best went to remonstrate with Graham, and was verbally abused. When Best returned with a sergeant and two other constables, Graham shot all four. (He has always been an expert deer-stalker and marksman). Best still lived, though mortally wounded and Mrs Graham ran out of the house to fetch him a doctor. Two strangers she met came to the farm to see if they could help. Graham killed them. Then he took off for the bush, returning at night to find the Home Guard occupying his home. He was wounded in an exchange of fire, and headed for the bush again. Five days later, manhunters spotted him, and he was wounded for a second time, but escaped yet again.

Finally, on October 15, a police officer found Graham hiding in farm outbuildings and shot him without warning. This prompt action was commended by the coroner.

'DO SOMETHING ABOUT SOLDIERS KILLING KIDS'

The Chronicle of Crime is unwilling to recommend the Hunnish provision of field brothels for British fighting men. But as the country is turned into a stronghold with black-outs, the Army must take full responsibility for the armed and fit young men it draws out of homes and families and deposits in alien places.

We feel compelled to demand action in the light of three murders over the last twelve months.

Samuel Morgan used weekend leave from Seaforth Barracks to rape and strangle Mary Hagan in an empty Liverpool blockhouse last November. He was caught because he dropped an army thumbstall by the body and the bandaging and acriflavine exactly matched field dressings issued to Morgan's unit, which Morgan used when he cut his thumb on barbed wire.

Morgan was hanged in April. Harold Hill awaits trial for the murder in November of 8-year-old Doreen Hearne and 6-year-old Kathleen Trendle. They were stabbed in the throat and chest and dumped in Rough Wood, about four miles from their homes in Penn, Buckinghamshire. Hill picked them up in his army truck, which he then drove back to base in Yoxford, Suffolk. Only a laundry-marked handkerchief dropped near the bodies, and a schoolboy's observation of the truck's markings, traced this mobile military murderer.

These boys in uniform should be our heroes. Is the army doing enough? Should they provide something more than chaplains and bromide in the tea for soldiers' morals?

Since the South African War, British soldiers have mastered their libidinous desires with the true Englishman's gentlemanly self-control, assisted by unobtrusive doses of a depressant drug in their tea. The term "the licentious soldiery" has not been applied to our brave boys since Queen Victoria's day.

Black-Out Ripper: Young Killer Airman

ON FEBRUARY 13, a good-looking young airman in a Piccadilly brasserie in central London offered Mrs Greta Haywood a drink at the nearby Captain's Cabin. There, in the darkness of the black-out he attacked her, but ran off when she screamed, leaving his gas-mask behind.

It yielded the fingerprints of a ruthless killer who had already struck that night, strangling Mrs Doris Jouannet at her flat in Paddington, and savagely mutilating her abdomen and breasts with a tin-opener.

The night before he had done the same to prostitute Margaret Lowe. Two days before that, ex-Windmill dancer Evelyn Oatley was his victim. On February 9, respectable chemist Margaret Hamilton was attacked in Montague Square and robbed of her handbag after being strangled with the scarf she was wearing.

The man committing these crimes had no convictions, so his fingerprints were not on file. Now the police know he was Aircraftsman 525987 Gordon Frederick Cummins, a 25-year-old trainee pilot.

After leaving Mrs Heywood, Cummins made another attack on a woman: Katherine Mulcahy (aka Kathleen King), who took him back to her Paddington flat.

Cummins used the cash he stole from his murder victims to support a fanstasy image of himself as a well-heeled man about town. His pretence of noble birth and good education made him unpopular with his fellows in the Air Force and earned him the nickname "the Duke".

Cummins offered no defence at his trial except a denial, and was convicted and hanged.

Victim: Evelyn Oatley

Victim: Margaret Hamilton

Victim: Doris Jouannet

Fire-Watcher Convicted for London Blitz Killing

HARRY DOBKIN'S trial this November 1942 brought the Russian-born Jewish fire-watcher a death sentence. Dobkin's marriage to Rachel Karpinski was arranged by a broker in 1920, and lasted three days! But in that time a son was conceived, and for the next 20 years Dobkin was harried for maintenance. When the child reached adulthood, Rachel's sister encouraged her to continue to press for support.

In April 1941, when he started fire-watching, Dobkin invited Rachel to meet him at a cafe. She was never seen again. Her sister had a premonition that Dobkin had murdered her, and wrote a long letter to the police.

On April 15 Dobkin reported a small fire in the vestry of the chapel in St Oswald's Place, Kennington Road. No serious damage clearance was done at the site until July 1942, when a burned human skeleton was found under a flagstone. Rachel Dobkin had been reported missing just three days before the fire in the chapel.

Mrs Dobkin's dentist identified the skull positively. Dobkin's persistent claim to know nothing about Rachel's disappearance, did not convince the jury, and he was convicted.

Harry Dobkin and Rachel Karpinski on their wedding day in 1920

Teenage Torture-Murderer Reprieved

RAYMOND L. WOODWARD JR, the garden-boy whose plea of guilty to murdering Constance Arlene Shipp drew an automatic death penalty in Massachusetts, has had his sentence commuted to life imprisonment.

15-year-old Woodward, is backward and unruly. In June last year he was put on probation for making an indecent suggestion to a woman. He attacked another woman two weeks later.

Before his court hearing for that crime he kidnapped, tortured and murdered 16-year-old Arlene Shipp, who was reported missing on July 15. For four days nobody thought of searching the rambling old parsonage opposite her home.

When they did, they found she had been kept alive and tortured for at least two days. There were 22 separate wounds on her body – cuts, blows and knife-thrusts – and she was finally killed by heavy blows to the head. Wood's fingerprints were found in the building and bloodstains on his clothes matched his victim's. He confessed, and would have been led to the electric chair but for his youth.

Lady in the Lake's Killer Caught

AFTER TEN YEARS the mills of God ground exceeding small for Monty Illingworth, who has finally been convicted of murdering his wife Hallie in 1932.

When Hallie disappeared from her home in Washington State, Monty reported that the 36-year-old waitress had deserted him and run away to Alaska with a sailor. Since Illingworth frequently beat his wife, nobody was surprised. He moved to California and remarried, and Hallie was forgotten until the summer of 1939.

In that year, two fishermen dredged up a blanket-wrapped bundle from Crescent Lake, Washington. Something like a foot protruded from it, but the whole thing weighed less than fifty pounds, and there was no sign of putrefaction. The fishermen believed they had found a shop window dummy. In fact, they had found the body of a woman.

The features of the corpse had been obliterated by the chemicals in the lake water, and there was no means of identification. However, the coroner estimated that "the lady in the lake" had been dead seven years. After three years it was determined that this must be Hallie Illingworth.

Monty was unable to produce any evidence supporting his story of Hallie's desertion. He was convicted of second degree homicide and given a life sentence.

Canadian Soldier Freed in Prostitute Slaying

CANADIAN SOLDIER Joseph McKinstry, who is stationed in England, has been found Not Guilty of murdering prostitute Peggy Richards. Her body was found in the Thames beside Waterloo Bridge in London on June 23. There was bruising on the body and marks of an attempt to strangle her.

McKinstry was questioned because he had gone to the police the previous night to turn in Peggy's handbag. He said he had met her in a pub near the bridge where he chatted her up, but the conversation had turned into an argument, in the course of which she had hit him with the bag before running off and leaving him holding it.

A witness testified that McKinstry had gone on to the bridge with the woman and paid her to have intercourse with him there. McKinstry agreed with this statement, but stuck to his tale of having left her alive.

No evidence was produced to disprove his story, and it seemed improbable that a murderer would have called attention to himself by turning in the handbag to the police. The jury found him not guilty.

Peggy Richards has paid the price for taking strange men to dark places where they will not be disturbed. Prostitutes like Peggy, who purvey sex standing up against walls, are no less at risk than the women who work in seedy flats in the West End. Vice in London seems more prolific than ever in the blackout.

Black Magic Suspected in Murder of Nassau Millionaire

Nassau police pull Gallic playboy Alfred de Marigny on suspicion of murder

THE DUKE OF WINDSOR'S bomb-free sinecure as Governor of the Bahamas has been troubled by a murder, and HRH has dirtied his fingers trying to help solve it.

Millionaire Sir Harry Oakes was found dead in bed on July 8. White feathers all over the place coupled with an unsuccessful attempt to burn the body suggested at first that this was a native killing with "obeah" (black magic) overtones, carried out in the course of a robbery.

But Sir Harry had been killed by a blow to the head while he was facing downward, and blood had trickled from behind his ear to his cheek. Yet the body was found lying on its back, and the blood couldn't have run uphill! Native robbers seemed unlikely to have gone to the trouble of moving the body back to the bed.

The Duke called in two Miami detectives, who concluded that Sir Harry's French son-in-law, playboy yachtsman and chicken farmer Comte Alfred de Marigny, was responsible. They found one of his fingerprints on a screen near the bed, and the Comte was arrested and put on trial.

Alas, the Duke's detectives

Comte Alfred de Marigny, "undesirable alien" in the Bahamas

were incompetent. Marigny's was one among a multitude of fingerprints found in the room, yet all the others had been cleaned-off without being examined! And Marigny's dinner guests gave their host a pretty good alibi for the night. Not surprisingly, The Comte was acquitted.

Strange rumours are circulating in Nassau: that Sir Harry was seen during the night being driven to the harbour by his friend Harold Christie, who discovered the body; that Christie, Oakes and the Duke of Windsor have shared mysterious business deals.

But His Excellency the Governor, wanting his own way as ever, has used his powers with petty vindictiveness, and deported Alfred de Marigny as "an undesirable alien". What, we wonder, is our ex-King covering up?

Son Blows Up Father in Wheelchair with Mine

ARCHIBALD BROWN was a tyrant. His treatment of his wife niggled his 19-year-old son, Eric, but neither the lad nor his older brother could stand up to the bullying bank clerk.

Mr Brown's conduct was not made sweeter by paralysis of the spine, a disability which ulti-mately confined him to a wheelchair. On July 23, Nurse Mitchell was out with her patient near his home in Rayleigh, England, when Mr Brown demanded a cigarette. As she walked around the chair after lighting it for him, she was suddenly thrown to the ground by a mighty explosion. The wheelchair and Mr Brown were blown to bits.

Eric, it transpired, had got hold of a Hawkins Grenade Mine, capable of destroying a tank, and booby-trapped the wheelchair with it!

A court in Chelmsford this November learned that his sole motive was to ease his mother's life. He has been found guilty but insane.

LONDON'S CHANGING GANGLAND

The war has brought changes to London's gangscape. Dominant feature of the pre-war years was the struggle between the Sabini brothers and a breakaway Yiddisher mob for control of the racecourse protection racket. One savage open battle under the noses of police, at Lewes racecourse in 1936, led to multiple arrests which weakened both gangs, but in no way diminished their hostility.

In 1941 the Italians and the Jews fought it out in a Soho drinking club, leaving Harry Distleman dead on the floor. To every villains' dismay, the police brought murder charges against Sabini "soldier" Tony Mancini — no connection with Cecil Louis England of Brighton trunk murder fame who used the identical name as his alias — and made them stick. The Appeal Court rejected the argument that no individual can be blamed for death in a general fracas, which has served gangsters well in the past. The Sabinis had to think twice about their habitual violence.

In the end war did what the law couldn't. All but one of the Sabini brothers were mopped up as enemy aliens last year and interned. The sole survivor went to prison. The reign of the Clerkenwell Italians is over.

Over, too, is the stranglehold of French and Quebecois pimps on the vice trade. When Roger Vernon and Pierre Alexandre were jailed for killing pseudo-Quebecois "Emil Allard" (actually Latvian Max Kassell — *see* 1936) they made space for the Maltese Alexandria-born brothel-owner Eugene Messina, who had come to Britain two years previously. Messina moved his brothers in, and they organized the street-walking trade into a most unrewarding business for punters, with all-night sessions prohibited and girls forbidden to allow any one client more than ten minutes in bed before they got back to ply for new trade.

But the Messinas are British enough to be liable for conscription, and melted back to the Mediterranean when war came. Other Maltese ponces, the Vassalo-Mangrion gang from Frith Street, are now trying to take over the "Messina girls" in the brothers' absence.

Heiress Bludgeoned with Onyx Candlestick

WHEN BEAUTIFUL heiress Patricia Lonergan failed to emerge from her bedroom all day on October 24, Captain Peter Elser, her visitor that evening, helped her little son's nursemaid break down the door in the superior apartment on 51st Street, New York.

Patricia lay naked on her bed, battered into insensibility with an onyx-and-brass candlestick, then strangled.

Mario Gabelline, her date of the previous night, was not suspected; neither was Captain Elser. But this was the work of someone who knew her well enough to be admitted to her bedroom.

Patricia's estranged husband Wayne was in Toronto, serving with the RCAF. He came to New York immediately, and spent some time answering police questions. After 84 hours, he broke down and confessed that he was the killer.

He first met Patricia while working as a bus driver at the New York World's Fair of 1939; marrying her after the death of her disapproving father, a German brewer who fled the Europe to avoid the war.

But Wayne was a bisexual delinquent wanting to live the high life. The birth of their son converted Patricia to more of a houseloving homebody. He left her and returned to his native Canada, frequently paying visits to New York.

He goes on trial next year. The courts will assess his claim to suffer from uncontrollable psychopathic personality problems against the District Attorney's stern observation that Patricia was leaving him out of her will.

Native American Soldier Slays Wigwam Woman

THE EXECUTION of half-Indian French-Canadian soldier August Sangret brings to an end the mysterious "Wigwam Murder" of last year.

Two soldiers discovered the body of Joan Pearl Wolfe in a shallow grave on Hankley Common, England in September. She had been battered over the head with a nearby log, and then stabbed with a knife that had a hooked blade.

Joan was a promiscuous young vagrant who hung round the army camp at Godalming. She spent most of last summer making love to Sangret, who constructed wigwam-like huts and shelters for her out of branches and furze. Sangret denied having seen her for some time. But it was known that Joan had found herself to be pregnant and demanded that he marry her.

His curved clasp knife was found secreted in a washroom where he had asked permission to relieve himself while being interrogated. There was blood on some of his clothing. He was hanged at Wandsworth on April 2.

(Left) Joan Wolfe's skull. (Right) A prayer Joan pencilled on a hut where slept with Sangret

Crime King Goes to the Electric Chair

Louis "Lepke" Buchalter, the infamous boss of Murder Inc

LOUIS "LEPKE" BUCHALTER has been electrocuted. The boss of the infamous "Murder Inc" murder squad was convicted in 1941 of ordering the killing of candy-store owner Jacob Rosen, who threatened to expose Buchalter's activities to the District Attorney.

Mindy Weiss and Louis Capone (no relations to Hymie or Al) carried out the actual killing, along with "Pittsburgh Phil" Strauss; they preceded their boss to the chair. Pittsburgh Phil was the most prolific killer in organized crime. Estimates of his murders range from 50+ to 100+. His girlfriend, Evelyn Mittleman, was known as the "Kiss of Death Girl", because of Phil's lethal response to men who made a play for her. But this is the first time that the head of a crime family has paid the law's penalty for ordering a killing.

To the end, Buchalter hoped that threats and blackmail would save him. He suggested to Governor Tom Dewey that he could ensure his victory over Mr Roosevelt in the November presidential elections. This was ironical, as the governor's political career took off from his successful prosecution of mobsters, which put "Lepke" in jail for narcotics dealing, making him liable for new charges when squealer "Kid Twist" Reles broke the "Murder Inc" story. But Republicans ignored hints that President Roosevelt's labour advisor Sidney Hillman is up to his neck in crime.

"Lepke's" final public statement that he has not talked to anyone was intended to secure his family against gangland retribution. While in Leavenworth Prison, Buchalter was astonished to encounter conscientious objectors serving sentences, and made a classic outsider's comment on the immorality of compulsory military conscription: "You mean they put you in here for not killing people?"

> ❝ **YOU MEAN THEY PUT YOU IN HERE FOR NOT KILLING PEOPLE?** ❞
> QUOTE **Louis 'Lepke' Buchalter**

SICILIAN 'MAFIOSI' HEAD NEW YORK MOBS

Buchalter's crime "family", with important labour racketeering interests and its lethal "enforcement" role, now passes to Albert Anastasia, "Lord High Executioner" of the so-called "Murder Inc". All New York's crime families are now under Sicilian leadership. In 1931 "Lucky" Luciano killed and replaced the elderly "Mustache Petes" who were warring for control of the old-style Sicilian Mafia. Luciano's new-style was coloured by experience with the inter-ethnic "Broadway Mob" of rum-runners Joe Adonis, Frank Costello, Meyer Lansky, Bugsy Siegel and Luciano himself. "Dutch" Schultz was a force to be reckoned with and Louis Buchalter had inherited "Little Augie" Orgen's labour rackets. The five "families" now are: Luciano's (with Vito Genovese managing on the outside for him while "Lucky" issues orders from Dannemora prison); Anastasia's; Joe Profaci's; Tommy Lucchese's (formerly Tom Gagliano's); and the slightly maverick but deadly efficient Joe Bonnano's. These men, with Joe Adonis and the relatively non-violent manipulators, Frank Costello and Meyer Lansky, are the all-important bosses whose agreement makes their policies law.

Heroic Ex-Naval Man Dragged to Death

SMASH AND GRAB raiders from south London became murderers when a retired naval commander bravely tried to stop their car.

Thomas Jenkins and Ronald Hedley tried unsuccessfully to rob a jeweller's shop in Birchin Lane in the City. As they rushed their getaway car through the tight right-angle turn into Lombard Street, Commander Ralph Binney tried to halt their progress. They drove ruthlessly over him, and his body was caught on the car bumper and dragged down Gracechurch Street and over London Bridge, to fall off, dead, in Tooley Street.

Hedley has been hanged for this hideous crime, and Jenkins is serving a very long prison sentence.

Improved store security may soon bring an end to "smash and grab" raiding.

Sydney 'Pyjama Girl' Identified after Ten Years

Linda Agostini, the "Pyjama Girl"

AFTER TEN YEARS OF confusion, the Sydney "pyjama girl" case has at last ended with the conviction of Italian waiter Antonio Agostini for manslaughter. In 1934, the body of an attractive young woman in yellow silk pyjamas with a dragon on the back was found in a culvert near Sydney, Australia. Her head had been severely battered, and subsequently she had been shot. Six people identified her as Mrs Anna Coots, missing wife of a local writer. Mrs Coots' mother, however, disagreed.

The body was placed in a metal coffin filled with formaldehyde and stored in the University Pathological Museum. In 1938 a police sergeant saw it, and believed it to be Linda Agostini, an acquaintance he had not seen since 1931. In the same year a forensic investigation by Dr Palmer Benbow proved that the body had at one time been in a shack near Albury. But Dr Benbow did not establish its identity.

Early this year the New South Wales police commissioner re-examined the file, and noted letters from Linda Agostini's mother in England. These described precisely the pyjamas in which the body had been found, and expressed grave suspicion of Linda's husband Antonio.

He was quickly traced to a camp for enemy aliens, and at length confessed to having killed Linda "accidentally" in the course of a quarrel. The jury believed him, despite pathologists' evidence that ship's hairdresser Linda had been battered to death before "the gun went off..." And Agostini has been given six years' hard labour.

Antonio Agostini, the Italian waiter arrested for the murder of his wife

Arrests Made in 'Cleft Chin' Murder

CLEFT-CHINNED hire-car driver George Heath, found dead at Staines, a town on the outskirts of London, on October 11, can rest in peace. His murderers have been caught.

Heath's stolen Ford V8 was spotted parked in Fulham Palace Road, and watching police nabbed the man wearing a US Army officer's uniform who got into it. Under interrogation he admitted to being Private Karl Hulten, AWOL. He said he had been with his girlfriend Georgia Grayson on the night of October 10–11.

"Georgia Grayson" is the stage-name of "exotic" dancer Elizabeth Jones. The 18-year-old stripper cracked under questioning and revealed that she and Hulten (whom she knew as "Ricky") had gone looking for excitement. She believed his claim to be an American gangster, and the two robbed and threatened a schoolgirl on a bicycle before Hulten shot Heath and made off with his car.

US military authorities have waived their right to court-martial Hulten or send him back to America for trial and he will appear at the Old Bailey with Jones in the New Year.

River Lea Sack Murder Cleared Up

THE LUTON SACK MURDER CASE is over. When a naked woman's body was found bagged up in the River Lea, near Luton, England at the end of last year, photographs of the face flashed on cinema screens in the area produced a rash of wrong identifications.

Early this year, a cleaner's tag was noticed on a piece of cloth inside the sack. This led to fireman Horace "Bertie" Manton, who assured police his wife had left him the previous year, and produced letters she had sent.

They contained the characteristic spelling mistake "Hamstead" for "Hampstead"; an error Manton reproduced when given dictation by detectives. He confessed that he had killed his wife in the course of a quarrel that was violent on both sides. Since he also admitted putting his hands around her throat, he was convicted of murder and sentenced to death. But he has been reprieved and now faces life imprisonment .

IN BRIEF

WAYNE LONERGAN *shown below* was given a life sentence for murdering his wife (*see* 1943).

HAROLD DORIAN TREVOR (*see* 1943) hanged for murder of Mrs Greenhill.

Evil Doctor Killed Jewish Refugees from Paris

Dr Marcel Petiot

THE AUTHORITIES in Paris are nearly ready to go to trial with their case against Dr Marcel Petiot. In March last year, police and firemen called to investigate foul smoke and odours from the doctor's house in Rue Lesueur, were appalled to find 27 dismembered and decomposing bodies in the cellar. Petiot explained that these were collaborators killed by the Resistance. The patriotic officials winked at his activities, but suspicion was aroused when the doctor and his family suddenly left Paris. Those who knew of the bodies in Rue Lesueur started to wonder whether Petiot had really been collaborating with the Germans and using his killing chamber on their behalf.

With the Nazi scourge swept out of Paris, Petiot surfaced as "Captain Valery" of the Free French, and claimed that the Gestapo had framed him. The bodies in the cellar, he told the newspaper *Resistance*, were actually German soldiers, of whom he had killed 63 during the course of the war.

But records showed that "Captain Valery" had been a patriotic soldier for a mere six weeks; that Dr Marcel Petiot had a criminal record going back to the War of 1914-18, when he was convicted of black marketeering. In 1928, as Mayor of Villeneuve, he was convicted of drug-trafficking. He was also suspected of murdering a woman patient, but the case was dropped when an important witness died suddenly.

It is now clear that Petiot's appalling scheme was the deception and murder of wealthy Jews trying to escape from occupied France. He offered, for a fee, to smuggle them abroad, and then killed them and stole their valuables. 47 suitcases whose owners thought the doctor was helping them to safety have been found in his possession. And he is believed to have stolen more than £1 million from his victims. If the case is proved, Dr Petiot will go down in history as an evil war profiteer.

Black Marketeers Start Killing Each Other

REUBEN MARTIROSSOFF was known to villains all over Europe as "Russian Robert". On November 1, his body was found covered by a blanket in the back of his small car parked in Chepstow Place, off Notting Hill in west London.

Through informants, police learned that Martirossoff had been telephoned by a Polish friend the night before, who arranged a meeting. From the limited information that the Pole was called Marian and had been a naval officer, police deduced that this must be Polish deserter Marian Grondkowski. When he was traced, Martirossoff's wallet and cigarette lighter were found in his possession.

Grondkowski blamed another Pole, Henry Malinowski. He said the two had met Martirossoff and gone with him to a pub to discuss their black market business. Afterwards, Martirossoff's car wouldn't start, and while the two were pushing it, Malinowski decided to kill and rob him after leaping into the back of the car when the engine turned over. Grondkowski helped him take the car and corpse to Chepstow Place.

Malinowski confirmed this story, except that he said Grondkowski was the killer. Both men have been found guilty of the murder and sentenced to death.

Police believe these two are also responsible for killing black marketeering taxi driver Frank "the Duke" Everitt, whose body was found in similar circumstances on Lambeth Bridge, and whose taxi was also abandoned in Notting Hill. It is hoped the opportunistic nature of Martirossoff's murder means it will not find imitators. Otherwise, rationing bodes ill for the murder rate in the capital.

Charged with Rape-Murder of WAAF

LEADING AIRCRAFTSMAN Arthur Heys did not return to RAF Beccles with fellow airmen after a dance. Instead he turned up at the women's quarters, where the duty corporal redirected him to his own billet.

On the way he ran into 27-year-old radio operator Winifred Evans. Her body was found in a ditch in the morning. She had been raped and suffocated.

Heys was identified by the duty corporal at a parade, and has not improved his chances of acquittal by smuggling a forged, anonymous letter to the police claiming that the writer, and not Heys, committed the crime. The writing has been identified as Heys's, and the letter contains details unknown to anyone but the police or the murderer himself.

'A Witch Shall Not Live!'

SEVENTY-FOUR-YEAR-OLD farm labourer Charles Walton lived with his niece in the village of Lower Quinton, near Stratford-on-Avon, England.

This is idyllic and typically English rural countryside, yet it is part of the country where witches are believed to meet at the Rollright Stones on Midsummer's Eve. According to ancient lore, a band of soldiers were turned into the stones after killing an old hag suspected of putting the "evil eye" on livestock.

So it's not surprising that Charlie Walton had a rather strange local reputation, and that his rather solid bank balance (apparently accumulated from saving his labourer's wages) has been attributed to fees charged for magical consultations.

White magic, you might think, but might villagers have asked Charlie to curse their enemies? There are those prepared to swear that he was an evil warlock, but nobody expected to find him ritually murdered.

Walton failed to come home for tea at his usual time on Valentine's Day. His niece went to see farmer Albert Potter, for whom the old man worked. She feared that he might have fallen and hurt himself.

Mr Potter had seen Walton trimming hedges on Meon Hill during the afternoon. There was nothing unusual about his peaceful afternoon's labour along the hillside. Hearing Miss Walton's news, he took an electric torch and went to search for him.

Charles Walton lay in a ditch. His throat had been slashed through with his own sickle. A cross had been carved on his chest, and a pitchfork had been thrust right through his neck and six inches into the ground. The killing bore all the hallmarks of an attempt to exorcise a witch and put an end to Charlie's supernatural powers.

Superintendent Robert Fabian of Scotland Yard could get no other explanation from villagers. After a very full investigation, "Fabian of the Yard" is prepared to leave it at that. Privately, however, he is sure that the trappings of superstition surrounding the death are meant to throw the police off the scent and conceal the true motive for the killing. Like most of the villagers, he believes that the old man was murdered by someone to whom he had lent money from his savings and who was unable to repay the debt.

Privately, for there is not enough evidence to bring charges. It is observed that Albert Potter's farm has been doing badly and he needed capital assistance, and that he found the body remarkably promptly in the dark, and that his accounts of seeing Walton at work during the day are inconsistent.

So who *did* exorcise the witch of Lower Quinton?

Birthday Party Ends in Tragedy for Family

THE TRATSART FAMILY'S night out in Lyons Corner House on Oxford Street in the heart of London's west end was sadly broken up when 19-year-old Jack, whose birthday they were celebrating, gave way to profound depression.

Convinced that nobody loved him, he drew a pistol and started shooting. Diners dived under tables, and when Jack was arrested, his father and sister were dead, and the gun had vanished. Jack refused to say what he had done with it, and only after prolonged searching was it found, in a hanging light bowl, where he had successfully thrown it.

The young man is clearly disturbed, and has been confined to Broadmoor at His Majesty's pleasure.

IN BRIEF

KARL HULTEN and **ELIZABETH JONES** (*see* 1944) convicted of murdering George Heath. Hulten hanged; Jones reprieved and given a life sentence. Hulten is the only US serviceman to have been released to British civil authorities for trial on a capital offence during the war. He could legally have been tried by US court martial.

Notice of Karl Hulten's execution posted at Pentonville Prison, London

Sadistic Killer Inflicts Appalling Injuries on Women

Neville Clevely Heath, handsome con-man and sadistic killer of Margery Gardner

NEVILLE GEORGE CLEVELY HEATH was handsome and charming: a perfect escort for ladies. His long record of petty criminality included housebreaking and jewellery theft. He habitually passed bad cheques and used false identities. During the war he claimed ranks and decorations to which he was not entitled, yet was so good a flying instructor that the South African Air Force continued to use his services, even when they knew he was not, as he claimed, "Lt Col Armstrong".

After his demob he led a raffish life in London, and met "Ocelot Margie" at the Panama Club in Knightsbridge. The two seemed perfectly suited, as she was a masochist and he had sadistic inclinations. They enjoyed at least one date on which the binding and beating was satisfactory to both parties.

On July 21, 32-year-old Margery Gardner's body was found in the Pembridge Court Hotel, Notting Hill. She had been tied up and gagged with a scarf. She had been savagely beaten with a riding whip: the lattice pattern of its weave had left clear marks on her body. Her breasts had been bitten till they bled. And some strong instrument – possibly a poker – had been forced into her vagina.

The room had been booked by "Lt Col and Mrs Heath". There was no sign of the colonel. He wrote to the police, however, disclaiming responsibility for the murder, and pretending that he had gone out so that Margery could sleep with another friend.

As "Group Captain Rupert Brooke", Heath turned up in Bournemouth. There he met 21-year-old Doreen Marshall who was convalescing at the Norfolk Hotel. She had tea and dinner with "Group Captain Brooke" on July 3, and then disappeared. On July 8, her strangled and mutilated body was found in Branksome Chine.

As "Brooke", Heath went to the police to make a statement about Miss Marshall. He was immediately recognized as Neville Heath, wanted in connection with Margery Gardner's murder.

At his trial he pleaded insanity. But an extraordinary impulse to do bizarre and wicked things is no defence in law if the defendant knows that what he is doing is wrong. Heath was convicted and hanged in October, going jauntily to the gallows with the springy manner of the habitual charming confidence trickster.

Twenty-one-year-old Doreen Marshall, Heath's second victim

Shady Ladies Come to Sticky End

TWO UNCONNECTED murders of London women this year seem likely to remain unsolved mysteries. Efficient 36-year-old Dorothy Wallis ran an employment agency in High Holborn. Her secretary was shocked when she came in for work at 9.00 am and found Miss Wallis's battered body lying in a pool of blood.

A witness who rang the office shortly before 6.00 pm the night before, heard the telephone answered by a man with an educated voice, who gently put the caller off. And neighbours heard screams around 6.30.

Miss Wallis's diaries contained a clue and a shock. The respectable spinster businesswoman habitually went out alone to bars and picked up strange men for sexual recreation. It seems her sins have caught up with her. But police have little hope of tracing her killer among London's army of discreet promiscuous men.

Margaret Cook, on the other hand, always seemed poised for trouble. The 26-year-old ex-Borstal girl had become an "exotic dancer" and exhibited her charms, shielded only by a g-string, in Carnaby Street's Blue Lagoon Club; Elizabeth Jones (see 1944) had also undressed to music here.

Margaret is known to have been warned that a new boyfriend had a gun. Unfortunately it is not clear who the boyfriend was, or who gave her the warning: only that Margaret dismissed the idea. This was unwise – Margaret was found shot dead in an alley outside the club. There seems no way of tracing her murderer. Although this is being called "the Blue Lagoon murder", one thing the police have ascertained is that it has nothing to do with the club staff or patrons.

Young Maniac Killer Scrawls Plea for Help

WILLIAM HEIRENS (17) knew he had to be stopped from killing women; knew he couldn't stop himself; and scrawled a message in lipstick on the wall of Frances Brown's sitting-room in Chicago: "For heaven's sake catch me before I kill more, I cannot control myself."

That was in October last year. Miss Brown was found in her bathroom with her pyjama top tied around her neck and a long bread-knife thrust below her ear. She was his second victim. His first victim, seven months earlier, was Mrs Josephine Ross whose throat he cut. His third and worst was 6-year-old Suzanne Degnan, who was taken from her home this January, dismembered, and dropped in bags around the sewers.

In June he was caught at last, trying to break into an apartment building.

An obsessive character, who scrupulously washed his victims' bodies after killing them, Heirens had long dressed in women's clothes in the privacy of his bedroom and became fascinated by pictures of top Nazis.

He has been adjudged insane and given three consecutive life sentences with a judicial recommendation that he never be eligible for parole.

> **" FOR HEAVENS SAKE CATCH ME BEFORE I KILL MORE, I CANNOT CONTROL MYSELF. "**
> QUOTE **William Heirens**

Maniac killer William Heirens (left) called to a bench conference in court

---

Condemned Man Hopes as Another Confesses

WALTER GRAHAM ROWLAND (39) who has one conviction for murder on his record already (he was reprieved) has been convicted again of battering 40-year-old Olive Balchin on a Manchester bomb-site.

But while he waits in the condemned cell, another man has confessed to killing Olive. David Ware, a prisoner in Liverpool, swears that he murdered her, and his statement has been rushed to the Home Secretary by Rowland's legal advisors.

Anxious Rowland must now sit and await his adjudication.

IN BRIEF

ARTHUR HEYS (see 1945) hanged for murder of Winifred Evans.

DR MARCEL PETIOT (see 1945) convicted and guillotined for multiple murders of Jewish refugees he pretended to help escape from occupied Paris.

King's Housekeeper Shot by Bigamist Boyfriend

THROUGHOUT THE WAR, exiled King George II of Greece lived quietly in Chester Square, Belgravia, London. This year he employed 41-year-old Elizabeth MacLindon as housekeeper to oversee some renovations.

His Majesty had no idea that he was visiting the scene of a murder when he passed through the house in June. Nor did the King's secretary when he made a cursory inspection the following week. But they were concerned that there was no sign of Miss MacLindon, and informed the police.

Miss MacLindon was discovered, shot dead, in a locked room. An unopened letter from her fiancé, Arthur Boyce, enquired why she did not trouble to answer the telephone.

Boyce was traced to Brighton and turned out to be bigamously married already. He had also shared lodgings with one John Rowland, owner of a .32 Browning automatic. This weapon had been lent to Boyce, and was now missing. But Rowland could produce a spent shell fired from it for comparison with the bullet that killed Miss MacLindon. The same gun fired both.

Boyce claimed he had given Elizabeth the gun for her own protection in the empty house. The jury declined to believe him, and he was hanged on November 1.

Desert Dream Leads to Bugsy Siegel's Slaying

A **FEW YEARS AGO** Bugsy Siegel had a fatal vision. In a two-bit desert town called Las Vegas, boasting a couple of gas stations and a diner, it struck him that desert land is cheap in the legalized-gambling state of Nevada. The mobs already make most of their income from illegal gambling – especially off-course betting on horse races. Siegel's partner, Meyer Lansky, acknowledges that he owes his wealth to gambling. So why not entertain punters openly, suggested Bugsy? The mob staked him $6 million dollars, and he hired construction boss Dell Webb to build a luxurious casino-hotel. When Webb demurred at working with mobsters, Siegel reassured him: "We only kill each other!"

The Flamingo' hotel-casino (named in compliment to Siegel's moll Virginia Hill's "flaming" red hair) has lost money ever since its disastrous opening. And the mob is unforgiving of those who lose them money: especially when, as in Siegel's case, they suspect some additional embezzlement. And so, as the elegantly-clad gangster sat alone in Virginia Hill's plushy Hollywood sitting-room, three .30 rifle bullets tore through his head, fired from outside the house.

Now its grand architect has paid the price, Las Vegas will no doubt revert to being a two-bit desert stop, and nobody will ever again imagine anything so preposterous as a gambling capital in the howling desert.

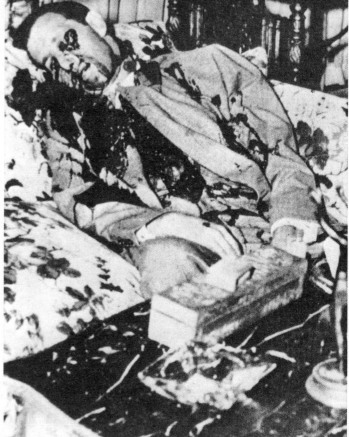

Bugsy Siegel shot dead in Virginia Hill's sumptuous sitting-room

OBITUARY

BENJAMIN 'BUGSY' SIEGEL (1906-1947)

Ben Siegel's fortune as a teenage delinquent was to be best-friends with criminal genius Meyer Lansky. Siegel was just a flashy good-looking hood whose mad ("bughouse") rages encouraged a capacity for savage violence.

Known as a "cowboy" who liked to do his own killing, Siegel was available for enforcement when Lansky teamed up with "Lucky" Luciano. But violent, publicity-loving Bugsy was rather an embarrassment to the new breed of hoodlums, who advocated discretion and a low profile.

So he was sent to California to tie up crime for the syndicate. He was a huge social success in Hollywood, cosseted by stars who thrilled at drinking with a man who might slip out and kill someone. Bugsy squired well-known actresses and adventuresses, finally fixing on Virginia Hill: an unsuccessful actress who bed-hopped around mobsters, and carried money or messages for them.

Naked 'Actress' Cut in Half: Hundreds Confess

THE MURDER of 22-year-old Elizabeth Short, "the Black Dahlia", has inspired more confessions than Los Angeles police can ever remember, and they are still pouring in!

Elizabeth came to California ambitious to be an actress. She had little talent, but secured work as an extra. Her personal gimmick was always to wear black clothes (whence her nickname). Her lifestyle was sleeping with any and every man who might advance her career. She was a heavy drinker, a habit acquired after the death of her husband in the armed forces.

Her naked body was found on a piece of waste ground, crudely mutilated and cut in half at the waist. The letters "BD" were carved on the thigh. Since then, scores of cranks have made worthless confessions to police.

The one correspondent the police want to hear more from sent letters cut out of newspapers, reading "Here are the Black Dahlia's belongings. Letter to follow." Enclosed were Elizabeth's social security card, birth certificate, and address book – with one page missing.

But the promised letter has not come, and the murder remains a mystery.

Two Reprieved in Chalk-Pit Murder

FORMER NEW SOUTH WALES Minister of Justice Thomas Ley fled Australian corruption charges in the 1920s. He settled in London with his mistress, good-natured Mrs Maggie Brook.

But paranoid jealousy possessed Ley as he approached 60. Last year he formed the delusion that bartender John Mudie enjoyed Mrs Brook's favours. In November he hired car-rental manager John Buckingham to abduct Mudie to Ley's house in Knightsbridge, where Ley and a builder called Smith beat and strangled Mudie, dumping his body in a chalkpit near Woldingham.

At their trial this year, Buckingham (who turned King's

Thomas Ley

Evidence) and Smith admitted bringing Mudie to the house and tying him up, but swore he was still alive when they left separately. Ley pompously professed ignorance of the whole thing, and bribed a petty criminal to appear with a preposterous story of having broken into the house to rob it, and tentatively pulled at the bonds of the still-living Mudie in such a way that it just might have strangled him!

Ley and Smith were both condemned to death. But as Ley has been found quite mad and transferred to Broadmoor, Smith, too, has been reprieved.

One Murder: Two Doctors' Suicides

FIFTY-SEVEN-YEAR-OLD Dr Robert Clements of England, killed himself after his fourth wife died. Not from grief at his bereavement, but because he could not face enquiry into whether he killed her. And his previous three!

Dr Clements normally married well and inherited largely when widowed. It happened again this year, when Mrs Clements died of what was diagnosed as mycloid leukemia. The doctor made the diagnosis and suggested it to an inexperienced young colleague, Dr James Houston, who willingly signed the death certificate.

But suspicious tongues wagged; the corpse's eyes were noted to have pin-point pupils; an autopsy showed she died of morphine poisoning.

So did Dr Clements, anticipating his arrest and trial for murder. And so, alas, did young Dr Houston, horrified at his own error.

Actress Pushed Out of Porthole at Sea

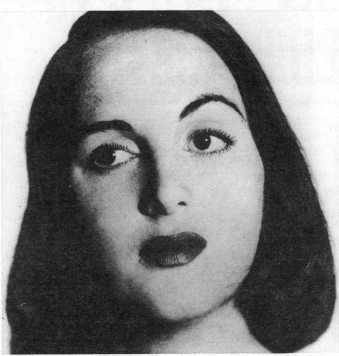

Gay Gibson: porthole murder victim

SHIPBOARD LOTHARIO James Camb is to be tried for the murder of actress Gay Gibson, missing at sea from the liner *Durban Castle*. The handsome 31-year-old deck steward enjoyed offering his sexual services to good-looking lady passengers, although company rules forbade him to enter their cabins.

At 3.00 am on October 18, the bell in the cabin-stewards' quarters summoned the night steward to Miss Gibson's first-class cabin. When he arrived, Camb half-opened the door and sent him away. In the morning, Miss Gibson was nowhere to be found, though marks on her bunk showed that she could have been strangled there or had some sort of seizure. After a good deal of hopeless lying about not being in the cabin at all, Camb has finally admitted that she died in his presence and that he callously disposed of the body by pushing it through the porthole.

He says she died of a seizure while making love. Police think he killed Miss Gibson while attemping to rape her. A jury will be left to decide the truth, next year.

IN BRIEF

WALTER ROWLAND (*see* 1946) hanged for the murder of Olive Balchin despite David Ware's confession that he killed her.

CHARLES JENKINS (brother of reprieved smash-and-grab killer Thomas Jenkins – *see* 1944), Christopher Geraghty and Thomas Rolt, vicious south London thugs, violently robbed a Charlotte Street jeweller; shot brave motorcyclist father of six, Alex de Antiquis who tried to block their escape. Jenkins and Geraghty hanged; Rolt under-age so imprisoned.

Fingerprinting the Town Traps Child-Killer

POLICE IN Blackburn, England, fingerprinted the whole adult male population of the town after 3-year-old June Anne Devaney was murdered in May. And it worked! They caught the killer.

Little June was taken from her bed in Queen's Park Hospital's children's ward by a man who left stockinged footprints on the polished floor, and a fingerprint on a heavy bottle he moved. Then he took the child out into the grounds where he sexually assaulted her, battered her to death, and left her body to be found.

Police took nearly 47,000 fingerprints in the search for this brute, and the people of Blackburn willingly co-operated. Set no. 46253 yielded the match, and 22-year-old flour-mill worker Peter Griffiths was arrested and charged.

He admitted to silencing the child by smashing her head against the wall when he crept away from the ward, and said: "I hope I get what I deserve."

He did. A jury found him guilty in 20 minutes, and he was hanged in November.

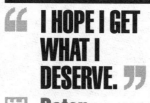

IN BRIEF

JAMES CAMB (*see* 1947) convicted of murder of Gay Gibson at sea. Reprieved because suspension of death penalty under consideration in Parliament. Some observers note that Camb's conviction is itself unsafe, as the evidence is equally compatible with his defence.

Peter Griffiths, child murderer

Chinese Bandits Invent a Crime: Plane-Robbery

IF TRAIN-ROBBERY is dead, maybe plane-robbery will take its place. A gang of Chinese criminals have invented the crime though first results are less than promising.

On July 16, a Catalina passenger flying-boat operated by Cathay Pacific Air Lines, came down in the Pearl River, en route from Macao to Hong Kong. The sole survivor, a passenger named Wong Yu, was taken to hospital, where he told a fellow-patient the story of the plane's last minutes. His listener told the police, who were far from slow to act.

Wong Yu, with three armed accomplices, Chiu Tok, Chiu Choi and Chiu Yeng, joined the passenger flight. Their plan was to force the pilot to fly to a lonely stretch of the Pearl River, where they would rob all the passengers and hold some of them for ransom.

This novel form of piracy was foiled by Scottish co-pilot McDuff, whose reaction to the armed men springing up was to seize an iron bar and "lay on" them, like his namesake in Shakespeare.

Wong Yu fired his gun at him, but killed the pilot, so that the plane promptly crash-dived into the river.

Neither Mao Tse Tung's Chinese Communists nor Chiang Kai Shek's Kuomintang believe in justice delayed. Wong Yu was executed within a week of confessing to this new crime. Let's hope he has no imitators.

Trade War Among the Vice Lords

THE VICE TRADE is growing more competitive and violent. The deaths this year of 60-year -old Helen "Russian Dora" Freedman in her Long Acre flat and Rachel Fenwick, knifed in her flat opposite Broadwick Street police station, are both being put down to pimps trying to enforce their dominion over the Soho prostitutes. So was last year's murder of "Black Rita" Barrett in her Rupert Street flat.

It became apparent that there is a prostitution-related gang war going on in London when three women – Marthe Watts, Janine Gilson and Blanche Costaki – stepped off the streets last year to charge five Maltese men – Messrs Vassalo, Borg, Mangrion, Saliba and Sultana – with demanding money with menaces. The five pimps were all convicted, but during the proceedings it became clear that the plaintiffs were acting under pressure from their existing "protectors", Eugene Messina and his brothers, who have returned to England since the war ended and are trying to reassert their control of London vice.

An attempt to quash the evil "white slavers", by bringing charges against eight Soho landlords for living off immoral earnings this year, failed. One woman working from one flat commits no offence, and neither does her landlord. Mr Justice Maude, dismissing the case, gave a strong hint that it is time for Parliament to change the law.

It is not clear whether the moralist of the bench is more interested in criminalizing prostitution, or harassing its greedy suppliers.

Thief Kills Policeman and Escapes Hanging

Thomas's hideout with Mrs Winkless in Stockwell lodgings

`PC Nat Edgar, murder victim

ARMY DESERTER Donald George Thomas is a lucky man. Police-killers are always caught; police-killers never escape the gallows. Police and the courts see to that.

But Thomas, who killed Constable Nat Edgar early this year, timed his conviction to coincide with the temporary suspension of capital punishment this spring, while Parliament debated its abolition. Thomas has been convicted, but lives to tell the tale.

PC Edgar spotted Thomas loitering outside 112 Wades Hill, Southgate in London,England, on February 13. There had been several burglaries in the area, so he questioned the 23-year-old and noted his name and address before arresting him. Whereupon Thomas pulled a Luger pistol and shot him.

Thomas was not to be found at the Enfield address he had given Edgar, but police traced him to Stockwell in south London, where he and his mistress, Mrs Winkless, were lodging with a Mrs Smeed. As officers burst into his room, he reached under the pillow for his gun, but was overpowered before he could reach it. The habitual criminal remarked coolly: "You were lucky. I might as well be hung for a sheep as a lamb."

In the event it is Thomas who has proved lucky. Concealed in his room were 17lbs of ammunition, a rubber cosh, and a book entitled *Shooting to Live with the One-Hand Gun*. It is to be hoped that this lethal young thug is not given any future opportunity to practice its evil and sinister agenda.

Old Lady Beaten, Tied: Put in Trunk to Die

HOUSEBREAKER George Russell has a long record of petty offences. But carelessness in leaving his fingerprints in the dusty house of reclusive widow Mrs Freeman Lee has brought him to the gallows.

Mrs Lee's body was found in her home in Maidenhead, England, at the beginning of June, when the milkman realized that she was not taking in her milk. The old lady was 93, so the house was quickly searched.

In the hall stood a large black trunk, with a woman's shoe beside it. Inside the trunk was Mrs Lee. She had been hit over the head and her hands were tied behind her back. Cause of death was asphyxiation, so she had apparently been bundled into the trunk alive, and died there for lack of air.

The neglected and cobwebby house had been ransacked, and Russell's fingerprints were on a cardboard box. Arrested in St Albans, he denied everything until a scarf of Mrs Lee's was found in his possession, and he was confronted with the fingerprint evidence. Then he broke down, and sobbed: "I was told she had a lot of money by another man. Did I murder this poor woman for something she was supposed to have, and had not? "

Apparently he did. He was hanged for it on December 2.

Police fetching the trunk with the body of 89-year-old Mrs Freeman Lee, to put in the ambulance

Was Haigh Really a Mad Blood Drinker?

ACID-BATH MURDERER John George Haigh asked a curious question after his arrest: "What are the chances of getting out of Broadmoor?" And soon after that, Haigh told of his nightmares filled with blood-dripping crucifixes; of the thirst to drink human blood which led him to kill. He claimed to have tapped each victim's jugular and drawn off a cup of blood before dissolving their bodies in acid.

Haigh was arrested on February 28, as police investigating the disappearance of Mrs Olive Durand-Deacon from Onslow Court Hotel, Kensington, London, lost patience with his evasions over testimony that she was last seen accompanying him to Crawley. And the murderer finally blurted out: "Mrs Durand-Deacon no longer exists. I've destroyed her with acid. You can't prove murder without a body."

He was wrong. The murder was proved and he has hung for it. But it was shocking to discover that this was his sixth such killing for gain.

In 1944 he killed 21-year-old Donald McSwan, shooting the young man in a basement in Gloucester Road, and dissolving his body in acid. The following year he killed McSwan's parents after pretending that Donald (who was on the run evading conscription) wanted to meet them. Then he forged power of attorney over the McSwans' property, and cleaned up a fortune.

He lost it at the dog-track, and in 1947 killed Dr and Mrs Henderson. Their house and car put him in funds again; which, again, he gambled away.

This year he persuaded Mrs Durand-Deacon, that he had a new process for manufacturing artificial finger-nails. She went with him to his workshop in Crawley, and all that police found of her after she had been shot and stirred in a vat of acid, was some fatty scum tipped out on waste ground, her gallstones and her false teeth.

This was enough to convict Haigh. And there is little doubt that in every case he wanted money, and not a cupful of blood!

POINTS OF LAW

Haigh's legal error is an old one. Since murder can only be proved if there is a *corpus delicti* (body of the crime), killers from as long back as Eugene Aram in 1759 have presumed that if their victim's body is missing or unidentifiable, they cannot be charged.

But "corpus" does not mean cadaver to the lawyer. it only means a sufficient "body" or weight of evidence to demonstrate that a crime took place!

And Haigh's remark "I have destroyed her body with acid" proved for a start that the crime of preventing a burial had occurred!

Howard Unruh under arrest after his mad rampage

Ex-GI Kills 13 People in 12 Minutes

THE US ARMY called machine-gunner Howard Unruh a hero, and decorated him for his service at the Battle of the Bulge. A comrade-in-arms, however, found Bible-reading Unruh's diary, which lovingly recorded the killing of every German he had shot.

Demobbed in Camden, New Jersey, Howard became reclusive and paranoid, building a large wooden fence to keep out the view of his neighbours.

On September 9, when pranksters stole his gates, Howard snapped. Dressed in a natty brown suit with a red bow tie, he walked on to the street and killed 13 people in 12 minutes.

Shoemaker John Pilarchik, working in his shop was the first victim. Barber Clark Hoover and the 6-year-old whose hair he was cutting were next. ("I've got something for you, Clarkie," was Unruh's remark to this childhood acquaintance.)

Unruh's insurance salesman was killed as he stepped from a drugstore saying, "Hallo, Howard". The Cohen family were pursued through their home where Mr Cohen, his wife and mother were killed. Strangers on the street were shot down, until shoppers huddled on floors indoors.

Back in his own house, Unruh said conversationally to a pressman on the telephone, "Well, they haven't done anything to me yet. But I am doing plenty to them."

Tear gas forced him out with his hands up to surrender to police. But there was a flash of anger when they asked if he was mad: "I'm no psycho! I have a good mind!" he snapped. But he was sent straight to New Jersey State Mental Hospital from which he is highly unlikely ever to emerge.

Lovers Prey on Lonely-Heart Widows and Spinsters

TWENTY-STONE Martha Beck met seedy Latin lover Raymond Fernandez through a Lonely Hearts Club in 1947. She fell for him, in his ill-fitting black wig, and he reciprocated her ungainly passion. Nor was Martha dismayed when Raymond revealed that he made his living by swindling and stealing from lonely widows he met through commercial introduction agencies. Martha went into the business with him, passing herself off as his sister.

And she added a new crime to the dodge of seduction and bigamous marriage. Murder.

Murder when Martha got jealous of her lover-boy tucked up in

Martha Beck (right) and Raymond Fernadez (middle) at a bench conference in court

> ## "YOU ARE A DOUBLE-CROSSING TWO-TIMING SKUNK."
> **Martha Beck**
> QUOTE

bed with younger, better-looking, thinner women.

In Michigan this January, Martha dosed 28-year-old Mrs Delphine Dowling with sleeping pills, and then Raymond shot her in the head. Delphine's 2-year-old daughter Rainelle was an additional problem. They bought her a dog when she cried for her mother. Then Martha drowned her in the bath.

When neighbours reported the

Dowlings' disappearance, police quickly spotted a grave-sized patch of wet cement in the basement, which yielded the missing couple. Michigan has abolished capital punishment for murder, so Beck and Fernandez cheerfully boasted about their many slayings.

But they certainly did not anticipate being extradited to New York to face trial for the murder of Alice Fay.

They have been convicted and

sentenced to death, and the love-letters exchanged between their cells have grown sour. Martha heard that Raymond has been joking about her size and blaming her for his fate, and she has written to him: "You are a double-crossing two-timing skunk."

Naughty Raymond was booked to accompany his fat vamp to the electric chair on August 20, but the pair have won a stay of execution pending their appeals.

Young Advertising Executive Kills Wife's Parents

TO ALL APPEARANCES, Danny Raven is a nice young Jewish boy, with a good job, and a sweet wife and baby. But on October 10 he had an altercation with his parents-in-law after the family went

to see Danny's wife and newborn son in the nursing-home at Muswell Hill, London.

When police visited Danny to tell him his parents-in-law had been found battered to death with a television aerial, they were surprised to find the young man spick and span in clean clothes late at night. On further investigation they found his half-burned bloodstained suit and shoes in the boiler. It didn't take much to guess why.

Twenty-three-year-old Danny is now in prison awaiting trial for the murder of Leopold and Esther Goodman.

Coarse Lesbian Cross-Dresser Batters Tramp-Woman to Death

THE MOST obvious trouble with "Bill" Allen was that she was still really Margaret. Dressing in men's clothes and swilling pints of beer in pubs didn't change this, and her one woman friend

Mrs Annie Cook broke off with her when "Bill" proposed a sexual relationship.

None of which explains why Margaret Allen killed bag-woman Mrs Nancy Chadwick, who came begging at her door in August last year. "I was in a funny mood," she told police when charged. "I just happened to look round and saw a hammer in the kitchen. On the spur of the moment I hit her."

And up to the point when she was hanged in January, she gave no further explanation of this motiveless murder. It will remain a gallows' mystery for all time.

Pieces of Black Marketeer Washed up in Essex

Donald Hume, spiv acquitted of murdering Stanley Setty

BRIAN DONALD HUME has been acquitted in a London court of murdering fellow racketeer, Stanley Setty. But, as accessory after the fact he goes to Dartmoor for 12 years.

Levantine "car dealer" Setty's headless, legless torso was washed up on Tillingham marshes in October last year. A stab wound in the chest showed how he died. Fingerprints showed who he was.

Trained pilot Hume was one of Setty's known associates, handling stolen cars. Police found that Hume had hired a light aircraft on October 5 and boarded it with two parcels. The shady crook claimed that the parcels contained parts of a printing press for counterfeiting ration books.

He now says that three powerful gangsters, known to him only as "Greenie", "Mac" and "the Boy", forced him to dump the parcels at sea for them. He concedes that a "gurgling noise" from one of them suggested that he was perhaps disposing of a dismembered Stanley Setty, whose disappearance was the subject of intense speculation in the underworld.

The jury at Hume's trial in January could not agree. With a new jury empanelled, the judge ordered a verdict of Not Guilty to the murder charge, and accepted Hume's plea of Guilty to the accessory charge.

It is understood that, the police are not making any particular efforts to trace "Greenie", "Mac" or "the Boy", who are more likely to be the creation of Hume's fertile imagination than genuine denizens of his slimy spiv world.

Van Driver Makes Impossible Confession to Murder

Timothy John Evans, brought to Paddington from Wales by detectives

WELSH POLICE In Merthyr Tydfil were astonished when 24-year-old Timothy John Evans turned up unannounced, and confessed to "disposing of" his wife Beryl down the manhole outside his London home, 10 Rillington Place.

Evans is a tiny man, and the solid iron manhole cover required a special key and three strong policemen to raise it! Needless to say, no trace of Beryl was evident in the shaft. But a search of the couple's flat in the end-of-terrace house yielded the gruesome discovery of Beryl and her baby daughter, both of whom had been strangled and their bodies left in the small washhouse at the rear. Confronted with his own tie, used to murder baby Geraldine, Evans confessed.

By the time Evans came to trial this February, he had withdrawn his full confession, and, to the acute embarrassment of his legal advisers, made an unwarranted attack on his downstairs neighbour, Mr John Christie, accusing him of killing Beryl in the course of performing an illegal abortion.

Christie, a temporary special policeman during the second World War, and a World War I veteran whose voice carries permanent damage from mustard gas, made an excellent impression on the court. His evident unwillingness to expose his unhappy young neighbour's mendacity was particularly affecting. As a simple warehouse clerk, Christie would, of course, have no capability of performing an illegal operation, and Evans's desperate lies were an outrageous injustice to a middle-aged man in poor health who has served his country well.

They did not save the educationally backward van-driver, who has been hanged for the murder of his nearest and dearest.

$3 Million Robbery at Brink's in Chicago

QUIS CUSTODET IPSOS CUSTODES? Usually means "Who'll police the cops?" But now it might mean "Who'll protect armed guards?" For Brink's, the firm whose armed men and armoured cars keep your valuables safe, has just lost nearly three million of its Chicago customers' money, cheques and securities to as cheeky and artful a band of thieves as ever forced open a window.

The job was well planned. The thieves wore Brink's uniforms, and aroused no suspicion entering and leaving. On January 17, they let themselves in by the stairwell entry; made their way up to the second floor, along the hallway, through the counting room, across the safety room, through two sets of cage doors, and into the vault. They had keys to all the doors, and just walked silently in on their thick-soled footware!

The five vault keepers were mighty surprised when what looked like half a dozen colleagues in Hallowe'en masks held them up. The gang was away within 15 minutes. And all the vault's contents went with them.

Baffled Brink's employee Thomas Lloyd (in shirtsleeves) shows a detective the strongroom where theives held him

The biggest robbery ever, it was carefully rehearsed. At some point the gang surveyed every lock in the place and got their own keys made. And the Good Lord only knows who will be up to catching crooks who've fooled the world's biggest and most highly respected private security firm!

Policeman Kills Girlfriend — Then Drives Over Body

GLASGOW Police Officer James Robertson is a bad liar. Come to that, he's a pretty poor murderer, too! When his car was found abandoned in a side street, and proved to be the one that had mangled the body of Mrs Catherine McCluskey in Prospecthill Road on July 27, Robertson said it had been stolen. Shortly after this he changed his statement, claiming that he'd found the vehicle again after it was stolen and just used it without reporting the theft

He claimed that on the night of Mrs McCluskey's death he'd stayed off duty between 11.00 pm and 1.00 am working on his car which was giving trouble. Yet he also said he'd logged the death of a woman in a hit-and-run accident at 12.50.

Robertson changed his story again, when faced with pathologists' proof that:

Mrs McCluskey had not been hit by any car she had been laid out with a blow to the back of the head then somebody had driven figure-of-eight patterns over her.

Now Robertson admitted that he knew Mrs McCluskey and was the father of her second child. He admitted seeing her on Prospecthill Road, but refused to give her a lift as he was on duty. Then he changed his mind, backed up and accidentally trapped her under the car. He had thereupon driven backwards and forwards to disengage the encumbrance!

Cross-examination by the prosecution made short work of that silly pack of lies. Robertson will hang on December 16.

Prostitute Tortures and Kills Elderly Punter

RED-HEADED Jean Lee (32) is an Australian call-girl. Her business boomed during the war, but then trade went slack. So Jean teamed up with Robert Clayton and Norman Andrews in the badger game. Trouserless punters would be "discovered" by her outraged "husband" (Clayton), who would demand cash compensation. Andrews would join him to beat up any who refused to pay up.

Seventy-two-year-old book-maker William Kent met the gang in a hotel, and went to his room where they tried to pick his pocket while he was drunk. But he held on firmly to his cash. So they tied him up, ripped his pocket out, and slashed him with a broken bottle when they found nothing worth stealing.

Mr Kent died of his injuries. Jean and her goons were arrested in a Sydney night club, where they had gone to celebrate their crime! The final celebration for this unsavoury trio will be from the end of three ropes!

IN BRIEF

DANNY RAVEN executed for the murder of his parents-in-law (*see* 1949).

Vice Girls Try to Discredit Ace Reporter

LAST YEAR, *The People* newspaper exposed five Maltese brothers Alfredo, Attilio, Carmelo, Eugene and Salvatore Messina as vice lords of Mayfair. They came to London in the pre-war years, after disputes among pimps culminating in the murder of "Red Max" Kassell (*see* 1931) made room in Soho for new faces. The Messinas left again to avoid the war. Now they are back in Mayfair, with a stable of French girls.

Reporter Duncan Webb's series of exposés calls for their deportation. Mr Webb has given his readers details of the addresses in Shepherd Market where the Messina girls are alleged to practise their profession.

His dossiers on this crime empire also have an avid reader-

ship at Scotland Yard. Superintendent Mahon of the Vice Squad, in particular, hopes they will yield some useful information. The same three women's names crop up consistently in these stories, however, leading to doubt as to how extensive the Messinas "empire" really is.

Two Messina girls complained this year that Webb had demanded money with menaces from them. As Mr Webb does not have an entirely clean record (see Box), police investigated these allegations. Other journalists who had been present throughout his encounter with Marthe Watts and Blanche Costaki supported his version of events, and it soon became clear that the prostitutes were trying to discredit the reporter.

Mayfair pimp Carmelo Messina

HOIST WITH HIS OWN PETARD!

Duncan Webb is featured as the ace crime reporter whose daring exposés of the Messinas have put his life in danger. As a stunt, he even has bullet-proof glass around his desk.

Readers with a prurient interest in Mr Webb's pet subject must be disappointed by his repeated insistence that he cannot say what goes on in harlots' flats, as "this is a family newspaper". He knows more than his oft-quoted phrase after receiving a prostitute's unequivocal invitation – "I made an excuse and left" – suggests.

In 1946, Mr Webb was convicted of common assault. On this occasion, he picked up prostitute Jean Crews in Regent Street and went to her flat where, in the words of the police report, "he had connections with her" for £2. Afterwards he refused to leave, and followed her out on the street when she and her sister went to telephone for help. A passer-by who lent them change was shown Mr Webb's press card, which, Webb suggested, was police ID. The unfortunate man was hit by the angry journalist for refusing to submit to "arrest".

The magistrate, however, refused to interpret Webb's act as the offence of impersonating a policeman.

Murderous English Robbers Give Themselves Away

SEVENTY-NINE-YEAR-OLD Frederick "Gossy" Gosling was believed to keep £1,000 in his little home above the shop in Clay Corner, Surrey. Brothers Joseph and Fred Brown, broke in and tried to rob him on January 11.

The following day, two men broke in again. This time Mr Gosling was tied up and gagged, and bruising over his face showed he had been beaten to make him talk. Mr Gosling choked to death on his gag. The robbers killed him for a mere £60 loot.

In a couple of days the police picked up the Browns, but quickly freed Frederick and charged third man, Edward Smith as Joe Brown's accomplice. On hearing that Gossy had choked to death, Smith said defensively, "If I wanted

to hurt him I could have hit him or something."

Since someone had done just that, the remark hanged Smith and Brown.

> **IF I'D WANTED TO HURT HIM I COULD HAVE HIT HIM OR SOMETHING.**
> QUOTE
> **Edward Smith**

Collaborateuse Stands Trial for Shooting Lover

AS A TEENAGER in occupied France, Pauline Dubuisson disgusted neighbours by her affair with a Wehrmacht colonel. After the war she suffered the public humiliation awarded *les maitresses des Boches*; then went to Lille University, where she had many liaisons, and kept a secret journal describing her lovers' sexual quirks.

Handsome student Felix Bailly realized his mistake in time, and broke off an engagement to her, proposing to marry a Paris girl. Pauline brooded for 18 months; then, in March, bought a gun and uttered threats. Bailly hired bodyguards, but she got past them into his flat and shot him. Then she tried to gas herself. She is still in a serious condition and will not face trial until November. Most inhabitants of the land of love feel no great affection for this *traitresse sexuelle*.

Pretentious Would-be Poet Planned Perfect Murder

HERBERT LEONARD MILLS, a 19-year-old of Nottingham, England, telephoned the *News of the World* on August 9 to say he had found a body. He told them, too, that his reaction on finding 48-year-old housewife Mabel Tattersal strangled in Sherwood Vale was to read a poem. Finally he asked the paper to pay him for a literary composition, which turned out to be a confession. He decided to commit a perfect murder.

He had met Emily in a cinema, flattered her by his "educated" attentions, and arranged a meeting. Then he strangled her. He goes to the gallows in December.

Anthony D'Anna (centre) denies leading the Detroit Mafia to Senator Estes Kefauver (rear view)

Senate Crime Committee Hears Gangsters Take the Fifth

TOP HOODS don't like coonskin-capped Senator Estes Kefauver (Dem., Tennessee). One after another, Mafia bosses shambled into the Capitol for the Senate Special Committee Investigating Crime, and Kefauver has grilled 600 witnesses over the last few months. Not that the Mafiosi said much, except that they couldn't say anything because it might tend to incriminate them, (or "discriminate against me," as Jake "Greasy Thumb" Guzick, Al Capone's old business manager mumbled.) High points of the testimony: Gangsters' moll, glamorous Virginia "Flamingo" Hill, relict of the late Ben Siegel, showing flaming temper as well as hair, when she loosed an uppercut at presswoman Marjorie Farnsworth, and screamed at other journalists, "You goddam bastards! I hope an atom bomb falls on all of you!"

"Prime Minister" of the underworld, Frank Costello, was so wary of the hearings revealing his appearance to all and sundry that only his tense hands were visible on the nation's television screens.

Gambler Willie Moretti, chattered with amiable eccentricity, until colleagues feared his mind was going. And not long after he left Washington with the Committee's praise for his co-operation glowing in his breast, a couple of bullets from a friend's gun occupied the same place, and Willie is no more.

> ## "YOU GODDAM BASTARDS. I HOPE AN ATOM BOMB FALLS ON ALL OF YOU. "
> ### QUOTE Virginia Hill

IN BRIEF

Raymond Fernandez and Martha Beck electrocuted for the Lonely-hearts murders (*see* 1949). Fernandez went to the chair first, as the weaker partner.

CASE ON OUR CONSCIENCE David John Ware – who made and withdrew a confession to killing Olive Balchin in 1947 – has been convicted of killing another woman in Bristol, admitting "I keep having an urge to hit women on the head." Ware has been found Guilty but insane. Problem for the authorities is: Walter Rowland was hanged for Olive Balchin's murder – Did he do it?

Child-Killer Escapes Broadmoor, Strikes Again

THE ENGLISH public's fears were realized this March, when murderer John Straffen escaped from Broadmoor Criminal Lunatic Asylum and, in a bare three hours of freedom, slew another little girl.

Twenty-two-year-old Straffen was committed to Broadmoor last year after killing two small girls near Bath. He said he did it to annoy the police. As he is a known child-molester, it is more likely that he committed his crimes from perverse sexual desire. Doctors who had found him mentally defective in 1947 testified to his continuing state of near-imbecility. As a result, he was found unfit to plead, since he would not be able to understand the circumstances and procedure of a trial.

His escape was a consequence of extraordinarily lax security at Broadmoor. Straffen was left sweeping a yard beside an unlocked gate while guards attended to the exercise of other prisoners. Staff have complained for many years that the institution is dangerously undermanned.

Public horror at this incident was such that Straffen was put on trial again, with Broadmoor doctors testifying that their treatment had improved his understanding

John Straffen taken by police to Reading Magistrates's Court, charged with murdering 5-year-old Linda Bowyer

to the extent that he could now follow the case in court. Straffen was convicted and sentenced to death.

Loathsome though this defective is, we must concur with the Home Secretary's view that it would be uncivilized to hang a man whose mental grasp is so feeble. Our relief at his reprieve is only tempered by anxiety that there be no further failure in keeping this creature immured and away from the public until the end of his natural life.

Wastrel Kills Parents: Tips them off Cornish Cliff

YOUNG MILES GIFFORD was an idle and irresponsible worry to his Cornish solicitor father. Psychiatric treatment when Miles was 14 suggested that he was responding badly to his father's attempts to instill discipline into him. Since serving in the Merchant Navy during the War, Gifford junior has done nothing but scrounge off his parents.

In August this year 27-year-old Miles met 19-year-old Gabriel Vallance in Chelsea and decided to marry her. When his father pointed out that he could not marry until he could support himself, Miles wrote to Gabriel, "Short of doing him in, I see no future in the world at all."

On November 7, Miles battered his parents to death in their home near St Austell, probably killing his mother only because he saw no alternative after having killed his father. He took the bodies in a wheelbarrow to nearby cliffs and dumped them into the sea. Then, purloining some of his mother's jewellery, he drove his father's car to London and met up with Gabriel. She thought he was joking when he said he had killed his parents, and happily went with him to the cinema and on to the Prospect of Whitby pub at Wapping.

But as a taxi returned them to Gabriel's Tite Street home, police cars surrounded the vehicle. Miles was arrested and charged immediately with stealing his father's car; subsequently with murder.

He goes on trial in the New Year, and it seems unlikely that a bucolic and conservative Cornish jury will pay much attention to medical evidence that this young man was disturbed and ruined at an early age by his stiff-necked upper-class father's unbending severity.

SHORT OF DOING HIM IN, I SEE NO FUTURE IN THE WORLD AT ALL.

QUOTE

Miles Gifford

English Family Massacred on French Camping Holiday

French officials remove the bodies of Sir Jack Drummond and his family

SIXTY-ONE-YEAR-OLD Sir Jack Drummond (perhaps Britain's leading biochemist), his pretty wife Ann (46) and their 11-year-old daughter Elizabeth have all been murdered at a farm near Lurs in Provence where they had pitched a tent and were preparing to camp for the night.

Sir Jack and Lady Drummond were both shot near the tent while half-changed into their pyjamas. Elizabeth had been chased to a river bank, and clubbed to death. The bodies were found before dawn by 33-year-old Gustave Dominici, son of the owner of La Grande Terre farm. But Gustave did not report his find until railway workers had also found the dead family and informed police. Gustave claims to have heard shots at about 1.00 am, and says he was too frightened to investigate. He also admits that Elizabeth was still alive when he stumbled over her body.

Grave suspicion rests upon him, but it has only been possible to charge him with failing to assist a dying person. French police are still investigating.

Murderous Hitch-Hiker Goes to Gas Chamber

DROOPING-EYED William Cook, 35, has been executed in San Quentin's gas chamber, thus ridding the roads of the southwestern USA of a lethal menace.

Cook pulled a gun on a motorist from whom he was hitching a lift to Joplin, Missouri, at the end of 1950, and stole his car. Abandoning the vehicle near the Texas/New Mexico border, he hitched another ride with the Mosser family. They spent their New Year taking him aimlessly around New Mexico and Texas, until he shot them all – two adults, three children and a dog – near Wichita Falls, and drove them across Oklahoma to Joplin where he dumped them down a mineshaft. Two days later he was seen in the Mossers' bloodstained, bullet-riddled car and a national search finally traced him via Arizona and California to Mexico. In transit he had also killed motorist Robert Dewey, near Yuma. And it is for this last murder that he has now been executed.

" **I'M GONNA LIVE BY THE GUN AND ROAM.** "
William Cook

Judge's Daughter Repeatedly Stabbed in Face

THIRTY-SEVEN separate stab-wounds on the face and neck of 19-year-old Patricia Curran left the Northern Ireland judge's daughter looking as though someone had discharged a shotgun in her face.

Patricia was found at White Abbey, near Belfast, after her mother had raised the alarm when she did not return from her classes at Queen's University as usual on November 12. The girl was unconscious and died soon after. Some of her torn clothes were removed, yet left neatly near the body. Chief Superintendent Capstick concluded that Patricia knew her assailant who, it seems, attempted to rape her. A small girl reported seeing Patricia walking home with a man, and following her description, the entire personnel of Edenmore RAF Station were interviewed.

Ian Hay Gordon, 21, who knew Patricia, aroused suspicion because of a black eye, which he explained as the result of "horseplay" in the barracks.

Judge Curran remarked that Gordon was obsessed with violence and had stated that the 37 wounds were unnecessary: four would have done the job.

Gordon has now confessed that he stabbed Patricia when she resisted his advances as he walked her home. Police are searching for the murder weapon, which he threw into the sea.

IN BRIEF

Huge Crowd in London Mourn Bentley's Hanging

Derek Bentley, the backward 18-year-old cash boy executed this year

THE EXECUTION of 18-year-old Derek Bentley in January has divided the country. Crowds nearly rioted, and had to be restrained by Derek's brave father. Many see the hanging as judicial murder: an act of frustrated revenge by authorities who cannot kill the real criminal, 16-year-old Christopher Craig. Others feel it was a salutary reaction to youthful violence, and necessary retribution for PC Miles' death.

On November 2 last year the two teenagers were spotted on a Croydon warehouse roof. Police climbed up and arrested Bentley, who was armed with a knife and an evil spiked knuckleduster. Craig, armed with a pistol, shot at the police for about 20 minutes. In the course of this, PC Miles was killed instantaneously by a bullet through the head as he came on to the roof. At that time, Bentley was already securely in the custody of Detective Constable Fairfax.

Craig taunted the police, saying, "Come on, you brave coppers! Think of your wives!" Finally, when he ran out of bullets, he hurled himself off the roof, breaking his pelvis. Bentley was contrastingly quiet and shocked after the death of PC Miles.

South London's climate of fear over "cosh boys" seemed to demand an execution in this outrageous instance of murder. Yet because of the two hoodlums' ages, the one whose finger was on the trigger inevitably lives. And so huge crowds accuse:

Lord Chief Justice Goddard of conducting a biassed trial and failing to urge on the Home Secretary the jury's recommendation to mercy

Home Secretary David Maxwell Fife of crowning his undistinguished political career with the judicial assassination of a feeble-minded lad whose B-film engendered notions of adventure never came close to making him a callous murderer.

Devout French Nun and Prostitute Are Sisters

TWENTY-THREE-YEAR-OLD streetwalker Léone Bouvier, sentenced to life imprisonment at Maine-et-Loire for shooting her lover, was watched through out her trial by her sister Georgette – who is a nun! Georgette's vocation wrecked Léone's hope of acquittal on the ground of their sad family background. (Her father is a violent drunk; her mother mentally disturbed). If Georgette became a model of virtue, why did Léone have to become the promiscuous woman of her village; a prostitute; and finally a murderess?

Probably, in fact, because her plain physique and dull mind led to unfavourable comparisons with Georgette all her life. Coarse coupling under hedges brought a simulation of love, and then for three years garage-hand Emile Clenet told her he really did love her and would marry her. So she spent every Sunday sleeping with him in cheap hotels – becoming pregnant, enduring an abortion at Emile's behest, and losing her job in the process. When Emile refused to help her financially, she had no alternative but prostitution. When he told her he was off to North Africa and never intended to marry her, she shot him dead. And serve him right, we say!

A raz-z-z-z-berry to cruel French justice, which purports to recognize *crime passionnel*, yet lets this unhappy and abused child go to penal servitude! The only word of sympathy for her has come from Georgette's Mother Superior, who calls Léone, rightly, "La Pauvrette" (Poor Little One).

Corpses in Necrophile Christie's Ghastly Kitchen

Reg Christie poses in his graveyard garden

JAMAICAN Beresford Brown had a nasty shock when he tore away a puzzling piece of wallpaper covering an alcove in the ground floor flat he'd just rented at 10 Rillington Place. Concealed in his kitchen were the half-naked corpses of three strangled streetwalkers!

Police started an urgent hunt for the flat's previous occupant, 55-year-old clerk John Reginald Halliday Christie – especially when they found Mrs Christie mouldering under the sitting room floorboards! And the garden yielded the skeletal remains of two more women (the thighbone of one having been incorporated as a strut in the fence!)

Picked up by an alert policeman on Putney Bridge, Christie confessed to killing women by offering them a Friars' Balsam inhalant into which he introduced household gas. When they were dead, he ravished their bodies. For this repulsive lecher, who collected pubic hairs in an old tobacco tin, couldn't function properly with real, living lovers.

Worst of all, Christie admits to murdering his upstairs neighbour Mrs Beryl Evans in 1949; a crime for which her husband, retarded van-driver Timothy John Evans, was hanged (*see* 1950).

Christie has now been hanged himself. But the case of Timothy Evans will have to be reopened to satisfy public concern.

Police recovering the skeletons of Christie's victims Ruth Fuerst and Muriel Eady

London 'Cosh Boys' Fight Ends in Murder

TEENAGERS Fred Chandler and John Beckley were ready for a fight when they jeered at the sharp drape suits worn by "The Plough Boys" – a gang of yobs from Clapham Common. What they didn't expect was that knives would be pulled on them.

The two were chased to Clapham Common North Side, where they flagged down a bus in which Chandler escaped. But Beckley was hauled off the platform, and stabbed to death before the eyes of horrified commuters.

Six youths were identified as participating, but in the end all but one escaped with common assault convictions. On the testimony of one commuter, and one commuter only, 20-year-old John Michael Davies was accused of delivering the fatal blow. He denies this, and states firmly that he does not own and was not carrying a knife.

His denial is supported by his own gang, and even by Fred Chandler. So the Home Secretary has commuted his death sentence. Derek Bentley (see above) has sated the establishment's lust for cosh boys' blood this year.

Lancashire Jury find Housekeeper Guilty of Murder

LOUISA MERRIFIELD, 46-year-old housekeeper-cum-companion of elderly widow Sarah Ricketts, is to hang for poisoning the old lady. Louisa's nasty 70-year-old husband Alfred has been released after the jury could not agree on his guilt.

The Merrifields went to work as resident companions to Mrs Ricketts in March. Within a week Mrs Merrifield told friends that she was being left Mrs Ricketts' house. Within two weeks she called in a doctor to confirm that Mrs Ricketts was mentally fit to write a will. Within three weeks Mrs Ricketts was preparing to sack the Merrifields. Within four weeks, Mrs Ricketts was dead by poisoning.

It was proved in court that a Manchester chemist had sold the poison to the Merrifields. Proved, too, that its acrid taste is effectively disguised by rum, which Mrs Ricketts took as a nightcap. Proved that Mrs Merrifield's handbag contained a spoon, still dirty with a mixture of Rodine and rum.

So this squalid woman, who falsely accused her husband of a liaison with aged invalid Mrs Ricketts, will hang at Strangeways in September.

Lesbian New Zealand Schoolgirls Murder Mother

NEW ZEALAND schoolgirls Pauline Parker and Juliet Hulme (16 and 15) were due to be separated when Dr Hulme, Juliet's father, decided to emigrate to South Africa; partly because of marital difficulties, but partly also to separate Juliet from Pauline – the latter's mother had alerted him to the way the girls bathed, slept and talked sex together obsessively, activities which he regarded as not healthy.

Pauline immediately declared her intention of accompanying her friend and lover, but Mrs Honora Mary Parker flatly forbade her to do so. Whereupon the adolescent lesbians determined to eliminate this obstacle to their furtive passion.

On June 22 the girls went for a walk together in Victoria Park, Christchurch with Mrs Parker. As Pauline and her mother argued, the girl persuaded the older woman to bend down, whereupon she hit her over the head with a brick stuffed in a stocking. Mrs Parker did not die instantly, so first Pauline then Juliet went on and on hitting her until, after 45 separate blows, the unfortunate woman finally expired.

The girls told a cock-and-bull story to police of Mrs Parker's slipping and hitting her head on a brick, against which it "kept bumping and banging" as they tried in vain to help her. The pathologist's report stopped that idea from gaining credence with the police authorities and they were charged with murder.

Their attempt to plead not guilty by reason of insanity collapsed when Pauline (said by psychiatrists to consider herself a genius and above the law) uttered coldly, "I knew it was wrong to murder and I knew at the time I was murdering somebody. You would have to be an absolute moron not to know murder was against the law."

The two teenagers have been found both sane and guilty, and detained at Her Majesty's pleasure.

> **" I KNEW IT WAS WRONG TO MURDER AND I KNEW AT THE TIME I WAS MURDERING SOMEBODY. YOU WOULD HAVE TO BE AN ABSOLUTE MORON NOT TO KNOW MURDER WAS AGAINST THE LAW. "**
>
> QUOTE **Pauline Parker**

Pauline Parker (left) and Juliet Hulme, lesbian schoolgirl murderesses

French Girl Made to 'Sacrifice' Her Child

VILLAGE POSTMASTER'S daughter Denise Labbé had a lot of lovers after she went to work in Paris, and bore an illegitimate daughter. But she was a nice simple girl, and adored little Cathy, whom she placed at her own expense in foster-care and regularly visited. Until she fell in love with St Cyr officer cadet Jacques Algarron.

This Mephistophelean would-be *übermensch* dazzled her with his self-aggrandizing satanical philosophy. He forced her to make love to other men; then plead for his forgiveness. He scratched and bit scars on her back, and got her to parade them at the beach. He openly slept with other women. And he promised they two should be the "exceptional couple"; hinted he would marry her, but on one condition – that she murder her own daughter!

Pressed by his threats and cajolements, Denise tried three times to do as he said. She could not bring herself to drop little Cathy from a high window. She threw her into a canal, but screamed for help in time to have her saved. Finally she drowned the child in a washtub. And the evil Algarron casually says it means nothing to him, now, and he would never marry her!

The two go on trial at Blois next year: Denise facing the death sentence; Algarron an inadequate maximum 20 years' hard labour.

Boston Brink's Robbers Caught after Informer Talks

AFTER FOUR YEARS, the gang that pulled the outstanding Brink's Security Co robbery in Boston (*see* 1950) has been caught. Dishonour among thieves trapped them. Gang member Joseph "Specs" O'Keefe felt he deserved more of the $2.7 million haul than was coming his way, and when he demanded another $63,000 the rest of the gang hired the underworld's top hit-man, Elmer "Trigger" Burke, to murder him. For once Burke failed.

A wild machine-gun chase through Boston streets wounded O'Keefe, but did not kill him. The greedy robber then ran to the law for protection. The great robbery gang turns out to be 11 middle-aged Bostonians, most of whom have only petty theft records. They planned for two years before making the robbery, and then agreed to lie low without spending the money for another six years, letting the heat cool off!

Young Doctor Convicted of Killing His Wife

NEUROSURGEON Sam Sheppard of Bay View Hospital, Cleveland, Ohio, gave a dinner party last June. Before the guests left, Sam fell asleep on the couch, leaving his wife Marilyn to see them all to the door after midnight.

Toward dawn, a neighbour received a call from Dr Sheppard who sounded distraught, saying, "I think they've got Marilyn." Blood bespattered the Sheppards' bedroom walls. Marilyn's battered body lay on the bed. The room had been ransacked.

Sheppard claimed he was roused from sleep by screams and ran upstairs, but was instantly concussed by a blow to the head. When he recovered he found Marilyn's body, and then heard noises from downstairs where he discovered an intruder, and chased him out through the garden toward the nearby shore of Lake Erie, only to be felled again.

It seemed odd a man should suffer two consecutive concussive blows to the head without being in far worse shape than the doctor. The idea of the clean "knock-out blow" doing no lasting damage is a myth of films and pulp novels.

Sam didn't help himself by

Dr Sam Sheppard (in sunglasses) answers questions

claiming that his marriage was hunky-dorey. Investigators turned up his infidelity to Marilyn.

After that things came together quickly. A mark on Marilyn's pillow suggested one of Sam's surgical instruments. The t-shirt he was wearing when he fell asleep had gone

missing – why, unless the owner wanted to hide tell-tale bloodstains on the garment?

So despite his continuing pleas of innocence, Dr Sam Sheppard has been convicted of second-degree murder and sentenced to life imprisonment.

Mother-in-Law to End All Mothers-in-Law

GREEK CYPRIOT Styllou Christofi (54) came to England last year to join her married son Stavros, a waiter in Britain since 1937. This year, Stavros' wife Hella (a pre-war refugee from Hitler's Germany) told her husband that she was taking their three children on holiday, and unless mother-in-law Styllou left their Hampstead home, she would not be returning.

Mrs Styllou Christofi, a ferocious and possessive peasant mother, did not disguise her jealous resentment of her daughter-in-law. When Stavros told his mother she was being given her marching orders, the virago took steps to secure her position.

While Stavros was out she bat-

tered Hella with the iron ashplate from the kitchen stove, and strangled her with a scarf. Then she dragged her outside into the back yard and poured paraffin over the body before setting it alight. A neighbour in his upstairs bedroom saw her start the fire, but assumed she was incinerating a tailor's dummy. Others came to Mrs Christofi's aid when she ran into the street crying, "Please come! Fire burning! Children sleeping!"

Her clumsy attempt to disguise her crime as Hella's accidental self-immolation did not deceive a soul. This evil harridan has gone to the gallows furiously resentful that Stavros is unenthusiastic about her particularly murderous form of mother love!

Hella Christofi's body is removed

WHEN MOTHER-IN-LAW WAS DAUGHTER-IN-LAW

Wicked Mrs Styllou Christofi has now killed her second Mrs Christofi! In 1924 she killed her own mother-in-law in Cyprus by forcing a burning brand down her throat! On that occasion she was acquitted by a jury of her peers. A British jury, however, is less tolerant of Greek Tragedy Passions.

Prostitute Hangs for Shooting her Chiselling Charmer

BRASSY LONDON BLONDE Ruth Ellis, a former night club "hostess" and manageress of The Little Club for convicted pimp Maury Conley, has been hanged for shooting her lover, amateur racing driver David Blakely, outside the Magdala Tavern, Hampstead. (Coincidentally this is in the same street where, last year, Styllou Christofi savagely murdered her daughter-in-law, Hella.)

David, a bit of a wastrel, was clearly tiring of the older Ruth, and ashamed of her in the presence of his middle-class family and friends. He was spending the weekend with motor engineer Anthony Findlater and his wife, who fielded Ruth's phone calls and cut off her attempts to contact David. This led the jealous woman to believe (wrongly) they were conniving at David's enjoying a sexual weekend with their baby-sitter, and after two days of growing frustration, she borrowed a gun and went round to watch the house in Hampstead.

When David drove out to the pub for beer and cigarettes, she waited for him; then chased him round his car and gunned him down, slightly injuring the hand of a passing pedestrian by accident with a riccocheting bullet. Then she gave herself up meekly, and it was with the greatest difficulty that her counsel persuaded her that a plea of Not Guilty would be a proper formality and not a lie.

For Ruth Ellis had moral standards, even if they don't accord with most people's sexual ethics. She undoubtedly played off David against another older lover, Desmond Cussen. She lied shamelessly about sleeping with the one while lodging with the other. But she didn't behave with the cowardice and long-term deceitfulness David showed toward her. Some 50,000 people recognized the good in Ruth Ellis, but their petition for clemency was ignored, and the gallows has claimed another woman.

Ruth Ellis (third from right) partying with alternative lover Desmond Cussen (third from left)

Ruth Ellis with David Blakely

Convict Carves Soap Gun and Escapes from Prison

CANADIAN PROSPECTOR, 45-year-old Wilbert Coffin, sentenced to death for the murder of three American hunters on St John's River, Quebec, broke out of jail this year when his appeal was turned down. Coffin admitted meeting the three men on June 10, 1953, and helping them with their broken-down truck. In July the hunters' bodies were found. They had been robbed and shot by rifle. This year Coffin fashioned a handgun out of soap, and used it to bluff his way past guards. Out of jail, he contacted his lawyer, however, and accepted his advice to give himself up. Coffin stoutly maintains his innocence, and says that two other Americans were in the vicinity of the murders, a lonely part of the country, travelling in a jeep. Such a vehicle was found abandoned near Bathurst, and there is widespread belief in Coffin's innocence among the public at large.

Agreement with Germans Saves BAOR Sergeant-Major

Sergeant-Major Frederick Emmett-Dunne (right) on his way to court-martial in West Germany

A QUIET WEDDING in Taunton last year prompted whisperings among former NCOs in the BAOR. When REME Sergeant-Major Frederick Emmett-Dunne married pretty blonde widow Mia Watters, the late Sergeant Watters' mess-mates began whispering about his suicide by hanging at the barracks in Duisberg. And the whispers reached Scotland Yard.

Home Office pathologist Dr Francis Camps flew out to Germany and examined Reginald Watters' exhumed remains. His report? "This man never died from hanging... he died from a severe blow across the front of the throat." Just such a blow as a sergeant-major trained in unarmed combat might inflict, in fact!

Emmett-Dunne was taken back to Düsseldorf to stand trial for murder. His original story of leaving Watters earlier in the evening before his body was found was now changed. He claimed that Watters had threatened him with a pistol, knowing (as the trial fully proved) that he was having an affair with German-born Mrs Watters. He had accidentally killed Watters in self-defence, and staged the suicide in panic.

The story didn't ring true at all, and Emmett-Dunne was convicted and sentenced to death. But Germany has witnessed a lot more state executions than anybody thinks reasonable during the last 20 years, and the West German government has no wish to continue a tradition of murderous authoritarianism. So the accord between the Bonn government and Britain stipulates that there shall be no executions on federal territory leased to British military authorities.

Emmett-Dunne is lucky. He has been brought home to serve a life sentence.

IN BRIEF

DENISE LABBÉ sentenced to life imprisonment after jury finding her guilty of murdering her infant daughter, made a strong recommendation to mercy (*see* 1954). Her diabolic lover Jacques Algarron given the maximum possible sentence for manipulating her to murder; ten years hard labour.

Houseboy Fires his Counsel and Proves his Guilt!

DISSATISFIED with the conduct of his defence, Bart Caritativo, on trial this January for the murder of wealthy Joseph and Camille Banks at Stinson Beach, San Francisco, fired his lawyers, writing, "I have lost the trust to my attorneys."

Prosecuting counsel were delighted. For Caritativo's memo reproduced the solecistic use of "to" also found in a suicide note that appeared to be signed by Joseph Banks, saying: "I am responsible to what you see and find."

Philippino houseboy Caritativo (49) became friendly with a compatriot who was housekeeper next-door to his employers some years ago. When she had the good fortune to marry her boss and become wealthy, Camille Malmgren remained a friend of Bart's. And their shared literary aspirations kept them close after Mr Malmgren died, and throughout Camille's relatively short-lived marriage to English alcoholic Joseph Banks.

A good-natured lady, Camille allowed Joseph to go on living in her house when the relationship was clearly dead. It came as a shock, therefore, when an estate agent, coming to survey the property before Camille moved abroad, found Mrs Banks in the bedroom with her skull split, and Mr Banks surrounded by whisky bottles in the living room. A knife was in his chest, and his suicide note apparently explained something of the tragedy.

But Banks would not have misused the preposition. Mrs Banks's will proved equally full of solecisms and spelling mistakes. And it left all her property to Caritativo. Handwriting experts believe he forged it. Pathologists say Joseph Banks was too drunk to have stabbed himself as the note implied. Caritativo went on trial. And ensured his conviction when he fired his counsel.

> ## I HAVE LOST THE TRUST TO MY ATTORNEYS.
> QUOTE **Bart Caritativo**

Finger-Printing Potters Bar Catches Teenage Killer

WHEN MRS CURRELL'S battered and strangled body was found by the 17th tee on Potters Bar golf course in Hertfordshire on April 30, the only clue to her murderer was a bloody palm-print on the iron tee-marker that had been used to assault her. Mr Currell was in the clear. He had reported his wife's failure to return from walking the dog the previous night.

The print did not show up on police files, so 9,000 Potters Bar men were laboriously fingerprinted. And 17-year-old local government clerk Michael Queripel was charged with the murder.

Queripel admitted seeing Mrs Currell and seizing her with the intention of rape. When she struggled, he struck her repeatedly with the marker. Then he tied her stocking round her neck. Finally he ran home, and cut his arm with a razor blade to explain the blood on his clothes.

His guilty plea cannot lead to a death sentence as, at 18, he is under-age, and he has been sentenced to detention at Her Majesty's pleasure.

Killing Mom – And a Plane-Load with Her

John Graham – matricide plus

The failing Denver drive-in restaurant Mrs Daisy King bought for her son, John, to manage

CREW-CUT 24-year-old American Jack Graham seems the perfect momma's boy. The mechanic's mother, Daisy King, rescued him after his conviction for embezzlement five years ago. She paid back $2,000, and arranged for him to repay another $2,000 from his earnings. She opened a drive-in restaurant for him to manage. By this year, Graham's debt was down to $100.

Graham seemed devastated when his mom died in the United Airlines Flight 629 disaster at Denver last year. But FBI men made some surprising discoveries. Traces of dynamite in the baggage hold showed that the plane had been bombed. The only passenger whose luggage had disintegrated was Mrs King. Her life had been insured for a staggering $62,500 in Jack's favour.

After hours of questioning last December, Graham confessed. He fell out with his mother when the drive-in stopped paying. He tried unsuccessfully to burn it down for the insurance. He wrecked a car for insurance. And finally he killed his mother (and the other 44 passengers and crew on Flight 629) to receive the pay-out on her life.

Graham withdrew and reinstated his confession several times before his trial this February, and tried to kill himself once. But his guilt was clear and his appeal has been rejected. He is scheduled to be executed in the New Year.

Cop Killer Took Family Hostage, Goes to Chair

PETTY THIEF Richard Carpenter lived by demanding the takings of small Chicago bars and grocery stores, using a pair of six guns as persuasion. In August last year, however, detective Bill Murphy recognized him on the subway and arrested him.

As they left the train, 26-year-old Carpenter shot Murphy dead and escaped. On the street he forced a driver to take him to central Chicago's Loop district, and disappeared among the crowds of shoppers and workers.

Now the city's most wanted man, he had to sleep on the run. He was spotted snoozing in the back row of a cinema by off-duty policeman Clarence Kerr. When Kerr tried to arrest him, Carpenter shot his second cop. But Kerr did not die and another policeman came to his aid, shooting Carpenter in the leg as the killer raced from the cinema.

That night, Carpenter forced his way into the home of truck-driver Leonard Powell, forcing him and Mrs Powell to go about their business at gunpoint. The Powells did not alarm their children by explaining his presence, and Powell went to work the following day as normal. When he came home that evening, Powell suggested that suspicion would be aroused if the family did not make their regular visit to his wife's mother. Amazingly, this ruse worked – Carpenter let them go and within minutes the house was surrounded by cops.

Carpenter could not escape. At his trial he could not exculpate his wanton murder resisting arrest. He died in the electric chair at Joliet prison this year.

Doctor's Eastbourne Widows Dying Like Flies

Dr John Bodkin Adams

LOTS OF RICH old ladies in England go to south coast towns to die, but they don't expect expensive private doctors to help them into the grave prematurely!

The death of Mrs Gertrude Hullett this July has, however, drawn police attention to the mortality rate among Dr John Bodkin Adams' patients. The roly-poly bachelor doctor, who lives with his mummy and looks as though he subsists on cream buns, drew attention to himself by asking the coroner for a "private post mortem" in this "very peculiar case", before his patient actually expired!

The shocked coroner called Home Office pathologist Francis Camps to perform a very public post mortem, and it transpired that

Adams' diagnosis of cerebral haemorrhage on the death certificate was misleading to say the least: Mrs Hullett died of barbiturate poisoning. And Dr Adams' prescriptions had made her an addict!

The coroner accused Adams of "an extraordinary degree of careless treatment." The police suspected something worse when they learned:

That Mrs Hullett left the doctor her Roll-Royce;

that this was the second Rolls Adams inherited from a grateful patient (deceased);

that Adams was mentioned in over 100 patients' wills, and has inherited thousands of pounds, and quantities of jewellery, antiques and silver from patients who died under his care;

that local gossip says he makes house calls with a blank will form in one hand and a bottle of morphine in the other;

that an outraged nurse said, "You realize, doctor, that you have killed her," as she watched a patient die.

Adams is now charged with the murder of Mrs Edith Alice Morrell, from whom he inherited a Rolls-Royce, a chest of silver and an antique cupboard in 1950, when she died after his reckless prescriptions of morphine. And if that charge doesn't stick, the police have nine more up their sleeve!

The chemist's shop in Eastbourne where Dr Adams' lethal prescriptions were made up

Coffee Meeting Housewives Plot Lazy Husband's Death

WHAT COULD be duller than Columbia, South Carolina, suburban housewives Joyce Turner, Audrey Noakes and Clestell Gay? Joyce's bar keeper husband Alonzo, apparently – an individual too lazy even to quarrel interestingly.

At the day-care centre Joyce ran, the three women – all in their thirties – would endlessly discuss Joyce's expressed intention of killing him. This June, an exasperated Clestell asked pointedly: "Well, are you going to do it or not?" Joyce promptly borrowed Clestell's .22 pistol, ran home and shot Alonzo as he slept!

Joyce's story of an intruder, motivated by Alonzo's alleged affairs, collapsed when police found the dead man was far too indolent to have bestirred himself for sexual adventure!

All three women have pleaded guilty to conspiracy to murder, and their nattering over coffee has brought them life sentences.

Car Helps Trace Killer Rapist – Medium Traces Girl's Body

WHEN MYRNA JOY AKEN disappeared from her home in Durban, South Africa this October witnesses said she had been seen in a light-coloured car. The car was traced to the owner of a radio shop who, when questioned, said he had lent it for the day to salesman Clarence van Buuren (33). Police went to van Buuren's home but, like Joy Aken, could find no trace.

Medium Nelson Palmer, called in by Joy's family to help with the case, said the girl would be found 60 miles away in a drain below the highway. And so she was, just outside Umtwalumi village! Palmer led the search party to Joy's naked, raped and shot corpse.

Nine days later van Buuren was picked up by police at Pinetown. In his statement, he claims to have asked Joy to come for a drink which she refused; on subsequently finding her bloody body in his parked car, he states that he panicked and dumped it in the culvert.

At his trial in the New Year he will have to explain his possession of .22 ammunition of the type that killed Joy.

IN BRIEF

WILBERT COFFIN (*see* 1955) hanged in Quebec for the murder of three American hunters in 1953. He still protested his innocence. The hangman's verdict? "This man, I swear, was innocent."

LONDON GANG WAR
Jack Spot (real name Jack Comer), East End Jewish ruler of Soho, received a knife wound requiring 78 stitches from Albert Dimes and a blow over the head with an iron bar from Bob Warren, both minor villains in the entourage of Billy Hill, who seeks to wrest away Spot's crown. The indignity of sustaining personal injury from such small fry does not improve Spot's standing with the ungodly.

Farmer Cross-Dressed in Dead Women's Skins!

GENTLE ED GEIN (51), a loner from Plainfield, Wisconsin, was unusual in the rural community. Too squeamish to hunt, he couldn't bear skinning and cutting up deer, he told everyone.

So it came as a considerable shock to policemen looking for missing storekeeper Bernice Worden to find her headless, gutted body hanging from the ceiling of Ed's garage!

But that was nothing as compared to what they found inside the house. Ed's squalid bachelor nest contained:

Chairs bottomed with strips of human skin!

The sawn-off crania of four skulls: two ornamenting Ed's bedposts, and two used as porringers!

A bag of women's noses preserved in salt!

A bag of women's vulvas preserved in salt!

Offal from Mrs Worden, awaiting cooking and eating!

Masks around the bedroom wall, which proved to be women's flayed faces!

A belt of women's nipples!

A long black wig, which proved to be a woman's scalp!

A bizarre "costume" of breasted waistcoat and greaves, made from the skins of dead women!

When questioned, Ed admitted to digging up the bodies of numerous women from the cemetery to assemble his collection. And in addition to Mrs Worden, he had killed bar proprietor Mary Hogan in 1954. (Her disappearance had been put down to her connections with the Chicago underworld.)

Ed ate parts of his corpses. Weirdest of all, at full moon he liked to dance dressed up as a woman in mask, wig, waistcoat and greaves, with a vulva held to him by panties!

And what, sheriff's officers wondeed with a shudder, lay in the half of the house Ed had sealed up? These rooms turned out to be those inhabited by his puritanical mother, preserved exactly as they had been at the time of her death.

Then people realized that Mrs Hogan and Mrs Worden slightly resembled the late Mrs Gein, who had always taught Ed that women were bad and sex was wicked!

Ed has been sent straight to the lunatic asylum without anyone pausing to consider a trial!

Weird cross-dresser Ed Gein, who wore the skins of women he exhumed or murdered

Kenneth Barlow and the wife he poisoned with insulin

Wife in Bath Died of Poisoning!

MALE NURSE Kenneth Barlow (39) acted in a way reminiscent of George Joseph Smith (*see* 1915) when he called a doctor saying his wife Elizabeth had drowned in the bath.

Barlow had pulled her out and given her artificial respiration, to no avail, he said. Then why, wondered police, were his pyjamas quite dry? And why, wondered the police surgeon, were Mrs Barlow's pupils dilated?

When it became known that Barlow had incautiously told friends that insulin injected into the bloodstream would be absorbed and so might make a perfect method of murder, the police decided to examine the body of the dead woman.

They made several significant discoveries: needle marks on her buttocks and traces of insulin beneath the skin around them. Despite his pleas of innocence, Barlow has been given a life sentence for Elizabeth's murder.

Gangland Slaying of Albert, the Lord High Executioner

THE LORD HIGH EXECUTIONER is dead, executed in his barber's chair at the Park Sheraton Hotel, New York City. No sooner had Brooklyn crime tsar Albert Anastasia settled himself with hot towels for a haircut and manicure than his bodyguard innocently left the room and two gunmen with scarves over their faces marched in to blast away the man who has blasted so many in his time.

A devoted follower of "Lucky" Luciano and Frank Costello, Anastasia seized headship of the Brooklyn "family" in 1951 by eliminating Phil and Vincent Mangano. He went too far the following year, killing non-Mafioso Arnold Schuster for betraying the non-Mafia burglar Willie Sutton. But for the time, Luciano, Costello and Meyer Lansky needed him to ward off rival Vito Genovese's retrograde attempt to make himself "Boss of all Bosses". Now, perhaps, they don't.

Albert Anastasia's body is taken from a Brooklyn funeral parlour for interment

OBITUARY

ALBERT ANASTASIA (1903-1957)

Albert Anastasia and his brother "Tough Tony" became prominent in labour racketeering soon after they entered the USA as immigrants in 1920. Albert quickly became known as a hit man. He spent 18 months in Sing Sing awaiting trial for killing a longshoreman. He was acquitted because the key prosecution witness disappeared – something that often happened to potential witnesses against Albert.

His love of being present at killings rather than leaving them to sub-contracted gunmen earned him the nickname "the Mad Hatter". Later he became the "Lord High Executioner" when he oversaw the work of Abe "Kid Twist" Reles and his "Murder Inc." group (see 1940).

Mafia Bosses Caught Out at Upstate New York Convention

IT MIGHT HAVE been a scene from the Keystone Kops! New York State police investigating a mysteriously large gathering of out-of-state cars parked near an isolated mansion in Appalachin on November 14 flushed out 58 of the nation's top Mafia bosses, gathered for a conference on Joe Babara's estate. Vito Genovese, Santo Trafficante, Joe Profaci, Joe Bonnano and Carlo Gambino were prominent among the elegantly dressed townees whose pointy-toed patent-leather shoes tripped away so unfittingly over the rough country ground. And as one by one they were hauled in by chortling cops, their reiterated explanation, "Just happened to be passing and dropped in to visit an old pal", made even the hoods realize they were looking particularly dumb.

The purpose of the meeting was to crown Vito Genovese "Capo di Tutti Capi"; a mighty chieftaincy that has been in abeyance since "Lucky" Luciano and Meyer Lansky firmly terminated the silly rivalry among ancient "Mustache Petes" for anointed headship (see 1931). But maybe Vito was set up. Too bad, so soon after he hired "Crazy Joe" Gallo and his brothers to murder rival Albert Anastasia!

Circumstantial Evidence Convicts 61-year-old Man

SOME CIRCUMSTANTIAL evidence is strong and some is weak. Sixty-one-year-old Leonard Scott Ewing of Bel Air, California has been convicted of his wife's murder although there is no real proof of his guilt, just a strong motive.

Leonard married wealthy widow Evelyn in 1949. Two years ago he cancelled premiums on her jewellery insurance and explained her sudden absence by saying she had gone away, but he knew not where. He declared that if she did not return after seven years he would begin a new life.

He waited one year before proposing marriage to another woman. Then Evelyn's spectacles and false teeth were dug up in a neighbour's garden. Scott, his finances under scrutiny, fled to Canada, where he was arrested.

Scott refused to testify and was found guilty of first-degree murder. Now in prison, he still asserts his innocence.

IN BRIEF

CLARENCE VAN BUUREN hanged for the murder of Joy Aken (*see* 1956).

DR JOHN BODKIN ADAMS, acquitted of murdering Mrs Morrell (*see* 1956) after defence counsel Geoffrey Lawrence brilliantly exposed blustering prosecutor Reginald Manningham-Buller's crass incompetence in putting forward tainted evidence from nurses that contradicted their own log of prescriptions. To police disgust, the DPP refuses to proceed with other charges against the doctor.

Glasgow Fiend Goes to the Gallows for Killing Eight

PETER MANUEL (31), charged in January with killing eight people and convicted of seven of those murders in May, was hanged at Barlinnie Prison in July. Thus ended a lifetime of theft, burglary, indecent assault and rape, and two years of wanton killing around Glasgow.

Manuel killed Ann Kneilands (17) in January 1956 when he dragged her to a wood and battered her around the head after assaulting her. This was the crime of which he was acquitted, the only hard evidence being his confession which he withdrew and reinstated from time to time after his arrest.

In September of the same year he broke into the Watt family house while Mr Watt, a master-baker, was on a fishing trip. There he murdered Mrs Watt and her sister and niece. Since it would have been just possible for Mr Watt to drive home in the night and commit the crimes, he was remanded for questioning in Barlinnie, where Manuel, too, found himself in custody for burglary. The good-looking murderer drew attention to himself by offering to produce evidence exonerating Mr Watt.

In 1957 Manuel was in Newcastle where police believe he murdered taxi driver Stanley Dunn. And last December he assaulted and murdered 17-year-old Isabelle Cooke, burying her body in a field near Uddington.

New Year's Eve found this brute in the Smart family home in Uddington, where he killed Mr and Mrs Peter Smart and their 10-year-old son. But at last a murder could be traced to him. Manuel subsequently tendered new £5 notes Mr Smart had drawn from his bank. Manuel confessed to the murders when he learned that his father was also in custody, being questioned about the presence in his house of property from the murder victims.

Manuel's victims: Left to right (top) Ann Kneilands, Marion and Vivienne Watt, Margaret Brown; (bottom) Isabelle Cook, Peter, Doris and Michael Smart

At his trial Manuel withdrew his confessions, arguing that Mr Watt was responsible for killing his own wife, sister-in-law and niece. He also dismissed his counsel and defended himself – with remarkable skill and aplomb, as the judge commented. But it didn't save him from the gallows!

Hung Jury in the Finch-Tregoff Trial

LOS ANGELES' sensational society murder case will go to a retrial because the jury cannot agree. Not in dispute, however, are the following points:

1. Dr Raymond Finch (42) was threatened with divorce proceedings by his wife, Barbara, who claimed he intended to kill her. She also claimed just about all his property by way of a fair settlement!

2. Dr Finch and his attractive secretary-mistress, ex-model Carol Tregoff (21), hired petty crook John Patrick Cody. Finch asked him to compromise Barbara. Carole asked him to kill her!

3. When neither compromise nor killing happened, Finch and Tregoff visited Barbara in July.

4. After the visit, Barbara was left with a fatal bullet wound in her back as a memento.

So did Barbara herself pull the gun on her unwelcome guests? Had they brought a knife and hypodermic syringes to kill her? Or was it all a tragic accident?

The jury couldn't decide. Let's hope the next one does better.

Nasty Teenage Lovers Rape, Murder and Mutilate Nine

CHARLES "LITTLE RED" STARKWEATHER is a backward, 5ft 2in refuse collector from Lincoln, Nebraska. At 19 he reckons the world ain't done him no favours. Up to the end of January the only person Charles cared for was wayward 14-year-old Caril Fugate, who slept with the bandy-legged, sandy-haired loner.

On January 21, Charles went to Caril's house while she was still at school, and Caril's mother, Velda Bartlett, put her foot down about Caril's misconduct. When Charles threatened her, Caril's stepfather, Marion Bartlett, came to her aid. Charles shot them both.

When Caril got home from school, the two choked her 2-year-old sister to death, and pinned a notice on the door reading, "Stay Away. Every Body is sick with the Flu", before retiring to bed to spend the next 48 hours watching television, eating junk food and making love – blissful pursuits to the heartless pair.

When food in the fridge ran low, and relatives and police came round at intervals to knock on the door, the couple made off in Starkweather's old jalopy. They broke into a farm and killed the farmer. They robbed two teenagers and stole their car after taking them to a barn where Starkweather raped the girl before shooting them; the jealous Caril mutilated the girl's body obscenely. They broke into a businessman's house where they tied up, killed and mutilated his wife and maid and killed him, too, when he returned from work.

Finally, they killed a salesman as he dozed in his car in a layby. This car proved hard to start. When a motorist stopped to help them, the pair's strange antics attracted the attention of a passing police squad car. Caril threw herself into a policeman's arms, declaring that her lover had forced her to accompany him on his murderous jaunt. At the trial each accused the other of instigating the mayhem. Caril has been sentenced to life imprisonment and Charles has a date with the electric chair.

Murderous teenagers Charles Starkweather and Caril Fugate

Camera Buff's Bondage Pictures Pay Off in Prison

CALIFORNIAN KILLER-SADIST Harvey Glatman trapped victims by pretending to be a professional photographer. The television repair man booked sessions with models Judy Dull (19) and Ruth Rita Mercado (24) for mock "bondage" shots for pulp mags. The gals got tied up for real – and raped, and strangled. The same fate met divorcée Shirley Bridport whom he contacted through a lonely hearts club. All three women wound up in graves in the desert.

He intended model Joanne Arena to join them there, but as he pulled a gun on her it went off. She used the chance offered by Glatman's momentary surprise to grab the gun and keep him covered till the highway patrol arrested him. Now he's been convicted, magazines are falling over themselves to buy his raunchy shots of the women he killed. Glatman just loves this belated recognition!

What Limey Gave the Master-Sergeant Arsenic?

USAF MASTER-SERGEANT Marcus Marymont has been convicted of poisoning his wife Mary Helen. The court-martial in Denham, England, heard that Marymont was dallying with 23-year-old Cynthia Taylor; heard that doctors found Mrs Marymont had been ingesting arsenic for a month; heard that Marymont had asked for arsenic at shops and cleaners in Berkshire and also back on his USAF base in Norfolk.

That's enough to send him back to Fort Leavenworth Prison, Kansas, for a life sentence. But nobody's admitted giving the sergeant the white powder. So where did he get it from?

IN BRIEF

NATHAN LEOPOLD, survivor of "thrill-killers" who murdered Bobby Franks (*see* 1924), paroled at the age of 51. Says former "boy genius", "I am a broken old man. I want a chance to find redemption for myself and to help others." To this end he will work as a lab technician for a church in Puerto Rico.

BRIAN DONALD HUME, paroled from conviction as accessory after the fact to Stanley Setty's murder (*see* 1950), now confesses he did it all himself! The three villains "Greeny, Mac and the Boy" were an invention based on detectives who questioned him!

'Boss of Bosses' Vito Genovese Jailed

DON VITO GENOVESE, self-proclaimed "Capo di Tutti Capi" (Boss of all Bosses) has been given 30 to 50 years for dope-dealing on the evidence of Puerto Rican hood, Nelson Cantellops. A bum rap, the gang boss complains!

Not since Tom Dewey put away Don Vito's predecessor "Lucky" Luciano for pimping (*see* 1936) has Uncle Sam had such a big Mafioso as his long-term guest. Genovese succeeded Luciano – paroled and deported to Sicily in 1946 – as head of the old Masseria "family" in Manhattan. But his rise to the top of the pile made enemies of other "family" bosses in a number of ways:

He deals in narcotics, which underworld "Prime Minister" Frank Costello and exiled king "Lucky" Luciano oppose, fearing heavy federal intervention.

He aims to be recognized as "Boss of all Bosses" – a silly personal ambition which led to gang wars in the 1920s and early '30s .

He needs Luciano's exile to be permanent to retain control of his family. It probably will be, anyway.

But Luciano's friends Lansky, Costello, Carlo Gambino and the late Albert Anastasia all hoped the Big Man might settle at least as close as Cuba. Luciano himself, bored with provincial Sicily, longs to swagger down Broadway again.

He arranged the murder of rival Albert Anastasia (*see* 1957) and an unsuccessful attempt on Frank Costello's life, which creased the "Prime Minister's" scalp.

His Appalachin convention embarrassed national crime bosses when they suffered a humiliating police raid (*see* 1957).

So Don Vito retires to Atlanta Penitentiary, where he hopes to go on running his crime syndicate from his cell. And the bum rap? He must be right! One can no more imagine Don Vito personally trafficking paper bags of dope with a nobody like Cantellops than one could imagine Luciano taking a nickels-and-dimes cut of the take directly from two Broadway prostitutes. But did Uncle Sam frame Don Vito? Or has he been finally suckered by Luciano, Lansky, Costello and Gambino?

Don Vito Genovese, top Mafioso, talks to reporters as he leaves court on bail before his trial

Sex Beast Traced and Caught in Arkansas

TWENTY-SIX-YEAR-OLD musician Melvin Rees has killed one woman, one entire family and possibly at least four other girls. The dark, lean saxophonist first came to official notice in 1957 when he used a gun to try and force his way into a parked car where Miss Margaret Harrold was sitting with her boyfriend, an army sergeant. Miss Harrold became hysterical when Rees started molesting her, and he shot her dead. The sergeant escaped and summoned help, but Rees managed to get away without being positively identified.

In January this year he used his car to force Mr Carroll Jackson off the road; then pulled his gun and made Mr and Mrs Jackson and their two children get in the trunk of his Ford. Stopping on the roadside near Fredericksburg, Virginia, he shot Mr Jackson, leaving one of the daughters to suffocate under the body. The other had her skull smashed, and was buried with her mother who had been raped and strangled in a cinderblock hideout Rees ornamented with pornographic photographs.

Rees was traced to Arkansas where he worked as a piano salesman. Police believe he was also responsible for sexually assaulting and slaying four teenage girls in Maryland while he was a university student there.

Melvin Rees (left) covers his face as FBI agents bring him in for murder

'Amnesiac' Blackmailer Hanged for Killing Policeman

GERMAN-BORN Gunther Fritz Podola (30) came to England from Canada this year. After stealing furs and jewellery from Mrs Verne Schiffman's South Kensington home, he telephoned her, pretending he had discovered compromising tapes and photographs in her mansion flat.

Fearing nothing on this score, Mrs Schiffman strung him along before informing the police. By the time Podola called her again, from South Kensington underground station, her phone was tapped, and detectives quickly surrounded the call-box.

Podola eluded them, however, and took temporary refuge in the foyer of an apartment building.

Here, he hid behind a pillar and shot dead Detective-Sergeant Raymond Purdy when the policeman approached him. Podola made good his escape and evaded capture for several days.

Police traced him to a small hotel where a group of officers broke down the locked door to the room in which he was hiding. Podola was hauled off into custody. The black eye and bruises evident on the accused's face were incurred, the police said, when the door flew open. Podola and his sympathizers said he was beaten punitively and as a result of this violence could no longer recall anything about the circumstances of Sergeant Purdy's murder.

Gunther Podola (right) brought to court by detectives

At his trial in September it was suggested that Podola was unfit to plead because he could not remember anything. The matter was put to the jury. They decided that a letter written by the accused while awaiting trial proved both his fitness to plead and that he was shamming. Podola was tried, convicted and executed. Before his execution, his memory spontaneously returned!

Düsseldorf Doubles Killer Gets Life Sentence

THE TRIAL IN GERMANY of 31-year-old Werner Boost for killing two courting couples and threatening a third has ended with his life imprisonment – for the occasion when he killed one of a pair of homosexuals embracing in a car.

Boost worked in collaboration with Franz Lorbach, who claims that Boost terrified and hypnotized him, forcing him to assist in the perverse murders. According to Lorbach, who has received a six-year prison sentence, Boost took pep pills and truth serum. He injected his victims with sedatives and then raped the women before killing them and their partners.

The two killed homosexual lawyer Dr Serve in January 1953, beating and robbing his male lover. In 1955 they killed Thea Kurmann and Friedhelme Behre, crushing their skulls before dumping the bodies in a water-filled gravel-pit. Early in 1956 they killed Peter Falkenberg and Hildegarde Wassing, and immolated their bodies in a haystack.

In June of the same year a courting couple successfully scared them off. This gave the authorities the lead they needed: they now knew the "doubles killer" was two armed men. Shortly after this, Lorbach was arrested. While he was safely in custody, a forest ranger spotted Boost stalking another courting couple.

Lorbach's confession allowed charges to be brought, but the lack of strong corroborative evidence allowed three years to pass before Boost could be convicted. He has only now been found guilty of murdering Dr Serve.

CANADA'S YOUNGEST RAPIST MURDERS GIRL

LYNNE HARPER, a 12-year-old of Goderich, Ontario, went trustingly on the crossbar of young Steven Truscott's bicycle when he offered her a ride. He willingly admitted this after Lynne's worried parents asked schoolchildren if they had seen her. He added that he had dropped her off at a highway where he saw her accept a lift in a grey Chevrolet.

But Lynne's raped and strangled body was found in woodland near the Air Force base where her father worked. Young Steven was found to have a sore penis and scratches consistent with defensive wounds inflicted by the struggling girl. Found guilty of her murder, he is the youngest living Canadian to have heard the death sentence pronounced. His age, however, makes his reprieve inevitable.

IN BRIEF

BRIAN DONALD HUME, self-confessed murderer of Stanley Setty (see 1950), has killed again: this time a taxi-driver in Zurich, Switzerland, where he was robbing a bank. The Swiss courts have no intention of seeing him freed for a third murder, and he has been imprisoned for life.

Ups and Downs of a G-Man's Career

TWICE G-MAN Melvin Purvis arrested surviving Capone rival, Roger "the Terrible" Touhy. Once he wrongly charged Touhy with a kidnapping perpetrated by the Barker-Karpis gang. Then he had him convicted of kidnapping "Jake the Barber" Factor, a Capone associate. But it seems Purvis was set up by Capone to ensure Touhy's long-term imprisonment on this bum rap.

Purvis's reputation also suffered after the Little Bohemia, Wisconsin, gunfight with the Dillinger mob, in which FBI men shooting wildly injured two civilians and killed a third. But the arrest of Dillinger (*see* 1934) reinstated Melvin as the nation's most daring G-man. It was Purvis's famous squeaky voice that prompted the gangster to go for his guns when he called, "Stick 'em up, Johnny, we've got you surrounded." And it was the gun he fired at Dillinger with which Purvis has now killed

himself at his home in South Carolina, rather than endure slow and debilitating illness.

Despite the nickname 'Nervous Purvis", the agent's personal courage was amply demonstrated when he faced the guns of "Pretty Boy" Floyd, "Baby Face" Nelson, Verne Sankey and Volney Davis.

The contrast with the Bureau's deskbound but publicity-hungry director was unacceptable to Mr Hoover. Purvis was the only local bureau chief in the country whose press releases started, "Melvin Purvis announces..." instead of "J. Edgar Hoover announces..." In 1935, when Purvis resigned, Mr Hoover had to deny publicly that the cause was a rift between them.

Such a rift certainly existed, however. Purvis's memoirs of his time in the FBI never mention the famous director! Hoover had Purvis's name omitted from the index of the standard history of the bureau.

Top FBI agent Melvin Purvis, head of the Chicago office of the FBI in Al Capone's day

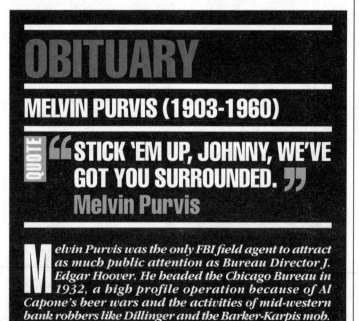

OBITUARY

MELVIN PURVIS (1903-1960)

QUOTE **" STICK 'EM UP, JOHNNY, WE'VE GOT YOU SURROUNDED. "**
Melvin Purvis

Melvin Purvis was the only FBI field agent to attract as much public attention as Bureau Director J. Edgar Hoover. He headed the Chicago Bureau in 1932, a high profile operation because of Al Capone's beer wars and the activities of mid-western bank robbers like Dillinger and the Barker-Karpis mob. In the Second World War, Mr Purvis served with the Army War Crimes Office. Afterwards, he practised privately as a lawyer, until the illness that led to his suicide.

Husband-Killer First Cleared Then Convicted

NINETEEN-YEAR-OLD Sharon Kinne reported two deaths last year. In March she rang Kansas City police, hysterically telling them that her husband of five years, electronics worker James Kinne, had been shot by their 2-year-old as the child played with a pistol.

James was indeed dead on the bed, shot in the back. And when police gave the little girl the unloaded gun to play with, she confidently released the safety catch. End of case.

With James's insurance money, Sharon bought herself a Thunderbird. In May she reported discovering Patricia Jones, wife of her car salesman, lying dead in a lover's lane. Sharon claimed that she suspected Patricia of having an affair, and so trailed her around bars and clubs until she came across the body, shot with a .22.

Sharon went on trial for Patricia Jones's murder this year after police established that:

Sharon has grown remarkably friendly with Patricia's husband
Patricia was seen getting into Sharon's Thunderbird on the evening of her death
Sharon persuaded a co-worker to buy her a .22 pistol without registering it in her name.

But confused ballistic evidence about practice shots fired by the missing .22's previous owner led to Sharon's acquittal. The 20-year-old was immediately rearrested, however, and charged with James's murder. Expert gunsmiths are unanimous in their rejection of Sharon's claim that a 2-year-old had the strength to pull the trigger of the handgun.

London Youths Kill Lad for 14 Shillings!

TWENTY-ONE-YEAR-OLD Alan Jee was one of the nicest young men you could wish to meet in South London. Polite, decent, hard-working, engaged to be married, and seemingly without an enemy in the world.

These attributes didn't stop four youths from attacking him as he walked through a dark alley in Hounslow after seeing his fiancée home. Francis "Flossie" Forsyth (18), Norman James Harris (23), Chris Darby (23) and Terence Lutt (17) jumped on him; threw him to the ground; robbed him of the mere 14 shillings they found in his pockets; and kicked him so savagely that he died in hospital two days later.

Chris Darby was found guilty of non-capital murder. The other three were found to be capital offenders, though Lutt's youth means he can only be detained at Her Majesty's Pleasure.

"Flossie" Forsyth's youth has led to some agitation against his hanging. But the brutal beating of Alan Jee to "shut him up", leaving blood all over Forsyth's shoes, invites truly humane people to feel more concern for innocent Alan, his family and fiancée.

The crowd at Wandsworth Prison for the hanging of vicious killer "Flossie" Forsyth

---

Headless Body Found in Midlands YWCA

TWENTY-ONE-YEAR-OLD Margaret Brown was working in the laundry-room of Birmingham YWCA hotel on December 23 when a heavy-set man burst in and attempted to molest her. Miss Brown screamed, scaring the man off. Staff then searched the building for him, and made a horrifying discovery behind the locked door of Room 4 in the annexe.

On the floor lay the body of 29-year-old shorthand typist Stephanie Baird. But not her head! That lay separately on a bloodstained bed! Post-mortem examination revealed that Miss Baird had been sexually abused after death. There was a note in her room, apparently left by the murderer, which read, "This was the Thing I Thought Would Never Come."

Not a fingerprint has been found to assist inquiries, but police are following up evidence that a "peeping tom" has lurked around the hostel for some weeks. A bus driver's report of a passenger dripping blood in his vehicle on the murder night may prove useful, too, as the blood group of the stains matches Miss Baird's.

Murdered YWCA resident Stephanie Baird

'Beast of the Black Forest' Got His Kicks from Porno Films

HEINRICH POMMERENKE, the "Beast of the Black Forest", has received prison sentences in Germany totalling 140 years after being charged at Freiburg with an astonishing catalogue of crimes:

10 rape-murders
20 rapes
35 assaults and burglaries.

This 23-year-old monster has been a sexual pervert ever since puberty, when he took to molesting girls outside a dance-hall in Mecklenberg. He began his career as a rapist in 1955, and in 1958 attacked two girls in Austria. His first murder victim was 18-year-old Hildegarde Knothe in 1959, whom he followed from a cinema to a park where he raped her before cutting her throat. In 1959 he discovered trains as a suitable site for sex murders. When he found student Dagmar Klimek sleeping on a transcontinental train bound for Italy, he assaulted her, pushed her out of the compartment on to the line, then pulled the communication cord and jumped out after her to rape and kill her where she lay. As his bestial assaults continued, his description began to circulate in the Black Forest area. He was picked up in Freiburg this year and made a full confession. He says that watching pornographic films made him "tense"! Well, he's got more than a century to cool off his lust, and it's safe again to take a walk in the Black Forest!

IN BRIEF

MICHAEL JOHN DAVIES paroled from his life sentence for the murder of John Beckley (*see* 1953). Davies still insists he was not the knife-wielder.

Woman Raped and Paralyzed by Gun Murderer

A MYSTERIOUS GUNMAN forced himself into the car occupied by Michael Gregsten and Valerie Storie as they sat in a field at Dorney Reach, near Slough, England. After forcing Gregsten to make a fantastic all-night drive around the edges of London, the gunman directed him up the A6 and into the layby on Deadman's Hill. There he killed Gregsten; raped Miss Storie; and fired several bullets at her, one of which entered her spine, paralyzing her.

She was found and taken to hospital the following morning. A police hunt for the brown-haired man with brown "staring" eyes she described turned up the peculiar near-fascist loner Peter Louis Alphon. He was reported by hoteliers as behaving suspiciously around the time of the murder, and identified by a Mrs Dalal of Richmond as the stranger who pulled up her skirt and threatened to rape her when she showed him a room to let, saying as he did so, "I am the A6 killer."

But Valerie Storie did not pick Alphon in an identity parade. Indeed, she picked out a seaman who was out of the country at the time of the murder.

The murder weapon was found abandoned on a London bus. Bullets fired from it were found in a hotel room next to the one where Alphon had stayed before the killing. Its occupant, incompetent burglar James Hanratty, was said to be wanted by the police, and the description of the A6 murderer now gave him staring saucer-like blue eyes, like Hanratty's.

Hanratty telephoned Superintedent Bob Acott to protest his innocence, but refused to give himself up, saying he would only be held for burglary. Police found him, nonetheless, in Blackpool. And Valerie Storie identified him positively after asking him to say, "Be quiet. I'm thinking." (Which he pronounced "finking", just as the murderer had done.)

Despite his insistence that he was in Liverpool at the time of the offences, Hanratty goes on trial in the New Year.

SUNDAY PICTORIAL

February 18, 1962   No. 2,444   5d.

THE A6 MURDER

GUILTY

HANRATTY JURY TAKE 9½ HOURS

JAMES HANRATTY
—the A6 killer
First picture

James Hanratty, charged with raping and maiming Valerie Storie and murdering Michael Gregsten

A6 murder victim Michael Gregsten, with his wife

'Identikit' Picture Traps Antique Dealer's Killer

A LL OF ENGLAND'S national newspapers carried on their front pages the awkward-looking drawing of a fierce dark-haired young man. The image was not up to the usual standard of press portraiture. The picture was put together from jigsaw puzzle-like sections for the approval of witnesses, the idea being to obtain a reasonable likeness of a suspect by assembling the right sort of nose, eyes, lips, and so forth.

This new technique, called "Identikit", helped to track down the man who killed Mrs Elsie Batten in Louis Meier's antique shop at Cecil Court, Charing Cross Road, on March 3. Eurasian Edwin Bush (21) argued with Mrs Batten about the price of a dress sword, then killed her and made off with it. Subsequently, he tried to sell it.

At his trial, Bush attempted to win sympathy by claiming that Mrs Batten had provoked him with her racist remarks. True or not, this did not win him a reprieve, and the first victim of the "Identikit" became the latest victim of the hangman.

Brenda's Murderer Caught in Prison after Confession

YOUNG 12-YEAR-OLD Brenda Nash was abducted close to her home at Heston, England, in October last year. Her strangled body was found in Hampshire two months later.

Meanwhile, police inquiries established that a man in a black Vauxhall car who ate peppermints had attacked another girl near Heston in September. A thorough check of 5,000 Vauxhall owners in Surrey and Middlesex drew attention to Albert Arthur Jones, who kept peppermints in his car. The day after Brenda's body was found, Jones's niece contacted police to say that her uncle fitted the description of the man they were hunting. This was still insufficient evidence to charge Jones with Brenda's murder. He went on trial in March for the assault in September, for which he received a 14-year sentence.

While he was in prison, a fellow-convict told the authorities that Jones had privately confessed to Brenda's murder. He was tried and convicted on this new evidence, the jury taking seven minutes to reach a guilty verdict. Jones has returned to prison for life.

Murdering judge Joseph A. Peel of Florida with his wife

Discovery in Wales of Murdered Woman

FORTY-ONE YEARS AGO, 26-year-old chorus-girl Mamie Stuart disappeared. She had married an older man, marine engineer Edward George Shotton, two years previously. In 1919 the couple left rented rooms in Swansea to live in a house called Ty-Llanwydd. One week after the couple moved in the house was left deserted. Concern about Mamie's whereabouts was expressed by her parents whose letters had gone unanswered.

In March 1920 some of Mamie's clothes were found, torn to shreds, together with her shoes, cut to pieces, in a small suitcase, itself locked inside an unclaimed portmanteau which had lain at the Grosvenor Hotel in Swansea since the beginning of the year. Two weeks later, a cleaner found Mamie's mildewed leather handbag, containing £2 in change and her old wartime ration card, tucked away behind a washstand in Ty-Llanwydd.

Shotton was traced and questioned, and turned out to be married already. He claimed that Mamie had left him after a quarrel. The garden of Ty-Llanwydd was dug up, but no human remains or further possessions of Mamie's were found to disprove his story. He was charged with bigamy, for which he received 18 months' imprisonment. There the story rested for some 40 years.

In November of this year, potholers found a woman's body, cut in three pieces, hidden at the bottom of a disused lead-mine in Glamorgan. The clothing matched the description of Mamie's, and superimposition of a picture of Mamie over the skull proved that she had at last been found.

Finally, the postman who had delivered mail to Ty-Llanwydd at the time the Shottons lived there reported to the police a curious but telling incident which he had kept to himself since 1940. He had come across Mr Shotton carrying a heavy sack out of the house. The startled householder had exclaimed in surprise, "Oh, my God! I thought you were a policeman."

And Shotton's explanation? Too late to ask: Edward Shotton died three years ago!

Judge Hired Killers to Eliminate Brother Judge

FIVE YEARS AGO the Hon. Judge C.E. Chillingworth of the Circuit Court, Palm Beach, Florida, disappeared. So did his lady wife. Bloodstains and footprints marking a scuffle showed they had not left their home voluntarily, but nothing more could be established.

Last year, 37-year-old Judge Joseph Peel Jr approached sheriff's aide James Yenzer, asking if he would arrange the murder of a crook called Floyd "Lucky" Holzapfel, who was blackmailing him. With a quietly raised eyebrow, Yenzer plied Holzapfel with drinks in a bugged hotel room. He learned that not only was Judge Peel somehow involved in the death of a police informer named Lew Harvey, but he had employed Holzapfel and another hood called Bobby Lincoln to kidnap the Chillingworths and dump their weighted bodies at sea. It seems that honest Judge Chillingworth knew all about shady Judge Peel's crooked friends, and might have had the scallywag disbarred.

Despite his claims that this is all an attempt to ruin his political career, Judge Peel has collected a couple of life sentences for unlicensed pruning of the Florida judiciary. As a result, he's been disbarred and his political career is finished. Holzapfel is lucky not to be going to the electric chair.

IN BRIEF

FINCH-TREGOFF (*see* 1958). After two trials in which juries could not agree, Dr Bernard Finch was convicted of first-degree and Carole Tregoff of second-degree murder. Both also convicted of conspiracy to murder and given life.

BIRMINGHAM YWCA MURDER (*see* 1960). Irish labourer Patrick Byrne, traced to Warrington, confessed under interrogation. His conviction for murder reduced on appeal to manslaughter as he may be insane. His life sentence is unaffected.

Luciano's Luck Runs Out

SALVATORE LUCIANA joined the Five Points Gang as a boy: immigrant juveniles under the direction of Johnny Torrio (*see* 1919) who continued New York's violent traditions of the Dead Rabbits and Bowery Boys. While still a kid he became friendly with Meyer Lansky, and during Prohibition he and fellow-Sicilians co-operated with Lansky's Jewish mob as the Broadway bootleggers. He now masculinized and anglicized his name to Charlie Luciano.

In 1929 he acquired the nickname "Lucky", when he survived being "taken for a ride", and walked back from the outskirts of New York with a badly cut face after abductors had seized him. Luciano's various stories that this was the work of rival gangsters probably disguised the humiliation of having been striped by an angry cop whose daughter he had seduced.

When Prohibition ended, Luciano used Jewish muscle supplied by Lansky and Bugsy Siegel to eliminate the old "Mustache Petes" whose competition for supremacy kept the Sicilian Mafia locked in internecine warfare. But this understanding didn't prevent him becoming the first really prominent victim of Tom Dewey's crime-busting campaign, when two hookers testified that a large part of their earnings was redirected to him. "Lucky" copped a massive sentence for poncing.

During the war he negotiated with government from his cell, and in return for supplying introductions to local leaders during the allied landings in Sicily – a deal which reinstated the Mafia, whose power in Italy Mussolini had succeeded in destroying! – he was paroled in 1946 and deported, never to return in his lifetime.

Luciano's supreme importance in the formation of modern syndicated crime was his recognition that co-operation is as important a business principle as competition. Although a full-blooded Sicilian Mafioso, his most important alliance was with Meyer Lansky. The two rated practical financial success more highly than ethnic rivalry or hollow prestige. Crime has not looked back since.

Charlie "Lucky" Luciano in his heyday, enjoying a meal in Rome after a round of golf

OBITUARY

SALVATORE LUCIANA AKA CHARLIE 'LUCKY' LUCIANO (1897-1962)

Born in Palermo, Sicily, Luciano was brought to America when he was nine. His first arrest (for shoplifting) came in the following year. A major figure in setting up the national crime syndicate, Luciano was nevertheless the first great Mafia Don sentenced to long-term imprisonment (see 1936). He died of a heart attack in Naples. After a black plumes funeral in Palermo, the body was flown to New York for burial in St John's cemetery.

'Kill Me, Please' said Victim – It's Still Murder!

HANGED IN South Africa, cowboy-clad Marthinus "Killer" Rossouw learned the hard way that you shouldn't do everything your boss tells you!

Rossouw (23) was employed by Baron Dieter von Schauroth as a bodyguard and general gofer. In March last year the playboy-farmer baron was found shot through the head near Cape Town. He appeared to have been robbed, and diamonds littered the scene.

Inquiries showed that the baron's marriage was unhappy; that he had recently insured his life heavily; and that he was suspected of being involved in illegal diamond trading.

Eventually, Rossouw confessed to killing the baron, but his story had a twist. Von Schauroth, he said, had asked him to do it, giving him a cheque for Rand 2,300 and handing him the revolver.

Although this appears to be true, Rossouw was foolish to obey the order. He has now paid the penalty for excessive obedience, leaving an interesting little dispute raging between the baron's insurance company and his widow. The former says von Schauroth committed suicide, invalidating the policy. Baroness von Schauroth points to the court decision that her husband was murdered, and demands payment.

Rent Boy Kills Punter Who Didn't Give Him a Job

SEVENTEEN-YEAR-OLD Manuel Garces from the slums of Valparaiso, Chile, sold himself to wealthy homosexuals in the hope that one of them would help him escape from poverty and squalor.

One of them, Enrique Mercier, an elderly and respected lawyer, seemed to offer the hope of a better life, promising to find the lad satisfactory employment. Later, Mr Mercier was found dead in his office, wearing only a shirt and socks. He'd been beaten over the head and his wallet taken.

The office building staff confirmed to police that male prostitutes had visited the old gentleman after hours. Manuel was caught when he tried to pass a stolen cheque belonging to the dead man.

The lad told police that Mercier had not kept his promise to help him. He has been given 15 years' imprisonment, which doesn't seem too harsh a sentence for a crime born out of disappointment.

Hoover U-Turn After Inside Informer Sings For His Life

FOR 30 YEARS, FBI chief J. Edgar Hoover has angrily denied that there is a Mafia or national crime syndicate. It's no secret that Attorney-General Robert Kennedy passionately disagrees with his top cop, and insists that the Justice Department will go after the big boys of organized crime just as strongly as Inland Revenue always has done.

But now Hoover's jumped at the opportunity to agree with his boss, without eating all his words. For Joe Valachi, fearing that Mafia boss Vito Genovese intends to have him killed in prison, is singing like a canary. He says the real mobsters call the outfit "Cosa Nostra" (Our Thing).

This term, used by Mafiosi in Sicily to distinguish their own particular "families", has been seized upon gratefully by Hoover, who says he has been aware of it all along, and is increasing surveillance of its activities!

Meanwhile, Valachi has helped those investigating the murky world of the crime bosses more than somewhat. In fact, he has

Joe Valachi takes the oath before giving evidence to a Senate sub-committee

given them a detailed insight into the world of the Mafia, naming 317 individual members of the organization, describing the breakdown of New York's "families", and the quasi-Masonic rituals of initiation. He's also done much to stir up the envy and internecine rivalry that "Lucky" Luciano and his allies hoped had been supplanted once and for all by their policy of pragmatism in crime.

Acquitted Husband Sent for Second Murder Trial

GOD FORGIVE YOU! He'll kill again!" cried Ted Garlick's mother-in-law when a jury decided Ted's suicide pact with her daughter did not amount to murder, even though Garlick had survived the gassing that claimed his wife.

The distraught lady was quite right. On October 12 this year, 16-year-old Carol Ann White disappeared after going out to ring her boyfriend from a call-box in West Drayton, England. Her purse was found under the telephone.

The following evening, Ted was walking his dog in the company of relatives when the animal

raced away into a field. Ted followed, and found Carol's body. The girl had died from multiple stab wounds.

Police discovered that Ted had been seen walking past the telephone box the previous evening. He broke down under questioning and confessed to the crime. He had chatted to the girl as she stood by the callbox. When she teased the 25-year-old about his sexual incompetence he had lost his temper and stabbed her repeatedly.

He has handed the murder weapon to the police, and goes on trial in the New Year.

Killer Ted Garlick with his dog Curly

President John Kennedy Assassinated in Dallas

Lee Harvey Oswald

WHILE A SMALL CROWD watched the presidential motorcade pass along Elm Street, Dallas, on November 22, shots rang out, and President Kennedy's head was seen to jerk back. Before his startled driver could accelerate away, Mrs Jacqueline Kennedy had crawled across the trunk of the limousine to protect her husband.

In hospital doctors struggled to save JFK's life, enlarging a bullet wound in his throat to perform a tracheotomy. But massive injury to the side of the president's head meant their work was in vain. Texas Governor John Connally, riding in the seat in front of the President, was also injured, suffering a cracked rib and broken wrist.

Many bystanders thought the shots came from a picket fence in front of the President and to his right. Senator Ralph Yarborough, riding in a car behind the president, smelled cordite and spotted a former army veteran throw himself to the ground as a bullet passed him. Police found a sniper's nest and an abandoned Mannlicher-Carcoma rifle at a window on the fifth floor of a warehouse to the rear of the cavalcade's route.

Within an hour, Lee Harvey Oswald (23), who had been working in the room that morning, was arrested after acting suspiciously in another part of town. Oswald has given no coherent explanation of his actions.

This young man has a very peculiar history. He was discharged from the US Marines when he defected to the USSR, where he married a Russian girl. Since then he has redefected, bringing his wife Marina to the USA. During the summer he was active in New Orleans on behalf of a pro-Castro group. But there are no reports that he has ever expressed particular interest in Mr Kennedy.

President Kennedy's coffin is borne from St Matthew's Cathedral to Arlington Cemetery for burial

Oswald Shot by Strip Club Owner

AFTER 24 HOURS in the hands of Dallas Police Department, officers were transferring Lee Harvey Oswald, President Kennedy's alleged assassin, from their headquarters building when Jack Ruby, proprietor of the Carousel Club, barrelled forward from behind onlooking detectives and fired a pistol pointblank into Oswald's abdomen.

The whole nation witnessed the scene on television, as Oswald, simply dressed in a dark sweater, light shirt and slacks, doubled forward clutching himself with an agonized expression on his face.

Ruby says he acted out of sympathy for Mrs Kennedy on learning that she would have to return to Dallas for Oswald's trial. This concern sits uneasily on a man who came to Texas from Chicago with an influx of hoods, and whose sleazy occupation running strip clubs hardly suggests that his is a sensitive soul.

But whatever his intention, Jack Ruby (born Jacob Rubinstein) has stymied the inquiry into the President's assassination. Guilty or not, Lee Harvey Oswald had to be the starting point for a serious investigation into the killing, and now he has died without answering vital questions concerning the gun and the sniper's position found at his workplace.

Greatest Train Robbery Ever Nets £2 Million

BRUCE REYNOLDS' south-west London mob collaborated with Thomas Wisbey's south-east Londoners this summer for a "big tickle" which had long been in the planning.

At dawn on August 8 the Royal Mail train from Glasgow was halted by a red signal at Bridego Bridge, Buckinghamshire. No sooner had the train juddered to a standstill than several men in balaclavas clambered into the engine compartment and the mail van. The driver was the only person to offer serious resistance. He was hit over the head for his pains in the sole incident of violence in the robbery.

The haul from this audacious robbery was handsome: some £2,631,634 in old notes on their way to the mint for destruction! The untraced "inside man" who advised the gang which train to target was certainly worth his cut

of this spectacular robbery, the biggest on record. From Bridego Bridge the robbers raced away in cars and trucks to a secret destination. A few weeks later, police discovered that this was nearby Leatherslade Farm, rented recently by a couple of Londoners, and a snug hideaway where the gang could lie low.

The brilliant plan collapsed at this point. Those responsible for cleaning up after the stay didn't do their job properly, and left finger-prints galore for police forensic.

Scotland Yard soon knew the men they were looking for. The first, Roger Cordrey (who fixed the signal by covering the green light with a glove and lighting a red lamp with a car battery) was picked up on a wild spending spree in Bournemouth. The rest have been netted steadily, and will go on trial next year.

Leatherslade Farm, the refuge of the train robbers immediately after the hold-up

Hungarian's Horrible Vengeance on Ex-Model Wife

HUNGARIAN REFUGEE Dr Geza de Kaplany, an anaesthetist in California, married beautiful Hajna Piller, daughter of the Hungarian fencing coach who defected at the Melbourne Olympics.

Within two weeks Hajna, who was pressed into the union by her snobbish mother, told her husband that he was an inadequate lover, and that she preferred the embraces of another.

The doctor returned to their San José apartment on August 28 and played loud radio music. By his own account he made love to Hajna before tying her up.

Then, dressed only in Bermuda shorts and sandals, he donned rubber gloves and took swabs of sulphuric, hydrochloric and nitric acid to where his wife lay helpless. He proceeded to destroy his beautiful wife's looks and her sexual

parts with the corrosive chemicals. As Hajna's low wailing rose to desperate screams, neighbours gathered outside; but it appears to have been the doctor himself who telephoned police.

When Hajna died in hospital, de Kaplany was charged with her murder. He refused an insanity plea, saying his motive was to spoil his wife's appearance and have her all to himself. But when a photograph revealing his wife's ruined features, destroyed left breast and corroded genital area was shown to the jury, the doctor threw a tantrum and changed his plea to not guilty by reason of insanity.

He claimed to suffer a split personality, citing as evidence the fact that he used different names when making appointments with two chiropodists. He was found guilty and sentenced to life imprisonment.

Prostitute Crucifies Lover while Posing as Inca Goddess

YERBA BUENA VILLAGE in Mexico fell victim to two confidence tricksters in January when Santos and Cayetano Hernandez assured peasants they could win them riches and favours from old Inca gods in return for money and sexual favours. For months the brothers lived and loved to their hearts' content, but doubt set in when no riches materialized.

Then the two brothers persuaded prostitute Magdalena Solis and her hustler brother Eleazor to come to Yerba Buena and pose as incarnations of gods. The cult revived. Sacrifices renewed. Sexual orgies were enjoyed by all. Two doubters were beaten to death.

But in June, Magdalena saw her favourite teenage lesbian lover enjoying sex with a male cultist. The "goddess" ordered the crucifixion of fickle Celina Salvana, and beat her unconscious while she hung on the cross. The girl was then killed and ritually burned.

Human sacrifice terrified a

teenage lad, who fetched a policeman. When cultists killed both informant and officer, they invited serious reprisals. Santos Hernandez was killed in the ensuing shootout. Cayetano had already been murdered by a cultist who wanted his place as high priest. The Solises have each received 30-year prison sentences for murder.

IN BRIEF

CONVICTED OF the murder of Carol Ann White (*see* 1962), Ted Garlick has been sentenced to life imprisonment.

MYSTERIOUSLY FOUND after New Year party in Sydney, Australia, the undressed bodies of government research scientist Stanley Bogle and Mrs Margaret Chandler.

Cause of death cannot be identified. Is this a KGB murder with secret poisons, or an undetected overdose of LSD used as an aphrodisiac?

Strangler Slays Thirteenth Victim in Boston

TERROR STALKS Boston, USA: an unknown man who gains admittance to the apartments of lone women, rapes them, and strangles them. Then he presents them as gruesome spectacles:

The victims' legs splayed obscenely apart; a dinky little floppy bow tied under their chins. Sometimes this bow is formed from the cord that strangled them, sometimes from their stockings or pantihose.

The strangler has killed women as old as 85 and as young as 19. He has variously stabbed and mutilated his victims, and raped them before or after they died.

The first five victims were aged from 55 to 75, suggesting a man with a mother fixation. But then the pattern changed. Sophie Clark was a strikingly tall and beautiful black girl of 25. His next victim was also young. Then he struck against 69-year-old Mary Brown with unbridled ferocity, crushing her head with a lead pipe and repeatedly driving a fork into her breast. The following victim, Beverly Samans, was a young woman. She was strangled after being tied to her bedposts, blindfolded and raped repeatedly. When she was dead, he used a jackknife to inflict 22 stab wounds on the body, leaving the knife behind with not a fingerprint to

Some of the victims of the Boston Strangler

THE STRANGLER'S VICTIMS

1962	Anna Slesers	55
	Mary Mullen	85
	Helen Blake	65
	Ida Jurga	75
	Jane Sullivan	67
	Sophie Clark	25
	Patricia Bissette	23
1963	Mary Brown	69
	Beverly Samans	23
	Evelyn Corbin	58
	Joan Graff	23
1964	Mary Sullivan	19

help detectives trace the killer.

Evelyn Corbin (58) was throttled by the killer's bare hands for a change. The bow that is his hallmark was tied around her ankle. And this year's victim, Mary Sullivan (19), killed on January 4, was again throttled manually after being tied up and raped. Her pretty body was left naked, and a card from her apartment reading "Happy New Year" was placed between her toes.

How does the killer gain access to these women? The city has dwelt under a pall of fear for 18 months; most solitary widows and spinsters have multiple locks and chains on their doors, and refuse admittance to any man without positive identification. Yet the strangler still gains entry and kills with impunity. What is his cover? Is he an an electrician? A plumber? A gas-fitter? A public health inspector? A brush salesman? A postman? Or, most sinister of all, could he present himself as a policeman, investigating his own crimes? The women of Boston, who have to live with the fear of becoming his victim, need to know!

'Measuring Man' of Boston Assaulted 1,000 Women

WHILE BOSTON TREMBLES at the degradations of the unknown strangler (*see* these pages), 33-year-old Albert DeSalvo has gained access to hundreds of lone Boston women's apartments by the simple expedients of a clipboard, a measuring-tape and a persuasive manner.

Claiming to represent a modelling agency, he invites ladies to undress and let him measure their vital statistics as a prelude to a possible lucrative and rewarding career in front of the cameras. Sexually insatiable, DeSalvo, whose wife divorced him for his inordinate demands on her body, then proceeds to rape them. He has already served one prison sentence for similar crimes. When apprehended previously, he boasted of once raping six women in a morning.

Active again during the past two years, DeSalvo was caught and sent to Bridgewater mental institution this autumn. Despite the strangler terror, De Salvo believes he has gained access to over 1,000 women in Boston with his modelling ploy. What price ambition? Any, it would seem.

Prostitute's Tainted Evidence Reduces Millionaire's Sentence

STRIKING RED-HEADED call-girl Gloria Kendall testified in New York this October that millionaire punter Mark Fein sought her help when he killed his bookie. Gloria, who uses 30 different names as a call-girl, and whose criminal record classifies her as a "common prostitute", says that Fein showed her the body of Rubin Markowitz, which had wounds to the head and chest. Gloria arranged for a couple of guys to box up the grocery-store clerk and bookmaker and feed him to the fish in Harlem River, whence police dredged him up. The bookie's little black book was found to include both Gloria's phone number and Mark Fein's name, which had a debt of $7,200 recorded against it.

Thirty-two-year-old Fein's counsel hastened to point out that Miss Kendall "aint no Goody Two-Shoes. Can you pronounce Mark Fein guilty of first-degree murder on the testimony of Gloria?" he asked incredulously of the jury. The jurors saw his point

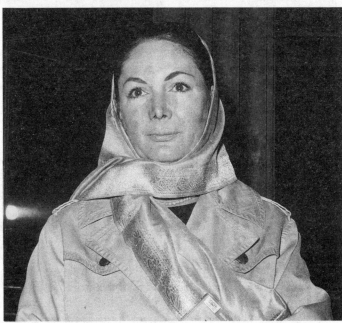

Hooker Gloria Kendall (aka Carmela Lazarus) arrives in court to testify against Mark Fein

and convicted Fein of second-degree murder, which sent him down for 30 years.

Nobody knows why he killed Markowitz over a gambling debt he could have paid ten times over.

Sharon Kinne Caught at Last — Arrested in Mexico

AFTER FOUR MURDER TRIALS, one terminating in her acquittal of the murder of Mrs Patricia Jones, the other three all mistrials when she was charged with killing her husband (see 1960, 1962), lethal 23-year-old Sharon Kinne has been caught with a smoking pistol in her hand. Literally!

In September this year Sharon went to Mexico City with a man.

Four days later she was out on her own when she met radio announcer Francisco Ordonez and went to a motel room with him. When the proprietor heard shots and hurried to investigate, he found Ordonez dead on the bed, and Sharon about to vamoose with her hot .22 in her hand. She shot the proprietor in the back as he tried to withdraw, but he seized her and was still holding her when police arrived.

Sharon explained that she had not understood Mr Ordonez' intentions when she accompanied him to the motel, and shot him when he tried to rape her . The Mexican court did not believe this story and sentenced her to ten years' imprisonment.

Meanwhile, the Kansas City D.A.'s office asked for the murder weapon. Ballistic tests proved it had also been used to kill Patricia Jones, whose husband had taken Mrs Kinne's fancy. Sharon cannot

be re-tried for that crime, but a foolish appeal against the severity of her sentence has enabled the Mexican courts to prolong her imprisonment by three years!

Multiple murderess Sharon Kinne

Wife Goes on Murder Jaunt 'For the Ride'

ON APRIL 7, laundry van driver John West was battered and stabbed at his home in Workington, England. A neighbour saw a car speed away from the scene of the crime. In a pocket of a raincoat left behind by one of the attackers police found a medallion inscribed "G.O.Evans", and the name and address, in Preston, of one Norma O'Brien.

When questioned by police, 17-year-old Norma agreed that three years previously she had met a "Ginger" Evans who wore such a medallion. Traced to his Preston lodgings with Mr and Mrs Peter Allen, Gwynne Owen Evans (real name John Robson Welby) admitted the theft, but accused Allen of the killing. Allen returned the compliment. The jury decided both were murderers, and both have been hanged.

Oddest feature of the clumsy crime: Mrs Allen and her children accompanied the killers from Preston to Workington in the stolen car, simply for the ride!

IN BRIEF

30-YEAR SENTENCES imposed on Great Train Robbers (see 1963) Ronald Biggs, Gordon Goody, Roy John James, Robert Welch and Charley Wilson have shocked public opinion, as these are longer than the normal period served by "lifers" who have murdered. Do our courts value property more highly than life and limb, we wonder?

The 'Measuring Man' Was the Boston Strangler

ALBERT DESALVO, arrested last year for multiple assaults on women, has been identified as the dreaded "Strangler" who has terrorized the city since 1962 (*see* 1964).

Diagnosed schizophrenic after his arrest as the "measuring man" (*see* 1964), DeSalvo was sent to Bridgewater secure mental institution. There the erotomaniac (dismissed from the army in 1955 for molesting a 9-year-old girl) talked at length about the stranglings with George Nassar, himself suspected of being the killer. Nassar thought DeSalvo suspiciously unforthcoming about the crimes. Police are now satisfied DeSalvo knows details that have never been released to the public, and conclude that he is the "Strangler".

Lawyer F. Lee Bailey, acting for DeSalvo, has apparently heard his client confess to all 11 strangler killings, plus two others. It seems unlikely that DeSalvo will ever be charged, however, because his schizophrenia makes a verdict of Not Guilty by Reason of Insanity a foregone conclusion.

Yet with all the confident assurance that the case is closed, some experts still voice doubts. They point out that:

1. It is extraordinary for this type of serial murderer to confine himself to lesser offences once the appetite for murder has been excited, and yet "Measuring Man" DeSalvo was active for nine months after the last strangling.

2. DeSalvo's exceptionally high rate of sexual activity is not characteristic of a ritualistic killer. DeSalvo wants sex morning, noon and night, saying, "Five or six times a day don't mean much to me." Psychiatrists believe sexual serial murderers to be withdrawn loners whose furtive sex-life will not be familiar to those who know them.

3. DeSalvo's knowledge of unpublished details of the murders came to light after he had held lengthy conversations with the former suspect who shopped him. It is argued that the strangler, whoever he is, would probably wind up in Bridgewater, and so DeSalvo might have learned these details from another inmate.

"Measuring Man" Albert DeSalvo, who has confessed to being the "Boston Strangler"

Swinger's Kids Mysteriously Abducted then Murdered

GLAMOROUS NEW YORK cocktail waitress Alice Crimmins (26) led a "swinging" lifestyle. Her husband Edmund separated from her because he couldn't keep up with all those lovers!

But he came round quickly on May 14 when she telephoned him to say their children, Eddie and Missie, were not in their beds. The kids' room was fastened on the outside by a hook-and-eye latch. Alice says this was to stop them raiding the fridge: police think the toreador-pants-wearing beauty really wanted to stop them interrupting her perpetually active love-life!

Someone appears to have got in and out of the window, taking the children from their beds. Missie was found strangled in her pyjamas on a building site nearby. Eddie, a week later about a mile away. So who killed the Crimmins children?

Burglar Confesses to Wylie and Hoffert Killings

TURNED IN TO New York police by drug addicts Nathan and Marjorie Delaney, heroin-habituated burglar Richard Robles (22) has confessed to the brutal murders of Janice Wylie and Emily Hoffert two years ago.

So the black man convicted of those crimes walks free.

Nineteen-year-old George Whitman Jr always said police had threatened and beaten a confession out of him. In an illiterate statement he wrote, "I was so squared if they told me name was tom, dick or harry I would have said yes."

Wylie and Hoffert were found in their apartment by their roommate on a day when both were off work. Wylie had been stripped naked and eviscerated. The two victims were tied together with strips of sheet.

Robles now claims that he enjoyed various sexual activities with Wylie, with her consent. Then, under the influence of heroin, an impulse to savage violence had overcome him.

> **I WAS SO SQUARED IF THEY TOLD ME NAME WAS TOM, DICK OR HARRY I WOULD HAVE SAID YES.**
>
> **GEORGE WHITMAN, JR**

London's Mysterious 'Nudes-in-the-Thames' Slayings Stop

GIANT HUNT FOR MANIAC SEX KILLER

Daily Mirror — Nude Number 4 found strangled in an alley—riddle of night visitor

The "Jack the Stripper" scare

THE WEST LONDON nude murders have suddenly stopped, after a massive police operation which entailed questioning all motorists discovered driving in Hammersmith and Kensington after midnight. The naked bodies of eight prostitutes have been found either in the Thames or on the foreshore near Chiswick, or dumped in garages and back alleys in this area of Britain's capital.

The scare began in February last year when a woman's body was washed up by Hammersmith Bridge. In April another appeared at Duke's Meadow. It was then recalled that two bodies had been found the previous November. As bodies continued to turn up, police observations prompted certain definite conclusions:

The killer was choking his victims when they practised fellatio on him. (Proved by missing teeth and semen traces in the throats.)

He was storing their bodies in or near a car-spraying works; proved by flecks of paint on them.

He was abusing the bodies again after death.

He drove a small van, seen a couple of times speeding away from the sites where bodies were found.

His occupation justified his driving around the West End at night.

The killer's secret lair, a sprayshop at Westpoint Trading Estate, West Acton, was stumbled upon with the discovery of Bridie O'Hara's body. The case was finally closed when a security guard for the estate – one of the three final suspects – committed suicide saying the pressure was too much.

Discovery of body in West London puts Police on trail of 'Nudes in the Thames' killer

THE NUDES IN THE THAMES

THE NUDES IN THE THAMES

1963
JUNE – Elizabeth Figg, found in the river
NOVEMBER Gwynneth Rees, found in the river

1964
FEBRUARY – Hannah Tailford, found by Hammersmith Bridge
APRIL – Irene Lockwood, found in Duke's Meadow
APRIL – Helene Barthelemy, found in Swyncombe Avenue, Brentford

1965
JULY – Mary Fleming, found in Berymede Road, Acton Lane
NOVEMBER – Margaret McGowan, found in Hornton Street, Kensington
FEBRUARY – Bridie O'Hara, found at Westpoint Trading Estate, West Acton

Tucson 'Pied Piper' Leads Schoolkids to Murder

RUNTY LITTLE Charles Schmid (22) raised his 5ft 3in stature by wearing cowboy boots packed with cardboard and crushed Coca-Cola cans. He dyed his hair jet black, employed eyeshadow to give himself a heavy-lidded smouldering look, and painted a mole on his cheek.

This bizarre posturing impressed high school kids, the only ones who would pay "Smiddy" any attention. He enjoyed being a charismatic personality among immature juveniles.

On May 31 last year Schmid told young John Saunders and Mary French that he felt like killing a girl. French decoyed 15-year-old Alleen Rowe to join them for a late-night drive in the desert. There Schmid raped her in front of Saunders, afterwards telling him to hit her over the head with a rock. Alleen ran off, but "Smiddy" chased her, caught her, killed her, and buried her with the help of French and Saunders.

In August this year, Schmid was consumed with jealousy when his 17-year-old girlfriend, Gretchen Fritz, boasted of having gone "all the way" with a boy in California. Gretchen and her 13-year-old sister Wendy disappeared. When Schmid boasted of killing them to Richard Bruns, the young man did not believe him. So "Smiddy" took him to the bodies in the desert.

Bruns, fearing his own girlfriend was next on Schmid's hit-list, went to the police in November. Schmid, French and Saunders are now awaiting trial.

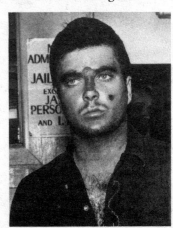

Charles Schmid

Hindley & Brady: The Moors Murderers

Police searching Saddleworth Moor, near Manchester, for the victims of Hindley and Brady

Robbery, Yes...Murder, No! Said Whistle-Blowing Sister and Brother-in-Law

SEVENTEEN-YEAR-OLD David Smith was not an especially law-abiding young man. When his sister-in-law's boyfriend, Ian Brady, talked about the Marquis de Sade and the appeal of his cruelty, Dave was impressed. When he talked about "rolling a queer", Dave was prepared to help pick up 17-year-old Edward Evans in a pub and bring him back to the ordinary little estate house on Wardle Brook Avenue, Manchester where Ian Brady said they would rob him.

But when it came to murder... David wanted no part! David was in the kitchen when his sister-in-law, Myra Hindley, ran in and screamed at him to help Ian. In the sitting-room David found Ian smashing a hatchet into Eddie's head. When he had killed the young man, he handed the weapon to Dave, saying, "Feel the weight of that!" And before they cleaned up, he said: "It's done. It's the messiest yet. It normally takes only one blow."

Dave slunk home to his young wife, Myra's sister Maureen, and the terrified pair armed themselves with a screwdriver to hide in a public telephone box until dawn, when they called the police to tell of the unbelievable horror Dave had witnessed. Doubting policemen surrounded the house. A detective wearing a delivery-man's white coat knocked on the door and with Edward Evan's body found upstairs, Hindley and Brady were arrested.

Clue to Evil in Childhood Prayerbook

A search of the house turned up a luggage deposit ticket carefully hidden in the spine of the innocent white missal Myra had been given for her first communion. The ticket led to two suitcases at Manchester station. The suitcases contained sado-masochistic paraphernalia of whips and bonds, pornographic books and pictures; and the horrifying solution to the mystery of Lesley Ann Downey.

Cruel Child Killers Made Gloating Souvenirs

Ten-year-old Lesley Ann had been missing for nearly a year. She had disappeared in December 1964 and not a clue to her fate had ever been found. Now there was proof in lewd photographs and the most appalling audio-tape ever recorded. Pictures of little Lesley Ann, looking uncomfortable as she had to stand undressed before the camera. A dreadful tape recording of the child pleading to go home because "her mum would kill her" for being late, while a relentless Hindley and Brady go on doing whatever they're doing to her; and making her do whatever it is they want her to do. Apart from Myra's threats to lose her temper and slap the frightened child, the most sinister words are the repeated command to Lesley Ann to "Put it in". In later years, however, Myra has insisted that this isn't "as bad as it sounds", implying that it refers simply to something like a gag.

After what seems like endless minutes of this sadism comes the eerily inappropriate sound of merry Christmas music: "The Little Drummer Boy" and "Jolly Old St Nicholas".

More Murders Become Moors Murders

Pencilled notes in Brady's handwriting proved to be plans for another murder: that of 12-year-old John Kilbride. It was from these notes, some snapshots and the testimony of friends and neighbours, that detectives were gradually able to piece together what had happened.

Ian Brady was an unusually successful child-abusing killer because he had a willing woman accomplice. Kids are told not to accept sweeties and lifts from strange men. Brady didn't drive. Myra owned and operated their mini-van, and she invited kids to come with her for picnics on the moors. No doubt other missing children from the Gorton district of Manchester had fallen prey to this monstrous couple. Sixteen-year-old Pauline Reade lived near David and Maureen Smith and disappeared in July 1963. Twelve-year-old Keith Bennett has been missing since June 1964.

It is quite impossible to contemplate the release of these murderers. Relatives of the victims have sworn to take the law into their own hands should the pair ever be paroled. The animosity towards Brady and Hindley also extends to their families. There were angry scuffles at the funeral of Myra's sister, Maureen, even though she had set aside family loyalty to expose the murders.

The victims were buried on Saddleworth Moor. Brady had been an obsessive lover of moor — and since his Scottish childhood. The couple transported soil from the newly-turned graves back to Wardle Brook Avenue, prepared to tell anyone that they liked to carry moor- and humus in the van for their garden. Carefully posed photographs of Myra on the moor at last led the police to the graves of Lesley Ann Downey and John Kilbride and the couple were charged with their murders.

Sullen Couple in a World of their Own

The murderous pair made no confession and coldly denied everything. Myra's one moment of emotion came when police told her the forensic laboratory had accidentally killed her pet dog. Myra screamed at them "You bloody murderers!" She

was oblivious of any irony.

The two were office workers at a Manchester chemicals firm. Commonplace 19-year-old Myra became privately obsessed with the brooding 24-year-old Brady, and confided to her diary how thrilled she was when he noticed and eventually dated her.

She had fallen in love with a child of the Glasgow Gorbals whose juvenile delinquent record gave way in early childhood to an obsession with sadism and Nazism. Myra's girlish infatuation willingly embraced her lover's peculiar ideas. She let him cane her. She accepted his nickname "Hessy" for her – a double pun on the names of pianist Myra Hess and Hitler's deputy, Rudolf Hess. She joined him in his appalling murders. The couple remained sullenly withdrawn right through their trial. The only spark of humanity was in Myra's admission, "I feel ashamed", when asked what she felt on hearing the tape of Lesley Ann Downey.

When the two were given life sentences at Chester Assizes in 1966, there were strenuous appeals for the revival of capital punishment in Britain.

Myra Hindley

Ian Brady

MYRA'S IMPRISONMENT

1972 Prison governor Dorothy Wing is reprimanded for taking Myra on a routine walk outside jail, as if anticipating parole.

1973 Prison officer Pat Cairns becomes Myra's lesbian lover and plots her escape. Caught and convicted.

1986 Myra confesses to Reade and Bennett murders.

1987 Myra and Ian separately help police searches. Pauline Reade's body found in August.

1988 Author Jean Richie wins Myra's trust, but writes very hostile and condemnatory book about her.

LORD LONGFORD – THE MOORS MURDERERS' FRIEND

Catholic peer and former Labour cabinet minister Lord Longford has often been attacked for regularly visiting Brady and Hindley in prison. As a Christian he recognizes his duty not to abandon those who have erred. He leaves judgement to God.

Longford regards Ian Brady as unbalanced and Myra Hindley as a woman overcome by an immature love that allowed her to be in thrall to Brady and his perverted desires. Especially controversial is his view that Hindley would not constitute a danger to the public if she were paroled. Indeed, some people believe that she should remain locked up for her own safety.

Police find the body of Pauline Reade, 20 years after the conviction of Brady and Hindley

Mayhem in London Outside Wormwood Scrubs

The scene of the slaying of police officers in Braybrook Street

THREE UNARMED London policemen have been gunned down in cold blood on Old Oak Common. The killings occurred when Detective Sergeant Christopher Head ordered his patrol car to stop so that he could investigate a blue Vanguard estate car parked suspiciously close to Wormwood Scrubs prison.

The occupants of the Vanguard, villains Harry Roberts, John Witney and John Duddy, were in fact contemplating burglary when approached by Head and Detective Constable David Wombwell. Roberts immediately opened fire, closely followed by his two accomplices.

The patrol car driver was shot dead before he could either help his comrades or escape the murderous villains. A passer-by took the number of the blue Vanguard, which was traced to a lock-up garage under Waterloo railway arches, rented to an individual called John Witney.

He confessed to having been in the company of Roberts and Duddy. The latter was easily tracked down in Glasgow, where he had family.

Ex-soldier Harry Roberts, experienced in jungle warfare, kitted himself out with camping gear and disappeared in the direction of Epping Forest. He was not caught until October, when a schoolboy found his camp in Hertfordshire woodland. Once surrounded, Roberts came quietly. The three murderers received life sentences at the Old Bailey in December.

Drifting Seaman Slays Eight Nurses: Rapes One, Misses One

ON JULY 14, passers-by were startled to see a young woman, precariously perched on the narrow window-ledge of a bedroom in the nurses' home at the South Chicago Community Hospital, screaming for help.

Inside the building, Pamela Lee Wilkeming, Nina Jo Schmale, Valentina Pasion, Patricia Ann Matusek, Mary Ann Jordan, Merlita Gargullo, Suzanne Bridget Farris and Gloria Jean Davie, student nurses in their early 20s, had been brutally murdered. All had been stabbed except Patricia Matusek, kicked in the stomach and strangled.

The girl on the window ledge, 23-year-old Corazan Amurao, was the sole survivor. She had hidden successfully under a bed as the killer took his victims one by one to their doom. She recounted what had happened that evening.

A lean-faced, pock-marked young man with a tattoo on his arm reading "Born to Raise Hell" rang the doorbell. When Miss Amurao answered it, she found herself facing a knife and a gun. The young man told her he only wanted money. Pushing his way in, he secured her and five other nurses with torn sheets. Around midnight, two other resident nurses returned, one accompanied by visitor Mary Ann Jordan.

When all the nurses were bound, the intruder became increasingly jumpy, until he took Pamela Wilkeming into an adjacent room. Her scream as he stabbed her was choked by the piece of sheet he drew round her neck. Twenty minutes later he returned for another victim; twenty minutes later for another. The remaining girls cowered under their beds, but only Miss Amurao escaped his search. The last victim, Gloria Jean Davie, was the only one he raped. He spent half an hour in normal and anal penetration, at one point politely asking her to put her legs around his back.

Miss Amurao's clear and accurate description led to the speedy arrest of the drug-abusing killer, who was picked up in hospital after trying to cut his wrists in a seedy

Richard Speck is led away after receiving the death sentence on eight counts of murder

flophouse. Ordinary Seaman Richard Speck (24) was easily identified by his tattoo, and his likeness to an "artist's impression".

The jury took just 50 minutes to reach a guilty verdict. Speck has been sentenced to death in the electric chair.

Berserk Ex-Marine Slaughters 21 on University Campus

CLEAN-LIMBED, crew-cut Charles Whitman (25) was every conservative's ideal of a perfect son. Eagle scout, ex-marine, he was a youthful version of the American dream.

The ideal broke down in the small hours of August 1, when the beefy blond engineering student stabbed his wife and his mother. He left notes to the effect that the murders were to save them the embarrassment of what he was about to do next – that was, to take an arsenal of weapons to the observation deck on the 27th storey of the University of Texas tower and spend the morning picking off passers-by. He had killed 21 people and injured another 28 by midday when three police officers broke in on Whitman and shot him dead.

Was it nature or nurture that ruined Charles Whitman? The young man hated his father, who was excessively strict. Whitman's first signs of disturbance dated from the time his parents' marriage broke up. On the other hand, pathologists found a tumour on Whitman's brain, pressing hard on the aggression centre.

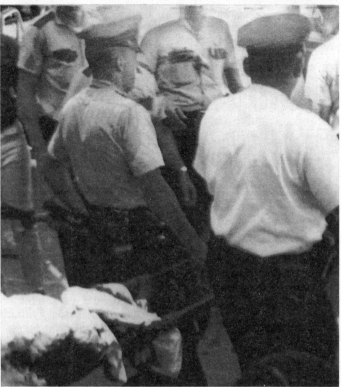

The covered body of beserk gunman Charles Whitman is carried from the University of Texas Tower

IN BRIEF

CHARLES SCHMID (*see* 1965) sentenced to 55 years' imprisonment for rape-murder of Aileen Rowe; John Saunders life imprisonment and Mary French 4 to 5 years for abetting the offence.

BRITAIN JOINS the civilized countries of Europe, as the death penalty for murder is abolished. Treason, piracy and arson in the royal dockyards remain capital offences, though it is hard to imagine anyone being hanged for the last two!

EDDIE RICHARDSON, Charlie Richardson and Frankie Fraser (*see* this page) jailed after "torture trial" describes their gang's kangaroo courts with physical torture of enemies and traitors.

Gangfight in South London, Who Rules Now?

WHO RULES the south London underworld? A gunfight at the Catford nightclub "Mr Smith and the Witch Doctor" tried to settle the question recently. The Richardson brothers of Camberwell inflicted their services as "protectors" on the club-owners only to find rivals hoping to displace them filling the bar in the small hours of March 8. Deciding enough was enough, gang leader Eddie Richardson hopped on a table at 3.00 am and announced no further drinks would be served without his permission. It was the signal for staff and innocent punters to depart in a hurry.

Then fighting broke out. Guns were pulled. The police arrived too late to stop the fighting. They found the smoke-filled, cordite-smelling club wrecked and empty. Most of the wounded, including Eddie Richardson, had been driven away from the mayhem in cars.

Outside were his chief lieutenant, "Mad Frankie" Fraser, nursing a broken leg, and Richard Hart, a distant cousin of the East End's notorious Kray twins, who lay dead on the street.

Careful police reconstruction of the physical evidence in the club led to "Mad Frankie" being charged with murder, but in the absence of corroborating evidence from eye-witnesses, he was only given five years for "causing an affray", as were Richardson and two others.

Sam Sheppard Walks Free After 12 Years

TWELVE YEARS AGO, Dr Samuel Sheppard was convicted of murdering his wife in Cleveland, Ohio. He told a cock-and-bull story about a "bushy-haired intruder" who broke in and knocked him out twice in the middle of the night (*see* 1954).

Two years ago, brilliant young lawyer F. Lee Bailey secured Sam an appeal, claiming that the trial was flawed by a "carnival atmosphere" and "prejudicial publicity".

This year the re-trial was heard, and Bailey won the doctor's acquittal. He pointed out that none of Sam's story has been disproved, nor was Sam "unharmed" by the assailant's furious assault: he attended his wife's funeral in a wheelchair and wearing a neck-brace.

In fact, the whole prosecution case was "ten pounds of hogwash in a five pound bag", according to Bailey. The jury agreed with him and Sheppard was acquitted.

Sexy Welsh Blonde Manipulated Men to Murder for her

BUSTY BLONDE Kim Newell knows how to get what she wants from a man. Sex first. Lots of it. And then, whatever else she wants from him. An abortion, say. Money. All he can lay hands on. Assistance in murdering an inconvenient woman.

Back in Wales, in her teens, Kim worked as a confectioner's assistant. She enjoyed a passionate affair with Eric Jones, 20 years older than her and 20 years richer. When Kim became pregnant, she demanded an abortion. Once he'd done that, she had an even better blackmailing hook driven in to him, although she didn't use it at first. She went to Berkshire where she took a job at Borocourt Hospital. Here, she met big, slow Raymond Cook, a draughtsman training as a male nurse.

Ray was 10 years older than Kim and a great deal wealthier, thanks to a better-educated property-owning wife who was 11 years older than he.

Kim claimed to love Ray. And to need his (wife's!) money in ever-increasing amounts. She persuaded Ray to live with her. When that cut his allowance off, she sent him back: to insure Mrs June Cook's life.

Then Eric Jones was summoned from Denbighshire and told the police would learn all about the abortion he'd once given underage Kim if he didn't come and give her another! He was also told to give Ray a hand in staging an accident to get rid of June.

On March 2, Cook took June drinking. On the way home in their red Mini, they were stopped by Jones, driving his blue Cortina, near Henley-on-Thames. June was dragged from the car, battered over the head with a jack, and pushed back into the driving seat. The car was driven cautiously into a tree at Rumerhedge Wood. Cook then got in the passenger seat to play injured. Astute village bobby PC Sherlock realized the "crash" had been far too gentle for the injuries June had sustained; he spotted, too, blood outside the car.

With Eric Jones's Cortina traced, and Kim Newell associated with him, the plot unravelled. The Lady Macbeth of Berkshire received the life sentence also awarded to her two dupes.

Kim Newell, charged with the Berkshire Mini murder, taken to court under police escort

Eric Jones, who was blackmailed into helping with the murder of Mrs June Cook

Rapist Schoolboy Left Toothmarks in Girl's Breast

FIFTEEN-YEAR-OLD Linda Peacock was found raped and strangled in the cemetery at Biggar, Scotland on August 17. Her right breast was so savagely bitten that clear impressions of unusual pitted canine teeth remained on her flesh, and the mark of a dropped filling.

When police checked a nearby school for delinquent boys, they soon figured that the young rogues were trying to cover for one of their number, Gordon Hay. The 17-year-old had been absent on the day of the murder, although he vigorously denied this. He was snared though by a match of the dental impressions which proved that his were the fangs that had buried themselves in poor Linda's bosom.

Since he is under 18, the vicious young man is detained at Her Majesty's pleasure. The appeal court has upheld this new form of forensic evidence – toothprints in erogenous zones.

Panties, 4,000 Miles from Home, Solve Two Murders

AMERICAN PATRICK D'ARCY'S first murder plot was as complicated as an Agatha Christie story. Only one little mistake led to its solution, and the discovery of his second murder – he left a pair of panties behind!

He apparently quarrelled with his beautiful 28-year-old girlfriend, Maria Domenech, when she discovered that he was married. She drew out her $6,000 savings in May, and went on holiday to Europe to forget about him. Travel agent D'Arcy got himself a passport in the name of Mr A. Young.

No sooner did Maria reach Paris than "Mr A. Young" joined her, and the two spent a pleasant evening together on May 21, travelling to London, and thence to Ireland, where "Mr Young" hired

a car in Dublin. On May 22, car headlights were seen at 4.00 am on the Moher Cliff, County Clare. At 8.00 am "Mr Young" checked into the nearby Shannon airport hotel, but left again at midday, returned the car in Dublin and flew to New York. Exit "Mr Young".

On May 24, Maria's raven-haired body was washed up on Doolin Strand, below Moher Cliff. The body was naked and unidentifiable except for a pair of black panties. Made in America, they supplied the vital clue. The corpse's fingerprints were sent to New York and, *mirabile dictu*, identified, since Maria was both a Puerto Rican immigrant and a City social worker – both categories whose fingerprints are filed.

The NYPD visited Maria's

mother, only to find she had disappeared, though a card from Maria posted at Orly Airport enabled checks on the girl's movements in Paris to begin.

Checks on her several boyfriends soon uncovered D'Arcy, who turned out to have been the lover of Mrs Domenech and her daughter! When he absconded, police found the telltale "A. Young" passport in his office, and the story of Maria's death fell into place.

By the time they caught up with D'Arcy in Miami this July, however, he had killed himself. So we shall never know how he killed and disposed of Mrs Domenech. Indeed, had he not left American panties on a corpse in Ireland, we would never have known that he killed at all!

F. Lee Bailey Suspended after Losing Murder Trial

AMERICAN ANAESTHETIST Carl Coppolino thought he'd found the perfect poison: succinylcholine, which occurs naturally in the body but relaxes muscles if injected in additional doses. Overdoses paralyze and kill.

When Dr Coppolino remarried after his wife Carmela's death in 1965, his jilted lover Marjorie Farber told police she had watched the doctor inject her own husband with poison, and then suffocate him when it failed to take effect. But state prosecutors were unable to prove the presence of toxins in the body, and jealous Mrs Farber's word was not enough to convict the doctor.

Detailed analysis of the late Mrs Coppolino's brain, however, revealed artificially manufactured succinic acid, and despite gruelling cross-examination by F. Lee Bailey, Dr Joseph Umberger convinced a jury of Coppolino's guilt – espe-

Dr Carl Coppolino is led away in handcuffs after his conviction for murder in Naples, Florida

cially when they learned Carmela was insured for $65,000!

A furious Bailey launched such a blistering attack on the prosecu-

tors after the case that he has been banned from practising in New Jersey for a year. His client has received a life sentence.

New Drug Law May Bring Mafia to Britain

BRITISH LEGISLATORS have been swayed by popular press hysteria over a handful of doctors over-prescribing heroin and cocaine to a few addicts, and a handful of drug-addicts who fill their prescriptions at all-night chemists in the Piccadilly area, only to sell the surplus on the streets to other addicts; a couple of these doctors are corrupt, and a couple are convinced their actions are medically sound.

Parliament's new Dangerous Drugs Act prohibits the prescription of these drugs on the National Health. From now on, addicts must be referred to treatment centres for "cold turkey".

It remains to be seen whether this will have a beneficial effect, or whether, as many observers fear, it will give organized crime, notably the Mafia, the toe-hold in Britain it has long been seeking, and lead to a massive increase in professionally "pushed" hard drugs, ultimately affecting juveniles and schoolchildren.

IN BRIEF

US Supreme Court decision to hear two cases designating capital punishment "Cruel and Unusual" has frozen action on Death Row. Killers like Richard Speck and Charles Schmid (*see* 1965/6) (awarded death sentence for murders of the Fritz sisters, *see* 1964) will now be held alive until the Supreme Court decides whether or not their execution would be constitutional.

Dr Martin Luther King's Assassin Caught in England

JAMES EARL RAY, killer of Martin Luther King Jr, was arrested in London in June, and returned to the USA in July to go on trial next year.

Dr King was shot in Memphis, Tennessee, on April 4 as he stepped onto the balcony of the Lorraine Motel. Ray was in the hotel opposite, firing from a bathroom window. He fled immediately, dumping his weapon in the door of a shop. His subsequent peregrinations were so complicated, sophisticated and well-financed as to encourage suspicion that powerful paymasters guided the actions of this petty crook.

A small-time robber, Ray escaped from Missouri State Prison last year. After his escape he armed and placed himself perfectly to kill Dr King, coming to Memphis in May to support a demonstration. Though just what sort of organization feels it protects its own interests best by murdering the civil rights leader is unclear, especially as his was a voice of moderation, a bulwark against the militancy among some younger members of the movement.

After the murder, Ray reached Canada with forged documentation giving him identities of existing people, some of whom resembled him. After arriving in England, he made a trip to Lisbon and was about to go to Brussels when picked up at Heathrow. These side trips have never been explained.

Yet those best placed to know insist that Ray was a lone madman. It is unlikely that the FBI will make any effort to establish the truth. Director J. Edgar Hoover's loathing of Dr King is well-known. He has gone so far as to bug his bedrooms, and send prurient information to Mrs Coretta King in the hope of damaging King's role in the civil rights struggle.

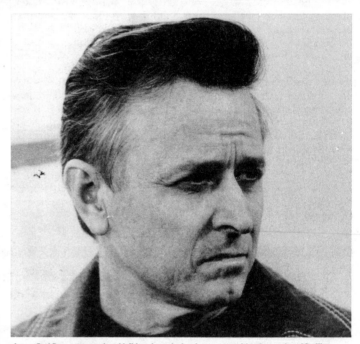

James Earl Ray, petty crook and jail-breaker who has been arrested for the murder of Dr King

English Schoolgirl Laughs at Victim's Funeral

PRETTY, PRECOCIOUS 11-year-old Mary Flora Bell is a self-assured liar, a playground bully, a schoolroom vandal – and a callous murderess!

On May 25, 4-year-old Martin George Brown's body was found in a derelict house in Scotswood, Newcastle, England. Next day, a nursery school which Mary and her friend Norma Bell (no relation) were later found vandalizing was broken into, and a childish note was left saying, "We did murder Martin Brown."

A few days later Mary called at the Brown's house and asked if she could see Martin. "No dear, Martin is dead," said the boy's mother. "I know. I wanted to see him in his coffin," was the little girl's chilling answer.

On July 31, 3-year-old Brian Howe went missing. Mary said she had seen him going to a vacant lot. Brian was found there, strangled, with cuts on his face and legs.

Mary told the police she had seen an 8-year-old with a pair of broken scissors beating Brian. This was interesting, as it had not been published that broken scissors were found by the body. Chief Inspector Brian Dobson was certain Mary was his killer when he saw her laughing and rubbing her hands as Brian's coffin was carried past her.

But it was 13-year-old Norma who cracked under questioning, and proved totally under Mary's influence, quite incapable of undertaking the murders herself.

Mary comported herself like a seasoned old lag, answering questions firmly yet evasively and demanding legal representation. This pretty little girl is evil incarnate and as such has shocked the great British public.

She has been found guilty of manslaughter and sentenced to life detention. No asylum will take her, and she has been sent to a special approved school.

> **" I WANTED TO SEE HIM IN HIS COFFIN. "**
>
> **MARY BELL**
>
> QUOTE

Swinger Alice Crimmins Convicted of Killing Daughter

SEXY TOREADOR-PANTS-WEARING Alice Crimmins (27) has been found guilty of the manslaughter of her daughter Missie *(see 1965)*. A neighbour saw the swinging ex-cocktail waitress on the night Missie disappeared, leading her son Eddie by the hand, accompanied by a man carrying a bundle. As the man threw the bundle into a car, Alice cried, "My God, don't throw her like that."

Pathologist Dr Milton Helpern testifies that Alice's account of the meal her daughter ate before her disappearance is a fabrication. The prosecution believes this unnatural mother killed her children because they were getting in the way of her promiscuous sex-life.

Swinging Skipper Killed in Kinky Scottish Cottage

MAXWELL GARVIE was a 30-year-old sexual swinger. The wealthy Scottish gentleman-farmer started Fordoun Flying Club and become its "skipper" ten years ago. When he decided sex was better than flying, he started a nudist colony in order to survey the talent and select his partners.

But his sexual tastes extended beyond straightforward wife-swapping. His bisexual fancy fell on young barman Brian Tevendale. Maxwell's particular delight was to have his wife, Sheila, make love to Brian immediately before possessing her himself. He also started a very experimental relationship with Brian's sister, Mrs Trudi Firse. Because of the goings-on, neighbours soon nicknamed the Garvies' farmhouse, "Kinky Cottage".

Sheila Garvie came to hate being passed from partner to partner by her husband, and resisted his new demand that he sodomize her. In time she fell in love with Brian Tevendale. In May the pair got rid of Max. He was shot, battered with a gunstock and then suffocated with a pillow in "Kinky Cottage". Exactly who did what was subsequently as hard to determine as who had done what with and to whom in Maxwell's bed !

Then, with the help of young Allan Stephens, Tevendale dumped the body in a culvert at Lauriston Castle. Max's car was left at the Flying Club to give the impression that Max had taken a trip abroad to look for further kinky pleasures with new partners.

The pair were informed on by Sheila's mother when Sheila wanted to live permanently with Brian. They have been sentenced to life imprisonment.

Bobby Kennedy Gunned Down in Moment of Triumph

A candlelit procession to commemorate Senator Robert Kennedy

SENATOR ROBERT FITZGERALD KENNEDY was assassinated on June 5 in the Los Angeles' Ambassador Hotel as he turned to leave an enthusiastic meeting of campaign supporters. His victory in the California primary had effectively assured him of the Democratic presidential nomination this year.

Over 300 people saw Sirhan Bishara Sirhan step forward and at pointblank range fire a volley of shots from an eight-chambered Iver Johnson pistol. Three of the bullets struck the senator; others went wide, wounding several innocent bystanders.

Sirhan claims that his motive was to strike a blow for the Palestinian people by eliminating a friend of Israel. He has even been hailed as a hero in some countries in the Middle East.

Americans are puzzled that the junior senator from New York should be such a target. Kennedy liberalism has never threatened displaced Arabs: it might even become a modestly supportive political power centre, untarnished by anti-Semitism. It is suggested that ten rather than eight shots have to be accounted for; that a security guard fired the fatal shot; that Sirhan's pocket litter included $400 cash and no identification – just what might be expected of a hired killer.

However, these points are too tenuous to arouse the kind of just suspicions of conspiracy that lie behind the assassinations of Bobby Kennedy's brother, John, and Martin Luther King. Still, even by terrorist standards, Sirhan's motive seems pretty dumb!

East End Gang Lords Jailed after Murders

> ## "TAKE NO NOTICE OF KRAY. HE'S JUST A BIG FAT POOF."
> ### GEORGE CORNELL

TWINS RONNIE AND REGGIE KRAY (38) have been convicted of murdering fellow-villains George Cornell and "Jack the Hat" McVitie respectively. The Krays' life sentences carry no eligibility for parole for 30 years.

With that, the gangsters' terror-hold on London's East End collapses, despite their acquittal on the charge of murdering Frank Mitchell, "the Mad Axeman", whose escape from leisure in HM's prison the Kray brothers had engineered.

George Cornell was a leading lieutenant of the Richardson brothers (*see* 1966) who escaped conviction at the "torture" trial. Previously, in negotiations between the Krays and the Richardsons attended by important American gangsters, Cornell remarked, "Take no notice of [Ronnie] Kray. He's just a big fat poof."

Although Kray makes no secret of his homosexuality, and is certainly overweight, this insult could not go unavenged. Shortly after the "Mr Smith and the Witch Doctor" affray, Cornell was drinking at the Blind Beggar pub on Whitechapel Road when Ronnie Kray marched in with "Scotch Ian" Barrie and shot him dead at pointblank range. Then he walked out again, confident that no witness would dare to name him.

The following year, minor criminal Jack McVitie cheated the Krays out of a few hundred pounds over a couple of deals, and boasted about it. They invited him to a party in Stoke Newington, where Reggie

Reg (left) and Ron Kray, the twin lords of protection racketeering in London's East End

tried to shoot him with a pistol that jammed, and then stabbed him with a carving knife.

Scotland Yard chiefs destroyed the murderous protection racketeers by giving Superintendent Leonard "Nipper" Read a task force to operate out of Tintagel House.

After careful investigations, the force arrested the Krays and all their henchmen in a dawn raid, then assured terrorized witnesses that there was no one left to kneecap them. Result: the Kray twins are enjoying a deservedly long holiday at Her Majesty's expense.

Cannock Chase Child Murderer Caught

Flowers left in memory of Christine Darby

IT'S TAKEN TWO YEARS, but the evil pervert who raped and strangled Christine Darby (7) is behind bars. It was clear in 1967 that a dangerous child-molester was operating from a grey car along the A34 between Stone and Walsall, Staffordshire. Investigators were hampered by the fact that each time the monster struck it was in an area covered by a different police force; separate incident rooms and awkward liaison between the various forces guaranteed confusion.

The deaths of little Diane Tift, Margaret Reynolds and Christine Darby gave urgency to the detectives' work, however. When, last year, accumulating evidence pointed to Raymond Leslie Morris of Walsall, it seemed as though charges might not be possible, as Mrs Morris alibied her husband, saying he had been home with her on the evenings of the murders.

Morris, a motor engineer with a fetish about his own competence and excellence at anything to which he turned his hand, gave the police no assistance. He simply stonewalled all their questions.

But Mrs Morris changed her story when pornographic pictures of little girls were found in Raymond's drawer: pictures he had taken, and in one of which his hand with clearly identifiable watchstrap was visibly pushing the child to take up the position he wanted. The child was Mrs Morris's five-year-old niece! She has now given evidence against her husband, and is starting divorce proceedings.

Raymond Morris can look forward to a miserable life in jail: as a "nonce" or "beastie" (child-molester), he risks being maimed by outraged fellow-prisoners.

California's Zodiac Killer Revels in Publicity

TELEVISION VIEWERS watching lawyer Melvin Belli's San Francisco breakfast chat-show heard the sibilant voice of a man who claims to have killed at least seven people. "I don't want to go to the gas chamber," he complained. "I have headaches."

Was this really the murderer? Some survivors who have heard his voice doubt it, but there is no doubt that the Californian couples killer loves publicity. He usually leaves his mark – a curious cross overlapping a circle – which gives him his nickname. One survivor says the emblem is painted in white on the black balaclava he wears. Other survivors describe a podgy bespectacled man with reddish hair. The

Melvin Belli (right) shows a colleague a letter purported to come from "Zodiac" and other evidence

killer has written to the newspapers, providing irrefutable proof of his identity by sending part of a victim's shirt. All courting couples hope that this lust for publicity will lead to the killer's capture – 'cause it just ain't safe to park on the coast these days!

Career of a Mafia Boss

GENOVESE FLED TO ITALY in 1937 when Tom Dewey's crime-busting put the heat on New York mobs. Despite Mussolini's hostility to the Mafia, Genovese ingratiated himself with the Duce; and then curried favour with American invasion forces at the war's end. Back in New York he built up his financial base by drug trafficking. He headed the old Luciano family, and killed Willie Moretti and Albert Anastasia (*see* 1957) to consolidate his influence over other New York families. But his attempt to have Frank Costello murdered failed, and the Appalachin hoods' convention (*see* 1957), which was supposed to crown him formally, ended in fiasco with a police raid.

Two years later, Lansky and Costello secured Don Vito's arrest (*see* 1959), after which the crime tsar ruled the underworld from prison. But his power had been seriously eroded.

OBITUARY

VITO GENOVESE (1897-1969)

Don Vito, last of the Mafia family bosses to claim the title "Capo di tutti capi" (boss of all bosses), has died of natural causes in Atlanta Penitentiary. His deplorable legacy is undoubtedly the introduction of drug trafficking as a major source of Mafia revenue. This will be more damaging than their old interests, prostitution and gambling.

Bible-Spouting Brute Kills Belles of Ballroom

G'lasgae lassies are nae sae keen tae gang oot dancing, the nicht. For they ken weel a strangler twirls his tootsies at yon Barrowland Ballroom.

HE STRUCK FIRST in February last year, killing Patricia Docker and leaving her naked body in a garage doorway in Carmichael Street, Glasgow. She had been strangled and kicked in the face, but not raped. A sanitary towel was found beside her, for she had been menstruating.

This August, Jemima MacDonald was found strangled with her own tights in a derelict building. She too had been menstruating. Both women had been dancing at the Barrowland Ballroom.

But on October 30 the killer was seen by someone who survived being with him. He travelled by taxi from the ballroom with his last dancing partner of the night, Helen Puttock, and her sister Jeannie MacDonald. He talked about sexual passages in the Bible and declared himself a non-drinker. Helen called the man John.

Jeannie walked to her home from the taxi, while John said he would see Helen to her husband's house. In the morning Helen was found outside, strangled, with her sanitary towel stuffed under her armpit. So "Bible John" is the young man Glasgow dreads. He seems to have a horror of menstruating women.

Och, laddie, ye're awfu' foul yersel', compared wi' healthy fertile lassies!

Charles Manson: Evil Master of Hippy Commune

Charles Manson in court

Shocking Sharon Tate Murder Solved

THE HORRIFIC DISCOVERY at 10050 Cielo Drive, Beverly Hills, appalled the world. The house was occupied by film director Roman Polanski and his beautiful young wife Sharon Tate and it changed instantaneously from a highly desirable residence to one of the world's most infamous murder sites.

When the cleaner came to work on the morning of August 10, 1969, she found:

In a car on the drive, the body of Steve Parent (18), delivery boy, pre-college student, hi-fi enthusiast, shot through the head.

On the lawn, Voytek Frykowski, 32, immigrant Pole, up-market gigolo, scrounger, dope-dealer, stabbed to death. Abigail Folger, 25, coffee-heiress, current keeper of Frykowski, stabbed and clubbed to death.

In the sitting room, Jay Sebring, 35, fashionable hairdresser; Sharon Tate, 26, eight months' pregnant, film actress. They were roped loosely together around the necks, Sebring shot, Tate stabbed.

On the door, written in blood, was the word "PIG".

LaBianca Killings

The murder of grocery chain proprietor Leno LaBianca (45) and his 38-year-old wife Rosemary at their home in the La Feliz district of Los Angeles the following night showed no obvious connection with the Sharon Tate killings.

Leno and Rosemary were stabbed. Leno's flesh was also incised with the word "WAR". A carving fork was protruding from his abdomen.

Violent housebreakers are common in urban America. The prosperous LaBiancas were typical bourgeois victims of such criminals, unlike the rather racketty "Beautiful People" living on Cielo Drive.

Written in Blood

What might have connected the two cases was the writing in blood. On the LaBiancas' wall: "Death To PiGS" and "RiSE". On their refrigerator door, "Healter Skealter".

A recent Malibu murder had also been accompanied by a blood graffito. Musician Gary Hinman, stabbed to death in his flat, had "POLITICAL PIGGY" written on his wall beside a Black Panther-style clenched palm-print "paw-mark".

But since an obvious perpetrator was under arrest for that murder – young actor Bobby Beausoleil, who had no good explanation for possessing Hinman's car – police were not inclined to look further.

Hinman and Beausoleil were young drug-using hippy types. The LaBiancas emphatically were not. The drug-using Tate-Folger entourage's social context was so superior to Hinman and Beausoleil that there seemed no likely connection.

Helter Skelter

In August and November, a commune of young hippies calling themselves "the Family" were raided, first at the Spahn Ranch near Hollywood, then at the Barker Ranch in Death Valley. The kids were (rightly) suspected of drug-dealing, auto-theft, sex with minors, shoplifting and cheque fraud. Many of the young girl hippies believed their charismatic leader, 43-year-old Charles Manson, to be an incarnation of Jesus Christ.

But police paid no attention to their painted graffito "HELTER SCELTER", which might have indicated that, like the visitors to the LaBianca house, someone could not spell "helter skelter" correctly.

Susan Atkins' Confession

In December, a "Family" member arrested for participating in murdering Gary Hinman, told her cellmate about the other murders. Twenty-one-year-old Susan Atkins shocked prostitute Ronnie Howard with her cold-blooded satisfaction over the slayings and clear hope of perpetrating more. For the first time in her life, Ronnie decided she must grass.

Susan quickly agreed to a plea-bargain with state prosecutors (which she subsequently abandoned) and told them how she and Leslie Van Houten (20), Patricia Krenwinkel (21), Linda Kasabian (22) and Charles "Tex" Watson (23) were sent by

"I have done my best to get along in your world, and now you want to kill me.... I don't care anything about any of you."
"Truth is... I ain't never been anything but a half-assed thief who didn't know how to steal without being caught."

Charles Manson

Charles Manson at the time of his sixth bid for parole, in 1986. It was turned down

Charles Manson to the Cielo Drive house (which they had formerly known when Beach Boy Terry Melcher lived there) with orders to kill all the occupants and write "something witchy" on the walls.

Watson killed Steve Parent, who was leaving the premises of 10050 after trying to buy hi-fi equipment from the houseboy, quartered in a separate building. Then the armed kids surprised the mildly stoned occupants of the house, Watson saying, "I am the devil and I have come to do the devil's work."

Sebring was shot when he protested; Frykowski and Folger chased onto the lawn and cut down when they tried to make a break for it.

Sharon Tate, the last of the victims to be killed, pleaded for the life of her unborn child. But Susan, nicknamed by the Family "Sadie Mae Glutz", was proud of her response, "Look, bitch, I don't care about you.... You're going to die and I don't feel anything about it."

Immediately after stabbing Sharon repeatedly, Susan licked blood off her hand, saying, "Wow, what a trip!"

Motive

According to Susan, the motive was to precipitate a black vs white war, following which Charles Manson would take command of the black victors and become king of the world. This Armageddon, called "Helter Skelter", was supposedly predicted in the song of that name recorded by the Beatles.

Prosecutor Vincent Bugliosi accepted Susan's story, and on this basis Manson, Atkins, Watson and four others were convicted of the Tate and LaBianca murders.

But Manson, a life-long unsuccessful petty criminal, says this story was all Susan's delusion. The true motive was cover for Bobby Beausoleil. Since Susan had left bloody graffiti at Gary Hinman's murder scene, it was hoped copycat killings might lead to Beausoleil's release from jail.

A still more plausible suggestion is that this might be true of the LaBianca killings, but Manson, who pimped his "Family" and dealt drugs in fairly sophisticated circles, may have accepted a contract to murder Frykowski and Folger, who were trying to monopolize marijuana dealing in South California.

This, too, would explain the group's subsequent murder of Spahn ranch-hand "Shorty" Shea, who knew too much.

BIZARRE TRIAL

As if the Tate murders weren't sensational enough, the goings-on at Manson's trial attracted more world headlines.

Led by Lynette "Squeaky" Fromme, pretty young hippy girls from "the Family" sat barefoot on the pavement outside the courthouse in vigil while the trial proceeded. They gave press interviews and displayed the fine embroidery-work worn by "the Family".

When Manson tried to disrupt proceedings and carved an X on his forehead, the girls, too, "X-ed themselves out of your world." When Manson altered his X to a swastika, so did the girls. When Manson shaved his head after his conviction, so did they.

TABLE OF MANSON FAMILY CRIMES

1969

AUGUST 4 – Murder of Gary Hinman by Bobby Beausoleil, accompanied by Susan Atkins and Mary Brunner.

AUGUST 8 – Arrest of Bobby Beausoleil.

AUGUST 9 – Murder of Steve Parent by Tex Watson. Murders of Jay Sebring, Abigail Folger, Voytek Frykowski and Sharon Tate by Tex Watson, Susan Atkins and Katie Krenwinkel; Linda Kasabian accompanying them.

AUGUST 10 – Murders of Leon and Rosemary LaBianca by Tex Watson, Katie Krenwinkel and Leslie van Houten. Manson headed break-in and tying-up of victims before leaving.

C. AUGUST 17 – Murder of "Shorty" Shea by Manson, Steve Grogan, Bruce Davis and probably others.

OCTOBER 12 – Manson and other family members arrested at Spahn Ranch on autotheft charges.

DECEMBER – Case breaks after Susan Atkins talks indiscreetly to fellow-prisoner.

Incompetent Brothers Kidnap Newspaper Magnate's Wife

IN BRITAIN'S FIRST major kidnapping, brothers Arthur and Nizamodeen Hosein, from Trinidad, grabbed Mrs Muriel McKay, wife of the deputy chairman of the *News of the World*. The incompetent villains thought they were kidnapping millionaire Rupert Murdoch's wife, having trailed the company chairman's official car to Mr McKay's home in Wimbledon.

Mrs McKay was snatched from the house on December 29. Demands for £1 million ransom were then made by telephone and in notes and a letter to the newspaper's editor. Unfortunately the kidnappers were as hopeless at collecting the money as they were at identifying their victim, and attempts to follow their directions to telephone boxes on the London-Cambridge road were aborted. A suitcase of money was dropped, but the Hoseins failed to pick it up. Watching police did, however, identify Arthur Hosein's car reconnoitring the area, and fingerprints on the ransom demand notes tied the 34-year-old trouser manufacturer and his 22-year-old brother inexorably to the case.

Arthur Hosein was trying to live it up as the "squire" of Stocking Pelham, Hertfordshire, where he had bought Rooks Farm. Lacking the money to support his grandiose self-image, he succeeded only in

Police gather at Rooks Farm to search for Mrs McKay's body

bringing on himself the derisive local nickname "King Hosein".

The brothers have made no confession, and no trace whatsoever of Mrs McKay has been found. There can be little doubt that she was murdered, and the Hoseins have been sentenced to life imprisonment for that offence, in addition to their convictions for kidnapping and blackmail.

But where is Mrs McKay? Local rumour has it she was fed to the pigs on Rook's Farm!

An evil-looking weapon left by the kidnappers at the McKay house

Kidnapper Nizamodeen Hosein

College Killer Hid Victims in Uncle's Laundry Room

NORMAN JOHN COLLINS of Michigan, the 22-year-old Ypsilanti co-ed murderer, was trapped by hair-clippings in his last victim's panties. Not his hair, not hers, but the hair of Norman's cousins, the Loucks kids.

While his uncle, policeman Dana Loucks, was vacationing with his family, young Collins had the use of his house. Before dumping the half-dressed body of 18-year-old freshman student Karen Sue Beckemann in a gully, the murderer kept it in the basement, little thinking that Mrs Loucks' habit of cutting the family hair down there would leave tell-tale evidence in the girl's panties.

Collins has murdered and mutilated seven girls since 1967 – all either college or high school students. He has shot, knifed, strangled and battered his victims, frequently even mutilating their sexual parts.

A good-looking motor-biker attending Eastern Michigan University, Collins regularly dated co-eds and led an active sex-life. Some, however, could tesify to savagery if a girl refused to sleep with him. Others knew that he had a peculiar phobia about menstruating women, and would curse a lover and throw her out if she were having her period. (The maniac "Bible John" who has been terrorizing Glasgow – *see* 1969 – appears to have the same sick fear of nature.)

Now that the physical evidence links him definitely to the killings, Collins, a previous suspect, goes to trial in the New Year.

Miners' Union Reformer Shot

WHEN JOSEPH YABLONSKI was shot dead in his Clarksville, Pennsylvania, home with his wife and daughter, suspicion fell on the United Mine Workers' Union. Yablonski had run for election against president Tony Boyle last year, claiming that Boyle embezzled union funds.

Boyle won the election, but Yablonski intended to contest the result, saying returns had been falsified and union funds steered into Boyle's campaign.

As it happened, Yablonski's killers had checked the premises a fortnight earlier, passing themselves off as unemployed miners. Suspicious, Yablonski had kept a note of their car number, which proved to belong to the daughter of Silous Huddleston, a close associate of one of the Union's strong-arm men.

At the same time, baby-faced burglar Wayne "Buddy" Martin was picked up and found to be carrying the telephone numbers of Huddleston's son-in-law, Paul Gilly,

Joseph Yablonski, union reformer and murder victim

and another burglar named Claude Vealey. Pulled in for questioning, Vealey soon cracked and turned State's Evidence against Gilly and Martin who, he said, had killed Yablonski.

Both men were convicted in separate trials and sentenced to

death. The FBI has traced the conspiracy back to implicate Huddleston's union friend, William Prater, and Albert Pass, treasurer of the East Kentucky branch.

Perhaps Tony Boyle will now be charged with murder and not just electoral fraud!

Wife Gives Ant-Poison to Unwanted Husband

THIRTY-ONE-YEAR-OLD South African Maria Buys had been quarrelling with her husband Christiaan for 15 years when she met young Gerhard Groesbeek in 1968. These marital quarrels were usually caused by Maria's flirtations, and usually concluded with a beating for her.

Maria decided that Gerhard was different and their relationship amounted to true love. She asked Christiaan for a divorce. This was refused. On Valentine's Day last year, Christiaan was taken ill. His persistent vomiting continued until

he was admitted to hospital, where he died on March 8.

The post-mortem revealed large quantities of arsenic. A thorough and prolonged examination of Maria's affairs revealed that she had bought large quantities of arsenical ant-poison.

After marrying Gerhard Groesbeek, she was tried at Bloemfontein in November last year, found guilty and condemned to death. But she was still alive when Gerhard went on trial this June as a co-conspirator.

Maria's firm statements saved her 21-year-old lover, showing courage worthy of a better cause. "I just wanted to avenge myself on Chris," she said. "I wanted to make him thoroughly sick so that he would divorce me." She concluded her statement with, "I poisoned him with arsenic."

Young Gerhard benefited from her openness and was acquitted. But Friday, November 13, 1970 was Black Friday indeed for Maria, who was hanged by the neck until she was dead.

Rage Diminishes Reasoning, Say South African Courts

FORTY-ONE-YEAR-OLD self-made Cape Town real estate millionaire Ronald John Vivian Cohen committed a common enough murder and was caught in a common enough way. He battered his beautiful young wife Susan to death with a bronze ornament, then claimed he had surprised an intruder who escaped after murdering Susan.

He also claimed his memory had gone blank after he seized the bronze statuette to beat off the intruder, and didn't know for sure what happened. Cynical police observed no sign of robbery; no sign of sexual assault; no sign of struggle in the murder room – hence, no motive and no intruder. A marital row had to be the cause.

Cohen's defence, that he remembered nothing of the incident, served him well. His lawyers argued successfully that his was a "momentary insanity" which diminished his responsibility. Cohen has received 12 years' imprisonment for an offence which has led many before him to the gallows.

Mafia Boss Shot for Denying Mafia's Existence

IN 1964, Joe Columbo replaced Joe Magliocco as head of New York's "Profaci" Mafia family. Other crime bosses were grateful to "rat fink" Colombo, who revealed that Joseph C. Bonnano, also known as "Joe Bananas", had hired Colombo's boss, Magliocco, to "rub out" the current crime syndicate rulers.

The "Banana war" took place and ended in defeat for ambitious Bonnano. Joe Colombo then founded the "Italian-American Civil Rights League."

This extraordinary association claims that there is no Mafia, and that public attention to organized crime induces prejudice against Americans of Italian birth. Despite the absurdity of a leading Mafioso peddling this twaddle, it appealed to Italian immigrants, and the League won considerable support from politicians and church leaders. Last year 50,000 people attended its Unity Day rally at Columbus Circle, and New York State Governor Nelson Rockefeller accepted honorary membership.

Older and wiser Mafiosi were displeased. They know that, for them, all publicity is bad publicity.

Joe Colombo's denial of the Mafia's existence simply drew mocking press attention to it. Carlo Gambino, one of the bosses saved when Colombo betrayed Magliocco, had no hesitation in ordering a "hit" on the President of the Italian-American Civil Rights League. The contract was passed to Joe Gallo, who delegated it to Harlem mobsters.

So it was that on July 28 this year, Joseph Colombo's career ended as he stood in Columbus Circle, preparing once more to tell cheering throngs that it is racism to claim that crime is organized and Italians play a large part in it. Jerome A. Johnson, a black man wearing a press badge, came up to the platform and gunned down the gang leader before he could warm to his message of assuring the world that no such gunnings-down happen in Italian circles.

Johnson was himself instantly killed by Colombo's hoods. Colombo has survived, but has suffered such severe brain damage that his former level of stupidity has nose-dived to that of a vegetable. He continues to exist at this level thanks to a life-support machine.

Joe Colombo (centre) appears before a federal court in April

Colombo's funeral in Brooklyn, seven years after the attempt on his life which crippled him

'Murder-by-Negligence' Doctor Murdered in Texas

THE STRANGE CASE of Dr John Hill has ended with his murder by a professional hitman – himself shot by police before he could say who employed him.

In 1968 Hill's wife Joan died in Houston, Texas, after he had taken her for treatment to a hospital in which he had shares. It was suggested that this was unnecessarily far from their home; that Dr Hill had deliberately ignored his wife's sudden and serious indisposition; that he might have caused it, since she was buried with unseemly haste and her death certificate was signed without close examination.

There was no doubt that the doctor's obsession with classical music and Joan's equal passion for equitation left them little time together, and it was whispered that John Hill really married Joan Robinson for her father Ash's money. This last point was given validity when Hill remarried within three months of being widowed. Millionaire Ash Robinson promptly had his daughter's body exhumed, and after inconclusive autopsies suggested possible liver failure or possible meningitis as causes of death, Ash's influence secured the doctor's trial for murder this February.

The method alleged was negligent delay in treating Joan's illness. So when the second Mrs Hill (by now herself separated from the doctor) blurted out that he had tried to poison her, a mistrial was declared. Before the case could be heard again, John Hill was dead.

Suspicion obviously points in the direction of the vengeful Ash Robinson, but nobody believes that Houston can bring this particular "Big Daddy" to book.

Mexican Migrant is America's Greatest Mass Murderer

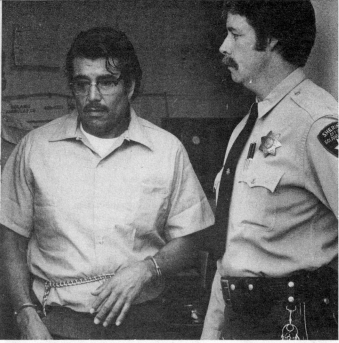

Juan Corona (left) is led from court

JUAN VALLEJO CORONA (38) crossed into California from Mexico 20 years ago as a migrant fruit picker. Big, burly and enterprising, Corona soon raised himself to the status of labour contractor, and by last year he was one of Yuba City's successes, with a wife and children, money in the bank and a barracks-like ranch. Here he housed the single men he employed, many of them derelicts and alcoholics and the antitheses of the healthy Mexican migrant specimens 200-lb Corona and his brother Natividad embodied.

Last year Natividad, who ran the Guadalajara Cafe in Marysville, fled back to Mexico after a migrant youth sued him for criminal sexual assault and was awarded $250,000 damages. This May, a Japanese fruit farmer found the body of hobo Kenneth Whitacre in a freshly-dug grave in his peach orchard. There was homosexual literature in the pocket. of the dead man, who had been sexually assaulted and then killed with a machete.

More graves were found on more farmers' land, prompting thorough police excavations, which unearthed the bodies of 25 recently killed men. Receipts for bills Corona had paid were in several of the graves. Some of the murdered men had been seen in his company before their disappearance. A search of his home turned up bloodstained clothes and knives, a machete and a pistol.

Most sinister of all, a ledger contained the names of many of the victims and the dates of their deaths. In all, 21 have been identified, leaving only four mystery men.

Corona's trial, with 25 indictments for murder, started in July. His claim that somebody else must have carried out the killings is unlikely to hold up against the evidence assembled against him!

Circumstantial Evidence Convicts NZ Double Slayer

ARTHUR THOMAS once courted farmer's wife Jeanette Crewe of Pukweka, New Zealand. But that doesn't explain why he chose to kill Jeanette and her husband Harvey on June 22 last year.

Both were shot with .22 bullets and dropped in the Waikato River. Jeanette was tied with wire and wrapped in bedsheets. Harvey was weighted down with a car axle.

Police tested every rifle in the neighbourhood. Thomas's was one of two which might have fired the murder bullets. At Thomas's farm they also found wire similar to that used to bind Jeanette, and axle stubs which could have come from the weight on Harvey.

So without any plausible motive, Thomas has been convicted of the murders and sentenced to life imprisonment.

Montreal Vampire Killer Caught in Calgary after Car Clue

FOUR YOUNG WOMEN strangled in Montreal all died with smiles on their faces and hideous bite marks on their breasts. Though Norma Vaillancourt, Shirley Audette, Marielle Archambault and Jean Way, killed at roughly six month intervals from July 1968, were all described as "raped", their serene expressions and the absence of signs of struggle belied this. Yet they were all killed, and all had hideously chewed nipples.

In May this year, an identical killing took place in Calgary. Victim Elizabeth Porteous had been seen with a young man in an identifiable car, however. A broken cufflink was found under her body.

After being convicted of the murder of Elizabeth Porteous, Wayne Clifford Boden, owner of car and cufflink, admitted to all the killings save that of Norma Vaillancourt (whose face was chewed up as well as her breasts).

It seems likely that his sadistic tendencies rose to lethal levels in the company of relatively willing masochistic partners.

IN BRIEF

LEOPOLD DIES. Thrill-killer Nathan Leopold (*see* 1924) died of natural causes in Puerto Rico where he worked as a $10-a-week hospital lab technician after his parole in 1958.

Since 1961 he had been married to florist Tudi Garcia de Quevedo.

The Director in Charge to the Last

IN 1917, YOUNG CIVIL SERVANT J. Edgar Hoover was posted to the US Justice Department under President Wilson's corrupt Attorney-General A. Mitchell Palmer. During the infamous and spurious "Red Scare" engineered by Palmer, young Hoover learned the value of holding extensive files on all hostile persons.

In 1921 he was transferred to the Department's sloppy and incompetent Bureau of Investigation under President Harding's even worse Attorney-General, Harry Daugherty. The Bureau had completely failed to stop sabotage and spying during the First World War.

When Calvin Coolidge set about cleaning up the scandals of the Harding administration, Hoover was appointed Director of the Bureau, and, like a good headmaster, boosted morale by upping intake and appearance. Agents were required to have degrees in law or accountancy and to dress smartly at all times. Rigorous standards of personal morality and integrity were enforced.

Not until the Roosevelt administration were agents allowed to carry arms and make arrests, however. Then, with the high profile encouraged by the President (*see* 1937), the Bureau was renamed the Federal Bureau of Investiga-

tion, and Hoover became a national figure, directing his "G-men" in highly publicized arrests of "Public Enemies", and issuing statements about law and order.

In the Second World War the FBI was entirely successful in suppressing German espionage and sabotage. After the war, Hoover concentrated his attention on his old foes, the "Communist subversives" until the tiny CPUSA was so heavily infiltrated that FBI informers almost outnumbered Marxists among card-carrying party members!

The findings of the Kefauver Committee (*see* 1951), led to criticism of Hoover for failing to tackle organized crime. In the 1950s and 1960s Hoover was antagonistic to the demands of civil rights activists, and reserved especial hatred for Dr Martin Luther King.

The Kennedy administration wished to dispense with his services, but the Director was too popular with the conservative public, and too entrenched with his infamous "files", which documented the peccadilloes of prominent politicians – not least those of President Kennedy himself! President Nixon, too, was unable to dismiss this tetchy and vindictive old man. So Hoover was granted his wish and died in harness.

J. Edgar Hoover, Director of the FBI for 50 years

Bodies Found in Black Leader's Garden in Trinidad

MICHAEL ABDUL MALIK, aka Michael X, aka Michael De Freitas, controversial black community spokesman when he lived in England, is a murderer!

A fire at his house in Trinidad while he was on a speaking tour in Guyana led emergency services to investigate a bed of lettuces in his back garden. Thinking Malik might have buried weapons there, police dug it up. They found the bodies of Gale Benson, daughter of the former Conservative MP for Chatham, and Joseph Skerrit, a young barber's assistant who had recently joined Malik's "commune". Both had been killed with machetes. Soil in Miss Benson's lungs showed she was still breathing when she was buried.

Miss Benson, it seems, joined the commune when travelling with another self-proclaimed black mes-

siah: the American Hakim Jamal. But Malik could not tolerate worshippers of anyone but himself. Nor did he like the sexual attraction between Miss Benson and another of his followers. So he called in a "hitman" from America to murder her.

Skerrit was murdered personally by Malik because he asked too many questions about the disappearance of "the white woman", and was afraid to participate in the robberies by which the "commune" maintained itself.

On hearing over the radio that the bodies had been found, Malik immediately shaved off his beard, left his Guyana hotel and fled to the jungle.

He was caught in a state of exhausted desperation before he could reach the Brazilian border. He now awaits trial in Trinidad.

Burglary at Democratic Party Campaign Headquarters

AN EXTRAORDINARY break-in at the Watergate complex in Washington DC, where the Democrats have their campaign headquarters for the election, has led to wild speculation about the burglars' motives.

Six men, all Cuban or with Cuban connections, were found in the building after they had foolishly taped open a locked door twice – thus ensuring that security staff, who had merely closed the door on the first occasion, took notice on the second and summoned the police.

The burglars were discovered in campaign chairman Larry O'Brien's office. They refused to explain themselves, and when brought before magistrates the following morning all gave their occupation as "Anti-Communist" and reserved their defence. Not surprisingly, Democrats accuse the Republican Committee to Re-Elect the President of law-breaking tactics. President Nixon firmly denies this, and it seems unlikely that what he rightly calls "a third-rate burglary" will make any lasting impact on American political life.

"Burglar" James McCord is questioned about bugging equipment found in the Watergate building

Chicago Deaf-Mute Charged with Killing Prostitute

IN 1965 illiterate Donald Lang (25) was the last person seen with streetwalker Ernestine Williams before her stabbed body was found in a Chicago alley.

It proved impossible to charge the black deaf-mute, who apparently could not follow the proceedings. He was confined for seven years in a hospital for the criminally insane.

Soon after his release this July, prostitute Earline Brown was found suffocated in Chicago's Viceroy Hotel. Lang was the last person seen with her. This time, bloodstains of the prostitute's group on his shirt provide compelling forensic evidence, and he will stand trial whether or not he can understand the proceedings!

Hertfordshire Poisoner Kills Workmates out of Curiosity

Poisoner Graham Young

WHEN HE WAS A CHILD, Graham Young poisoned his stepmother and made his father seriously ill in the hope of being returned to the care and control of his grandmother. He spent seven years in a secure institution for that crime.

Released, Young got a job with Hadlands, a photographic instruments firm in Bovingdon, Hertfordshire. Mysterious illnesses occurred soon after, and two popular workers, Bob Egle and Fred Biggs, died of disorders which doctors could not diagnose.

When police came to the factory to question staff over the case, 23-year-old Graham drew attention to himself by asking whether they had considered thallium poisoning as the cause of death.

They hadn't, but the young man's diagnosis was spot on! A search of his room turned up a library of books on poisons and further enquiries brought his past record to light. Graham found himself charged with murder.

His only motive seems to have been the interest of finding out whether and how the poisons would work. He also enjoyed a sense of power in being the only one to understand the mysterious "Bovingdon bug".

IN BRIEF

TONY BOYLE, president of America's Union of Mine Workers, convicted of ordering the murder of Joseph Yablonski (*see* 1970).

ROBBER BERTIE SMALLS gives information on hundreds of crimes, incriminating scores of major villains, in return for special treatment in prison. Dubbed "Supergrass", he may point the way to increasingly successful crime control.

DETECTIVE INSPECTOR ROBSON and Detective Sergeant Harris of Scotland Yard have been convicted of corrupt association with criminals, following accusations in *The Times*. Worse may lie in store, as *The People* accuses Commander Alan Drury, former head of the Flying Squad, of holidaying with pornography racketeer Jimmy Humphreys!

1973

CRIMES OF THE TWENTIETH CENTURY

President Nixon Falls after Televised Claim of Personal Honesty

> **YOUR PRESIDENT IS NOT A CROOK.**
> RICHARD M. NIXON

PRESIDENT NIXON has resigned rather than face certain impeachment for "High Crimes and Misdemeanours". For the first time in history, an American president has been exposed as a lawbreaker.

If tried, Mr Nixon would almost certainly be convicted of obstructing justice. He has been exposed by a taped conversation with his aide R.H. Haldemann which makes it clear that he knew full well the Watergate burglary (*see* 1972) had been carried out on the orders of the Committee to Re-Elect the President and also approved measures to prevent law enforcement agencies from bringing the Watergate burglars to book.

Yet over the past year, Nixon has flatly denied any such involvement, over and over again; even going so far as to make the melodramatic televised declaration, "Your President is not a crook."

One by one he has thrown overboard loyal and not-so-loyal staffers to save his own skin. Attorney-General John Mitchell, Special Presidential Counsel John Dean, Special Counsel Chuck Colson, Head of Staff Bob Haldemann, Home Affairs Adviser John Ehrlichmann – and a host of lesser Washington figures – face trial for varying degrees of complicity in the conspiracy

Now the truth is known: the President was a crook. And after a tearful farewell and a helicopter flight from the White House to a retirement in disgrace in California, he's gone.

President Nixon assures the American nation that he is not a crook

VEEP WAS A CROOK, TOO!

Mr Nixon's best safety-net was his constitutional successor: coarsely bullish Vice-President Spiro Agnew. But when the ex-Maryland Governor pleaded "No contest" to charges of accepting bribes – both when in Maryland and while in the White House – it became possible to contemplate Nixon's going with equanimity, the new veep being decent and honest ex-Congressman Gerald R. Ford.

Essex Barn Murder: Ince Cleared – Two Men Confess to Being There

GEORGE INCE, three times identified as perpetrator of last year's shocking murder at the Barn Restaurant, Braintree, has been cleared after a jury heard Mrs Dolly Kray, sister-in-law of the notorious gangster twins Ron and Reg (*see* 1969), confess that Ince spent the night in her bed.

The alibi carries conviction, for it cannot have been lightly given. Her husband, Charles Kray, is in jail with his brothers and she knows that the underworld vindictively upholds the male chauvinist view that a convict's wife should not have a sex-life while her villainous spouse is locked up!

The murder occurred when two armed men forced their way into the house of restaurant owner Bob Patience on Guy Fawkes' Night last year, stole money from the safe, and shot Mr Patience and his wife and daughter. Mrs Muriel Patience died of her injuries.

This November, petty criminal John Brook showed an acquaintance the gun he said had killed Mrs Patience. When Brook's associate Nicholas Johnson was arrested, he admitted being present at the robbery, but accused Brook of the shooting. The two men go on trial next year.

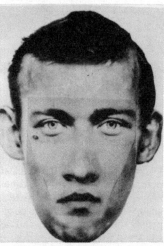
Photofit picture of George Ince

Killer Thought Human Sacrifices Prevent Earthquakes

I'S BEEN A ROUGH 18 months for Santa Cruz, California, which has been terrorized by mass-murderers Ed Kemper (*see* below) and Herb Mullin.

Mullin, religiose son of a Marine colonel, may have blown his mind smoking dope and taking acid. Anyway, last year he heard voices telling him that human sacrifices would save southern California from the massive earthquakes that naturally occur along the Pacific coast. So he killed 13: a tramp; a lone girl; a priest; four campers; two potheads; a mother with two children; and an old man digging his garden.

Though Mullin has been in and out of mental hospitals, diagnosed paranoid schizophrenic, a jury that wants him locked up forever has refused to find him insane and de-clared him guilty of ten counts of murder. Once the schoolboy most likely to succeed, Herb Mullin now goes to prison for life.

Mass murderer Herb Mullin under escort. He was found guilty of murder, on ten counts

Playing with Kids, Texas-Style, Sets Murder Record

PASADENA POLICE were shocked when 17-year-old Wayne Elmer Henley telephoned to say he'd just shot 33-year-old electrician Dean Corll. For Corll was known locally as "a real good neighbour and a real good guy", who especially loved small children, giving them candy and rides in his van.

Turns out that what Corll really loved was big kids. He bribed Henley and his buddy David Brooks to lure drunk teenage boys to his Houston boatshed, where they would be handcuffed and tied up while loud music drowned their screams. A tarpaulin would catch their blood while Corll indulged his enjoyment of torture. He would spend up to a day in this before killing them.

The gruesome ongoing party stopped when Henley brought a girl by mistake. Corll threatened to kill the boy if he didn't rape and murder 15-year-old Rhonda Williams. Henley could not comply, and shot Corll instead!

Twenty-seven boys have been found in shallow graves around Corll's boathouse. Juan Corona's US mass murder record (*see* 1971) has been broken.

Gentle Californian Giant Decapitates Momma

AT 6FT 9INS, gentle Ed Kemper was too tall to be a policeman – he'd have scared the public. It didn't help either that he spent his adolescence in a secure mental hospital for shooting his grandparents!

Ed loved cops, and hung around the police station in his home town, Santa Cruz, California. Santa Cruz police just didn't believe it when Ed telephoned from Pueblo, Colorado, this April to confess to being the co-ed killer who ravished, decapitated and mutilated six college students in the previous year. But when Ed persuaded them to look in his house, they locked him up in a hurry.

Ed's mom was decapitated in her bed. Her battered head was on the mantelpiece, and it seemed Ed had thrown darts at it. The larynx, from which the termagant had screamed abuse at Ed and her suc-

Ed Kemper (left) seems pleased to be under arrest in Colorado, awaiting extradition to California

cessive husbands, had been cut out and thrown in the dustbin. In the sitting room, also decapitated, was her best friend, Sarah Hallett.

Now cops believed Ed's stories of picking up college girls as hitchhikers in his car, which had a passenger door that would not open from the inside; believed that he'd raped them, cut bits off them, kept heads in his wardrobe for days, eaten parts and masturbated into human carrion. Now they knew they had a gentle, charming, intelligent, likeable monster on their hands. Ed has been arraigned on eight counts of murder, and hopes to receive the death penalty.

Lord Lucan Disappears After Slaying of Children's Nanny

Lord Lucan

PROFESSIONAL GAMBLER Lord Lucan has disappeared. Confusion surrounds the events of Thursday, November 7 at his former home in Belgravia, currently occupied by his estranged wife and their two children. Ascertained facts are as follows:

9.00 PM 29-year-old Sandra Rivett, the children's nanny, leaves the room where Lady Lucan and the elder child are watching television to make a cup of tea in the basement kitchen.

9.20 Lady Lucan goes to see why Sandra is taking so long and is struck over the head. She recovers to find a man struggling with her, and as she restrains him, by crushing his testicles, recognizes the assailant as her husband.

9.30 Lord and Lady Lucan retire upstairs to discuss the fact that Sandra Rivett is dead in the basement. While Lord Lucan goes to wash, Lady Lucan runs from the house and raises the alarm at a nearby pub, saying an intruder has attacked her.

9.45 Neighbours accompany her to find Lord Lucan has left. Miss Rivett's battered body is found stuffed in a US mail sack, a bent bloodstained bludgeon made of lead piping with an elastoplast grip lying beside it. Lady Lucan now says the intruder was her husband.

9.50 Lord Lucan telephones his mother to say that while passing the house he saw a stranger grappling with Lady Lucan and rushed in and drove him off, only to have Lady Lucan believe it was he who had attacked her.

11.30 Lord Lucan drives to friends in Sussex and tells them the same story. He also writes letters repeating it to other friends. He declares his intention of "lying doggo", and insists on driving away, at 1.15 am.

NOVEMBER 8 Lord Lucan's car found abandoned near Newhaven. In the boot, an empty US mail sack and a bludgeon made from the same lead piping as the one that killed Sandra Rivett. The obvious conclusion is that the earl hid in the house intending to kill his wife on the nanny's usual night off (Thursday). When Miss Rivett came downstairs, he mistook her for Lady Lucan and killed her.

Lord Lucan's friends deny this possibility, insisting that he will return and give a full account of himself. But they, like Lord Lucan himself, strike many people as a dislikeable bunch of aristocratic gamblers. Their snobbish contempt for the police and the fate of Miss Rivett is hindering the inquiry.

Their attitude is well illustrated by the outraged response of one of them to the suggestion that Lucan might have been attractive Miss Rivett's lover – "Sleeping with the *nanny*!". Their good opinion of the noble lord is not shared by the public.

Suggested change in Lucan's appearance

Unspeakable Brutality in Utah Robbery-Murders

AIRFORCEMAN DALE PIERRE and friend William Andrews robbed a hi-fi store in Ogden, Utah this April, and treated the proprietors and three of their friends with quite unspeakable cruelty.

The victims were herded into the basement, tied up and robbed. They were forced to drink Drano, a vitriolic compound of caustic acid used to clear blocked plumbing. A teenage shop assistant was raped, and all the victims were shot in the head. Finally, one who was only superficially injured was half strangled, and finished off by having a ball-point pen thrust into his ear.

Doctors saved the lives of two of them, who identified Pierre and Andrews when stolen property turned up at the USAF base. A half-empty bottle of Drano was found with stolen hi-fi equipment in Pierre's rented garage. Relatives and friends of the victims are furious that the US Supreme Court allowed the prohibition of capital punishment two years ago.

Black Muslim Youths Kill 15 'White Devils'

SINCE NOVEMBER last year, a group of eight Black Muslim youths calling themselves "Death Angels" have been killing white citizens in San Francisco. The climax of their efforts was "the Night of the Five", January 28, when J.C. Simon suggested that his comrade "Angels" join him for a really hectic night of shootings.

It was apparent to police that young black gunmen were deliberately shooting innocuous white passers-by; for which reason the killings were nicknamed the "Zebra Murders" – black on white.

The disapproving Black community supported the setting up of white vigilantes. The Black Muslims themselves espouse no such doctrine of destruction and violence. In April, Anthony Howard came forward in response to a reward offered, and informed on his fellow "Death Angels".

One hundred police officers raided an apartment block, making seven arrests. As a result, Larry Green, J.C. Simon, Jesse Cook and Manuel Moore will stand trial for the "Zebra Murders".

Drifting Jailbreaker Kills 18 Before Shot Escaping

PAUL KNOWLES escaped from police cells in Jacksonville, Florida, on July 26. Though only charged with brawling, he was on parole from a longer sentence for theft – one of many in his 28-year-old life. That night he robbed elderly Alice Curtis, leaving her to suffocate on the gag he forced down her throat.

There followed a four-month spree during which he drove from Florida to Connecticut and back, killing 17 people on the way. His normal method was to knock on a house door and then force his way in at gunpoint. He raped or robbed most of his victims; once, also, he killed two children who were friends of his family and could therefore identify him.

He spent a few days with English journalist Sandy Fawkes, who picked him up in a bar. She found him good company out of bed, but a poor lover, and they went their separate ways after his abortive attempt to rape a friend of hers.

One week later he was caught trying to crash a roadblock. On November 18 an FBI agent shot him dead as he tried to grab a sheriff's gun in an escape bid.

Killer Paul Knowles (centre) under arrest

New York Family Failure Kills his Parents and Siblings

YOUNG RONALD DEFEO JR disappointed his parents. Ronald DeFeo Sr was a self-made man whose successful car business had earned him a large house in Amityville, Long Island. He hoped that young Ronald would follow in his footsteps.

Unhappily the boy required psychiatric treatment when he was 15, and proved incapable of holding down a job. Like many of his generation he used recreational drugs, but he had no real taste for the hippy "alternative" lifestyle.

On November 13 he appeared in a bar asking for help. Friends who returned to the house with him found the entire family – Mr and Mrs DeFeo and their four other children, aged 18 to 9 – shot dead in their beds.

Ronald's story of his father's underworld associates having sent a "hitman" did not long survive the discovery of boxes of rifle ammunition in Defeo Jr's bedroom.

This unhappy failure to live out the American dream goes on trial next year for the slaughter of his entire family.

The house in Amityville where Ronald DeFeo wiped out his family

IN BRIEF

SENTENCED TO life imprisonment despite his plea for death, Ed Kemper (*see* 1973), California multiple murderer.

JOHN BROOK convicted of murder, and Nicholas Johnson of manslaughter in the Barn Restaurant case (*see* 1973).

FOR HELPING homo torture murder freak Dean Corll (*see* 1973), David Brooks gets one life sentence (eligible for parole in 11 years). Wayne Henley gets a total of 594 years! Henley is not charged for ridding the earth of Corll.

SOHO GANGLAND wars continue. Alfredo "Italian Tony" Zomparelli, released from prison after conviction for the Latin Quarter affray with Knight brothers (*see* 1970), stabbed to death by persons unknown in Golden Goose Arcade, Wardour Street.

Adolescent Psychopath 'Franklin Bollvolt I' Freed to Kill

Patrick Mackay, aka Franklin Bollvolt I

PATRICK MACKAY (22) loved dressing up in spiked helmet and cardboard armour and parading before his mirror as "Franklin Bollvolt I, Dictator of the World". Seven years ago, psychiatrists called him "a cold psychopathic killer".

This April he proved it when the fully-clothed body of Fr Anthony Crean was found in the bath at his cottage in Gravesend, England, beaten to death with a hatchet.

Two years ago Fr Crean had sought the withdrawal of charges against Mackay for forging a cheque. Mackay recently visited the priest in a state of agitation after friends suggested the older man's interest in him was homosexual.

Fr Crean was confronted by an angry giant, who pursued him to the bathroom, cut him down, and gazed for an hour at his bloody handiwork as he ran water into the bath. Mackay confessed to this killing and much more.

In addition to many muggings, he confessed to the murder of Isabella Griffiths last year in Chelsea, and to that of Adele Price this February in Belgravia. Both old ladies were killed in their flats. To fellow convicts Mackay boasted of another eight killings, and detectives concluded:

Mackay certainly killed: Miss Mary Haynes (73), robbed and murdered in her Kentish Town flat; Frank Goodman (62), Finsbury Park tobacconist, robbed and murdered in his shop.

Mackay probably killed: Stephanie Britton (74) and her grandson Christopher Martin (4) in Hadley Green, Hertfordshire.

Mackay may have killed: Heidi Mnilk (17), stabbed and thrown off a train from London Bridge; Mrs Ivy Davies (54) in Southend; an unidentified tramp he claims to have thrown off Hungerford footbridge across the Thames.

Mackay did not kill: Sarah Rodwell (92), robbed of her pensioner's Christmas bonus on the doorstep of her Hackney home.

Pleading guilty to the manslaughter of Fr Crean, Mrs Griffiths and Mrs Price, and asking for 26 more robberies to be taken into account, Mackay has been sent to a secure unit for life.

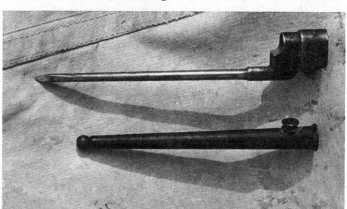

A lethal weapon Mackay may have used for murder

Nazi insignia found among Mackay's "Dictator of the World" costumes and props

Murder-Suspect Doctor Plucked off Plane at Take-Off

THE AIRLINER TAXIED out on to the Kennedy Airport runway; the flight to London was about to begin its long sprint before lifting away into the sky over New York when the pilot was ordered to return to the terminal and hand over passenger Charles Friedgood!

Sophie Friedgood, the middle-aged surgeon's wife of 28 years, died in June, and her husband certified the cause as stroke. The authorities then learned that the doctor had a young mistress with two children who was pressing him to divorce Sophie and marry her. When traces of the poison demerol were found in Sophie's body, police acted. The doctor also has to explain why he was trying to cross the Atlantic with $600,000 of his late wife's cash, bonds and jewellery in his hand-baggage, all secured on her forged signature!

Girl Promised Sex for Murder of Lover's Wife

LOVELY SOUTH AFRICAN model Marlene Lehnberg (19) made poor, one-legged Cape Coloured Marthinus Choegoe an offer he couldn't refuse: a car, a radio and sex with her, if he would kill Susanna van der Linde, whose husband Marlene wanted to marry.

Choegoe did the deed in November last year, stabbing Mrs van der Linde with a pair of scissors. He was soon arrested, because witnesses clearly recalled a man with a limp.

Marlene stood trial with him this March. Apart from her tantalizing incitement to murder, she may have helped in person, as crippled Choegoe could barely strike hard enough to kill.

Lehnberg and Choegoe were convicted and sentenced to death, but then won a reprieve.

London Sieges Inspire New Metropolitan Police Techniques

Police surrounding the Balcombe Street flat where IRA gunmen holed up

SOFTLY, SOFTLY CATCHEE MONKEY! is the watchword of London's Metropolitan Police, as villains and terrorists try new escape techniques: keeping pursuers at bay by holding hostages at gunpoint under siege. The only practicable response is long, slow negotiation, meeting the kidnappers' more reasonable demands until the hostages are safe.

The Spaghetti House siege of September 27 was set up after croupier Franklyn Davies learned that managers of the Spaghetti House chain of restaurants met on Saturdays in the Knightsbridge branch, carrying money.

Davies recruited Wesley Dick, Anthony Munroe and Samuel Addison. The four gunmen burst into the Knightsbridge eating place and forced the assembled managers into the basement. One, however, managed to slip away and raise the alarm. Teams from passing police cars trapped the kidnappers immediately, and for five days negotiations continued until they gave themselves up.

The Balcombe Street siege was the work of Martin O'Connell, Harry Duggan, Edward Butler and Hugh Doherty: IRA thugs who confuse their hate-filled taste for bloody thrills with the political aspirations of those who want to

bring about a united Ireland.

The gang had already car-bombed Dr Gordon Fairley and shot dead the journalist Ross McWhirter. On December 6 these young fools re-enacted 1920s Chicago gangplay, driving past Scott's Restaurant in Mayfair and firing machine-guns at it.

Police were promptly after them. Cornered in Balcombe Street, Marylebone, the terrorists found a flat there not being used for prostitution, and held middle-aged Mr and Mrs John Mathews hostage for six days. While they were being talked out, police acquired fingerprint evidence linking IRA suspect Brian Keenan with their activities.

Ross McWhirter, IRA victim

Crime Boss Murdered

Sam Giancana: the mobster who knew too much for his own good

SAM "MOMO" GIANCANA, boss of Al Capone's old Chicago territory, has been shot by intruders at his home in Oak Park, Chicago. Sam worked for Capone in the 1920s, and was imprisoned for offences from bootlegging to burglary.

His post-war rise to Chicago gangland supremacy was important for his straight contacts. Frank Sinatra introduced Sam to Hollywood starlets, and enlisted his support in the presidential election of 1958. It is believed the Mafia corrupted the result in Cook County, Illinois, swinging the photo-finish election from Richard Nixon to JFK.

The Kennedy presidency saw further Giancana-related Mafia connections with the administration. After the "Bay of Pigs" fiasco the CIA talked to John Rosselli and Sam Giancana about rubbing out Fidel Castro. The Mafiosi long to recover their Havana gambling and prostitution interests, but rightly thought the CIA men were nuts, and strung them along as they heard dotty schemes only a professional spy could take seriously: these included exploding fountain pens and potions to make Castro's beard fall out!

Meanwhile, Sam Giancana shared a mistress with Kennedy! Lovely Judith Campbell bounced between Sam's bed and JFK's, carrying messages, until J. Edgar Hoover warned Kennedy that this indiscretion was known about.

Giancana was indignant that JFK's Attorney-General brother Bobby turned federal heat on organized crime, just when Sam hoped he had the administration in his pocket, so he broke his ties with Sinatra and Kennedy.

He was due to tell a Senate Investigating Committee about these shenanigans. Now he will never do so. The CIA publicly, and the mob privately, both plead complete innocence of his murder!

IN BRIEF

SANDRA RIVETT'S inquest jury finds Lord Lucan guilty of her murder (*see* 1974). The gambler's influential friends have protested, and coroners' juries may lose their historic right to name persons responsible for wilful murder.

RONALD DEFEO convicted of slaughtering his family (*see* 1974). The murder house on Ocean Street, Amityville, Long Island sold, but buyers move out after a few weeks, complaining of a sense of evil and mysterious happenings.

Kidnapped Patti Convicted of San Francisco Bank Robbery

NEWSPAPER TYCOON William Randolph Hearst's granddaughter Patti, kidnapped by the "Symbionese Liberation Army" in February 1974, and recruited into their ranks from captivity, has been found guilty of participating in the San Francisco bank robbery on April 15, 1974. Security cameras showed her waving a machine gun.

The tiny group of terrorists, led by Donald DeFreeze, self-styled "Field Marshal Cinque", began operations in November 1973, when Russell Little and Michael Remiro murdered school superintendent Marcus Foster in Oakland, California, for the "Fascist" offences of forming a school police and introducing pupils' identity cards. The two were arrested in January 1974, and their confederates' demands when they kidnapped Patti included their release, as well as the distribution of millions of dollars of food-aid to the poor.

On May 17, DeFreeze, his deputy William Wolfe, and three women who were the real driving force of the group, Patricia Soltysik, Nancy Ling Perry and Camilla Hall, were killed in a desperate shoot-out with police. Patti, however, escaped with William and Emily Harris and Wendy Yoshimura, and stayed in hiding until they were finally arrested in San Francisco last September.

At her trial this March, defence psychiatrists testified that she was "brain-washed" by her captivity, and could not be held responsible. It was said De Freeze and Wolfe had raped her.

The Symbionists denied this, claiming that Patti had been in love with Woolfe, and the prosecution produced irrelevant smear evidence to show that she had been sexually active since she was fifteen.

The court expressed great sympathy for her parents, while sentencing Patti to seven years' imprisonment, despite the manifest evidence that psychological dependency on captors is a normal reaction of kidnapped people.

Patti Hearst led to trial for bank robbery

Gary Gilmore after going on a hunger strike to support his demand to be executed

Utah Robber Demands Death from Judiciary

SECOND-RATE CROOK Gary Gilmore (36), who has spent half his life in jail, used his parole this year to bungle more crimes. During a spate of nickels-and-dimes robberies, he killed a filling station attendant and a motel manager. This no-hoper would attract no attention were it not that he was given a formal death sentence, and to everyone's horror demands that it be carried out. No criminal has been executed in the USA for nearly ten years, but the reactionary Nixon appointees on the Supreme Court hope to return the country to less civilized habits. It is no surprise that a crass little psychopath like Gilmore should share their preference for death over life.

IN BRIEF

CONVICTED OF MURDERING his wife Sophie, and given New York's maximum penalty for murder – 25 years to life – Dr Charles Friedgood (*see* 1975).

Southeastern States' Mafia Boss Murdered

FLORIDA MAFIA CHIEFTAIN John Roselli ended his days in the Atlantic, sealed up in a heavy oil-drum weighted with chains.

This should have been his final disappearance, but gases emitted by the decomposing body brought it to the surface and to the world's attention.

In his youth, Roselli was the mob's man in Hollywood. He shook down the studios for a million through a Mafia-controlled union. He also swindled Groucho Marx and Phil Silvers out of a lot of money in a bent card game.

After moving to the southeast, he worked closely with Sam Giancana in efforts to recover Mafia interests in Cuba. This led to the notorious conversations with the CIA which Roselli revealed to a senate committee last year. With government spies proposing *Boys' Own* paper stunts, such as poisoned cigars, against Castro, it's a safe bet that the Mafiosi took the government's money with a straight face and made no attempt to carry out these hits.

Talking to the senators proved to be a mistake, however. Sam Giancana was killed before he could give evidence before the same committee (*see* 1975). Roselli managed to testify but then made a serious professional error by rejecting advice to hire bodyguards. The man who knew all about sitting targets became one himself.

Senior Yard Men Convicted of Porn Corruption

A HIGH-LEVEL INVESTIGATION into corruption among former members of the Obscene Publications Squad has unearthed the worst scandal Scotland Yard has endured since "The Trial of the Detectives" (*see* 1877). From top to bottom, detectives allocated to suppress Soho's sex bookshops have been taking money from the pornographers.

"Licences" to sell pornography were granted for £14,000; £200 a week ensured freedom from prosecution. Worst of all, senior men who collected the fat bribes stuffed envelopes of used notes into the pockets of honest junior officers to make them feel implicated and unable to protest.

Twelve officers and ex-officers arrested in February have been charged, the most senior being ex-Commander Kenneth Drury, former head of the Flying Squad, ex-Commander Wallace Virgo of the Area Command, and ex-Detective Superintendent William Moody, former head of the C.1 Obscene Publications Squad. Five of the first six tried this year were convicted: the sixth has resigned from the special force.

Happily, the porn kings have not come out of this enquiry unscathed. Bernie Silver and Frank Mifsud have both been charged with arranging the murder of Tommy "Scarface" Smithson when they set up their operation in 1956. Mifsud was acquitted and Silver convicted, though the Court of Appeal overturned the conviction. He has since been jailed for living off immoral earnings. Jimmy Humphreys has been convicted of arranging the beating-up of Peter Garfath for having an affair with Mrs Rusty Humphreys.

Class-conscious John Mason – who remembered haughtily the ineptitude with which one of the corrupt policemen had handled his asparagus tongs during a meal – and old Reptonian Gerald Citron were convicted of the offence they were all guilty of: selling obscene publications!

Murderous Black Panther Caught

THE MYSTERIOUS "Black Panther", whose 17 sub-Post Office robberies across northern England and the Midlands has left three people dead, and whose spent bullets prove him to be the kidnapper and murderer of Lesley Ann Whittle, has been caught. Thirty-nine-year-old joiner Donald Neilson is a "survival" freak whose happiest times were spent in the army. So keen was he on army-style life that he forced his family to wear combat fatigues and join him in adventure games.

Neilson, a short man who changed his name from Nappey because he considered it undignified, was arrested when two policemen in a patrol car saw him loitering suspiciously in Mansfield Woodhouse, Nottinghamshire. He pulled a gun on them and tried to force them to drive him away, but they stopped outside a fish-and-chip shop when his attention wavered. Two civilians waiting in the queue in the shop helped overpower the villain. Back at the police station, two black hoods found in Neilson's possession proved that this was the "Black Panther".

He has been urgently sought since January last year, when he snatched 17-year-old Lesley Ann from her home in Shropshire, under the misapprehension that she was a rich heiress. He held her in the labyrinth of drains and culverts under Bathpool Park, near Kidsgrove. His elaborate attempts to collect ransom money, with dynotape messages left in telephone kiosks, failed, however, serving only to draw attention to the park. A security guard who tried to apprehend Neilson was murdered around this time.

When his lair was unearthed in March 1975, Lesley's body was found there, hanging by a wire noose. By her were a sleeping bag and survival equipment. But police discovered no evidence as to the identity of the "Black Panther" until Neilson's capture this December.

He goes on trial next year.

"Black Panther" Donald Neilson

Neilson's uniform

The wire noose with which Lesley was killed

New York 'Son of Sam', Couples Murderer Caught

THE MONSTER who has terrorized New York city for 13 months is in custody. The couples killer, whose bizarre letters declared that he killed on father "Sam's" orders, turns out to be 24-year-old Jewish mailman, David Berkowitz, and the demonic Son of Sam who controlled him is a dog!

David Berkowitz (centre, clean-shaven with dark hair) smirks as he is arrested for the "Son of Sam" killings

Berkowitz was caught because he left his car blocking a fire hydrant on August 10 while he killed 20-year-old Stacey Moskowitz and injured her boyfriend Robert Violante in their parked car in Brooklyn. Detectives investigated reports of a short suspect with scruffy blond hair behaving suspiciously in the vicinity, and connected a yellow Volkswagen with him. Husky Berkowitz, with short curly brown hair and Ford car, clearly did not fit the bill.

But routine checks on ticketed parking offenders near the murder sites put NYPD detectives in contact with the traffic bureau at Yonkers where Berkowitz lived. Police telephonist Wheat Carr, daughter of Sam Carr whose dog Berkowitz identifies as his evil genius, was shocked to learn that the neighbour whose bizarre misconduct had led her family to wonder whether he might be connected with the murders was perfectly placed for the Stacey Moskowitz killing.

Soon Berkowitz was surrounded in his apartment. When police broke in they found weird satanic messages scrawled on the walls. Drafts of new "Son of Sam" letters were in his room and car. At his arrest, a smirking Berkowitz asked, "What took you so long?" He has confessed to shooting 13 young men and women, killing six. He claims that the devil in the shape of Sam Carr's black labrador prompted the slayings. Brooklyn and Queens are relieved that the worst couples killer in living memory is off their streets.

The .44 pistol that gave the "Son of Sam's" killings the alternative name of the ".44 murders"

Black Landlord's Eviction by Manslaughter

FOR THREE YEARS Battersea landlord Berman Benjamin Bailey tried to clear tenants paying statutory controlled rents out of his house in Marjorie Grove. He bullied and hectored. He said to crippled Harry Cadwell, who has lived there since 1938, "This is a black man's house. I want you out."

County court orders served on Bailey enjoined him against harassment and interference. When his considerable contribution to bad race relations got him nowhere, Mr Bailey took a final, murderous step against the tenants he wanted to be rid of.

One December night, he or his agents crept into the house, poured paraffin over furniture in the hall and set light to it. Ironically, the innocent victims of this inferno were Mrs Icylma Amos and her two little boys and Mr Gladstone Fuller, four of the black tenants he claimed to prefer to whites.

Bailey has been jailed for ten years for manslaughter.

George Davies is Guilty – OK? So Change the Graffiti

THE CAMPAIGN IS OVER. The walls can be washed clean, and bleeding-hearts who think cops always lie and villains are injured innocents may wear sackcloth and ashes. For George Davies has been caught red-handed, brandishing a gun outside the Bank of Cyprus in Seven Sisters Road, Holloway, which he and five others proposed to rob on September 23.

Two years ago, Davies was convicted of robbing the London Electricity Board in Ilford, and given a 17-year sentence. Since then the Davies family and friends have conducted an extraordinary campaign to secure a reversal of the conviction. The slogan "George Davies is Innocent – OK?" has appeared on large surfaces all over London. The Test wicket at Headingley was destroyed, as if anti-apartheid campaigners were objecting to a tour by South African cricketers. The Home Secretary has

George Davis (in pinstripe jacket) after his release from prison in May 1976

been badgered and pestered, until last year he allowed George's release on parole.

George Davies, having used his

freedom in the activity he knows best, may now Go Straight Back to Jail, Without Passing Go, and Without Collecting £200.

Murdered Gangster's Head Found in London Public Lavatory

A COUNCIL WORKER has made a gruesome discovery in a North London public lavatory: it's a severed head in a balaclava helmet which was left there in a carrier bag.

It belongs to murdered thief Billy Moseley, whose decapitated, handless body was found on Rainham marshes three years ago! Three men have only recently been convicted of his murder after Britain's longest criminal trial.

The first conclusion the police reached in 1974 was that armed robber Ronald Fright had killed

Moseley because the thief had had an affair with his wife. Fright had uttered serious threats against Moseley, who was last seen alive going to a meeting he had arranged with him, an appointment Fright says he never kept. The villains, the story ran, must have overdone the punitive torture handed out to Moseley for his indiscretion.

However, the authorities also linked the case with the murder of jewel thief Mickey Cornwall, found buried after a short-lived affair with Kathy Duncan, who happened to be the daughter of an associate of

Bob Maynard, Billy Moseley's best friend.

So Reg Dudley, Bob Maynard, Kathy Dudley, Ronald Fright and greengrocer Charlie Clarke found themselves in the dock facing trial for various degrees of involvement in one or other of these murders. The jury decided to acquit Fright and Kathy, and to send down Dudley, Maynard and Clarke for the murders. This decision has deeply displeased the underworld. Friends of Bob Maynard's furiously object that he would never have harmed a hair of Moseley's head, the two having been brought up as brothers. Kathy Maynard and the womenfolk of other villains have marched through North London in protest.

It has been suggested that Moseley's head was removed from storage in deep-freeze to prove that the men in prison had no control over it. But who in the world would want to lovingly preserve Billy Moseley's head for all this time?

Who Cleared Killer Electrician for Bank Work?

DAVID WALSH was just the bloke who had come to service the adding machine when he first appeared in the tiny branch of Williams and Glyn's bank at Prestbury, England, this February.

Next day he was a bit more forceful. At lunchtime, with only 21-year-old cashier Nicholas Jebb and 19-year-old teller Susan Hockenhull on duty, Walsh pulled a knife. He killed Mr Jebb with it, and held it to Miss Hockenhull as he made off with £2,400 and the girl as a hostage.

The following day, he telephoned the police to say she was on the moors, north of Lake Rudyard. So she was, but as he had left her tied and gagged in freezing wind and rain, she was dead.

Convicted of murdering both bank employees in October, Walsh becomes the first person in England successfully prosecuted for wilful murder of an adult by exposure to the elements.

What banks and banking staff unions want to know is why a machine service company sent them a man with serious convictions for theft and violence plus a heavy load of debt!

IN BRIEF

BACK TO BARBARISM – petty criminal Gary Gilmore got his way (*see* 1976) and was executed by firing squad in Utah, taking the USA out of the roster of civilized nations which have abandoned the death penalty.

MURDEROUS POST-OFFICE robber and kidnapper Donald Neilson, "the Black Panther", convicted of four murders and sentenced to life imprisonment.

913 Cultists Commit Enforced Suicide in Guyana Jungle

" DIE WITH DIGNITY! "
REV JIM JONES
QUOTE

EVEN IN AMERICA, the Reverend Jim Jones was obsessed with suicide, telling congregations at his "People's Temples" to prepare for a "White Night" in which they would all react to persecution by killing themselves.

Feeling persecuted last year, Jones came to an agreement with Prime Minister Forbes Burnham of Guyana, and leased a section of South American jungle to form the commune-colony of Jonestown. About 1,000 cultists moved there from San Francisco.

Rumours that dissidents were held against their will leaked back to California. Congressman Leo Ryan went on a fact-finding mission on November 14.

All started well. Cultists enthused about the Reverend Jim, and Ryan expressed his satisfaction with all he had seen. Trouble came, however, when the Congressman and his entourage were about to leave. Cultists on a flatbed truck suddenly opened fire on the visitors, and Congressman Ryan, three journalists and a departing cultist were killed. Jonestown was now doomed. But the Reverend Jim did not wait for the Marines to land. He set his suicide plan into operation.

Security guards rounded up the 913 cultists. Loudspeakers intoned, "We're going to meet again in another place", while mothers and babies, children and adults were forced to queue, collect a paper cup of purple Kool-Aid laced with cyanide, drink it, and die. While Jones screamed "Die with dignity!" if any hesitated, nearly

The terrible spectacle of nearly 1,000 bodies at Jonestown

1,000 people meekly killed themselves, leaving a clearing full of bodies for horrified emergency forces to bury when they arrived.

Hardly any survived, so it is not known whether Jones himself put the bullet through his head that finally killed him, or whether one of his guards saw to it that he accompanied his flock to oblivion.

Charismatic charlatan Jim Jones

Partner's Split Leads to Boy-Friend's Murder

TWENTY-THREE-YEAR-OLD Melanie Cain is co-founder of New York's My Fair Lady Agency. Her partner, ex-racehorse trainer Howard "Buddy" Jacobson (48), pretended to be only 29 while he was her boyfriend. This year Melanie tired of Howard's sleeping with other models, and left him for restaurateur Jack Tupper, who lived in the same apartment block. Jacobson threatened Tupper, tried to bribe him to leave Melanie, and then cut off the water to his apartment.

In August Melanie went to lease a new apartment so that she and Tupper could escape Jacobson's persistent harassment. She returned to find Tupper gone and Jacobson and his son tearing up the rug in the hallway. Wet red stains on the underlay had been daubed over with white paint as had bloodstains on the wall. The following day Tupper's body was found burned in a vacant lot, where a witness testified to seeing Jacobson and an employee dump a crate and set fire to it.

Howard Jacobson now faces trial for Tupper's murder.

Deadly Butler Takes Ex-MP for a Ride

WALTER SCOTT-ELLIOT was once a Labour junior minister. He was also rich, with an equally rich wife, and could well afford a stylish butler like Archibald Hall for his London home.

On December 9 last year Hall gave Mr Scott-Elliot a heavy dose of sleeping pills and tranquillizers. But even so, it was odd that the old man accepted his butler's telling him they were suddenly going for a drive to Scotland. Odder still that he should accept a bewigged woman he'd never seen before as his wife!

What Hall didn't tell his employer was that Mrs Scott-Elliott lay dead in the car boot. Burglar and con-man Hall had introduced his confederate Michael Kitto into the Scott-Elliot's flat to examine the premises during the night, under the impression that Mrs Scott-Elliott was in hospital. When she turned out to have been discharged unexpectedly, the two suffocated her.

The plan was to bury her in a Scottish burn where Hall had successfully hidden an earlier victim: a villain whose violence threatened his security in a comfortable job.

Mr Scott-Elliot proved too much of a handful, so he was killed in Cumbria, and left there with his wife. Then Mary Coggle, the confederate who had masqueraded as Mrs Scott-Elliot, turned awkward and demanded the lady's fur coat. So she too was killed. Finally Hall's half-brother, whom he had never liked, joined him and Kitto. The half-brother's body was in the car boot when North Berwick police discovered that its number-plates were false. Hall ran, but was quickly picked up. He is now serving a life sentence for his crimes.

Red Brigades Terrorists Murder Italy's Ex-Premier

ALDO MORO, five times Prime Minister of Italy, was kidnapped on March 16 when his car was ambushed as he drove to a special session of Parliament.

The left-wing "Red Brigades" terrorists claiming to be holding him sent messages to the government, accompanied by photographs of Moro holding the day's newspaper, to prove that he was alive. They demanded the release of 14 of their leaders, on trial in Turin. When the government refused to accede to this blackmail, Sr Moro was shot. His body was left in a car parked near the Communist Party headquarters and the offices of the Christian Democrats. The "unholy alliance" between these two parties has aroused the ire of the extremists of the left, whose crimes are taken more seriously than the atrocities perpetrated by neo-Fascists and Mafiosi over the years.

IN BRIEF

MURDERER CHARLES FRIEDGOOD (*see* 1975) has provoked a new law in New York state. Henceforth, it is illegal for a doctor to certify the death of his own next of kin.

Killer Clown Stuffed Boys Under his House

FOR SIX YEARS building contractor John Wayne Gacy has gone to gay zones around Chicago, picking up young men and driving them back to his home on Norwood Park. There he would tie them up, torture them, and finally kill them. He pushed the bodies in the crawl space under his floor until that got full. Then he started burying them in his garden.

At the same time, Gacy presented a popular and acceptable public profile. A Democratic Party ward worker, he was photographed shaking hands with First Lady Rosalynn Carter. As Pogo the Clown he put on whiteface and costume to delight kids in hospital or at parties he threw in his mausoleum. But Gacy the secret slaying sodomite got careless.

Last year a young man complained that Gacy pulled a gun on him when he came to apply for a job. Gacy wriggled out of that saying the man was blackmailing him. This March he let 27-year-old Jeffrey Rignall go after chloroforming and torturing him for a day, figuring that a man who didn't know his name or address when he came round in Lincoln Park wouldn't be able to identify him. Rignall watched out for weeks until he saw Gacy's car and turned the number over to Chicago police – who did precisely nothing.

Des Plaines police were more determined when missing 15-year-old Robert Piest was shown to have been in Gacy's company. They watched Gacy, questioned him, followed him; and finally two policemen received his hesitant confession. With 27 bodies under his house, three buried in his garden, and four more thrown in Des Plaines River, Gacy is under arrest as America's worst mass murderer.

First Lady Rosalynn Carter unwittingly shakes hands with America's worst mass murderer, John Wayne Gacy

Secret Weapon Assassination of Cold Warrior

Magnified photograph of the poison pellet

GEORGI MARKOV was a refugee from Bulgaria. When he annoyed the Communist authorities he fled to Italy. Ten years ago he was granted political asylum in Great Britain.

Since then he has been broadcasting to his native land on the BBC World Service – too effectively for the regime, it seems.

On September 7 he was walking along the Strand in London, on his way to read the evening news bulletin from Bush House, when he felt a stinging sensation in the right thigh. It appeared he had been prodded sharply by the umbrella of a man in a bus queue, who apologized profusely for the injury in a strong foreign accent before hailing a taxi and disappearing in the traffic.

Mr Markov's leg grew stiff. By 11.00 pm he felt feverish and went home. The following day he was in hospital, where the puncture in his thigh puzzled doctors. Also giving concern was Mr Markov's white blood corpuscle count which rose alarmingly. Two days later Markov was dead.

During the post-mortem examination the pathologist extracted a miniscule pellet measuring 1.52 mm across from the dead man's leg. The pellet was found to be hollow with two microscopic holes bored in the sides. Forensic tests determined that Mr Markov had been poisoned with ricin, a rare derivative of castor oil seeds. Research on this substance has mainly been carried out in Hungary and Czechoslovakia.

The metal from which the pellet was made is an alloy of platinum and iridium; the workmanship that went into making the pellet is far beyond the engineering skills possessed by an ordinary jeweller. A similar metal was found in the back of Vladimir Kostov, another Bulgarian defector, who was shot with an umbrella-gun in Paris last year. Mr Kostov survived, so the poison dosage must have been increased for Mr Markov.

No prizes for guessing who is behind these James Bond-type killings of dissident Bulgarians.

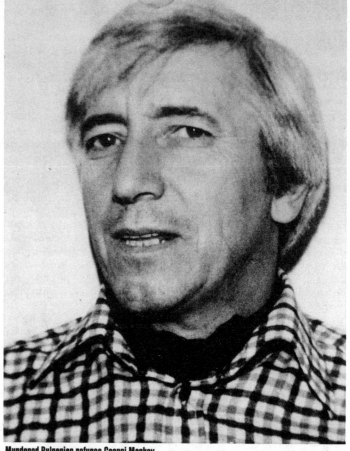

Murdered Bulgarian refugee Georgi Markov

IN BRIEF

IRA HIGH PROFILE murders this year include Airey Neave MP, killed as a car-bomb was detonated by a tilt device when he mounted the ramp to leave the House of Commons underground car park; and Earl Mountbatten of Burma, killed in his booby-trapped motorboat while on holiday in Northern Ireland.

Airey Neave, MP, IRA victim

Killer Confesses, the Speaking Ghost was Right

MEDICAL ORDERLY Allan Showery would never in a million years have been convicted of murdering 48-year-old Teresita Basa on the original evidence turned up by police. A Filippino doctor's wife told police that, five months after Manila-born Teresita was found stabbed, burned and wrapped in sheets in her apartment, the dead woman's ghost came to her in a vision and named Showery as her killer!

Teresita, like Showery, was an employee at Edgewater Hospital. Embarrassed detectives paid him a visit to ask him what he had to say to the supernatural accusation. They were very surprised to find some of Miss Basa's jewellery hidden in his apartment.

Still, Basa's lawyers said murder on ghost testimony was easy to defend. They were disgruntled when Showery confessed, accepting 14 years' imprisonment for the murder!

France's Top Criminal Gunned Down by Police

JACQUES MESRINE has been shot down in the street by Paris police. The French designated this kidnapper, bank robber, burglar and, by his own account, murderer, their own "Public Enemy No.1".

Mesrine fought in Algeria in the 1950s, and joined the near-terrorist OAS when De Gaulle, in their view, "betrayed" the right by granting Algeria independence. Since Mesrine's first wife was a beautiful black Martiniquaise, his right-wing extremism may have been more exaggerated individualism than colonialist racism.

In 1962 he attempted a bank robbery. Released from prison after a year, he oscillated between trying to go straight and reverting to crime, until 1968 when he accompanied his girlfriend, Jeanne Schneider, to Montreal. There they kidnapped millionaire Georges Deslauriers, and were the last people seen with wealthy Madame Evelyne le Bouthillier before she was found dead by strangulation.

Extradited from the USA, they were tried for these crimes. Mesrines was imprisoned for the kidnapping. He escaped from prison, and instantly killed two rangers when they spotted him in woods near Montreal. Taking a new mistress, he travelled to the USA, Venezuela and Madrid, living by bank robberies.

In France from 1972 he became a franc millionaire by robbing banks, and built up a reputation as a daring jailbreaker and chivalrous criminal. In prison in 1977 he wrote a book called *The Killer Instinct*, and in court demonstrated insouciantly how easily he could unlock his handcuffs.

After a side trip to London, and an abortive plan to kidnap the judge who had sentenced him, he was surrounded in his Paris flat by the police. Mesrine was shot down as he tried to leave. The police danced in the streets at having killed their glamorous foe.

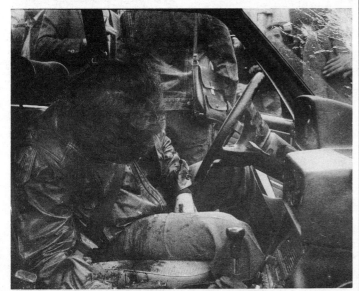

Jacques Mesrine, shot dead in his car as he prepared to leave his Paris flat

Huge Drug Snatch Leads to Lengthy Paper-Chase

IN SEPTEMBER last year, several Scotland Yard men passed themselves off as a fishing party in sleepy Talland Bay, near St Austell in Cornwall. There, as expected, the yacht *Guiding Lights* crept in by moonlight, and dropped anchor for its crew to spend nearly three hours ferrying two and a half tons of cannabis resin (street value £2,250,000) to be hidden under the false floor of Talland Bay Cafe.

Then *Guiding Lights* eased gently out to sea again, to be intercepted by waiting revenue cutters and diverted to the port of Plymouth.

Prominent drug dealers Ron Taylor and Roderick Eagleton were arrested with two associates. Other gang members were picked up from addresses in London.

So much money is washing around from this gang's recurrent drug runs that it will be another year before accountants finish tracing the profits through secret Swiss bank accounts!

Rapist-Murderer Demands the Death Sentence

AMERICAN STEVEN JUDY'S first conviction for rape came ten years ago, when he was just 12 years old! He knocked at a neighbour's door, forced his way in when he found she was alone, raped her at knife-point, stabbed her, and beat her about the head with a hatchet. Miraculously, she survived and testified against him.

The child received nine months' treatment in a secure mental home and was turned loose again. Six years later he served a six-month prison sentence for viciously beating a woman in Chicago.

This April the 22-year-old bricklayer drove his girlfriend to work in his red and silver pickup, then noticed attractive housewife Terry Chasteen driving along the highway near Indianapolis. He promptly drew alongside her, flashing his lights and pointing to her tyres. When she stopped to see if she had a flat, he raised her bonnet and disconnected the ignition. Then, like a good Samaritan, he offered her a lift to the nearest filling station.

Trusting Terry and her children got in his truck, and found themselves driven off the highway to remote White Lick Creek. There, Judy stopped, turned to Terry and said, "I guess you know what's going to happen now." Terry reluctantly sent the children off to walk in the woods, and submitted to undressing and being raped. As Judy hurt her, she screamed, and he strangled her. When the children came running back, he drowned them in the creek.

His pickup, which had been seen parked near the scene, was identified and he was swiftly arrested. This horrible danger to womankind goes on trial next year.

Stephen Judy

John Lennon Assassinated in New York

FORMER BEATLE John Lennon was shot down outside his home in the Dakota Apartment Building, New York, on December 8. His killer, freaky 25-year-old Mark David Chapman, called out "Mr Lennon" as the singer walked past him. Then Chapman fired five times, four bullets striking Lennon at pointblank range.

Chapman's life has veered between rebellion and drug abuse in his early adolescence, and born-again Christian work for the YMCA. After failing at college in Arkansas, he went to Hawaii and attempted suicide. A period in a mental hospital appeared to effect complete recovery, and he worked successfully with geriatric patients for a while afterwards.

He came to New York with the deliberate intention of killing Lennon, believing this would fulfil something of J.D. Salinger's fictional "Catcher in the Rye's" crusade against "phoneys".

Mark David Chapman has the paranoid's crazy conviction that he is far more important than the facts warrant. This hopeless man believes he has won some kind of immortality by killing one of our time's most creative minds.

Lovely Dorothy Stratten, raped, sodomized and murdered by her estranged husband

'Playmate of the Year' Slain by Pimp Husband

BEAUTIFUL DOROTHY STRATTEN appeared as "Playmate of the Month" in August *Playboy* last year and was heading for stardom as "Playmate of the Year 1980".

But she couldn't take her husband with her. Paul Snider was a pimp when he met Dorothy Hoogstraten in Vancouver and persuaded her to let him send photo spreads to *Playboy*. The magazine employed her, and Snider came along as her manager. When he obviously wasn't wanted there, he married her to tie her to him. Dorothy fell in love with film producer Peter Bogdanovich, then... well, then I guess Paul just couldn't take it any more.

When Dorothy called to talk about divorce, he tied her up, ravished her, shot her, ravished her corpse all over again, and shot himself. It's a sad old world if you get out of your depth in the glamour spin.

IN BRIEF

FACING THE JURY for rape-murder, Steven Judy (*see* 1979) said, "You'd better put me to death because next time it might be one of you or your daughters." They obliged.

HENRY MACKENNY, John Childs and Terence Pinfold, convicted of a series of London contract killings, for which their normal fee was £2,000. Known as the "teddy bear murderers", because their first killing was to acquire a teddy bear factory, they dismembered bodies and burned them in a tiny household grate.

ARTHUR THOMAS (*see* 1971) pardoned and awarded over NZ$1 million after evidence against him was shown to have been planted.

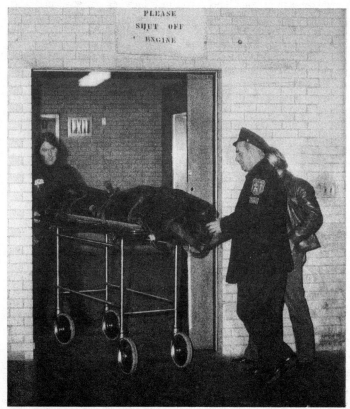
John Lennon's body is wheeled into the mortuary

Jeremy Thorpe Cleared of Murder Conspiracy

Jeremy Thorpe arrives at the Old Bailey with his wife, Marion

LEADER OF BRITAIN'S LIBERAL PARTY Jeremy Thorpe, exposed last year as a one-time latent homosexual, offered no defence to the charge that he and three others plotted to assassinate his accuser, male model Norman Scott. Instead, his counsel argued that the main prosecution witnesses – Scott himself, former Liberal MP Peter Bessell, and amateur hitman Andrew Newton – were so unreliable that the prosecution had not made its case. The jury concurred.

In 1960, young Scott stayed with Mr Thorpe at his mother's house and other places, receiving presents and affectionate letters from him. According to Scott, frequent homosexual acts – (at that time illegal) – took place. According to Thorpe this is untrue, although he confesses to homosexual leanings toward Scott.

Over the next 14 years whenever Scott's fortunes fluctuated he returned to Thorpe with appeals for money or help, always with the implicit threat that he might (through weakness rather than malice) expose their alleged relationship. The jury was asked what they made of the camp ending to a letter in which Thorpe (who nicknamed Scott "Bunny") promised help in the words, "Bunnies can and will go to France."

In the end, according to Peter Bessell, Thorpe urged him and Liberal party activist David Holmes to eliminate Scott. Through the agency of Cardiff club owner George Deakin, Andrew Newton was contacted, and in return for a promise of £10,000 agreed to make the "hit". He bungled it, however, shooting Scott's Great Dane dog, Rinka, on Exmoor in southwest England, but then failing to kill Scott because his gun jammed.

Despite this, part of his fee was delivered by carpet merchant John le Mesurier, an acquaintance of Holmes and Deakin. These last three men stood in the dock as Thorpe's co-conspirators.

In the event, Mr Bessell's off-colour business past made him an unreliable witness, and the flakiness of Scott and Newton made their uncorroborated testimony suspect. Conclusion: there was no case to answer.

Yet Mr Holmes, according to his counsel, would have pleaded guilty to a charge of conspiracy to frighten Scott. And Newton certainly drove Scott and Rinka to lonely Exmoor, where he killed the dog before driving away.

So, in the first murder charge ever brought against a major British political leader, we are still left asking – what happened?

Virginian Headmistress Harris Guilty of Homicide

DR HERMAN TARNOWER, author of *The Scarsdale Diet*, liked classy women, but he liked to treat 'em like broads, not like class. Sure, they could come on expensive holidays. Sure, he bought 'em expensive presents. But they always knew he was doing the same for other women.

Mrs Jean Harris, headmistress of classy Madeira School for Girls in Virginia, was Hy's main girlfriend for ten years.

But over the last three she became increasingly angered by his relationship with 12-years younger Lynne Tryforos; Mrs Harris was 44 in 1977.

On March 10 this year, she drove from Virginia to Scarsdale to have it out with Hy. She took a gun – to shoot herself, she says. When she found Lynne's clothes all over Hy's bathroom, Mrs Harris flew into a rage and pulled the gun. It went off, injuring Hy's hand, but classy Hy just said calmly, "Jesus, Jean! Look what you've done!" There was a short struggle, and the gun went off again. Twice.

Mrs Harris says she meant to kill herself. The jury, learning of a bullet in Hy's back, doubted it. She has been convicted of second-degree homicide.

Jean Harris about to be whisked away from court after hearing a "guilty" verdict from the jury

OBITUARY

WILLIE 'THE ACTOR' SUTTON (1901–1980)

*A*merica's best-loved bank robber has died in retirement in Florida. Willie Sutton became known as "the Actor" because of the disguises he used to penetrate banks. He robbed more and robbed 'em better than Dillinger. He was also admired for jailbreaks from Sing Sing and Holmesburg. For all that, he spent 33 years inside between 1926 and 1969.

Asked why he robbed banks, Willie said: "Because that's where the money is." And his autobiography, Where the Money Was restored his popularity, so that he enjoyed respect in his legit retirement.

Peter Sutcliffe:
The Yorkshire Ripper

Hard-Worked Police Unfairly Criticized in Yorkshire Ripper Case

Peter Sutcliffe, the Yorkshire Ripper

CLUES AND SUSPECTS

Sutcliffe emerged as a suspect under the following leads, only to be lost among thousands of others:

- Owner of a car with wheel and axle dimensions matching tyre-tracks left by the Ripper
  (First investigation – 1 of 10,000 possible suspects. After linkage with NVR computer – 1 of 2 million possible suspects!)

- Recipient in wage packet of new £5 note given to one victim
  First investigation – 1 of 8,000 possible suspects (all interviewed within a few months). After sophisticated re-run of notes' issue techniques had been carried out – 1 of 30 possible suspects; arrested before this re-investigation was complete.

GOOD OLD-FASHIONED police work ended the five-year terror of the Yorkshire Ripper. The cunning sex maniac avoided his favourite red light districts throughout 1979 and 1980, striking down five women in respectable residential areas.

However, in January 1981, when he returned to pick up a prostitute in Sheffield, the dogged Yorkshire police surveillance of working girls and, more importantly, their clients, paid off.

Sergeant Robert Ring recognized 24-year-old Olive Reivers as soon as he saw her with a man in a car down a dark lane. Olive had been cautioned for soliciting and had a forthcoming court appearance for a second offence, so the man's tale that he was "Peter Williams" out with his girlfriend cut little ice with the vigilant Sergeant Ring.

When the number plates on "Mr William's" car proved to be stolen, he confessed that he'd not wanted to be recognized kerb-crawling. His claim, "I'm bursting for a pee," won him a couple of minutes in the bushes, then it was back to the cells for an interrogation which soon had the local force calling in the Ripper Murder Squad.

The next morning, when Sergeant Ring reported for duty and found this petty thief still being questioned, he remembered that quick pee, and raced back to search among the bushes in Melbourne Lane. There he found a ball-pin hammer and sharp knife: the deadly trade-mark weapons with which, for five years, lorry-driver Peter Sutcliffe struck down women in Yorkshire and Lancashire, and mutilated their bodies.

The Yorkshire Ripper case was over.

Start of the Scare

Public anxiety began early in 1976, when prostitutes Wilma McCann, Barbara Booth and Emily Jackson were savagely murdered in Leeds. Detective Chief Superintendent Denis Hoban speculated that this was a man obsessed with wicked women: "Other women could be in danger," he advised the public - "not ordinary women in the street, but probably women who follow this way of life. Any street-girls, models on the seamier side of Leeds, and the prostitutes who may know or suspect a client that may be this way inclined and violently opposed to their way of life, should come forward and see us."

In fact, just such an obsessive was Barbara Booth's murderer: a student with a bizarre mission to suppress girls who smoked and chewed gum in public! As is normal with such delusional killers, he was picked up quickly and made no denial of his crimes.

Meanwhile, the more sinister sadistic maniac Sutcliffe had already attacked and injured two perfectly respectable women and in June 1977 would provoke the most extreme rage and panic by his murder of pretty 16-year-old shop assistant Jayne MacDonald on her way home after a night at a "bierkeller" disco.

Thirteen thousand people were interviewed in the aftermath of this murder. Nearly 4,000 written statements were taken, and 400 people seen near the playground where Jayne was killed were traced and interviewed within weeks.

But the sheer weight of evidence (*see* Box) handicapped

"Any street-girls, models on the seamier side of Leeds, and the prostitutes who may know or suspect a client that may be this way inclined and violently opposed to their way of life, should come forward and see us."

Detective Chief Superintendent Denis Hoban

police, and a cruel hoaxer misdirected the investigation for over a year.

The Hoax Tape

In June 1979, Assistant Chief Constable George Oldfield received an anonymous tape recording through the mail. "I'm Jack," a man's voice began. "I see you're having no luck catching me. I have the greatest respect for you, George, but Lord, you're no nearer catching me now than four years ago when I started."

Oldfield and the police have been criticized for letting this taunt dominate their investigation, but there were powerful forensic reasons for doing so. The tape was mailed from Sunderland by a man who also sent letters signed "Jack the Ripper". Initially dismissed as a hoax, these came to seem central clues in 1979 because:

An envelope from the hoaxer had been sealed with saliva from a blood group B secretor. This matched semen found in the orifices of Preston prostitute Joan Harrison, whose murder the hoaxer also claimed.

Light machine-oil traces on one of the envelopes exactly matched light machine-oil traces left by the Ripper on victim Jo Whittaker's body.

Highly original detective work was called into play. The tape was sent to brilliant dialectologist Stan Ellis at Leeds University. He reported that the speaker's accent came from Castleton, a small village near Sunderland.

Every man who lived in the village or who had grown up there was questioned. Yet each and every one of them had cast-iron alibis eliminating them from one or more of the murders. Alas, the misleading tape itself apparently exonerated Sutcliffe, who spoke with a Bradford accent.

The Ripper

When caught, the Ripper proved to be a good-looking, young lorry-driver, highly esteemed as a reliable workman by his employers. His Czech wife, Sonia, was unaware that he loved visiting sleazy red-light districts.

Formerly employed as a grave-digger, Sutcliffe claimed that God's voice, emanating from a grave, ordered him to kill prostitutes. This silly story, contradicted by the obviously sexual nature of his activities, did little to help his case. Compulsive he may be, rather than deluded, but nutty as a fruitcake given the nature of his compulsions.

Never fear, the Yorkshire Ripper, is locked up securely for life.

Victims: Left to right (top) Helen Rytka, Tina Atkinson, Jo Whittaker; (centre) Emily Jackson, Wilma McCann, Jean Jordan; (bottom) Irene Richardson, Yvonne Pearson, Jayne MacDonald

VICTIMS

1975
JULY • Annie Rogulskyj, waitress, Keighley. Severely injured.
AUGUST • Olive Smelt, office cleaner, Halifax. Severely injured.
OCTOBER • Wilma McCann, prostitute, Leeds. Murdered, mutilated.

1976
JANUARY • Emily Jackson, housewife/prostitute, Leeds. Murdered, mutilated.
MAY • Marcella Claxton, prostitute, Leeds. Severely injured.

1977
FEBRUARY • Irene Richardson, prostitute, Leeds. Murdered, mutilated.
APRIL • Tina Atkinson t/n Pat Mitra, prostitute, Bradford. Murdered and mutilated.
JUNE • Jayne MacDonald, shop assistant, Leeds. Murdered, mutilated.
JULY • Maureen Long, prostitute, Bradford. Mutilated, survived.
OCTOBER • Jean Jordan, prostitute, Manchester. Murdered October 1. Corpse mutilated October 9.
DECEMBER • Marilyn Moore, prostitute, Leeds. Battered, survived.

1978
JANUARY • Yvonne Pearson, prostitute, Bradford. Murdered and mutilated.
Helen Rytka, prostitute, Huddersfield. Raped, murdered and mutilated.
MAY • Vera Millward, prostitute, Manchester. Murdered, mutilated.

1979
APRIL • Jo Whittaker, office worker, Halifax. Murdered and mutilated.
SEPTEMBER • Barbara Leach, student, Bradford. Murdered and mutilated.

1980
AUGUST • Marguerite Walls, civil servant, Leeds. Strangled.
SEPTEMBER • Dr Uphaya Bandara, mature student, Leeds. Survived battery and strangling.
NOVEMBER • Jacqueline Hill, student, Leeds. Murdered, mutilated.

1981
JANUARY • Olive Reivers, prostitute, Sheffield. Saved by arrest, unassaulted.

Australian Dingo Baby Mother Charged with Murder

LAST AUGUST the world was stunned to learn of the dingo that entered the Ayers Rock campsite in Australia and stole 1-year-old Azaria Chamberlain. Trackers recovered nothing save Azaria's bloodstained clothing. Hearts went out to her parents, Pastor Michael Chamberlain and his wife Lindy.

But soon evil rumours began to circulate: that Azaria was spastic, and her parents destroyed her rather than cope with her handicap; that the Chamberlains' Seventh Day Adventist Church demanded Azaria (a name meaning "Gift of God") as a human sacrifice.

(In fact, the Adventists' extraordinarily high standard of personal integrity is enviable. All who met Michael and Lindy Chamberlain were impressed by the strength and courage the couple drew from their religion.)

The local coroner did his best to quash this vile gossip, expressing the hope that anyone reopening the case might "rot in hell". Despite this, people who fear the extermination of dingoes in consequence of the baby's death, and others with a prejudice against minority religions, have forced the authorities to hold a second inquest.

Every single person who heard Lindy Chamberlain cry "The dingo has got my baby!" totally believes her story of seeing the wild dog backing out of the tent shaking its head to control something in its mouth. Not a camper from Ayers Rock doubts that the dingo stole the child.

But pathologist Professor James Cameron of the London Hospital flew out with two British colleagues to testify that Azaria's clothes show no traces of dingo saliva, and speculative experiments suggest that they were removed from the baby by human hand and not canine teeth. This evidence must be inconclusive, as Azaria's outermost garment, a matinée jacket, has not been recovered.

Even so, Lindy has been charged with murder and Michael as accessory, and these unfortunate parents go on trial next year.

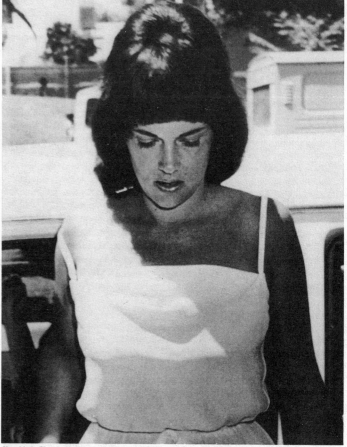

Mrs Lindy Chamberlain, charged with murdering her baby daughter

---

Castrated Child Killer Shot in Court by Mother

GERMAN CHILD-MOLESTER Klaus Grabowski submitted to castration in 1975 after he nearly strangled one of his victims, but then had himself treated with hormones and recovered his virility.

In May last year he lured 7-year-old Anna Bachmeier into his flat to play with his cat. There he strangled her with her tights. When police learnt that the convicted paedophile lived so near the missing child, they questioned Grabowski, who soon confessed and led them to the buried body.

But his trial this March was going his way, with prosecutors barred from asking why he had removed Anna's tights, and his story of little Anna's threatening to blackmail him receiving a sympathetic hearing. The judge was evidently taking a liberal and lenient line, viewing Grabowski as a penitent pervert, and the jury was not hearing enough about the accused's deliberate restoration of his sex drive.

As he looked likely to receive a light sentence for manslaughter, Frau Marie Anne Bachmeier, the little girl's mother, took matters into her own hands. In open court she shot the murderer dead, and calmly awaited her own arrest.

New York has its own 'Jack the Ripper'

HIGHLY INTELLIGENT, amoral and sadistic, that's how Blue Cross computer-operator Richard Cottingham struck the court, when he stood charged with the murder and assault of 19 New York women this May. Yet the arrogant amoralist remarked to one of his victims, "Prostitutes need to be punished," echoing Victorian Britain's infamous "Jack the Ripper" letter, whose author declared himself "down on whores".

Cottingham was traced through fingerprints found on the handcuffs he used to secure two of his teenage prostitute victims. Unsolved prostitute murders going back to 1979 were then traced to him. He has been sentenced to 197 years' imprisonment for 15 murders. Most shocking of all is that such a maniac should rampage through America's largest city without anyone even noticing his presence. Just how heartless can New Yorkers be about the precarious lives of its prostitutes?

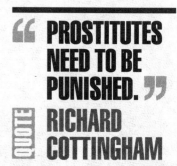

" PROSTITUTES NEED TO BE PUNISHED. "

QUOTE **RICHARD COTTINGHAM**

Atlanta Child Murders Stop after Suspect's Arrest

Wayne Williams

ATLANTA, GEORGIA has been terrorized by a serial murderer who has killed a black juvenile almost every month since 1979. All but two of this beast's victims were boys; the one victim to have been sexually assaulted was a little girl.

The black community nationwide has been stirred to fury, maintaining that:

1. The killer must be a white supremacist.
2. Atlanta police are not really concerned about murdered black children.

The first point is challenged by police, who note that the victims were abducted from black communities, where any suspicious white man would have been observed. The deduction is supported by the FBI Academy's Behavioural Sciences Unit, whose studies of habitual violent criminals show that sex maniacs almost invariably strike within their own racial group. These killings suggest the work of a black teenager commanding some respect from his victims.

The protestors' second point might well have been true originally, but with mounting nationwide campaigning and fear of riots was certainly invalid by this year. Senior detectives from all over the country have been pulled in to help, and President Reagan – hardly the black community's most sensitive friend – pledged $1.5 million of federal funding for the inquiry.

In July, two policemen patrolling a bridge over the Chattahoochee river at night heard a splash, and saw a man drive away in a station wagon. Another patrol stopped the vehicle before it could leave the bridge. The driver turned out to be 23-year-old Wayne Williams, an ambitious would-be photographer. When Williams denied stopping on the bridge, the officers advised him that he would be brought in for questioning if anything suspicious was found in the river; the body of 21-year-old murder victim Jimmy Payne had been found at the spot previously.

Two days later 27-year-old Nathaniel Cater's body was recovered from the Chattahoochee, and Williams was arrested. Dog hairs and carpet fibres found on ten of the child victims are identical to those in Williams' flat. The murders have stopped since his arrest. Although Williams has been charged with killing two adults, he is really on trial as the Atlanta child killer.

Police load the body of one of the Atlanta child victims into a hearse

Dr Jay Smith (left), suspected of Satanism, bondage orgies and murder

'Prince of Darkness' was Satanic Head of Murder High School

ENGLISH TEACHER Bill Bradfield of Upper Merion High School, Pennsylvania, has been convicted of theft and deception, following the discovery that he was the beneficiary of $730,000 worth of insurance and the recipient of $25,000 of investments taken out by his deceased colleague Susan Reinert.

Everyone knows, however, that the authorities are preparing a murder case against Bradfield. Susan's body was found in her car in 1979, dead by asphyxiation. She had apparently been kept in chains before her death.

Deeply implicated in some way is school principal, Dr Jay Smith, who is believed to have conducted Satanic orgies. Chains matching abrasions on Susan's body were found in his cellar. His comb was found in Susan's car, and a brooch of Susan's was found in his car. Dr Smith is being held in custody for firearms, drugs and theft offences, but sooner or later it is expected he will be shown to have played a major part in killing Miss Reinert.

IN BRIEF

THE TAYLOR-MILLS drug-smuggling gang members *(see* 1979), convicted at the Old Bailey, have received sentences ranging from two to ten years, and fines totalling £675,000. Ronald Taylor, however, bailed against police advice, was not with them.

He is reported to have taken his millions to Spain.

Irish Attorney-General Resigns after Pal is Arrested

Attorney-General Patrick Connolly (left) returns to Dublin to tender his resignation

AN UNEXPECTED crisis hit Taoiseach Charles Haughey's Fianna Fail government in Ireland when police arrested 36-year-old murderer Malcolm MacArthur – in the Attorney-General's private flat! To make matters worse, Attorney-General Patrick Connolly blandly flew off on a long-planned holiday in America!

Playboy MacArthur, who has dissipated an inheritance of £80,000, ran out of funds while junketing in Tenerife this July, and came back to Dublin determined to fill his pockets by armed robbery. The University of California graduate stayed with his old family friend Connolly, and went to historic Phoenix Park to steal a getaway car.

Bridie Gargan, a 25-year-old nurse, was sunning herself beside her Renault when the ham-fisted would-be crook forced her into the car with a dummy handgun and hit her over the head with a hammer. As he raced along in the Dublin traffic, an ambulance driver spotted the hospital sticker in his rear window, and assumed he was a doctor taking a sick patient to hospital. With its siren blaring and lights flashing the ambulance cleared a path for him through the crowded streets to St James's Hospital. On arrival MacArthur whizzed in at the vehicle entrance and whizzed straight out again at the exit! Two miles away he abandoned the car and Miss Gargan, who died in hospital four days later.

Despite Mr Haughey's instant despatch of a private jet to fetch the errant Attorney-General back from America, and his immediate acceptance of the impolitic Mr Connolly's resignation, the indiscretion contributed to Fianna Fail's loss of the autumn election.

Wife Picked Paraquat for Poison Pie

IT GIVES A WOMAN a nasty turn if her husband comes home unexpectedly to find her curled up in the arms of his best friend. It's still more startling if your lover races down your garden path, vaults the gate and pelts off along the street stark naked. And it puts your marriage at risk if your husband then gives you a beating. So thought Essex girl Susan Barber (28) when husband Michael surprised her in bed with Richard Collins in May last year. But Susan was not to be put off her stroke! With Michael at work the next afternoon, she called in Richard for another love session.

Afterwards they went down to the garden shed and collected some Gramoxone, a weedkiller containing the deadly poisonous paraquat. Now paraquat tastes disgusting, but Susan still managed to make a really tasty meat pie with just enough paraquat to kill Michael slowly.

After an illness which seemed much like pneumonia, Michael died in hospital. Nobody suspected a thing: the cause of death was said to be Goodpasture's Syndrome, a condition much rarer than the common cold but perfectly natural. One pathologist dissented: he reckoned the body showed traces of paraquat. He sent samples from Michael's digestive tract to the National Poisons Unit for analysis. Back came the reply – nothing untoward to report. Dr David Evans was mystified. It

Poisoner Susan Barber partying with one of her lovers after the death of her husband

looked as though the widow had got away with murder.

Richard didn't last long in Susan's bed, though. Soon she was broadcasting for lovers on CB radio. Her call sign was "Nympho' – and she wasn't exaggerating! Her casual lovers on one-night stands were taken aback to find that Susan's idea of a good time included calling up a stranger on CB to listen to their love-making.

The fun stopped this year. Dr Evans followed up the case and discovered that someone at the poisons lab had just lost the first set of the victim's samples and sent back the negative report! Now it's been proved that Michael ate paraquat pie. Susan's got a lifetime in prison, and Richard's earned a couple of years in jail for helping her.

Doping Tourists in India

FRENCH VIETNAMESE supercrook Hotchand Bhawanni Gurmukh Sobrajh – but just call him Charles – preys off tourists and drug buyers in the Far East. He dopes tourists and steals their money and papers. He buys, sells and steals drugs. He's not averse to jewel theft either. And if people get in his way, they're liable to end up dead!

This noxious 38-year-old representative of the "me generation" carried his "good old-fashioned greed" too far in Delhi this year when he met a party of French tourists in the Bikram Hotel. The suave Paris-educated con-man warned them of the horrors of dysentery, and generously distributed medicine among them.

Only Charles's medicine was a sedative, aimed to k.o. the lot of them while he rifled through their luggage. Unhappily for him, he got the dosage wrong. They fell ill, and with 20 French tourists collapsing all over the hotel lounge, Sobrajh found himself under arrest.

For two of his past murders in India he's received seven years' hard labour and life. Now eight other countries want a shot at putting this lethal smoothy on trial!

Digging up one of Sobrajh's victims in Thailand

Charles Sobrajh under arrest in Delhi

Ginger, You're Barmy! We Say to Murderer

HORRIBLE JOHN "Ginger" Bowden, a 26-year-old drunk from Camberwell, London, has a record as long as your arm for robbery, assault, blackmail and wounding. At liberty, for a change, over the last couple of years, he and his mates Michael Ward and David Begley took to preying on lonely old people and down-and-outs.

This January they struck up acquaintance with former amateur boxing champion Donald Ryan. They took him back to Mrs Shirley Brindle's council flat in Camberwell and there felled him with a machete, dropped him in a scalding bath, and cut him into pieces with an electric carving knife.

After the loathsome Bowden had a good giggle at the murdered man's head, they scattered parts of him around waste ground and then put the head in a dustbin before going back to sleep among the blood and residual gore.

On receiving a minimum 25-year sentence, Bowden yelled at the judge, "You old bastard! I hope you die screaming of cancer!" His lordship was too polite to return the compliment, so we'll do it for him: "Same to you, Ginger."

> ## YOU OLD BASTARD! I HOPE YOU DIE SCREAMING OF CANCER!
>
> QUOTE **JOHN BOWDEN**

Berserk Police Killer Shoots Himself in a Hide

FOR 17 DAYS in June and July 38-year-old Barry Prudom ran amok in northern England. In Doncaster, he shot PC David Haigh who stopped him for a traffic check. Haigh's notebook recorded his car number, so police knew who they were looking for.

In Girton, Lincolnshire, he shot George Luckett dead and severely injured his wife, making off in their car to north Yorkshire where he injured PC Kenneth Oliver.

In Old Malton he shot Sgt David Winter three times at point-blank range, after thinking, "I'll have this bugger".

In Malton he held elderly Mr and Mrs Maurice Johnson and their son Brian hostage for a couple of days. He established amicable relations with them, and even described his previous murders.

On July 4 he retreated to a hide outside the Johnson's house. There he shot himself after police had surrounded it and opened up with stun grenades, rifle and shotgun fire. And nobody knows why he did it all.

IN BRIEF

WAYNE WILLIAMS (*see* 1981) convicted of two murders. The complete cessation of Atlanta child killings since his arrest convinces police he was also responsible for them.

West Coast Hillside Strangler Convicted – by an Eyelash

IT'S TAKEN FIVE YEARS, but at last both the "hillside stranglers", who tortured, raped and murdered nine Californian women and girls in 1977, and a tenth the following year, have been convicted.

Judge Ronald George, who refused to allow prosecutors to drop charges against Angelo Buono (47) two years ago, was accused of conducting a "judicial extravaganza". But the mothers of 15-year-old Judith Miller, 14-year-old Sonja Johnson and 12-year-old Dolores Cepeda – all bound, raped, sodomized, strangled, and left naked in lewd postures on parkland – will not feel the millions of dollars, nor the time of 400 witnesses in the USA's longest criminal trial has been wasted. Buono goes to life imprisonment without possibility of parole.

The trial of Buono's cousin and accomplice, Kenneth Bianchi (31), was equally odd. Bianchi spent 1975-78 with upholsterer Buono, a beer-swilling slob who entertained prostitutes in his grungy Los Angeles home. When, in 1977, they started their killing spree with a prostitute, Bianchi's fastidiousness came into play, and the naked body was carefully washed before being obscenely exposed on a hillside.

Eight killings later, Bianchi moved to Bellingham, Washington. When he killed two young women in Bellingham, he was quickly identified as the last person seen with one, and LA police suspicions of him in the Hillside stranglings were revealed.

But Bianchi claimed to suffer from split personality, asserting that his alter ego "Steve" committed crimes, which central personality Ken deplored. Several psychologists supported this claim, and only later was its fraudulence exposed.

Bianchi feared Washington state's death penalty by hanging, and wished to serve his imprisonment in California's more comfortable jails.

Confessed "hillside strangler" Kenneth Bianchi testifies in a Los Angeles hearing against his accomplice, cousin Angelo Buono

So when guaranteed immunity from a capital conviction, he pleaded guilty to the Bellingham killings; then proceeded south to testify against Buono.

Buono's conviction proved difficult because, reversing character, he scoured his filthy house before forensic teams examined it. Not a trace remained of the blood and semen that had once stained the premises. Or the dead girls' belongings. Except... a single eyelash! Just one eyelash, identifiably belonging to one victim remained in the house. And that sent Buono to prison for life.

While Bianchi, to his disgust, (and the public's satisfaction) has been returned from warm California to cold Washington.

Woman Shampooed to Death and then Walled up

LONG-DISTANCE lorry-driver Luigi Longhi has the weirdest sexual fetish. He becomes aroused shampooing women's hair! In May 1981, Longhi picked up hitchhiker Heike Freiheit in Germany, and persuaded her to come to his Padborg apartment for a jolly good shampoo. It proved so satisfying that both fell asleep after the foamy climax. But Heike awoke to find herself tied up and gagged, with Longhi lustfully lathering her again.

When he ran out of shampoo, he rubbed her scalp with cottage cheese, honey and salad dressing. When she drummed her feet on the floor to summon help, he strangled her and stuffed her in a space behind the wall, where a workman repairing the roof found her this year.

Longhi has been sent to indefinite psychiatric confinement.

Blocked Drains at London flat Give away Killer

The kitchen of the top floor flat, 23 Cranley Gardens

THE DRAIN-CLEARER called to 23 Cranley Gardens, Muswell Hill, London, this February didn't care for the job. The outside underground pipe was clogged with meat. And somehow... it seemed... almost human. Still, knocking-off time was approaching, and he went home shelving his worries for the night.

Next day, almost all the meat was gone! But a little bit remaining seemed to be a definite finger. Police learned from other tenants that the top-floor flat occupant, 37-year-old Job Centre clerk Dennis Nilsen, had been up and down all night, flushing loos and prodding around in the drain.

When Nilsen got home from work he didn't beat about the bush. He showed detectives human remains bagged in polythene in his flat. He showed them the big saucepan in which he cooked himself curries – when it wasn't in use for boiling down his victims' heads!

He confessed to 15 murders, in Muswell Hill and at his previous flat in Willesden.

Nilsen, a gay, drew his victims from the grey netherworld of homosexual runaways and drifters. He picked them up in pubs; invited them home for more drinks; and strangled them with ties, often preserving the bodies for a few days and even sketching them.

£26 Million Bullion Robbery from Brink's-Matt

THE ROBBERY to dwarf all others took place on November 26 at Brink's-Matt Security Warehouse, London's Heathrow Airport. Yet it was the accidental work of small-timers.

The robbers were brutal and careless. With guns and balaclava helmets, they broke into the warehouse, overpowering the guards, but accidentally revealing, since they addressed them by name, that they had an inside accomplice.

They poured petrol over their captives' genitals and threatened to drop lighted matches on their flies. But this abominable treatment so shocked one of their victims that he could not recall the code number to release magnetic shields from the safes. Frustrated and furious the robbers idly looked into what they took to be a pile of shoeboxes lying around the warehouse.

Shoeboxes, my eye! They'd found a huge consignment of gold bullion in ingots! A mob who anticipated a few hundred thousand from their dirty work have made off with £26 million, and become the biggest and most successful thieves since Sir Francis Drake!

One-Eyed Matricide Hillbilly Confesses to Texas Murders

Henry Lee Lucas: multiple murderer

SQUALID, SMELLY little Henry Lee Lucas (46) has only been arrested for two murders in Stoneburg, Texas. But, with his grubby confederate, Floridian Ottis Toole, he just may be the biggest multiple murderer ever!

Early this year, 83-year-old Mrs Kate Rich of Stoneburg disappeared. The friendly widow had no enemies and little worth stealing. Her only shady acquaintance was Henry Lee Lucas who once worked a couple of days for her, with his young common-law wife Becky.

Lucas amiably insisted he knew nothing about Mrs Rich's disappearance. Nor, it seemed, about Becky's! Snake-handling Pastor Moore swore to Henry's good character, and supported his story that Becky had left him. But when police checked Lucas on the national crime computer, they found a record as long as your arm, including autotheft, sexual assault and – wait for it – matricide! This man spent seven years in prison for killing his prostitute mother!

Under pressure, Henry at last confessed to killing Becky (and ravishing her body) when she wanted to leave him; killing Mrs Rich (and ravishing her body) because he felt like it. He proved this by taking police to the crime-sites. But now he is confessing to more and more rapes and murders, often in association with Becky's uncle, Ottis Toole. And police all over the country are sending in reports of unsolved crimes which they hope this horrible little man may clear up.

Who Played 'Tie-Me! Beat-Me!' Games with Reagan's Pal?

THE MURDER OF beautiful model Vicki Morgan by her homosexual lodger Marvin Pancoast has unleashed a flood of gossip and innuendo around the White House. It appears that Ms Morgan was the sado-masochistic playmate of President Reagan's friend and kitchen cabinet member, the late department store millionaire Alfred Bloomingdale.

"Trustworthy and distinguished citizen" Bloomingdale joined the presidential Foreign Policy Advisory Committee. Ms Morgan's $10 million "palimony" claim in 1982 shows that she thought Bloomingdale's "trustworthiness" lay in giving her a monthly allowance of $18,000, in return for which she serviced his "distinguished" appetite for "flog-and-snog" orgies.

The courts cut Vicki's claim down to size, and never questioned the lots of naughtiness that she and Bloomingdale got up to before his death.

Pancoast was being evicted from Vicki's house for failing to pay his rent, though his statement,

"I was tired of being her slave boy," might suggest that he too was dragged into kinky games – and didn't like them. Anyway, he beat her to death with a baseball bat as she slept.

Most people couldn't care less about this homosexual drifter's wayward crimes. They're more interested in the videotape his attorney, Robert Steinberg, says Pancoast owned. This supposedly shows Vicki and Bloomingdale playing very naughty games with very distinguished people.

America wants to know who else in the Reagan circle is wallowing in wallopings?

> ## " I WAS TIRED OF BEING HER SLAVE BOY. "
> ### MARVIN PANCOAST

QUOTE

Vicki Morgan, pervert's partner and murder victim

Marvin Pancoast, murderer

Alfred Bloomingdale, millionaire pervert

Sexy Surrogate Mum Shoots her own Kids

POSTWOMAN, 29-year-old Diane Downs made headlines as one of America's first "surrogate mothers", letting a childless husband impregnate her and carrying his child with the approval of his wife.

Fellow-workers in Arizona knew her as an insatiable lady, who slept with any good-looking man she could. When Lew Lewiston de-

cided that an affair with Diane was too demanding, and concentrated on putting his marriage straight, Diane moved to Oregon, hoping absence would make the heart grow fonder.

When it didn't, she decided that her children, Dannie (3) Cheryl (7) and Christie (8), were the real obstacle to her commanding Lew's love. So she shot them, shot herself in the arm, and then drove to hospital with a story of a "shaggy-haired gunman" who had attacked the whole family.

Christie and Danny survived Diane's best efforts to kill them, and under patient and supportive questioning by sympathetic officials revealed that there had been no gunman, just their own dear mom who had done the shooting. The judge who sentenced Diane hopes she will never be released.

MP Links Rose-Grower's Murder to *Belgrano* Scandal

LABOUR MP Tam Dalyell wants Mrs Thatcher's government to come clean about the sinking of the Argentinian battleship *Belgrano* when it steamed away from the "exclusion zone" around the Falklands during the conflict in the South Atlantic. He believes a puzzling murder in Shropshire holds a vital clue.

Seventy-eight-year-old Miss Hilda Murrell was one of the country's leading rose-growers. On March 21, when she returned to her country cottage after shopping in nearby Shrewsbury, an intruder seized her, forced her into her own car, and drove her seven miles to a copse, where she was stabbed and left to die.

No valuables were stolen from Miss Murrell's house. Police assume that she disturbed a burglar before he found anything worth taking. But Mr Dalyell says

her papers had been rifled, and a manuscript she was composing had disappeared.

He notes that Miss Murrell's nephew was a naval intelligence officer at the time the *Belgrano* was sunk, and believes that he may have given his aunt information which would expose the government's lies to Parliament and the public.

Mr Dalyell and the police are in agreement on one thing. Both believe Miss Murrell interrupted a break-in, and was overpowered and driven out to the country where the panic-stricken intruder stabbed her. Only the police think the burglary was just "Bill Sikes" looking for swag, and Mr Dalyell thinks the burglars were government agents.

He's not alone in suspecting this. Anti-nuclear campaigners believe that her missing article, exposing the inefficiency and danger

Hilda Murrell, murder victim

of the proposed Sizewell B nuclear reactor, proves that Secret Servicemen acted to silence a critic of the nuclear energy policy by which the government sets such store.

Police are anxious to interview a man wearing a dark suit and trainers who was seen jogging away from the place where Mrs Murrell's body was found.

While sensible observers agree that the police conclusions are far more persuasive than conspiracy theories, they concede that the hectoring and priggish stridency and inflexibility of Thatcherism on almost any issue invites paranoid suspicion of misconduct.

Racist Neo-Nazi Fascists Shoot Talk-Show Host

DENVER TALK-SHOW HOST Alan Berg's station promoted him as "the man you love to hate", but they never imagined that uttering controversial opinions on the airwaves merited death: Berg was cut down by a hail of gunfire as he stepped from his car this June.

Berg's possible enemies, it was suggested, ranged from Libya's Colonel Gaddaffi to the KKK. But in October, FBI agents raiding a cache of arms in Idaho came across a machine-pistol which had fired the bullets into Berg.

The group hiding the arsenal was a neo-Nazi organization styling itself the Bruders Schweigen (Silent Brotherhood).

In a December shoot-out with police, their leader, Robert Jay Matthews, was killed. Their "assassination squads" targeted liberals, Jews and homosexuals. Eleven of the fascists face indictment next year for a range of offences, including Berg's murder.

Blue-Blood Brewster Babe Keeps Little Black Books

SYDNEY BIDDLE BARROWS is an American aristocrat. Descended from Elder William Brewster, spiritual leader of the Pilgrim Fathers, she belongs in the Blue Book of Boston as a scion of the original American families. Gracious, educated, and well-bred, Sydney Biddle Barrows is everything you don't expect of ... .a procuress!

When Sydney used her good manners and social expertise to gain employment answering the telephone for an escort agency, she was surprised, if not shocked, to

find the business was really up-market prostitution. And she was shocked, if not surprised, to find it was very badly run. "As I saw it," she says, "this was a sector of the economy that was crying out for the application of good management skills – not to mention a little common sense and decency."

So Sydney brought her business training to bear on the problem. In New York she ran escort agencies, employing classy girls to service "scores of prominent businessmen" whose names were recorded in little black books.

Arrested in December, Sydney will be charged with promoting prostitution; the clients' names will remain suppressed, though. Impenitent Sydney insists that her $2,000-a-night call-girls are no worse than married women who withhold favours from their husbands. She also believes that her ancestors would have understood, "in a more

enlightened era... that the private behaviour of consenting adults is not the business of the state."

Sydney Biddle Barrows, classy bawd

IN BRIEF

'COLONEL' BRIAN ROBINSON and Michael McAvoy, south London villains, have been convicted, along with their inside informant, security guard Anthony Black, for involvement in the Brinks-Matt bullion robbery (*see* 1983). Police investigations continue to trace the missing bullion, which appears to have been distributed to receivers and smelters all over the country.

White House Farm Murderer not Mad Model 'Bambi' After All

IN AUGUST, English papers reported that ex-model Sheila "Bambi" Caffell went berserk and slaughtered her adoptive parents and twin boys at the White House Farm, Tolleshunt d'Arcy in Essex. Police were called before dawn by Sheila's distraught brother Jeremy with the news that his father, Nevill Bamber (61), had telephoned saying something was very wrong.

When the police broke in, they found Nevill's body in the kitchen, shot in the face and neck amid signs of a terrific struggle. Upstairs the 6-year-old twins had been shot in bed, as had Mrs June Bamber. Beside her on the floor lay "Bambi", clutched in her hand the .22 semi-automatic rifle which had wrought all this carnage and finally shot her twice in the throat.

Jeremy told of his sister's persistent mental disorders. He was sick on the spot when officers said what they had found. His evident grief spoke for itself, so it came as a shock when two months later he was arrested for the murders.

Nevill's nephew David Boutflour never thought "Bambi" could have done it. She was too small to have battered her father down before shooting him. Two discoveries convinced David that the police had missed vital evidence.

A forced lavatory window disproved the theory that the mayhem was the work of someone living in the house.

The rifle's silencer was found, wiped and put away in the cupboard downstairs where it belonged.

They reopened the investigation when Jeremy's girlfriend, Julie Mugford, went to the police with her story after a quarrel with him. She claimed that Jeremy, though given a small farm of his own by his father, yearned to inherit the large White House Farm and live extravagantly; that he had made various plans to destroy his family

Jeremy Bamber and girlfriend Julie Mugford at the funeral of the family he murdered

– which she took to be jocular fantasies – until the murders actually took place; and that he envied "Bambi" the flat in London Nevill had given her. Forensic scientists have now established that "Bambi" was shot twice, first with the silencer on the rifle then with it off. Since she could not have shot herself, taken the silencer downstairs, returned to the bedroom and shot herself again, Jeremy finds himself arrested and awaiting trial for appalling murders he still denies.

The murder weapon with tell-tale silencer

Satanic 'Acid King' Killer Hangs Himself

RICKY KASSO, 17-year-old "Acid King" of Northport, New York, got his kicks from drug abuse and satanism. The two mixed badly when young Gary Lauwers fell into his hands on June 16 last year. Kasso had long suspected Lauwers of stealing "angel dust" from his pocket, and beaten him up for this on several occasions. But on June 16, the two boys seemed friendly again as they left a party to go into the woods and take some mescaline.

Somehow the quarrel revived, and in a drugged frenzy Kasso stabbed Lauwers repeatedly, screaming, "Say you love Satan!" and explaining to horrified companions "He's gotta say he loves Satan."

Gary's body was found on July 4. It took a year to assemble enough evidence to arrest Kasso, who declared he would kill himself if ever he were incarcerated – and he did. On July 6 this year, the "Acid King" was found hanging in his cell.

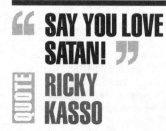

> **" SAY YOU LOVE SATAN! "**
>
> QUOTE **RICKY KASSO**

Policeman Stabbed to Death, but Killer Walks Free

BRITISH JURIES do not take kindly to policemen dressed as terrorists invading private property without a warrant. So the officers investigating the missing Brinks-Matt bullion (*see* 1983) discovered this January.

Deeply suspected of receiving stolen ingots was businessman Kenneth Noye, whose house in Kent was used by special forces during the war and is believed to contain underground bunkers.

Mr Noye does not welcome visitors. His locked gates open only to people who identify themselves before closed-circuit television cameras. Rotweiller dogs roam the grounds. Keen to inspect this suspect territory, Detective-Constable John Fordham and Detective-Sergeant Neil Murphy spearheaded a covert police operation. Dressed in camouflage jackets with balaclava helmets covering their faces save for sinister eye-holes, the pair went in over the wall.

The operation went wrong at once as the dogs noisily discovered them. Murphy signalled on his radio that the break-in was compromised, and made his way out. Fordham stood still to prevent the dogs attacking him, and was on the premises when Mr Noye came to investigate the brouhaha, carrying an electric torch and a kitchen knife. With him were his wife and a friend, both armed. As a result of the encounter, DC Fordham was stabbed to death.

The police assumed they had a straightforward case of murder by a suspect evading arrest. The jury, noting that the policemen were illicitly on private property, were impressed by a photograph of a man standing in shrubbery dressed in the gear worn by Fordham and illuminated by a torch. Such a sinister figure, they felt, might unnerve the toughest householder. Any unguarded move by such an intruder would certainly justify a quick and violent response. If the responding householder was carrying a weapon – well, the intruding policeman just asked for all he received! The killing of DC Fordham goes down in the records as an accident.

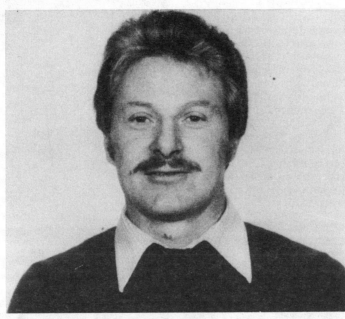

Victim of his own daring: Detective-Constable John Fordham

Murdering Canadian Minister's Appeal Refused

COLIN THATCHER, Minister of Energy and Mines in Saskatchewan, was a blustering bully. In 1981 his wife Jo Ann divorced him, winning the largest settlement ever awarded by a Canadian court.

Just over a year after these proceedings, a mysterious attempt to murder Mrs Thatcher occurred. Somebody fired a shot through her window in Regina, hitting her in the shoulder.

In January 1983, somebody finished the job off, bludgeoning Jo Ann down in her garage and then shooting her through the head. This same somebody dropped a credit-card slip signed Colin Thatcher.

Incredibly, such was the former minister's political power that it was not until last October that he stood trial. His bluster did little to impress the court, though, and he was convicted. His blustering appeal failed this May, and so he will remain in prison for life.

Entrepreneur Eliminates Family to Escape Disinheritance

STEVE BENSON'S Florida businesses always failed. Not that it mattered: his adoring mother, Margaret, poured out money from the family's tobacco fortune to keep him going. But when she learned that Steve (34) had transferred $325,000 from the businesses to buy himself a house, she told him she was cutting him out of her will.

On July 9, the police in Naple, Florida, were called to investigate a massive explosion outside the Benson mansion. They found Steve sitting in a state of shock beside the smoking remains of Margaret's car, and the remains of Margaret, Steven's sister Carol Lynn Kendall, and her son Scott. Inside the car experts found remains of two pipe bombs, with Steven's palm-prints on one of them. He goes on trial for murder next year.

An emotional Steve Benson in court

London's Railway Rapist Caught after Terrorizing 26

AFTER A PUBLIC APPEAL in May and June for information about missing TV company secretary Anne Lock, a man has been arrested and charged with her murder, and the rape-murders of Alison Day and Maartje Tamboezer, and some 26 rapes committed around London since 1982.

Short, spotty John Duffy was a railway carpenter. One of the first clues to uncovering this persistent rapist was the fact that he always struck close to railway stations. Deduction? For some reason – probably connected with his work – he knew their layouts and the secluded lanes behind them where he trapped his victims.

He nearly always tied his victims' hands behind their backs – fingers straight, thumbs aligned, in a "praying" position. He also used a type of brown string manufactured from paper which was almost exclusively used by British Rail.

The rapist also combed the pubic hair of his victims after assaulting them, and used tissues to wipe his semen from their vulvas. This was clearly a cunning man, who was trying to destroy tell-tale biological evidence that could lead to his conviction. In his murders he similarly tried to destroy vital clues: for example, by throwing Alison Day's body in the River Lee, and stuffing tissues into Maartje Tamboezer and Ann Lock's vaginas which he then ignited.

Despite these extreme measures, his semen has been identified on Maartje Tamboezer, and fibres from his clothing have been found on Alison Day's waterlogged sheepskin jacket.

Suzy Lamplugh, the missing estate agent's negotiator

DON'T START THE HUNT TOO SOON!

Police started a "missing persons" investigation unusually early on Suzie Lamplugh. Their reasons for caution when young women go missing were well illustrated over the first weekend of the hunt.

Another young lady was reported missing, and the press linked this story with Suzie's disappearance. Her name was headlined all over the country – to her extreme embarrassment when she surfaced from a naughty weekend on Monday morning, and had to confess that she and her lover had not emerged from the bedcovers to look at newspapers or television news for the whole time she was desperately being sought!

London Police Fear Missing Estate Agent is Dead

THERE NOW SEEMS LITTLE HOPE that 25-year-old Susannah Lamplugh, the estate agent's negotiator who disappeared from her work on July 28, is alive.

Pretty yuppie Suzie left Sturgis Estate Agents in Fulham Road at lunchtime, taking the keys of 37 Shorrolds Road with her; she apparently intended to show a client, named on her jotter as "Mr Kipper", round this property.

When she had not returned from the address late in the afternoon, police were informed. They quickly recognized that Suzie was not the type to run away and disappear for private reasons; and her handbag, left on her desk, seemed mute evidence that she intended to return. A massive search was immediately launched.

Ms Lamplugh's car was discovered parked in Stevenage Road – a mile away from Shorrolds Road and in the wrong direction from her office. Witnesses declared they had seen her in her car or with a man – possibly carrying a bottle of champagne.

All leads were followed, but even a police visit to Belgium to investigate a Mr Kuyper whose abandoned car was found in London proved fruitless. There can, alas, be little doubt that the unfortunate Susannah Lamplugh has been kidnapped and killed.

Man Goes on Trial for Murdering Nicola and Karen

FOR ONE OCTOBER night and a day, police and citizens of Brighton, England, searched Wild Park for missing children Karen Hadaway (10) and Nicola Fellows (9). When they were found, in a "hide" among thick undergrowth, both had been strangled and partially undressed; Nicola had also been raped.

An important clue proved to be a man's sweatshirt abandoned close to the murder site. Its owner, 20-year-old Russell Bishop, joined searchers with his dog on October

10, and was the second person on the scene when Matthew Marchant found the bodies.

Thereafter, Bishop described accurately the positions in which Karen and Nicola lay, although both Mr Marchant and Police Sergeant "Smudger" Smith who had urged Bishop to hurry across and see what Marchant had found, confirmed that he never went close enough to the overgrown hide to be able to see more than a flash of bright clothing. Bishop goes on trial next year.

Jet Set Rent Boy was Rough Trade Killer

MICHELE DE MARCO LUPO is London's leading sadistic rent boy. You wanna be flogged by a man in a mask? He's your guy. He'll flog men, women – anyone, for high prices. Wealthy international masochist swingers pay his expenses and more to have him fly the Atlantic and lash their eager little bottoms.

But simple binding and beating does not fully satisfy him – sexy gay Michele wants to go further

than commerce or the law allows.

He did so with railwayman James Burns, strangled in a derelict house in Warwick Road on March 16. He did so with James Connolly, strangled in a Kennington railway shed on April 3. He did so with IRA suspect Damien McClusky, strangled in an empty basement in Cromwell Road. He did so with an unknown tramp, encountered on Hungerford footbridge and strangled. But David Cole, picked up at Nine Elms, and destined to be Lupo's next victim, got away. He led police officers investigating the Burns and Connolly cases around gay bars till he spotted Lupo.

Lupo confessed at once, and told a great deal more into the bargain. How he loves sinking his teeth into the bottoms of his corpses. This particular little habit will undoubtedly lead to his conviction when he goes on trial next year.

Police comb the site of the murders

Wild Park, with footpaths running to the murder hideout

Miss Whiplash Found, Bound and Drowned in Bath

MRS CHRISTINE OFFORD was a specialist prostitute. Calling herself "Miss Whiplash", the 35-year-old ran a "torture dungeon" in Queens Gate, London. There punters could be tied up and gagged and flogged and have clips put on their nipples, and endure all the other extraordinary procedures that masochists enjoy undergoing at the hands of booted and corseted young ladies.

For her private and personal pleasure at her £100,000 home in Hounslow, however, Miss Whiplash much preferred caressing and making love to other women. Fellow prostitute Margaret Dunbar (29) was Mrs Offord's main lover and she was not pleased when Christine ended their lesbian liaison of several years last year.

Margaret decided to hire Robert Casaubon-Vincent and

Barry Parson of West Sussex to "rough up" her lover, and so bring her back into line

These two toughs went way over the top. They tied up Miss Whiplash, then threw her in the bath at her Queens Gate home before crushing her throat with one of the iron bars in her dungeon.

It was all most unfortunate, according to the women's friend, Mrs Pamela Shaw – at least as far as Margaret was concerned. "It happened when she was high on drink and drugs and she only intended slight harm," she assured the court.

Nevertheless Miss Dunbar has been sent down for seven years along with her hired thugs.

IN BRIEF

CONVICTED OF MURDERING his adoptive parents, sister "Bambi", and her twin sons: Jeremy Bamber (*see* 1985).

CONVICTED OF MURDERING his mother and nephew: Steven Benson (*see* 1985).

DR JAY SMITH, suspected Satanist principal of Upper Merion High School, convicted of complicity in the murder of Susan Reinert (*see* 1981). His alleged motive: silencing a teacher who knew of his satanic-sadistic orgies.

"DINGO BABY" Azaria Chamberlain's matinée jacket found: does not support Dr James Cameron's contention that a dog never touched the baby. Lindy and Michael Chamberlain have immediately been granted free pardons from the murder and accessory convictions standing against them since 1982.

Berserk Gunman Rampages Through Quiet English Town

THE SLEEPY BERKSHIRE TOWN of Hungerford will never forget August 19. On that warm summer afternoon, 27-year-old Michael Ryan charged along its streets shooting at all and sundry with a Beretta pistol, a carbine, and a Kalashnikov automatic rifle.

Ryan, a bachelor loner who lived with his mother and was obsessed with guns, started his carnage with an attack on pretty housewife Susan Godfrey, who had taken her children for a picnic in Savernake Wood. Dressed in combat fatigues and armed to the teeth, Ryan strapped her children in her car before making her walk into the woods with a groundsheet. Why he then killed her, only he knew. The probability is that he tried to rape her and lost his temper when she resisted.

On his way back to Hungerford he shot up a service station. Then, on the streets of his home town, he shot dead 13 people, critically injured two more; and wounded a further 11. His mother and several close neighbours were among the dead. Another neighbour, 77-year-old Mrs Dorothy Smith, survived. Ryan fired at her and missed after she shouted at him, "Is that you making all that noise? You're frightening everybody to death. Stop it!" The resolute old lady spat back at his retaliatory fire with, "You stupid bugger!"

A policeman in a patrol car

Police marksmen join the hunt in Hungerford for rampaging gunman Michael Ryan

managed to radio for help before being killed. Ryan ultimately shot himself after holing up for an hour in John O'Gaunt School and negotiating with encircling police.

Home Secretary Douglas Hurd was as shocked as the public to learn that Ryan's gun licence covered his entire armoury – including the military Kalashnikov. New laws are promised to keep such instruments of death out of irresponsible private hands.

Smoke pouring from the house Ryan shared with his mother. He set fire to it after murdering her

Diane Downs Escapes for a Naughty Weekend

MURDERING MOTHER Diane Downs (*see* 1984) escaped from Oregon Women's Correctional Center this July after her appeal was turned down.

Good-looking Diane's impenitent ruthlessness, and total inability to accept responsibility for her actions, make her an extremely dangerous woman. Authorities feared that she might have engineered her escape in order to seek out and injure crime historian Ann Rule, whose excellent book *Small Sacrifices*, published this year, exposes Diane's wickedness.

There was also the danger that she might seek out her surviving

children, Christie and Danny, now happily adopted by the lawyer who prosecuted her.

All were given police protection in safe places until, 11 days later, the escaped murderess was traced to a nearby house where she had set up with temporary boyfriend Wayne Sheifer and three of his men friends.

Diane issued statements about the reason for her escape, giving as her main motive the wish to look for her daughter Cheryl's "real" killer. She undoubtedly acted from a normal desire for freedom; a normal need for a male lover; and an abnormal love of notoriety.

Baltic Baroness Battered Blind Ex, Say Police

ARRESTED THIS DECEMBER in Shropshire, England, Baroness Susan de Stempel, great-granddaughter of slave-trade opponent William Wilberforce, is charged with murdering her first husband, Simon Dale.

Architect Dale married the ex-debutante, several years his junior, in 1957. With her own money she bought Heath House in Shropshire, a splendid Georgian brick mansion. The house was dilapidated, with only three habitable rooms when Mrs Dale set about having it expensively restored and refurbished.

Meanwhile, her husband's eyesight was failing and his eccentricities increasing. He became convinced, for example, that Heath House was the true seat of King Arthur, and that excavations in house and grounds might uncover the Round Table.

In 1973 Susan divorced him, alleging that he dug a hole under a yew tree saying it would be her grave. Dale remained in Heath House, to his ex-wife's chagrin.

In 1984 she married Michael de Stempel, a German with an obscure Baltic title awarded by the Czars in the 19th century. He refused to consummate the marriage and, after an attempt to have it annulled, the pair divorced in 1986. De Stempel alleged that his wife had forced him to sleep in a tent in the garden.

With all her capital tied up in Heath House, the Baroness (as she continues to call herself) was short of cash. In September the almost blind Michael Dale was found battered in his kitchen. He had been dead for about two days, his supper of toad-in-the-hole burned to a cinder in the oven. The police swiftly decided that the Baroness, despairing of slow and expensive legal procedures to recover the house, had conspired with her children to get rid of the old man by beating him to death with a very unaristocratic jemmy.

Marie Hilley Dies – for Real, this Time!

CONVICTED ALABAMA murderess Marie Hilley absconded from prison while out on a weekend's furlough in February, and was subsequently found dead of exposure. Marie had "died" before and resurrected herself as her own imaginary twin, but this time her death was for real.

Marie's career in crime began in 1975, when she poisoned her 45-year-old husband Frank. She then proceeded to live it up on his insurance. In 1978 her daughter nearly died of arsenic poisoning, after Marie had heavily insured the girl's life. Investigation of this misadventure led to further delvings into Frank's death, revealing arsenical poisoning as the cause.

When it looked as though she was cornered, Marie jumped bail and fled to Florida where she married a boat-builder in 1980. Then she went away and announced her own death, returning to Florida to console her husband as her "twin" sister Teri! It was as "Teri Martin" that she was arrested in 1983, and subsequently convicted.

Is Gloucester Killer Suzy Lamplugh's Murderer?

RAPIST JOHN CANNAN had only been out of one of Her Majesty's residences for her less savoury subjects for three days last year when estate agent Suzy Lamplugh disappeared (*see* 1986).

Now that Cannan has been charged with the murder of Bristol newlywed Shirley Banks, the question of whether he was also responsible for the abduction of the missing Ms Lamplugh arises.

Mrs Banks disappeared after going shopping in October. Weeks later her naked body was found decomposing by a stream in the Quantock Hills, 45 miles away.

Cannan was questioned because of his long record of sex offences. The tax disc of Mrs Banks's car was found in his possession, and her car was traced to his garage where he was crudely repainting it.

Good-looking ladies' man Banks has a string of legitimate girlfriends, some of whom tell of the sudden violence that can replace his smooth charm.

In prison he was nicknamed "Kipper", because of his love for Seventies-style clothing and kipper ties. Suzy Lamplugh's last appointment, according to her jotter, was with a mysterious "Mr Kipper".

John Cannan, charged with killing Shirley Banks and suspected of being "Mr Kipper"

IN BRIEF

CONVICTED OF homosexual murders and sentenced to life imprisonment (in solitary confinement as an AIDS sufferer): Michele Lupo (*see* 1986). So much for Lupo's priggish and uptight health freak's anti-smoking stance!

ACQUITTED OF the murders of schoolgirls Karen Hadaway and Nicola Fellows: Russell Bishop (*see* 1986). Witnesses to Bishop's movements cast reasonable doubt on his access to Wild Park at the time of the murders, despite suspicion engendered by his own constantly changing story and some circumstantial evidence against him.

EXECUTED FOR horrifying Utah audioshop murders (*see* 1974): Dale Pierre.

DISAPPEARED FROM their home in Jersey: wealthy Lloyd's underwriter Nicholas Newall and his wife Elizabeth. Cleaned-up bloodstaining in their house suggests foul play some time after the couple's last known meeting with their sons Mark and Roderick.

London's Stockwell Strangler Convicted, Given 40 Years

THE TERRIFYING STRANGLER who invaded old people's bedrooms in Stockwell, south London, for three months in 1986 has been given the longest minimum sentence ever imposed in Britain. Half-Antiguan Kenneth Erskine will not be released for 40 years, when he will be 66.

This horrible creature sodomized and strangled four elderly men and three elderly women. Another potential victim, Fred Prentice of Mortlake, 73, managed to escape his clutches. He struggled and activated an alarm, causing the intruder to flee.

Mr Prentice's description was not essential to the police invetigation. Apart from the statistical knowledge that the strangler was probably black (*see* below on psy-chological profiling), a negroid hair had been found in the room of murdered Mrs Eileen Emms. Subsequently, a fingerprint left in Mrs Jane Cockett's room identified Erskine, who had a previous conviction for burglary.

But the real difficulty was in tracing him. Police trailed him to more than 300 squats and bedsits in London, and still never found his main place of abode. Erskine was caught because, although he had at least £3,000 from break-ins, he went on collecting unemployment benefit. He was arrested at the Social Security office. Erskine proved stupid to the point of half-wittedness, and so uncontrolled that at times his arms had to be restrained to stop him masturbating in open court.

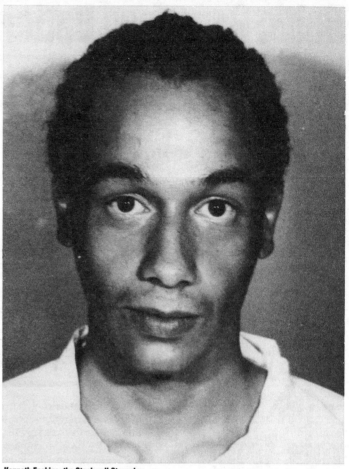
Kenneth Erskine, the Stockwell Strangler

Psychological Profiling and Computers Transform Detection of Serial Murder

JUST EIGHT YEARS AGO all England reeled before the seemingly unstoppable Yorkshire Ripper (*see* p. 280). Two juries this year convicted men whose crimes presented similar difficulties. Both Railway Rapist John Duffy and Stockwell Strangler Kenneth Erskine attacked victims unknown to them, and did not steal identifiable property for marketing. Two factors make it unlikely that a serial killer will ever again be at large for long in Britain.

It is well-known that police questioned Sutcliffe nine times before his arrest during a routine check of prostitutes working the car trade. But the truly massive collection of card-index files made simultaneous recovery of the various entries identifying him impossible.

These days, computerization would instantly identify him as a prime suspect. Sutcliffe would turn up again and again in the investigation: as one of scores of car-owners frequently spotted in red-light districts; one of hundreds of possible recipients of the new £5 note passed to one victim; one of thousands of car-owners whose tyre and axle sizes fitted tracks left beside another victim.

Psychological profiling, developed by the FBI Academy at Quantico, has also proved amazingly fruitful. Instead of accepting the introspectively derived psychoanalytic categories of human personality, the Quantico Behavioural Sciences Unit works from statistically quantified interviews with convicted violent criminals and the practical experience of evidence left at scenes of crimes.

Following this technique, Professor David Canter of the University of Surrey correctly advised police that the Railway Rapist would prove to be a small, physically unattractive, unhappily married man from Kilburn or Cricklewood, doing semi-skilled work for British Rail, and interested in the martial arts. The planning of his crimes showed an "organized" personality, compared with Erskine's opportunistic "disorganized" violence.

FBI statistics also show that sexual offences against old people number among the very, very few types of sex crime more commonly perpetrated by black than white offenders.

New Scientific Technique Catches the Right Man

IT'S NOT JUST your fingerprints that give you away now: your blood, sweat and tears can all be identified precisely, not just categorized into groups. Laboratory "blooding" or "genetic fingerprinting" can take cells from your body, or drops from its fluids, and show a pattern of darks and shades, similar to a supermarket bar code, which identifies you and you alone. It's the end of the road for the anonymous rapist – unless he uses a condom!

Twenty-eight-year-old Colin Pitchfork has just had to surrender to the irrefutable evidence of science. Back in 1983, 15-year-old Lynda Mann was raped and strangled on Black Pad footpath near Narborough, Leicestershire, England. Blood tests on eight suspects proved inconclusive.

In 1986, 15-year-old Dawn Ashworth suffered a similar fate in Narborough's Ten Pound Lane. A simple-minded mental hospital kitchen worker confessed under questioning. His semen, sent with that found in Dawn's body to Dr Alec Jeffreys' laboratory, produced the genetically fingerprinted report that he was innocent, and that Dawn's killer had also killed Lynda.

Blood and saliva samples were taken from all males in the area. At first the operation seemed a failure, because tests did not throw up the murderer. But this was only because crafty killer Colin Pitchfork persuaded a friend to go in his place. When the deception was exposed, Pitchfork was well and truly caught. He confessed.

His trial this January lasted a mere half a day. He has been sentenced for two murders, two rapes and the conspiracy to avoid giving specimens.

American Televangelist Humbug Jim Bakker Jailed for Fraud

Fraudulent televangelist Jim Bakker (right) with wife Tammy and their lawyer

JIM AND TAMMY FAYE BAKKER stand high on the list of glitzy super-spectacular entertainers whose televised pseudo-pentecostal religion is deeply offensive to the truly spiritual. Not surprisingly, there was a distinct lack of Christian charity flowing among the reputably godly when the Reverend Jim was exposed as having a torrid affair with luscious church secretary Jessica Hahn.

Since most televangelists are blatantly in the religion game for the money rather than for God, it came as no surprise that Jim met the problem with cash, trying to buy Jessica's silence for $265,000.

Investigation of the source of the bribe exposed the man as a major fraud. He and Tammy Faye had been enjoying a luxurious lifestyle courtesy of his flock, whom he had systematically fleeced of their savings. Convicted on 22 counts of fraud, the slimy reverend was carted off to a 45-year jail sentence. Nobody, but nobody, was moved by the whinging wimp's tears of remorse as he went.

Greedy Whizz Kid Financier's ZZZZ has Gone Bust

HORRIBLE REPRESENTATIVE of President Reagan's untrammelled free market in finance is whizz kid Barry Minkow, off to jail for 25 years on 57 counts of fraud.

By 1986 the rug-cleaning business ZZZZ Best he started in his parents' California garage six years ago, when he was 16, was valued at $200 million on the stock market. When the crash came just a year later, its assets fetched a paltry $62,000. How were all those real smart brokers and bankers fooled into believing that Minkow's business was such a winner? The short answer is by old-fashioned scams and their own greed.

Kid Minkow used credit card fraud, kited account cheques, even faked burglaries to bring in some instant cash.

The decent hard-working folks of America long to see the end of this rats' nest of junk bonds, insider trading and general greedy fraudulence which passes itself off as "free enterprise capitalism"!

IN BRIEF

JOHN DUFFY, the Railway Rapist (*see* 1986), convicted of two murders and five rapes.

Acquitted of Ann Lock's murder because the decomposed state of her body prevented such scientific evidence as would preclude "reasonable doubt".

Other rape charges remain open on file against him.

Murder Causes Race Uproar in Massachusetts

The body of murderer Charles Stuart recovered after his suicide

EIGHT-MONTH PREGNANT Carol Stuart's murder in Boston last October provoked white fury against black street violence. The handsome, rising young Stuarts – Charles a furriers' manager, Carol a lawyer – were good Catholics expecting their first baby.

According to Charles, the couple were waiting at a set of traffic lights in the black neighbourhood beside the hospital where Carol took pre-natal classes when a robber hit them. Twenty-nine-year-old Charles, severely injured with a gunshot wound in the abdomen, managed to croak a call for help into his car-phone. The mugger, in black jogging-suit with a red stripe, had also shot Carol in the head and taken her jewellery.

Carol and her baby died in hospital. Charles was lucky to survive. Politicians, churchmen and opinion formers denounced urban black criminality. A petty black crook was implicated by his juvenile nephew (who loved boasting of Uncle Willie's crimes). Black spokesmen were embarrassed and tongue-tied, though Uncle Willie denied complicity and the nephew later retracted his story.

This year, Charles's brother Matthew revealed that, when the Stuarts were supposedly being attacked, he actually met Charles's car by prearrangement to collect Carol's rings and a pistol. He had retained her engagement ring and thrown the pistol in the river, from where police retrieved it.

Charles's main error actually made his story plausible: the shot supposed to give credence to his yarn injured him more seriously than he had intended. Charles left home in a hurry as Matthew's story was about to break and threw himself into the river before he could be arrested.

The black community is understandably furious that a white yuppie combining wife-murder with a cheap insurance scam should be instantly believed when he randomly accuses a black man of his own vicious crimes.

TV Sculpture Tracks Family-Slayer After 20 Years

JOHN HARDY was a decent middle class accountant, with wire-rimmed spectacles and receding hair; so was John List. John Hardy was a faithful married Lutheran, quietly introverted, rarely talking much above a whisper; so was John List. John Hardy had no children; nor had John List – well, not after the autumn of 1971. Prior to that he had two girls and a boy. He lost them, and his wife, and his mother, in one fell swoop. And the world lost John List for 17 years!

The entire List family had to leave their Rutgers, New Jersey, home suddenly to nurse a sick relative in North Carolina, so letters from List informed the children's schools, the bank, the public utilities, the church, and anybody else who needed to know.

The Lists' mansion on the edge of town stood silent and deserted, with random electric lights burning as a precaution against burglary.

The occasional failure of those light bulbs led neighbours to reflect that the Lists had been away from home an inordinate length of time. After a month passed, police broke into the List mansion.

There, in the freezing ballroom, neatly laid out, were the three children and Mrs List, all shot. Upstairs in a cupboard, List's mother Alma, also shot.

Investigations revealed that List was almost broke as a result of bad investments, and that he had "borrowed" from his mother to compensate. It was inferred that, unable to control his womenfolk without the aid of purse-strings, he shot his wife and mother, killed his children as they came home from school, and fled. Very successfully: his car was in the airport carpark. Mr List had disappeared.

Crime-reconstruction television company Cosgrove-Muerer broadcast a sculptor's impression of how List must look today, with further receded hair and flaccid muscles. And behold, many people recognized retiring Mr Hardy of Richmond, Virginia., who denied it, of course. But his fingerprints match List's old army records, and he's now under arrest for murder as John List.

Jack the Ripper Identified at Last

CRIME-SOLVING TV company Cosgrove-Muerer (*see* John List story on these pages) has proposed a solution to the 100-year-old mystery of Jack the Ripper that satisfies experts from Scotland Yard and the FBI. The company hired FBI psychological profilers Roy Hazelwood and John Douglas (*see* 1988) to examine the evidence and produce a profile, as they would in a modern case.

The agents agreed that of all the suspects ever suggested, the only one who can be the true Ripper is the Polish Jewish immigrant identified by CID chief Sir Robert Anderson at the time of the murders, as author Martin Fido proposed a year ago. A panel of experts, including representatives from Scotland Yard and the Milton Helpern Forensic Science Institute, unanimously concur.

IN BRIEF

BOB STUTMAN, head of the New York branch of the Drug Enforcement Administration, offers his "personal guarantee" that Britain will have a serious 'crack' problem (*see* 1985) by 1991.

His word should be heeded. In 1986 he correctly predicted that America would be "swamped with crack" in three years, and look back on the drug problems of 1986 as "the good old days".

Baroness Moves from Frying-Pan to Fire

Baroness Susan von Stempel is driven away after her court appearance

SHROPSHIRE BARONESS Susan von Stempel and her children have been acquitted of conspiring to murder her ex-husband, Simon Dale (*see* 1987). So the slaying of the virtually blind architect in the kitchen of the house from which Susan was trying evict him remains unsolved.

Many other interesting facts came to light during the case, though. Detectives noticed that the Baroness's cottage was stuffed with valuable antiques and furniture. These proved to be the property of her late aunt, Lady Illingworth, and were left to Susan, or so she claims, at the old lady's death in 1986. The signature on Lady Illingworth's will appears to be a forgery, perpetrated by the Baroness de Stempel.

Susan's hugely rich "Aunt Puss", as Lady Illingworth was known, left Claridge's to live with the de Stempels in 1984. Within a year she was no longer rich, her funds transferred to the Baroness. "Aunt Puss" was herself transferred to a hostel, with the misinformation that she was a sex-obsessed alcoholic, liable to wander off. When "Aunt Puss" died, she wasn't given the Catholic funeral she had wanted. Susan had her cremated – and then declined to pay the bill or collect the ashes.

Baron de Stempel was around when Lady Illingworth was defrauded, so he too stands in the dock with Susan and her brood.

Madman 'Yosser' Kills Copper, then Himself

The scene of the shootings of Inspector Codling and Sergeant Bowden

ANTHONY HUGHES (42) of Baguley near Manchester, England, seemed so dangerously barmy that neighbours nicknamed him "Yosser", after the tragic victim of unemployment and bad social services in Alan Bleasdale's TV series *On the Blackstuff*.

However, Hughes can seem far from tragic. He has served long prison stretches for armed robbery and a particularly nasty incident when he posed as a policeman to rape a 19-year-old girl and told her he was the Yorkshire Ripper.

At 2.00 am on September 14 he was in Birch Service Station on the M62 when Inspector Raymond Codling and Sergeant James Bowden, performing routine vehicle checks at the place, asked him a pertinent question about his motor bike. Hughes responded by shooting both men, killing Inspector Codling instantly. Then he rode furiously to Manchester in search of a Catholic priest. Finding Fr Maurice Keenan away from home, Hughes shot himself dead

Despite mild agitation for the restoration of capital punishment in the light of this bloody and senseless crime, it is obvious that no deterrent of any kind would have been the slightest use with someone as deranged as Hughes, and no retribution could be inflicted on a suicide.

Ted Bundy: The 'North-Eastern' Murderer

Multiple murderer Ted Bundy's furious reaction to being sentenced to death in the electric chair

Bundy Fries in Florida to Crowd's Cheers

TED BUNDY WAS born illegitimate in 1946. His grandparents didn't help his sense of stigma by pretending he was his mother's little brother. When she married decent Mr Bundy, who gave little Theodore his surname, the boy was long-ing to break away from his working-class background.

His mother expected higher education would lead him to great things. Ted achieved little at Washington State University, but he did win an up-market girl-friend in rich Californian Stephanie Brooks. Bundy skied and improved his sense of class with her, and adopted her liking for verbal Briticisms. When she graduated and went home, he followed her, intending to study Chinese at Stanford.

The move was a disaster. Washingtonian Ted looked gauche, immature and pushy when placed alongside the so-phisticated Brooks family. Stephanie broke off their un-derstanding. A devastated Bundy dropped out of school and sank to menial work as a dishwasher and warehouseman.

Yuppie Topside – Kinky Underside

Politics lifted him. Back in Washington State he worked as a roady for a popular black lib-eral Republican candidate for the Lieutenant-Governorship. Accepted by powerful state party members, he reverted to a pre-sentable existence in three-piece suits. His chameleon good-looks fitted any circles. He became the lover of a prominent local Republican's young divorced daughter. He also used his po-litical connections to go back to college and study psychology.

This was the best period of his life. He was an A-grade stu-dent. He worked well for the telephone Samaritans. His future seemed assured – yet his sex life was deteriorating. To keep his relationship with a di-vorcée alive he played bondage games; but during one of these sessions he tried to strangle her and the woman broke off their affair. Another lover suffered a similarly unnerving experience.

While his smart Young Mr Republican appearance was to the fore, he re-encountered Stephanie, who willingly ac-cepted formal engagement now her beau had all the attributes of a gentleman.

But the betrothal was only a self-aggrandizing power-play for Bundy, who abruptly broke it off once Stephanie was hooked, heartlessly refusing to return her calls.

In December 1973 he started his worst secret vice. Over the next four months, seven young Washington girls were sexually assaulted and murdered in their beds by an intruder, or disap-peared mysteriously. All had long, centre-parted hair like Stephanie's.

Ted in a Sling

In the summer of 1974, Janice Ott and Denise Laslund disap-peared from Lake Sammanish Park, Washington. Janice had been seen talking to a young man with his arm in a sling, call-ing himself Ted, who asked her to help him load a sailboat on to the roof of his car.

Another girl had been ap-proached by the same man. She had refused to go further when he changed his story at the car, saying the boat was at his house and they would have to drive there.

These stories produced other tales of a good-looking young man with a brown VW and an injured arm who asked college girls to help him gather dropped books. When one real-ized he wanted to lure her into his car, he laughed and took his arm out of the sling before dri-

> "Take care of yourself, young man. I say that to you sincerely. It's a tragedy to this court to see such a total waste of humanity. You'd have made a good lawyer. I bear you no animosity, believe me. But you went the wrong way. Take care of yourself, partner."
>
> **Judge Edward D. Cowart, sentencing Bundy**

...ing away. Several friends of Ted Bundy's realized with horror that he fitted descriptions of the "north-eastern murderer".

Arrests and Escapes

But before he could be investigated, the murders stopped. The reason? Ted had transferred to the University of Utah to study law. Here, he raped and strangled the Midvale police chief's daughter, and abducted Laura Aime. He also travelled out of state to Colorado and killed at least four more women.

Back in Salt Lake City he met the one that got away, Carol Da Ronch, who identified him after his attempt to kidnap her failed.

In August 1975, Bundy was picked up for erratic driving in Salt Lake City. When a ski-mask, an ice-pick and a crowbar were found in his car, he was suspected of attempted burglary. When a hair matching Midvale victim Melissa Smith's was also found, together with road-maps of the Colorado murder area,

Bundy was in serious trouble.

Carol Da Ronch positively identified him and he was convicted of her attempted kidnap, and sent to Aspen, Colorado, to face trial for murder.

Bundy opted to defend himself, and was granted access to the civic law library. Finding himself unguarded there one day, he leaped from a 20-foot window and escaped. He was recaptured shortly afterwards at a mountain-lodge.

Bundy's escape, good looks and articulacy contributed to his elevation into something like a criminal media star.

Closely watched and chained when outside prison, he none the less escaped again. He dieted down till he could get through the 18-inch square lighting panel in his cell and crawled out along the wiring ducts.

The Florida Murders

With well prepared documents as Chris Hagen, Bundy might have stayed out of trouble.

Instead he went to Tallahassee, Florida; lived by credit card fraud and shoplifting; battered two students to death and seriously injured two others in Chi Omega Sorority House on January 15, 1978, maiming another sleeping girl student on his way home.

In Pensacola in February he raped and strangled a 12-year-old. But in Jacksonville he was picked up after trying to abduct another child. Ted Bundy was then sent to prison for good, never to enjoy freedom again.

Jailhouse Lawyer Par Excellence

For ten years, he was the smoothest jailhouse lawyer in America. He defended himself, revelling in plaudits from other lawyers and the press. However, Bundy couldn't buck the evidence, and he knew it.

Television screens saw elegant bow-tied Bundy fervently claiming to be the innocent victim of a series of coincidences. They didn't see the

screaming maniac trying desperately to avoid having toothcasts taken for comparison with the savage bitemarks left on one of his victim's buttocks and breasts.

Most of America, disgusted by the self-satisfied murderer's courtroom performances, rejoiced when delays and appeals ground to a halt and Ted Bundy went to the electric chair.

On that day, January 24, 1989, crowds outside the prison cheered his death. Fireworks went off. Demonstration-style banners reading, "Roast in Peace" were waved in jubilation – and probably relief – that his reign of terror was at an end.

BUNDY'S CRUCIAL FAILURE

Bundy's giveaway crime was the attempted abduction of Carol Da Ronch. In November 1974 he presented himself to her as a plain-clothes policeman in a Salt Lake City shopping mall. He said someone had attempted to break into her car, and persuaded her to accompany him to the station to make a statement. When he pulled handcuffs on her in his car she struggled, and both cuffs snapped on one wrist. When he pulled a gun, she tumbled out of the car. When he lashed at her with a crowbar, she held it off and kicked him hard where it hurt, before running into traffic to be rescued by a startled passing motorist.

A victim who could positively identify Bundy had, for the first time, escaped an obvious abduction attempt.

Demonstrators wave placards, cheer and shout outside the Florida prison where Ted Bundy is executed for his crimes

Bishop Convicted of Assaulting Child

RUSSELL BISHOP, acquitted of the murder of two little girls in England in 1986, has now been given life imprisonment for the attempted murder of a third.

On February 4, Mr and Mrs David Clifton were enjoying the exhilarating view from Devil's Dyke, Sussex, when a naked little girl with tears streaming down her face appeared, bleeding from gorse scratches, and announced, "I've been kidnapped."

The 7-year-old child (whose name may not be published) was roller-skating near her home in Brighton when Bishop grabbed her and bundled her into the boot of his red Cortina. As he drove to the lonely beauty spot, the girl had the presence of mind to remove her roller skates in the hope of making a better escape. She also banged on the boot lid with a hammer she found.

On reaching Devil's Dyke, Bishop squeezed her throat till she passed out. Eventually she came round in the gorse where Bishop had thrown her, presumably leaving her for dead. Doctors say that the child was extremely lucky to survive Bishop's strangulation.

At Bishop's trial the child gave very clear and courageous video evidence against her attacker. Forensic scientists found hammer marks where she testified to striking Bishop's car boot lid, and a thread matching the fabric of her jumper in the boot. Most damning of all, DNA "fingerprinting" confirmed that her saliva and Bishop's semen were both on a pair of men's track suit trousers discarded at the scene of the crime.

Bishop's sullen claim that they were not his, and that the police had framed him by stealing a used contraceptive from his house to contaminate them, cut no ice with the court. He goes to jail to join the "nonces" so despised by hardened criminals.

Haysom-Soering Case Concluded after Extradition Battle

AT LONG LAST Virginia prison gates clang shut on arrogant Jens Soering, son a German diplomat. His co-criminal, American student Elizabeth Haysom, started her two 45-year stretches in 1988.

In 1986 the pair were picked up in London for passing dud cheques to retailers Marks and Spencer before returning their goods for cash at different branches. They were very well equipped with false identification and cheque books for this simple scam.

A search of their lodgings produced an astonishing cache of letters. These two, it seemed, had fled America after murdering Elizabeth's parents. Jens had carved them up with a butterfly knife while Elizabeth went to the theatre to establish an alibi for herself and her lover. Virginia police confirmed this and Elizabeth was sent back to America to stand trial.

But Jens fought extradition through the House of Lords and the European courts. His aim? Ideally, to be tried in his native West Germany, where he would be lightly sentenced as a juvenile and soon regain his freedom. In any case, he did not want to risk going to the electric chair, an unpleasant prospect which Virginia held out. Now, after a judicial compromise with the German authorities, who will not extradite for capital punishment, he's got life.

But why did they kill the elderly Heysoms in the first place? Astonishingly, it seems, because Mrs Nancy Heysom enjoyed a covert lesbian relationship with her bisexual daughter and hoarded mildly pornographic pictures of Elizabeth naked!

The young couple's supercilious arrogance has forfeited their hope of public sympathy.

Ozzie Vampires Lure and Kill Man

AUSTRALIAN TRACEY WIGGINTON is a lesbian vampire. Her girlfriends, Lisa Ptaschinski, Kim Jervis and Tracey Ann Waugh, have little scabs on their wrists showing where they open their veins to let Tracey suck their blood.

Tracey has been drinking animal blood since her teens. As an adult she clumped around Brisbane in hob-nailed boots and T-shirt and jeans. Until she wanted something special, that is, when she could make herself as attractive to men as her friend, pretty little Tracey Ann Waugh.

After a champagne supper the four went hunting, Tracey and Kim Jervis bringing along ninja butterfly knives. When they saw waiter Edward Baldock making his drunken way home, they stopped the car and came on to him like vamps. Wigginton, Jervis and Waugh were all over him, and invited him to have sex on the river bank.

Down at the river, Kim and Tracey Ann got cold feet and stayed behind. Tracey Wigginton and Lisa Ptaschinski made their way down to the bank, where Ted stripped and cautiously put his wallet in his shoe. They undressed to disarm his suspicions, and as he approached them, Ted spotted a credit card he'd overlooked, and slipped it, too, in his shoe. Then he prepared for prolonged ecstasy with the slender, naked girls.

Tracey alone enjoyed it. With the two knives she flailed at Ted Baldock, stabbing him over 50 times, and almost cutting his head off. Then she buried her mouth in his throat and sucked his blood. After she'd washed off Ted's gore in the river, the girls went home.

The police caught up with them when it was realized that the credit card Ted put in his shoe belonged to Tracey. She confessed and pleaded guilty to his murder in October. The other three go on trial next year.

Accused: Tracey Ann Waugh.   Accused: Kim Aileen Jervis.   Accused: Lisa Marie Ptaschinski.

Guilty: Tracey Avril Wigginton.

Murdered: Edward Clyde Baldock.

The Australian lesbian killers, with Wigginton shown at bottom left, and victim Edward Baldock

Boxer Terry Marsh Acquitted of Attempted Murder

FRANK WARREN may have enemies, but which of them wanted him dead on November 30 last year? An Old Bailey jury decided that it wasn't former light-welterweight world champion Terry Marsh.

Warren, who has grown rich as an unlicensed boxing promoter, offending the British Board of Boxing Control, was Marsh's manager. He steered him to the world title, but then everything fell apart.

Frank had just arranged another big fight for his new champion when Terry gave the *Sun* newspaper an interview. In this he revealed that he suffered from epilepsy. The implication that Warren knew of his condition and was still willing to let him fight was damaging and caused quite a stir.

Not surprisingly, relations between the two men soured irrevocably.

But why should Terry want a professional "hitman" to pump bullets into Warren as he approached the Broadway theatre, Barking, last year? According to Terry's estranged wife, Jacqui, because he believed Warren had used him; made himself rich and then thrown him away once he had no further use for him. She made a statement to the police to this effect, then retracted it. So Terry walks free.

Warren's underworld connection through his uncle Bob - once a thug in the pay of Billy Hill (*see* 1956) - has been aired, as have his troubles with other promoters, but none of it explains who was out to get him on that autumn evening.

Vain murderer Michael Shorey, who killed his girlfriend and her room-mate

Former world champion boxer Terry Marsh, found not guilty of assaulting his former manager

God's Gift to Women Kills Lover and Friend

HANDSOME 35-year-old Michael Shorey pulled girls as and when he felt like it. The streetwise West Indian accounts clerk was a sharp dresser with a neat line in chat. He picked up *East Enders*' TV star Sandy Ratcliff in a bar for a £10 bet, and became her lover when she was at a low ebb.

But he was already engaged to 31-year-old Elaine Forsyth, and he couldn't take it when Elaine had enough of his lies and swaggering and broke it off. He strangled her with a sash cord. And when Elaine's flatmate, Patricia Morrison, came in, he strangled her, too. Then he left both bodies in a car.

He was caught when he asked a friend to help him get bloodstains off a carpet. Despite Sandy's tentative attempt to give him an alibi, he's received a life sentence for failing to swallow his pride.

IN BRIEF

JONATHAN MOYLE, 28-year-old Briton, found hanging in his hotel wardrobe in Santiago, Chile, was treated as a suicide by local police, but a judicial investigation has agreed that he was murdered. Political or arms-dealing connections are suspected.

Publishing Millionaire Robert Maxwell Stole Millions

TYCOON ROBERT MAXWELL, who died suddenly at sea on November 5, stole at least £526 million! His rickety publishing empire was over £1 billion in debt, and his welter of trusts and offshore deposits will take accountants years to disentangle. Principal victims of "Cap'n Bob's" frauds were:

- *DAILY MIRROR* PENSIONERS: £150 million of their fund's vanished! Another £150 million is securing Maxwell's loans.
- MIRROR GROUP AND MAXWELL COMMUNICATIONS CORPORATION SHAREHOLDERS AND EMPLOYEES: With share-prices of these two Maxwell giants in free-fall, nobody with a stake in them is secure.

- *NEW YORK DAILY NEWS*: Just months after the ebullient Brit barged in, promising to revive the ailing tabloid's fortunes, its future is in doubt again.

Robert Maxwell's career was checkered with dubious incidents. In 1971 inspectors from the Department of Trade and Industry declared that he was unfit to manage a public company, but it's taken 20 years to prove them right! Within a month of the great socialist capitalist's death, he was shown up as a failed gambler, whose business bubble burst the instant his smooth-talking face was no longer available to offer lies, excuses and promises.

Millionaire fraud and thief, Robert Maxwell

MAXWELL'S CAREER

1923	Born Jan Hoch in Czechoslovakia.
1939	Flees to Hungary.
1940	Joins Czech Legion in France.
1941	Transfers to British Army and changes name to Leslie Du Maurier.
1945	As Lt Maxwell awarded MC and promoted to rank of Captain.
1945-7	Works for Information Services Control in occupied Germany.
1948-50	Distributes German scientific publications in UK and USA.
1951	Founds Pergamon Press. Buys ailing book distributor Simpkin Marshall.
1954	Simpkin Marshall folds. Maxwell blamed.
1964	Elected Labour MP for Buckingham.
1971	DTI inquiry says Maxwell is "not a person who can be relied upon to exercise proper stewardship of a publicly-quoted company".
1981	Takes over British Printing Corporation.
1982	Takes over Oxford United football club.
1984	Buys the *Daily Mirror*.
1987	Founds London *Daily News*, which folds the same year. Buys into French television. Buys £15 million yacht *Lady Ghislaine*.
1989	BPC changes its name to Maxwell Communications Corporation.
1990	After aggressive world-wide takeovers, Maxwell's profits do not cover interest paid on loans.
1991	February – makes rescue bid for *New York Daily News*
November – Drowns off *Lady Ghislaine* near Canaries. Inquest reports heart attack prompted fall overboard.

DIY Builder Fights Planning Decision with Bullets

A PLANNING OFFICER'S intransigence led Albert Dryden to commit murder in front of television and news cameras – the first such killing in Britain.

Albert wanted to use his £15,000 redundancy payment, from the closure of Consett steelworks, to build a bungalow in the country for his mother, but Derwentside planning officer Harry Collinson told him this was out of the question. The official jokingly remarked that anything built on the plot of unspoilt agricultural land Albert had bought couldn't be more than three feet high. Bearded eccentric Albert took this as permission. He dug a deep pit,

and built his bungalow in it!

When Collinson ordered him to destroy the monstrosity, Albert tried every legal stratagem to save his handiwork. Inevitably, he lost. Just as he was on the point of giving up the struggle, a badly worded official letter gave him the impression that he had won five weeks' grace. So when Harry Collinson turned up with demolition workers, Albert was waiting for him.

As the dispute had reached the local papers, pressmen, police and a television crew were present at the encounter. They watched in horror, then fled, when Albert shot the bureaucrat with an antiquated pistol before giving himself up.

Bearded weirdie Albert Dryden shoots planning officer Harry Collinson in front of press cameras

Missing Oxford Student Slain by New Zealand Lover

W HILE ENGLAND FEARED that Rita Maclean's disappearance at the start of her Oxford term meant another Suzie Lamplugh-style disappearance (*see* 1986), police decided that her New Zealand boyfriend, John Tanner, knew more than he was telling.

John was the last person to see Rita alive – at the buffet on Oxford station where he said good-bye before returning home to Nottingham. He claimed that Rita went to

drink coffee with a man he didn't know, who offered her a lift back to her digs in his car.

With no subsequent sighting of the missing student, and a letter at her digs showing Tanner had written to her as soon as he got home, police couldn't act. There were no signs of grave-digging in the garden and no smell of rotting flesh in the lodging-house. Then Inspector Parker found a loose board in the basement.

When that was opened up, there was Rita's body in the crawl-space. Giveaway putrefaction had been prevented by a cool, damp through-draught.

With the body exposed, a penitent Tanner cracked and confessed. He killed Rita in fury when she said they must break off their relationship. Young love came to a sad end in sudden death.

'Pussy, Pussy! Eat up Your Nice Mrs Perry!'

J OHN PERRY'S first two marriages ended in divorce. When the 52-year-old aircraft fitter from the Welsh border married pretty young Filippino Arminda, she knew nothing of his reputation for marital violence. But John soon reverted to type, and Arminda, too, had divorce papers served on him. The two quarrelled over Arminda's affair with Barry Burns – then she disappeared.

Four days later, when Inspector Ross Duffield called to ask where Mrs Perry was, John replied at once, "I've done a good turn. I've fed her to the animals." He showed the astonished policeman the bags of cooked flesh in the garage. In an armchair sat Katie, the tabby cat, replete after her meal of Arminda.

Katie, the tabby cat who ate Mrs Perry

Schoolmarm Seduces Pupil, Makes him Kill Husband

S WINGING PAMELA SMART, rocking "Maid of Metal" on local radio when she was at college in sunny Florida, found herself a 22-year-old housewife, married to an insurance salesman in freezing New Hampshire by 1989. She was also media advisor to the local school board, and a counsellor at Winnacunnet High School.

Husband Greg, once a passion-

ate punk rocker like Pamela, was settling down to provincial yuppie-dom and commonplace infidelity, with a little fling on an out-of-town trip just before Christmas 1989 – barely six months into the marriage. He made the mistake of telling Pamela all about it during a quarrel. In no time the slender siren lured 15-year-old schoolkid Billy Flynn into her office and

showed him naughty pictures of her in her undies. Then she took him home when Greg was away, and showed him naughtier videos. Then she took him to the bedroom, so starting Billy on a sex-drenched life that came up to every teenage lad's dreams. When he was well hooked on her body, Pamela told him there'd be no more "fun" for Billy-boy – unless he killed Greg!

Driven by desire, Billy persuaded two friends to help him. They stole a gun and shot Greg dead in a faked burglary on May 1 last year. But they talked, and first they, then the steamy seductress,

went on trial. A year later, pretty Pamela has been locked up for life without the possibiity of parole.

IN BRIEF

TRACEY ANN WAUGH acquitted in the Australian lesbian vampire case (*see* 1990). The other two defendants convicted.

Jeffrey Dahmer: 'Milwaukee' Cannibal Monster

Jeffrey Dahmer, the chocolate-factory worker who ate parts of his 17 victims

Gay Cannibal Monster Caught in Milwaukee: Parts of his 17 Victims Stored in his Flat

ON JUNE 4, 1978, Jeffrey Dahmer graduated from high school. Two weeks later he committed his first murder.

Stephen Hicks was hitching home from a rock concert at Chippewa Park, Ohio, when Dahmer picked him up and invited him in for a few beers. When Hicks said he had to leave, Dahmer, who had been left on his own in an empty house by his divorcing parents, snapped. He hit Hicks over the head with a barbell and strangled him with its handle.

He hid the body in the crawlspace under the house for a few days, then stripped off the skin and flesh with chemicals, smashed the skeleton to smithereens with a sledgehammer, and spread the bone fragments and viscous matter on open soil, leaving nothing like a newly-turned grave to attract attention.

Life with Grandma

Following failure at college and a dishonourable discharge from the army, Dahmer, a young alcoholic homosexual, went to live with his grandmother in Milwaukee's upmarket suburb of West Allis.

She encouraged his interest in tropical fish, unaware of his passion for haunting sleazy gay bars and bath-houses after his low-grade work in a chocolate factory finished.

He was barred from one bath-house for drugging his sexual partners in cubicles. By this time Dahmer had discovered he preferred an unconscious partner. When, in November 1987, he killed Stephen Tuomi in a room in the Ambassador Hotel, he discovered he liked it even better if his partner was dead.

He took Tuomi back to Grandma Dahmer's basement for disposal. He also fried and ate one of Tuomi's biceps.

Early in 1988 he killed two more rent boys picked up in gay clubs. But the increasingly smelly garbage he was depositing, the remains of his victims, made even his grandmother wish he would move out.

In September he moved to a cheap apartment of his own on Milwaukee's downmarket West Side.

The Sinthasomphone Scandals

The day he moved, Dahmer offered 13-year-old Laotian refugee Somsack Sinthasomphone $50 to pose for photographs. Somsack was given drugged coffee, indecently fondled and photographed in lewd postures.

But the child wandered woozily out of the deathtrap apartment, and Jeffrey found himself arrested and charged with enticing a minor for immoral purposes.

Between his conviction in January 1989 for assaulting Somsack and sentencing two months later, Dahmer killed another young man. He painted the skull of this victim, retaining it as a potential ornament for a necrophiliac "shrine" he proposed erecting in the living-room of his home.

His prison sentence was suspended, on condition that he lived for a year in a correctional institution from which he could still work at the chocolate factory and support himself.

With that punishment completed, Dahmer took a flat in Oxford Apartments, a flat that would become infamous. As virtually the only white man around, he began to make his rooms the smelliest on the block, with decaying flesh stashed away. He killed four more young men in 1990, paused for six months, and

"Intoxicated Asian, naked male (*laughter*), was returned to his sober boyfriend (*more laughter*)." Policeman reporting the incident which was in fact kidnapping and sexual assault with actual bodily harm, and escalated to murder following his decision to return the young man to Dahmer.

Police carry away bagged human remains from Jeffrey Dahmer's flat

killed another three in the spring of 1991.

Then, on May 26, quite by chance, he picked up 14-year-old Konerak Sinthasomphone, the younger brother of his former victim, Somsack. Like his brother, Konerak was not entirely overcome by Dahmer's drugs, but after suffering brutal abuse wandered unsteadily onto the street when Dahmer slipped out to buy beer. Since he was naked and bleeding from the buttocks, he attracted instant attention. Nicole Childress and Sandra Smith ran to help him and call the police.

When three cops turned up, Dahmer reappeared. He handled the police with aplomb, taking them to his room and showing them Konerak's clothes and suggestive polaroid photographs he had snapped of him. He claimed that Konerak was his steady boyfriend, and a lot older than he looked – 19, in fact. He said the two were into S-M. The cops believed him.

Nicole Childress and Sandra Smith didn't. They protested (rightly) that Konerak was obviously a child and that his bleeding anus indicated something worse than mutual spanking games. The cops brushed them off and threatened to arrest them if they went on protesting.

Their precinct colleagues brushed off Sandra's mother, too, when she telephoned her continuing anxiety. They assured her it was just two adult faggots who enjoyed beating each other – and all quite legal, however distasteful. Milwaukee police would live to regret their recorded calls and responses. As soon as they left, Dahmer made up for lost time and murdered Sinthasomphone.

Sandra and Nicole, like almost all Dahmer's victims, were black; Dahmer and the cops were white. After Dahmer's arrest, mass protests would draw attention to the tendency of police to disregard information given to them by black citizens.

The End

Despite the failure of Milwaukee's finest, Dahmer had only two months and four more victims to go.

On July 23 he picked up 32-year-old Tracy Edwards – a heterosexual who was not willing to join in sex-play or drink drugged coffee. But Dahmer got a handcuff on one of Edwards' wrists, and used that and a knife to hold him prisoner for four terrifying hours.

Edwards escaped when Dahmer's attention flagged. He stopped two policemen in a patrol car and asked them to release him from the handcuff. After hearing his story they went back to Oxford Apartments to investigate this strange homosexual kidnapper.

Dahmer offered the sullen explanation, "I just lost my job and I wanted to drink some f-ing beer." He resisted their attempts to come into his flat. An attempt to arrest him resulted in a struggle which ended with Dahmer screaming on the floor. A thorough inspection of the flat uncovered:

A human head in the fridge
3 heads in the floor-freezer
a human heart in the fridge-freezer compartment

a blue barrel jammed with body parts and bones
two skulls in a computer packaging box
three skulls and some bones in a filing cabinet
two skulls in a kettle
a penis and some hands in another kettle

The Milwaukee cannibal's career was over, and Dahmer was dragged away in custody, howling like a mad dog.

DAHMER AND RACE

While Milwaukee policemen's regrettable failure to take the complaints of black witnesses seriously may justify the race protest demonstrations led by the Reverend Jesse Jackson in the wake of the murders, the secondary suggestion that Dahmer himself was racially motivated seems ill-founded. Dahmer's victims break down into the following categories:

1 American Indian
1 Half-Jewish Puerto Rican
1 Hispanic
1 Asian
2 White
11 Black

This mix is very close to the demographic population of the poor districts of Milwaukee and Chicago where Dahmer made his pick-ups. So it seems certain that he took his victims opportunistically at random. With all his faults Jeff Dahmer is no racist, although he found the worst possible way of demonstrating his freedom from prejudice!

THE Milwaukee JOURNAL
Tuesday, July 23, 1991 – Latest Edition
Body parts litter apartment

Sensation in Milwaukee with the discovery of a homosexual cannibal serial murderer

Prostitute Robbed and Murdered her Punters

AILEEN "LEE" WUORNOS (38) lived in run-down trailers in Florida with her girlfriend, Tyria Moore, socialized at run-down bars, and made her money by soliciting worn out men. Guess it all got a bit too dismal, and Lee just had to hit back. She went from being a no-hoper to America's first sexual serial murderess!

When the half-clothed bodies of men with condoms beside them continued turning up along highway I-52, Florida police concluded that some prostitute must be killing her punters. The victims included: social services investigator Dick Humphreys; truck driver Buddy Burress; repair shop owner Richard Mallory; rodeo rider Chuck Carskadoon; concrete loader David Spears; and Bible-toting preacherman Peter Siems. Some of the families of these guys are angrier about the fact that Aileen has exposed their loved ones' appetite for paid-for sex than that she killed them!

Picked up at a bar, Aileen confessed to six slayings, though she gave details of seven, and there may have been more! Her victims were big middle-aged men. Aileen says they tried to rape her, but defence psychiatrists say they represented her father in her mind.

Aileen's childhood was a disaster: brutally thrashed and sexually abused, she learned before puberty that boys would give her money if she let them "put their things" into her. She spent the money she got from schoolgirl prostitution on endless cigarettes. Unhappy little Aileen was despised by the kids who used her. She fell into the hardened prostitute's icy self-contempt and defensiveness toward the world before she had full-grown pubic hair.

The fact that Aileen robbed every man she killed went against her. Last year, juries in her trials for four of her murders rejected her pleas of insanity and gave her a date with Ol' Sparky.

This year another county's court found her insane and unfit to plead! Now what's Florida going to do with its madwoman under sentence of death?

Killer-hooker Aileen Wuornos

Victim David Spears

Wuornos' first victim, Richard Mallory

South London Drug Wars, Brindle Brothers Acquitted

THE ACQUITTAL OF BROTHERS Patrick and Anthony Brindle this May, charged with murdering prominent drug dealer Ahmed "Turkish Abbi" Abdullah in March 1991, closes a bloody act in south London's raging gang war.

Its worst episode was the murder of the Brindles' brother David at a pub in Walworth in August last year. Two gunmen's incompetent scatterfire killed one innocent customer and wounded others. One killer is supposed to have yelled, "That's for Abbi!" as they shot Brindle in the back.

The Brindles have a sister married to Abbi's cousin, Dogan Arif, said to be South London's drug czar, even though he is residing in a high-security cell.

"Mad Frankie" Fraser, the Richardson brothers' old henchman (see 1966), is the Brindles' uncle. "Mad Frankie" caught a bullet himself last year, as he passed the Turnmill Disco in Clerkenwell. True to form, he told police he was Tutankhamen, and refused to talk about his injury!

FEMINISM AND MURDER

American feminists have got themselves in a state about murderous women. Pamela Smart (*see* 1991) – well, she's easily excused for murdering an unfaithful husband. But the politicized gals ain't quite sure whether to praise or blame her for educating young Billy Flynn in bed. Is she catchin' up on beastly men by playin' their game of sex with kiddies, or is she lettin' the side down?

Betty Broderick (*see* these pages). Okay, Dan was a heel and deserved all he got, but what had his second wife, Linda, done? And can the great mystique of mother-love survive evidence that Betty put her own hurt pride and greed before the kids she mightily distressed?

Neither Betty nor Pamela rates high with the Red Lesbians, who think women must substitute lesbian Marxism for marriage and the "American Dream". Aileen Wuornos is their heroine: lesbian in her personal tastes; financially exploiting men's nauseating wish to have sex with women; killing some.

As for her robberies – well, to a Marxist "property is theft", and lesbian feminists believe every prostitute is unhappy and exploited and wants out. So Aileen was just cute to liberate those guys' wallets.

Andrei Chikatilo, whose 53 known killings give him No. 1 spot in the world serial killer league

Freak Blood Grouping Saved Russia's Record Mass Killer

BACK IN 1984, when 48-year-old Andrei Chikatilo was arrested in Rostov, police believed they'd got the serial killer terrorizing the city. However, tests showed his blood belonged to group A; the sperm found on bodies recovered over the past few years was AB.

Yet as early as 1978 he was a murder suspect. A small girl's body was found in the river Don, and blood-spattering in a squalid shack where Chikatilo used to entertain prostitutes proved she had been killed there. Another resident of the street, who had once been convicted of sex-murder as a juvenile, confessed under interrogation, and was executed for Chikatilo's crime.

It was red faces all round for Red officialdom when it was revealed that Chikatilo is that one-in-a-million individual, one whose semen registers a different group from his blood.

In Brezhnev's USSR the scandals would have been covered up. (Sexual serial murder was purely a product of decadent capitalism!) But Chikatilo was arrested in 1991, under Gorbachev. He has committed at least 53 murders, a world record for modern times.

He was convicted in Yeltsin's Russia, and sentenced to death.

America Divided over Ex-Wife's Revenge on Husband

THROUGHOUT NOVEMBER and December last year, America watched Betty Broderick's second trial in San Diego for the murder of her ex and his wife.

Dan Broderick III was a brilliant lawyer earning $1 million a year. In 1983, aged 38, he started a secret affair with receptionist Linda Kolkena, and told Betty, his wife of 14 years, she was "old, fat, ugly, boring and stupid." Two years later he finally admitted to extra-marital sex. He was unrepentant and aggressive into the bargain, depriving Betty of custody of their four children and kicking her out of the marital home. His legal skills enabled him to get the better of her in every way. Betty retaliated by making his life a misery, leaving profane tirades on his answerphone. Finally, in 1988, she went at dawn to shoot Dan and Linda as they slept.

Half the women of America feel Dan got what he deserved. Others are less sure, given Betty's insistence that money matters more than parenthood. Anyway, she was convicted of second-degree homicide in January, and her case looks like becoming a recurrent controversy on Oprah Winfrey's show.

Look Out, Look Out, There's Counterfeit Sperm About!

DR CECIL JACOBSON of Virginia has been convicted of an amazing new scientific crime: sperm fraud! At his fertility clinic, "the baby maker" offered childless cou-

Sperm fraud Dr Cecil Jacobson

ples artificial insemination by donors from a "carefully regulated" programme, matching physical, mental and social characteristics. But it wasn't true. After 15 babies were born, all bearing a striking resemblance to Dr Jacobson, he confessed. The semen used in the clinic was his own: freshly drawn just before the patient came in for insemination. Dr Jacobson collected a raft of convictions for misuse of communication systems, and the like. Meanwhile, the legislature wonders how to draft new laws prohibiting men from lying about their sperm!

> " GOD DOESN'T GIVE YOU BABIES. I DO. "
> QUOTE CECIL B. JACOBSON

Nurse Murders Four Children: Damages Nine

Beverley Allitt (centre), the nurse who killed children in her care

STATE ENROLLED NURSE Beverley Allitt attacked her first victim within a week of starting contract work in Ward Four at Grantham Hospital, Lincolnshire, England. Baby Liam Taylor died on February 23, 1991, of an inexplicable heart attack.

Two weeks later, on March 5, 11-year-old Tim Hardwick died; epilepsy was diagnosed.

On April 4, 9-week-old Becky Phillips died at her parents' home after a short stay in hospital; cot-death, the doctors decided. Becky's parents were so grateful to Beverley for her caring support of the child that they made her godmother to Becky's twin, Katie. When Katie was hospitalized, her godparent struck again, failing to kill her, but causing permanent brain damage.

One week later, blood from 5-month-old Paul Crampton, who suffered three near-fatal attacks in March, was analysed. It was found to contain a massive overdose of insulin. Grantham Hospital was alerted, and a close watch was kept on Ward Four.

Despite this, Beverley killed again before the month was out, injecting 15-month-old Claire Peck with potassium. Finally, in May, Nurse Allitt was arrested and the killings stopped.

After her arrest Allitt developed anorexia and lost five stones in weight. She spent the entirety of her trial this year in Rampton Secure Mental Hospital.

Her real problem, however, is the extreme attention-seeking disorder Münchhausen's Syndrome. Bev graduated from florid lying through self-injury and hypochondriac illnesses to inflicting illness and death on those in her care.

Now she stands as England's greatest 20-century female mass murderer.

Homosexual Hoover was Mafia Puppet all Along

J. EDGAR HOOVER, architect of the FBI, was a closet gay and occasional cross-dresser. What's more, sneering Mafia bosses knew this and threatened him with exposure! So says respected British investigative writer Anthony Summers in a new book. Summers establishes, with responsibly documented statements, that Hoover:

Was widely known to be homosexual, favouring his gay lover Clyde Tolson, whom he promoted to FBI Deputy Director over the heads of better and more experienced officers

may have known and feared the widespread belief that he had African blood

was seen in drag on a couple of occasions at private hotel-room sex-parties, where his bulldog features, hideous in wig and dress, were introduced as "Mary"

was fully understood by many Mafiosi to be in the pocket of Mayer Lansky, who acquired pictures of Hoover enjoying sex with a man in the late Thirties, and used it to force the Director to lay off organized crime.

The inference that Hoover was controlled by the Syndicate makes sense. His puzzling failure to stop the "Crime Commission's" nationwide racketeering has usually been put down to fear that his Bureau would fail in tackling it (*see* 1951, 1962, 1972). Hence his preference for targeting easy Mid-West bankrobbers.

The FBI has gone from strength to strength in combating organized crime since Hoover's death, culminating in the conviction of godfather John Gotti last year, at the fourth attempt.

Gotti comes as near as today's climate allows to being New York's "capo di tutti capi", so his is the most important criminal conviction since Vito Genovese (*see* 1969). Don Vito, it is thought, was secretly got at by Lansky and Frank Costello, with "Lucky" Luciano's approval. You have to go back to Tom Dewey's conviction of Luciano in 1936 to find a comparable effective crime-busting op.

Summers implies there was a carrot as well as a stick. Hoover was a compulsive gambler, following the horses being as near as he came to having a cultural life. It is suggested that "Prime Minister of Crime" Frank Costello unobtrusively paid him off by:

Giving him hot tips on fixed races accepting his illegal high off-course bets never demanding payment when Hoover lost!

Whatever else is remembered about Director Hoover, he now goes down as one of the most evil-smelling humbugs of all time!

NEW LIGHT ON JFK

Anthony Summers' revelations about J. Edgar Hoover make sense, at last, of the steady drip of information linking the Mafia to President Kennedy's assassination. Since the same informants indicated that the Mafia had damaging evidence of JFK's promiscuous sex-life, it wasn't obvious why they should want to destroy the president they had the bite on.

But once Attorney-General Bobby Kennedy succeeded against all odds in forcing Hoover to turn the FBI on the Mafia, almost any price would be worth paying to win back Hoover's neutrality. And as Mafia associates always said, the best way to disarm Bobby was to kill Jack.

Children's Crime Provokes Near Riot in Liverpool

ALARMING SCENES of mob fury took place in Liverpool this February when police took boys in for questioning in connection with the murder of 2-year-old James Bulger.

The infant was abducted from a shopping centre. Security cameras showed that two boys, aged about 10 or 12, led him away when his parents had taken their eyes off him. Witnesses believe they saw James in some distress, being led by other children in the direction of the railway bank where his body was found, savagely mutilated.

Although violent crimes are sporadically committed by children (the horrific rape and murder of 4-year-old Tracey Wair by a 12-year-old boy in 1977 is a good example), they do not often attract massive public attention. Mary Bell (*see*

Police hold back an angry crowd as two boys are charged with the murder of James Bulger

1968) was the last major case in Britain. Her sensational trial aroused vehement feelings that she was a thoroughly abnormal child. The James Bulger murder has unleashed a torrent of guilt and anger about deteriorating moral standards in society being responsible for such crimes.

Outrage at James's fate is understandable, but it seems irresponsible to assume the suspects to be guilty and also to attribute to them motives that have not yet been fully explained or explored in a court of law. The circumstances of James's death will remain a mystery until that case is conducted.

Convicted Rape-Simulator's Case Re-Opened

IN 1991 YVONNE SLEIGHTHOLME of England, who went blind while awaiting trial, was convicted of killing her ex-lover's wife. In December 1988 Mrs Jane Smith was found dead by her farmer-husband outside their house. Her body was half-dressed and had injuries consistent with a sexual assault.

At her trial Miss Sleightholme claimed that Smith had hired three killers to carry out the murder, fearing expensive divorce proceedings, although he had only been married seven months. Smith tearfully denounced her story as "wicked, wicked lies," and the jury agreed.

This January Yvonne's appeal against conviction was dismissed, the appeal court finding there was no error in the judicial summing-up at her trial. But, with new solicitors, Yvonne is determined to try again, claiming new evidence uncovered must be heard.

Extradition Proceedings After RN High Seas Arrest

EXTRADITION PROCEEDINGS in Gibraltar and Paris have been started to bring brothers Roderick and Mark Newall back to the Channel Islands to face charges in connection with the death of their parents (*see* 1987).

Lloyd's underwriter Nicholas Newall and his wife Elizabeth disappeared from their Jersey home after their sons had visited them for a champagne dinner to celebrate Mrs Newall's 48th birthday. The brothers allegedly left their parents alive and well after midnight.

There were no signs of forced entry, nor of theft; but equally, no signs that the Newalls had left of their own volition: their passports were in the bungalow and their breakfast table was laid.

Roderick Newall (centre) is taken to face extradition proceedings in Gibraltar

From minute bloodstains found in the house, police deduced that the Newalls had been killed there, after which the place had been scrupulously cleaned up and the central heating turned up high to dry out all traces of mopping-up. It looked like an inside job, done by somebody who knew their way around the house.

Mark and Roderick inherited their parents' wealth when it was assumed the couple were dead. Within a few months, Roderick resigned his army commission and put to sea in the family's 66-foot

yacht, *Austral Soma*. In August last year the Royal Navy frigate *Argonaut* apprehended 26-year-old Roderick at sea and took him to Gibraltar. Here, "new evidence" was presented to the courts in a move to extradite him. Roderick fought the proceedings, desperately trying to have a tape-recording excluded which apparently implicated another person as well as himself. Since his arrest he has made three suicide attempts.

This year, extradition proceedings were started against Mark, too, now resident in Paris.

Murder in Broad Daylight by Contract Killer

SELF-MADE MILLIONAIRE 55-year-old Donald Urquhart was gunned down as he walked along Marylebone High Street in London in broad daylight with his Thai girlfriend, Pat Iamspithone. After the attack the killer made off on a Yamaha motorbike.

Forensic science laboratories link the killing with last year's murder of south London off-licence owner Roger Wilson. However, this might mean only that the same professional killer was hired for the two murders.

Underworld gossip hints that the killer's name is known, and that he received £20,000 for the murder. The police suspect that Urquhart courted danger by going into the illegal gaming machines business currently controlled by south London gangsters.

INDEX

A

Abberline, Frederick 115
Abdullah, "Turkish Abbi" Ahmed 308
Acott, Superintendent Bob 236
Adams, Fanny 36
Adams, Dr John Bodkin 227, 229
Adams, Katherine 104
Adams, Kitty 101
Addison, Samuel 269
Adonis, Joe 168, 194, 202
Agostini, Antonio 203
Aguirr, Martin 115
Aime, Laura 301
Aken, Myrna Joy 227
Albert Victor, Prince 83
Aldridge, Cecilia 43
Alexander II, Tsar 66
Alexandre, Pierre 186, 201
Algarron, Jacques 222, 225
Allaway, Thomas Henry 155
Allen, Emily 126
Allen, John ('Ned') 48
Allen, Margaret "Bill" 213
Allen, Peter 243
Allen, William 37
Allitt, Beverley 310
Alphon, Peter Louis 236
Altendorf, Paul 144
Amos, Icylma 272
Amurao, Corazon 248
anarchists 92, 125, 128, 152
Anastasia, Albert 168, 194, 197, 229, 232, 255
Anderson, Andrew 173
Anderson, Moncrieff 181
Andrews, Norman 215
Andrews, William 266
Angel, Miriam 78
Anselmi, Albert 178, 179
Apsley Castle affair 70
Archambault, Marielle 261
Arena, Joanne 231
Arifsaid, Dogan 308
Arkall, Father Henry 62
Armstrong, Major Herbert Rowse 152, 155
Arran murderer 82
Ashford, Mary 11
Ashford, William 11
Ashworth, Dawn 297
Astor, John Jacob 107
Atherstone, Welding 129
Atkins, "Irish Rose" 190
Atkins, Susan 256, 257
Atkinson, Tina 281
Atlanta Child Murders 283, 285
Audette, Shirley 261
Aumuller, Anna 137
Avory, Mr Justice 163
Ayres, Herbert 173

B

Bachert, Albert 98
Bachmeier, Anna 282
Baguley, Ada 187
Bailes, Maria Ellen 125
Bailey, Berman Benjamin 272
Bailey, Edward 79
Bailey, F.Lee 244, 249, 251
Bailly, Felix 217, 219
Baird, Stephanie 235
Bakanowski, Father Adolphus 62
Baker, Arthur Reginald 113
Baker, Frederick 36
Baker, Mary 12
Bakker, Jim and Tammy Faye 297
Balchin, Olive 207, 209, 217
Balcombe Street siege 269
Baldock, Edward 302
Ball, George 136, 139
Bamber, Jeremy 290, 293
Bandara, Dr Uphaya 281
Banks, Camille and Joseph 225
Banks, Shirley 295
Banner Cross murderer 58
Barbe, Warren Gilbert 160
Barber, Susan 284
Barker, Ma "Arizona Kate" 183, 187
Barker, Sidney 44
Barlow, Kenneth 228
Barn Restaurant case 264, 267
Barnett, Henry C. 104, 113
Barney, Elvira 174
Barnum, P.T. 44
Barrett, "Black Rita" 210
Barrett, Michael 38
Barrie, "Scotch Ian" 254
Barrow, Clyde 181
Barrow, Eliza 133, 134
Barrows, Sydney Biddle 289
Barthelemy, Helene 245
Bartlett, Adelaide 76
Bartlett, Marion and Velda 231
Barton, John 28, 35
Basa, Teresita 276
Bass, Sam 59
Bates, Albert 177
Batt, Charles 35
Batten, Elsie 236
Beachy, Hill 29
Beard, Arthur 149
Beard, Dr Thomas 44
Beausoleil, Bobby 256, 257
Beck, Adolph 111, 116
Beck, Martha 213, 217
Beckemann, Karen Sue 258
Becker, Lieutenant Charles 135, 141
Beckley, John 221, 235
Bedbrook, Mr and Mrs (Lamson case) 68
Beer Wars 178
Begley, David 285
Behre, Friedhelme 233
Bell, Mary Flora 252

Bell, Norma 252
Belli, Melvin 255
Bellingham, John 10
Benbow, Dr Palmer 203
Bender, Johann 49
Benhayon, Henry 80
Beni, Jules 25
Bennett, Herbert 109, 111
Bennett, Keith 246
Benson, Gale 262
Benson, Harry 57
Benson, Steven 291, 293
Bentley, Derek 220
Benwell, Frederick 84
Berard, Alexander 129
Berg, Alan 289
Berger, Theodore 116
Berkowitz, David 272
Berlin, Lucie 116
Berman, James "Abbadabba" 182
Bernays, Guillaume 69
Beron, Leon 132
Berry (hangman) 74
Bertron, Suzanne 186
Bessell, Peter 279
Besumer, Louis 146
Bianchi, Kenneth 286
"Big Mary" 73
"Big Nose Kate" 79
Biggs, Fred 263
Biggs, Ronald 243
Bihari, Paul 143
"Billy the Kid" (William H.Bonney) 58, 66, 67
Bingham, Edith 133
Binney, Commander Ralph 202
Birchall, Reginald 84
Bird, Greenup 35
Birkenhead, Lord (F.E.Smith) 149, 154
Birkett, Norman 176
Bisbee Massacre 71, 73
Bishop, Russell 293, 295, 302
Black, Anthony 289
Black Hand 110, 123
Black Panther 271, 273
Blakely, David 224
Blind Beggar Gang 87
Blixt, Claus 95, 97
Bloomingdale, Alfred 288
"Blue Lagoon" murder 206
Blume, Johanna 123
Boden, Wayne Clifford 261
bodysnatching 59
Bogart, "Darky the Coon" 129, 176
Bogdanovitch, Peter 278
Boggia, Antonio 25
Bogle, Stanley 241
Bolber, Dr Morris 188
Bonati, Minnie 165
Bonnano, Joseph C. ("Joe Bananas") 202, 260
Bonnie (Parker) and Clyde (Barrow) 181
Boost, Werner 233

Booth, Anna 146, 151
Booth, Barbara 280
Booth, John Wilkes 32
Borden, Emma 91
Borden, Lizzie 90-1
Boston Strangler 242, 244
Botkin, Cordelia ("Red Hot Mama") 104
'Bottle Imp' 61
Bottomley, Horatio 155
Boulton, Thomas 74
Boutflour, David 290
Bouvier, Leone ("La Pauvrette") 220
"Bovingdon bug" 263
Bow Street Runners 9
Bowden, Sgt James 299
Bowden, John "Ginger" 285
Bowers, Dr J.Milton 80
Bowyer, Linda 218
Boyce, Arthur 207
Boyd, Ben 55
Boyle, Tony 259, 263
Bradfield, Bill 283, 287
Bradfield, Christine 136, 139
Bradley, Francis 34
Brady, Ian 246-7
Brady, Patrick 182
Brain, George 190
Braintree (US) robbery murder 152, 165
Branson, William 146, 151
Bravo, Florence 54
Breaks, Harriet "Kitty" 149, 151
Bremner, Edward 183
Brennan, Molly 53
'Brides in the Bath' 140
Bridport, Shirley 231
Briggs, Thomas 30
Brindle, Shirley 285
Brindle brothers 308
Brink, J.W."Doc" 24
Brinkley, Richard 123
Brink's robbery (US) 215, 223
Brink's-Matt robbery 287, 289, 291
Britton, Stephanie 268
Brixton Taxi case 157
"Broadway Mob" 202
Broderick, Betty 308, 309
Brodovitz, Henry 113
Brodsky, Jane 132
Brook, John 264, 267
Brook, Maggie 209
Brooks, David 265, 267
Brooks, Stephanie 300
Broughton, Sir "Jock" Delves 196
Brown, Beresford 221
Brown, Earline 263, 265
Brown, Eric 200
Brown, Ernest 177, 181
Brown, Frances 207
Brown, Fred and Joe 216
Brown, Grace "Billie" 120
Brown, Hannah 17
Brown, Margaret 235

INDEX

INDEX

INDEX

ACKNOWLEDGMENTS

The publishers wish to thank the following sources for their kind permission to reproduce the photographs in this publication:

Archive Photos; Associated Press; The Bettmann Archive; The Black Museum, Scotland Yard; Jean-Loup Charmet; E. T. Archive; Mary Evans Picture Library; John Frost Historical Newspapers; Hulton Deutsch Collection; Illustrated London News; London Features International/Michael Ochs Archive; Mander & Mitchenson Theatre Collection; Mansell Collection; Peter Newark's Pictures; Popperfoto; Press Association; Raymond's Press Agency; Reed Consumer Books Picture Library; Reuters/Bettmann; Rex Features; Roger-Viollet; S&G Press Agency Ltd; Frank Spooner Pictures; Syndication International; Topham Picture Library; UPI/Bettmann.

Every effort has been made by the publishers to credit the copyright holders of the photographs and apologizes for any omissions.